"What'd I Say"
The Atlantic Story

Compiled and Edited by C. Perry Richardson

Art Direction and Design by Marc Balet

Editorial, Design, Picture Research and Interview Assistance:
Janet Elen Richardson,
Stephanie Chaplin,
Marlon Richards, Sheryle Tamagini, Julio Mario Santo Domingo, Jeremy Schildcrout, Yves Beauvais, Bob Kaus, Joey Helguera, Kati Meister, Darius James and Barney Hoskyns.

Timeline: Stephanie Chaplin, Janet Elen Richardson and J. C. Costa

Interviews: C. Perry Richardson
  Pete Frame and Kevin Howlett
  Brendan Hughes and Uri Fruchtmann
  Darius James and Sheryle Tamagini

Further Consultant Editor: Bob Kaus

Picture Research: Kati Meister

Index: June Wilkins

Copy Editor: Rosemary Fallowfield

Acknowledgements:
The Publishers would also like to thank each of the contributors, photographers, agencies and archive sources as well as the following people for all of their help in making this book possible: Leila Logan, Frances Chantly, Ian Ralfini, and everyone at Atlantic Records. Edward and James Richardson, Ian and Bron Gillan, Mike Curle, Michael Halsband, Willie Nininger, Steve and Jenny Black, Tony Ferris, Paul Martin, Gail Gerber, Terry Southern, Richard Charkin, Thierry Ansellem, Andrée Buchler, Charles O'Donnell, Nicola Joss, Jenni Trent-Hughes, Kris Wrech, Chuck and Susan Zuretti, Brian Mandell, Matt Netherway, Andrew Peppin, John Hardingham, Ron Pickless, Phil Barker, Rachel Shapland, Darrin Ehardt, Richard Heddington, Nick Stevens, Ray Cole, Peter Burns, Bill Millar, Marv Goldberg, Charlie Gillett, Nick Tosches, Stanley Booth, Mike Golden, George and Anna Condo, Anita Pallenberg, David Macmillan, Daine Spoelberch, Emanuele di Savoia, John and Aglae Seilern, Sandro and Charuvan Sursock, Julio Mario Santo Domingo Sr., Mica Ertegun and Selma Ertegun.

Publishers: Julio Mario Santo Domingo and Charles Perry Richardson
Copyright © A Publishing Company Limited
London. Geneva. New York.

All rights reserved. No part of this publication may be reproduced, stored in a retrieval system or transmitted in any form or by any means, without the prior permission in writing of the Publishers as above.

This edition first published in Great Britain by The Orion Publishing Group Limited, Orion House, 5 Upper Saint Martin's Lane, London WC2H 9EA

First Orion Edition 2001

ISBN: 0-75281-792-2

A CIP catalogue record for this book is available from the British Library.

Origination by Chromolitho Ltd., Optica Ltd., Formatrix Ltd., Bridgewater Ltd.
Final production by Aylesbury Studios Ltd.

Printed and bound in Italy by Milanostampa

**This book is dedicated to the memory of
Luis Felipe Santo Domingo**

"What'd I Say"
The Atlantic Story
50 Years of Music
Ahmet Ertegun

with

Greil Marcus · Nat Hentoff
Lenny Kaye · Robert Gordon
Robert Christgau · Vince Aletti
Will Friedwald · David Fricke
Barney Hoskyns

Table of Contents

The Forties
Duke Ellington, Johnny Hodges, Rex Stewart, Harry Carney, Adele Girard, Barney Bigard, Joe Marsala, Lou McGarity, J.C. Higginbotham, Ralph Hawkins, Pete Johnson, Art Hodes, Zutty Singleton, Teddy Wilson, Jelly Roll Morton, The Blue Devils, Baby Dodds, Bunk Johnson, John Hammond, George Avakian, The Count Basie and Bob Crosby Bands, Big Joe Turner, Leadbelly, Henry 'Red' Allen, Mezz Mezzrow, Little Miss Cornshucks, Boyd Raeburn, Ginnie Powell, Sylvia Syms, Lester Young, Dizzy Gillespie, Charlie Parker, Norman Granz, The Kid Ory Band, Jimmie Noone, Mutt Carey, George Lewis, Ernie Fields, Thelonious Monk, Howard McGhee, Roy Eldridge, Teddy Hill, Lionel Hampton, The Harlemaires, Joe Morris, Lloyd 'Tiny' Grimes, Oscar Pettiford, Eddie Safranski, Willie Bryant, Ray Carroll, 'Jumbo' Jack Walker, Jesse Stone, Melrose Colbert, Erroll Garner, Frank Culley, Amos Milburn, Sarah Vaughan, Johnny Griffin, Al Hibbler, The Delta Rhythm Boys, Doc Pomus, Blind Willie McTell, Professor Longhair, Eddie Condon, Ruth Brown, The Rockin' Highlanders, Granville 'Stick' McGhee, Brownie McGhee. ... 4

The Fifties
Fred McDowell, Jimmy Yancey, 'Mama' Estella Yancey, Meade 'Lux' Lewis, Eurreal Wilford Montgomery, Connie Kay, Joe Bushkin, Sam 'The Man' Taylor, The Clovers, The Cardinals, The Diamonds, Harry Van Walls, Big Joe Turner, Lil Green, Ray Charles, Ruth Brown, LaVern Baker, Clyde McPhatter, Jesse Stone, Bobby Robinson, The Chords, The Drifters, John Lee Hooker, Ivory Joe Hunter, Joe Mooney, Lee Konitz, Lennie Tristano, Shorty Rogers, The Modern Jazz Quartet, Charles Mingus, Jimmy Witherspoon, Wilbur De Paris, Sydney De Paris, Pete Johnson, Chuck Willis, Champion Jack Dupree, T-Bone Walker, The Cookies, The Bobbettes, Warne Marsh, Chris Connor, Phineas Newborn, Bobby Short, Mabel Mercer, The Coasters, Jerry Leiber, Mike Stoller, Guitar Slim, The Raeletts, The Sensations, Mort Schuman, Ben E. King, Bobby Darin, Jimmy Giuffre, Chick Ganniman, Thelonious Monk, Art Blakey, John Coltrane, Ornette Coleman. ... 48

The Sixties
The Mar-Keys, Carla Thomas, William Bell, Solomon Burke, Charles Mingus, Sonny Stitt, The Modern Jazz Quartet, Ed Blackwell, Don Cherry, Mr. Acker Bilk, Mel Tormé, Buster Smith, King Curtis, McHouston 'Mickey' Baker, Nat Adderley, Carmen McRae, Mose Allison, Hank Crawford, Herbie Mann, Stephane Grappelli, Ornette Coleman, John Coltrane, Betty Carter, The Drifters, The Coasters, Otis Redding, Booker T. & the M.G.s, Doris Troy, Rufus Thomas, April Stevens, Nino Tempo, Phil Spector, The Righteous Brothers, David Porter, Isaac Hayes, The Mad Lads, Barbara Lewis, Esther Phillips, Don Covay, The Astors, Joe Tex, Titus Turner, Sam and Dave, Wilson Pickett, Arthur Conley, Percy Sledge, Eddie Floyd, Mary Wells, Allen Ginsberg, Sonny and Cher, The Young Rascals, Bobby Darin, Buffalo Springfield, Shelley Mann, Roy Ayers, Freddie Hubbard, Max Roach, Rahsaan Roland Kirk, Elvin Jones, Charles Lloyd, Aretha Franklin, Dan Penn, Spooner Oldham, Patti LaBelle & the Bluebelles, The Bar-Kays, Sir Mack Rice, Johnnie Taylor, Don Byas, Albert King, Otis Rush, The Bee Gees, Roberta Flack, Dusty Springfield, Dr. John, Yes, Boz Scaggs, Archie Bell & the Drells, Iron Butterfly, Julie Driscoll & The Brian Auger Trinity, Vanilla Fudge, Led Zeppelin, Cream, King Crimson, Eddie Harris, Les McCann, Gary Burton, Yusef Lateef, Shirley Scott, Joe Zawinul, Jimmy Scott, Keith Jarrett, Blind Faith, Freddie King, Lulu, Jerry Jeff Walker, John Hammond Jr., Clarence Carter, R. B. Greaves, Crosby, Stills & Nash, Woodstock, The Allman Brothers Band. ... 128

The Seventies
Aretha Franklin, Brook Benton, Derek & the Dominos, Delaney & Bonnie, Eric Clapton, The Velvet Underground, Duke Ellington, The Allman Brothers Band, Crosby, Stills, Nash & Young, The Sweet Inspirations, Mongo Santamaria, Ronnie Hawkins, The Dixie Flyers, Dr.John, Emerson, Lake & Palmer, Steve Stills, Donny Hathaway, Ray Charles, MC5, Led Zeppelin, The Rolling Stones, The Persuaders, Blue Magic, Ike & Tina Turner, Clarence Reid, Betty Wright, King Curtis, John Prine, Loudon Wainwright III, Manassas, Art Ensemble of Chicago, Bette Midler. Buddy Guy, Junior Wells, Doug Sahm, Willie Nelson, The J. Geils Band, Chick Corea, Dave Brubeck, Carmen McRae, Billy Cobham, Bad Company, Black Oak Arkansas, The James Gang, Genesis, King Crimson, Yusef Lateef, The Modern Jazz Quartet, Rahsaan Roland Kirk, Roberta Flack, Average White Band, Hall & Oates, Roxy Music, Maggie Bell, Yes, The Bee Gees, The Manhattan Transfer, Abba, Ben E. King, The Trammps, Hot Chocolate, The Small Faces, Ringo Starr, Dave Edmunds, Alice Cooper, Esther Phillips, Jean-Luc Ponty, Peter Gabriel, Roy Buchanan, Bryan Ferry, Firefall, Jimmy Webb, AC/DC, Blackfoot, Peter Tosh, Jay McShann, Charles Mingus, Larry Coryell, Lenny White, Sonny Sharrock, Foreigner, Slave, Brides of Funkenstein, Boney M, Mass Production, Cerrone, Sister Sledge, The Spinners, Chic. ... 245

Table of Contents

The Eighties
Pete Townshend, The Blues Brothers, The Rolling Stones, AC/DC, Stevie Nicks, Robert Plant, Crosby, Stills & Nash, Phil Collins, Bette Midler, The Manhattan Transfer, Abba, Chic, Sister Sledge, Roxy Music, Jim Carroll, Foreigner, Laura Branigan, Zebra, Tangerine Dream, Genesis, Sippie Wallace, Ray Charles, The Honeydrippers, Ahmad Jamal, Peter Tosh, Bob Geldof, Roger Daltrey, Yes, Twisted Sister, Savatage, Ratt, Julian Lennon, Jean-Luc Ponty, Billy Joe Royal, John Parr, Debbie Gibson, Mink de Ville, Mike + the Mechanics, The Firm, INXS, The Modern Jazz Quartet, Illinois Jacquet, LeVert, Skid Row, White Lion, Winger, Mr. Big. — 361

The Nineties
Rush, Phil Collins, En Vogue, Juliana Hatfield, Marc Cohn, Alannah Myles, Everything But The Girl, Roberta Flack, Anita Baker, Tori Amos, Stone Temple Pilots, The Lemonheads, INXS, The Modern Jazz Quartet, Nino Tempo, Bobby Short, Genesis, Mike Jagger, Stevie Nicks, Crosby, Stills & Nash, Pete Townshend, Bad Religion, The Melvins, Hootie & the Blowfish, Robert Plant and Jimmy Page, The Three Tenors, John Michael Montgomery, Confederate Railroad, Tracy Lawrence, Neal McCoy, Wessell Anderson, Cyrus Chestnut, James Carter, All-4-One, Seven Mary Three, Collective Soul, Donna Lewis, Jill Sobule, Fountains Of Wayne, Duncan Sheik, Poe, Edwin McCain, The Bottle Rockets, Tim McGraw, Clannad, Rick Braun, Gerald Albright, Mike Stern, Madeleine Peyroux, Moondog, Trans-Siberian Orchestra, The Manhattan Transfer, Bette Midler, Robin S., Changing Faces, Timbaland & Magoo, Junior M.A.F.I.A., Quad City D.J.s, Mark Morrison, Lil' Kim, Aaliyah, Big Wreck, Olu Dara, Lili Haydn, Youssou N'dour, Chris Stills, Victoria Williams, Widemouth Mason, Catatonia, Scott Weiland, Davíd Garza, Michael Crawford, Regina Carter, Martin Sexton, Randy Crawford, Kris Kristofferson, plus ONE, The Buena Vista Social Club, Kid Rock, Uncle Kracker, Bif Naked, LeAnn Rimes, Emmylou Harris, Sinéad O'Connor, Rod Stewart, P.O.D. Sugar Ray, The Corrs, Brandy, matchbox twenty, Jewel. — 431

Essays
Atlantic Records 1947-54 By Greil Marcus — 64

The Jazz Heritage of Atlantic Records By Nat Hentoff — 84

The Second Taste 1954-1962 By Lenny Kaye — 122

Southern Soul By Robert Gordon — 190

The Move Into Rock By Robert Christgau — 290

Lost In Music: Alantic's Disco Years By Vince Aletti — 340

The Great Age of Excess 1972-1986 By David Fricke — 388

Jazz By Will Friedwald — 418

The Soul in the Machine 1986-2000 By Barney Hoskins — 450

Index — 516

Timeline (TL: in picture captions refers to timeline decade) — 526

Picture Credits — 560

Bibliography — 565

Ahmet (front), Nesuhi and Mrs. Hayrunisa Ertegun

"If it had not been for the fall of the Ottoman Empire, my father would, of course, never have been able to travel in the way that he did on behalf of the new leadership of Turkey, as Ambassador to Paris, London and finally Washington, D.C. It may well be that Nesuhi and I would have found it extremely difficult to travel to America, and would certainly not have been allowed to stay behind and pursue a career outside of the family's legal and diplomatic professions. In 1936 Ataturk decreed that every citizen of Turkey had to choose a surname. Prior to that time people had simply been known as 'Son of James', 'Son of Richard' or whatever. This, of course, led to some spectacular names being chosen. Our family name up to that point was Munir, so my father selected the surname Ertegun, which roughly translated means 'living in a hopeful future'.

"My mother, Hayrunisa Rustem, was very musical. If it hadn't been for the mores of Turkish society, she probably would have been a star. She had a beautiful voice, played every instrument by ear, was a terrific dancer and loved music. Wherever we were, she always bought all the popular hits of the day: Josephine Baker, Mae West, the Mills Brothers, the Boswell Sisters, among many others, so we always had a lot of music in the house. I can honestly say that, from the age of about five, I fell in love with jazz music. My elder brother Nesuhi introduced me to a wide array of these wonderful artists. Nesuhi and I used to sneak records into our rooms at night and fall asleep listening to them. As I grew up, I began to discover a little bit about the situation of black people in America, and experienced an immediate empathy with the victims of such senseless discrimination. Because although the Turks were never slaves, they were regarded as enemies within Europe because of their Muslim beliefs. When my father announced that we were moving to Washington, D.C., however I said, 'Oh thank God, I'm going to the land of cowboys, Indians, Chicago gangsters, beautiful brown-skinned women and jazz.' Of course, when we arrived in America I was sent to a tough, British-type prep school and I saw no cowboys, Indians, gangsters, beautiful women or jazz musicians. But, soon enough, I found all of them.

"Making records was something I'd wanted to do ever since I was a young kid. Finally, when I was fourteen years old, my mother bought me a record-cutting machine, which was more than a toy; it was an amateur recording machine which cut acetate discs. I had an instrumental recording by Cootie Williams of 'West End Blues' to which I wrote some lyrics. I put the instrumental version on a Magnavox record player, turned on the recording machine, and sang my lyrics into the microphone with the record playing behind me. That was my first experience with over-dubbing. I was amazed at how good it sounded and managed to astonish all my friends because I would play them this record and they had no idea that it was me singing. So it worked extremely well in a primitive way."
Ahmet

Below, clockwise from left: Ahmet, Sadi Koylan, Nesuhi and Delia Gottlieb

From left: Nesuhi, Ahmet with friend and photographer William Gottlieb

From left: Sadi Koylan, William Gottlieb and Nesuhi

Opposite, fom left: Nesuhi and Ahmet Ertegun

Musicians from the Ellington and Marsala bands playing at the Turkish Embassy – from left: Lawrence Brown's trombone, Johnny Hodges (partially hidden), Rex Stewart, unidentified saxophonist, Harry Carney, Adele Girard, Barney Bigard and Joe Marsala

"In 1932, when I was nine years old, Nesuhi took me to see Cab Calloway's Orchestra at the Palladium in London. Then we went to hear Duke Ellington. It was an incredible experience for me, because while I had heard jazz on records, the sound of those bands live was unbelievable.

"Cleo Payne worked as a janitor at the embassy. He was an ex-fighter and another terrific character. As well as giving me boxing lessons, he'd take me around the black section of Washington. For my little sub-deb party, he got this really funky family band with a lady pianist that reminded me of Lil Armstrong, who played with Louis Armstrong's Hot Five."
Ahmet

Playing ping pong at the Turkish Embassy. From left: Lou McGarity, J.C. Higginbotham, Ralph Hawkins, Pete Johnson and Art Hodes

From left: Ahmet, Duke Ellington, Bill Gottlieb and Nesuhi, 1941

"In the forties, Washington was like a Southern town, and black people were completely excluded from most of the amenities afforded by the city to the white population. There was total segregation. Black people had their own movie theatres in their own section of town and were not allowed in white movie theatres. The exception was the burlesque theatre, where black people had to sit in the balcony, while whites sat downstairs.

"Black and white musicians did play together, but it was not easy. It was more possible in New York, particularly in Harlem, but in Washington at that time it was virtually impossible. I went to college in Annapolis, Maryland, and one night three of my school friends and I went to hear a band at a black nightclub, and we were arrested coming out of the place. I asked the judge, 'Where is the law written which states that we cannot go to this club?' And he replied, 'It's not written, but it's understood.' I, of course, insisted that he couldn't arrest us on those grounds, and it became obvious that they just wanted to throw a scare into us and would not be prosecuting on that occasion – particularly not the son of the Turkish ambassador.

"All the big bands toured at that time – Louis Armstrong, Chick Webb, Benny Goodman, Duke Ellington, Tommy Dorsey, Jimmie Lunceford – and they'd often play Washington on a Saturday night. Nesuhi and I made the most out of the extra-territorial situation offered by the embassy by inviting musicians who'd played in town the night before over for Sunday lunch. They all loved the idea of having lunch at an embassy, particularly one as well-appointed and in such grand surroundings as the Turkish embassy in Washington. After lunch, jam sessions would inevitably develop and we had some fantastic times with so many great musicians – Johnny Hodges, Benny Carter, Rex Stewart, Joe Marsala, Lester Young, as well as the boogie woogie piano player, Meade Lux Lewis.

From left: Zutty Singleton, Joe Marsala, Teddy Wilson, Nesuhi, Ahmet and Adele Girard in front of the bust of Ataturk in the Turkish embassy

Back row, from left: Sadi Koylan (cousin), Nesuhi, Selma Ertegun (sister), Dr. Vahdi Sabit (original Atlantic Records investor), Vesamet Kutlu (family friend) and Ahmet. Front row, from left: Ahmet Emin Yalman (editor of Turkey's leading newspaper), Ambassador Munir Ertegun (father), Hayrunisa Ertegun (mother) and Celal Bayar (President of Turkey)

"I remember that my father would occasionally receive letters from outraged Southern senators saying something to the effect of: 'It has been brought to my attention, Sir, that a person of colour was seen entering your house by the front door. I have to inform you that, in our country, this is not a practice to be encouraged.' My father would respond with a terse one-sentence reply such as: 'In my home, friends enter by the front door – however, we can arrange for you to enter from the back.'" Ahmet

Jelly Roll Morton

"One of my acquaintances and influences from that time was Jelly Roll Morton. I recently donated a complete collection of Jelly Roll Morton's works and piano rolls to the Library of Congress in my brother Nesuhi's name. For me, Jelly Roll is still, to this day, one of the greatest musicians of all time.

"Jelly Roll had hit rock bottom when he came to Washington – didn't have a place to stay, didn't have anything. There was a lady who had a soda fountain/coffee shop kind of place on U Street, which was the main street of the ghetto. She had an upright piano on the second floor, so Jelly Roll would play that piano and they'd sell beer to the people who would go up and see him and hang around while he played for them. He made a little money doing that and managed to get hold of an old Lincoln limousine, which he used to drive up to New York on the weekends for Sunday jam sessions at Nick's on 7th Avenue. Nick's was a jazz club and it featured Dixieland and New Orleans type of music. Although the personnel would change from week to week, Jelly Roll Morton's band at Nick's was always a fabulous band. It was mostly Big Sid Catlett on drums, Sidney Bechet or Albert Nicholas on clarinet, Sidney De Paris on trumpet, various trombonists, Pops Foster or Wellman Braud on bass. Braud was the original Ellington bass player and Foster played with Louis Armstrong. Danny Barker or Al Casey used to sit in on guitar. It was always one hell of a band.

"Then, of course, between numbers Jelly Roll would talk about how he invented jazz and taught all these guys to play – how he, bascially, was the origin of everything! The guys in the band would either laugh at Jelly Roll or get angry. Either way, laughing or cursing, Sunday jams at Nick's were some of the most incredible sessions I've ever heard.

The Blue Devils

Baby Dodds

"Nesuhi and I would go looking for old records by the great bands – Louis Armstrong and His Hot Five, King Oliver, Jelly Roll Morton, The Chocolate Dandies, McKinney's Cotton Pickers or The Blue Devils – all of these historic bands. Of course you couldn't find them anywhere. There were a couple of record shops that reissued them from time to time – like HRS, which stood for the Hot Record Society. It was on 7th Avenue and 54th Street, and was run by a man named Steve Smith. The other shop was the Commodore Music Store on 42nd Street, across the street from the Hotel Commodore. That was run by Milt Gabler, who later became the A & R head of Decca Records. In those days, however, he had this record shop on 42nd Street which he ran with his brother-in-law, Jack Crystal, whose son, Billy, became one of America's most successful comedians and comic actors. At the Commodore Music Store, Jack and Milt also sold cut-out records, but these were not cheap. The going price for rare Bessie Smith records could be as much as $3 or $4 for a single 78 rpm record which ordinarily would retail from 35¢ to 75¢.

Bunk Johnson

"There was always somebody who sold black music to black people. Sometimes it was a drug store that had a record department or it could be a grocery store or whatever, but there was always a place to buy black music. Nesuhi and I also used to go house to house, ring the bell and say to the people when they came to the door, 'Have you got any old records for sale?' They'd say, 'Oh, we've got a whole bunch of old records down in the basement.' They'd bring up these 78's, some of which would be fifteen, twenty years old, that they didn't know what to do with and didn't play any more. We used to buy almost everything they had because these collections were exactly what we were looking for and almost always contained some absolutely unique recordings – early Fats Waller, some wonderful blues records, as well as one or two Caruso or maybe Paul Whiteman records.

"We would also go looking for places which sold records to jukebox operators, which were like one-stops. They'd buy up 10,000 old records and put a sign up: 'Records For Sale, 5¢ Each'. So we'd go through all of those and find a Fletcher Henderson record, an early Duke Ellington or whatever, for 5¢ – the value of which would be $3 or $4, sometimes as much as $15." Ahmet

John Hammond

"John Hammond, whom I first met in 1939 or 1940, was an American aristocrat with leftist leanings, who from childhood had developed a great love of black music and culture. He recorded Bessie Smith's last session in 1932 and, I'm sure, was the first to push the record companies he had dealings with to record Billie Holiday, Ella Fitzgerald, Lionel Hampton, Teddy Wilson, and other great artists.

"In talking about John Hammond, I must mention George Avakian, who was also a great pioneer in recording jazz music in the early thirties. I remember one night in

George Avakian

Nesuhi and Ahmet

1941 or 1942 they both came to Washington to spend an evening listening to records with my brother and me. We had a lot of records they had never come across – all collectors had treasures others had been unable to find. We had a lot of the rare, rare recordings by Jelly Roll Morton and King Oliver. We played them some Frankie Teschemacher, some Boyce Brown and a lot of very rare blues records. One of these was called 'Tea Roller's Rub', which is about a man who rolls marijuana cigarettes. It was recorded in maybe 1928, was a big regional hit and was also a precursor to some of the rap music people have produced recently. Throughout the whole time George Avakian was there, I couldn't understand why he seemed to be so incredibly nervous. Finally he told me, 'You know why I'm so on edge? It's because I'm Armenian and if my father ever found out that I had come down to have dinner at the Turkish embassy, he would get extremely upset.'" Ahmet

"One of the most important things that John Hammond did was to organize the *Spirituals to Swing* concert at Carnegie Hall in 1938. He managed to co-ordinate an unprecedented presentation of black music. He brought in the Boogie Woogie Boys – that's what they used to call them, but they were great gentlemen. Albert Ammons, Meade Lux Lewis, and Pete Johnson, who was a great boogie woogie piano player, but also an incredible blues player. He brought in Benny Goodman's big swing band, and the Kansas City bands of Joe Turner and Count Basie. It was an historic concert.

"John himself was never commercially involved. In other words, he was actually slightly above working for a record company or getting paid for what was really a work of love. I don't think, however, that in today's terms he would run too much risk of being branded solely as a record producer. I remember on one occasion I was recording an artist in the adjoining studio to him. I popped over to see what was going on next door and he was recording Dinah Washington – actually she was singing and he was reading *The New York Times*. He did have a tremendous ear for talent and discovered so many important artists: Bob Dylan, Aretha Franklin, Phineas Newborn – I mean the list goes on and on. He was very much in the middle of all things jazz and a lot of pop as well. He was a wonderful person and a great friend and I certainly miss him. You know I really think John was probably the most important person in the development of jazz in America, in the sense that he not only understood the music, but was also able to champion the cause of black people in America. Mrs. Roosevelt tried to effect similar changes. Terrible as the situation still is today, I don't know how many young people appreciate quite how absurd the circumstances were just fifty years ago. When Benny Carter – who was an exile of sorts and a friend of my brother's in Paris – was forced by the war in Europe to return to the States, he formed a big band and started touring. One of the first dates they played was in Washington, so we invited him to have dinner the following night. 'What restaurant could we go to?!' The only place in the capital city of America at that time that would allow black and white people to sit together – and then only because of practical reasons that left no other choice – was the Union train station restaurant. It may sound funny now, but it wasn't funny then. It was very demeaning, and you know what, demeaning was something black people faced every day. So I think that it's not easy for white people to understand the rage that still exists.

John Hammond

"At that time, Nesuhi had been invited to give talks at a bookshop in Washington on the origins of jazz and blues. I still find it interesting that although a lot of white mainstream society have found black music threatening, women working in bordellos never have had that reaction. The number one favourite song of all strippers became 'Black And Tan Fantasy' by Duke Ellington. Even today, if you go into strip joints, you'll hear them play very earthy black music, which is what they like to dance to. Both Nesuhi and I saw that so much of what America had to offer came from, or quite simply was, black culture, and we were fascinated by its roots and development. For example, the story of how, in the mid-18th century, the vanquished French in Canada, the Acadians, were piled aboard horrifically overcrowded ships bound for the Southern states by the victorious British. Those who survived and migrated to New Orleans determined that light-skinned female slaves, although not suitable to marry, were certainly good enough to open up bordellos. As a result, a curious French influence was brought to bear on the music which, a century and a half later, was being played in the bordellos of New Orleans, and it was under those circumstances that artists such as Jelly Roll Morton, Louis Armstrong, and others learnt and discovered their musical style. This artform that developed has, of course, been the origin of so much else, that I think you could make a very good case for the argument that a lot of American culture has actually come out of the bordellos. It was after one of these talks by Nesuhi that a young guy came up to him from the audience and engaged him in such informed and absorbing conversation that they came back to the embassy to continue their discussions and listen to some more music. That was the first time that I met my business partner-to-be and good friend, Herb Abramson.

"Another great friend of ours from that time is William Gottlieb. Bill was then a journalist on *The Washington Post* and another avid fan of this wonderful music. One night Bob Crosby was playing at the Capitol, Washington's white venue, and Count Basie's band was playing the Howard, Washington's black theatre. So our friend Bill Gottlieb asked the owner of the Howard if Crosby could fall by after his show at the Capitol and join Basie onstage. The owner said, 'Sure – of course!' Then he went over to Crosby, who loved the idea, and announced it to his audience. Crosby came right over that night and it was one hell of a session, to a packed audience of black and white fans." Ahmet

The Count Basie and Bob Crosby Bands join forces at the Capitol Theatre in Washington, D.C. From left: Count Basie, Ray Bauduc (Bob Crosby's drummer) playing Jo Jones's drums, Herschel Evans (sax) and Bob Haggart (bass)

Big Joe Turner performing at the first Washington concert staged by Nesuhi and Ahmet

"As Nesuhi and I had become friends with Duke Ellington, Lena Horne and Jelly Roll Morton, we decided to put on the first integrated concert in Washington. We had black and white musicians onstage, people like Sidney Bechet, Joe Turner, Pete Johnson, Pee Wee Russell, and others – and also we had an integrated audience. We had a lot of trouble finding a place in Washington where we could stage this event. The first concert we held was at the Jewish community centre, which was the only place that would allow a mixed audience and a mixed band. After that the National Press Club broke down and let us use their auditorium. Leadbelly used to come to some of our jam sessions at the embassy and he sang at the first concert we gave at the National Press Club. When he peeked out from the wings backstage and saw the size of the crowd, he said, 'Man, you gotta give me double the price, otherwise I'm not going on.' So of course we did – we gave him everything we could, and you know, we certainly weren't pretending to be experienced promoters, we were just doing it for the love of the music."
Ahmet

Washington concert poster

Bunk Johnson and Leadbelly performing at the first concert staged by Nesuhi and Ahmet at the National Press Club, Washington D.C.

From left: J.C. Higginbotham, Art Hodes, Henry 'Red' Allen and Mezz Mezzrow on stage at the first Washington concert organized by Ahmet and Nesuhi

"In 1943, when I was 19 or so years old, I went to a nightclub in the northeast black ghetto section of Washington and heard a singer whose name was Little Miss Cornshucks and I thought, 'My God!!!' She was better than anything I'd ever heard. She would come out like a country girl with a bandana around her head, a basket in her hand, and so forth, which she'd set aside fairly early on into the show. She could sing the blues better than anybody I've ever heard to this day. I asked her that night if she would mind if I made a record of her for myself. So we went to what probably was at that time the only recording studio in Washington. This was the first time that I had ever been to a recording studio. I got the saxophone player from the club where she was singing – a tenor man from Kansas City – and also the piano player, whose name, I believe, was Johnny Malachi, who later made some records. We cut 'Kansas City' along with some other blues and she also sang a song called 'So Long'. She had such a wonderful sound and I remember just thinking, 'My God! My God!' And I didn't have a record company, I just made those records for myself.

"I loved that experience, and then that same year I met Boyd Raeburn. He had an avant-garde Stan Kenton type of big band, which made several records – 'Boyd Meets Stravinsky', that sort of thing. He also had a beautiful wife whose name was Ginnie Powell. Ginnie and I became great friends and she suggested, 'You know, you should make some records with me and the band.' So I had no record company or anything, but at the same time I met a young guy by the name of Bob Clark. I was in a record store when this character breezed in and told the owner that he wanted one of everything. I thought, 'Are you crazy?' I mean, I'd never heard of such a thing. I asked him, 'Don't you care what kind of music it is?' He replied, 'No, I just want one of everything.' So they sold him one of everything they had in stock, which was about four or five thousand records. He was the son of a man who owned a chain of hotels, and I became friends with this crazy guy who also wanted to be in the record business, but also had no idea about anything. So I mentioned that I had this great orchestra and he put up $3,000 or $4,000. We went into a recording studio in New York and recorded the Boyd Raeburn Band with Ginnie Powell singing on all of the sides. I took the demo record I had made to my friend John Hammond, who at the time was working with Mitch Miller at Mercury Records. When I played it for them, John and Mitch said, 'My God – that is terrific – did you produce that? Why don't you come and work for us?' I said, 'Thank you very much, but I don't want a job, I just want a distributor.' Somehow we never did get a distributor. In the meantime, Bob Clark had become friends with Boyd Raeburn, who wasn't getting too many bookings – life was tough and the band wasn't getting paid. They were living in the Forrest Hotel, a dumpy little place in Times Square. So Boyd Raeburn said to this guy Clark, 'What do you need this Ahmet character for? You put up the money and we'll do this together.' So they came to me and said they wanted to go into business with each other and I said, 'Fine. That's okay with me.' I gave them the masters and I was out of it. Needless to say it didn't go very far, because in all probability Clark's father stepped in. I don't know what happened, but the records were never released. Then maybe two years after we started Atlantic, Boyd Raeburn called up – he still had the masters, so we made a deal and released them."
Ahmet

Boyd Raeburn

Ginnie Powell

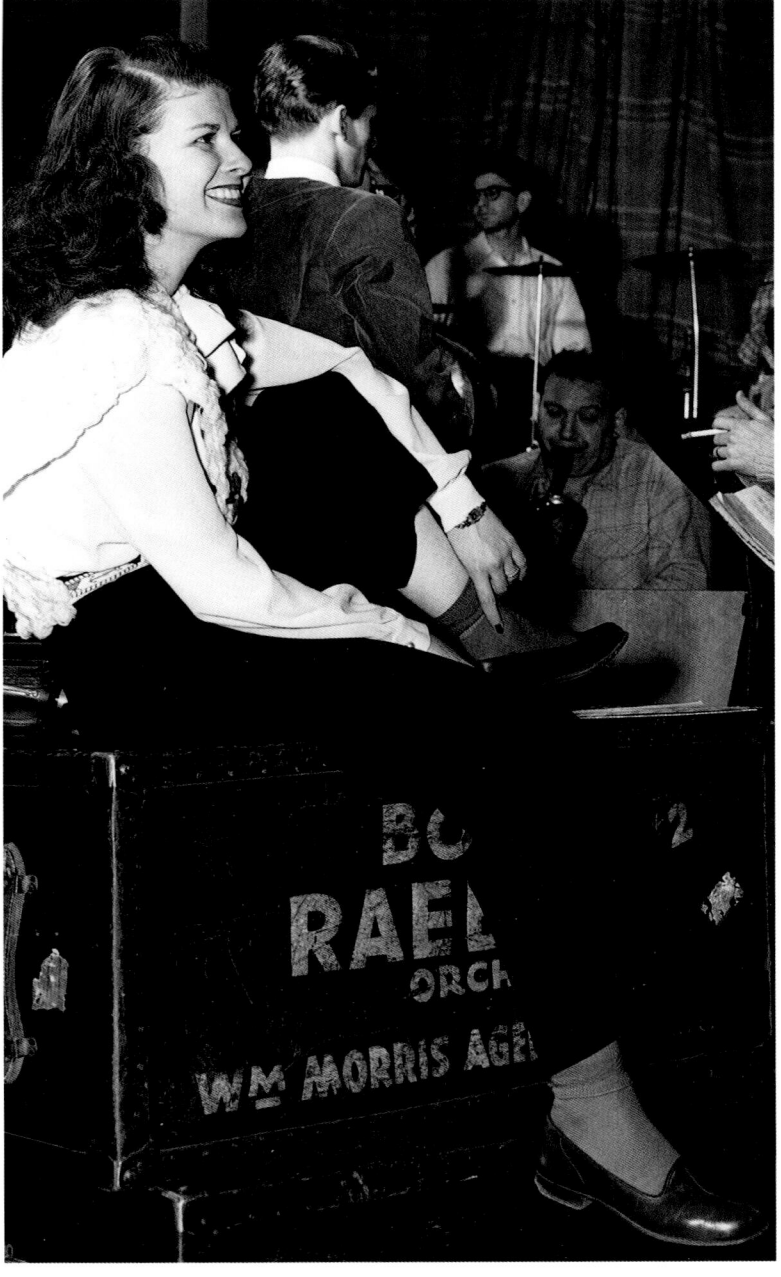

Opposite: Little Miss Cornshucks

Mezz Mezzrow

"Mezz Mezzrow was a great friend of ours, he was a character. They used to call grass 'The Mezz' after him – he smoked marijuana, purveyed it for people and gave it to a lot of other musicians. I once asked Lionel Hampton, 'Why did you have him on that date?' And Lionel said, 'Man! He brought the shit!'

"Mezzrow wanted to live a totally hip black life; to us everything black was hip and everything white was square. That's how most jazz musicians felt – even in the South, during the days of segregation.

"Mezz played the saxophone better than he played the clarinet, which had a shrieking kind of tone, but he was still the favourite of a lot of critics. Hugues Panassie, a French jazz critic who wrote the first serious book on jazz, didn't like any of the white players except Mezzrow."
Ahmet

From left: Billy Taylor, Bill Gottlieb, Sylvia Syms and Ahmet

Lester Young

From left: Ahmet, Rudi Blesh, Dizzy Gillespie, Mr. and Mrs. Jorge Guinle, Charlie Parker

Norman Granz

"All the kids wanted to do was act, walk and talk like the hip musicians they idolized. Suddenly, all over every American city, white saxophone players were holding their saxophones sideways like Prez. Every city had three or four guys who played like Lester Young. Prez was the epitome of cool. We didn't call it that in those days, but that's what he was. He was natural. He wasn't trying to be hip. It became hip because he was doing it." Ahmet

Marili Morden, Jimmie Noone and Nesuhi in Los Angeles, 1943

"Around the end of 1943, Nesuhi had met and married a girl named Marili Morden, who lived in California. She owned a specialty record store in Los Angeles called the Jazzman Record Shop, so he spent an increasing amount of time on the West Coast, discovering and promoting the music which they both shared such a passion for, New Orleans jazz. Nesuhi would tell the story of how, in 1944, Orson Welles, who at that time had a coast-to-coast radio show, called him up and told him that he wanted to have a real New Orleans band on his show. So Marili and Nesuhi thought, fantastic, here was a chance to get more exposure for the music that they loved. They convinced Kid Ory, who had been working at the post office, to make a comeback. They got the clarinettist Jimmie Noone,

Mutt Carey

who had been playing with his group on Hollywood Boulevard; Mutt Carey on trumpet, who had been working as a porter on the railroad; Zutty Singleton on drums; and Ed Garland on bass. So Kid Ory arranged for this new band to meet up at the CBS studios to rehearse. Some of the guys hadn't seen each other since they'd all been in New Orleans in 1918. They all fell into each other's arms and then they said, 'What do we play?' Someone said, 'How about "High Society"?' So Noone went into that chorus solo, they played a little and then the big man, Welles, came into the studio and Nesuhi took him around to each of the guys in the band to introduce him. They got to Kid Ory and Nesuhi said, 'This is Kid Ory.' Kid looked at Welles and said to Nesuhi, 'What was that name again?' Nesuhi thought, 'Oh my God, he's gonna get us all thrown out.' So he enunciated very clearly, 'Or-son Welles.' And Kid said, 'Oh yeah sure, I've heard of you.' But Orson was great, he liked the band and fixed for them to go on the show. They scored a triumph, mail started to pour in and Welles said, 'I want to keep them on, I've got about thirteen weeks to go, can you arrange it?' Nesuhi said, 'Sure.' So they played for three weeks. A couple of days before they were due to start the fourth week, Jimmie Noone got up one morning, was shaving in his bathroom, when he collapsed and died; that was in April 1944.

"So Nesuhi called up Orson and told him he couldn't have a band for the show that night because Jimmie Noone had died. Orson called back a little later and said he wanted to do a tribute that night to Noone; that if Nesuhi could find another clarinet player and bring in the band, they would do something. Nesuhi called in Wade Wailey, a player of much less ability than Jimmie, but the best he could find on that day. Of course the band was very depressed, but Orson asked Nesuhi to tell him all he knew about Jimmie Noone – where he was born, how he started, who he played with, that kind of thing; Orson didn't take any notes, just listened. Then that night he went on the air with no script, but talked about Jimmie Noone. It was one of the most moving things that anyone could hear in their life. When Orson finished, Nesuhi was in tears, the band was in tears and then he said, 'Now we're going to play the blues, for Jimmie.' And the band played beautifully."
Ahmet

Opposite: The Kid Ory Band appearing on the Orson Welles radio show, Los Angeles, 1944 – From left: Ed Garland (bass), Buster Wilson (piano), Marili Morden, Jimmie Noone (clarinet), Mutt Carey (trumpet), Zutty Singleton (drums) Kid Ory (trombone), and Bud Scott (guitar)

From left: Duke Ellington with Max Silverman at the Quality Music Store, Washington

"Toward the end of 1944, my father died and was buried at Arlington National Cemetery. In 1946, Harry Truman decided that his body should be taken back 'in state' to Turkey through recently liberated waters aboard the USS Missouri, the battleship upon which the official Japanese surrender had taken place several months earlier. This voyage therefore became a further focal point of the Allies' victorious achievements. An old friend of mine, Leyla Umar, now a distinguished and much-lauded journalist in Turkey, remembers the day that the USS Missouri arrived at the port of Istanbul. The docks were festooned with flowers, thousands of people had turned out holding up banners in support of the Allies and the new leadership of Turkey. Leyla was at that time 15 years old and, along with her classmates, had been granted special dispensation by the nuns, who ran the convent school she attended, to race down to the port and join in the festivities to celebrate the safe and joyous arrival of this special convoy.

"My family returned to Turkey soon after this and Nesuhi and I were left with a straight choice; also return to Turkey to finish our studies, become lawyers and enter the diplomatic corps as was traditional in our family, or remain in America and pretty much support ourselves. Nesuhi had been forced by the outbreak of war to abandon his studies for a Ph.D. in Philosophy at the Sorbonne and now felt very strongly that he wanted to remain in America. I was still working on my master's degree at Georgetown University. Having lived in embassies all my life, I had now moved in to occupy a tiny apartment on a very small student's allowance. No more chauffeured cars, servants, cooks and per diem, so I thought that I should get a job as well. I'd never worked a day in my life, but Eugene Meyer, then owner of *The Washington Post*, offered me a job as a cub reporter, and other friends of my father's offered me positions on Wall Street, but I was really not interested. So I decided that what I did want to do was make records, because that's what I knew about. I thought it would be fun and I could make some money on the side. Just a temporary thing to help put myself through college, before returning to Turkey as expected." Ahmet

"While Nesuhi and I were searching around for rare records, we'd stumbled upon a radio repair shop on 7th and T, right in the heart of the black section. It was called the Quality Radio Repair Shop. It sold new radios, used radios, and repaired radios. Then in the back they had records for sale at 10¢ each, three for a quarter. The shop was owned by Max Silverman, who later described in an interview how he would witness this limousine pulling up and two young men jumping out wearing camel's hair overcoats, all dressed up in a natty way, intent on going through all the records in the shop. Max said he knew that every record we were buying was worth a lot more than we were paying, but he didn't know which ones were worth what and so he couldn't stop us raiding his stock.

"Then one day Max found out that there was this book called *The Hot Discography*, written in 1934 by the son of the painters Sonia and Robert Delaunay, the originators of the Orphism school of painting.

The George Lewis Band, from left: Percy Humphrey, George Lewis and Bill Mathews, at the Paddock Club, New Orleans

Max eventually got hold of a copy of this publication, only to discover after much study that it was still impossible to deduce from this book which record was worth what. We, of course, were doing this all the time, so we got to know very well what was rare and what wasn't. Max soon began to phase out the radio repair business to concentrate more on records. Before too long, he changed the name to the Quality Music Shop and it became a pure record store with a very good jazz department where you could always get the latest releases.

"I was still attending graduate school at Georgetown and in the evenings I would go to Waxie Maxie's, which had become Max Silverman's nickname. The name of his shop had also changed from Quality Music to Waxie Maxie. It was around this time that Max had gone out of the used record business and into the new record business. One of his first hits was 'I Wonder' by a certain Private Cecil Gant. It was pressed on cardboard, with a little lamination on top. As this record was a big hit and you couldn't get it anywhere else, Max was selling his copies for $1.25, while the big pop numbers were selling for 75¢. Max also developed a radio programme, so all the independent record company owners used to come by the shop to make deals with him, including giving him free records in order to get their new songs on the air. I was down there practically every evening and the record shop now stayed open until midnight. Around 11 o'clock sometimes we'd close up and go catch the end of the last show at the Howard Theatre, just around the corner from the store. Then we used to hang out with whichever artists were there and we'd go to after-hours clubs, one thing and another. Max's wife was ready to divorce him because he didn't get home until 4 o'clock every morning.

"So Max and I became very good friends, and in going to the store every evening, I was also really learning about the music business. We began to understand what people were buying and why they were buying it. You could see how some numbers would come in and run out right away. We'd have only fifty copies of a certain record and there'd be hundreds of people coming in looking for it, so Max would be on the 'phone, screaming at the distributor to send him 5,000 more copies. There were really only three majors at that time: RCA-Victor, Columbia and Decca. They only pressed the top artists, who were mostly all mainstream pop singers. Coleman Hawkins had a minor hit with the song 'Body and Soul'. There was a shop called the Rainbow Music Store across the street from the Apollo, and because they couldn't get hold of this record, they re-recorded the song with Coleman Hawkins, but then discovered that he didn't have the right to do that. So they called the piece a new composition, titled it 'Rainbow Mist', and suddenly they were in the record business. And in fact, the record sold very well. So by the end of the war a great explosion was happening, made up of wonderful artists wanting to get their work onto record. And there was a whole network of newly formed, small, independent record companies providing the opportunity that the war and the policy of the major companies had denied to this wealth of talent. Most of these companies were located in Los Angeles and New York, such as Swingtime Records in L.A., owned by Jack Lauderdale, who first recorded Ray Charles. There were others around the country like Dot Records in Tennessee, owned by Randy Woods and King Records in Cincinnati, run by Syd Nathan. Several of these independent record companies were black-owned. Otis and Leon Rene had a company in California called Exclusive, Peacock was out of Houston, and Vee-Jay Records, for example, was in Chicago." Ahmet

Ernie Fields and members of his Orchestra, from left: Elton Watkins, Leroy 'Tex' Cooper, Ernie Fields, Butch Lockett, Robert Brooks and Al Duncan

Minton's Playhouse, Harlem, 1947. From left: Thelonious Monk, Howard McGhee, Roy Eldridge and Teddy Hill

"By that point, a great network of independent record producers had been established pretty much throughout the whole country. I also met a lot of the independent record company owners, some of whom were ex-jukebox operators. I remember on one occasion some people took over wasteland in Pittsburgh, Pennsylvania as settlement for a debt. Someone discovered that on this desolate landscape there was a record pressing plant. So it was decided, 'Hey, let's make some records.' Some of these new owners had nightclubs in the black sections, like the Chess brothers who ran a black nightclub in Chicago. I began to realize that a large number of owners, however, didn't know anything about the music. They couldn't tell a trumpet from a saxophone. I felt that I knew what black life was in America, what black music was in America, black roots, gospel music, black blues from the Delta to Chicago, Texas blues that went to the West Coast. I was struck by the fact that so many of these owners seemed to be accidentally in the record business because there was a void and a need for that void to be filled. They were just recording whatever came along or else they'd hire somebody who knew a little something. Very few of these people, however, seemed to know too much about: a) the musicians; b) the music; or c) the taste of the public. So it occurred to me that I probably could do better and that this was a business that I could really get into.

"By 1946, Herb Abramson and I had been friends for some time and he was already working part-time at National Records as head of A & R, while studying dentistry at New York University on a grant from the Army. At National, Herb had already been recording Billy Eckstine, the Ravens and Joe Turner, among others, but also wanted to have his own company – so we thought that maybe we should start a record label together. We didn't have the finances, so we finally talked Waxie Maxie into backing us to start two labels, one called Jubilee and the other Quality. We thought we would do gospel on Jubilee and that Quality was going to be a jazz and R & B label. We made a recording of Sister Ernestine Washington, who was a gospel singer and sang at various New Jersey churches. We recorded her with Bunk Johnson's New Orleans band, which had George Lewis on clarinet. Bunk Johnson was a legendary New Orleans trumpet player who was supposed to have been one of the teachers of Louis Armstrong. He had a great following, played very archaic music, but was well known for a gospel style. We also recorded a regional black orchestra called Ernie Fields and his Orchestra, that had a fairly popular singer.

"We cut four sides in total I think, put out a couple of records, which of course didn't sell at all. Max Silverman, our financial supporter, decided that he didn't want to carry on in the record business with Herb and myself. In fact, Herb kept the Jubilee label open and sold it soon after that to Jerry Blaine, an independent record distributor in New York, who took it on and made it a lot more successful." Ahmet

Lionel Hampton

Gladys and Lionel Hampton

"Meanwhile, I was still intent on starting my own label. I'd known Lionel Hampton for some time and managed to persuade him to provide the financing to start another record company. The total of the investment that I thought I needed had steadily decreased, but he had agreed to an amount of, I think, $15,000. I had told him that I had to start a record company and he'd said, 'Man, don't worry, we'll pull it together, I'll get you the money.' We decided on the name Hamp-Tone Records. Next we had to go and see Lionel's wife, Gladys, who was the equivalent of the bank. She held all of Lionel's money, and if anything, looked after him a little too tightly. As a result, however, Lionel is rich today, but Gladys was always a very tough lady. She had a boyfriend who was a saxophone player, the only white guy in Hampton's band. So Gladys and this white saxophone player used to share the star dressing room while Hampton would be in a small room next door. We went to the New York theatre he was playing in that week to settle the final details of the deal. He walked up to the dressing room with the big star on the door, knocked and went in while I waited outside in the corridor. It quickly became apparent that the walls in this particular theatre must have been extremely thin, because I soon began to hear raised voices, mainly Lionel's wife screaming, 'You're what?! You're going to give this kid how much?! You're going to give our money to this little jerk who's never worked a day in his life?!' So that was the end of that. Not so long ago Lionel came to see me, walked around the Atlantic offices and said, 'To think – all of this could have been mine.'" Ahmet

"When Nesuhi and I made our respective decisions to stay in America, we had sold pretty much our entire collection of some 15,000 records in order to help supplement the very small allowance we were still getting from our family. By this time, in 1947, those funds had run out and I was spending more and more time in New York. I was still determined to start my own company and knew that Herb was the perfect person to go into partnership with. He agreed to sell his share in Jubilee Records to Jerry Blaine in order to be able to put up $2,500, but I could not convince anyone else I knew, or any of my father's friends, to invest in me. They all knew my background and refused to show any confidence whatsoever in my ever being able to run any kind of business. Finally, in desperation, I turned to my dentist, Dr. Vahdi Sabit, who actually fell for the line that I was peddling at the time, which was something like, 'If we could only sell one record to each record shop … ' He turned out to be a gambler and mortgaged his house in order to put up the $10,000 that we needed, became a partner with Herb and myself, and we started recording in 1947.

"The name Atlantic was probably about our eightieth choice, because every name we came up with – Horizon, Blue Moods, all kinds of names like that – had already been taken. We'd call the union and the union would say, 'We already have a record company registered by that name.' I'd heard of a label that called themselves Pacific Jazz at that time. So in desperation, I said, 'Look, they call themselves Pacific, let's call ourselves Atlantic.' That's how that happened. It wasn't a name we were crazy about – it was so generic. There are so many Atlantics, A&P and all of that, but finally we said, who cares what we call it? So then as soon as we had set up, we discovered that the American Federation of Musicians had declared that there was going to be a one year all-out strike beginning the 1st of January, 1948. Caesar Petrillo, a very tough guy from Chicago, the tsar of the union at that time, had decided that there would be no further recording with union musicians. This meant that there would be no recording at all, because the union would not give a licence to anyone who would record non-union musicians. So we decided that for the remainder of '47, all we would do was make recordings in order to be able to have enough music to release in 1948. We thought the majors would take their artists to Europe and record there, but of course we couldn't afford to do that. The first tracks that Atlantic recorded were cut on November 21st 1947, and were by a group called The Harlemaires. We began the session with a song entitled 'The Rose Of The Rio Grande.'" Ahmet

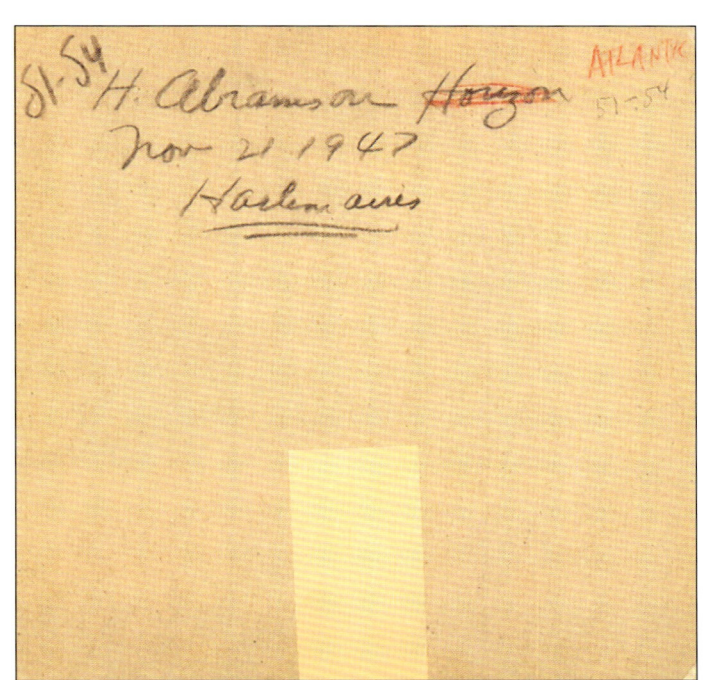

'The Rose Of The Rio Grande', by the Harlemaires

The Harlemaires, featuring Billy Butler on guitar and Chester Slater on piano TL: 40s

Opposite: Herb Abramson

From left: Lionel Hampton and Joe Morris

From left: Sir Charles Thompson (piano), Tiny Grimes (guitar) and Red Prysock (saxophone)

"Our headquarters were in a broken-down hotel on 56th Street, between Sixth and Broadway, called the Jefferson, which was condemned as unsafe soon after we moved in. I had rented a tiny suite on the ground floor, slept in the bedroom, and the living room was the Atlantic office. I had a cousin who was a Turkish poet named Sadi Koylan. He used to hang out in Greenwich Village with a lot of the intellectuals of the day. He was a great poet, a radical person and terrific guy. At that time he had a room in some little flophouse, so to save the rent on that, he moved in with me because we could fit two beds into my room. He lived with me for quite a few years because he was like a brother to me. He published in Turkey and used to write only in Turkish, so of course there wasn't much call for that in New York. So in this atmosphere Atlantic was born. That first set-up was incredible. People like Rudy Toombs and Doc Pomus used to come by and audition their songs. We used studios like WOR, Belltone and Apex. We would go in, set up, work with the various engineers, and in this way between the 21st of November and 29th of December we recorded 65 tracks. We were grabbing at straws because of the threat of the coming strike and we recorded lots of semi-names, unknown artists. Our first releases, in 1948, were four singles by Tiny Grimes, Eddie Safranski, Joe Morris and Melrose Colbert. We'd found a trumpet player who had been with the Lionel Hampton band, named Joe Morris, and his partner was Johnny Griffin. The Joe Morris Band featuring Johnny Griffin was a little bebop band, but we had them do some funky kind of blues things, too. We also released 'Lowe Groovin'' in 1948, named for the Washington DJ, Jackson Lowe. He played it quite a bit, and Waxie Maxie helped us a lot, too, by playing our records on the radio show sponsored by his Quality Music Shop. Critics have said that this and other stuff that we produced at that time didn't fit into jazz, bop, or even race categories – that it represented the first tentative steps toward an easily identified R & B sound. We were just trying to create our own mix of music that we enjoyed.

"Tiny Grimes had this terrific little quintet. The first records, like 'That Old Black Magic', were made with John Hardee, the great jazz tenor man. He was replaced by Red Prysock, who played in a very swinging, less jazz, more funk style. With Grimes and Prysock, we cut tracks like 'Annie Laurie' and 'Midnight Special'.

"Eddie Safranski was the bass player with Stan Kenton's orchestra. We made a record with him and all the jazz stars who were in Kenton's band at that time. We called them the Poll Cats because they had all just been winners of the *Down Beat* poll." Ahmet

Joe Morris (left), Ahmet with Oscar Pettiford (right) and friend

Opposite: Eddie Safranski TL:40s

The Willie Bryant Band, Savoy Ballroom, New York

"At the first concerts Nesuhi and I staged in Washington, we hired Willie Bryant to be the MC. They used to call him the 'Mayor of Harlem'. He was a tall, very light-skinned, good-looking man. He had been onstage as a young teenager in a Broadway play titled *Mamba's Daughters*, starring Ethel Waters, which was one of the first important black musicals. That was in the early 1930s, but after its great success he couldn't get another part. Although he himself was not a musician, he became a swing band leader, because that was about the only thing a black performer could do during that era. He used to do an imitation of Cab Calloway, and although the band made quite a few records, they did not become very famous. As the war started up and so many people were drafted, kids began playing in small bands. The swing era was virtually over and the R & B craze had started. Race records moved out of the back of the record shop and came up front, and new stars were developed like Dinah Washington and Billie Holiday. A different era had begun, featuring smaller bands. Bebop had emerged and Willie Bryant couldn't be a bandleader anymore. So having been a hit actor and more or less a hit bandleader, he became the MC at the Apollo Theatre, a gig he shared with Ralph Cooper. The next thing that happened was that records became really hot. At least in part because of the upturn in the economy due to the war, a lot of records were selling in very large quantities to black audiences. Due to the lack of shellac during the war years, the majors had virtually stopped making any hillbilly or race records. Towards the end of the war, therefore, a wide range of tiny independent record companies opened up across the country, providing the specialized and new forms of music that so many people wanted to hear. Disc jockeys became an extremely important link in the growth and distribution of this music. So Willie Bryant naturally became a disc jockey, forming a team with a white announcer by the name of Ray Carroll. Together they pioneered a very successful show called Willie and Ray – they played jazz and rhythm and blues. Along with another extremely popular DJ, Symphony Sid they really became the kings of radio until Alan Freed moved in – but that was quite a bit later.

From left: Willie Bryant, Mahalia Jackson and Ray Carroll, New York

"Their gopher was a man called Jack Walker. Jack had been well-educated, was extremely well-spoken, highly intelligent and did many different things. Willie and Ray would do their shows at night, and Jack used to bring records in for them to play, go out and get coffee and sandwiches, and eventually became a disc jockey in his own right. They used to call him 'Jumbo' Jack Walker, and at one point a little later in our story, I even hired him to be the director of publicity at Atlantic Records for a while. He also used to edit *Out World* magazine, which was started in competition with *Ebony*. He was a wonderful character who was tragically the victim of a pointless random killing. The radio station which he broadcast from was in Harlem, and one night this psycho came in off the street and just shot him dead. It was Jack who had told me, when things started to change in Harlem, 'Ahmet, don't hang around Harlem anymore, 'cause they're wild – they can't tell friends from foes. If they see a white face they'll kill you.' And that was the end of my life in Harlem. But back in '44 and certainly for some time after that, I used to spend half my life up there. One night, after Jack had finished his show at the Palm Cafe, where I used to go to eat spaghetti, he said, 'Listen, there's a new rib joint up the street, let's go get some ribs.' It had been opened by Sidney Poitier who'd made one film, then hadn't got any other parts. He'd come to New

The Apollo, Harlem

York to try to get into something, and I guess nothing was going on, so he opened this rib joint. It was a tiny place, like a small tunnel, and Sidney was behind the counter. We were sitting there eating, when a comedy-type couple came in, a tiny man and a big fat woman. As he walked in the door, the man said, 'My God, look, that's Sidney Poitier, the famous movie actor.' So the woman said, 'Shit, if he's an actor, how come he ain't in Hollywood?'

When Prince Michael of Greece came to America, he wanted to go to Harlem. I called up Jack and he arranged to have a couple of off-duty cops come along, and we all went and had dinner at one of the restaurants uptown. Then we went to Small's, to Baby Grand, to all the clubs and had one hell of a night. That was one of the last things I did with Jack.

"Now about Jesse Stone. Jesse had been in the business for many years with his own big band in Kansas City. Then he came off the road and settled in New York in the forties. He worked the Apollo, and wrote all kinds of songs for artists and orchestras, including 'Idaho' and 'Sorghum Switch', which was a hit for Jimmy Dorsey. RCA signed him up to do something like Louis Jordan was doing for Decca. After that, he signed to MGM, but still did some freelance arranging – which was how he'd met Herb Abramson at National Records. We offered Jesse a contract, but he didn't want it. He wanted to keep doing what he was doing and remain freelance. He wrote many wonderful songs and also became one of our musical arrangers, along with Leroy Lovett and Howard Biggs, who also made several hits for us. As well as all of the success that we achieved with Jesse, he also helped us complete one after another of the many records we made at that time which did not sell at all." Ahmet

'Jumbo' Jack Walker

Jesse Stone

Melrose Colbert

"We recorded Melrose Colbert who had been singing with the Earl Hines orchestra. We made some records with her and then, oddly enough, she went to Chicago and made exactly the same records on Aristocrat, which was a Chess label. So the first argument we had with anybody was with Leonard Chess as to how we can have the same songs by the same singer on two different labels. None of them ever sold, so in fact it was an argument about nothing.

"One time I'd got on the plane to go to L.A. and just before takeoff, the last passenger who got on sat next to me and it was Erroll Garner. We hugged one another and started talking about this and that. There were these two guys dressed in business suits with briefcases – they looked like stockbrokers – sitting across the aisle from us. So once we were up in the air one of these guys came over and said to Erroll, 'Excuse me, sir, I don't mean to interrupt your conversation, but if you don't mind I would just like to shake your hand and thank you for all of the wonderful, wonderful hours of great pleasure you've given to so many people with your beautiful music.' So Erroll said, 'Oh man, this is great, thank you.' Then the guy said, 'Do you mind, my friend is also a great music lover and would love to come over and say hello to you. Can I ask him?' Erroll said, 'Sure.' So the guy says, 'Jim, come over, shake hands with Oscar Peterson.' Erroll turned to me and said, 'What should I do?' I said, 'Shake the man's hand, Oscar.'" Ahmet

Erroll Garner TL: 40s

Overleaf: 52nd Street, New York

TONY'S Jimmy RYAN'S BAR LEON & EDDIE'S
ONYX
HARRY the HIPSTER

Frank 'Floorshow' Culley, later known as Frank 'Coleslaw' Culley TL: 40s, 50s

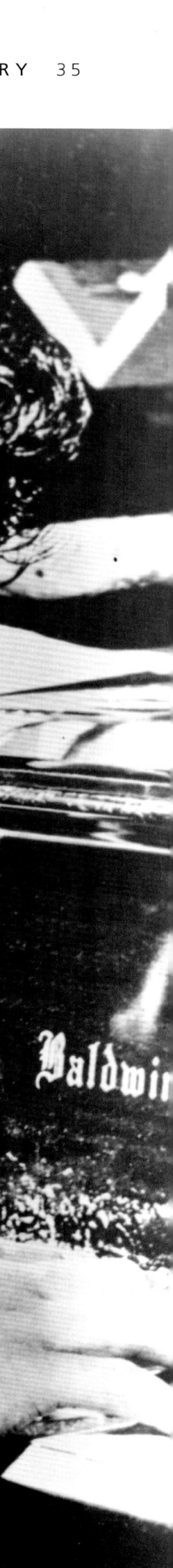

Amos Milburn TL: 40s

Joe Morris TL: 40s 50s

"When I first started the label, I thought we'd make records for two or three years and that would be it. We did it for one main reason – we wanted to make the kind of records that we would want to buy. First and foremost, we were having great fun, and we never imagined that we would be able to make a real living out of doing what we loved so much. I realized right away, though, that there were two important things: one, making a great record; two, getting it played on the radio. If you could do that, you could figure out the rest. Some of our records were selling a little bit and I was amazed that we were somehow not going bankrupt straightaway. Then we also realized that although you couldn't record in America because of the strike, people were recording in 'Europe', but Europe turned out to be New Jersey. All the musicians would come up and say, 'Look – we know there is a strike, but nobody has to know – we'll go and make records anytime you want and we'll record for half scale.' We were very lucky that we were able to survive. We were one of the last independents to come into the picture, so a distribution network had already been set up, ready-made for us to plug into. Even so, the competition was very tough and we'd spend hours on the telephone selling records to our distributors, then go to see disc jockeys to try to get our records on the air. I got thrown out of so many stations!" Ahmet

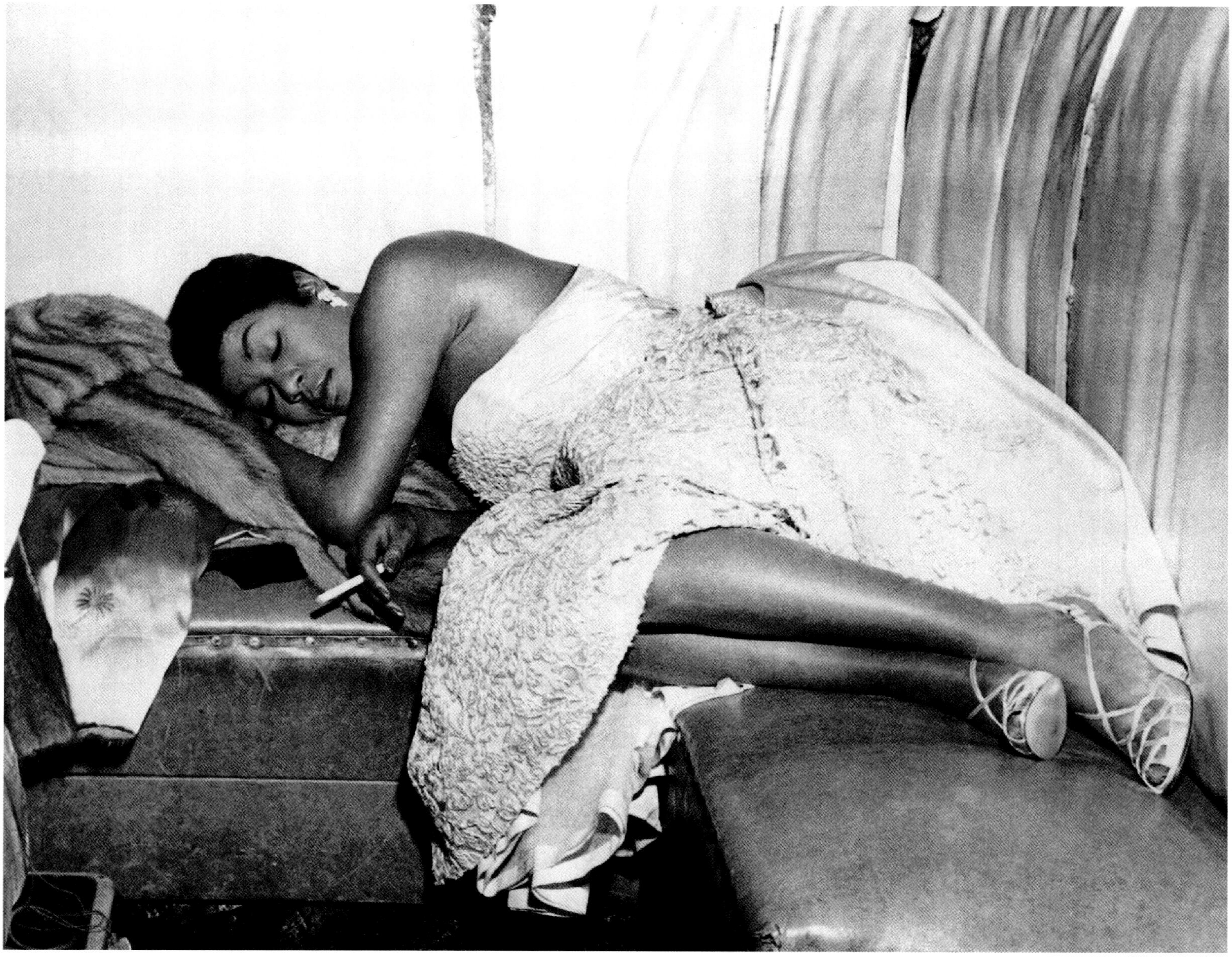

"Sarah Vaughan was of course one of the greatest jazz singers of all time. We were not able to sign her at the time but she did give us some tracks that we were finally able to release in the early 50's.

"Eventually the date arrived when the Hotel Jefferson was to be officially condemned and we were cleared out. We moved to a tenement building on 8th Avenue and 54th Street, the same block as Stillman's Gym, which was the place where all the boxers trained. We were very short on help. There was just Herb, Herb's wife Miriam, and me. Occasionally, if we had a particularly heavy box of records to send out, we would give one of the less successful heavyweight fighters a dollar to come and carry our shipment to the local post office. At that time, I frequented an Armenian restaurant called Izmir on Lexington Avenue around 23rd Street. It was run by this wonderful lady from Istanbul named Mrs. Hovakimian, who was a great cook. She would let students and other young people eat on credit until they managed to get the money together to pay her. She had a son nicknamed Blackie, who had shortened his surname to Hovak. His only interest seemed to be music, and he would sit at the cash register reading *Down Beat*. His mother begged me to give him a job, so I hired him as our first stockroom clerk. Blackie was a really handsome young guy, always looking very sharp, and super cool. He was interested in Latin music and jazz, and he knew about all the mambo bands in East Harlem. So he would go uptown with me, and we'd go to clubs, where he was well-known and was a great help with the music and the musicians. On Fridays, Blackie would go to the bank with me when I cashed the cheques for everybody's salary. One day, we were walking back from the bank when I dropped a 50¢ coin, which fell under the tyre of a parked car. I was leaning down to pick it up when Blackie said, 'Man, why are you doing that? That's so square; you look so bad going down onto the dirt like that – just leave the money.' I said, 'Are you crazy? That's half a dollar; you could get lunch for half a dollar!' So I picked up the coin, while Blackie kept complaining, 'That is so uncool, so uncool.'

"Then, a couple of days later, he drove up in a Cadillac Eldorado convertible. Now, we were paying him something like fifteen dollars a week, so I said, 'Where'd you get the car?' He said, 'That's my short, man.' They used to call a car 'the short'. So I asked him again, 'Where'd you get it?' He took me aside where we couldn't be overheard and said, 'Let me tell you something, man. Do you think I'd be working here, packing records and all this shit, if it weren't for my mother? I've got other shit going.' I said, 'What other shit?' He said, 'Man, I've got fifty chicks working for me.' I said, 'Fifty chicks!' He said, 'Yeah, that's right … don't tell my mother about the car!'" Ahmet

Above: Sarah Vaughan TL: 50s and right, Johnny Griffin TL: 40s 50s 60s

Al Hibbler TL: 50s

"Al Hibbler made a great many hits for Atlantic. He was a blind singer with Duke Ellington's orchestra when we signed him up. Before I signed him I went to see Duke, whom I had known since I was twelve or thirteen years old. I said, 'Duke, I know he's your band's singer, but do you mind if we record him as a solo artist?' He said, 'Oh no, that's okay, you can do that, that's fine – but let me just warn you about one thing – if Al Hibbler could see, he'd be a train robber!' Anyway, Al was a wonderful man, very, very hip and even though he sang in this funky R & B style his taste ran to jazz." Ahmet

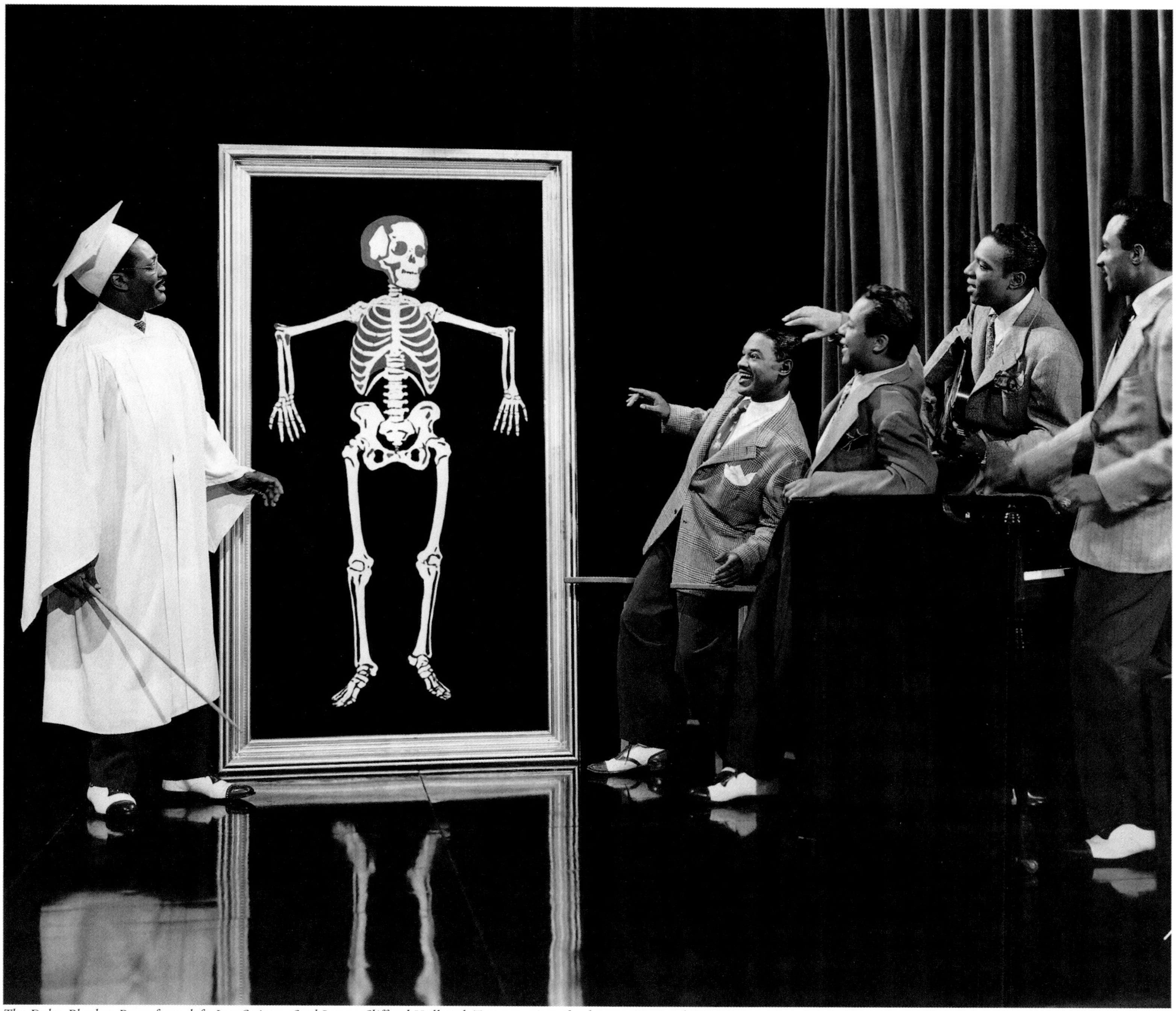

The Delta Rhythm Boys, from left: Lee Gaines, Carl Jones, Clifford Holland, Traverse Crawford, Rene De Knight TL: 40s

"We were always looking for guitar players who could play the blues, and in New York at that time it wasn't easy. There's a great difference between Duke Ellington or Billy Eckstine and Muddy Waters or Big Bill Broonzy; it's a totally different culture. Of course, the Duke Ellingtons of this world, the Louis Armstrongs, the Jelly Roll Mortons, they all knew about the blues, they could play the blues. They wouldn't play it the way Muddy Waters played it, but they played it, they heard it, they felt it. To them it was simple, it was basic, it was primitive, and they figured that they had moved on to much wider harmonies and more intricate melodies. To them it was going backwards to play like Muddy Waters or that style of blues. Louis Armstrong once described the blues as some sort of homecooked meal, whereas what he was doing was equivalent to having a meal in a fine restaurant – grand cuisine. Personally, I prefer the homecooked meal. There are millions of shadings in between, so what I'm saying, of course, is over simplification. Also Louis Armstrong really changed everything – he was the bridge between different black cultures and between black and white. He was impossible to hate or refuse. He taught everyone how to swing.

"Even so, Harlem was a sophisticated place: they were the dicty, the society people and tended to make fun of the Southerners. I couldn't find any real funky blues singers or players in New York because that was not where they were: Muddy Waters was not down the street. So in 1949, Herb and I made our first field trip down South to record funk and blues." Ahmet

From left: Doc Pomus with Duke Ellington and friend, New York

"I had collected records by Blind Lemon Jefferson, Blind Willie Johnson, Blind Willie McTell – a lot of the early blind blues singers. I was walking along a main street in the black section of Atlanta – to me this is the most incredible story of my whole career – and there was a blind man who was sitting on the corner of the street with his back to the side of the building singing gospel songs, with a hat in front of him for people to drop money into. I stopped to listen to him because he was playing incredible slide guitar and singing so beautifully. I handed him some money so that the fellow could tell it was bills, not coins, and he said, 'Oh thank you – thanks.' So I said, 'Have you ever heard of Blind Willie McTell?' And he said, 'Man, I am Blind Willie McTell.' I said, 'I can't believe it. You are … ?' He said, 'Yeah, that's who I am.' And I said, 'I would love to record you. I'm from a record company in New York.' So he said, 'How's everybody at RCA-Victor doing?' I said, 'No, I'm from another record company,' and he said, 'No man, if you're from the New York record company, that's Victor – RCA-Victor – that's who we used to record for.' But that was twenty years earlier, so I said, 'No, we are not them, and I would like to make some records with you.' We went to the studio that same day, but he only wanted to play gospel songs. I said, 'Oh man, but we wanted some blues.' He said, 'Well, I don't sing blues any more, I've found God.' I said, 'But you make great blues music – this is not a bad thing – if you could just sing some blues.' 'Well,' he said, 'don't put my name on it.' So I said, 'Okay, we'll call you Barrelhouse Sammy.' So we made some blues records and they came out under that name until after he died, when we released them with his actual name. It would have been criminal not to let people know who he was.

"While we were down South, someone mentioned Professor Longhair, a musical magician who played in a style all his own. We asked around and finally found ourselves taking a ferryboat to the other side of the Mississippi, to Algiers, where a white taxi driver would deliver us only as far as an open field. 'You're on your own,' he said, pointing to the lights of a distant village. 'I ain't going into that nigger town.' Abandoned, we trudged across the field, lit only by the light of a crescent moon. The closer we came, the more distinct the sound of distant music – some big rocking band, the rhythm exciting us and pushing us on. Finally we came upon a nightclub – or rather a shack – which, like an animated cartoon, appeared to be expanding and deflating with the pulsation of the beat. A big man at the door barred our way and told us we couldn't go in. I was going to say, 'We're from Atlantic Records,' but then I remembered that hardly anyone had even heard of Atlantic, so I said, 'We're from *Life* magazine.' And he said, 'Oh really?' I said, 'Yeah – and we've come to hear Professor Longhair.' So the guy said, 'Well, I don't think you should be coming in here.' So I said, 'Well, just put us in a corner, hide us, we want to hear the music.' I mean it was blaring out of there – drums, a mike on the piano and on the vocals – the place was packed, people hanging out of the windows and everything. Finally the guy on the door said, 'Okay, I can put you right behind the bandstand.' I said, 'Fine – put us anywhere, it doesn't matter.' So he walked us in, and a lot of people actually scattered because they figured the law had arrived. We were put in a corner and I was amazed to see that there wasn't a full band, there wasn't even a drummer, there was only a single musician – Professor Longhair. He was using the upright piano as both keyboard and bass drum, pounding a kick plate with his right foot to keep time, playing two and four against the thing, creating these weird, wide harmonies and singing in the open-throated style of the blues shouters of old. 'My God!' I said to Herb, 'We've discovered a primitive genius.' I'd never heard music like that and I've never to this day heard anybody else play the piano quite like that. So after the set he came over and I said, 'You know what, you're going to be recording for Atlantic Records.' So he said, 'I'm terribly sorry, but I signed with Mercury last week.' Then he added, 'But I signed with them as Roeland Byrd. With you, I can be Professor Longhair.'" Ahmet

Professor Longhair TL: 40s 50s 80s

Opposite: Blind Willie McTell TL: 40s

Eddie Condon TL: 40s, 50s

"Eddie Condon had his own club in New York and a great Chicago-style band with musicians like Buddy Rich and Bobby Hackett. Chicago-style is a totally different type of music to Dixieland, but Ernie Anderson, who was at one point Louis Armstrong's advisor, was also Eddie Condon's publicist. He was a man who did a lot to help a number of jazz musicians. *Time* magazine, which was as big a news magazine then as it is today, had produced a series of movie shorts to be played in the cinemas before the main feature films came on. They were called 'The March of Time' and were a kind of news magazine programme, each lasting about fifteen minutes. Everybody loved them and they were shown in just about every movie theatre. Ernie Anderson said he knew the people at *Time* magazine, and that they were going to do a 'The March of Time' about the music business. They had to feature one label and he thought that if we recorded Eddie Condon, he could get us to be that label. For us, this was a huge thing. I knew that we weren't going to be able to sell many records of Eddie Condon's band, because it was strictly a jazz group, but I thought it was a perfect opportunity to make some recordings featuring a new artist we'd signed named Ruth Brown and put her out to a large audience. So we cut two sides with the band alone, and two with Ruth singing. I asked Dick Cary, who played with Eddie, to write some arrangements for her, and all the musicians on the session were famous, big band players. One of the songs we did with Ruth was 'So Long'. It was her first record, and it was a big seller. Then, in 1950 she had a smash with the Rudy Toombs song, 'Teardrops From My Eyes', for which Jesse Stone wrote a beautiful arrangement featuring two horns playing two patterns over a steady four-four beat from the bass and drums." Ahmet

"I was working in the Crystal Caverns club in Washington, D.C., when one night Duke Ellington and Willis Conover, who was the *Voice of America*, came in and sat ringside. I couldn't believe it! So I went out and they all had such lovely expressions on their faces. Duke and Willis were just smiling as I was singing. When I got through, Willis Conover got up and went to the pay phone and telephoned Ahmet Ertegun and told him that he and Herb had better get down here and listen to this girl at the Crystal Caverns!" Ruth Brown

"When I went to the club to hear her I thought, 'My God! This girl's terrific! We have to sign her!' Particularly because she sang 'So Long' a bit like Little Miss Cornshucks. She was managed at the time by a wonderful woman, Blanche Calloway, Cab Calloway's sister. Capitol also wanted to sign her but, fortunately for us, Blanche approached Waxie Maxie as the maven of records, who knew everything about the different labels and what they were doing. Well, of course, Max Silverman, being a close and old friend, gave us a very high endorsement and as a result, we were able to sign her." Ahmet

"The arrangement was made for me to go with Atlantic Records. We were en route to

Ruth Brown TL: 40s, 50s

New York when we had an automobile accident in Chester, Pennsylvania, which put me in the hospital for a year. I was getting ready to be twenty years old, and I'll never forget it, they came to the hospital for my birthday and they brought the contracts, a pitch pipe and a music book with them. They were going to teach me how to sight read. So I signed with Atlantic Records from a hospital bed in Chester, Pennsylvania." Ruth Brown

"At first the songs Ruth most enjoyed were more like Doris Day imitations and pop songs. It seemed she didn't really like to sing the blues. But she sang a great version of 'So Long', and while initially she may not have had an outstanding voice, she certainly did have great rhythm – so we called her 'Miss Rhythm'. She became the biggest-selling artist of her genre throughout the fifties and many of her hits were rhythm tunes." Ahmet

Above and below: The Rockin' Highlanders. Above, from left: Herb Gordy, Jerry Potter, Leo Kelly, Tiny Grimes, Joe Sewell TL: 40s

"We did everything ourselves, and once a week I would 'phone up all of the distributors and take orders. Try as we might, our New York-style records weren't going over that well in the South. One day I was on the 'phone with William B. Allen, who was our distributor in New Orleans, and his total order came to maybe thirty singles, which retailed at 79¢ each. So I said, 'Can't you push these a little more?' But he said, 'No, that's all we need; nobody's looking for these records.' Then he added, 'Oh, by the way, there's a record selling like crazy down here, but we can't get any more copies. It's on the Harlem and Cincinnati labels. But if you can find any, I'll take 30,000.' I said, '30,000!' I mean, I had never heard anything like it, so I asked him to send me a copy. It was a song called 'Drinkin' Wine Spo-Dee-O-Dee', by Stick McGhee, and it turned out that Mayo Williams, who used to work for Decca, had made it on the side and shipped it around for cash. So we decided to record our own version. I said to Herb, 'It's very easy to remake this, but we've got to find the right blues singer.' The only blues singers we knew in New York were Sonny Terry and Brownie McGhee, but they were doing Carnegie Hall-type blues – more like folk singers, doing hollers and that sort of thing. Eventually though, I called Brownie and told him I was looking for somebody to sing a song called 'Drinkin' Wine Spo-Dee-O-Dee'. He said, 'That's my brother's record!' And I said, 'No kidding! Do you know where I can get hold of him?' He said, 'He's right here.' So Stick came on the line, and I asked him if he had signed anything when he recorded the song. He said, 'No man, I never signed anything. They gave me $75 and a couple of hot dogs.' So I asked him, 'Will you come with us and make the record over? We'll give you $500 and a fair deal, and we've got all the musicians lined up.' On the Cincinnati version, there were no drums and the whole thing was pretty bare. So Stick McGhee came in and we added drums, bass, and boom, and this and that, and most of all, good players. Brownie sang background vocals and these musicians played fantastic twelve-bar blues. Stick was great but sometimes he would sing 13 bars, sometimes eleven and a half, so it took us a long time but finally we got it right – and that was the first big hit that we ever had. We sold at that time, I would say, 700,000 copies of 'Drinkin' Wine Spo-Dee-O-Dee', and the bootleggers sold a million.

"No distibutor in Texas wanted our label, so I went to Houston to try to get one for us. I walked into a record store, which was the major jazz and race record store in the city, and there, right in the very front of the shop, was a stack of about 300 copies of our record, 'Drinkin' Wine Spo-Dee-O-Dee', which lots of people were coming in and buying! I picked up a copy and it had the Atlantic logo and label, but it wasn't our pressing. So I asked the owner, 'Where did you get this?' He wouldn't tell me. So we started talking and the guy, Abe Atlas I think his name was, said, 'Look – you want to have lunch with me later, fine – but I can't tell you where they came from.' I said, 'Okay, fine, I'll wait.' He said, 'I've got to go out.' So he goes out, gets in his little truck with a speaker

fixed to the roof, and drives off around the city selling tickets that night for Jazz at the Philharmonic. After he came back I asked him, 'How much do you get paid to do this?' He said, 'Oh they don't pay me anything but Norman Granz told me that he'd introduce me to Ella Fitzgerald and Buddy Rich.' I said, 'That's why you're doing this?' He said, 'Yeah.' We hung out together all that day and we kind of became friends, but he still wouldn't tell me where he got the records. That evening we tried to go backstage at the concert, but they wouldn't let him in – he'd been driving around all day promoting and selling tickets for their show and they wouldn't let him in! I said, 'Wait just five seconds.' Then I said to the person at the door, 'Would you please tell Mr. Granz that Ahmet Ertegun is here?' So they came back and said, 'Oh yes, will you please come in.' I said to Abe, 'Will you wait for just one minute?' Then I went

Miriam Beinstock (formerly Miriam Abramson)

in and saw Norman Granz and said, 'Look – this isn't fair – this fellow's been working for you all day … ' And so I got Abe in, after which he turned around and said to me, 'That son of a bitch promised me he would get me in and you're the one who did this – you know what, I'm going to tell you tomorrow where to get the records.' I said, 'Great.' So the next day I go to the record shop and he says, 'Okay. In Paris, Texas, there are these guys who make bathtub gin, bootleg rye whiskey and also have a record pressing plant. It's up in the mountains above the city; they've got five or six guys with rifles and automatics on guard 24 hours a day, but here's the address and here's a map of how to get there.' I thought, 'I'm going to go up there and get killed!' So that was that – there was no RIAA, the police couldn't have cared less, that's how it went. In spite of all this though 'Drinkin' Wine Spo-Dee-O-Dee' was a massive hit for us." Ahmet

Ahmet

Herb Abramson

Overleaf: Stick and Brownie McGhee TL: 40s

Fred McDowell TL: 50s

Above: Meade Lux Lewis TL: 50s

Below: Eurreal 'Little Brother' Montgomery TL: 50s

"Herb and I made one of our field trips to Chicago in July of 1951. We recorded the great slide guitar blues player, Fred McDowell. We also recorded pianist Jimmy Yancey's last session, just two months before Jimmy's death. His left arm was partly paralysed, so he brought along Israel Crosby, who played the boogie woogie bass lines for him on the upright bass. Jimmy's wife, Mama Yancey, also sang on the session. We were so excited to have made those tracks with them, but at the time, no one seemed to want to buy the records. We couldn't believe it. All we could do was keep them safe until people were more interested.

"That same day, we also recorded blues pianist Eurreal 'Little Brother' Montgomery. He was another one of the authentic talents that I feel very honoured to have worked with. A few months later, we went back to Chicago, where we did several tracks with another great boogie woogie pianist, Meade Lux Lewis, including 'Honky Tonk Train Blues'." Ahmet

Opposite: Far left, Jimmy Yancey, and left, his wife Estella (Mama) Yancey TL: 50s

Connie Kay TL 50s

Joe Bushkin TL 40s 50s

"Connie Kay played drums on a whole range of recordings for us before we signed him later with the Modern Jazz Quartet.

"Joe Bushkin is a wonderful musician, who made a couple of albums with Atlantic and has remained a life-long friend.

"The musicians we worked with were people like the saxophone player, Sam 'The Man' Taylor. We used people who could swing but who also were funky. We couldn't get as funky as the people in Chicago did, but we got our own kind of funk, which crossed over." Ahmet.

Opposite: Sam 'The Man' Taylor TL: 50s

Times Square looking north from 43rd Street

Ahmet

The Clovers TL: 50s

"Basically, I started writing songs because the music publishers wouldn't provide any material to this little hole-in-the-wall company called Atlantic. So I really had no choice but to write the material myself, and in any event, at that time the publishers didn't have these types of songs anyway. I don't play an instrument, and many songwriters at that time didn't either. Guys like John Davenport and Eddie Cooley, who together wrote 'Fever', and Rudy Toombs, used to bring in songs and just clap the back beat and run through the number vocally. I would go to the recording booths in the arcade at Times Square. They were a little like passport photo booths today, except that they had doors you could close. You'd put in a quarter or 50¢ and make your own record. They were pretty flimsy pieces of vinyl, but you could use them as a demo for a song.

"The Clovers were a Washington group; they were found by a fellow named Lou Krefetz who worked in the Washington area for an independent distribution company. He brought them to us, and Max Silverman let us use his store to audition them. I wrote a lot of their songs, lots of hits. Once they'd become successful, Lou Krefetz gave up his job at the distribution company and became the group's manager. He was a very colourful guy, very active in the music business and he knew everybody. He was a good promotion man as well. At one point after the group had broken up, he became our sales manager. The Clovers had lots of hits through the 50's.

"The first song I wrote for them was called 'Don't You Know I Love You', which became one of the largest R & B hits in 1951. Jesse Stone helped with the arrangements, and we brought in Randy Weston on piano and Frank Culley on saxophone – which was the first time a tenor sax had been used with a vocal group. That same year I wrote the song 'Fool, Fool, Fool' and practically forced the Clovers to record it. Then another miracle happened and I was so amazed – all I could hear was this song blaring out of music shops and radio stations. It became another number one, and the Clovers didn't even want to record it!" Ahmet

The Clovers, from left: Harold 'Hal' Lucas Jr., Matthew McQuater, John 'Buddy' Bailey, Harold Winley and Bill Harris TL: 50s

Harry Van 'Piano Man' Walls TL: 50s

"Harry Van Walls had originally been a sideman to the great saxophonist Frank 'Floorshow' Culley from Harlem. Although Harry worked with us so wonderfully on so many records, I still think that one of his great moments was when he played the introduction to the Rudy Toombs song, 'One Mint Julep' recorded by The Clovers, in 1952." Ahmet

The Cardinals, formerly known as The Mellotones, from left: Jack Johnson, Ernie Lee Warren, Meredith Brothers, Leon Hardy and Sam Aydelotte TL: 50s

"The Cardinals were originally called The Mellotones, but under either name they were not what the public was waiting for. The only chart success we managed with them was a song called 'Wheel of Fortune', which was a minor hit in 1952.

"We cut three singles with The Diamonds, none of which had any chart success. One of the songs was 'A Beggar For Your Kisses', an original single of which today, I'm told, is worth in excess of $300." Ahmet

The Diamonds, clockwise from left: Harold 'Sonny' Wright, Daniel Stevens, Myles 'Mousey' Hardy and Ernest 'Rocky' Ward TL: 50s

Above and below: Big Joe Turner TL: 50s

"I had heard that Joe Turner had joined Count Basie's band and that their first engagement was at the Apollo theatre. Now Big Joe Turner had been on various record labels, including National, where Herb had recorded him. I knew Joe from the jazz concerts Nesuhi and I had run in Washington. Count Basie was about to open at the Apollo and at the last minute his blues singer, Jimmy Rushing, got sick. So they rushed out and got Joe Turner, who had never even rehearsed with Count Basie before. I went to this first show and Joe knew most of the songs, but not all of them. Then on top of that, the Basie Band had intricate arrangements that were not exactly 12-bar blues. In between the blues, there would be maybe 18, 20, 24-bars. Joe couldn't read music, so there was really no way he could have gotten all of this right without some rehearsal. So he was singing with the band, but he would come back in the wrong place, and the band would clash with what he was doing. Then the band finished and he was still singing! The Apollo audience was the toughest and very critical – so at the end of this tragic moment for Joe they started hooting, howling, whistling, jeering and laughed him off the stage. After this was over I ran backstage to console him, but they told me, 'No, Joe's already left, probably gone up to the corner somewhere.' Sure enough, there he was on the next corner in Braddock's Bar. I said, 'Look, Joe, forget about that – you shouldn't be a sideman with an orchestra anyway, you're a star in your own right – we want to make you a big star. Come and make records with us.' For his first Atlantic session, I wrote a song for him based on blues changes called 'Chains Of Love'. We had Harry Van 'Piano Man' Walls, whom I loved, playing on it. Jesse Stone made a wonderful arrangement with organ chords, Joe sang beautifully, and it was a big hit.

"Van Walls had never heard of 'Chains Of Love' before that session, but he played an introduction that was so beautiful, I said, 'Look – I know you didn't write the song, but I'm going to give you half of it – you're going to be my co-writer on this.' So he didn't know, didn't give a damn, said, 'Okay, fine.' Then about five or six years later, he called me up from some little club he was playing in New Jersey – I think on the beach at a place in Wildwood. He said, 'Listen – would you come down to hear this band I've got now? By the way, would you bring me $500?' I said, 'What for?!' He said, 'Because I want you to buy back my half of that song.' I said, 'Van, don't do that.' He said, 'No, if you don't buy it, I'm going to sell it to somebody else.' So I went down there and bought back the other half of the song that I'd given him. He made a few hundred dollars and was happy, but I was not happy about it. I said, 'Don't you know this is wrong?!' He said, 'Look, man, I don't care about these things, I need the money now and that's that.' So now it's back as my song but some people still go around saying that I stole the song from him." Ahmet

Ahmet

Lil Green TL: 50s

"Lil Green was an original artist with great style that we just couldn't translate into chart success at the time. Her last session for us was in 1951, when we recorded 'Every Time', and a song written by Doc Pomus, 'I've Got That Feeling'." Ahmet

Harry Van 'Piano Man' Walls TL: 50s

Ray Charles Robinson TL: 50s

"In 1952, we signed up a man who was going to become one of the most important people in the history and development of Atlantic Records. One evening I was over at Herb and Miriam Abramson's house when they said, 'We've got to play you this,' and they put on a record of Ray Charles. I said, 'My God – he's fabulous!' Ray was on a Californian label by the name of Swingtime, which was owned by Jack Lauderdale. At that time, I had a friend named Billy Shaw, who was an agent who booked a lot of R & B talent and did very well, but Billy didn't think he could book him. Finally, he said to me, 'Look, why don't you record him? I would be able to book him if you made some good records.' I said, 'I guarantee we'll make great records with him – how do I get him?' He said, 'You buy his contract. Lauderdale is ready to sell. He wants $2,500.' I said, 'Done deal.'

"So we brought Ray to New York where he also got a job playing piano with the Joe Morris Band. At that time, Joe had Cecil Payne, Philly Joe Jones, Johnny Griffin, and Ray on piano. And that was some band! Anyway, we took Ray into the studio and as usual, I was producing the record. I wrote a couple of songs, Jesse Stone wrote a couple of songs, Ray brought in a couple of songs written by other people, and we recorded all of this stuff with a pickup band. I wrote a song called 'Heartbreaker' for one of Ray Charles's first sessions with us. Around the same time, I also wrote 'Mess Around' for him. Because of a studio tape that was floating around, a lot of fuss has been made about my singing this song to Ray so that he could memorize it and get the off-beat. We were just running through it, that's all. What was incredible about that session was that although Ray, I'm sure, knew about boogie woogie piano playing, he had not at that time heard Cow Cow Davenport, one of the pioneers of that style. So in explaining 'Mess Around', I was trying to put across to Ray the very precise phrasing of Cow Cow Davenport, when he suddenly began to play the most incredible example of that style of piano playing I've ever heard. It was like witnessing Jung's theory of the collective unconscious in action – as if this great artist had somehow plugged in and become a channel for a whole culture that just came pouring through him. I was trying to produce Ray the way we were recording Joe Turner or the Clovers. The records didn't do that well, but well enough so that he could go out on the road. That was when he started writing, so we didn't have to find material for him anymore. He would rehearse all his songs and when he said, 'I'm ready to record,' we'd go into the studio, and he'd have 'Hallelujah! I Love Her So' and all these terrific songs that he'd written. By the time we did 'What'd I Say', which became like an anthem all over the country, Ray had become our first big, big star – and of course he still is a huge star today." Ahmet

"I really think that they were phenomenal about hearing talent – most of us who came to Atlantic, what we were doing was raw, it was raw stuff, it really was. I think they had this feeling for the music and they never got in the way of my music, never, at no point from start to finish. They would submit songs to me but they never once said, 'Record this'. There was never a time there was any pressure like, 'The producers brought this song down and this is for you to do.' There was never any of that." Ray Charles

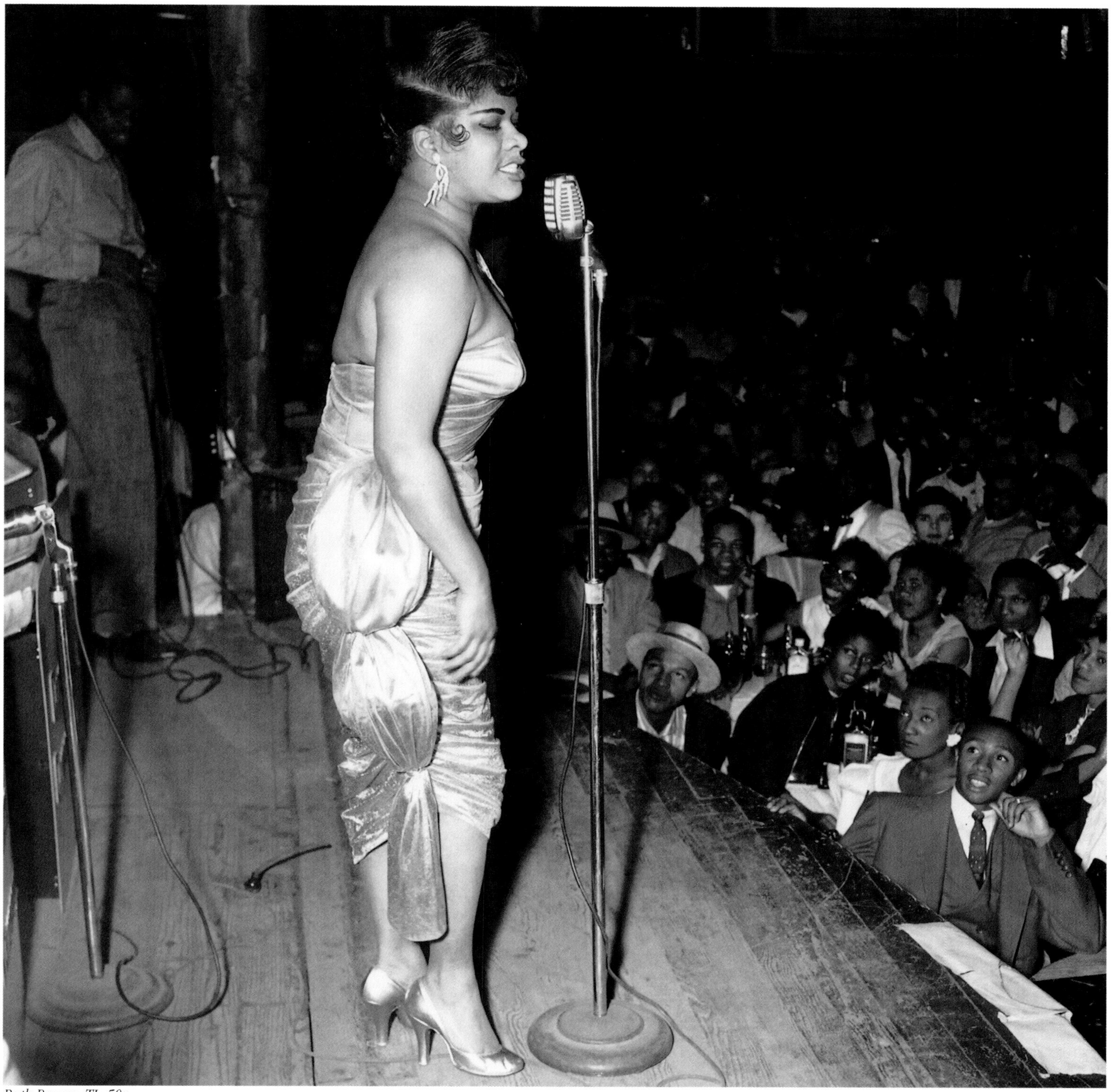

Ruth Brown TL: 50s

"The record Ruth is probably best known for is 'Mama, He Treats Your Daughter Mean'. When we gave her the song, she wasn't crazy about it. We had to cajole her, convince her, and promise her we'd treat her right. We tried it at four different speeds and rhythms and she could hit all of them! Finally we got it to where it had to be and she saw that it was right on the money. By this time we were working with a fabulous band of house musicians: Mickey Baker on guitar, Connie Kay on drums, Lloyd Trotman on bass, and Harry Van Walls or Ernie Hayes on piano. When Jesse Stone wasn't free, we could call on arrangers such as Budd Johnson or Howard Biggs. We'd also found Sam 'The Man' Taylor, who played terrific blasting saxophone, and if we needed a tenor sax with slightly softer tones, Budd Johnson would step in. Then Ruth Brown told us that her boyfriend was going to come in and accompany her on saxophone at the next session. The boyfriend turned out to be Willis 'Gator Tail' Jackson, another great player whom we used regularly after that." Ahmet

"At that time in the South, there was no Holiday Inn to check into. You had to arrive early enough to go down to the main drag in town, where the favourite black barber, beauty parlour, or restaurant was, and hope that you could find someone who would take you into their home. Nine times out of ten someone had something like a little tourist home outside in their yard that you could stay in. In the Northern cities, black and white were mixing a little

Willis 'Gator Tail' Jackson on saxophone TL: 50s

bit more, but in the South, it was still strict segregation. They had ropes down the middle of the theatre, blacks on one side and whites on the other. There were balconies where the spectators sat and where no dancing was allowed, and the dance floor below. Sometimes the black people would be upstairs, the whites down, other times it would be vice versa. You had to go into all of these small towns and believe me, I played every one of them. If it had a warehouse, if it had an Elks Lodge, a barn with a tobacco truck rolled up with two bricks under the wheel, I performed in it. I think that's why a magazine once claimed that 'in the South, Ruth Brown is better known than Coca-Cola'." Ruth Brown

THANKS DOWN BEAT READERS ↓ For voting "Mama, He Treats Your Daughter Mean" the TOP Rhythm and Blues record of 1953. *Ruth Brown*

"We signed LaVern Baker, who was called Little Miss Sharecropper. Like Little Miss Cornshucks, LaVern originally had a 'down home' style, wearing baggy, cotton sack dresses. And like Cornshucks, she could really sing. For me at that time, Cornshucks, LaVern, Dinah Washington and Little Esther Phillips were the truly great voices." Ahmet

LaVern Baker TL: 50s

"Herb had qualified as a dentist, curiously enough, even with everything else he'd been doing. The government had paid for his training – and they called him up! He was going to have to do two years' military service. So he, Miriam and I started to look around for someone who could take over for him while he was away. The first choice for all of us was our old friend Jerry Wexler, who worked at *Billboard*, where incidentally, he coined the term 'Rhythm and Blues'. He'd turned us down before and would only come and work with us on condition that we make him a partner. So we did – we gave him stock, a good salary, and he came and joined us in 1953." Ahmet

"I'd had the temerity to say to them, 'Look, let me buy into the partnership, I'll be glad to join you.' Well that made them practically roll around on the floor with laughter. But then a year later, they gave me the opportunity to come in as a partner. How they came to imagine that I would have the qualifications for this I have no idea! They could have been just as wrong as maybe they turned out to be right, but sometimes you go along with friends." Jerry Wexler

"Jerry's wife, Shirley, conducted the negotiations with Herb, Miriam and me regarding Jerry's deal. As a result we ended up paying him a salary which came to around $300 a week. In turn he gave us $2,063.25 and we gave him 13 percent of the company. At that time, Jerry drove an old fluid-drive Dodge, the kind of car which you had to be an optimist to even get into. So Herb, Miriam and I took that $2,063.25 and put it towards a company car, a green Cadillac convertible with fins, and gave it to Jerry." Ahmet

Ahmet with Clyde McPhatter

"I always thought I'd be incredibly great – a real hotshot at making records – because I could analyse other people's mistakes and see how bad they were and I could guess at how much better I could do. The minute I was thrown into the pot I knew how wrong I had been – I was terrified and saw immediately that there was far more to it than I could even begin to imagine. Ahmet was paying me a salary of $300 a week, a considerable amount in those times, and something that contributed greatly to my motivation from day one was the outright fear that this great situation would fall apart! My first session for Atlantic was with the wonderful Clyde McPhatter, where we cut 'Money Honey', 'Gone', 'Watcha Gonna Do' and 'Boogie Woogie Roll'.

"It became my business and Ahmet's to know every disc jockey in every territory who had any weight – I'm talking about the rhythm and blues radio stations – and to work very hard to cultivate them and try to make them become friends of our music. There would be quid pro quo in various forms – some of which were even legal – but the idea was called 'taking care of business'. We would make a Southern trip and we'd see a transmitter, go into the station and there'd be a disc jockey we might know. So we'd bring

From left: Herb Abramson, Jerry Wexler, Ahmet, Clyde McPhatter

out the latest acetate, which hadn't even been pressed yet, and say, 'Here's one to try out.' There were no rules in those days – like you couldn't play it because it wasn't on a playlist. They would just put the record on and we'd leave behind a bottle of Jack Daniels or a polyester sports shirt!" Jerry Wexler

"In late '53, I took Jerry to New Orleans to visit retailers, distributors and disc jockeys, as well as to record Joe Turner at Cosimo's Studio, where we cut 'Midnight Cannonball'. Jerry had never been to the Crescent City before and those old twin-engined aeroplanes used to drop into air pockets hundreds of feet deep all the way down there. It never really bothered me, so I would have my head in a book or drift off to sleep. On this trip, every time I came round Jerry would be on the edge of his seat seemingly attempting to anticipate the next 400-foot drop, apparently with limited success. Consequently, when we arrived I was ready to hit the town, but he could hardly walk. When I got back to the hotel the next morning, however, he'd come round and in amongst everything else that we were doing we still found time to try out some different routines. One of these was a little number we'd pinched from the legendary impresario and champagne lover, Wilson Mizner. We'd walk into a pawnbroker's and make a big show out of cashing a company cheque that we were supposed to split fifty-fifty. Then we'd get the pawnbroker to dole the money out onto the counter as a stack of twenties and a stack of singles. Then I'd point to the stack of twenties and say, 'I'll take an inch from here.' Then to the stack of singles and say to Jerry, 'You take an inch from there.' 'That's fair,' he'd say. The pawnbroker couldn't stand it, 'That's not fair!' he breaks in. 'The guy's robbing you!' In high dudgeon Jerry insists, 'This man is my friend. He would never do that. He takes care of me.' 'He's fucking you!' the guy finally cries out. So then with a great show of indignation I take out my wallet and throw it at Jerry. 'Are we talking leather?' he demands, removing his shoe and throwing it back at me. Pulling himself up to his full height, he turns to the pawnbroker and tells him, 'You see, now we're straight. I told you we split everything fifty-fifty!'

"Clyde McPhatter was one of the original members of The Dominoes. And for me, when Clyde sang, everything changed. He was a singer from heaven, with the most beautiful, lyrical voice. One day, I went down to see The Dominoes perform at Birdland, but when I looked up at the stage, Clyde McPhatter wasn't in the group. So during intermission I went backstage, and the guys in the group told me that he had been fired five days before. I said, 'Clyde was fired? Are you kidding?! Where does he live?' They said he lived in New York, but they didn't know exactly where. So I rushed off to the telephone booth at the club, called information, and got two or three listings under McPhatter. The first one I tried turned out to be Clyde's father, who was a preacher. Clyde came on the line and said hello in that big high voice he had. I said, 'My name's Ahmet, and I'm from Atlantic Records.' He said, 'Oh yeah, I heard you used to come around.' So I said, 'I understand you're free. Can

Herb Abramson

you come see me tomorrow morning?' So the next day he came to my office, we signed him up, and of course he became ten times as big as The Dominoes ever were.

"After signing Clyde we then had the task of forming a group. After a false start which really didn't work for us, Clyde said that he had some friends with whom he had sung in church and who were called the Thrasher Brothers. So the new quintet was made up of Bill Pinkney and Gerhard Thrasher, tenors, Andrew 'Bubba' Thrasher, baritone, Willie Ferbie, bass and Clyde as lead tenor. Bill and Clyde came up with the name The Drifters, and we started to rehearse with Jesse Stone, who not only arranged, but also wrote their first big hit, 'Money Honey', in 1953." Ahmet

Clyde McPhatter TL: 50s, 60s

Atlantic Records 1947-54
By Greil Marcus

Atlantic Records was formed in New York City in 1947 as a partnership between two dedicated jazz fans: sometime dental student and full-time recordman Herb Abramson (1920-99) and sometime graduate student in philosophy and would-be-recordman Ahmet Ertegun (1923-), son of the former Turkish Ambassador to the United States. A left-wing Jew, an heir to the secular, modernist revolution that took power in Turkey the year he was born, and $10,000 in seed money from one Dr. Vahdi Sabit, the Ertegun family dentist – it was perfect. It was too good to be true. It was America, where you need both money and love to make the world go 'round.

The money was gone overnight. The company was incorporated in October; a musicians' union ban on recording was due to begin on the 1st of January, 1948. The two men recorded anyone who could breathe on a beat, and beat the deadline with over 200 titles in the can. They spent the next year releasing them; none were hits. The all-class, no-cash label went through a long time of try-anything and what-have-we-got-to-lose confusion in the years that followed, with Ertegun leading treks through the South scouting for talent, sometimes recording it on the spot, with hundreds of one-shots on jazz, blues, and emerging rhythm and blues performers – Sarah Vaughan, Blind Willie McTell, John Lee Hooker, Art Pepper, Bobby Short, Professor Longhair, The Clovers, The Delta Rhythm Boys, Erroll Garner, Leadbelly – and also Eddie Safranski's Poll Cats (yes, polka), a full-length version of Romeo and Juliet, and recordings of 256 children's stories. In 1949 the company released 187 records – and with 'Drinkin' Wine Spo-Dee-O-Dee' by Stick McGhee (1918-61) and His Buddies, a fabulous country-blues band's ode to rotgut, and 'So Long', a wistful, only barely cheesy R & B ballad by Ruth Brown (1928-), it commenced to score.

A reputation, a company personality, began to emerge. It was a reputation for hustle disguised as style and cool (courtesy of the jive-talking, Kant-reading, always perfectly dressed Ertegun), fairness (the company, in a practice that scandalized its competitors, be they majors like Columbia or fellow independents like Chess, paid not only the legally-mandated publishing royalties to song publishers, but performance royalties to artists), business sense (courtesy of Miriam 'Tokyo Rose' Beinstock, then Herb Abramson's wife, and Atlantic's intimidating manager), attention to detail (a clear, crisp sound, the recruitment of the best players in New York for sessions with even the least practised singers, the belief that a horn break deserved to be heard as sharply as lead vocal), and perhaps, most of all, enthusiasm, fans' enthusiasm. It was that and a reputation for hits. On the black charts, of course – but even as white artists' covers of recordings by black artists soared past the originals on the pop charts, out in the real America the originals sooner or later often piled up more sales. And on jukeboxes, which also paid up, the originals almost always outspun the covers – especially those of Atlantic. Because they were so carefully made, with air in the sound, it took forever for their sound to go stale. They stayed in the air, and made it fresh.

Now, on the 15th of February, 1954, Atlantic is about to seal this era, to catch it whole and sum it all up; the sound to be made today will also break into the future. In the studio, which is still the office – 234 West 56th Street, with the desks stacked and the chairs pushed into the hall – is almost the full complement of the Atlantic team (missing are Miriam Abramson, working out of another office, and Abramson, finishing his Army service; he'll be back, then soon enough gone for good). Present are Ertegun and Jerry Wexler (1917-), a New York Jew and former *Billboard* writer, now a budding producer and writer who joined the label as a partner in 1953 (he paid $2063.25 for 13 per cent of the company; Ertegun immediately put the money down on a green Cadillac and gave it to Wexler, since Cadillacs were what recordmen had to drive if they expected anyone to take them seriously). There is Jesse Stone (1901-99), a music man with experience far beyond that of anyone else in the room, Atlantic's musical director and chief arranger, songwriter, rhythmist, a man who has been with the label from the very first, but who cut 'Starvation Blues' for Okeh in 1927, who had schooled himself in Bach, Bartok, and Stravinsky and taken songwriting lessons from Cole Porter – Jesse Stone, indomitable, dapper, the grandson of a slave, a slave who told his grandson he had owned "the first Cadillac in Kansas". Tom Dowd is there, the whiz-kid engineer – once a physicist, now one of the first true soundmen – who will fashion Atlantic recordings for the next thirty years. There are the Blues Kings, with Stone on piano, Mickey "Guitar" Baker (later of Mickey & Sylvia and 'Love Is Strange' fame), Lloyd Trotman on bass, Connie Kay (later of the Modern Jazz Quartet and Van Morrison's Astral Weeks) on drums, Wilbur De Paris on trombone, Sam "The Man" Taylor on tenor sax, and Mack Easton on baritone sax.

And there is, ultimately, at the centre of it all, Joe Turner, "The Boss of the Blues". Big Joe Turner, who, as Nik Cohn lined it out in *Rock Dreams*, "can tear down walls with his bare hands, can chew pig-iron and spit it out as razor blades, can kill a man with a smile; can holler like a mountain jack, can swallow hogsbacks whole, and make love all night long; can do whatever you can do – Big Joe can do it better". And that was just what his records sounded like.

He was born in Kansas City, as Joe Tucker – "Joe Turner" was the name of a feared, racist Nashville sheriff, and also the name of a song from which, Leadbelly once said, all blues came. By means of a moustache Turner drew on his face with pencil, by the age of sixteen he was sneaking into Kansas City's wide-open night-spots, most notably a place called the Backbiters Club. ("It was Prohibition," Jesse Stone would tell Nick Tosches, "and Pendergast," the consummate midwestern political boss, "was running the whole town like an after-hours joint.") On such brilliant records as the 1951 'Honey Hush' (Turner's first for Atlantic, and his first number one) he sounded as if he knew it all and as if he'd seen it all, and even if he never learned to read, by the time he hit twenty he'd seen enough for a bluesman's life time. From club to club in K.C. he ran errands, ran whiskey, bounced drunks, tended bar, and sang his head off. When Pete Johnson, his first pianoman partner, hit a roll, Turner would sing from the bar – whole numbers, the drinks flying all the while.

He and Johnson played John Hammond's legendary *Spirituals to Swing* celebration at Carnegie Hall in 1938; that same year he cut his first record, 'Roll 'Em Pete'. He and Ertegun went way back. It was seeing Cab Calloway and then Duke Ellington perform live at the London Palladium in 1933, when he was ten, that changed Ertegun's life, that made him a seeker after sound and glamour; in Washington, D.C., he began to get a feel for what he called the "secret language" of African-American culture, and along with his older brother, Nesuhi Ertegun (1919-89), he learned it. They became jazz fanatics, amassing over 25,000 78s, attending shows, meeting musicians, and soon enough, in the face of the complete racial segregation that ruled in the nation's capital, putting on integrated shows, on the stage and in the audience, sometimes with their friend Herb Abramson, first in the Turkish Embassy, then at the Jewish Community Centre. Along with Sidney Bechet, Joe Turner was on their first bill. Abramson had produced hits for Turner when he was running the National label in 1945-47. Since then Turner had rattled back and forth across the country on nine different labels; by 1950 he had fifty records out and his career was slipping. Ertegun saw him at the Apollo Theatre in Harlem one night in 1950, ruining himself in front of the Count Basie band; instead of turning away Ertegun went after him, told Turner that he and his cool, hot label could change everything, and signed Turner to a one-year contract with two one-year options; in Turner's world, about the same thing as an annuity.

Ertegun had had a little record-making machine as a kid in D.C.; naturally, he recorded himself singing his favourite blues and jazz songs. With Atlantic beginning to sail he took himself to Times Square record-your-own-voice booths and cut the songs he composed in his head; songs like 'Chains Of Love', which would be Joe Turner's first record for Atlantic. But it wasn't nostalgia he was working on by signing Turner. He knew he had his hands on wasted talent, something someone else was sure to see soon enough, as this new sound that no one had a real name for yet, what Alan Freed was calling "Rock'n' Roll", what Jerry Wexler wanted to call "Cat Music", what down in Texas they were calling "Western Bop", demanded more and more voices. As Bill Graham would say years later, it was a matter of getting up earlier than the other guy – or, with Ertegun (who like Jackie Gleason's Minnesota Fats in *The Hustler* could go until dawn, drinking, greeting, jiving, listening, drinking some more, without a thread out of place), of never going to bed at all.

So they are set for 'Shake, Rattle And Roll'. Jesse Stone has written the music and the witty, perfectly balanced blues verses, making a story of domestic lust, lustful impatience, sexual wonder and sex – grinding – that at once goes far beyond the salaciousness of the R & B hits of the time and is somehow as clean, healthy (and perhaps as dutiful) as hard work. Stone's chorus is a great shout: "And it's shake! Rattle and roll! Shake … " They all had to know it was the hook that would sell the song. "For a fact rock'n'roll ain't no different from the blues," Joe Turner would tell Peter Guralnick years later, "we just pepped it up a lot … it's all trends." But this song – or what, that day, all the people in the studio, in the office, did with it – was different. Or it was on the verge of difference, reaching for it, pulling back.

Back in 1949, travelling through the South, Stone and Ertegun were trying to understand why their records – so well-made, up-to-date, even innovative in their way – didn't sell. Watching the crowds night after night in the clubs they hit, Stone understood it: people were dancing in a new way, young people especially, and they couldn't dance to the classy, urbane Atlantic beat. So for an instrumental version of Stone's old number 'Sorghum Switch', retitled 'Coleslaw' for honking tenor sax man Frank Culley, Stone, in his words, "designed" a special bassline; he put country blues into the city sound, and it clicked. Now he leads off 'Shake, Rattle And Roll' with a repeating piano line that runs like a clear, beckoning stream. It's light, bouncy, and it pulls your legs out from under you. The horns come in, and they are not jazz, not R & B, they are pure pop – they are, literally, popping the beat, counting it off like shouts. There are hooks everywhere. You're hooked. And the man who knows what he wants and knows how to get it has made his move.

Clyde McPhatter

Joe Turner is a great actor more than a great singer in 'Shake, Rattle And Roll'. You can see everything happen. When he sings the line Jesse Stone got from drummer Baby Lovett – "I'm like a one-eyed cat, peepin' in a seafood store", those still stunningly outrageous phallic-vaginal metaphors that don't have to sound like anything but what they say they're about – you can see Turner, all 250 pounds of him, crouching on his knees, peeping through the glass. He is all blues, all roll, but the chorus isn't: sung by Turner with Ertegun, Wexler, and Stone shouting their heads off behind him, it has a flashy, white, drunken frat-boy edge, a feeling not that far from the Swingin' Medallions' 1966 'Double Shot (Of My Baby's Love)'. The beat jerks; Turner is weary and sly and weary and ready, taking it slow, not rushing anything, and on the chorus you hear a cheerleading squad. The sound doesn't exactly fit, and yet it's wonderful. It's as if the singer, with all of his wisdom, all of his knowledge of the ways of the world, is ready to pass it on, and has welcomed his whole new audience – the millions of young people, black and white, that Stone knew, and Wexler knew, and Ertegun knew perhaps most of all, was out there somewhere – onto the record with him. On the black charts, it was number one for eleven weeks.

Today, it seems to matter less that later in 1954 Bill Haley and His Comets, a white country outfit jumping the R & B train, cleaned up with 'Shake, Rattle And Roll' (in two senses: all trace of sex was removed from the lyrics and the record was a huge pop hit) than that in 1955, with a demo cut with the Blue Moon Boys, Elvis Presley, not changing a word, demonstrated just how completely the song – the idea, the catchphrase, the rhythm, the ethos – had entered American culture, making the tune his own, making it personal, making it teenage, making the song about the discovery of sex, not a lifetime of it. Against the Turner-Stone-Ertegun-Wexler original, neither Haley's nor Presley's version may matter at all – save that royalties from Haley's hit and Presley's later recording of the number on RCA have likely helped ease the travail of Jesse Stone's very long life. Today the first 'Shake, Rattle And Roll' still sounds like a door being flung open. But it doesn't quite sound as if people have made it to the other side.

As it happened, other people had already made it to the other side. In the same office, in the same studio, on the 9th of August, 1953, almost exactly six months before Joe Turner cut 'Shake, Rattle And Roll', Clyde McPhatter and The Drifters had made 'Money Honey', a Jesse Stone composition, an Ertegun-Wexler production – they had flung open the door, shattered it, only to see it somehow reassemble itself and close once more, but in a flimsier state, so that, next time, one good wolf's breath could blow it down again. You can listen to 'Money Honey' today and hear this event clearly – but it wasn't clear at the time. That the sighting of a new world should follow and not precede the landing is just one of the paradoxes of a time when no one knew what rock'n'roll was and there were no rules. Rock'n'roll was invented, but it was also discovered; when people discovered it, they didn't necessarily know what they had.

"Here's the sort of record we need to make," Wexler in his autobiography, *The Rhythm and the Blues*, written with David Ritz, recalls Ertegun telling him early on. "There's a black man living in the outskirts of Opelousas, Louisiana. He works hard for his money; he has to be tight with a dollar. One morning he hears a song on the radio. It's urgent, bluesy, authentic, irresistible. He becomes obsessed. He can't live without this record. He drops everything, jumps in his pick-up, and drives twenty-five miles to the first record store he finds. If we can make that kind of music, we can make it in this business." The imagined audience is bizarrely constricted, still governed, perhaps, by a jazz fan's fantasies – never mind black and white, there are no young people of any kind, they don't exist – but the spirit, the will to tap a hidden need like a surgeon might open a vein, is absolutely right. From his own perspective, Wexler puts it somewhat differently: "I dug cross-cultural collaborations and craved commercial success, which is maybe why Ahmet and I got on so well. We could have developed a label along the lines of Blue Note, Prestige, Vanguard or Folkways, fastidious documentaries of core American music. Bobby Weinstock, Alfred Lion, Moe Asch, Orrin Keepnews, Manny Soloman, and the other keepers of the flame were doing God's work. Ahmet and I, however, didn't feature ourselves as divinely elected. We weren't looking for canonisation; we lusted for hits. Hits were the cash flow, the lifeblood, the heavenly ichor … It may not be God's work, but God sends His rewards! … the wherewithal of survival. While we couldn't divorce ourselves from our tastes and inclinations, neither could we deny our interest in income. Nor could we stand still; we believed to our souls that the way of the independent label was either growth or death."

There is the urgency that kept Ertegun up all night; there is the perspective that let Wexler know when he needed to go to bed. The result, after the initial dry spell of carefully crafted but generic early R & B pieces, was haphazard then consistent hit-making – but, in the slowly forming pop arena, not necessarily great or even interesting music. Ruth Brown kept the label going in the late 1940s and early fifties, but she couldn't wear Dinah Washington's sash and today nearly all of her recordings seem up-ended by limited talent. Her upper register was entrancing; her lower register, to which she turned after establishing a theme, to nail the theme, to show she really meant it, is histrionic or lugubrious. The Clovers, a vocal group that got great songs from the label ('Devil Or Angel', 'Fool, Fool, Fool', 'Your Cash Ain't Nothin' But Trash', 'One Mint Julep'), were a rehearsal for the long run of Coasters' hits that along with those of Ray Charles would in the late fifties make Atlantic the most dominant independent label in the history of the American recording industry – but the group had no emotional depth and no edge. The Cardinals charted high – especially in 1952 with, of all things, a black group's cover of a white pop hit, Kay Starr's 'Wheel of Fortune' – and they were perhaps the worst doo-wop combo ever to cut more than one 45. Nothing was certain; little was known. What did a hit mean? The chance to make another record.

Clyde McPhatter (1932-72) was nothing like Atlantic's previous artists; he was the new world. He was the first Atlantic singer to project as much personality as talent, the first to leap off his records with the irresistible physicality and undeniable individuality of Little Richard, Elvis Presley, Chuck Berry, and Jerry Lee Lewis, all of whom came later. Unlike Joe Turner he was young and he was beautiful. On his best records – on 'Honey Love', 'Let The Boogie Woogie Roll', 'White Christmas', 'Such A Night', and 'Money Honey' – when the singers around him let the beat hang in the air and McPhatter let his voice catch in just that way, he was the sexiest thing on earth.

Ertegun got McPhatter the night McPhatter was fired as lead singer of Billy Ward and the Dominoes, a vocal group riding high on the string of hits that followed the scandalous 1951 success of 'Sixty-Minute Man'. With the Dominoes, McPhatter was all about the ineffable – there are no more sublime moments in all of pop music than his reading of 'When The Swallows Come Back To Capristrano', or, even more perfectly, the other-worldly opening bars of 'Don't Leave Me This Way'. In the early spring of 1953 Ertegun was in Birdland, a Manhattan club owned by gangster recordman Morris Levy, there just to see McPhatter do the Dominoes' huge hit 'Have Mercy Baby' – but McPhatter had broken a band rule and he was gone. Within an hour Ertegun was huddled with the singer, figuring out a new group. After a false start they settled on the Thrasher Wonders – Bill Pinkney and Andrew Thrasher, tenor, Willie Ferbie, bass, Gerhart Thrasher, baritone – and with McPhatter in the lead named the whole the Drifters.

McPhatter's Drifters had a short run. He was drafted in May of 1954, and when he returned he went solo; he lost his music and never found it again. He died a forgotten drunk. But in his one short year of greatness he became a dynamo unlike anything pop music had seen before. He came out of himself, he soared, he ran wild with his own songs, and Stone's, and Ertegun's and Wexler's – even Irving Berlin's. As you listen now, a new man appears before you when McPhatter sings; a whole story tells itself. The slyest smile in the music communicates the notion that the singer is getting away with the greatest prank in history while the whole world watches, the whole world asking – "Who was that masked man?" – when the record ends, then playing it again and again as if by doing so the world could find out. The man before you is charming, urbane, utterly cool, yet at any moment a sense of weightlessness, of pure fun, can break out and engulf the entirety of the performance. The man is a trickster, for 'White Christmas' (which would hit the R & B Top Ten in 1954, '55 and '56, and remains on Christmas time radio to this day), the other Drifters begin respectfully, with a straight arrangement patterned after that of the Ravens, who hit the black charts with the tune in 1948. They finish a verse – and then the Imp of the Perverse arrives, singing like Rumpelstiltskin promising to spin straw into gold, leaving the nation dumbfounded with his whirling falsetto, open-mouthed in the face of a reversal of the country's shared cultural symbolism that in pop music would not be matched until Jimi Hendrix played 'The Star-Spangled Banner' at Woodstock in 1969. ("I mistakenly feared Irving Berlin's people would never approve it," Wexler writes. "They loved it.")

'Money Honey' is comic, though humour was hardly all Jesse Stone was writing – his 'Losin' Hand', an early Ray Charles side for Atlantic, is as chilling a blues song as anyone needs to hear. But here the humour is all in the bottled-up urgency McPhatter gives Stone's lines, and the humour is deadly serious. "Without love, there is nothing", McPhatter would sing softly on one of his solo hits; the message here is that without money there's no love. But there is the thrill of the chase.

Big Joe Turner

Part of the thrill of the record is in waiting to see if each next verse can top the one before it, tell a better story, and every time it does. The real thrill is in the fact that with 'Money Honey' you are hearing pure, complete, finished, fully realized rock'n'roll, and with the special energy that only comes when people sense that they are putting something new into the world, something that will leave that world not quite as it was.

As always the desks are piled up, the chairs shoved out, and somehow there is room for the five singers, for the band Ertegun and Wexler have assembled, for them and Stone and Dowd. "Ah-Ooooom," the singers begin, low and comic and ominous, and then, singing very high, McPhatter begins the quest that will occupy him for the rest of the song: the quest for his rent. He takes the first verse full of enthusiasm; there's a stumble on the drums going into the chorus, as there will be on every verse, but he leaps over it. The second verse is congenial – hey, he's trying to get the money from his girlfriend – but on the third verse she takes over, McPhatter bears down, almost scared, and everything tightens, goes hard and mean. McPhatter shouts for the break, Sam "The Man" Taylor comes in for his solo – but then he burns it, rocketing the music out of anything it's prepared you for, the beat now rushing upstream with too much power, and then McPhatter screams.

There's nothing like this scream – not in McPhatter's music, nor in any of the music to follow his, as the enormous impact he would have on Jackie Wilson, Elvis Presley, Sam Cooke and countless others filtered down over the years to the hundreds and thousands of singers who wouldn't recognize his name. It's a scream of surprise; it's the scream of a man watching the door blow out, the scream of a man who's made it to the other side and is ready to pull everyone over.

Almost half a century later, you can hear this event as it happened. In 1953, it wasn't plain that it had. Nevertheless the music was abroad in the land; like so many other records made in the late 1940s and early fifties by Atlantic, Sun, Chess, King, Alladin, Imperial or Specialty, 'Money Honey' would sneak through the cracks in the official media curtain that shrouded the country, and it would change the country in its own way.

Soon enough, Ertegun and Wexler would buy out Herb Abramson and Miriam Beinstock, and Dr. Sabit, too: his $10,000 had bought him half of the company. Nesuhi Ertegun would join as a third partner. By 1958 Jesse Stone had begun to drift away but, by then, the stage was set and the crowd that had assembled for the first performance refused to leave.

Big Joe Turner performing with, from left: Herb Ellis (guitar), Tommy Bryant (bass), Roy Eldridge (trumpet), and Sonny Stitt (tenor sax) TL: 50s

Ahmet

"They could segregate everything else, but they couldn't segregate the radio dial."

Ahmet

"After the last session Jerry and I cut with Joe Turner in New Orleans, we called another one in New York with Jesse Stone arranging. Jesse brought along a song he'd written with Joe in mind, which I believe is made up of some of the greatest lyrics ever written: 'You wear low dresses, the sun comes shining through / I can't believe my eyes all that mess belongs to you / I'm like a one-eyed cat peeping in a seafood store / You make me roll my eyes and then you make me grit my teeth.' On top of the verses he'd added a chorus, 'Shake, rattle and roll'. Jesse, Jerry and I sang the chorus. Harry Van Walls laid down some passionate boogie woogie piano – and the record created a storm. It quickly became a huge R & B hit and crossed over into the pop charts, but it immediately got covered by the white act Bill Haley and His Comets. They changed the lyrics and set it in the kitchen instead of the bedroom, and their version sold more than a million copies on Decca. Jerry wanted to call this new departure 'cat music', but of course the term 'rock'n'roll' took hold as the popular description for this music. For Joe Turner, it was just another record and he didn't care what they called it." Ahmet

Jesse Stone TL: 50s

Elvis Presley: TL: 50s

"Although black music was parochial and stayed in the black community for decades, maybe centuries, when it eventually did emerge, it captured the sensibility of the whole world. If you go with the notion that black music is the hallmark, the benchmark of our culture, then Elvis Presley was the communicator, the Messiah, the funnel that taught the world the joys, the euphoria, the pleasures of black music." Jerry Wexler

"We were all greatly impressed by the records Sam Phillips was putting out on the Sun label. I listened to some of those early Presley records and thought, well, here's a guy who's really unbelievably talented, a great singer who understands black music. So we went after him. At a dinner in Los Angeles, I met Elvis's manager, Colonel Parker, through Freddie Beinstock and Gene Auerbach, who were Elvis's publishers. I offered $25,000 to Parker for Elvis's contract, which was almost everything we had in the bank. It was a huge amount for us then, especially when you consider that we started the company with about $11,000. Colonel Parker was asking for $45,000, which was more than we could afford at the time, particularly as we never borrowed money from any bank, so eventually he signed with RCA-Victor for $45,000.

"I used to go to the Apollo Theatre every Friday because they'd have a new show each week. So we'd catch the first show, which was around noon. Bobby Robinson had a shoeshine parlour in the next block up from the Apollo. He had the electric brush going and I, along with a lot of other people, used to get a shoeshine there every week. Bobby was West Indian and was very funny. One day I said to him, 'You know, they've got 45 rpm records out now, so what you ought to do is get all the hits, put them up on the wall, put a speaker outside and play the records. It'll attract the people lining up for the Apollo to come and have a shoeshine.' All the record shops at that time played records on a speaker outside, so that people would hear them, go in, and buy the records. As a promotional thing, we'd say to the store owners, 'If you play this record on the speaker, we'll give you 25 records free.' Bobby took to this idea, so I gave him quite a few Atlantic records to start him off with. It worked so well that after a few weeks, he gave up the shoeshine stand entirely and turned it into just a record shop. Then a few weeks after this, he 'phoned me up and said, 'Ahmet, I'd like to get a list of your distributors.' I said, 'A list of our distributors?' He said, 'Yes, I'm going into the record business.' I said, 'Oh man look, you can't just go into the record business. To make records you have to have a bookkeeper, you have to have somebody to answer the 'phone, you have to have artists – where are you going to find the artists?' He said, 'Man, I got the artists, I got everything!' So I said, 'Well, you've also got to get disc jockeys to play the records, you've got to get promotion people, you can't just make a record.' But he said, 'No, you've got to give me a list of your distributors.' So I gave him a list of our distributors and I gave him a list of our disc jockeys. But then I said, 'Listen Bobby, you are making such a mistake. You've done so well out of the record shop, you're going to sink all your money into this ridiculous idea. You're going to lose all the money that you've made at the shop. Please, please don't do it, you're making such a big mistake.' So he put out 'Kansas City', which sold more records than I had ever sold up to that date. It sold two or three million records – I hadn't even sold a million yet. 'Kansas City', in fact, was a Leiber and Stoller song." Ahmet

Ahmet, Miriam Beinstock, Jerry Wexler

Opposite: Bobby Robinson, Ahmet, Clyde McPhatter

The Chords, clockwise from left: Claude Feaster, William Edwards, Carl Feaster, Jimmy Keyes, Floyd McRae and Rubert Branker TL: 50s

"With 'Sh-Boom' by the Chords, the major labels began to take notice of the red and black logo of Atlantic. 'Sh-Boom' was, to my mind, one of the great R & B records, but all we could do was watch some pip-squeak white cover band, the Crew Cuts, obliterate our sales. Today we're told by the self-appointed mystic keepers of history that 'Sh-Boom' was a seminal record – isn't that lovely? With the passage of time, the covers have become an absurdity. It's a rare example in our commercial culture of art winning out over commerce – if you wait long enough!" Jerry Wexler

THE ATLANTIC STORY 73

Jerry Wexler

"I co-wrote the song 'Honey Love' with Clyde McPhatter and it was banned for what were viewed to be suggestive lyrics. Imagine being banned from juke boxes, in juke joints – beer and reefers everywhere – I looked on it as an honour." Jerry Wexler

Tom Dowd

"One of the first engineers whom we worked with was to become a lifelong friend, a genius of the recording studio, and someone who has always been able to encourage the best out of just about every form of music and every kind of artist – his name is Tom Dowd. On one occasion, Tom came in to help us record an idea of Herb's, which was to produce a children's magic story album. Herb had thought up this process where you could have separate grooves, all starting at the beginning of the record – so the needle would randomly pick up one of these grooves every time you played the side. On side one, there were four versions of the first part of the story, then on side two, there were four versions of the second part of the story, and so on. We created it so that each part worked with every other part, which meant that practically every time you played the record, you would get the surprise of a different story. We called it *A Magic Children's Album* because there were, I think, 356 possibilities of how the story could unfold. Anyway, we recorded it and it sold pretty well." Ahmet

"In 1954, I became exclusive to Atlantic, which was then at 234 West 56th Street. The studio was the office and the office was the studio. Before a year had elapsed, they moved to 157 West 57th Street and gave me the entire top floor. We expanded the studio as far as we could without violating the fire laws of the stairwell. I designed and built a console so that we could record stereo and mono simultaneously. Ahmet and Jerry were not too keen on pop dates being in stereo and mono and we were still doing seven, eight, even nine-piece bands in our studio – anything bigger than that, with strings and so forth, we'd have to go outside. Sometimes when we were recording at Capitol or some other studio, I would bring the stereo equipment and record the session separately, while Ahmet and Jerry would be in the control room doing mono. The first time I met Jesse Stone had to be in '48. I saw him on one or two other dates in '49/'50. Then Ahmet asked me to engineer Ruth Brown's track 'Mama, He Treats Your Daughter Mean'; we cut that in a stage studio on 5th Avenue at 57th Street and Jesse and I became fast friends. We established a dialogue – shortcuts: drop this note, don't play here, play here, play soft. I know from '49 until about '57 a lot of the dates were with Jesse. Ahmet and Jerry would pick the songs, and Jesse would go and see the group play live, figure out what their best key would be, and then write an arrangement for five, six or even seven pieces." Tom Dowd

"We were still very short on personnel, so we hired a wonderful lady by the name of Fran Wakschal who worked with us for 49 years." Ahmet

Fran Wakschal

Fran Wakschal

"I came to work in 1949. It was my first job directly out of school – right out of my mother's womb and into Atlantic. Ahmet and Herb Abramson had a big corner office and faced each other across their desks. They both interviewed me and I got the job. I sat at a desk in a small area outside their room. I was the receptionist, the stenographer, I was the computer, I was the cleaning lady. I was everything – it was a one-girl office. Another person who worked in the office was Blackie the shipping clerk, who used to have to come in early in the morning. We were next door to Stillman's Gymnasium on Eighth Avenue and there used to be some unsavoury people sleeping in our lobby. I wouldn't come into the office until Blackie arrived so that he could escort me upstairs. Herb's wife, Miriam, did the record ordering and managed the office. That was it in the office. They had a partner, Dr. Sabit, the dentist. He was not a music person but he was a lovely, lovely man and he used to come in quite often to see what was happening. Right from the start, we always had a lot of fun in the office. It was really a very exciting place. I remember the first party they had when they did their first album – *This Is My Beloved*. They had a reception at Le Coq Rouge. All the disc jockeys were there and I was thrilled." Fran Wakschal

"There was a very popular book of poetry at that time called *This Is My Beloved*, the lead poem of which had been the favourite poem of GIs during the war. It was kind of erotic for the time – not really sexy, but romantic and slightly erotic. People loved that poem, so we got the rights to record it. I'd become very good friends with Vernon Duke, who was the composer of 'April In Paris', 'Autumn In New York', 'I Can't Get Started', and was one of the top composers of that era. So he agreed to write the score for *This Is My Beloved,* and we persuaded the actor John Dahl to read the poetry. The record sold extremely well. It sold so well that five or six years later we did it all over again. Somebody came to us and said that Eva La Gallienne, the famous actress who was then in her sixties, had always wanted to make records of Shakespeare. So Herb and I thought, what if we made *Romeo and Juliet* with orchestral music in the background and famous actors and actresses as the cast. Then we started to figure that if every library and every college bookshop took one copy, then we could carry on throughout the whole series – The Complete Shakespeare! This was a very tough one for us because it required a fairly large orchestra to play Mendelssohn's score. The conductor we found was a young guy who was very hot on the project, but was also extremely tyrannical, particularly in terms of the timing of music to text being absolutely exact. So finally, after weeks of rehearsal we had reached the point where we were about to record – the orchestra and the cast were all in place, the microphones and recording levels had all been checked and set, there was a hush in the studio, I pressed the button, the recording light came on, the conductor flung his arms above his head and one of them came out of its socket. The only sound was him screeching at the top of his voice and we had to rush him to the hospital and pay all these physicians. Eventually he was well enough to finish what turned out to be a fascinating recording. Unfortunately, it didn't sell very well but it was a good idea. Herb Abramson had an idea every three minutes. For example, we recorded a square dance album. Chubby Jackson, who had been a bass player for the Woody Herman Orchestra, formed a square dance band. So we made an album with them, with a caller saying, 'Hold your partner, dosey doe … ' and all of that." Ahmet

"Originally, there was no studio at the office on 54th Street, but then we moved to 234 West 56th Street, which had been a speakeasy before. It was called the 23456 Club and had a cased elevator the likes of which you can't believe. It was so slow. First Atlantic took one floor, and then when we expanded, we had two floors – with a studio on one and the shipping room and offices on the other. But before we got the studio at 234 West 56th, they did a lot of outside recording at Ampex and Beltone studios. Ahmet has told the story of his distributors ordering from one to five copies at a time of different records, and I used to have a lot of fun doing the royalties. We didn't have computers, and our distributors were all over the country – individual distributors that I used to have to invoice and bill. There were no calculators either, just an adding machine – and loads of paper! Which was fine until it got to summer – the fan got turned on and all the invoices went flying!

Ahmet was very fond of Max Silverman. Waxie Maxie would always come into the office and it seemed as if everything they ever did, Max was there. It was really the happiest of times. Ahmet was amazed that they were surviving. He used to check the order books all the time. He used to get on the 'phone and ask for money – 'Distributors, you're five minutes late!'

"Ahmet, Herb and then later Jerry when he joined us would play tapes until around two, three in the morning and then they still did what they had to do in the office. Music was going on all the time. It was quite a thing for me, when I heard Atlantic records on the radio. I felt such pride to be associated with the company that produced that sound." Fran Wakschal

"My brother Nesuhi was living in California, running his labels Jazzman and Crescent, which were dedicated to New Orleans jazz. He was also making modern jazz records for Contemporary Records, which was owned by Lester Koenig. At the same time, he was teaching the first accredited courses on jazz and American folk music at UCLA.

"Now Atlantic's competition at that time were other independent labels; and some of them were starting to be astounded by the success we were having. Lew Chudd, who owned Imperial Records, which had Fats Domino among others, said, 'Hell – if one Turkish kid can make it, maybe this other one can too – I mean, they're brothers for Chrissakes!' So he offered Nesuhi a partnership in Imperial Records, and Nesuhi telephoned to tell me that he was going to take up this offer. I said, 'Are you kidding?! You can't do that! We can't be competitors. Come and join us, we'll make you a partner.' So, eventually, I convinced him to leave California, move to New York, and become a partner with us." Ahmet

"Bringing Nesuhi in was one of the great moves. It elevated Atlantic into an all-round eclectic record company, because he developed one of the great jazz lines of all time." Jerry Wexler

Ahmet and Nesuhi

The Drifters, clockwise fom left: Gerhart Thrasher, Tommy Evans, 'Carnation' Charlie Hughes, Johnny Moore and Jimmy Oliver TL: 50s

"I was brought in to help run the company, but mostly to make albums which would develop the jazz line of Atlantic. Curiously though, one of the first connections I made with Atlantic was when I was in California and a song had come up called 'Adorable', on a very small R & B label. Ahmet and Jerry thought that this song was fantastic and should be covered immediately, meaning the next day. So they called me and said, 'Would you mind doing this song with The Drifters, and you can do anything else you want with the session.' So I said, 'Okay.' At the time, I had befriended two very young writers whose names were Jerry Leiber and Mike Stoller. They'd just begun to write songs, and because I was going to do a session with The Drifters, I went to see Leiber & Stoller in their office. They said they had three or four songs, one of which was called 'Ruby Baby', and it became the biggest hit from that session." Nesuhi Ertegun

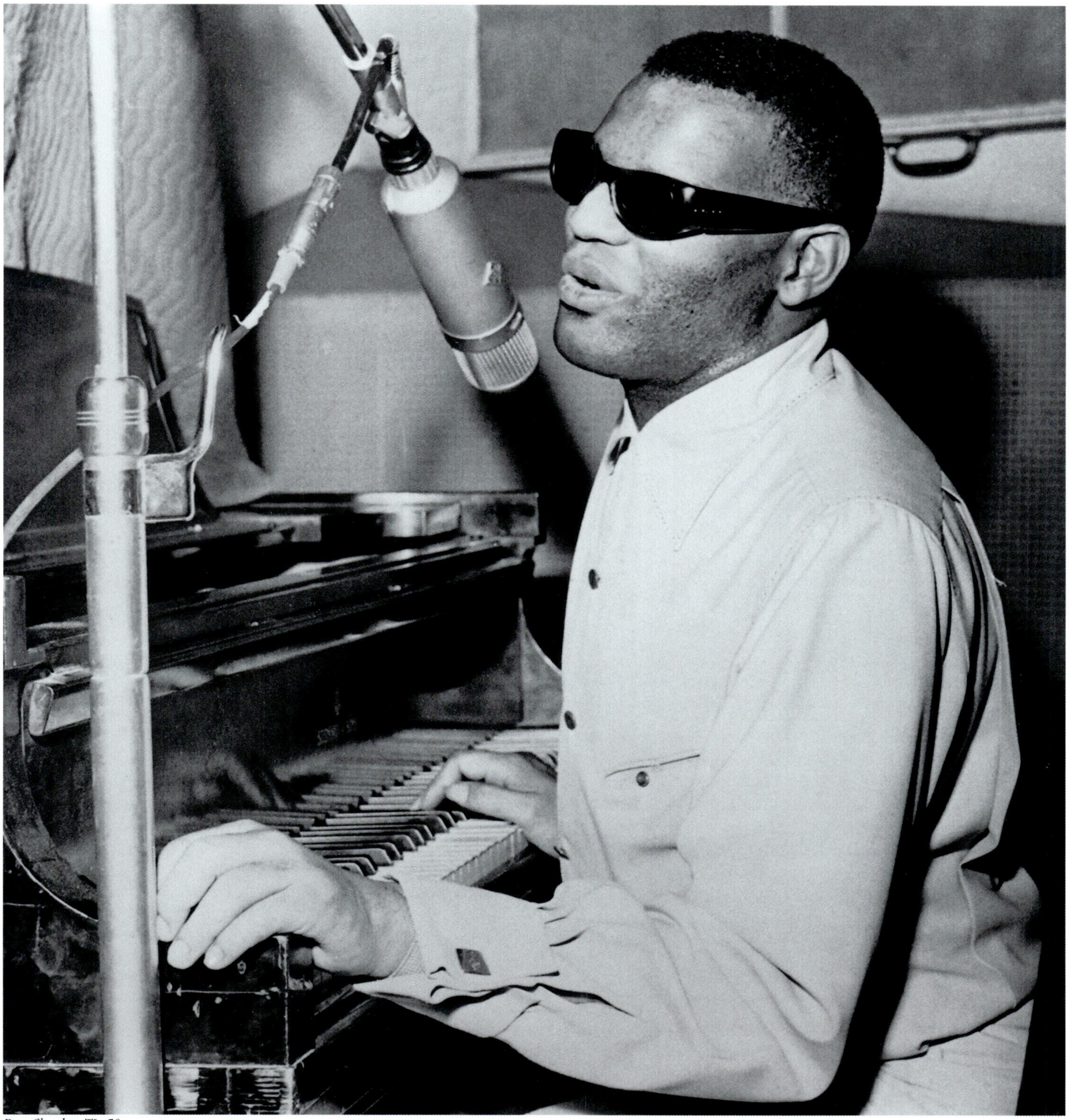

Ray Charles TL: 50s

"Ray summoned us to Atlanta. He was playing at a club called the Peacock and staying across the street in some very inexpensive motel that went with the nightclub. We went up to see him and he was very mysterious, just said, 'I've got something you boys need to hear.' Wouldn't tell us anything about it, but then suddenly said, 'Come on now!' and took off down the stairs. He had the route plotted out to the club, we couldn't keep up with him, and when we got there this seven-piece band was all set up on the stage. So then he sat down at the piano and they started playing some incredible songs – everything had been rehearsed, finished, ready to go. The next day we all went to WGST, the radio studio of Georgia Tech University, and cut these great songs. There never used to be studios like there are today in most towns. Then you had to go to a radio station where you'd be in the control room and have to stop every hour because they had to read the news. There'd be some old duffer who knew nothing about records and we'd say, 'Okay, be ready in two bars, saxophone coming up,' and a minute later he'd turn round and say, 'What, Sonny? What'd you say about a saxophone?'" Jerry Wexler

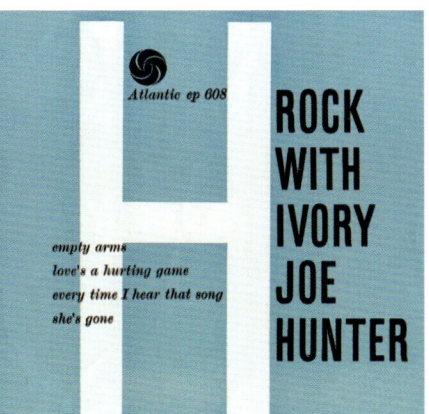

"When I wrote this song, 'I Got A Woman', I decided now is the time. Either you're gonna sink or swim. So at that point I just said, 'Hey, this is what I'm going to do and if I'm going to be accepted, good, and at least if I'm not going to be accepted, I'll know that too'." Ray Charles

"'A Tear Fell/ You Mean Everything To Me' was one of the first sessions we cut with the great Ivory Joe." Ahmet

Ivory Joe Hunter TL: 50s

THE ATLANTIC STORY 81

Lee Konitz TL: 50s

Lennie Tristano TL: 50s

"Joe Mooney was another one of my all-time favourites, and a great friend. He was a blind singer/organist, and he was really a kind of one-man band. He had a pop vocal style, but he was also a great jazz musician. His fans included Lee Konitz and Lennie Tristano.

"Shorty Rogers was one of Nesuhi's first signings. He was not only a terrific musician, but also a composer, arranger, and bandleader of considerable power."
Ahmet

Opposite: Joe Mooney TL: 50s

From left: Harry Geller and Shorty Rogers TL: 50s

Above: The Modern Jazz Quartet, and below, from left: Percy Heath, Connie Kay, Milt Jackson and John Lewis TL: 50s

"I first met Ahmet in 1946, when I was working for Dizzy Gillespie, and we went to Washington, D.C. to play the Howard Theatre. Ahmet came backstage to see Dizzy and that was our first introduction. He was what you might call a very enthusiastic young man – I've met an awful lot of people, but that first meeting with Ahmet has stuck with me over all the years. I didn't meet Nesuhi until 1954, when we went to California for the first time. The photographer and director, Bill Claxton, gave a big party for the Quartet, where I met Nesuhi. Later when he came to New York we became very close friends. Nesuhi always did great, great work and had the most tremendous, natural artistic sense. The decision to record for Atlantic was made by Monte Kay, who remained our manager from the beginning of the Quartet to the time he passed away. He and I were close friends even before the Quartet, because he was passionate about American music in the same way as Nesuhi and Ahmet. Monte appreciated, therefore, that Atlantic would be a great place for us to be, with both Ahmet and Nesuhi there." John Lewis

"The audience for jazz records was far from being entirely black. If anything, it was more white than black, unlike R & B. It was a very different audience, and jazz, of course, never sold as much as R & B. Over 20 years, I probably spent more time in the studio with The Modern Jazz Quartet than with anyone else. My first session with them was *Fontessa* in 1956. We cut the whole album in two and a half hours. The strength and essence of MJQ is the seeming conflict between John Lewis and Milt Jackson – the juxtaposition of Lewis's classically oriented, strong jazz roots against the total improviser, Jackson. Then, of course, there is the great rhythm section of Connie Kay and Percy Heath." Nesuhi

"I loved Charlie Mingus – he was a person who was ahead of his time and did not suffer any idiocy gladly. I remember once he was playing at the Five Spot. He started to play his number, but everyone was still talking. So he just stopped and said, 'We're going to play another song now, and we call this 'Reverse Psychology'. What we're going to do is play four bars, during which I'd like you to stay quiet. Then we're going to stop for four bars, and you can resume making noise and spilling your beers. That way, maybe we'll all get along.' So that's exactly what he did, and everybody became quiet." Ahmet

"Everybody said keep away from Mingus – he's unpleasant, he's destructive, violent, but I found that all of that was untrue. I worked with him for something like 20 years, and he was the easiest artist I've ever worked with. Some of my favourite records out of any that I've ever been involved with were the ones with Charles Mingus. I believe he's one of the great composers in jazz. He had this other extraordinary quality, which Duke Ellington also had – namely that people playing with him performed much better than when they were not playing with him. For me, every session with Mingus was a very important event, because I felt I was in the presence of one of the great cultural forces of the century." Nesuhi

Opposite page: Charles Mingus TL: 50s

The Jazz Heritage of Atlantic Records
By Nat Hentoff

Duke Ellington's highest praise for particular jazz musicians – a tribute he rarely used – was that they were "beyond category". The jazz heritage of Atlantic Records is composed of just such musicians – whose work has endured internationally because it transcends passing trends and fads. Charles Mingus, for one. The most compelling and inventive bass player in jazz history. A volcanic ensemble leader and the most original, far-ranging jazz composer, aside from Duke Ellington. "I'm trying," Mingus once told me, "to play the truth of what I am. The reason it's difficult is because I'm changing all the time." Mingus's continually surprising and challenging growth as a musician and a man (and in jazz, the two are the same) is available on Atlantic Records. John Coltrane is another musician who never stopped exploring the possibilities of the music – and himself. Alice Coltrane, his wife and a musician herself, recalls that "when John left for work, he'd often take five instruments with him. He wanted to be ready for whatever came". The Modern Jazz Quartet which also created music beyond category on Atlantic Records was not as fiery and explosive as the music of Mingus. Nor was it as trance-like as Coltrane. But its carefully shaped performances – with exceptionally subtle dynamics – also reached deeply into the roots of jazz, including the blues. Its improvisations were the jazz equivalent of chamber music, but it was chamber music with the rhythms of spontaneity. And Ornette Coleman, whose instruments included the alto saxophone, heard sounds and speech-like melodies that no one before had put into music. "My music," he told me, "is more like breathing – a natural, free time. People have forgotten how beautiful it is to be natural." These musicians, and other unique story-tellers – for jazz is a way of telling stories through the expression of memories and desires – have made Atlantic a unique presence in the recording field. Obviously there have been other labels that have produced enduring jazz performances, but what makes the Atlantic story singular is the breadth of the catalogue – from Ray Charles, another geyser of surprises, to Ornette Coleman.

A corollary mark of the label's unmistakable identity was the presence at Atlantic for many years of Nesuhi Ertegun, who headed the jazz division. During those years, when I spent nearly all of my time in the jazz community – in nightclubs, at rehearsals, in recording studios and in writing about the music – it was clear to me that Nesuhi was the most respected figure in jazz recording, among musicians and, indeed, among his competitors. He had – to begin with – unerring taste. With that taste went standards. His love for the music prevented him lowering his standards. And he had genuine respect for the musicians he signed for the label. I have been at sessions at other companies where the A & R man (the director of the sessions) harassed the musicians, continually interposing ideas that were embarrassingly irrelevant and ignorant. But, Nesuhi, as John Lewis of the Modern Jazz Quartet said, "let us decide what we wanted to play". At sessions I used to watch Nesuhi ensure the flow of the music while dealing with all manner of temperaments. Mingus, often sceptical of the intentions and knowledge of record company executives, focused his energy at Atlantic on the music because he trusted Nesuhi. So too with Coltrane and the other musicians. They knew that Nesuhi knew how to listen. He learned how to listen when he was quite young. Nesuhi was the son of a Turkish diplomat, who – among other posts – served in Washington, D.C. as ambassador to the United States. And in Washington, Nesuhi and his brother, Ahmet, became absorbed in blues and jazz. The brothers became regulars at the Howard Theatre in Washington, a citadel of black entertainment, and also became familiar with record stores in the black community. Moving to Los Angeles in 1944, Nesuhi ran the Jazzman Record Shop, a place that – in its choice of pure jazz recordings – reflected his integrity. Before Los Angeles, Nesuhi had become immersed in the work of such musicians as Louis Armstrong, Fats Waller, Duke Ellington, Lester Young and Billie Holiday. He then added a strong concern with authentic New Orleans jazz, and his shop in Los Angeles became a leading source of such recordings, as well as scholarly historic information from the enthusiast who ran the store. He also created his first label, Crescent, and recorded the legendary New Orleans trombonist Kid Ory, who had retired because he could not find any work. In addition, Nesuhi taught a jazz course at UCLA for four years – the first accredited course on jazz at any college in the United States. All of this intense background in the music, from New Orleans on, gave Nesuhi the scope of knowledge that few, if any, other jazz producers equalled. In 1955, he joined his brother Ahmet as a partner at Atlantic. As a producer he was able to fuse the enthusiasm of his youth and the extensive jazz knowledge that he had since acquired. There was also his abiding curiosity. He was not afraid of being surprised, or even startled, by sounds he had never heard before.

A characteristically bold Mingus recording at Atlantic was *Pithecanthropus Erectus*, the subject of which was nothing less than the rise and fall of man. Then there was Mingus's *The Clown*, which included the ominously evocative 'Haitian Fight Song' and the powerfully lyrical 'Reincarnation Of A Lovebird'. A sideman on those dates explained the tension that helped ignite the music: "You had to keep stretching yourself while you were with Mingus. He just wouldn't let you coast. Even in public – you've seen it – he'd yell at you in the middle of a solo to stop playing just licks and get into yourself. Christ, he had more confidence in what we were capable of than we had." And Nesuhi had confidence in Mingus.

John Coltrane was a study in apparent contradictions. His music was like a religion to him. He would not compromise it in any way. At the same time, off the stand, he was shy, self-critical and sensitive to the criticism of others. It is no wonder he felt vulnerable. As Jimmy Giuffre once said, "It was as if he was standing naked on the stage, the music coming directly from the man, not the horn." At Atlantic, Coltrane felt protected at a critical stage of his career so he could take risks and grow. In the box set, *Heavyweight Champion: The Complete Atlantic Recordings*, the evolution of Coltrane ranges from *Giant Steps* and *My Favorite Things* to performances with Ornette Coleman. As jazz critic Stephen Thomas Erlewine writes, "The scope of this music is, quite simply, breathtaking – not only was Coltrane developing at rapid speed, [but] the resulting music encompasses nearly every element that made him a brilliant musician, and it is beautiful." Coltrane's recordings, like those of Mingus, the MJQ, and others on Atlantic, will last as long as music is being heard.

John Coltrane

Along with his openness to new dimensions of music, Nesuhi had another quality that performers prize – patience. Roberta Flack was a case in point. The Washington-based singer and composer blended jazz, soul and pop, and she had a small but growing audience. Jazz historian Dan Morgenstern wrote that she had a "totally unique personality with a supreme gift of communication. Roberta Flack sounds like nobody else, and sounds like she meant to stay that way." Nesuhi recorded her on Atlantic, but it took a while for her to accumulate significant sales. "We knew she was going to happen," said Nesuhi. "So we kept on working on her, but it took two years for it to come." By careful planning of club dates and targeted publicity to writers and radio stations, this woman with "a supreme gift of communication" did indeed break through.

Another illustration of Nesuhi keeping his eye on the prize is the history of Ray Charles at Atlantic. In view of his current world-class stardom, it may be difficult to imagine that Charles once had a limited audience. Actually, Nesuhi recalled later, "Ray was an unknown R & B artist with a few songs, but we knew he was infinitely more than that. I made an LP called *The Genius of Ray Charles*. It was his first album that was not just his music or his group. I had the whole Count Basie band, half of the Duke Ellington band, plus Ray's own band. I had over 40 people in the studio when we made that album. It worked." Jerry Wexler wrote in *Rhythm and the Blues: A Life in American Music*, "The session was the most expensive in Atlantic history." At first, "disorder ruled; panic was in the air; and everyone was on edge." Quincy Jones, who had been commissioned to write all the arrangements didn't come through; but Nesuhi, having been given "the bad news before the Monday record date", did not panic. As Wexler remembers,

"In a flash, Nesuhi hired Al Cohn, Ernie Wilkins and Johnny Acea to write over-the-weekend scores, which were still coming in on Monday morning – and still being copied – while the players assembled in the studio. As the cats were playing one song, sheets of papers notating the next song were flying everywhere, and special couriers were arriving on motor bikes with last-minute changes." As Nesuhi said, "It worked."

One decision Nesuhi made that particularly impressed me was the signing of Ornette Coleman. John Lewis recommended Coleman, but there were many musicians who mocked the young man with the plastic alto saxophone and his music – music that had strange rhythmic accents and spiralling melodies with asymmetrical lengths. Some of the older players put Ornette's music down as not being jazz at all, and there was controversy wherever he played. Ornette had first recorded for Contemporary Records in Los Angeles, but Contemporary, a fine label, was not otherwise much involved in what could be called postmodern jazz. As for the other labels, the majors were only fitfully involved in jazz. The jazz companies were largely specialized. Commodore mainly recorded Chicago jazz including Eddie Condon's minstrels, plus some Billie Holiday. Prestige emphasized classic bop – Miles Davis and Sonny Rollins, among other improvisers. Mercury had Dinah Washington and Sarah Vaughan and was also distinguished by the presence of the brilliant young trumpeter, Clifford Brown. Some smaller labels kept the jazz faith. Atlantic's main competitor for taste and integrity was Blue Note Records, which ranged from Sidney Bechet, the New Orleans tornado-like soprano saxophonist, to Thelonious Monk. But Atlantic had the most diverse array of musicians – from Ray Charles to the Modern Jazz Quartet to Charles Mingus to John Coltrane and Ornette Coleman – as well as Lennie Tristano, the coolest (almost literally) of all jazz performers.

Charles Mingus

The history of Ornette Coleman's impact on the jazz world is particularly revealing of Atlantic's influence. John Lewis tells the start of the story; "After I suggested to Nesuhi out of the blue, that he record Ornette, he did something more, showing again that he was one of the most generous people I've known. In this case he not only arranged for a record date with Ornette, but he also paid for him to come to the Music Inn in Lenox, Massachusetts, where the MJQ was in residence. And he recorded Ornette there."

Ornette's first session for Atlantic, *The Shape Of Jazz To Come*, heralded the extent of Ornette's influence. It included the poignant, penetrating 'Lonely Woman' and 'Peace'. All of his recordings for Atlantic reverberate with the power of his approach to jazz. "Music," Ornette told me, "is for our feelings. I think jazz should try to express more kinds of feelings than it has up to now ... you're actually hearing and trying to express the warmth of a human voice." Indeed, it was feeling – joy, the deepest blues, anger, ironic wit and the sounds and rhythms of the human condition – that Nesuhi had to have in the music he recorded. The reason these Atlantic jazz sets have never gone out of fashion is because they are not about fashion. They are about what it is to be alive. As John Coltrane put it, "This music is the whole question of life itself."

All of Nesuhi's artists would have grown in stature and influence had they not been on Atlantic, but the care and feeling he put into their recordings gave their careers much added momentum. And Ornette's future has surely been affected by Atlantic. As *Jazz: The Rough Guide* – an authoritative, annotated discography – puts it: "Ornette Coleman's influence continues to show itself all over the jazz spectrum. Musicians not only listen to his music and learn from it; they also seek him out to study with him and discuss their musical ideas ... Ornette has made his music as serious as his life!"

When Nesuhi Ertegun died in 1989 at the age of 71, the tributes recognized the depth as well as the extent of his achievements. In *Cashbox*, Lee Keske wrote: "The history of jazz is dotted with people who, although not musicians, are essential figures in the music's advancement; people who, motivated simply by a love of the art form, helped to set it on its feet. Nesuhi Ertegun was one of those figures ... A giant in the business."

For a jazz musician who wants his music to be accessible to listeners long after he's gone, the quality of the person who produces his records is crucial. It is that person who will prove the best setting for those pieces the player has found and has personalized from all the music that has been out there in the first place. And it goes beyond the music itself when the producer, such as Nesuhi, takes the responsibility to guide the entire work as the consumer sees it. He directed the entire packaging of the album – the cover, the photography and the sleeves – and he even supervised the liner notes. The albums looked inviting before you even took the record out. The highly distinctive personalities of Mingus (the man and the music) compelled attention in the packaging of the Mingus sets (*Pithecanthropus Erectus*, among them). The cover of Ornette Coleman's *The Shape Of Jazz To Come* also intrinsically heralded the prosaic music within.

For a time Nesuhi left the active production of jazz recordings. As head of WEA International – which he built into one of the most powerful distribution networks around the world – he spent four out of each seven days outside the United States. But he yearned for the sounds and good feeling of the recording studio, and in 1988, Nesuhi started a new label, EastWest Records, distributed by Atlantic. The importance for him of being directly involved with jazz musicians is emphasized by a statement of his at the time: "I've had an urge to go back to the studio lately. It's been six, seven, eight years since I was last in the studio, and I've missed the feeling." With the Modern Jazz Quartet as his first project, Nesuhi said, "It'll be the beginning of a new chapter for me and for them. And this hopefully will be only the beginning of my return to the studio." He planned to keep the new label small, "with not many releases, very selective, extremely particular on quality, presentation. We're in no rush – we're not after the Top 40 hits." Nesuhi's new label would have been a challenge to the industry, setting new standards of quality and integrity. But Nesuhi died of cancer the next year.

One of the tributes paid him came from Paul Russell, managing director of CBS United Kingdom: "He had a tremendous wit, charm, and enthusiasm ... He made you feel special when you talked to him, no matter who you were." That was my experience too. I looked forward to conversations with Nesuhi. As a journalist I found him refreshingly candid. He never tried to put a manipulative spin on an answer to a question. Like a jazz musician, Nesuhi played it straight, no chaser. In these years since his death, his legacy has continued – not only with regard to the still fresh recordings he produced but also with regard to the standards he set for those who have followed him at Atlantic in recording such one-of-a-kind musicians as James Carter, Cyrus Chestnut and Wessell Anderson. Carter, a fiery yet lyrical master of the alto, tenor and baritone saxophones, has strong roots in jazz while helping to shape the future, as in both *Conversin' With The Elders* and *The Real Quietstorm*. He has played with Lester Bowie, Wynton Marsalis and The Lincoln Center Jazz Orchestra, among other engagements. The *Los Angeles Times* says that Carter's music "resonates with the sounds of jazz history." Nesuhi Ertegun would understand what James Carter means when he says: "When you play, you have to play with the spirit in the music. You can't just play the notes according to some method or some book." Also keeping alive the jazz spirit on Atlantic is pianist Cyrus Chestnut, whose playing resounds with the exuberance of gospel music and the further understanding of the human condition through the blues. Though attuned to contemporary jazz, Chestnut is an admirer of the timeless "Fats" Waller. He has worked with Jon Hendricks, Terence Blanshard, Donald Harrison and Wynton Marsalis. "It is my hope," he says, "to be an interpreter of life." As bassist Steve Kirby – who has played with Chestnut – points out, "He likes his music to be danceable, even if it's just a little riff. Cyrus Chestnut is indeed an interpreter of life, its full range. Like James Carter, he will be a long-lasting inspiration to other jazz players." Wessell Anderson plays the kind of warm, personal alto saxophone that is characterized by the title of two of his Atlantic albums, *Warmdaddy On The Garden Of Swing* and *The Ways Of Warmdaddy*. An alumnus of one of Wynton Marsalis' groups, he now heads his own unit. The emotional force of his singular style has been captured by Howard Reich in the *Chicago Tribune*: "[He is] an important new voice in jazz ... the intense, fervently wrought tone of his high register alto, long-held blue notes, chant-like phrases, wide open melodic leaps, lean and modern harmonies ... make Anderson's solo passages alluring." With these musicians, and others, the heritage of Nesuhi Ertegun continues. He went far into the depths of jazz and thereby became a creator himself, helping to forge the discoveries of many musicians into albums that assured their music would survive. In the process, as he moved with ease from Ray Charles to Ornette Coleman, Nesuhi understood what Sidney Bechet used to say: "There's this mood about the music, a kind of need to be moving. You can't just set it down and hold it. Those Dixieland musicianers tried to do that; they tried to write the music down and kind of freeze it. Even when they didn't arrange it to death, they didn't have any place to send it. That's why they lost it. You just can't keep the music unless you move with it."

Ahmet and Nesuhi

Nesuhi, with no lack of love for the jazz of the past, did keep moving with the music. And he became, in essence, one of the musicians. A description he would prize.

Nesuhi Ertegun and Miriam Abramson

"234 West 56th Street was a wood-framed brownstone from the late 19th century. The shipping room was on the fourth floor and we were on the fifth. The floor sagged and creaked, and the sloped ceiling had a skylight in the middle of it. The whole office wasn't more than nineteen feet by twenty-eight. The office *was* the studio and I had to make do. I was determined to get the clean, crisp sound that we all wanted to achieve. The whole operation was marked by a curious mixture of determination and improvisation. Lines of authority were blurry, but the bosses would compare notes and thrash out differences. From time-to-time though, they'd decide to organize. That was always a joke. There was always talk about saving money, but budgets were never established. I remember one meeting where Ahmet and Jerry insisted that we work the studio faster and develop more precise methods of operation. They asked for suggestions. I suggested that Ahmet and Jerry be fired for having absolutely no operating methods themselves. They busted up laughing. So much for procedural discipline." Tom Dowd

Clockwise from top left: Buddy Johnson, Norman Orlein, Ella Johnson, Joe Turner, M. S. Tather, Mrs. Alan Freed, Ahmet, Alan Freed and Jerry Wexler

Jerry Wexler, Ahmet and Miriam Abramson

Jimmy Witherspoon TL: 50s

"In the fifties, the label's classic jazz roster was dominated by trombonist Wilbur De Paris, who led a phenomenally entertaining unit usually spotlighting Omer Simeon's clarinet and the trumpets of both Doc Cheatham and De Paris' younger brother, Sidney. Here was no group of funny-hat Dixielanders grinding out tired rehashes of 'Tiger Rag'; here was an exciting, polished ensemble, under the thumb of a leader and producer who had the intelligence to create such unusual packages as an album of Cole Porter songs and a full-length collaboration with blues singer Jimmy Witherspoon." Will Friedwald

Wilbur De Paris and his band, from left: Wilbur De Paris, Freddie Moore, Eddie Gibbs, Don Kirkpatrick, Omer Simeon and Sidney De Paris TL: 50s

Ahmet, Joe Turner and Jerry Wexler

"I taught Joe Turner 'Corinne Corinna'. He vaguely remembered 'Corinne' as an old folk song. Anyway, it was my idea to do that and 'Midnight Special' – a song which was done either by Leadbelly or the Golden Gate Quartet – in a new version which we called 'Midnight Special Train'. They suited Joe, and had enough pop quality in them to make them hits. You couldn't just do 12-bar blues over and over again." Ahmet

Pete Johnson TL: 50s

Big Joe Turner TL: 50s

THE ATLANTIC STORY

LaVern Baker TL: 50s

"Chuck Willis was a great, great artist. He'd made records for Columbia on the Okeh label, had some hits there, and when his contract was over, we signed him up. So he was an established artist when we took him. His biggest hit for us was 'C.C. Rider', which was Chuck's total reworking of the classic song, 'See See Rider'. The first recording of the song I know of was by Ma Rainey in the twenties, and there were several recordings of it in the thirties by different singers. It's a different kind of blues. In fact, several years later, we had another hit with LaVern Baker's take on the traditional version of the song." Ahmet

Opposite: Chuck Willis, 'The Sheik of the Shake' TL: 50s

"LaVern Baker had a huge R & B hit with 'Tweedlee Dee', which started to climb up the pop charts at the same time. However, almost immediately, Georgia Gibbs recorded a white cover version for Mercury, which used almost exactly the same arrangement. It stole LaVern's glory by going all the way to #2 on the pop chart. LaVern was beautifully good natured, so when she was about to travel to Japan on tour and she was a bit nervous about flying, she took out a $1 million insurance policy and sent it to Georgia Gibbs with a note saying, 'Here – if my plane crashes you're gonna need this more than I do!'" Ahmet

Georgia Gibbs TL: 50s

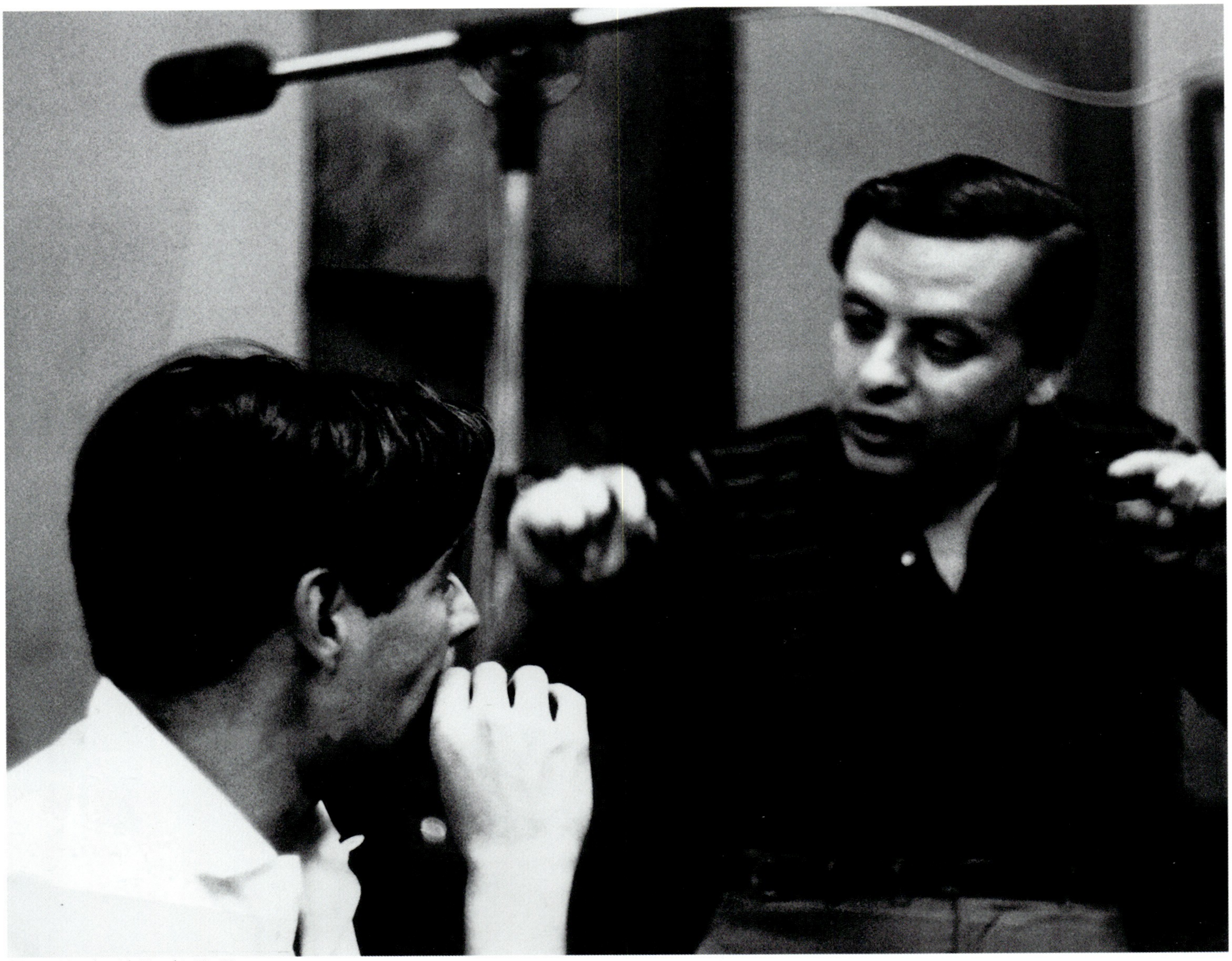

Warne Marsh with Nesuhi TL: 50s

"What did I learn from Lennie Tristano? Integrity. There's no bull with him as to what the music is supposed to be. You simply study what is recognized as having been great so far in jazz. A student first gets an education by listening to Louis, Prez, and Bird – before any theory. From there, Lennie applies the basic ingredients – harmony, ear training, rhythm, the understanding of what goes into improvising, without actually telling the student what to play. The big thing I got from Lennie was the feeling that music was worth so much to him, and it could mean that much to me if I played only what I wanted to play." Warne Marsh

THE ATLANTIC STORY 95

Above and below: Chris Connor TL: 50s 60s

"Chris Connor was considered a jazz singer. Why they called some music 'cabaret' and other music 'jazz', I don't know. Some say one, some say the other. I mean, Tony Bennett is a jazz singer and Bobby Short is a jazz piano player. There's a very fine line." Ahmet

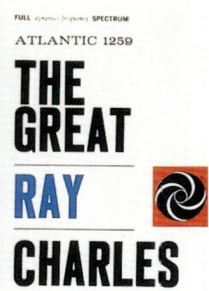

Wilbur De Paris at the Boston Symphony Hall with his pet poodle Zizi TL: 50s

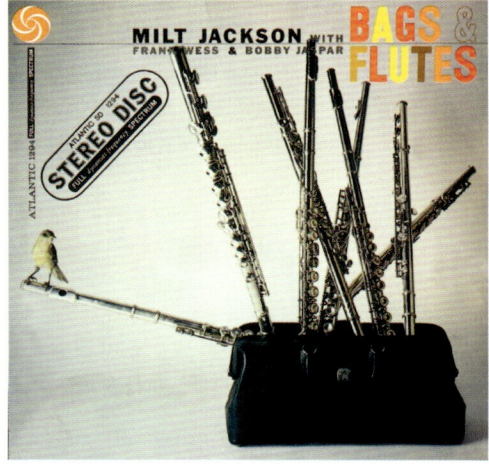

"Playing old numbers doesn't make it jazz. Our approach as Negroes is going to make it different. For instance, my playing of Jelly Roll's 'The Pearls' is slow, because I know that Jelly had to confine it to the three minute, 15 second time limit when he recorded it, so he had to speed it up from its original tempo. I knew Jelly well, lived right next to him in New York, and we've got an intuition for that music. We are playing exactly as the earlier musicians would be playing if they were playing today. That's why I call my band Wilbur De Paris and His New New Orleans Jazz." Wilbur De Paris

Phineas Newborn TL: 50s

"I'll tell you how we got Phineas Newborn. John Hammond called me and said, 'There's this great piano player who's up from Memphis and I would like you to hear his recordings.' So I went up to the office of Willard Alexander, who booked big bands – he's from the era of Benny Goodman, Tommy Dorsey, all those big bands. We signed him up. Phineas came from a very musical family – his father was a bandleader – and he had an unbelievable technique. I'd not heard such playing since the days of Art Tatum. Phineas made some really, really powerful records for us. Some people used to call him 'Phine-ass'." Ahmet

Bobby Short on Park Avenue in New York, in front of Ahmet's Rolls-Royce and chauffeur Frank TL: 50s

"My first wife was a native Californian. She used to tell me about a club, which was at the same place where Spago is now, on Sunset Boulevard in L.A. She said there was a terrific pianist/singer named Bobby Short, whom I'd never heard of. Her friends also told me that he was fantastic and that he came from New York. So I went and heard him play. I was knocked out and signed him up. And that was in 1953 or 1954, and he has remained a wonderful friend and contributor to the success of Atlantic over the years.

"Mabel Mercer had been a music hall dancer and a main attraction at Bricktop's in Paris in the thirties. She came to New York and eventually had her own club. She recorded some terrific albums with us in the fifties, including: *Songs By Mabel Mercer* and *Mabel Mercer Sings Cole Porter*. Later, in 1968, she and Bobby Short did a wonderful live album together from New York's Town Hall. Mabel Mercer was a singer's singer – Frank Sinatra, Lena Horne and Nat King Cole – they all admired her greatly." Ahmet

Bobby Short TL: 50s

Opposite: Mabel Mercer TL: 50s 60s

The Coasters, from left: Carl Gardner, Bobby Nunn, Leon Hughes and Billy Guy TL: 50s

"Firstly, we had to be amused. I mean, if Stoller laughed, my God, the walls would come tumbling down – I figured I had it made. There was a combination of things that went into that in terms of attitudes. First of all, we identified very much with the black point of view. As far as we were concerned, we were black. We did not identify strongly with a white sensibility. I had grown up on the edge of the black part of town, and had worked for years as a kid delivering groceries and coal, mostly in black neighbourhoods. My friends were mostly all from that area, so I practically grew up in that part of town. Then there was the fact that we were adolescents: we started writing when we were seventeen, and adolescents can be very anti-social. They do all sorts of things that are really unfathomable. They're also mischievous – they're resistant to orthodox authoritarian rules, values, convention. So a lot of the attitudes had to deal with thumbing your nose at an adult world by means of these little vignettes – but a lot of it had to do with this being a white kid's take on a black person's take on white society." Jerry Leiber

"After 'Ruby Baby', we became aware of Leiber and Stoller again through a band called The Robins, who'd had a hit with one of their songs, 'Riot In Cell Block No. 9', which was a very clever lyric. We tried to acquire that record from the Spark label, which was run by Leiber and Stoller. Although that didn't work out, the following year we were able to lease the masters of another Robins' song, 'Smokey Joe's Cafe', and at the same time, we made a deal with Leiber and Stoller to work as independent producers for Atlantic. I believe that was the first time any label had signed independent producers. In fact, up to that time, records never had a credit for a producer. The major record companies had musical directors who would hire arrangers, conductors and musicians, but at Atlantic we would call in arrangers to write up very rough charts – which we would then change because they would never be quite right. We were, in fact, very actively producing, because we were moulding the record. Leiber and Stoller were so great for us because not only did they write so many terrific songs, but they also knew exactly what they were doing as producers. At the time we made the deal with Leiber and Stoller, two of the Robins recruited two other singers and put together a new group which they called The Coasters, since they were all from the West Coast. So they became the first group which Leiber and Stoller produced for us under this new arrangement. The Coasters, of course, had many hits, and we also got Leiber and Stoller to produce The Drifters and Ben E. King, among others." Ahmet

"In the mid-to-late fifties, around four o'clock in the afternoon, kids would come up in the elevator at 234, go to the receptionist and say, 'Is Joe Turner going to record soon? When are you going to record Ruth Brown? I wrote a song for them.' These kids would be doing their homework, listening to DJs Willie Bryant, Ray Carroll and 'Jumbo' Jack Walker. When they'd hear a Clovers, a Drifters or a LaVern Baker record, they'd write the reply to that song. They didn't write a song and say, 'Somebody should do this song,' they wrote a particular song for a specific artist. They'd sit down at the piano and one kid would play and one would sing. We didn't sign the song, we didn't steal from them, we didn't give them $50. We'd just ask them to come back after school in maybe two weeks' time, and meet the artist – who would maybe say, 'Yeah, that's a good idea.' Carole King, Gerry Goffin, Neil Sedaka, Howie Greenfield – they were all going to school at the same time, they all knew each other, and they were all writing songs. So we're getting white answers to black records with black concepts, but with white dialogue for black artists. So while everyone else is doing the doo-wops, standing on the corner, beer barrel stuff, we are going through this transition." Tom Dowd

Ahmet dancing with top Galanos model Rosalie Calvert

The Coasters TL: 50s

"The Clovers had their first pop chart hit in 1956" Ahmet

THE ATLANTIC STORY

Jerry, Ruth Brown, Clyde McPhatter, LaVern Baker, Ahmet

"Danny 'Rum Joe' Taylor was a wino, a sweetheart and a sometime songwriter. He was petite, jockey-sized, with a cap, and always had a flagon or a half pint of hooch in a brown bag under his arm. He'd go to the top floor, walk into the first office and say, 'My man, I gotta, gotta, gotta,' because he had a terrible stutter, but then he'd start singing something like 'Thinking Of You Baby'. Someone would give him five dollars and say, 'Here Danny, come back when you're finished baby, but I want the song, don't give it to anybody else.' Then he'd go down to the next floor and he might pick up $30 from the whole building. He hit Atlantic once or twice, and we loved him, we weren't gonna screw him around. One day he walked in and Jerry was on one 'phone and Ahmet was on the other. Ahmet catches Danny's eye and says, 'You ask Jerry for $25, and I'll give you $15.' So Ahmet is making out like he's talking on the 'phone, and Danny goes over and sings a song through for Jerry, who says, 'All right, how much do you want for that?' Danny says, '$25.' Jerry's eyes get like saucers, the veins start to stand out on his face and neck, '$25!! You gotta be out of your goddamn mind! $25! That's not a $5 song!' Danny says, 'Ah, Ah, Ah-Ahmet needs $15.'"
Tom Dowd

"The Bobbettes were a group of kids who wrote the song 'Mr. Lee' about their least favourite teacher at school." Ahmet

"The Cookies were terrific. In fact Ray Charles loved them so much he took them and made them his Raelettes." Ahmet

Left: The Bobbettes, including: Jeannie Pought, Emma Pought, Heather Dixon, Helen Gathers, Laura Webb, and behind from left: Big Joe Turner, Sammy Price and Ahmet TL: 50s

Opposite: The Cookies, from top: Margie Hendrix, Ethel 'Earl-Jean' McRea and Pat Lyles TL: 50s

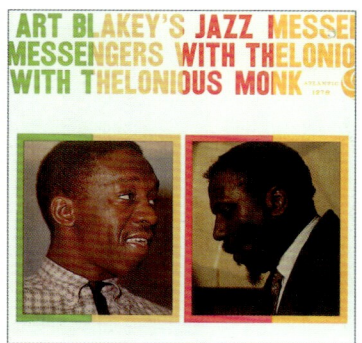

Art Blakey TL: 50s

"We began to rehearse – catastrophe. They couldn't play it, because Monk's music is very difficult rhythmically. Not to play the notes, but to play them with the right accents is extremely difficult. So we tried and tried for one hour, two hours; nothing was happening. At one point, Blakey and I thought we should talk to Monk, so we took him into a corner and Blakey said, 'Monk, do you have some music for these compositions of yours?' 'Sure, man, I got music, it's there in that briefcase.' So I said, 'Bring it out – please – help them.' He said, 'No way.' I said, 'Monk, you're a genius – these are musicians, they need some help, show them the music.' He said, 'They must memorize it, they have to – I will never show them the music.' So I said, 'Well, that means no record.' Six hours went by, we didn't record one minute of music. At the second session there were a lot of guests, including the Baroness, the lady in whose house Charlie Parker died. She was born Rothschild, was extremely interested in jazz, quite wealthy, and had tremendous friendships with a range of black musicians. She was probably, ironically, one of the best friends Charlie Parker had. She was also very, very close to Monk and his wife; they were great friends. So we were trying and trying again, and then suddenly the musicians got the idea of the rhythmic pattern and they felt at home. He never did show them the music, and maybe he was right and in the end they played better that way. As it

Nesuhi

began to go so well, he would play a few violent chords on the piano, then go to the Baroness and they would waltz. I was terrified that they'd hit a microphone or a wire or something. During the long stretches where there wasn't any piano, he wasn't just sitting there, he was dancing, and enjoying it going so well. I think we made an historic album.

"About 5 o'clock in the morning, I left the studio with my notes and everything. The sun was just coming up, and there outside the studio I was met by the sight of Monk, the Baroness, the entire Art Blakey band – all attempting to push the Baroness's Rolls Royce because it wouldn't start. It was the most fitting climax to two days of insanity! " Nesuhi Ertegun

Jazz fan holding magazine with Art Blakey on the cover

Opposite page: Thelonious Monk TL: 50s

Overleaf left: Champion Jack Dupree TL: 50s
Overleaf right: T-Bone Walker TL: 50s

Guitar Slim TL: 50s

Opposite: Ray Charles and members of his Orchestra TL: 50s

"Ray Charles introduced us to Guitar Slim, who was a true R & B artist. We recorded him in New Orleans. We also recorded him in New York, but I remember one session in New Orleans where he came with a retinue of about twenty-five people, including several chicks. I was sitting talking to one of the girls and I said, 'What are you doing here?' She said, 'I don't know, he paid my ticket from L.A.' He could hardly tune his guitar, but he had a band composed of young avant-garde beboppers who were all very adept. They were laughing at him; I mean, it was the weirdest scene. It was an absolutely insane session. I don't think we ever got anything right. But that band were really trying to get him, they kept catching him out. He'd play twelve bars, and the next section he'd play twelve and a half bars, and then he'd play thirteen bars, then he'd play eleven bars – the band didn't know what he was going to play. But in spite of that, he was a terrific performer and a great character." Ahmet

The Crowns, clockwise from left: Dock Green, James Clark, Charles Thomas, Elsheary Hobbs, Ben E. King TL: 50s

From left: Sarah Vaughan, George Treadwell, Ruth Brown and Dizzy Gillespie

From left: Mike Stoller, Lester Sill and Jerry Leiber

"We would invariably take the first tapes of what we'd done to Ahmet, Jerry and Herb, so that they could make comments and give their opinion – but mostly because we were so excited about what we'd just come up with. They were usually extremely enthusiastic, but I remember with 'There Goes My Baby' we played the tape for Jerry Wexler, who was eating a tuna fish sandwich at the time. He was so appalled by the record, that he automatically started yelling, forgetting that he was eating a sandwich – bits of which consequently ended up all over the wall as he kept shouting, 'Goddam awful trash! How can you play a tape like that for me?! That tune is being played in three different keys, it sounds like three stations playing at the same time coming through on one very bad car radio!' Just then, Ahmet came into the room puffing a cigarette saying, 'What was that? What was that?' Jerry yelled back, 'It's trash!' Ahmet said, 'Play it for me.' After which he nervously looked around the room and said, 'I think it's interesting.' Jerry was almost apoplectic! He stalked out of the room and didn't want anything to do with it – but on that occasion Ahmet was right." Jerry Leiber

"The Drifters' manager, George Treadwell, hired the band that I was in, called the Five Crowns, to take over The Drifters' name. We thought they were all joking, but we found ourselves downtown discussing contracts, engagements – all of which was Greek to me. In the space of one week this kid out of Harlem had gone from semi to pro status – and with Atlantic Records, probably the hottest label of that time, which was frightening!" Ben E. King

"One of the funny things with 'There Goes My Baby' was that I started playing a counter-line, something akin to a Borodin, Rimski-Korsakov kind of line. We decided to use strings on it, and we had four violins and a cello coming to the studio. I asked Stanley Applebaum to write it out for the strings. I felt more comfortable having an experienced hand writing out the arrangement. There was also one tympanum left from a prior orchestra date in the studio, but the drummer didn't know how to attempt it, so he played one note through all of the chord changes, which sounded very weird." Mike Stoller

"'Searchin'' took one or two takes and had this really funky, cranky, trashy sound that we loved. A tune like 'Searchin'' really was about media – the song's characters came from popular radio programmes. Essentially this kind of song is in the tradition of American folk song-writing. It's about tall tales – it's like Paul Bunyan or Paul Henry, the Northwest Mountie. The law is the law, and this man's going to get you, but it turns out it's not about the law, it's about this guy and he's after this girl, and you know what? He's gonna find her!" Jerry Leiber

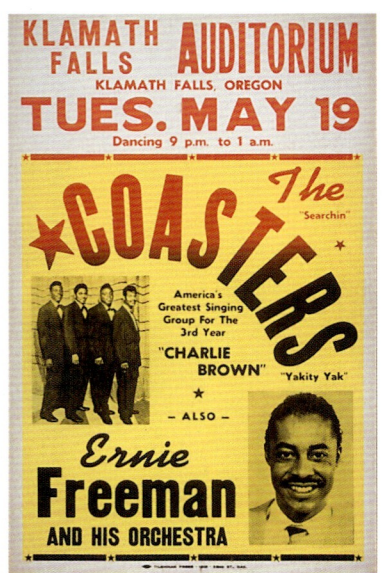

The Coasters on the Hy Lit TV show, New York. From left: Carl Gardner, Cornell Gunter, Will 'Dub' Jones and Billy Guy TL: 50s

The Sensations, from left: Richard Curtain, Alphonso Howell, Yvonne Baker, Sam Armstrong TL: 50s

Clyde McPhatter TL: 50s

Bobby Darin TL: 50s

"Bobby Darin would come up to see Herb, to talk to him about how his record was doing and so forth. While he was waiting, he would hang out in the office next to mine, where there was a piano. He would sit down and play Ray Charles tunes and work on his own ideas for songs. I thought, 'My God, this kid is terrific – he's a wonderful musician, he sounds like an R & B singer, and he's really hitting it.' So I would go in while he was playing, and listen to him, and it wasn't long before we became great friends.

"After Bobby's first releases for us weren't successful, Herb came to me and said he was going to release Bobby from his contract. But I was convinced he had great potential, and I insisted that we keep him on the label. In those days, our office doubled as our studio. We had a tiny control room and a fairly primitive setup, but it worked and had a great sound. In one session with Bobby, I produced several sides, including 'Splish Splash' and 'Queen Of The Hop', both of which he had written. When 'Splish Splash' was first released, a lot of people thought he was black, and we sold a lot of records as a result – as I said before, you can't segregate the radio dial. So 'Splish Splash' was an immediate smash. Next we put out 'Queen Of The Hop', and then cut and released 'Dream Lover'. Bobby Darin was a wonderful artist and an incredible performer, and we continued to make many great records with him." Ahmet

Tom Dowd

"Herb was drafted in 1953, fulfilling his obligation to the government, which had funded his dental school studies. By the time he came back from Germany two years later, the Atlantic executives were Herb's wife, Miriam, Jerry Wexler, my brother Nesuhi, and me. We all owned stock in the company, and we bought out my dentist, Dr. Sabit. We figured that for his original $10,000 he got back between 2.5 and 3 million dollars. So he was very happy, quit dentistry, and moved to the south of France with his wife. In any case, while Herb was gone, things had changed. Atlantic had flourished and become much bigger, almost to the point of being a different company. So we decided to start a different label, called Atco Records, which Herb would oversee. A few years later, Herb left the company, and he went on to form several other labels, as well as running a recording studio." Ahmet

"I convinced Ahmet, Jerry, and Miriam that our main engineer Tom Dowd should be employed with us as a full-time employee – he'd still been working freelance. Dowd told me in '57 that the Ampex tape machine company was now making available eight-track recording on one inch tape, which had been developed by Les Paul." Herb Abramson

Bobby Darin

"I'm listening to this Les Paul record and I'm thinking, how the hell does he do it?! I made a trip up there and I saw parts of Ampex machines laying all over the floor to feed this one transport, and all of a sudden it dawned on me what they were doing. They made such good records and the place looked like a bad radio repair shop – it was astounding!

"So I went back to the city, picked up the 'phone, dialed Ampex and very politely enquired as to how much an eight-track 300 cost and they said, I think, about $11,700. So I went back to Ahmet and Jerry and said, 'Herb's eight-track idea will cost about $11,000 but you'll have this and that … ' They said, 'Dowd, you're crazy – with that kind of money we can make ten more sessions, sell a million more records.' So I said, 'Okay, we don't do it today, we do it tomorrow, it'll take a year to deliver it, we can save $30 a day and we'll do it.' So they said, 'Okay we'll try it.'

"So now I began to worry! I ordered the thing from Ampex, they reckoned about eight-ten months to make it, so after five-six months I'm on the 'phone three times a week to make sure they're going to stick to that schedule and not take eight-ten years. So finally we got delivery of our eight-track child, and one of the first artists to benefit from Ahmet producing with this innovation was Bobby Darin with 'Splish Splash' and 'Queen Of The Hop'." Tom Dowd

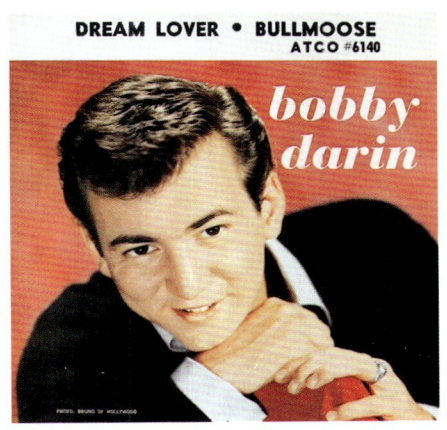

"Chuck Willis had a huge hit after his untimely death in 1958 – 'Hang Up My Rock And Roll Shoes', which was recorded during what would turn out to be his last session. It was our first experience of a great artist being taken away from us, suddenly out of the blue. It was a terrible tragedy and a devastating shock to all of us. Chuck had grown up as a poor boy in Atlanta, not part of that city's black society. When he became ill with a stomach disorder and needed an operation, he insisted on going back to Atlanta. He died on the operating table. At his funeral, thousands upon thousands of people turned out. He was a great, great artist and a truly wonderful person."
Ahmet

Chuck Willis TL: 50s

LaVern Baker TL: 50s 60s

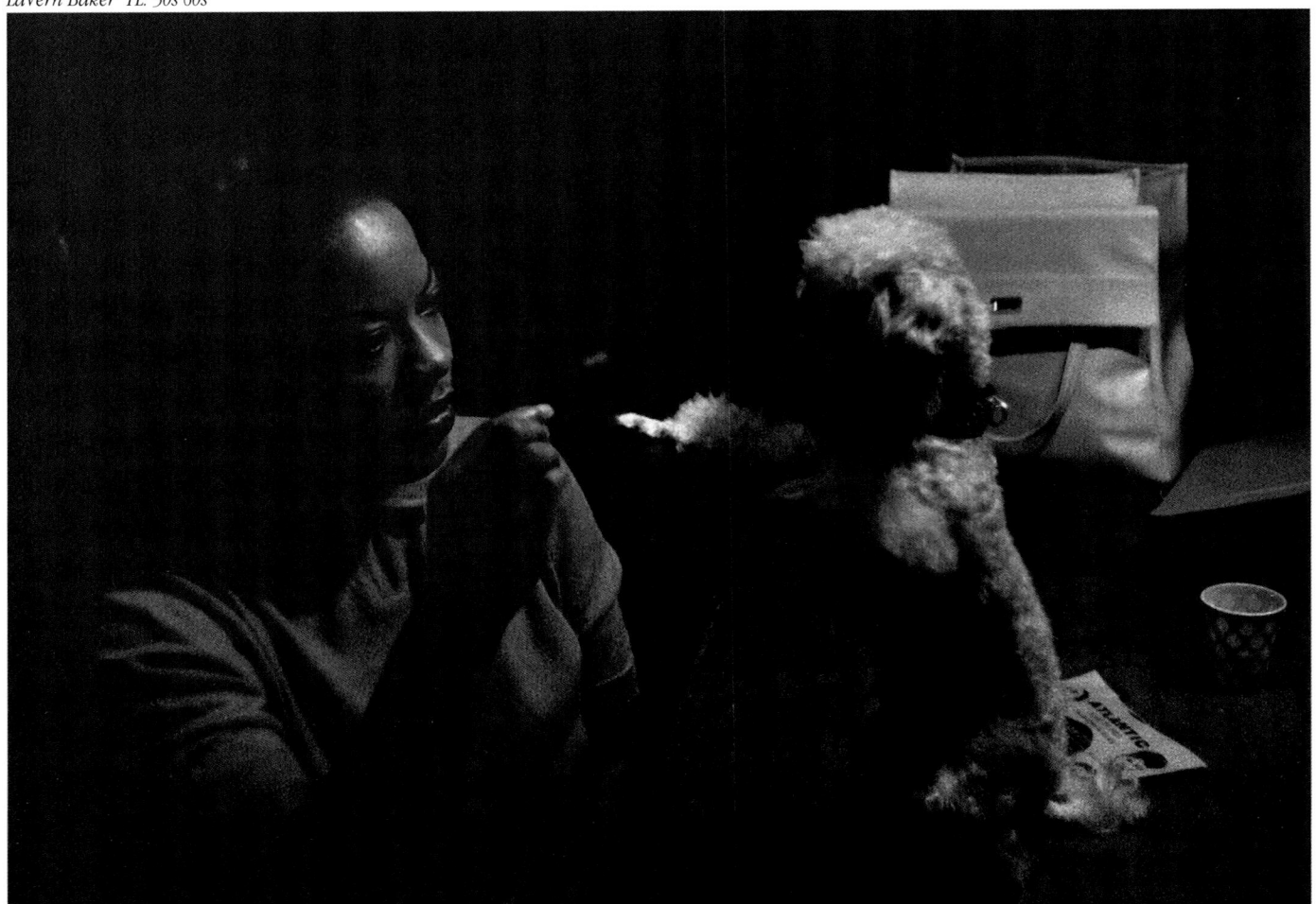

"When we started the jazz programme at the Music Inn in Lenox, Mass., with the Inn's owners, Stephanie and Philip Barber, quite a few musicians came there on scholarships. We had very few black applicants, so I was sent on a trip around the country to try and let people know that this programme was going on. Most black people in both cities and rural areas had no idea what jazz was, which was so strange to me because that music was almost the private domain of the areas where black people lived – jazz was their music, and had been for a long time. In fact, in the general mass public of the U.S., there is a kind of primitive naivety about many aspects of American culture. For example, while I was teaching music at Upper City College in New York, I had a talented student trumpet player in one class, and I asked him, 'Are you working on this material that I'm giving you?' He replied, 'Well, I can't do it at home because my parents are very religious; they think that jazz is the devil's music and it will only do harm.' I couldn't believe that his parents were that primitive, that this stuff was still going on. I'd heard of this kind of thing before the war, but I really thought that shit was over with – but it wasn't. He was just one example. There were many others who also couldn't convince their parents, the generation before them, that jazz was something extremely valuable."
John Lewis

The Modern Jazz Quartet, from left: John Lewis, Percy Heath, Connie Kay and Milt Jackson TL: 50s

John Coltrane TL: 50s 60s

"At our very first solo session with John Coltrane, we recorded a song called 'Giant Steps'. I think that this really represents a new chapter, not just in the history of the saxophone, but in the history of jazz development. I think that Coltrane's solo on 'Giant Steps' had more influence than any other recording he ever made. Some were more famous, but I think that this solo was the most influential since Charlie Parker. There was Parker and then the Coltrane era which, in my view, started with 'Giant Steps'." Nesuhi Ertegun

Ornette Coleman TL: 50s 60s

"It was Percy Heath, Connie Kay and John Lewis from MJQ who said, 'You should check out this guy, Ornette Coleman – try to find him.' I was able to get him on the 'phone, so I introduced myself and asked him, 'Are you interested in making records? Are you playing anywhere?' He said, 'No – I can't get a job. I'm working as an elevator man, but I can put up a rehearsal for you.' I said, 'Fantastic!' So he said, 'Well, come tomorrow at 3 o'clock,' and he gave me an address which was a garage in a very poor section of the city. I walked in there, and four musicians appeared – Charlie Haden on bass, Billy Higgins on drums, Don Cherry, and Ornette. There were also a lot of their friends there as well, children too, and that foursome began to play non-stop for two hours. I couldn't believe what they were playing, I was utterly astonished. I'd never witnessed so much energy before from any musician or any jazz group.

"The records were not popular, did not sell well at all, and received bad reviews. The critics hated him. I kept making the records because I knew they were important. People would say to me: 'You don't really like that, do you? He's a fraud.' I find this completely absurd. I love the music and I think that Ornette is a real intellect, an extremely profound character. To me, Ornette is basically a blues player – he worked in Texas R & B bands as a kid. He's full of blues and it shows through in his music." Nesuhi Ertegun

Ray Charles TL: 50s

"For 'The Genius Of Ray Charles' sessions I had the entire Count Basie band without Count Basie, seven of my favourites from the Duke Ellington band, and I had Quincy Jones do the arrangements. All of these famous musicians were not entirely sure that this blind piano player, who was the star, really deserved all of this. They were kind of looking down their noses a bit, making little wisecracks, and I could see that the atmosphere was not too cool. Ray called me over and said, 'The fourth bar, the third trumpet player, there's a bad note.' I said, 'Are you sure?' He said, 'I'm telling you, there's a bad note.' So I called Quincy over and he said, 'Impossible, I didn't hear it.' I said, 'Well, there's only one thing to do, have the trumpets play one by one.' So they each played, and sure enough, the third trumpet player was hitting a wrong note. Quincy Jones was astonished. He said, 'I've never seen ears like this!' The whole band applauded and it changed the session, saved it – from then on they worked like they never had before." Nesuhi Ertegun

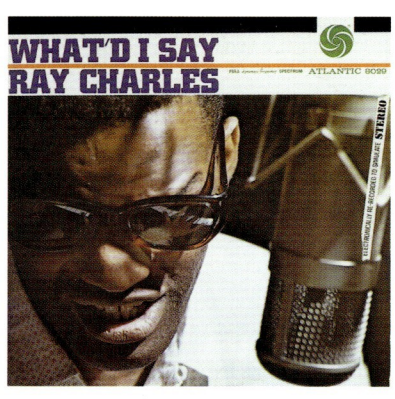

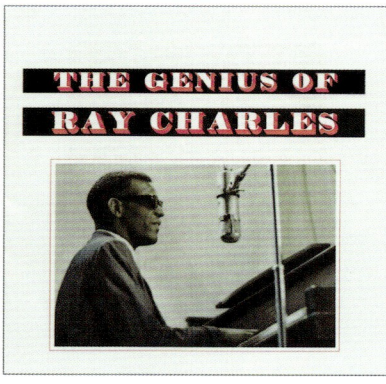

"Yeah, well, they talk about that story, but there's nothing unusual about it. After all, I can hear and I think I know a little bit about music, so if you hear well, you're going to notice a bad note and if you know music you're going to know what note it is. I'm a composer, so that means I can arrange, right? I know what the chord is when it's played – it's that simple. If you know what it takes to get what you should be hearing, you know when something's wrong. Then it's just a matter of saying, 'Hey, the guy who's playing the third trumpet part, or whatever, is playing the wrong note' – and it's not always that he's wrong, the note itself could be wrong on the paper. I mean, people do make mistakes – so it's just a matter of pointing it out and not letting it go on the record if you hear it." Ray Charles

"We were playing deuces [two sets a night] in those days, working from maybe 9 p.m. 'til 11.30, then half an hour intermission, then back again at midnight 'til 1 a.m. One particular night, I'd played everything, so I said to the musicians and the girls, 'Look, just follow this' – and I started playing 'What'd I Say', which is why if you listen to the verses, they're very disconnected. There's no storyline there as such – it's just completely ad-libbed. Every time we'd start to play this song, the place would go wild. People would say, 'Where can I buy this record?' So I telephoned Ahmet and said, 'I've got this song I want to record.' Ahmet just said, as always, 'Whenever you want to come in, you come in.' That was always the attitude: 'Whenever you want.' So we went in, and by then we had it down because, of course, we'd been playing it every night. See, then you didn't do all of this rehearsing in the studio, you did your rehearsing, your playing, getting the songs how you wanted them to be, before you got to the studio. So when you got to the studio, for the most part it was just a question of getting into the mood or the groove that you wanted." Ray Charles

"I'd get to 234 West 56th Street about 6 p.m. They would have stopped their appointments at 5-5.30 p.m. We'd roll the chairs out onto the stairwell, and push the two desks into a corner – one on top of the other. Then I'd start setting up microphones for what we were going to do. The musicians would walk in and say, 'Whose desks are those?' and we'd explain, 'Well, it's an office when you're not recording.' So they'd look at you like you were crazy, but that was it, and in fact, it worked very well. The biggest thing I ever had in there, at 23456, was probably Ray Charles – with the Raeletts, four horns, the piano, a bass, drums and Ray – ten, 11, or 12 people. I mean, if someone sneezed, it would be picked up on all the microphones." Tom Dowd

Ray Charles with the Raeletts, including Dorothy Jones, Margie Hendrix, Ethel 'Earl-Jean' McRea, Pat Lyles TL: 50s

Ray Charles TL: 50s

Milt Jackson TL: 50s

"I was booby trapped into doing the first Milt Jackson and Ray Charles album. Milt came by to a Ray Charles session and introduced himself to Ray. They got on great and Ray said, 'Milt and I are gonna make an album together. We'll be here next week sometime, I'll call you and let you know when.' I called Nesuhi and told him, 'Hey, you won't believe what just happened. Jackson came by, hung out with Ray, and they're gonna make an album together.' Nesuhi was really joyous and said, 'Oh Christ, how did you do it?' I said, 'I didn't do it, they did it.' So I got the piano tuner in, but I didn't know who the hell the bass player was gonna be, who the drummer was gonna be. Eventually the day arrived, and everything was ready. They both came in off the elevator, but Ray was carrying an alto sax, and Milt is holding a guitar. I said, 'What's this?!' Ray said, 'We're gonna record.' Oh shit! Ray with his alto and Milt with his guitar. But you know what? They still made a great record!" Tom Dowd

Wilbur De Paris TL: 50s 60s

From left: Diana de Cordoba, Ahmet, Mica Ertegun, Julio Mario Santo Domingo and Robin Butler at El Morocco, New York

Above and below from left: Jimmy Giuffre, Bob Brookmayer, Jim Hall TL: 50s

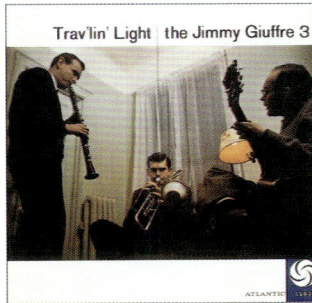

"One night, there was a dinner at the Algonquin to bid goodbye to a girl I had been dating before I met my wife Mica, and there were 15 or 20 of this girl's friends there. I had hired a limousine to take her to the airport, but everyone wanted to come along and see her off. So I telephoned the limo company and asked them how much it would cost for a bus instead of a car. They told me that a limo was $2.50 an hour, and a bus was $3.00 an hour. So for the next year or so, I hired a bus instead of a limo. I put a bar in it, made space for a three-piece band, and we'd have parties. One night, we parked this thing outside El Morocco, and as our friends arrived at the club, we invited them into the bus. Eventually, the manager of El Morocco came out to find out why practically no one was in his club that night – and he saw most of his patrons on board the bus. He calmed down after a while, we invited him on board and gave him a drink. He saw not only all his regular customers, but also his barman, the hatcheck girl, at least two of his waiters, and one hell of a band!" Ahmet

From left: Ahmet, Max Silverman, Miriam Beinstock, Nesuhi and Jerry Wexler

The Second Taste 1954-1962
By Lenny Kaye

Rock and roll. Can't have one without the other. The internal combustions and contradictions of white and black and country-city blues, teenage and wild adult and world-weary, a music that celebrated and revelled in its own inner tensions and dysfunctions and confusions and cataclysms. The solidity and the momentum. Let us rock, and then, honey, let's roll.

How did Atlantic respond to this new music? What did they even think of it, much less divine how to tap its power? What, in fact, was it? Early rock'n'roll sounded a lot like the gutbucket sound of Atlantic that Jesse Stone helped chisel out of his namesake granite. 'Shake, Rattle And Roll', with its two-four hand-clapping snare and sing-along chorus even helped crown it; but this was a don't-look-back hybrid. These weren't "just" R & B records, or "just" jump jazz, or hot blues, a fact increasingly apparent as records leaped over categorical boundaries. These were popular, Top Ten (including the all-important television) media sensations, a cultural impulse that pried open the midpoint of the American century and unleashed a rush of reborn release, as the word "pop" continued its inexorable manifest all over the globe.

In an eight-year span from the mid-fifties to the early sixties, a period palaeolithically referred to as Early Rock'n'Roll, Atlantic moved from being an independent perch over Patsy's, one room and one shipping room, scuffling to keep enough records in motion that they could make it to the next payday, to one of the most proven and respected of hitmakers. More, they did it on their terms, creating records that bore out their own philosophies while trying to intuit the vagaries of the pop flea market.

Now, with perfect timing, the tradewinds had shifted toward them, whipped by storms and geologic tremors, the prevailing currents favouring Atlantic's brand of high-end R & B. Financially and creatively established, with networks of distributors and front-line experience in recording and promoting, not to mention the all-important track record, the label was poised to make the great leap into the most challenging demographic of all: Everybody. But their artists weren't teen idols, like Elvis. They weren't even white, which had a lot to do with being Pop in 1954; crossover black performers were more like *cafe au lait* ("The only group the Ink Spots influenced were the Brown Dots," Ahmet liked to say), the rougher edges of their songs smoothed and covered by white song stylists who had bigger hits; and if the blues could claim to be a black music (Atlantic had never delved much into the white-country version, even though it was the heyday of Hank Williams), it was also not an especially adolescent music, except as filtered through Chuck Berry, and he was signed by Chess.

The actual birth of this rock'n'roll had occurred in a small Memphis manger belonging to Sun Records, whose mining of the R & B mother lode was a little more rural and a little more seat-of-the-pants than Atlantic's relatively urbane sophistication. The Ertegun epicentre was Manhattan and all manner of immigrant musics passed through its portals, stretching towards cosmopolitan Harlem. Despite this, the five boroughs had no indigenous gene pool to draw from, and there was no easily discerned New York style. This wasn't Mississippi or New Orleans or Chicago. Atlantic's forays into the South, Ahmet and Herb Abramson trekking through the Louisiana fields to find Professor Longhair performing as a one-man band at a house party, were more like field expeditions: bring 'em back alive. Atlantic was a city-bred label, attuned to the big beat of the city street, and if that city was New York, a crossroads far more ju-ju potent than that at which Robert Johnson sealed his pact with the devil, the company could custom-colour their signature sound. "Our musicians read music," Ahmet said. "We almost had to force the blues on them."

It was more than ironic coincidence that five days after Sun's Sam Phillips uttered the immortal words, "Hell, that's different. That's a pop song now," to Elvis and Scotty and Bill, the cover of the 10th of July, 1954 issue of *Cashbox* featured the triumvirate of Jerry Wexler, Ahmet Ertegun, and Miriam Abramson, Herb's wife representing him while he served in the armed forces. It was a telling moment in Atlantic's ascendance: *Cashbox* was an industry trade bible and the bones had rolled seven-come-eleven for Atlantic with Joe Turner.

"Cat Music", was how Jerry imagined sloganing the new, overt sound, but the rolled r's proved linguistically irresistible. Atlantic was closer to the source than they imagined, their rhythm and blues – Wexler had christened that genre when he worked at *Billboard* – already possessing the hooks and chants that would increasingly dominate pop music in the golden land of the hit single. And when the time came for Atlantic artists to stretch out, to reveal their inner heart, the essential liveness of their performance skills, they would prove able to deliver the deeper and subtler arts of emotion.

The Chords' 'Sh-Boom' on the Cat label is regarded as one of the opening shots in the R & B crossover, at least until they too were beset by the cover-record virus via the Crewcuts. Possessed of a nonsense syllable refrain that carved a place in one's memory bank with a single hearing, it nonetheless proved white America had its ear to the ground of black America, and vice-versa, and both of them wanted a slice of that pop pork pie. 'Money Honey', as much burlesque swing as 'Sh-Boom' is practically ska-like with its backbeats, might have provided the opening crescendo had not the group identity diffused personality. The nascent rock'n'roll breakthrough called out for an individual star, and Elvis became that first man on the moon. Atlantic bid $25,000 for the Hillbilly Cat, but was relieved when RCA topped their offer. It was a lot of money for a fledgling company, and there was more where that came from, wasn't there?

As the music business stared around dazedly at the atomic bomb that had gone off in its midst, grabbing at all manner of teen juvenile delinquency, Atlantic stuck to its guns. They avoided any aura of fad, and their music didn't so much change as shift shape, highlighting aspects that were there to begin with, as well as a growing confidence in their studio acumen. The records got more punchy, the charts more succinct, their own motivations and aspirations clearer. Rehearsing and preproducing, they believed a record should be "in tune and on time", and they paid particular attention to pitch and intonation. Atlantic's standard of musicianship was too high to take the mark of every street corner; besides, Ahmet and Jerry and Jesse and Herb and Tom Dowd had a corner of their own, and the passing parade looked just fine, thank you.

Ray Charles

LaVern Baker was their diva, a salty shouter whose 'Jim Dandy' raised up a rollicking folk hero, and left no question whose rescue Jim was coming to. Known as "Little Miss Sharecropper" when she worked the midwest blues circuit as a teenager, she was in the tradition of the Mas — Ma Rainey and Ma-halia Jackson. Her husky shasay recorded for Atlantic for nearly eleven years, with the jolly 'Tweedlee Dee' her breakthrough as 1954 drew to a close.

Jerry Wexler's maiden voyage as a producer was with LaVern, and he proved a quick study. He favoured a middle ground in his studio style, neither documentarian nor abstract visionary. He believed a producer should "set the table", bring "notions" to the studio, guide musicians around blind alleys and stiff backbeats, find the pocket and look for the groove; he liked the one and the three — the odd numbered beats — figuring they would take care of the two and four when they got there. Words of wisdom.

He also proved to be a sympathetic ear to innovation, allowing different styles of music to repercuss one on the other in unpredictable combinations, always concerned with locating the song's right key. Texas-born Ivory Joe Hunter had a tumbling descending piano line on his 'Santa Fe Blues'. Cannibalized, it became the rippling spine of 'Since I Met You Baby', an Ertegun-Wexler production that resisted cover versions to become a smash in 1956 with a vocalization that seemed straight out of Floyd Tillman's C & W stylings, an ironic turnabout since Tillman had covered Ivory Joe's first attempt at the song, then titled 'I Almost Lost My Mind' (1950). Throughout the remainder of his life, Hunter would attempt to bridge the gap between R & B and C & W, foreshadowing Ray Charles and, in the last year of his life, receiving the ultimate accolade of a Grand Ole Opry tribute to his artistry.

The beturbaned Chuck Willis was called "King of the Stroll", as well as "Sheik of the Shake", after his cantering 'C.C. Rider' took him up the charts in early 1957, a marimba solo in an ancient blues, no less. His 'Hang Up My Rock And Roll Shoes' has become a defiant statement that has outlived Chuck's untimely passing at the age of thirty a few months later, garnished by a middle eight blown by the original Daddy G. himself on tenor sax, Gene Barge.

It was with Clyde McPhatter that Atlantic had two separate gilded eras. His lithe voice was so unique that, when he returned from the army in 1956, rather than bring him back with The Drifters, Atlantic recorded him as a solo artist. His biggest hit was 1958's 'A Lover's Question', a record that would stylistically lead to Smokey Robinson and Curtis Mayfield, but for me, 'Treasure Of Love' is the one to swoon over; triplets fractioning a shuffle beat, gold ducats pouring as the vocal harmonies swell to meet the chorus.

Oddly, for a company that utilized group vocals so well, Atlantic was never known for its doo-wop combinations. They signed few, especially in an era that found harmonizing groups "hitting notes" wherever a convenient echo might be found, but the quartets and quintets they did have were seminal. Beyond the beauty of the songs, the scat-like harmonies set a standard for impeccable voice-stacking. Still the company's sounds hearkened back toward The Ravens and The Orioles, rather than forward to The Five Satins. The Clovers created two master works of the genre with 'Blue Velvet' and 'Devil Or Angel', moving from the blues towards a more settled crooning sensibility (though Leiber-Stoller restored their sass with 'Love Potion No. 9'), even as doo-wop was infiltrating New York's Italian/Jewish neighbourhoods, each group as much teen clique as singing combo.

"You ain't no child no more," Joe Turner warned. Atlantic's sensibility was definitely mature; but the generation gap could melt both ways. The Drifters' 'Honey Love', with its three squeezes per pre-chorus, wasn't much beyond the age of consent, and who was this 'Mr. Lee' the Bobbettes sang so coyly about? The core musicians – "We were the first record company to put pictures of sidemen on record sleeves," said Jerry – decorated blues progressions with a variety of inventive beats and almost jocular settings. Let them loose, as Cosimo Mattassa did with his New Orleans crew in Tommy Ridgley's 1954 'Jam Up', and you got a jitterbug holler that has the feel of a pre-dawn after-hours club, which is about the time that the stay-out-late Ahmet liked the best.

It helped him work on what he called his "second taste", a bubbling under of his own personal preferences to feel the public pulse. At home he might listen to Ella Fitzgerald, Louis Armstrong, Earl Hines and Fred Astaire. When out, roaming through parties and bars and a variety of high and low societies, he caught the rhythms and moods of the human animal at its most primal. The next day he would show up at the office around three or four or five in the afternoon and snap his fingers to what he had heard the night before. He recognized that the deep longings – for love, for sex, for money in the pocket and hope in the future – as expressed in song were usually unchanging in content; but styles did turnabout on themselves. It was often better to go for the classic look. A great record made an impact like a well-dressed man: the cut of a chorus, the sharp crease in the rhythm section, the fine fabric of the horns.

His cohort in this, Jerry Wexler, added a sense of magic realism to the Atlantic equation. A self-confessed record fanatic, matching Ahmet's enthusiasms with his own, he nonetheless had become intrigued with the machinations of the business as a reporter for *Billboard*. His world only began in the studio; he went to war each day with the rack jobbers and the song pluggers and the tune touts, the telephonic grind of co-ordinating pressing plants and distributors and artist appearances. He believed in "Hits" as a validating concept, as the justification and recognition of quality music's due. He liked to see those Lincolns and Jacksons rub together, as they did in Ray Charles' 'Greenbacks'. Originally making music for "adult negroes", Wexler's intense belief in music "that we personally dug" selling to a mythical Aunt Martha tuned to a radio somewhere, kept step with the vast changes within the music business. As rock'n'roll emerged into the world's spotlight, its implications spiralling far beyond anything the record industry had deemed possible, an independent record company couldn't operate with the same sense of out-of-the-wayness that gave it room to grow in the first place. Many of Atlantic's contemporaries were already beginning to feel growing pains, and few would survive the sixties.

Atlantic itself had no choice but to spread the company's creative centres of power. No longer could Jerry or Ahmet supervise each record, though they kept things small enough so that they might, if need be. Along with Nesuhi, Ahmet's older brother who joined Atlantic as a partner in 1955 to oversee their jazz roster, there was more happening than they could keep resolutely in-house.

Among those they felt had the same turn of mind as themselves were two West-Coasting songwriters – actually, a custom song shop operation that wrote, recorded, talent-scouted, arranged and peddled in a one-on-one motion that could make a one-hit wonder – named Jerry Leiber and Mike Stoller. The lyrically insightful Leiber had matched Stoller's boogie-woogie piano stylings catchphrase for catchphrase, and they'd produced records for many R & B artists and labels, including their own Spark, which featured a group they'd discovered and coached called The Robins. With 'Smokey Joe's Cafe' as a calling card, and a string of Elvis Presley vehicles ('Hound Dog', 'Jailhouse Rock'), Atlantic was more than happy to give them one of the first independent production deals in the music business, which not only allowed them to take on outside work, but gave them free rein with some of Atlantic's floating groups (like The Drifters) or let them guide their own, like The Robins, who would become The Coasters, or – separating from The Drifters – Ben E. King.

Bobby Darin with his wife, Sandra Dee

The urbane landscape Leiber and Stoller designed when they arrived at the Brill Building at 1619 Broadway, the beehive of this pop metropolis, made the neon city come alive. Their Drifters music was a Latin-tinged dreamscape cued for strolling under the bright lights of the avenue that ran outside their Times Square offices, of watching their baby go by on Baion Beach, of lying on the roof or under the boardwalk, living this or any other magic moment life cares to offer up. By this time, The Drifters had become a trademark, featuring a succession of lead singers in Rudy Lewis and Johnny Moore, the best of Don Kirshner's Aldon writers (Goffin-King, Mann-Weil) as well as some of Doc Pomus-Mort Shuman's most memorable compositions, and equally adept producers after Leiber and Stoller moved on, like Bert Berns.

The "social satire" that intrigued Leiber came to roost most especially with The Coasters. His and Stoller's gift for realistic *mise en scène* is such that you can almost hear the ball bounce on the schoolyard court in 'Charlie Brown', the itchin' 'Poison Ivy's guitar scritch, the vaudevillian Coasters able to leap from garbage can ('Wake Me, Shake Me') to nickelodeon ('Along Came Jones'), 'Searchin'' and 'Young Blood' and 'Shopping For Clothes', each a playlet sit-com. Even with their dramatic pauses for impact, all broad black and blue humoresque accents, the beat cracks on the snare and gets you in motion, and Leiber-Stoller's work represents a moment of strange delicacy, balanced between the ribald and the deadly serious, chuckling about "the joke that the poor tell on themselves", as Jerry once put it.

As Leiber and Stoller's productions increased in complexity, they attracted some of the best minds in the music business, all starting to sense the power for creation in this new music. A young Phil Spector played guitar for 'On Broadway'; Carole King watched the session. This was definitive pop music, constructed as records, no longer artefacts but art-cats. Along with a strong ethic in the power of individual performance came Atlantic's belief in the power of the musician's instinct, always pushing the tape level to catch the wobble behind the note, the string moving just that extra millimetre higher, the rhythm in sharp focus even as you can hear a musical mind setting up the next phrase of the chords. The needs of the song were always held paramount, and the catchy three or four note melodies and backbeat then parted to make way for the singer: always the singer.

Ben E. King's '(A Rose In) Spanish Harlem' tells it like no other, a meeting of these like instincts before each would go off to form their own record companies. King had been a member of The (Five) Crowns when they had been chosen to assume The Drifters' mantle in June of 1958; it meant playing twice-yearly at the Apollo, among other things, and it was his voice that scored the reincarnated group's first hit, 'There Goes My Baby'. Still one of the strangest sounding records ever made, its echo chamber dialled to a dismembered delay that rendered King's elegy about his love walkin' by into a funereal two-step, its string arrangement seemingly piped in from the session next door and randomly blended (Leiber said it was like listening to two radio stations at once, not a bad way to have a crossover hit). King returned to the stately Baion beat for his pledge of Hispanic fealty, and the strings flourished around him, taking on the blues "with eyes as black as coal", and then heading downtown to add a symphonic sweep of theme that was as nouvelle as any Truffaut film, the fantasia of these white go-go boys with the turn of phrase, the perfect romantic yearning, and the slippery sound of a record moving silkily up the charts.

The meticulous orchestrations were a far cry from Atlantic's R & B beginnings, where, as Ahmet recalled, "There was no mixing. What you played was what you got." They weren't making records in their offices anymore. They were Top 40 craftsmen, and as such, the Atco label, a custom imprimatur arranged when Herb Abramson returned from the army in 1956, provided a home for Atlantic's more diverse pop and novelty sounds. The Coasters would find themselves on Atco, along with a newcomer who was attempting to redefine the word "brash", Bobby Darin.

He wanted to be an "all-round entertainer" in the Italian sharkskin mode, but first he had to jump past the teen idol tag that his first hit, 'Splish Splash', had given him. Ertegun had produced it New Orleans-style along with Bobby's second score 'Queen Of The Hop', at a single session, but Darin's craving for the big band soon found him taking on such undeniable classics as 'Beyond The Sea' and 'Mack The Knife'. "Bobby was a great showman, and I knew the minute we ran down the orchestrations that we had a hit," said Ahmet of the Kurt Weill classic.

And hits respect no musical boundaries. Mr. Acker Bilk was a British Dixieland clarinettist whose 'Stranger On The Shore' became a surprise million-seller in 1960; as did Bent Fabric with 'Alley Cat'; Nino Tempo and April Stevens with 'Deep Purple'; and on and on. There was even a song by a Memphis girl named Carla Thomas, whose wistful 'Gee Whiz' led Atlantic to the beginnings of Stax and the Memphis sound, soon to become absorbed into Atlantic's oversoul as the sixties moved into high gear.

Ray Charles pointed the way. Atlantic purchased his contract from Swingtime Records in 1952, and Ahmet and Jerry soon realized that Ray knew his own music better than anybody. They simply made sure the tape recorder kept unreeling during crucial moments, giving Ray all the elbow room he needed, and found that his own seven-piece band (no guitar), honed on the road, Jack, backed him better than any studio aggregate. In Atlanta, in November of 1954, recording between newscasts in the Georgia Tech radio station, they were rewarded with 'I Got A Woman', a gospel R & B shout-it-out that swung to and fro with infectious glee.

Ray wasn't much for labels. "The greatest single artist I've ever worked with," (Ahmet), he liked to feel at home in all musics, and he absorbed them all. Charles had learned about western swing playing in cowboy bands; he had crooned like Charles Brown; and preached salvation (albeit musical) like any day-of-reckoning preacher. But when he twirled his fingers into the opening riffs of 'What'd I Say' four piano-roll choruses before that sly vocal comes in doin' the dog all night long, you just had to Let Ray. Or was that Raeletts?

Get right next to the speaker and you can hear Ray clap to himself as he keeps time in the chorus breakdown, his hands off-mike but present, the microphone placement that is Atlantic Records. In an instant, the music called Soul comes into being. Hallelujah!

Bobby Darin TL: 50s 60s

"I was at my friend Lotte Lenya's house for lunch one day when she asked me why I'd never made a record of her first husband Kurt Weill's work. I tried to explain that we were a small company that specialized in R & B. She couldn't understand and said, 'What blues? What R & B? Isn't it all pop music?' I said, 'No, it's all different – but maybe we'll try; if we can, we will.' Now Louis Armstrong had made a terrific record of 'Mack The Knife'. Literally a couple of days after my lunch with Lotte, Bobby Darin, who was a tremendous Armstrong fan, came up to me with this record and said, 'I know this sounds pretty weird, but I think I could make a great version of this – I should do it.' So we made a big band arrangement with a kind of Sinatra feel. We used Don Lamond, a great drummer from Washington, and Richard Wess completed the arrangement, although Bobby had a lot of influence over that, too. The minute I heard the track go down I said, 'This is magic!' I mean, the arrangement bubbles, it swings so much, it's just so in the pocket. Two or three takes was all it took, and Bobby sang his heart out, with so much feeling. It won the Grammy as Record of the Year, and Bobby was also named the Best New Artist of 1959 – which were Atlantic's very first Grammy Awards. Bobby became a huge star – playing all over, playing Las Vegas. He was a potential next Sinatra, which was a far cry from 'Splish Splash'. He kept some of that funky rock-'n'roll as well, but actually, I think, he didn't quite know where he was – we were doing something in between but it all worked, and he hit the big time."

Ahmet

Bobby Darin with Ahmet

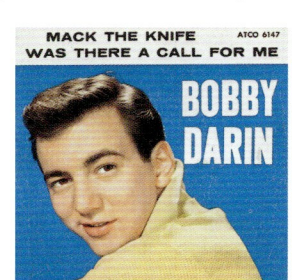

Ben E. King TL: 50s 60s

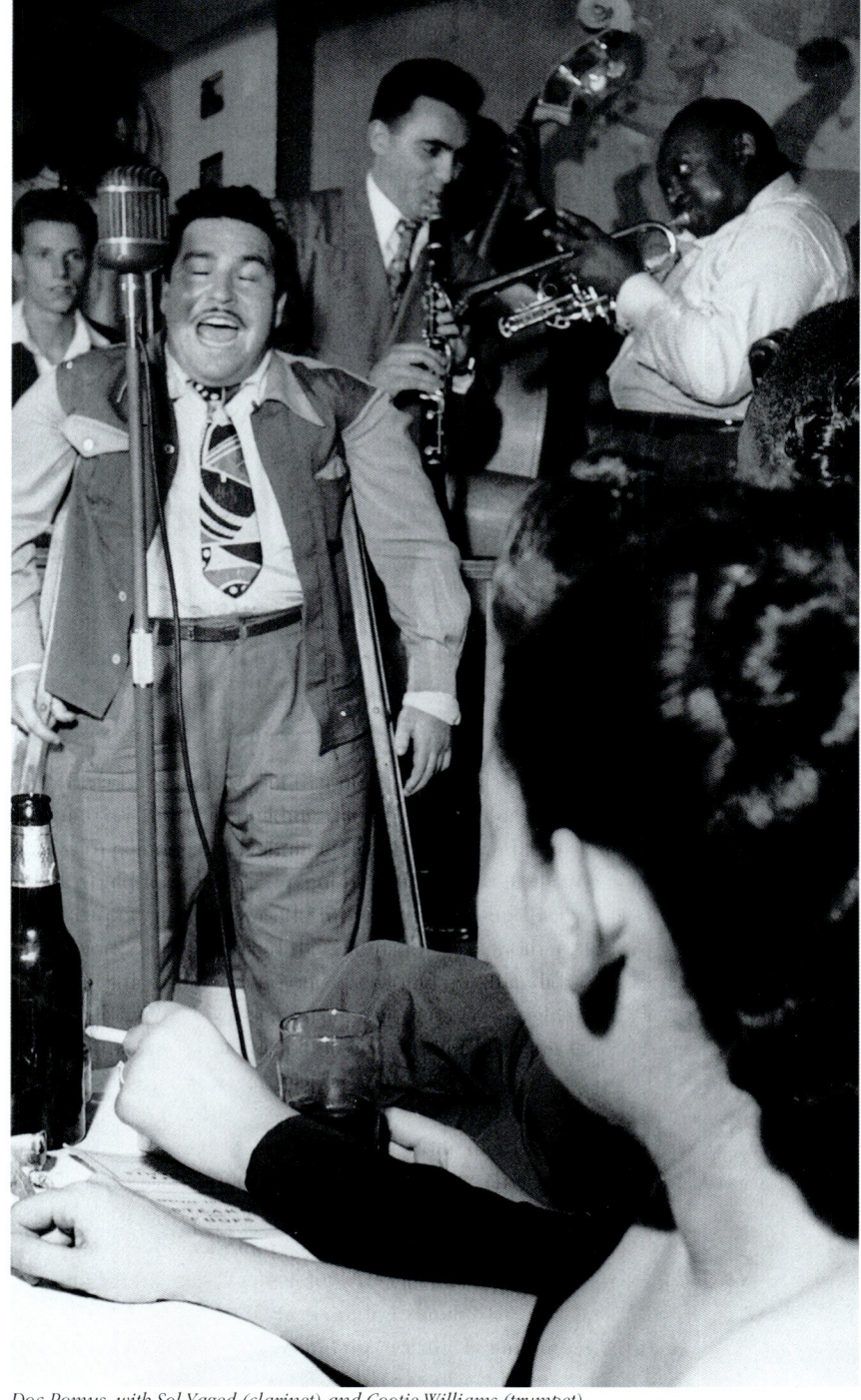

"We were at 1619 Broadway. Right about that time we started getting hits, and the owners of the Brill Building decided to give us this great office filled with paintings by Dubuffet. Mort Shuman and I sat in that office and would look at those paintings all day and at the plush, deep-piled carpets and the wonderful grand piano, and we never did a bit of work. So we insisted that we had to get another office. There was one little room that no one else would use, that did not even have space for a couch – just a small piano and two upright chairs. It was so bad that we would desperately try to finish up just so that we could get out of that room." Doc Pomus

"I never told them what to write – I would just say, 'Bring me something for The Drifters.' After hearing only four bars of 'Save The Last Dance For Me', I knew it was going to be a huge hit – I loved it. I've always been especially fond of Doc and Morty, and I don't think that Doc would have minded this story being told here: Doc was confined to a wheelchair most of his life, so he couldn't dance. He was married to this gorgeous blonde woman, and this was the beginning of the sixties. So he'd say, 'Yeah, we go out, that's cool – I like to watch her.' That's the song." Jerry Leiber

Doc Pomus, with Sol Yaged (clarinet) and Cootie Williams (trumpet)

"The Drifters signed a contract to make maybe $100 a week. We couldn't help noticing that everywhere we played was packed out, so we thought that maybe we could get a raise. Back in New York, we made an appointment to talk with George Treadwell, our manager. I was elected spokesperson because I guess they knew I'd be fired. I stood there with the group and made my little speech, after which he looked at me and said, 'I want you to stand aside and speak for yourself.' I said, 'Okay,' and I stood to one side and I did exactly the same speech all over again, to which he replied, 'Well, if you're unhappy, then you can leave.' So I took a gamble, left the office and was standing outside in the corridor waiting for the other guys to join me and, of course, nobody else came out." Ben E. King

From left: Mort Shuman and Doc Pomus

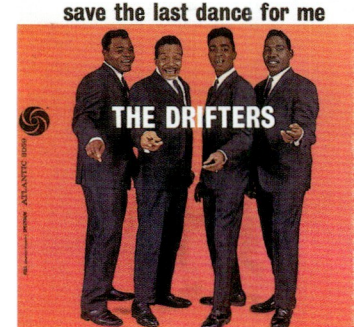

The Drifters, from left: Ben E. King, Charles Thomas, Dock Green and Elsbeary Hobbs TL: 50s 60s

The Coasters, from left: Will 'Dub' Jones, Carl Gardner, Cornell Gunter and Billy Guy TL: 60s

"I remember on one session Mike Stoller was in the studio and Jerry Leiber was with me in the control room. Suddenly, Jerry yelled through the intercom, 'What the hell's going on? I don't like what I'm hearing! This isn't what we rehearsed!' All the musicians are thinking, 'Who's this son of a bitch? We're playing the right notes.' So Mike would very calmly say, 'Well, let's hear the bass.' And Jerry would snap back, 'That's not the problem!' So they would get this thing going to the point where the musicians had an empathy for Mike and wanted to kill Jerry. Eventually they would get to listening to, for example, the guitar part, and Jerry would say, 'That's the problem.' Now if you had gone out there and said, 'I can't stand the guitar part,' George Barnes would hand you the guitar and tell you, 'Here! Play me what you wanna hear,' and if you couldn't play it he would say, 'Well, then shut up and leave me alone.' By this point, however, everybody in the studio loved Mike and hated Jerry, so Mike could very easily effect the changes and it worked perfectly. I think that those two always got the best out of everything, none of their sessions were more than three hours, and they were getting four sides every time." Tom Dowd

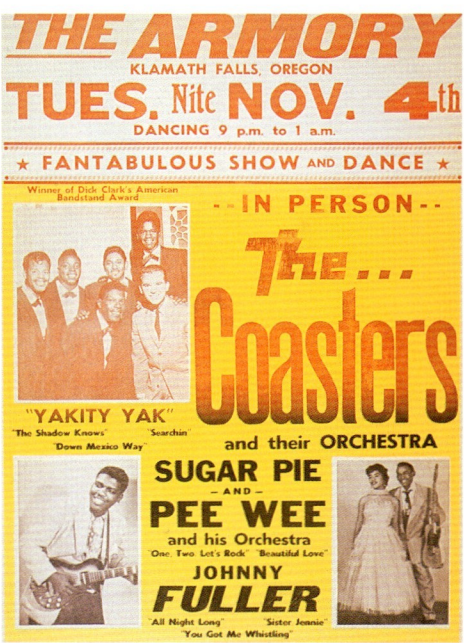

From left, clockwise: Songwriters Jerry Leiber, Lester Sill, Mike Stoller, and Atlantic's Sales Manager and Manager of The Clovers, Louis Krefetz

"We had always liked Latin rhythms. What started this thing was our love of the Baion rhythm. We used it constantly for a few years after the first success of 'There Goes My Baby'. We orchestrated it with different kinds of percussion – conga drums, bass drums, and what we called 'African hairy drums', which was literally what they were – large drums that still had the hair of the animal on them. Then we added triangle to that typical Brazilian rhythm and began to play around. We'd go up to the music rental shop, a place called Carroll's in New York, and we'd look around, see what they had – we'd play instruments, test the sounds, and then we'd try them out on sessions. For a while that particular rhythm became everybody's idea of what rock'n'roll was." Mike Stoller

Ben E. King TL: 60s

"We used to let Phil Spector hang out with us. I only ever wrote with Mike Stoller: if I had a song idea, I'd take it to him; if he had a tune, he brought it to me. That's how we worked. It was only much later that I worked with anyone else. On this occasion, though, Phil had been on and on at me to write a song with him, so finally I said, 'Okay, come over for dinner, afterwards we'll see what happens.' I didn't have an idea. So he came over and, sure enough, started fiddling with the guitar and played something that reminded me a little bit of Ibert's *Ports of Call, L'Escales*. It had that particular Spanish sound, so I kept pushing him in that direction – building the chords, a third up, a third up. He wrote the tune, but I was pushing him in the direction of a contour that was really an imitation of *L'Escales*. While he was doing this I got the idea, which was literal. It was Spanish, 'Spanish Harlem', and I wrote it – wrote it on the spot." Jerry Leiber

"At the same session where I recorded 'Spanish Harlem', we had about half an hour left and were sitting around with nothing to do. Jerry and Mike asked me if I had any songs, so I said I had one called 'Stand By Me' that The Drifters had just turned down. They said, 'Okay, let's hear it.' So I played a little bit of it on the piano. They said, 'Great, great!' All of a sudden they were turning over snare drums and making all kinds of weird noises – which was how that little scratch sound happened. These guys were so far ahead of themselves!" Ben E. King

The Mar-Keys, from left: Don Nix, Donald 'Duck' Dunn, Terry Johnson, Wayne Jackson, Packy Axton and Steve Cropper TL: 60s

"Jim Stewart and Estelle Axton, brother and sister. The first two letters of Stewart and the first two letters of Axton, you got Stax – and that's how the Stax name was born." Rufus Thomas

"We had been looking for sources for releases other than what we could produce ourselves, because we had begun to achieve a certain size. It's very hard to stay middling in this business. We either had to get big, stay very small, or go out of business – and we liked big! At the same time, we didn't want to get trashy, based on volume and so forth. We were pressing at a plant in Memphis, and the owner, Buster Williams, called me up one day and said, 'There's a record popping off down here that we just can't keep in stock. Maybe you ought to come down and see about it.' That record was ''Cause I Love You' by Carla and Rufus Thomas, which served as our introduction to Stax." Jerry Wexler

The Mar-Keys TL: 60s

"It is still such a shame when you look back on it – about certain people having to ride in the back of the bus, or having to go to a certain line to get food, or having to drink out of a different water fountain. It was sort of a way of life that had already been set up, so when you learn that as a kid you take it for granted. Onstage and in the studio, however, there really was no colour except in the sound of the music, because rhythm and blues, which was black, ethnic-rooted music, was very different from the upper crust of the top pop or country and western type of music."
Steve Cropper

Carla Thomas TL: 60s

"I was always a very sentimental kid, but I think all teenage kids get sentimental. I was a typical teenager and back then the phrase 'gee whiz' was popular, so I called the song 'Gee Whiz', which maybe was based on something I'd seen in the movies that had made me shed a tear." Carla Thomas

William Bell TL: 60s

"William Bell was thinking about becoming a doctor and was going to join the army, but they didn't get back to him. Meanwhile, he had written a great song in New York, called 'You Don't Miss Your Water'. Chips Moman finally convinced him to go into the studio and record it, with bass, drums, organs and horns. The artists and the times created an environment which these great musicians, writers and producers could all share in at Stax." Jerry Wexler

"Jim Stewart was a country fiddler, a diminutive man who worked in the mortgage department of a bank. That's how he found this old vacant theatre, which was used originally for movies, then for country and western shows, then as a makeshift church. His sister set up a record store in the lobby, and the studio was in the auditorium. Even after their early hits, Jim still held on to his day job. Jerry Wexler would try to reach him at the studio, but found he'd been given the number at the bank. After going through three secretaries, Jerry finally figured out that Stewart, the force behind these hot black records, was a plain vanilla mortgage clerk." Tom Dowd

"I liked Jim; he was personable and warm. When he came to New York, he'd stay with us in Great Neck. He became family. His sister was a mover and a shaker, but I respected her strength and made sure we got along." Jerry Wexler

"I would say that if anyone wants to go into the recording business and they don't run a record shop, then they need to be very close to one. There's no better testing market. Our record shop was in the foyer of that old cinema we got hold of and converted into our studio. *Billboard* and all the other trade magazines never did know that the Satellite Record Shop had any connection with the Stax label. They'd call me once a week for my report on what was selling – that was the wrong person to call! You ever heard of hype?!" Estelle Axton

"Bert Berns came along and was terribly important. He was hustling tunes around for $50 a week. Bert came into my office and I was sort of captivated by him – the way he played his songs and the way he did a demo. It soon became clear to me that this was a very talented songwriter, musician, and producer who was just marking time without even a decent job. He brought me quite a few songs, and then he brought me one called 'Twist And Shout'. Phil Spector was working for us then as an apprentice producer, and I went into the studio with Phil and a group called the Pearls, whereupon we proceeded to butcher this song. All Bert Berns could do was sit in the control room, not allowed to make a single comment, while we absolutely murdered the song. Not long after that Bert re-recorded it with the Isley Brothers and got every single thing out of what was in that song." Jerry Wexler

Bert Berns

Estelle Axton and Jim Stewart of Stax Records

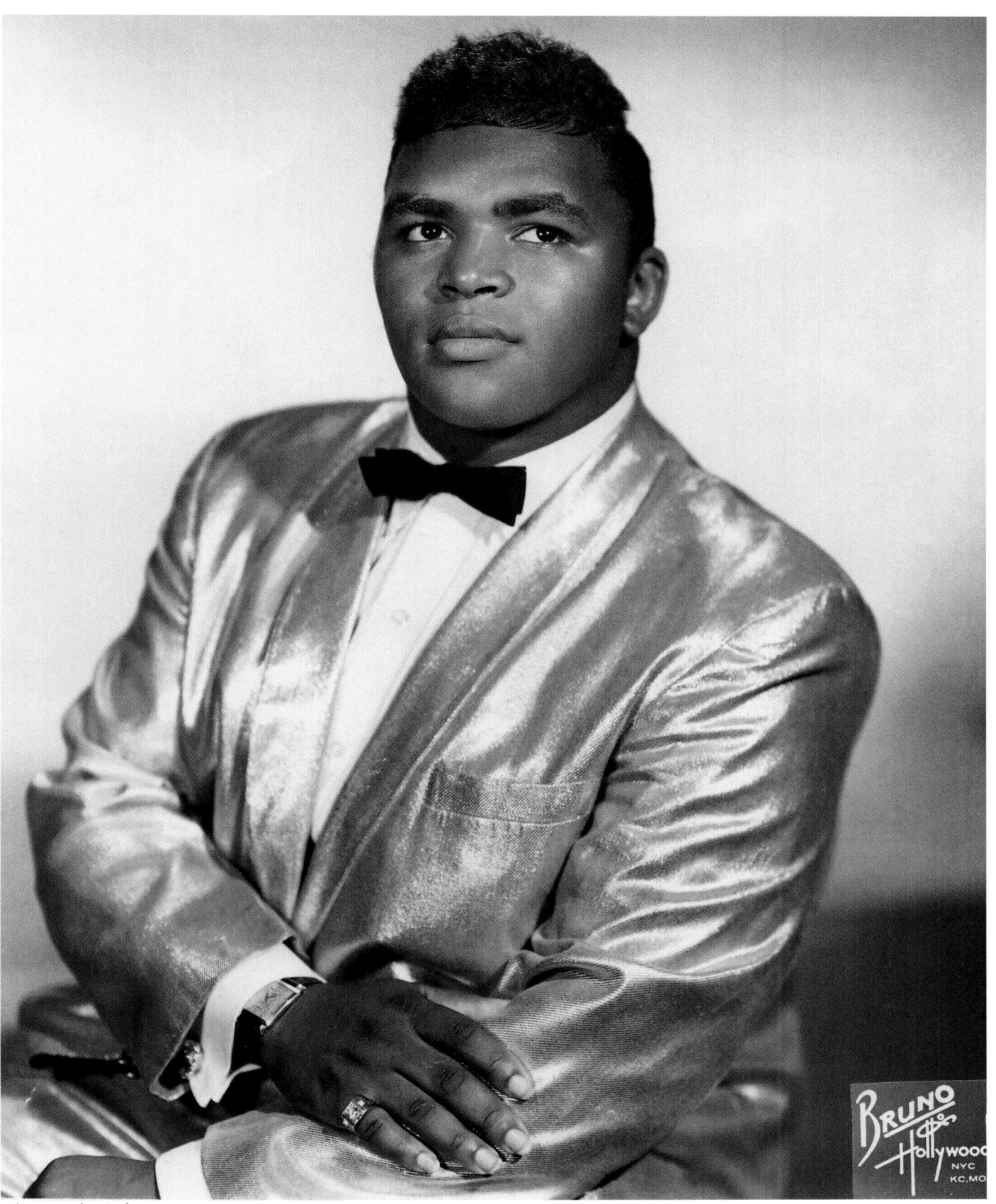

Solomon Burke TL: 60s

"We released an album called *Rock'n'Soul* and that was the beginning of a lot of the movement – the use of words and phrases such as 'soul music', 'soul movement'. People would ask me how and why I would sing country and western songs, ballads and things like that with the feeling and expression of soul. We were the first black artists ever to have a country and western song played nationally on radio and television and reaching the charts. We had crossed the colour barrier, and it was a very exciting situation to see these things happening in the early sixties. Atlantic Records has certainly opened doors and minds to a lot of new things. There will always be a red and black label, and when people pick it up they'll always remember that there was an era called soul – and it still exists. Soul is a feeling, an emotion, an expression. Soul is not something that's just sung, it's something that's utilized by you – spiritually, mentally, physically, financially, sexually. However you want to use it. If you're a cook, a driver, a painter, a carpenter, a singer, an actor, an actress or royalty. I mean, if you do it soulfully, then it's soul.

"We're on the bus going down South and nobody understands what's happening. I'd been on these tours four or five times, so I'm really hip to what's going on, and I know that you can't eat in certain places and you can't go into the bathrooms. They all said, 'Are you kidding? I'm from Chicago and I'm from New York and nobody's going to tell me I can't go anywhere because I'm black.' Personally, I didn't care – I said, 'Don't worry about it folks, I'm telling you you'd better get your sandwiches from me. You buy your sodas and hot dogs, I'll give you potato chips free! Only charging $5!' They'd laugh, 'We ain't going to buy this crap from you.' Further on down the road we'd stop the bus again, they'd jump off and run into another restaurant, then a few minutes later come back with a sad face. I'd say, 'Get your hot dogs, sodas and sandwiches from me, only $6 now – potato chips are still free, you know.' Going on down the road about one, two o'clock in the morning after constantly looking for some place to eat, they finally sent Dion into a restaurant. I was almost wiped out. I could have gone bankrupt right there. Dion comes out of the restaurant and he's got two guys carrying cardboard boxes full of sandwiches, chicken, and you could see the French fries falling off the edge of the boxes – sodas and hot chocolates with the whipped cream dripping down, and all kinds of pies. It was just too much for Charlie who, like the rest of us, was supposed to keep down until they got to the bus. He got so happy that he jumped off and ran across, almost shouting, 'Let me help you, Dion, with all of this food,' and when he did that, the two guys threw the food at him, ran back, got shotguns, and started shooting at the bus. Dion had chocolate all over him – oh, it was a terrible situation. We got away with our lives. We were blessed. Everything worked out. I charged $9 for the sandwiches, a dollar for the potato chips. Everybody ate and lived happily ever after." Solomon Burke

Ornette Coleman TL: 60s

"On one of our trips to San Francisco, Ornette Coleman came up from Los Angeles to see if he could pursuade Percy Heath, our bass player in the MJQ, to record with his group at the time. I thought that the way Ornette played was very interesting and unique. To me, it related to two great writers that I'm still very fond of, Dylan Thomas and James Joyce. For me, the fractured or deconstructed way that Ornette makes his music creates a merger with lots of American music. It was very interesting and exciting to me that he would play many nonsense things that would have nothing to do with anything you could hold on to, but then every now and then would come a phrase which you remembered from other music, and that would always make me laugh. For me, James Joyce also has long periods where his writings sound nonsensical, but then there is a whole other period where it becomes quite understandable – and that would somehow make everything else clear and hold the whole thing together." John Lewis

From left: Ed Blackwell and Don Cherry

John Coltrane TL: 60s

"I worked on John Coltrane's *Giant Steps* and *My Favorite Things*. John would get there a good hour before the session was due to start. He'd stand in the corner, change a reed, a mouthpiece, an instrument, and he'd play arpeggios, practising things by himself. Then finally he'd get down to something that he wanted to do, and he'd go over the same thing four or five times – there'd just be minute differences. While this was going on, he'd be standing in the corner playing with his eyes closed, listening to himself. The other musicians would arrive and say, 'Hey John, how are ya?' and would start setting up their instruments. He wouldn't even know that they had arrived because he was so focused and intent on what he was doing. Finally, when he stopped and turned around, he'd say, 'Hi guys,' and then they talked. They might have been there for five or 25 minutes, but they lit up to culture, to where he was coming from, their minds already set on page one. During our recordings with John, he was clean, sober, and prompt. I can't speak for his conduct three to four years later, because he changed dramatically, for whatever reasons, I don't know. When he was with us, though, he was a very intense, very conscientious human being." Tom Dowd

From left: Nesuhi, Arif Mardin and Tom Dowd

From left: John Lewis and Milt Jackson TL: 60s

"I first met Nesuhi Ertegun at the 1958 Newport Jazz Festival. I was a student at Berklee College of Music in Boston, and I had written two arrangements for the International Youth Big Band, which was made up of musicians from almost every country. I think that Nesuhi had heard these arrangements and was impressed. We all knew who he was. I had just come from Turkey; it was my first year in the States. My father knew his father, and his mother was my mother's grandmother's neighbour in Istanbul – so we all knew each other. I've always had a strong feeling that it was Nesuhi who arranged for me to receive the first BMI scholarship for jazz, through which I went to a seminar at a place near Tanglewood in the Berkshires, called the Music Inn. This three-week jazz seminar featured John Lewis, Max Roach, Lee Konitz – all of these great artists teaching young students. So Nesuhi heard some of my other pieces that I wrote for the faculty. Then, in 1962, my wife and I moved to New York. I was trying my luck, and I would see him socially at cocktail parties and so forth. Then one day out of the blue, he called me up and said, 'I've got something important to discuss with you.' So I went to his office thinking he was going to give me an arranging job. But he said, 'Would you like to be my assistant?' And I said, 'Yes.' I was unemployed, my wife was working at the United Nations – she was bringing in the money and I was embarrassed about that – so I took the job right away, and I became sort of a gofer." Arif Mardin

Charles Mingus TL: 60s

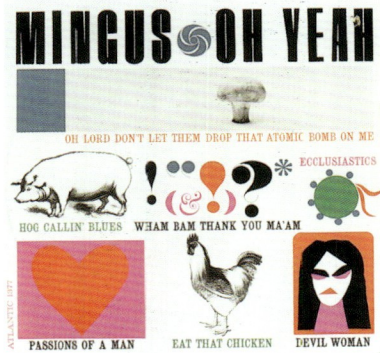

"Good jazz is when the leader jumps on the piano, waves his arms, and yells. Fine jazz is when a tenor man lifts his foot in the air. Great jazz is when he heaves a piercing note for 32 bars and collapses on his hands and knees. A pure genius of jazz is manifested when he and the rest of the orchestra run around the room while the rhythm section grimace and dance around their instruments."
Charles Mingus

"When I was 19, playing with Tiny Bradshaw, I heard the records Charlie Parker had done with Jay McShann, and I was anxious to meet him. So when we hit Kansas City, I rushed to Eighteenth and Vine, and there, coming out of a drugstore, was a man carrying an alto, wearing dark glasses and a blue overcoat with six white buttons. I rushed over and said belligerently, 'Are you Charlie Parker?' He said he was, and invited me right then and there to go and jam with him at a place called Chauncey Owenman's. We played for an hour, until the owner came in, and then Bird signalled me to cease with a little flurry of notes, so no words would ensue. He said, 'You sure sound like me.'" Sonny Stitt

Sonny Stitt TL: 60s

Ahmet with some of Atlantic's Twist collections

"I was one of the first people to go to the Peppermint Lounge, which suddenly became the place where all the society people wanted to go. Prior to that, I used to go almost every night to El Morocco. I remember saying at the time, 'Who the hell wants to go to the Peppermint Lounge?' Anyway, I went down there, walked in, and saw all these people – who would dance the foxtrot very sedately or the tango or whatever at El Morocco – all twisting to this little Italian twist band. They were doing an imitation of the original twist, which was done by Hank Ballard on King Records before Chubby Checker did it. The Peppermint Lounge band was called Joey Dee and the Starliters. My reaction was, 'My God!' I mean, you couldn't get in the place. It was like the beginning of the Studio 54-type situation – crowds at the door, only letting people in that they knew, and so on. Then inside you'd see the Duke of Marlborough, or whoever, twisting around on the floor in the middle of all this. All the models were there as well – I mean, everyone. So we started going there every night, and I had discussions with Joey Dee who said, 'Yeah, man, I'd love to sign with you.' But the next thing I knew, before we could even come to sign a contract, they'd gone with Roulette. The club was run by people who were probably connected, and so that was that. So I had seen the whole twist thing breaking out, had been there right at the beginning of the craze, and now everybody else was having hits with twist records. Eventually we put together compilations of a lot of records that we'd already put out and we called these albums *Do The Twist With Ray Charles*, *Twist With Bobby Darin*, and so on. We were able to reissue the same records because the people who were buying twist songs had never heard these records before. It wasn't a record-buying crowd, it was a dance crowd. There were no dance records as such in those days, not like we have now. We didn't have any dance charts. The discotheques were just beginning. There was Le Club in New York, there was New Jimmy's, The King Club, Regine's in Paris. They were already taking a lot of people away from clubs such as El Morocco, where there was live music, to a place where they were just dancing to records. Of course, there had always been songs about dancing, like 'Begin The Beguine', but this was the beginning of a new craze." Ahmet

From left: Vic Dickenson, Edmund Hall, Mr. Acker Bilk, Bud Freeman and Sidney De Paris TL: 60s

"We threw a celebration for Mr. Acker Bilk, who was reduced to tears when he saw the band we'd assembled, a pantheon of his heroes. The eminent George Wein was piano man and leader." Jerry Wexler

"I recorded many things that I knew would not be commercial successes, but I thought were important enough to be recorded. In order to make that possible, you also, of course, had to make records that sold. So I tried to make my share of hits. I picked up a couple of things from Europe that became huge sellers, which I didn't produce, but heard and knew had a commercial possibility. One was by an Englishman, Mr. Acker Bilk. I picked up 'Stranger On The Shore'. Everybody at Atlantic made fun of me; I was the joke of the company. They were saying, 'Is this the corniest record or what?' I'd reply, 'This record is good and will be a commercial hit.' It sold millions." Nesuhi Ertegun

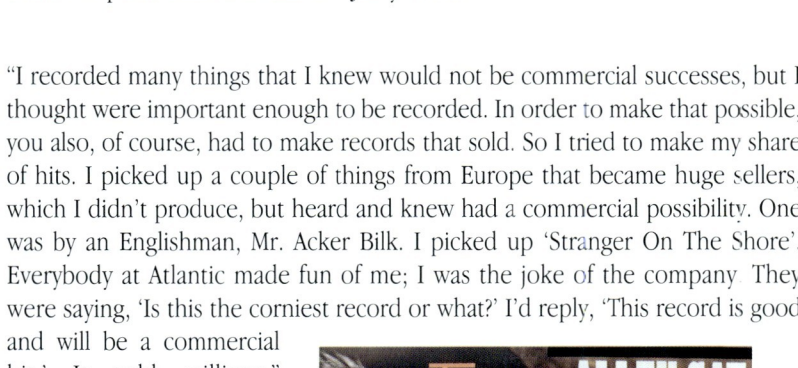

Mel Tormé TL: 60s

"Another commercial success of mine was a record by a Danish pianist, Bent Fabric. His real name was Bent Fabricius-Bjerre, and he owned the company that distributed our records in Denmark. One day he said to me, 'I made this record and it's a flop in Europe. It's always been my ambition to have one record released in America – would you put it out?' I said, 'Sure.' I listened to it and it was a charming, catchy little song – no masterpiece, but a nice song. To this day, Bent Fabricius-Bjerre receives royalty cheques from Atlantic because his song 'Alley Cat' still sells. I think it's the biggest-selling sheet music of the last twenty years." Nesuhi Ertegun

"They used to call Mel Tormé 'The Velvet Fog'." Ahmet

King Curtis TL: 50s 60s

"King Curtis told me a great story which I think every musician should know. He came from Texas up to New York, and one night there was a jam going on at Birdland. A group of wonderful musicians were playing 'Cherokee', which ordinarily is played in the key of B flat. Curtis was watching all of these great musicians and finally they said to him, 'Okay, boy, come on then, you can come up and play.' So he took his saxophone, got up, hit one note, and it was in the wrong key. They were playing in B major, which is very difficult for saxophones or B flat instruments. Furthermore, it's a very complicated song, so the chords were extremely difficult. Curtis looked around and one of the older men turned to him and said, 'Why don't you learn to play in all keys and then come back here?' Curtis told me, 'I thought I was pretty good. I'd been playing around, I could play and I could honk', but he went back home, practised more, and then came back." Arif Mardin

McHouston 'Mickey' Baker TL: 50s 60s

"Charlie Parker played in Buster Smith's band in the thirties and always acknowledged Buster's influence on his playing. He was not only an incredible influence on Charlie Parker, but also on Count Basie and the Blue Devils – he was a truly legendary figure in the development of jazz. We were very fortunate to produce the only record he ever made as a solo artist." Ahmet

"Mickey Baker was an extremely talented, terrific guitar player. He played as a session man for us with The Drifters, Ruth Brown and also on Joe Turner's 'Shake, Rattle And Roll'. He made his first solo record for us in 1959, and for me, it still stands up as a wonderful album." Ahmet

Opposite: Buster Smith TL: 50s 60s

Nat Adderley TL: 60s

"Nat Adderley was at the peak of his powers from the early to mid-sixties. He'd get this terrific, low, sub-tone register out of his horn. The quintet he had with his brother Cannonball was, of course, very successful for many years. We were extremely fortunate to be able to make several albums with Nat at Atlantic.

"Nesuhi made many albums with Carmen McRae. She was greatly influenced by Billie Holiday, and ranks as one of the all-time greatest jazz singers – along with Ella Fitzgerald, Dinah Washington, and Sarah Vaughan." Ahmet

Carmen McRae TL: 50s 60s

Mose Allison TL: 60s

"Mose Allison was signed by Nesuhi. He's a very special kind of singer, bordering on jazz – with terrific songs like 'Your Mind Is On Vacation But Your Mouth Is Working Overtime'. A great artist." Ahmet

"The blues is not only vocal music, it's instrumental music as well, and Hank Crawford writes and plays blues songs that reach you as quickly as Ray Charles singing them. Crawford is a gifted musician – as a soloist, as an arranger, and as a leader. Everything he does is funky, in the best sense of that overworked word. The line from Fillmore East and West to Ray Charles is clear enough. The line from Ray Charles to Hank Crawford and the blues side of jazz is just as clear. All you have to do is listen." Ralph J. Gleason

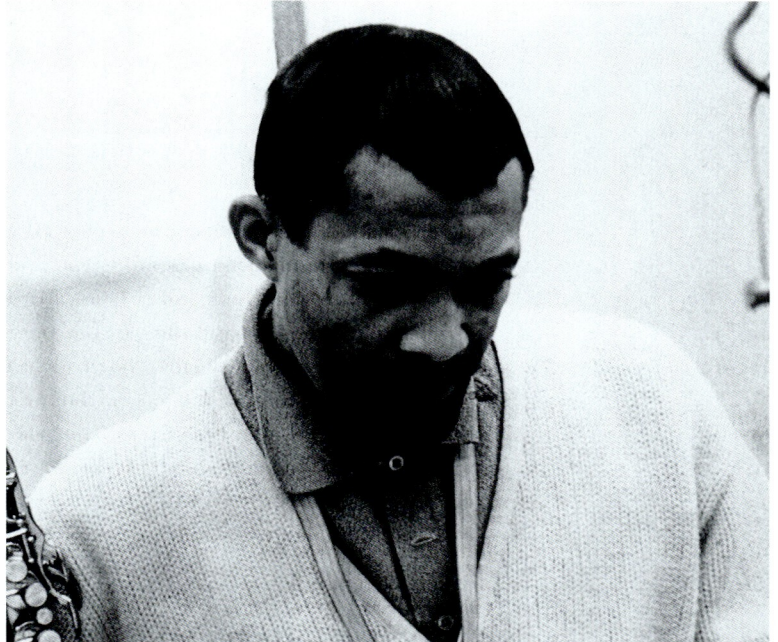

Hank Crawford TL: 60s

"Hank played baritone when he first started working with Ray, but he's an alto player first, and also an incredible arranger. So he was not only able to be a singular voice on his instruments, but he wrote those arrangments for Ray, and then went on to come up with his own sound. Those first Atlantic records where he had a seven-piece band without a piano – they're incredible records." Jerry Wexler

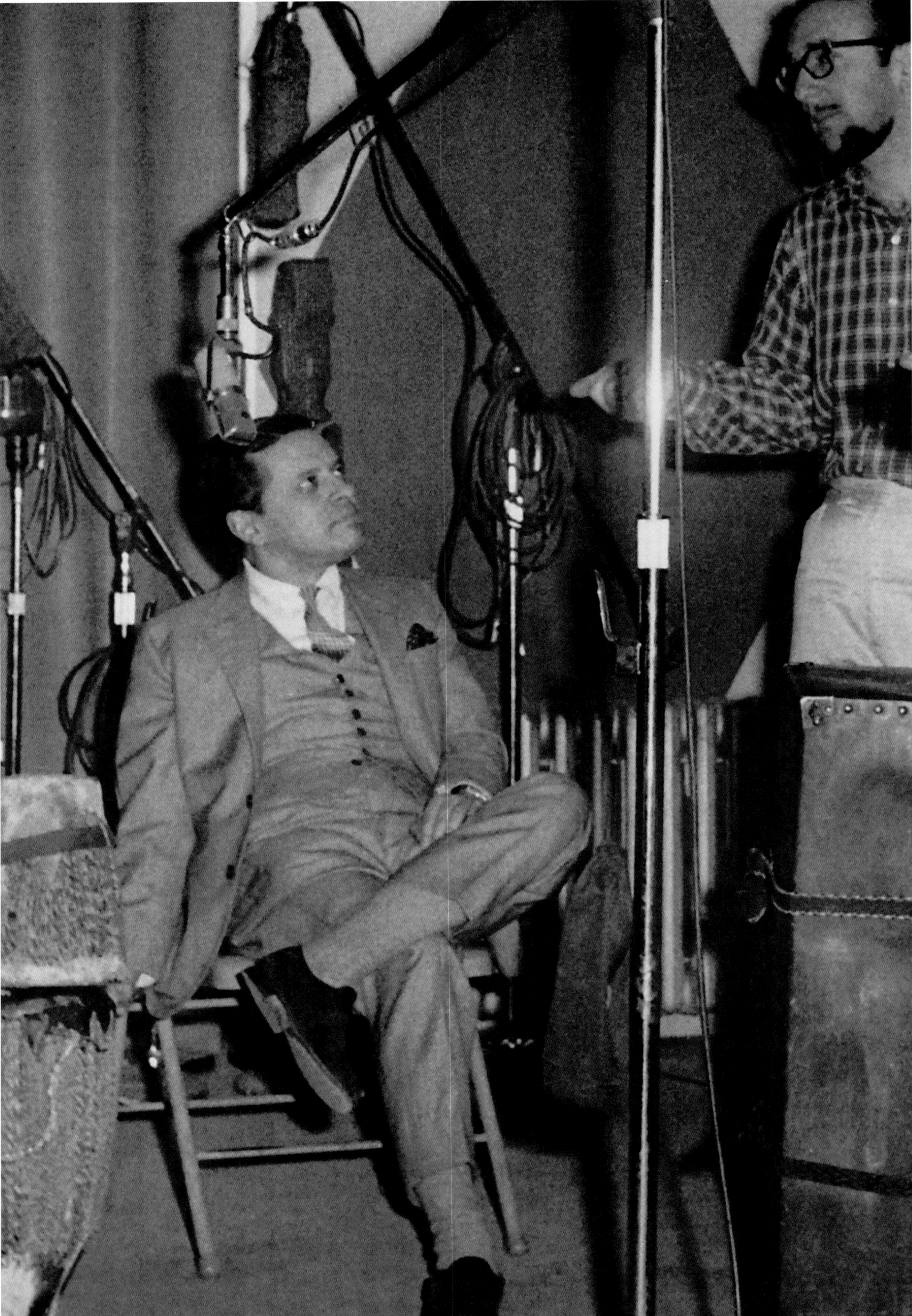

THE ATLANTIC STORY 145

Stephane Grappelli TL: 60s

Above: Herbie Mann and opposite with Nesuhi TL: 60s

"This is such incredible music! Why? Because you improvise! And when you improvise, you're a composer – you're composing as you play. You can't learn it. It's like Louis Armstrong said, either you've got it or you don't." Stephane Grappelli

"Although there are certain limitations to the flute, Herbie Mann is a master of the instrument. He went through many incarnations and he crossed over. He did some R & B sides, some bossa nova. I think we made over fifty albums with Herbie, more than with any other artist. One reason being that he kept getting different kinds of groups around him and was very clever at being able to increase the range of what he could do. He brought the music, therefore, to a wider audience, without commercializing it. See, there's no such thing as popularizing jazz, because the minute any jazz becomes popular, all the jazz musicians say it's not jazz." Ahmet

THE ATLANTIC STORY 147

"We worked with Phil Spector once more by accident. We were going into the studio to record The Drifters, and one of the songs was 'On Broadway'. We bumped into Phil going down the street and he asked where we were going. I said, 'We're cutting The Drifters. If you want to, why don't you drop by, have a drink afterwards or something?' He came by with his guitar, sat in on the session, and played the solo on the song."
Mike Stoller

The Drifters TL: 60s

Left: Betty Carter TL: 60s

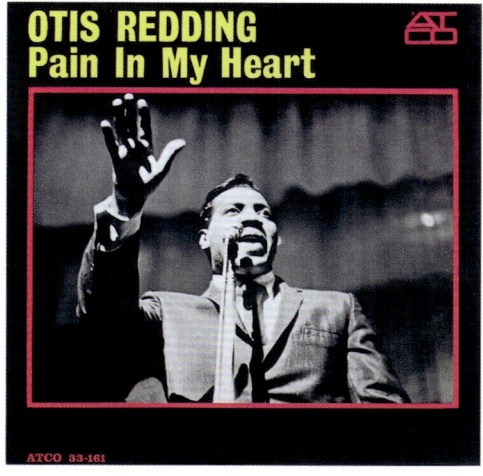

"We were just jamming on some blues, Jim Stewart heard us playing and just pushed the record button. He said, 'That's great! You know something like that could really be a record.' He was talking this whole thing up and he asked, 'You guys got anything you can do as a B-side?' Booker and I looked at each other and said, 'Well, we got this little riff we've been working for a couple of weeks.'" Steve Cropper

"The idea of that little combination of those three chords came into my mind when I was driving down one day from Indiana to Memphis. Funny how that happens sometimes when you're on the road. Musical ideas can just pop in – but it's just those chords, in that timing – the bass line – that simple. It's always been generally believed that MG represented 'Memphis Group'. On the day that we were cutting 'Green Onions', Chips Moman had a little MG convertible parked out front. He loved that little car and that was originally where we got the name from – it was always parked right outside Stax, his little red MG." Booker T. Jones

"Although Lewis Steinberg was part of the M.G.s for that first record, I think most people would agree that the classic line-up of the M.G.s was two white and two black guys. Me on bass, Steve Cropper on guitar, Booker T. on organ and Al Jackson Jr. on drums. The studio was the theatre, built on a downhill slope. The control room was where the screen was and they'd bring the movie curtain down to create a separation. At first they used the movie speakers and they were great! They could crank that shit up, play it back – boy, that sounded good – never heard a bass sound that big. The drums originally were down in the corner, until they moved them to the middle. There was always a horn section but before they had four or eight track recording put in, we'd all play live. There was always a delay with the horns. People used to think they were lazy, but it was because by the time the drum sound got over to the corner where the horns were playing, the beat was late. So they had to learn to anticipate the beat a little bit – amazing! The horns would be sitting down, and Jim would come around and thinking they were just being lazy, he'd say, 'C'mon – goddamn – you got to stand up and play!'" Donald 'Duck' Dunn

"We financed an instrumental session with Johnny Jenkins and the Pinetoppers at Stax through our Southern promotion man, Joe Galkin. At the session, Joe inveigled Jim Stewart into giving Jenkins' occasional vocalist, Otis Redding, a few minutes to cut one song. I think Otis was actually there that day as a driver for Jenkins. As an inducement Joe said, 'Well, you can put him on Stax and have the publishing,' – which he had no right to do. The next thing we knew it was presented as a Stax record. I didn't make a big fuss about it. I didn't want to be adversarial with Stax, because we had this great collaboration going, on a handshake. We didn't even have a contract – it was very tight." Jerry Wexler

"What was happening at that time came from the streets. I mean, it came from everywhere, but it came up from the streets. Otis Redding was our roadie – he just walked in the door one day." David Porter

"Booker T. & The M.G.s and the songwriters down there were responsible for a very important series of hits with various artists, and that was the fountain from which sprang a great part of our success.

"Otis Redding used to call me 'Omelette', but not as a nickname – he thought at first that this actually was my name." Ahmet

Opposite: Otis Redding TL: 60s

Booker T. & The M.G.s, from left: Booker T. Jones, Steve Cropper, Al Jackson Jr., Lewis Steinberg TL: 60s

Booker T. & The M.G.s, from left: Donald 'Duck' Dunn, Booker T. Jones, Steve Cropper, Al Jackson Jr. TL: 60s

Solomon Burke TL: 60s

"So Solomon is playing at the Apollo Theatre in New York and I walk into his dressing room and he's sitting with the most beautiful girl – she must have been 17 – gorgeous, a star. He says to this girl, 'This is the man who runs my record company!' So we're chatting, and then one of the roadies comes running backstage and says to Solomon, 'Hey man, your wife is coming upstairs!' Solomon says, 'Shit!' and says to the girl, 'You go over there and sit next to Ahmet.' His wife comes in, looks at this girl, and says a very cold hello to me. Solomon says, 'Ahmet, I have some personal matters to discuss with my wife. Do you mind going and taking your friend with you?!' So I walk out with this girl and say, 'I'll take you home, where do you live?' She says, 'I live in San Diego.' I said, 'San Diego?!' So we go back to my office and I ring up Solomon and say, 'I've got this girl here, she lives in San Diego, what do you want me to do? I can't leave her on the street!' He says, 'When I gave her to you, she became yours, you can do anything you want.' And that was that – I had to buy this girl a plane ticket back to San Diego."
Ahmet

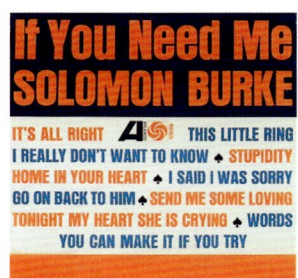

Doris Troy TL: 60s

Rufus Thomas TL: 60s

"I'd seen the dance called 'the dog' – my daughter Carla showed it to me. I'd been working at a club in a little place called Millington, Tennessee, about 15 miles outside of Memphis. We were playing a rhythm song that night and a girl was doing that dance. Now, if you've seen the dance and you know how it goes – well let me tell you, she was really good! As she was dancing and we had this rhythm pattern going, something flipped in my head and I started singing, 'Do the dog, do the dog.' I could think of three dogs, so I sang, 'Do the hound dog, do the bird dog, do the bulldog, any kind of dog, just do the dog.' That's how that song was born in that club. That's what made the song so good, because the dance really was far out! Now I came to England during that time and let me tell you, those English girls, man, they could really do that dance!!" Rufus Thomas

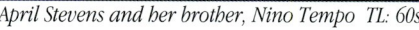

April Stevens and her brother, Nino Tempo TL: 60s

Glen Campbell

"There were two people that I always had to have on any session that I made in Los Angeles. The first was Glen Campbell on guitar, who was the only person I knew there who could play the blues and read music. And he really could play the blues. He was a truly great blues guitar player, like Clapton or B.B. King. He was the funkiest guitar player in Los Angeles, bar none. He was a very young, shy guy and had to be from the South because of the way he played the blues. The second person I had to have on those sessions was Nino Tempo. At that time, they were my two important people because they both could solo – so I had the option of either a guitar or a saxophone solo." Ahmet

Nino Tempo and friends

"Nino Tempo kept telling me that I had to hear his sister, April Stevens, sing. She'd had a hit several years before – a breathy, sexy song. She was a fine singer and Nino was also a very good singer, but they both had different conceptions about songs. We ended up making an album where the title song was a kind of rock'n'roll version of the thirties swing tune called 'Deep Purple'. It was a big, big number one hit." Ahmet

Ahmet with April Stevens, Nino Tempo and un-identified Cashbox magazine representative

Jerry Wexler (left), Ahmet (centre) and wife Mica (far right), and friends twisting the night away

Bobby Darin on stage at the Moulin Rouge TL: 60s

Bobby Darin and his wife, the actress Sandra Dee

"I'd met Phil Spector through the Ben E. King sessions, where he had somehow managed to wind up playing guitar. So when, a little later, I went to California, we met up again. He had this Thunderbird and we'd roar around in it all over the city. The publishers were big-time out there and generally much older than we were. They all wanted us to hear their new material, though, so I said, 'Look, there's only one way we're going to listen to it and that's if you bring it down to the car.' We had this 45rpm record player fitted up under the dashboard. 'You come down to the car, you sit in the back, and we'll play it.' So they would – they'd climb in the back and Spector and I would take off at 90 miles an hour up Sunset Boulevard. They'd be screaming in the back, 'Let me out of here – I don't care if you ever record one of our songs – just let me out of this car!!

"So I hired Phil Spector as my assistant, because I thought he was a very hot, terrific kid. He must have been about 20 years old then and he really was crazy, but charming, super-intelligent and extremely talented. One day I was going up to see Bobby Darin and I said to Phil, 'Come on, we'll both go.' At this point, Bobby had married the beautiful young film actress Sandra Dee. He had a huge, great mansion and was really living the Hollywood life. Phil and I walk in and Bobby, Sandra, and a few of their friends are sitting around by the pool. Bobby and I give each other a hug and I say, 'I'd like you to meet my new co-producer, Phil Spector.' So Bobby says, 'Hi, kid.' Phil says, 'Hello, Mr. Darin.' We had a couple of drinks, and eventually Bobby picks up his guitar and says, 'I want you to hear some of the new songs I've written.' So he starts to sing, *'Jailor bring me water, Jailor bring me water, Jailor bring me water, Cos I think I'm gonna die. Jailor bring me …'* Someone once wisely said,

'There's no such thing as a bad idea.' Now I knew that Bobby would play 12 or 15 songs, out of which maybe one would be a possibility, so I say, 'That's terrific.' Then he plays another horrible song, and again I say, 'That's terrific.' After about the fifth or sixth terrible song, I'm still saying that they're all fabulous. Finally, Phil, who I see has become increasingly twitchy, breaks in and says, 'Hold it, hold it. Are you kidding? I mean, are you crazy or am I?! These songs are crap!' So Bobby says, 'Who the hell is this kid?' And Phil says, 'You can't record this shit!' And Bobby starts screaming at him to get the hell out of his house. So a little later, I have to explain to Phil about a different way of doing things. A few months later, Bobby comes up to me and says, 'Ahmet, you know I love to work with you, but maybe we need some new blood. There's this kid, Phil Spector – do you think you could get him to work with us?' I say, 'That's the guy you threw out of your house!'

Lenny Bruce

"Anyway, Bobby and I loved each other and were always close friends. In Hollywood, when he was making pictures, he had all of these managers, agents and so forth, who only knew about major labels, saying to him constantly, 'How can you be signed to Atlantic?! Everything's great in your career, and yet you're signed with this unknown, tiny little record label!' Even through all of this, Bobby and I always had this very great warmth between us. Eventually, though, he succumbed to Hollywood pressure, and when his contract was up, he went to Capitol.

"I would say that Phil Spector has a very, very different perception of things than most people. It's a very special take he has on what's going on around him. We had such great times together. He also, however, had this great obsession with power, and with being in complete control. This obviously affected his style of producing. On the records he made, the artists were secondary. It was all about the songs, his style of recording, his wall of sound. Sonny Bono learned that from him and came close to duplicating it.

"Phil Spector and I were friends with Lenny Bruce. I spent one incredible night with Lenny in London. He'd been breaking it up in the club where he was playing. His insults and everything rubbed some English people the wrong way, but all the English comedians were studying him. I met him at Ronnie Scott's when Miles Davis was playing there. Then we went to a blues club where there was a great band blasting away. It was winter and everyone was bundled up in their big sweaters and coats. There were no tables or anything, just this big floor space, and everyone was lying down sleeping while this band was playing

Phil Spector

and it was so hysterical. Lenny found a spot to lie down, so I went and lay down next to him. We're all lying on the floor and this band is blasting away, '*Going to Kansas City, sorry but I can't take you ...* ' Nothing was happening, so I looked around and said, 'Let's get out of here.' Behind us were six or seven English comedians who were following us and trying to pick something up from Lenny. They couldn't understand at all why we'd be lying down there. This was a time when there was a lot of doping, everyone was doing some kind of dope. Nowadays the performers don't do much dope, but the audience does. Anyhow, we went to club after club after club. At the end of all of this, we dropped Lenny off at his hotel and went home. I later learned that he had injected himself, apparently overdosed, and had been rushed to the hospital. A rather macabre end to an extraordinary night." Ahmet

Phil Spector, centre, with The Righteous Brothers, from left: Bill Medley and Bobby Hatfield TL: 60s

"The Righteous Brothers were on Moonglow. We were distributing that label, so I did two or three sessions with them and then Spector took over. I'll never forget them, though. The first time I met them was when they came into the rehearsal studio in downtown Hollywood. They both arrived with no shoes on, they just came in barefoot. So I said, 'Look man, this is not the beach.'" Ahmet

Isaac Hayes and David Porter TL: 60s

"We worked our tunes up, got a rhythm section, got the horns and everything together. At first we didn't even have an office. We'd go to David's house or my house or to the piano in the studio. We slept on the floor at night. I'd get an idea and start playing something, and David would say, 'Yeah, man, okay,' and he'd start coming out with the lyrics. Then we'd teach them to the artists." Isaac Hayes

"We were always writing with the styling in mind, and the artist's personality. We would try to make the song fit the artist like a tailored suit." David Porter

"Barbara Lewis had a string of hits with us through the sixties, beginning with 'Hello Stranger', which was a smash number one R & B hit. She was from Michigan, a charming young lady, and she had this great voice that could range from soul to pop." Ahmet

"We were pranksters. The Mad Lads brought that high school thing into the company. Stax was like a family, and we were sort of like the kids in the family." John Gary Williams

The Mad Lads, from top:
William Brown, Julius Green,
John Gary Williams and
Robert Phillips TL: 60s   *Opposite: Barbara Lewis TL: 60s*

Jim Stewart of Stax

"In what was then called German Town, at two o'clock in the morning, you might find Little Richard, Lloyd Price and Elvis Presley hanging out together in the same club. But generally Memphis at that time was a brown bag town, so if Booker or Al asked me out, they'd take me to a black bottle club. If Steve or Duck asked me out, they'd take me to a white bottle club. But I couldn't take Steve with me to Al's club and I couldn't take Al with me to Steve's club. Very weird. One time I got chased into Memphis because they were delinquent in delivering a record for about a month, and Jerry Wexler was getting very upset, as we were banking on this flow of product and we weren't receiving it. They kept on saying they weren't sure about their equipment. So one day Wexler hit the 'phone and he said, 'Hey Dowd, how fast can you get down to Memphis?' I called him back and said, 'Seven o'clock local time.' So when I got there, Jim Stuart took me straight to the studio, where they were recording on well-maintained, but very old, equipment. I had my secretary send down the parts that they needed, and refitted all of their machines. The band came into the control room and asked if I could tape what they were doing. We went on that night until eleven, twelve o'clock, just jamming and talking. Every time I went there we all had lots of fun, just nothing but good times. Anyhow, the next morning, I went by the studio before leaving town and Rufus came walking up. He said, 'I figure everything must be working, all the cars are in the parking lot.' I said, 'Yeah, it's working.' That's when I first met Rufus. He said, 'I got this little ditty I wrote, wanna record it.' He sang this song once or twice, and I said, 'Okay, I'll tape it.' I made one cut on it, put it under my arm, and went back up to New York. When I got to Atlantic, I said, 'Hey Jerry, everything is working; here, listen to this, I did it yesterday.' Halfway through the song he yelled out, 'Right, 'Walkin' The Dog' – it's a fucking hit.'"
Tom Dowd

Booker T. & The M.G.s at the Stax Studio, from left: Steve Cropper, Donald 'Duck' Dunn, Booker T. Jones and Al Jackson Jr. TL: 60s

Tom Dowd

From left: Arif Mardin, Ben E. King, Lover Patterson (original manager of The Crowns), Ahmet and Bert Berns TL: 60s

"Bert Berns was a meat-and-potatoes, four-chord, basic kinda guy with a street feel that other people would have killed for. I think his talent far exceeded mine, but he couldn't really hear past four chords, and comparatively I was sophisticated. So I would come up with a fifth chord and he'd give me that look and say, 'What is that, bebop?!'" Jerry Ragovoy

"Johnny Moore had been to dinner the night before with Rudy Lewis. They'd talked about the session, Rudy seemed absolutely fine. Then later that night the news came through that Rudy had died from an overdose of drugs. Everyone was shattered. Jerry tried to cancel the date but the strings, everything had been booked and he could only put it forward by 24 hours. We all decided to go ahead. We re-scored the song, Johnny had to sing an octave lower than he usually did, but took the lead vocal. You can hear the sorrow coming through in their voices - it was an extraordinary recording." Tom Dowd

"I had turned The Drifters over to Bert, but I was acting as Executive Producer. They usually picked the songs, but somebody brought me 'Under The Board-walk', which I presented to the group and to Bert. They all said, 'Peeyoo!' but I said, 'I tell you what, fellas.' … I mean, I was still the boss … 'You can do any other songs you want on this session, but you've got to do this song. If you don't do this song, there will be no session.'"
Jerry Wexler

The Drifters, from left: Gene Pearson, Johnny Terry, Charles Thomas, Johnny Moore and Abdul Samad TL: 60s

David 'Fathead' Newman TL: 60s

"It's stunning to me that both David Newman and Hank Crawford, two such great players, were in Ray Charles' band at the same time. I'm a great fan of theirs and have been from the first time that I heard Ray Charles. The only other band that I know of which had such great original voices as Ray had with David and Hank was Duke Ellington's band. It's one thing to say you have an alto and a tenor player in your band, it's another entirely to be able to say you have David and Hank. David plays alto, tenor, and flute and has an absolutely original, incredible sound on each instrument. You don't get that kind of sound and feeling from a person who doesn't have that inside. I mean that's not something you fake." Arif Mardin

Ahmet and Esther Phillips TL: 60s

"Esther Phillips is one of my all-time favourite singers. Originally, she came out as 'Little Esther' when she was 12 years old. She had a very tough life. She'd become a junkie by the time she was 20, but then she rehabilitated herself and went on to have a very successful career." Ahmet

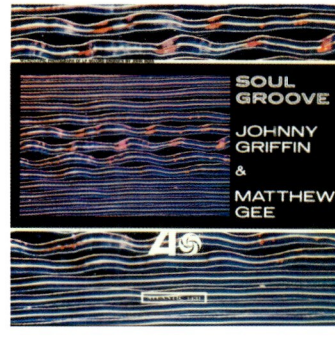

Don Covay with Jerry Wexler TL: 60s

"Some people say that soul is a vibe, some people say it's a spirit, a groove. It's been called many different things, but it's really the reaching out of spirits. Almost like a minister, you're touching the spirits that are in the audience, that are out there. That's the soul of the music being taken further, and when it came to the South, it became the Stax and the Atlantic Records sound. It's the feeling that makes people really get involved. It's part of expressing what is really going on inside you, but bringing it out in such a way as to make the community, the people, the audience feel – 'That's me!'" Don Covay

The Astors, including: Curtis Johnson, Eddie Stanback, Sam Byrns and Richard Harris TL: 60s

Joe Tex and members of his Orchestra TL: 60s

"I said, 'Joe, do me a favour. I want to record you one time the way I really want to, and if I don't make it with you, then I'll let you go.' So he started trying to do this song called 'Hold What You've Got'. I said, 'Look, I want a country chord. Just strum across the strings and give me that ... ' and everyone in there looked at me as if I was crazy. I said, 'Joe, you'd better do it my way.' He said, 'Okay, hit that chord and we start it.' Before I knew it, we had something that was so good that the only problem was getting the tracks to hold together. Then I overdubbed arpeggios on the piano and guitar, doing harmonies together, which had never happened before. Nobody had ever done that. I sent a copy of it to Jerry Wexler at Atlantic Records and he called me back and said, 'That's a smash, I want to put it out.' It had such a sound, it just popped off a radio at you. You just knew that you liked the sound before you even heard what the record was going to say. Joe Tex called me and said, 'Buddy, you promised you'd let me go. How about sending my release?' I said, 'Joe, we've got a hit.' He said, 'You put out that piece of junk?' I said, 'Yeah,' and he hung up on me – just hung up the 'phone. A few days later, he called back and said, 'Look here, you told me you'd be letting me out of my contract. Now I want out of my contract today!' I said, 'Joe, we've got a smash, we've sold a quarter of a million records.' He said, 'Man, you done told me ... what?!'

"All of the years I was having the big records with Joe he had road musicians, and most of the time road musicians don't play real good in the studio. He would fight me to use his band, and what I would do with Joe was I would let him do it, and when he left, immediately have my players come in and start replacing every track. The only thing I would use would be his vocal, so he would call me and say, 'What did you do? That sounds fantastic! That doesn't sound like it did when I left.' I'd say, 'Oh, just a few little electronic tricks.' I never did tell him what I was doing." Buddy Killen (producer and publisher)

"Titus Turner, Jesus! One of his songs said, 'If I don't love you ... grits ain't groceries, chicken ain't poultries, and Mona Lisa was a man.' That's a great line." Ahmet

Titus Turner TL: 60s

Solomon Burke TL: 60s

"Once, Solomon Burke was playing at the Apollo and Old Man Schiffmann, who ran it, called me up and said, 'You know, we're having problems with Solomon – can you talk to him?' I said, 'What's the matter?' He said, 'He's selling popcorn between shows, walking up and down the aisles with Dr. Solomon's Magic Popcorn. We have a concessionaire who has the exclusive for popcorn in the theatre.' So I called Solomon over and said, 'Solomon, you can't sell popcorn in this theatre, as they have a contract with this guy, and anyway, it looks terrible – you're the star of the show and you're walking up and down the aisles selling popcorn.' Then he looks kind of sideways at me and says, 'Okay, it's exclusive popcorn.' I said, 'Yeah, popcorn, hot dogs, they're exclusive.' He says, 'Have they got a pork chop sandwich concession?' I said, 'I don't think so.' The next thing I know, he's got a little hot plate set up backstage, and he's frying up this food and selling Dr. Solomon's Amazing Pork Chop Sandwiches." Ahmet

"'Mr. Pitiful' was a name given to Otis by Moohah, a W.D.I.A. disc jockey. He called him 'Mr. Pitiful' because of the begging and pleading way he crooned. I was in the shower one morning getting ready to go to the studio. I had to pick Otis up on the way and I started humming, 'They call me Mr. Pitiful.' I was thinking how Otis would sing that line – so I picked him up, gave him this idea, and we finished it in the car in about ten minutes on the way to the studio. We had another song all ready to go, but we showed this new thing to the guys and they all jumped in straight away. We cut it in about two or three takes, and there was 'Mr. Pitiful' – that's just the way things happened in those days, it was really effortless in a way. I mean, you just had to be there – getting up and being there was the job of the day, the rest just sort of fell into place!

"Not taking anything away from the other musicians, but Al Jackson was probably the most valuable musician in the entire Stax entourage. His beats were just impeccable. He knew exactly what groove would work with certain songs. 'I've Been Loving You Too Long' was pretty much there with Otis, but the thing with the stop time – the stop changes, which give it that elastic breath that it has – that was all Al and Otis who worked that out together. All I had to do was lay my hands on the guitar and something would come out of it. There was no thinking involved, it was just such a great bed of music that practically any notes you played on it sounded right." Steve Cropper

Otis Redding on stage with musicians from The Stax Soul Tour, and below with Steve Cropper TL: 60s

Sam and Dave, from left: Dave Prater and Sam Moore TL: 60s

"I went to a black nightclub in Miami where these two guys got up on stage and sang a song which I'd written for Ben E. King, called 'Don't Play That Song'. They were singing and performing that song so well that we decided to sign them. They were Sam and Dave. They became one of the most fabulous in-person acts of all time, and of course, recording down there in Memphis, they had some of the great writers and producers to work with." Ahmet

Wilson Pickett TL: 60s

"I really didn't know that much about Wilson Pickett other than that he had been with The Falcons and had also sung some gospel music. I just went up and started pulling out some of those things and listening to him singing lead on those old spiritual records. Invariably, on every song he sang, he went into this whole chant about the way to the midnight hour, 'See me Jesus in the midnight hour'. So I thought if that's what's on his mind, then that's what we'll have to write. So that's where the idea came from, and I hit him with it without even referring to the fact that I'd heard him do it on these spiritual songs — I didn't even bring that up. Just changed the words to 'Wait for your love in the midnight hour' instead of 'Waiting for Jesus in the midnight hour', which is really saying the same thing. At the time, there was a dance called 'the jerk'. Jerry Wexler was jumping around the studio, because we kind of had it going one way and he said, 'No, you've got to get it in this beat with this new dance!' I don't know if he even knew what to call it, because jumping around the studio he looked like a fighter shadow-boxing, but what he was trying to show us was this new dance they were doing up in New York. So Al and I started following him by putting down this delayed backbeat, which was actually something we'd used many times before — one being very dull and correct, and two being laid back and just behind the beat. This time, though, we'd got so involved watching Jerry dance around the place that he really pulled us into it, and that produced the rhythm on 'Midnight Hour'. It felt so good when we went and listened back to it, that we kept it that way." Steve Cropper

Allen Ginsberg TL: 60s

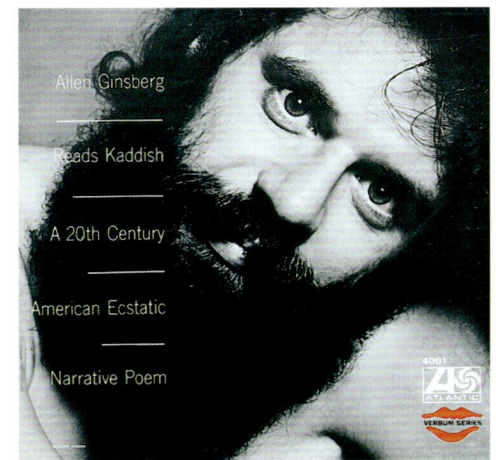

"Sonny Bono used to work for our distributor, Jack Lewerke. I used to let him help me get musicians for sessions, and then have him play tambourine or something on the record so that he'd earn scale. He was working as a promotion man for Merit Distributors, who were distributing Phil Spector's records. Sonny was very much in awe of Phil, as most people were at that time, and he also served as Phil's assistant some of the time.

"So Sonny and I were friends, and as well as everything else that he was doing, he also used to work occasionally for me as my assistant – on Righteous Brothers sessions, for example. He convinced my brother Nesuhi to sign him up and make a record. He sang with his girlfriend, and they called themselves Caesar and Cleo. They made a couple of records – I think my brother produced one and Jack Lewerke produced another – both of which flopped, and that was the end of that. In the meantime, I had recorded Nino Tempo with his sister April Stevens, and the two of them sounded pretty good together. So at the time of these sessions, Nino and I were driving down Sunset Boulevard with the radio on in the car and he said, 'Do you know this record? How can I get a sound like the drummer on this record?' I asked him who they were, and he told me Sonny and Cher. I said, 'Wait a minute, Sonny and Cher?! That's Caesar and Cleo.'

"A week later, a couple of friends of ours, Charlie Greene and Brian Stone, called me up and told me they were managing Sonny and Cher. I said, 'Really?' They said, 'Yeah – they're not getting on too well with Mo Ostin of Warner Bros. They have forgotten to pick up their option, we haven't said anything, time has passed, and now they're free.' I said, 'Well, we'll sign them up.' At that time I had no relationship with Warners, and no thought of ever selling my company. So I signed up Sonny and Cher, and our first record with them 'I Got You Babe', was not only a territorial hit, it was a nationwide hit and an international hit – I mean, like nothing we had ever experienced before." Ahmet

From left: Jack Nitzsche, Cher and Sonny TL: 60s

The Big Sensation in U.S.A.

SONNY AND CHER
I GOT YOU BABE

"One day, when I was in Los Angeles, Jack Lewerke, who in fact was not only our distributor there but also a wonderful friend of mine, gave a dinner party. Among the guests was a very beautiful woman, who looked as if she could have been a showgirl in Las Vegas – a very tall, statuesque lady. When I asked what she did, she replied that she was interested in metaphysics. I said, 'Oh, you mean Plato, Aristotle, that sort of thing?' She said, 'Oh, no, no. Dr. Wilson, who has the Church of Metaphysical Science.' I said, 'Oh, really, what is that?' and I made some joke. Whatever I said made everybody else laugh, but she started to cry and said I was insulting her religion. I said, 'Oh, I'm terribly sorry, please forgive me.' And she said, 'I'll only forgive you if you promise to go to the church with me tomorrow.' So I agreed to go to the church, took her home that evening, picked her up the next morning and asked, 'Where is the church?' She replied, 'At Gravmann's Chinese Theatre, which is up on Hollywood Boulevard.' It's Sunday morning, we go up there, and when we arrive it becomes evident that she must be quite an important personage in the church, as we are greeted in some style and immediately ushered into a private box – the only other occupant of which was the actor and fellow church member, Mickey Rooney. I must say that Dr. Wilson delivered a good sermon – it was a cross between the usual kind of born-again Christian doctrine and Dale Carnegie advice as to how to be successful in life.

"So after that I went out with this woman a few times and we became friends. One day she said to me, 'You know, I have a daughter who is a great singer.' I said, 'Listen, if we're going to be friends let's not talk about daughters who are going to be singers, uncles who write songs, and so forth. It never seems to work.' She said, 'Okay.' Then I didn't see her any more and time passed.

"So one thing leads to another, and when 'I Got You Babe' became such a huge international smash, Sonny and Cher came to New York. My wife, Mica, arranged for Cher to appear in a big spread for *Vogue* magazine, through its editor Diana Vreeland, who was a great friend of ours, and who also fell in love with Cher straight away. So during this session, Cher turned to me and said, 'You know what, I was very surprised to find out that you were friends with my mother.' I said, 'What are you talking about? I don't know your mother.' She said, 'Yes, you do,' at which point her mother walks in, and who is it, except this woman who was interested in metaphysical science. She said, 'I told you I had a daughter who sings!' I said, 'Oh good Lord!'" Ahmet

Andy Warhol with Ahmet

Baby Jane Holzer, with Cher, Ahmet and Sonny

The Stax Tour, from left: Arthur Conley, Al Bell, Wayne Jackson, Otis Redding, Steve Cropper, Sam Moore, Eddie Floyd, Joe Arnold and Dave Prater

"For about five years, I went in and out of Memphis at least once a month. I was considered the city cousin. So when it came to going to Europe, I was head honcho to take them there and break the ice. Some of them had never been more than 50 miles out of Memphis, and they went absolutely bonkers in London. One Sunday, at the old Mayfair before the first concert, I grabbed Jim Stewart, Al Bell, Steve Cropper and Duck Dunn and said, 'You guys have got to go through this tradition.' They looked at me like I was crazy, but we went down to the restaurant where there was this man pushing around a cart – he's wearing a wig of long white curls, stockings with knickerbockers, buckles on the shoes, the whole bit. He comes by our table to make the announcement, 'We have Yorkshire pudding and roast.' Jim Stewart just looked at me and said, 'Tom, what language is he talkin'?' I said, 'Jim, this is the deep English accent.' He said, 'Well, could I get a hamburger?' And Duck Dunn looked me straight in the eye and said, 'Tom, they got any fatback cacciatore?'" Tom Dowd

Otis Redding with Sam and Dave

From left: Steve Cropper, Al Jackson Jr., Booker T. Jones and Sam Moore

Otis Redding at French Customs TL: 60s

"The first time I met Otis the hairs stood up on the back of my neck. He was an incredible person and I believe that most people had that reaction to Otis. Even the French customs officials couldn't help but love him. Everyone did. We'd finish a session at Stax, doing some wonderful stuff, say with Sam and Dave, Wilson Pickett, whoever, having a tremendous time, but the question on everyone's lips was always the same - 'When's Otis coming back?' I consider myself very fortunate to have known him." Wayne Jackson

"They didn't want us out of the studio, they wanted us back there making records with other people. I think it was Phil Walden and Atlantic who just insisted. At that time we knew it was getting kind of big, but we didn't have any idea as to how big! Until Otis replaced Elvis as number one male vocalist – we all noticed that!" Donald 'Duck' Dunn

"British DJs like Roscoe, Johnny Walker, Dave Cash, had been playing American music, in particular American black music. *Ready, Steady, Go* was the first TV show that put the same music on television. We would use it behind the dancing, behind the charts, and behind the fashion. Then we started booking the acts as they came over and had them appearing live. One of the extensions of that was that we did some 'specials', and one of these was with Otis Redding and his band. The whole thing was totally live and, of course, with an audience. Good energy, and so exciting."
Vicky Wickham

"Soul lyrics, soul music, came at about the same time as the civil rights movement, and it's very possible that one influenced the other. Many black artists were friends with Stokely Carmichael – he was very popular and fortunately he befriended me. When I'd run into him backstage, he'd talk to me like a brother, which was very comforting." Ahmet

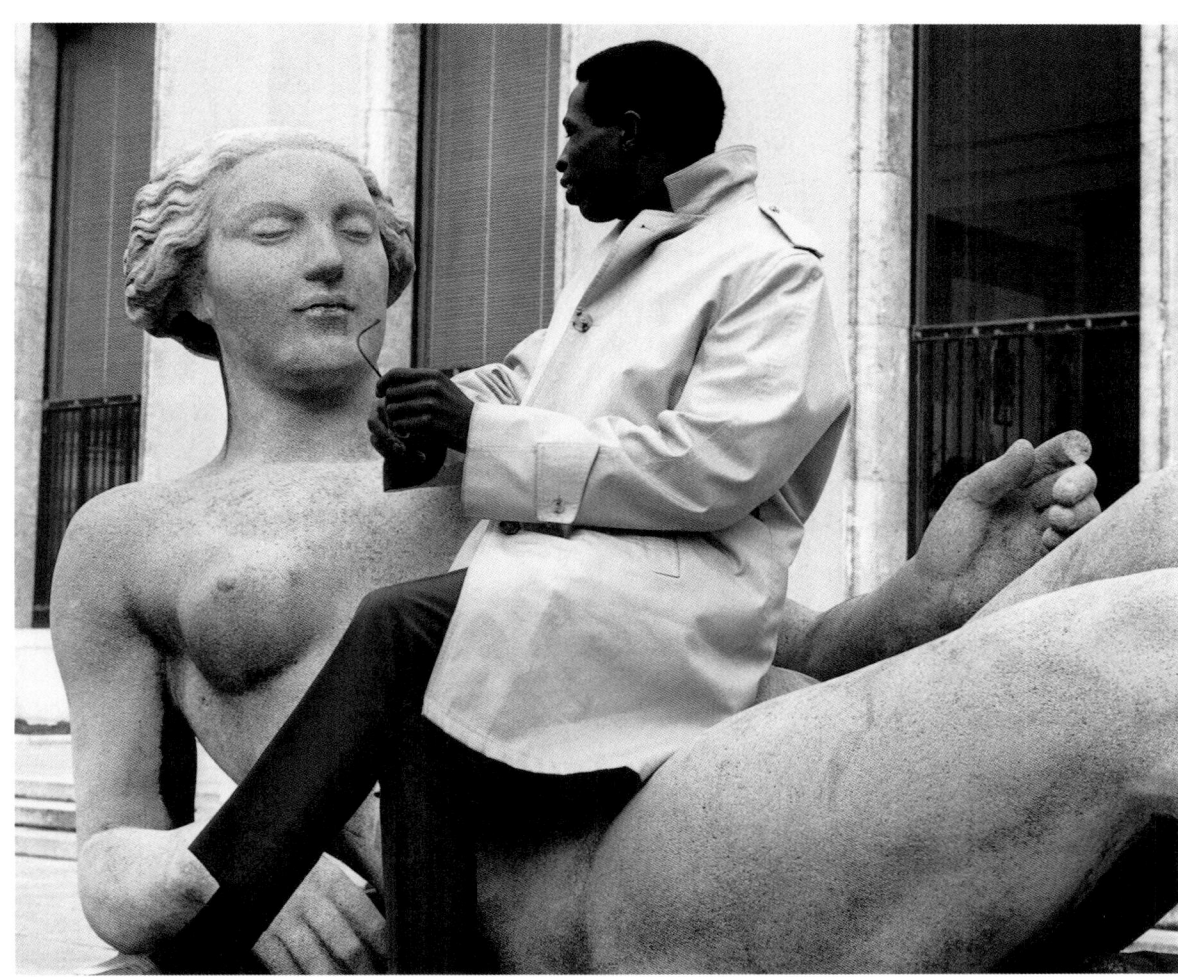

Arthur Conley TL: 60s

Above and below left: Percy Sledge TL: 60s

Arthur Conley TL: 60s

The Mar-Keys TL: 60s

Carla Thomas TL: 60s

"Quin Ivy produced 'When A Man Loves A Woman' with Percy Sledge and the Muscle Shoals musicians at a small studio in the next town along from us, Sheffield, Alabama. He played me the finished tape and said, 'What d'you think, what d'you think?!' I looked at him and I said, 'Hit record, number one record, big hit record, giant hit record!' He said, 'Are you kidding me?' I said, 'No, no, I'm telling you it's a smash. Maybe the biggest record I have ever had anything to do with. I mean, it's got to be a massive, massive smash.' He said, 'Well, God, can you help me make a deal on it?' I said, 'Yep, I sure can,' picked up the 'phone right away and called Jerry Wexler on his home number. It's Sunday, Jerry's in the pool with all of his big artists and big producers having a ball. He comes to the 'phone and says, 'Hello, Rick, you know you're bothering me. I've got all these friends here.' I said, 'You told me that if I heard something that I thought was a hit, I was to call you. I'm calling you – I've heard something that I think is a hit.' He said, 'Really?' I said, 'Yes – it's Percy Sledge, it's a local thing.' He said, 'No kidding!' I said, 'Look, Jerry, it's a number one record.' He said, 'That's pretty big – that's a huge statement to make.' I said, 'I know it is, but I'm telling you, I'll bet my life on it – just put it out, hide and watch, don't even worry about it.' So then, obviously, my points with Wexler went from zero to a thousand over a two-week period. I became his golden-haired boy."
Rick Hall

Wilson Pickett TL: 60s

"I can recall, as if it were yesterday, that first meeting with Wilson Pickett. He had on a black-and-white houndstooth coat, which in those days was fairly exceptional. He had his hair slicked down and was a very, very handsome black man. The way he was built, he looked like he should have been a running back for the New York Giants. He looked like a black panther – gorgeous, shiny, but if you touch him he'll bite your hand off. I picked him up from what was, in those days, a tiny little airport out here. It was like landing in the middle of a cotton patch. He got in the car, looked at me, I looked at him. Later he told me that he was thinking, 'Jesus, this is a little white boy, a little redneck boy, what's Jerry Wexler done to me?' I was thinking, 'Man, I wonder if I can control this at all!'" Rick Hall

Above: Linda Carr on the Stax Soul Tour, and right with Lee Dorsey TL: 60s

"Joe Tex was one of the most exciting entertainers up on stage that I'd ever seen. He worked with the microphone, and you'd think it was going to fall all the way, but just inches before it was about to hit the floor, he'd catch it with his foot, flip it back up, and go right into the lyric. He'd do splits, flip off the stage, then back onto the stage. He just danced all over the place. He was really an exciting man on stage." Buddy Killen

Joe Tex TL: 60s

Arthur Conley TL: 60s

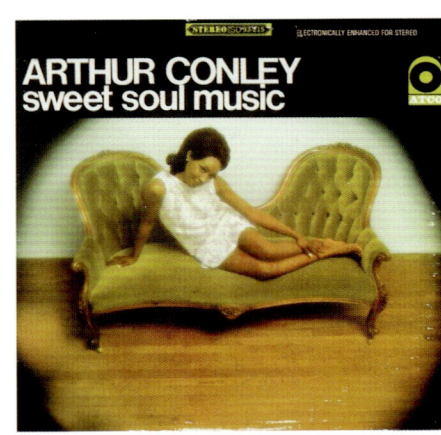

"Otis Redding had discovered Arthur Conley in a nightclub in Memphis. 'Sweet Soul Music' – we worked that out in my office one night. The intro, which is the old Marlboro theme, happened while we were watching TV one night and I said, 'We could use this horn line, the missed notes, as an opening for a record one time.' So we just stuck the Marlboro bit at the beginning of 'Sweet Soul Music'. We borrowed it and it worked!" Phil Walden

"There was such resistance to R & B music in England in those days. In fact one classic thing I remember was that a famous Radio 1 executive producer actually 'phoned up the head of A & R at Decca, Dick Rowe, who was my boss, and said, 'Why the hell is this guy Hall plugging this black singer called Otis somebody-or-other? Why isn't he pushing The Bachelors to me?' Virtually no help, I'm afraid, from 'Aunty' [BBC]. The people who used to help us were the pirates, especially Radio London. Anyway, the outcome was that, four weeks later, 'My Girl' was at number seven on the national charts, and I think the sales figure was about 107,000. It stayed in my mind because it made Otis's coming to England much more practical for promoters." Tony Hall

Otis Redding TL: 60s

Booker T. Jones TL: 60s

Sam and Dave TL: 60s

"We were in the studio working and no one else was there. So that you didn't have to walk out and down the corridor, they had built a rest room into the studio. So I was in the rest room, it was about 1.30 or 2.00 a.m., and Isaac [Hayes] was impatient because we'd been writing for several hours and nothing was happening. We hadn't come up with anything that we felt good about. He was at the piano and he was screaming, 'C'mon man – I'm tired, I want to go home.' I shouted out, 'Hold on, man, I'm coming, hold on …' and that was it! I came out of the rest room and said, 'Sac – we've got a smash!' He said, 'What?!' I said, 'Hold On, I'm Coming' – that's the title.' I laid on the floor, he started playing, and I just started singing. There was no music or lyrics on paper at that time, but we worked the whole structure out in about ten minutes. Isaac said, 'You know, I've got a little piece of a horn part that I think will work with it.' We took that lick and put it onto the melody we had, and that was 'Hold On, I'm Coming'. It was one of the quickest, smoothest tunes we ever wrote, and it was just magic."
David Porter

Carla Thomas TL: 60s

Eddie Floyd TL: 60s

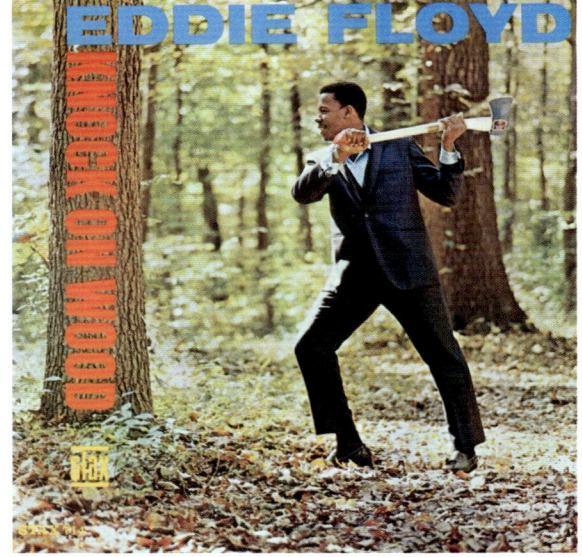

"'Knock On Wood' is actually another Steve Cropper song – 'In The Midnight Hour', in reverse. He just turned the chords around! He would concentrate on the riffs and on his part and I'd concentrate on the melody. We went into the studio the next day to run it down with the other guys. Duck Dunn contributed the bass line just the way he decided to do it. When we did it first, it was straight all the way through, too – I can't even imagine it now without the drum break. It was the drummer, Al Jackson, who came up with that idea. We needed something, because I'm singing, 'It's like thunder, lightning'. In fact, the reason for those lyrics was that on the night we were writing the song, it was thundering with lightning outside, but later, at the session, Al was thinking about somebody knocking or pounding at the door. Everybody thought it was just funny at first, but then when we tried it with the rhythm, it really worked!" Eddie Floyd

King Curtis TL: 60s

"King Curtis was very important – he was like a rock. His rhythm sections became the engine for many sessions. We're talking about Bernard Purdie, Cornell Dupree, Chuck Rainey, Ray Lucas – he even had Jimi Hendrix in his band. For me, a melody designed to be sung by a human voice, played by saxophone or trumpet, usually reminds me of Muzak. I'm not talking about Gershwin or Porter standards, I'm talking about pop songs. Curtis, however, was able to transcend that and make the melodies sing. So he covered a lot of melodies, and we relied heavily on him for his musical expertise." Arif Mardin

"Mary Wells achieved her greatest success with Smokey Robinson at Motown. Later, she had a Top Ten R & B hit with us called 'Dear Lover'. She was extremely well-liked, had a fanatical following – a wonderful person." Ahmet

Mary Wells TL: 60s

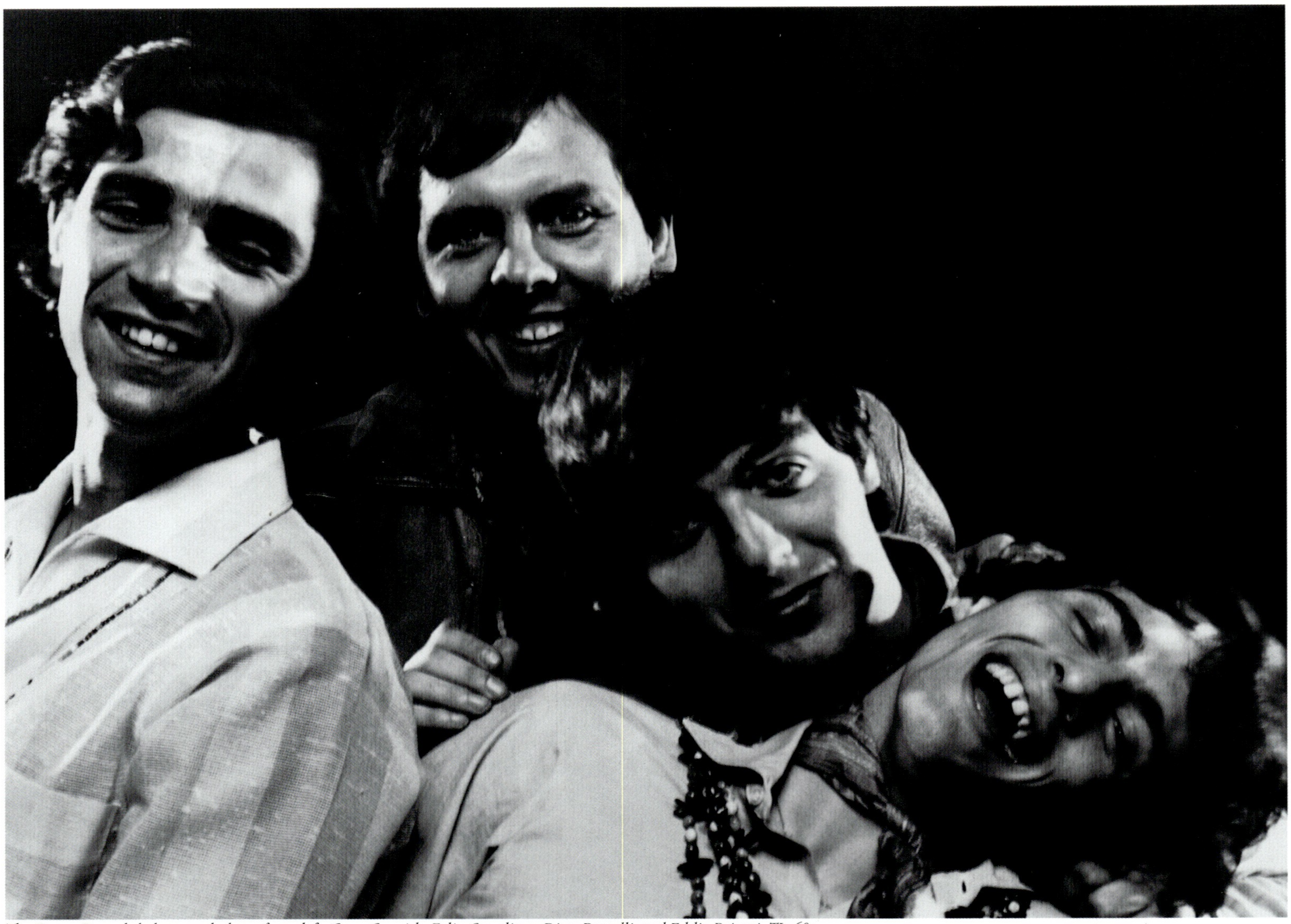

The Young Rascals below, and above from left: Gene Cornish, Felix Cavaliere, Dino Danelli and Eddie Brigati TL: 60s

"Our manager, Sid Bernstein, was the man who brought The Beatles to the States for their first appearance at Carnegie Hall and for their Shea Stadium concert in 1965. The night of their show at the stadium, he decided to put a huge flashing slogan with our name up on the scoreboard, so that a captive audience of about 75,000 people was warned: 'The Rascals Are Coming!' I'll never forget it, because Brian Epstein was there. He was very calm, cool and collected, and I don't think he ever raised his voice. He just said, 'That's very nice; if it's not off in approximately ten seconds, there will be no show,' – and bang, it was gone.

"We chose the location of our club residency very carefully. It was in a society-oriented place called Southampton, Long Island. We'd have people coming in like Bette Davis and Elaine, who owns the famous restaurant in New York – it was high-end clientele. I think they were crazier than other people, but they also brought in individuals from the business world. One man brought his contact in the music business – the man who became my manager, Sid Bernstein. Phil Spector came out to see us, and we had two or three labels that wanted to sign us. Now we get to the part that is most interesting to me, which is why we chose Atlantic. It was the only label that allowed me to produce, the only one that didn't just go completely through the roof. When I walked in and said, 'No, I don't want your A & R person, I want to do it,' what Atlantic did was to allow this to happen. I really have to say that the way they did it was brilliant. They gave us two people whom they called supervisors, but the two supervisors happened to be two of the best people in our industry – Tom Dowd and Arif Mardin. So, I mean, I thought I had died and gone to heaven – I had complete creative control, contractually, yet I had two absolute gentlemen working with me, two extremely talented people who loved to make music." Felix Cavaliere

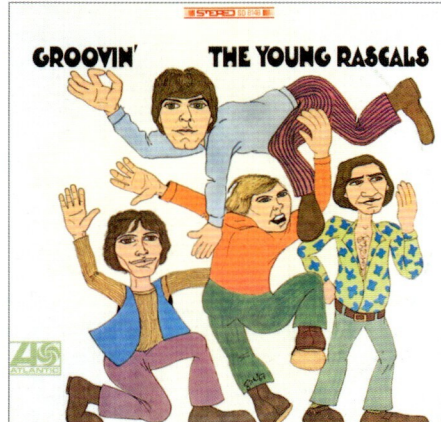

"They really started out as a garage band – youthful, very much influenced by R & B, with hard rock drumming. Felix Cavaliere and Eddie Brigati – they loved Smokey and all of that Motown music of the day. I think, though, that one of the very important things The Rascals brought to pop music was their love of jazz. They always used jazz musicians: Hubert Laws would usually play the flute solos, we'd have Richard Davis on bass, so there was always this influence. Felix would have the basic arrangements, the construction, the eighth notes, and the chords. Even with 'Groovin'', he had almost everything ready – we had a kind of conference, I suggested a few things here and there, like the piano. I actually played the vibraphone part on the record – three notes – ding, ding, ding!" Arif Mardin

Bobby Darin TL: 60s

"When Bobby Darin moved to Capitol, it didn't really pan out too well for him. He had a couple of semi-hits and then came back to Atlantic. The first song we came up with for him was 'If I Were A Carpenter' by Tim Hardin, which gave him another smash hit. In a way, Bobby had a tragic life because of a heart problem he'd suffered with since childhood, but he dealt with it so brilliantly. He was, I believe, one of the really great singers, performers, and creative artists of our times." Ahmet

Cream, from left: Ginger Baker, Eric Clapton and Jack Bruce TL: 60s

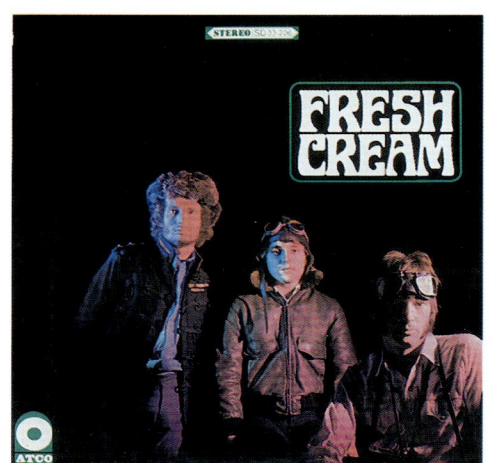

"There was a great wave in the sixties of a British awareness of American music, and of the British redefining American blues and American R & B. The Beatles were recording songs by the great R & B artists as well as their own compositions. The Rolling Stones took the world by storm doing their version of blues music. The Who were doing a combination of American music with English stories. One of the first people who really struck me as being a tremendous talent was Eric Clapton, who played better than anybody I'd ever heard. I first ran into him at a party we were giving for Wilson Pickett at the Scotch of St. James' club in London. There was a band playing when we got there, but then they stood down, and some other musicians got up onto the stage to jam. I had my back to the bandstand and was talking to Wilson Pickett when I heard this guitar solo behind me. I said, 'Wilson, your guitar player sure can play the blues, that sounds fantastic.' He pointed away from the stage and said, 'My guitar player is having a drink at the bar.' So I turned around and I beheld this young kid with an angelic face, a beautiful young gentleman, playing like B. B. King, and I couldn't believe it! That was the first time I met Eric Clapton. I think he's one of the greatest musicians of the century." Ahmet

"I was in Mexico at a sporting event when Jerry Wexler called me up and said that the managers Charlie Greene and Brian Stone were trying to reach me. They'd talked to him about a very talented new group called 'Buffalo Springfield' that was working in the Los Angeles area and had already built up quite a following. There was a lot of interest in them from other companies, but they were interested in going with Atlantic. So I told Jerry that instead of coming back to New York, I'd travel from Mexico City to Los Angeles and see them. When I got to L.A., I discovered that there was, indeed, considerable interest in this band from other companies.So I felt that I still had to sell myself or sell our company to the group. I guess they were quite impressionable young people because they were amazed that I knew

From left: Jack Bruce, Ginger Baker and Eric Clapton

Buffalo Springfield, from left: Richie Furay, Stephen Stills, Neil Young and Bruce Palmer TL: 60s

a lot of the music they were talking about, and they certainly seemed to feel that I was, in any event, a different kind of record executive. I would sit on the floor with them and chat, we'd play all kinds of records, I'd make comments, and it all seemed to make sense to them. We got on very well, they seemed to be happy with me, so we were able to sign them.

"Buffalo Springfield was very special in so many ways. First of all, the songs they wrote didn't resemble anything that anybody else was doing. They also had three outstanding lead singers who were also great guitar players – Neil Young, Stephen Stills, and Richie Furay. I mean, a rock'n'roll band is lucky if it has one good singer and one guitar player who can really play – that alone can make them a great band. The power in Buffalo Springfield was too incredible. They were one of the greatest rock'n'roll bands I've ever heard in my life.

"I recorded many of the early Buffalo Springfield tracks at Gold Star Studios, which was a very funky studio where a lot of hits were made. What they did in person, however, we somehow never seemed able to bring out on record. You couldn't capture the enthusiasm which they built up when they were playing for an audience, with all of these people dancing around them. They also became much more cerebral when they were in the studio, because they wanted to make a statement. Ultimately, they didn't do well enough for everybody in the band to be happy, and they broke up. They only lasted a couple of years, but in those two years, I would have sued to hear them play. I think they were one of the most important American groups in the development of what we call rock-'n'roll today." Ahmet

Buffalo Springfield, from left: Bruce Palmer, Stephen Stills, Richie Furay, Neil Young and Dewey Martin

Shelly Manne TL: 60s

Roy Ayers TL: 60s

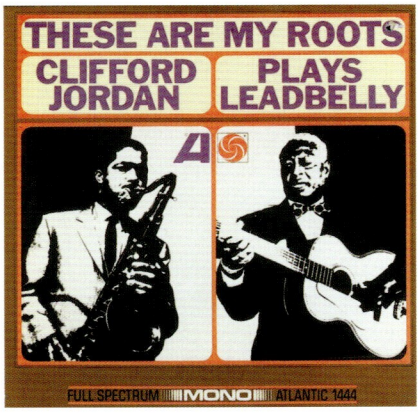

"Shelly Manne was an extremely talented swing drummer. He played with Coleman Hawkins, Stan Kenton, and Charlie Ventura. But he also played with Ornette Coleman, something quite different. We first recorded him in 1947 with Eddie Safranski and he recorded an album with us in 1966.

"Roy Ayers had worked with Herbie Mann, most notably on *Memphis Underground*, before going solo and recording some excellent jazz albums for us in the late sixties." Ahmet

Above: Freddie Hubbard TL: 60s 80s, and below, Max Roach TL: 60s

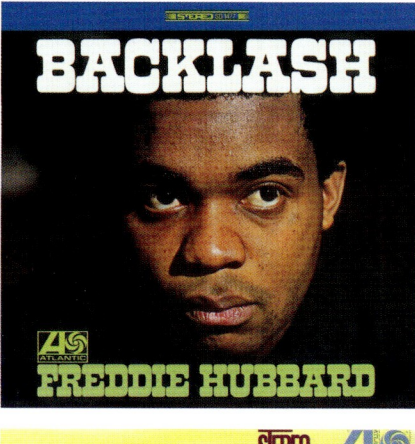
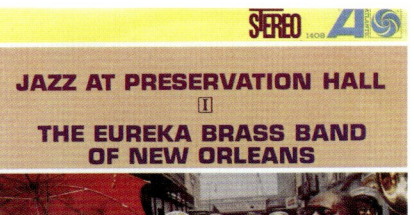

"Freddie Hubbard recorded several LPs for the label, introducing his classic composition, 'Up Jumped Spring', on the 1966 album, *Backlash*.

"On an appropriately appellated set called *Max Roach Presents The Legendary Hassan*, the great pioneer bop drummer spotlighted an obscure keyboard wiz who helped bridge the gap between Monk and 'outside' pianists like Cecil Taylor. Roach made other fascinating albums for the company, particularly *Lift Every Voice and Sing*, which combined his quintet with a gospel choir." Will Friedwald

"Nesuhi started going down to New Orleans. He would send a production crew or go himself. A highpoint for us was the series *Jazz At Preservation Hall*." Ahmet

Roland Kirk TL: 60s

"I have a tremendous hang-up with people not wanting to accept me as a man. Sometimes people can be too helpful. Like when I go on an aeroplane, some hostess always wants to carry my saxophone bag. Or if I go to a barbershop, a coloured barbershop, the barber always asks somebody else if I'm sure I want that much hair taken off my head. When I go to a white hotel, they're always afraid I'm going to fall out of a window or that I can't answer a 'phone without knocking something over. If a person will just accept me as a man, then I'll accept him as a man." Roland Kirk

Elvin Jones TL: 60s

Charles Lloyd and right, Jack DeJohnette TL: 60s

"Elvin Jones – one of the greatest drummers ever and a wonderful, gentle person. The whole family is like that, always so kind and shining. His brother, Hank, has always seemed to me to be like a prince, an earl, and all of them like a royal musical family.

"Nesuhi produced and I mixed *Forest Flower*. I remember Charles Lloyd would sit there as I mixed this record and say, 'Make it sound good!'" Arif Mardin

Aretha Franklin TL: 60s

"I signed Aretha Franklin, whom I thought was about the most exciting singer I had heard since Billie Holiday. Unfortunately, we had no concept of how to sell to the black market – it was a sing-along-with-Mitch-type company." John Hammond

"I was always a fan of hers and I'd been watching her for many years, so I knew that her contract with Columbia was about to run out. It was a dream of mine to sign her up for Atlantic Records. We had a mutual friend who was a gospel disc jockey in Philadelphia, named Louise Williams. She and Aretha were pretty close pals because Aretha was always very close to the gospel wheel all around the country. So I just said to Louise, 'Anything you can do to help me, to let me know when the right time might be,' and so on. I was in Muscle Shoals, I think with Wilson Pickett, when Louise called me and said, 'Here's this number, Aretha's waiting for your call.' As far as how to record her was concerned, it was just more or less a question of keeping on doing what we had been doing with our rhythm and blues artists. To let this sound emerge, be heard, and not try to make it palatable for a white audience – just let it out. So while being meticulous about those matters, but at the same time getting into the depth, the soul of the artist, the idea was to record her with great musicians, put her at the piano, and let her sing and play for herself." Jerry Wexler

"In about two hours, 'I Never Loved A Man' was in the can. It was a killer. There was no doubt about it. People started dancing and singing – I mean, musicians dancing with each other, just acting the fool. Everybody was happy, because it was a hit record. Everybody in there was a fan of rhythm and blues, and they knew that this particular morning, a star had been born. Then, when they played the second side of that first single, 'Do Right Woman', back to me – with Aretha singing and playing piano, and her sisters doing the harmonies so beautifully – I just about had a heart attack because it was so fine. The finesse on the piano, that voice singing exactly the right melody ... a perfect record in my estimation is 'Do Right Woman' by Aretha Franklin." Dan Penn

Aretha Franklin signing her contract with Atlantic. She is pictured with Jerry Wexler and her husband, Ted White

"I think my dad felt that I was gifted or uniquely talented as a child. He would coach me in different things. He would give me different records to listen to and see if I could emulate them on the piano – and various vocalists to listen to, such as Clara Ward and other similar artists. The first record I made with Atlantic was in Muscle Shoals, Alabama, and it was 'I Never Loved A Man'. Atlantic was a very hot label when I signed with them. I'd been with Columbia for five years previously and had not had a hit during that time – what I had were turntable hits. I got a lot of airplay, a lot of critical acclaim, but no hits. Most of the material was very stylized, and I think that made the difference. Mr. Wexler usually wanted to know what it was I wanted to do, and then he would submit things. We would have long listening sessions and sometimes dinner at his home, and thereafter, we would make our own selections." Aretha Franklin

"Nino Tempo used to talk to me about Aretha Franklin all the time. She was his favourite singer. After five years with Columbia, she had not had any big hits and became available, so we signed her up right away. I was in Europe when Jerry called me up and announced that he had just completed the deal with Aretha. I said, 'My God! That's fabulous!' First, Jerry took her down to Muscle Shoals to record. Then they brought the musicians to New York and made historic records, music that will never die. The team of Wexler, Mardin, and Dowd – they were each at their height, you know, and those records will stay as a testament to the great music made in those years." Ahmet

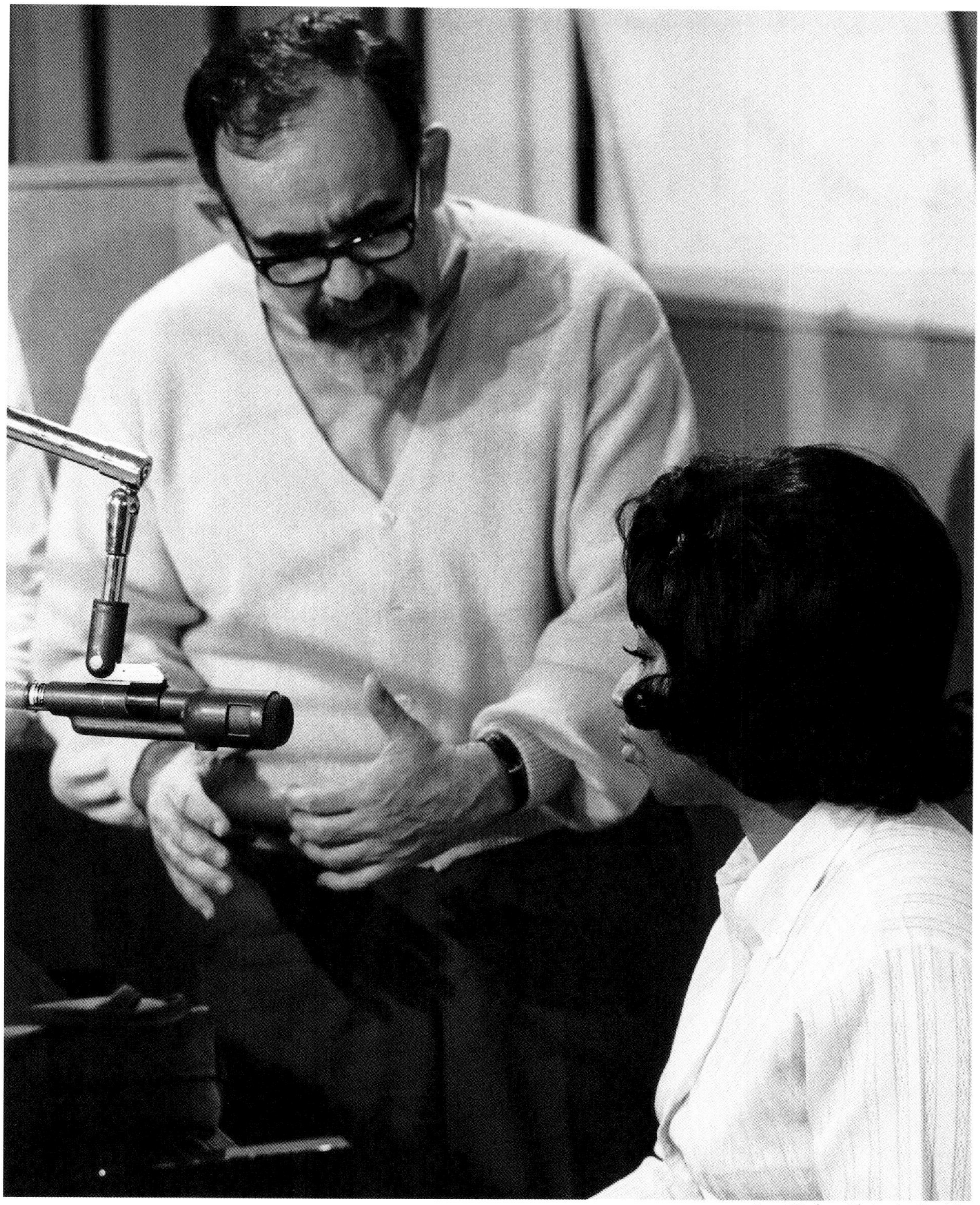

Jerry Wexler with Aretha Franklin

"Aretha hit a magical 'come here' kind of chord, and I remember watching this room full of great Southern musicians running to their instruments. They didn't waste any time, they ran. Chips Moman nearly broke his neck just getting to his guitar." Dan Penn

"I knew they'd cut some wonderful records in the Atlantic studio in New York, so of course that was a plus. It was as if we didn't have to be concerned about adapting, but could just play like we did at home. So the music part was no strain to us, but the traffic on the street – the foot traffic – that's the biggest difference. A lot of people on the streets walking around and a lot of people on elevators. You know you just didn't have to contend with elevators back home – there's maybe one in the whole town, and it probably went three storeys high." Spooner Oldham

Dan Penn

Spooner Oldham

Southern Soul
By Robert Gordon

"For me," says Ray Charles, "it was always a matter of what kind of music made my brain jump up and down and say 'Wow! Oh!'" For Ray, and for Ahmet Ertegun and Jerry Wexler, what made their brains jump up and down had navigated Atlantic Records through the 1950s establishing them in the sixties as survivors of the indie label boom. Their "Wow! Oh!" made Atlantic's 1960s soul the lasting music it has become. "The people at Atlantic can tap their feet to the music," Ray Charles continues. "Most record guys can't keep time, they just keep money. The people at Atlantic can snap fingers on to and fro. My experience with them has always been number one, jam up."

Between 1962 and 1967, Atlantic increased its sales by 500 per cent and people everywhere danced 'the dog' and 'the sideways pony'. "Southern soul is dance music," says Ahmet. "'Drinkin' Wine Spo-Dee-O-Dee', our first hit more than a decade earlier, is a rollicking thing, more like folk blues. Over the years, the rhythm got more and more modern, and that's really what distinguishes Southern soul." In its era of soul music, Atlantic signed Solomon Burke, Wilson Pickett, Sam and Dave, and Aretha Franklin. The label had hits, and it also nurtured many other studios and labels whose artists had hits. Atlantic created production deals and distribution deals, having their greatest successes with the Stax label and studio in Memphis and Fame Music in Muscle Shoals, Alabama. Stax was home to Rufus Thomas, Booker T. & the M.G.s, William Bell and Otis Redding, while Fame boasted Percy Sledge and a rhythm section that was as comfortable behind Clarence Carter as it would later be behind Boz Scaggs and Paul Simon. For Atlantic, Southern soul began with a country song in the Northeast. In the fall of 1960, Solomon Burke, in his twenties and fresh from his first music biz retirement, recorded 'Just Out Of Reach' under Jerry Wexler's direction. Though he couldn't yet know the song's success, Solomon's mind was on money. "When the session was over and we started to listen to it," Wexler told Peter Guralnick in *Sweet Soul Music*, "Solomon cut out; he wasn't going to listen. I said, 'Where are you going?' He said, 'I'm going back to Philadelphia. I'm on a snow-removal gig at $3.50 an hour.'" Burke's hit, significantly, broke in the Southern states, where a crazy promo man named Joe Galkin recognized its potential. Galkin had abandoned a successful job plugging songs in New York for a new life in the South, and his success with 'Just Out Of Reach' proved him a man of transregional taste. "Joe Galkin pointed me South at a critical moment when new sounds were exploding," writes Jerry Wexler in *The Rhythm and the Blues*; "a roots music that seemed to refer to the past, present, and future all at once." What is soul music? It is the vehicle that, when we shut our eyes transports us from the corporeal to the ethereal and back again. It is the sonic intersection of the spiritual with the physical. Whether it is about love or lust, about salvation or surrender, about anger or bliss, a soul song is capable of lifting us to another place. It takes you there. Wow! Oh! The South was a natural place for soul music to develop. The floodlands of the Mississippi delta made it rich for farming, but a conflict rose between those whose backs picked the cotton and those whose backs wore it. The region was fertile ground for their interaction but also a place of distinct class and racial segregation. The underlying dis-ease birthed the occasional riot and a wealth of artistic expression. The creation and exploitation of delta blues music in the 1920s and 1930s and of rock'n'roll in the 1950s, were reflections of Southern society. In the 1960s, Memphis was still a sleepy town. Quarantined by miles of rural farmland, it caught little of the European sophistication nor sociological advances that were a pre-requisite given in other parts of the country. Coming to Memphis from New York was, for Tom Dowd, Atlantic's engineer, producer, and physicist, "like turning back the hands of time. In the South, you'd be hearing country music, religious programmes, rhythm and blues records," says Dowd. "I'd be getting broadcasts I'd think were comedy records. In New York the groups that turned on the young people were Vanilla Fudge, Joey Dee and the Starlighters, Mountain. They were in your face, they were pop and they were brashy. Down here, the same age group was into mellow things, more soulful, emotional-type music. But communication was beginning to make major breakthroughs, so you were no longer in cloistered little segregated areas." One thing Memphis understood was shipping; the crops raised in the region had to be moved out. One maverick businessman perceived that Memphis and music also worked as an export and, in time to press the first Sun Records on credit, he established the first independent pressing plant away from the coasts. Not only could Buster Williams's Plastic Products press the vinyl, but his Music Sales could distribute the records to jukeboxes all over the South — jukeboxes which his Williams' Distributors owned. This monopoly made Buster a popular guy in the biz. Atlantic was one of Plastic Products' biggest accounts. So when, in mid-1960, Buster's plant manager Leon McLemore noticed the quantities he was moving on a new single, he 'phoned Jerry Wexler at Atlantic. The song was "Cause I Love You', a duet between Rufus Thomas and his teenage daughter Carla. The label was called Satellite but would soon change its name to an acronym of the owners' last names: Stax. Soulsville, U.S.A. It began in such innocence. A brother-sister team in Memphis stumbled onto a trove of talent, lucked into some good sounding records and, through Atlantic's established distribution, reached a national audience. Jim Stewart and Estelle Axton were clerks at a bank when they founded the label. Jim played country fiddle and Estelle didn't even have a record player. But Sun Records had recently sold Elvis' contract to RCA, and many people in Memphis thought it would be easy – or possible – to make music. When Atlantic came knocking, it was as unreal as Superman with a bag of cash. Stax was just settling into a former movie theatre-turned-church, building a studio, offices and, for cash flow, a record store in what had been the lobby. The Thomas' duet was the first single from this new location. ("The room was cavernous as far as recording studios go," says Dowd. "You never worried about a sound bouncing back at you. It died up in the drapes someplace.") Stax suddenly had money to upgrade some equipment and, more importantly, the possibility of some real distribution. Teenaged Carla Thomas returned to the studio to cut 'Gee Whiz', a ballad she'd written in her school notebook. She sang it as purely as mathematics homework, but with passion. It became a national best seller.

Steve Cropper

On an early visit to Memphis, Jerry invited Rufus and Carla to dinner. He was informed that no restaurant would seat an integrated table, and they had to settle for room service at his hotel. Apparently, racial mixing even in private was not tolerated: the house dick and his goon squad nearly broke down Jerry's door. Civil rights volunteers were being murdered not far away, and Wexler, fearing his life would end in the trunk of a car with Mississippi tags, dashed off a last communiqué to Ahmet, which he sprinted past the goons to mail. In this discordant society, Stax was defining itself as a house of harmony. The label's sound and direction were defined by their next hit single, 'Last Night' by the Mar-Keys. This song is bedrock Stax, a bridge between two societies. The Mar-Keys sax player, Packy Axton, was Estelle's son and Jim's nephew; he had begun to frequent Memphis nightclubs, which featured some of the swingin'est blues, jazz, and R & B then being played anywhere. He and Charlie Freeman and some like-minded high school classmates soon had a band, and found themselves with not only a tune of their own, but a tape of it too. The sound was black but the band was white. Estelle, proprietor of Stax's record store, was the label's *de facto* promo department; she was also a proud mom, and she made sure the record got released. Uncommonly funky, 'Last Night' is so simple it's silly. It's a bunch of horns and a cheesy organ. A sense of fun permeates the song, the glee of kids sneaking out at night. It plays just behind the beat, in the style of the region's nightclubs. With Atlantic's distribution, the song hit #2 on the R & B charts, #3 Pop, and the Mar-Keys found themselves in cities they were studying in geography class. With a string of hits, Atlantic began regularly including a Stax release in its schedule. The steady work helped a core of musicians coalesce in the Memphis studio. They were all kids who'd been inspired by the city's R & B scene, but who, until playing together at Stax, hadn't had a real opportunity to meet – the clubs were segregated. Stax was as much a community centre as it was a recording studio. For organist Booker T. Jones, it was an after-school hangout, a sort of continuing education class as he browsed through records and listened to the studio banter. Jones brought drummer Al Jackson Jr. into the fold. Jackson had been raised on Memphis bandstands; his father was one of the city's most popular bandleaders. And Jackson brought bassist Lewis Steinberg, with whom he'd been performing regularly as part of a popular area band. These black musicians shared a musical vocabulary with white guitarist Steve Cropper, who had dropped out of the Mar-Keys to devote more time to the studio, and with bassist Donald "Duck" Dunn, another Mar-Key who eventually settled into the studio. On the one hand, these musicians were all around the same age, from the same small city, and had been exposed to the same repertoire on radio and in clubs; on the other, they came from different backgrounds, sang different songs in church, and danced different dances. Some guys brought more of a blues feel, others brought country. If they couldn't dine out together, they could make good music together. "The rhythm section was the heart of the matter," says Wexler, "the chief reason Memphis mattered. Once I heard [Stax's house band], I realized it was the converse of what we were doing in New York." Head charts: The sound didn't come from written arrangements, it came from the soul. Head charts in the south were worked up on the floor, the parts written in your head. Head charts freed up each musician to try what felt right. It was easier for parts to change, for the song to evolve. More spontaneity and emotion stuck to the tape. No pencils were sharpened on the summer's day in 1962 when Stax's house band came into their own. Booker T., Al Jackson Jr., Steinberg and Cropper assembled for a session behind Billy Lee Riley, who'd had several rocking songs on Memphis's Sun label. But Billy Lee got sidetracked on the way, and while the house band waited, they messed around with a riff. What with fresh tape for the session – well, why not record? The instrumental was catchy, even with the menacing feel in its tone. 'Green Onions' reflected society's veneer and the rumble beneath it. And it established a name for Stax's house band: Booker T. & the M.G.s.

That autumn, Joe Galkin, sent another jam-up group to Stax. Johnny Jenkins and the Pinetoppers were popular on the Southern fraternity and chitlin circuit. Jenkins had a snazzy stage style and their gigs kept the dance floor packed. As their time at Stax wound down, the magic had not materialized. Trying to save the session from naught, Galkin said, "Okay, then – let's do something with this guy." "This guy" was Otis Redding, the band's driver and second vocalist. He stepped to the mike and they quickly laid down a no-nonsense Little Richard imitation. For a flip side, Otis had a ballad, which the band quickly worked up. 'These Arms Of Mine' was graced again by a simplicity, by a schoolyard charm that made itself plainly understood to kids of all ages everywhere. In thirty minutes, a session had been saved and a career launched – a fraction of the time a New York producer would have needed to look up the arranger's 'phone number and arrange to have some charts delivered. People talk about a family feel at Stax, but the image is not so much a bunch of kids under the strict eye of their parents; rather, it's more like grown siblings who've moved out of mom and dad's place but still fall by regularly for that solid meal. "From what I gathered on my first encounter with the chaps, which was on a Saturday," says Dowd, "we made friends; we talked sports and scores, old records, and somewhere along the line I said, 'Well, the only thing I miss about not being home this weekend is I'd play golf.' And Duck and Steve kind of looked and said, 'Okay, you'll play golf in the morning.' About 6.30 the next morning, we played ten or 11 holes, all of a sudden Steve says, 'Well, we'd better be heading back to the studio, we just about have time to get coffee and doughnuts.' And I think, well, it's Sunday, but okay. So I see that when people come out of church, they stop by Stax, talk about this and that. Al Jackson Jr. would show up and Isaac Hayes and David Porter. The horns moseyed in, and we're talking – I'd only met these people the day before. Rufus Thomas comes walking in the door, says, 'Hi, everybody!' Rufus is a pepperpot and a leprechaun, he's just gorgeous. He says, 'Everything working?' And they said, 'Yeah, it's working now.' Rufus says, 'I got a song!' Rufus runs this song by them once or twice, I'm up in the control room and I'm laughing at the lyrics, and Steve looks up and says, 'You ready to record?' And I say, 'You got it, let's go!' Boom, right? And I walked out, I had it under my arm that Monday morning when I went back to New York – 'Walkin' the Dog'."

Wilson Pickett and friend

Atlantic's muscle, strong enough to break hits, could also kill songs. Wilson Pickett had experienced the receiving end of Atlantic's punch, and when he visited Wexler's office in the spring of 1964, he wanted to join forces. A year earlier, Pickett's demo tape of 'If You Need Me' had landed on Wexler's desk; the song was great, but signed elsewhere, so Wexler rushed out a cover version by Solomon Burke – and prevented Pickett's from breaking. "You're not sore?" Wexler asked, and Pickett replied, "That's in the past." After several old school sessions in New York, Pickett wanted to cut at Stax. "Pickett was a pistol," according to Wexler. "His temperament was fire, his flash-and-fury singing style a study in controlled aggression, his blood-curdling scream always musical, always in tune … From the get-go Pickett's image was unapologetically macho. A man and a half."

They went to Memphis, and at Stax they cut, among other songs, 'In The Midnight Hour', '634-5789', and 'Ninety-Nine And A Half (Won't Do)'. When the band had trouble finding the right beat for 'Midnight Hour', Wexler fell back on Atlantic basics: ass-shaking. He ran out of the producer's booth and started dancing. "I was shaking my booty to a groove made popular by The Larks' 'The Jerk', a mid-sixties hit. The idea was to push the second beat while holding back the fourth – something easier demonstrated than explained." The little neighbourhood was producing not only singers but also songwriters. Before hooking up with Isaac Hayes, lyricist David Porter sacked groceries at the market across from Stax. "Before David and I were recognized as songwriters," says Hayes, "we were teased a lot. We had our little attaché case and David had this raggedy car, foam rubber seat cushion falling out everywhere. And the guys on the street would tease us. 'Hey hitmakers, how many songs y'all write today?' But when we started catching on, everybody wanted to write songs." The team of Hayes and Porter came to national prominence after Ahmet and Jerry signed to Atlantic Sam and Dave – a soul duo so hot they made sweat steam. Arriving at Stax, Sam and Dave hit with Hayes-Porter songs: 'Soul Man', 'When Something Is Wrong With My Baby', and 'Hold On, I'm Coming'.

By late 1965, Southern soul had become an integral part of national radio programming. At Stax, concern about losing the label's identity resulted in the termination of their production deal with Atlantic; the Stax sound would now be reserved for Stax artists. Stax's distribution agreement with Atlantic remained intact, to the mutual benefit of each. Stax was not, of course, the only studio in the south. In Muscle Shoals, Alabama, three hours from Memphis on small roads, a scene had gelled. There, Rick Hall's Fame Music had enjoyed a few successes, especially with Jimmy Hughes's 'Steal Away' and Arthur Alexander's 'You Better Move On'. Joe Galkin, once again, had made sure Wexler and Ertegun noticed this action. In February of 1966, an Alabama hospital orderly hooked up with a local disc jockey who had access to a twenty-five dollar Sears record maker. The orderly sang as if he were unburdening all men: 'When A Man Loves A Woman'. The disc jockey brought it to Rick Hall, who 'phoned Jerry Wexler, who 'phoned Ahmet Ertegun in Europe to say he'd found a single that was going to pay for their whole summer. Vocalist Percy Sledge became a new star, Atlantic found a new Southern recording base in Muscle Shoals, and Wilson Pickett was put on a 'plane headed Rick Hall's way. In Muscle Shoals, Pickett added to the mix songwriter and guitarist Bobby Womack; he cut 'Funky Broadway', 'Land Of 1,000 Dances' and 'Mustang Sally'.

"The trick," says Wexler about Southern soul, "was to keep the session open, the creative juices flowing, the improvisatory feeling of on-the-spot, here-and-now creation vital and fresh." Muscle Shoals guitarist and producer Jimmy Johnson states it more simply: "We gave Jerry the relaxed feeling he wanted, and Pickett gave him hits." And the hits kept coming: Clarence Carter cut 'Slip Away' and 'Patches' at Hall's Fame studio. Ahmet brought R. B. Greaves there and produced 'Take A Letter Maria'. Even The Rolling Stones wanted the vibe: they came and cut tracks for *Sticky Fingers*.

Things were sweet between Atlantic and Muscle Shoals when Wexler brought Aretha Franklin to Fame at the start of 1967. She had just left Columbia Records, where she'd been unable to find her voice. Wexler, however, could hear in his head what the Southern soul sound would do behind her powerful urban gospel vocals. Previously, black artists had worked there and little racial tension had surfaced. This time, however, a conflict arose and the whole session exploded before the second day could begin. When Wexler flew back to New York, he had one finished song, 'I Never Loved A Man (The Way I Love You)' and the rhythm tracks for 'Do Right Woman – Do Right Man'. "I ran off two dozen acetates of 'I Never Loved A Man' for my key DJs," says Wexler. "Before long, it was burning up the radio, 'phone lines were jumping, the thing was a smash, and there I was with my adenoids showing: we had a stone hit, but only half a single." Aretha finished the tune and the album in New York. From then on, the Muscle Shoals and Memphis musicians got on the plane. The blend worked: Southerners, Northerners (including Atlantic's sax exemplar King Curtis), and others (Bobby Womack, Eric Clapton). By 1968, Aretha's first four Atlantic albums enjoyed nine Top Ten pop hits and seven #1 R & B hits, including her treatment of Otis Redding's 'Respect', to which the Big O is said to have commented, "That little girl's just stolen my song." "Aretha was continuing what Ray Charles had begun," says Wexler, "the secularization of gospel, turning church rhythms, church patterns and especially church feelings into personalized love songs. Like Ray, Aretha was a hands-on performer, a two-fisted pianist plugged into the main circuit of Holy Ghost power."

Atlantic's work in the South was not over. Relations with Stax had remained cordial; during the 1967 Stax/Volt tour of Europe, Tom Dowd escorted the musicians to England, then flew back to chaperone Jim Stewart and Al Bell on their first transatlantic flight. The era's excitement was garnered by Arthur Conley in a gallop of horns and rhythm when he cut the ebullient 'Sweet Soul Music'. There was enough work for several rhythm sections. In addition to Booker T. & the M.G.s in Memphis, there were the Hodges brothers at Hi Records, Stan Kesler's groups, and Chips Moman's American Studio rhythm section. "We ran a variety of artists through American," says Dowd. "I mean, it was bizarre. Jerry Wexler, Arif Mardin, myself, we might show up one day with Lulu or Dusty Springfield and a week later come in with Herbie Mann or Wilson Pickett. We had an accumulation of musicians who were masters of their instruments, who were gracious and took our bizarre direction easily." In Muscle Shoals, Atlantic helped establish a new studio, Muscle Shoals Sound, which featured Rick Hall's former musicians; like river silt levelling a hole, another rhythm section fell into place at Fame. "These Southern musicians might have just come off a country date, off a blues date or a pop gig," says Dowd. "And they'd say, 'Hey man, you hear that lick you played in there? I got an idea … ' and Boom! They'd make a record out of the thing. And put it out. It was so dramatic, 'We gotta make a record out of this.' They were doing it because they had a good groove and they felt good doing it. One or two passes and it stuck. Hit records. Inspiration."

The mood shifted around late 1967, when Atlantic sold out to Warner-Seven Arts. Stax was informed that their masters were not their own; they were the property of Atlantic. Two weeks later, Otis Redding was killed in a plane crash, along with four of the young Bar-Kays. Stax sold out to a conglomerate. Rev. Martin Luther King Jr. was assassinated in Memphis.

Memphis found a way to keep making soul hits, and so did Muscle Shoals. Stax enjoyed various stages of success for another decade after its final split with Atlantic; Rick Hall continues to operate Fame Studio today. Session musicians who made their mark through Atlantic remain in demand, whether they've moved to the coast or to Nashville, or maintain home in Memphis or the kudzu countryside. The Southern soul era was a time when the nation's musical trends were not determined in the population centres and the corporate offices, but established instead by the sounds of small town Southern streets and neighbourhoods. Atlantic Records was hip enough to hear the potential and flexible enough to work with such satellites. People who'd never dreamed of the spotlight got to enjoy it, some for fifteen minutes, some forever.

Atlantic had started the decade with the post-doo-wop sounds of Ben E. King's '(A Rose In) Spanish Harlem', ended it with the Soul Clan's 'Soul Meeting' (Solomon Burke, Arthur Conley, Ben E. King, Don Covay and Joe Tex), and anticipated the disco seventies with Archie Bell & The Drells' 'I Can't Stop Dancing'. A more urban sound was on the horizon, the age of higher tech reflected through the new emphasis on machines. Disco made it difficult for the Southern revue to survive; horn sections were decimated by the flick of a new keyboard's switch. But Southern soul has settled into its lasting place in popular consciousness, inspiring prayer and making brains go: Wow! Oh!

Soul music, it takes you there.

Solomon Burke TL: 60s

"I don't know when Solomon Burke became King Solomon. He's a person who has the ambition and ability to become many different people. He's a preacher and also a party-type of guy who likes to go out, hang out – the opposite of what most preachers do. He's a musician, he's a businessman. At one point, he bought a drugstore. There was a sign outside that used to say 'Roots, Fruits and Snoots'. One time I ran into him and said, 'How's it going, Solomon? How's it going with the drugstore?' He said, 'It's going good, man, except the chemist, he's very expensive. I have to pay this guy a lot of money.' 'Well,' I replied, 'you've got to have someone who's qualified to fill prescriptions. I mean, you're not going to get such a person on minimum wages.' 'No,' he insisted, 'I've got to find a way around this – the guy's really eating into my profits.' So then the next time I saw him, a couple of weeks later, I asked him again, 'How's it going – how's the drugstore?' He said, 'Oh, I've got a thing worked out. I've got this young track star from the high school who says he can run a hundred-yard dash in 10.3 seconds.' So I said, 'No kidding – what does he do for you?' He said, 'He took the place of the chemist.' I said, 'How does that work?' So he said, 'Well, you see, people bring in a prescription and the kid will say, 'If you come back in an hour, we'll have this ready for you.' Then when the customer leaves, he sprints down to the next drugstore, gets the prescription filled there, dashes back with it, we slap our label on, and that's how we save on the chemist.'" Ahmet

Patti LaBelle and the Bluebelles, including, Cindy Birdsong and Nona Hendryx TL: 60s

"We started jamming a little riff, extending the song, ad-libbing and stuff, and we came up with the rhythm to settle it down. Jim Stewart walked back into the studio. 'What's that y'all doing?' 'Oh, it's just something we made up.' 'Do it again.' So we did it again, man, and he just flipped. 'That's a hit, let's cut it.' So we cut that version and we said, 'Now there's still something missing here.' We got to thinking – and I always would do the comical things on the trumpet, so I did 'Mary's Little Lamb', and they said, 'Why don't you put that on the front of it, man?!' It started happening from that point on. We cut 'Soul Finger' in about fifteen minutes." Ben Cauley of the Bar-Kays

The Bar-Kays, including: Jimmy King, Feyland Jones, Ben Peebles, James Alexander, Carl Lee Cunningham, Ben Cauley and Ronnie Cauldwell TL: 60s

Sir Mack Rice TL: 60s

"I was living in Kansas City. I got to St. Louis and I decided to toss up a dime. I said, 'Should I go towards Detroit for Motown or should I take the Southern route to Stax?' Stax won out." Johnnie Taylor

Johnnie Taylor TL: 60s

Above and below: Claude Nobs at the Montreux Jazz Festival of 1967

"Having been brought up in Montreux, I was working for the Swiss Tourist Board, and my dream was to stage an international jazz and blues festival in my small hometown. I managed to arrange a ticket to the States and decided to go to Chicago first. The only telephone number I had for anyone in that city was for the great bluesman Willie Dixon. He agreed to meet up, and I went to see him play at a little place the night I arrived. It was so incredible to me, and I suppose I was something of a curiosity – this young Swiss guy who was so excited to see one of his heroes perform, and who was also able to talk to him about his music, about rare tracks he'd recorded, and about other wonderful blues and jazz artists as well. So he took me around all of these clubs in Chicago, and by six o'clock in the morning, I was completely wiped out! Later that day, I travelled to New York to try and meet with Nesuhi Ertegun, whose name I had seen on so many terrific jazz albums. He had also written some of the most interesting and informed liner notes on the back of records with such stunningly beautiful covers. I had also discovered that this same person co-owned the company concerned, which was, of course, Atlantic Records. So I got to New York, found Atlantic's offices, went up to the reception desk, and informed the person there that I had come to see Mr. Nesuhi Ertegun. I was directed to his secretary, who quite reasonably asked me if I had an appointment, to which I replied, 'No, I'm afraid I don't.' She further enquired as to whether I knew Mr. Ertegun, to which I had to reply, 'No, I've never met him.' She, of course, told me that I should send in a letter which would explain why I wanted to meet with him. So I said, 'But I've come all the way from Switzerland!' She looked at me for a full ten seconds and then said, 'Okay, hold on.' She went into Nesuhi's office, came back out a minute later and said, 'Okay, he'll see you.' So I walked in, and the first thing he did was to get up, come around from behind his desk, hold out his hand to shake my hand and say, 'Hello, how are you?' But he spoke in Swiss-German. I was completely knocked out, because Swiss-German is a rare language for any other nationality to speak at all, never mind to be fluent in – as I discovered he most certainly was. We hit it off right away, and on leaving his office, I bumped into Roberta Flack and invited her to perform at the Golden Rose in Montreux for 500 dollars. She checked with Nesuhi before she agreed and, in fact, he quickly convinced other artists to come and play. He really helped so much to make the Montreux Jazz Festival possible and to help it develop into the magical event that it has become. Nesuhi always just had so much style and natural grace – such a wonderful character, so kind, perceptive, and a genuinely great music man." Claude Nobs

"Otis was magic. There was something pure about his personality: calm, dignified, vibrant. Stardom never changed him. He had a strong inner life. He was emotionally centred. His manners were impeccable. His humour was sly and roguish. He dealt with you as a human being, not as a white or a black or a Christian or a Jew. His intelligence was keen, his curiosity high, and despite stories to the contrary, he was anything *but* the cliché of the 'backward country boy come to the big city'. Otis knew what was happening." Jerry Wexler

Otis Redding and above with Don Byas TL: 60s

Albert King TL: 60s

Opposite: Otis Rush TL: 60s

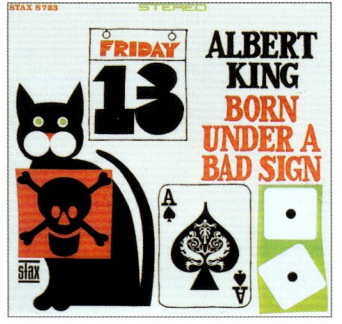

"Everyone has the blues ... they just don't know what the hell to call it. But it is the same old-fashioned country blues." *Albert King*

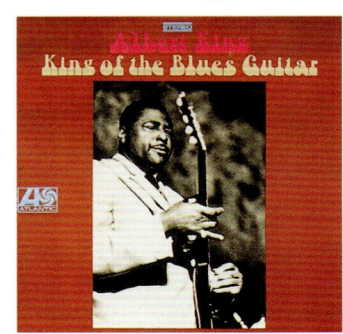

"The Bee Gees were a transplanted British group who came back from Australia, where they'd had some minor success as a singing group. They became a huge success with their first recordings on Atlantic. They were originally managed by Robert Stigwood and The Beatles' manager, Brian Epstein. Epstein wanted to put them on Capitol since he already had The Beatles there. Stigwood wanted to put them on Atlantic – he had found the group and was much closer to them than Epstein. At the time, Stigwood wanted to embark on a theatrical career. He was hoping to get the English rights for *Hair*, which was a big hit and had been produced by a very good friend of mine, Michael Butler. In fact, I had helped talk Michael's father into backing him to buy the rights, and to put the show up on Broadway. So I talked Michael into giving Robert the English rights to *Hair* at about the same time as this decision was being made concerning the Bee Gees. Robert broke up his partnership with Epstein as co-manager, and that's how we got them.

Sonny and Cher TL: 60s

"When Sonny and Cher hit very big, they were signed to play the Olympia in Paris. I happened to be there, so I went to see Bruno, who was the manager of the theatre. He congratulated me on how well all of our Atlantic artists had always gone down at the Olympia and said how he was was very excited about this new act, Sonny and Cher – whom he'd never seen but had heard were fantastic. I had some publicity photographs of them with me, and I said, 'Oh they're big stars, they're great, they've just happened, and she's a beautiful young girl.' So I showed him these photographs. He stopped dead in his tracks, looked up at me, and said, 'My God! But they're white!' I said, 'Well, what's wrong with that?' 'No, no,' he said. ' I don't want them! We can't have them, can't use them!' I asked him, 'Why not?!' He said, 'Listen – we had a white performer just recently and the audience threw rotten eggs, they booed him off the stage!' So I reassured him, and then I called up Sonny, who said, 'Well, tell him we have Harold Battiste as the leader of the orchestra, and that several other people in the band happen to be black as well.' So I said, 'Okay – and you know what you do? You come on, stay at the back of the stage to begin with, behind the band, and open up with 'Walkin' The Dog'. Sonny had a fairly limited vocal range, but he could do that song, so I said, 'And just try to sound like Rufus!'

"I tell you what: in Europe, if the performer is an American, black girl singer, no matter what she sounds like, people are going to go wild. If the same girl was white, they would be gone – turn around and walk out. At the same time, if you see a black band, there is usually one thing present which isn't necessarily the case with a white band – a particular kind of rhythm, a sense and style of beat derived from gospel and blues – which makes a lot of difference. But I've heard a few very poor black singers get ovations." Ahmet

The Bee Gees TL: 60s

Above and below right: Otis Redding at the Monterey Pop Festival TL: 60s

"There are a lot of black musicians who are loved by both black and white people, but who are never very politically vocal. White people have a tendency to say that these musicians do a lot to help gain equality for black people because they like them. You could say that about Duke Ellington and Louis Armstrong, who never were very political. I mean, everybody loved Louis Armstrong, except that some black activists thought he was clowning too much for the white folks. They said that about Fats Waller also, thinking that these performers were creating a stereotype. I fervently believe that the two greatest artists of the 20th century were Picasso and Louis Armstrong. Louis Armstrong changed the way everybody played and the way everybody sang. He came from deep blues roots, but he taught everybody how to swing. There's the perception that people who are beloved by white people do a lot to counter racism, because you can't hate all blacks but then love ten of them – it changes everything. It doesn't become a class thing anymore, either. Otis Redding also had the kind of presence that could inspire the world. The fact that he chose to keep living in the South also made a great difference to a lot of people down there at that time." Ahmet

"We'd just returned from Europe, so our show was together. We flew to Los Angeles, then up to Monterey, and boom! – into a completely different world. If you believe in Aquarius-type predictions, then that was it. That was the most 'Age of Aquarius' that I have seen on this planet. It was a totally new audience, I didn't know any of those people there, and I didn't know there were any freaks in the world." Booker T. Jones

"It was bizarre, it really was bizarre. I mean, none of the guys had any idea that anything like that existed. That was the first time we'd been around marijuana. The air was just full of this gross smoke, but they were having a great time. There were happy faces and there was nothing bad going on that I know of. Those kids sat there in a rainstorm waiting for Otis to come on, because the show was running late. I think originally we were meant to go on at about 11, but we didn't get to go on 'til midnight. The guy who owned the park said, 'The electricity is going off at 12.' Otis's manager, Phil Walden, said, 'I've got news for you, you ain't touching that switch – those guys are going on! We didn't fly all the way up here for nothing.' That's the way it was. The owner said, 'Well, cut the show down, do three or four numbers.' Phil said, 'No, we're doing the whole show.' I don't know, we killed 'em, that's all I can tell you." Steve Cropper

"After the now historic Monterey Pop Festival, Otis came to L.A., called me up and said, 'Let's go out to dinner together tonight.' I said, 'I want to take you up to see a friend of mine.' So we went to the Doheny Castle, which was Phil Spector's house

Esther Phillips TL: 60s

Otis Redding TL: 60s

at the time, and Phil, Otis, and I sat down, just to hang out and talk. Then Phil went to the piano and played a medley of the songs that I'd written. Otis was very surprised at how many there were, even though he had recorded 'Lovey Dovey' as a duet with Carla Thomas. Then the three of us went out to dinner, had a lot to drink, got a little high, and went to a club in the Watts district where Esther Phillips was singing. We stayed until at least five in the morning, and Esther and Otis sang together for around two to three hours. It just happened like that. Phil and I still talk about that night.

"Otis, as an artist, was similar in a way to Ray Charles – self-produced, made his own arrangements, had his own concepts. He was a man who was definitely larger than life, a man with a huge heart and a very personal style on stage. He was the son of a farmer from Georgia. I went down to his farm a few times, to a couple of big parties he threw there. It was such a great experience knowing him." Ahmet

"I've never gotten over Otis's death, and I couldn't even listen to his records for years. It was not an easy time. I don't know if anything ever bothered me like that. It was pretty awesome. It was very hard to work on the tracks after he was gone. I mean, I knew it had to be done, and Atlantic was demanding that I get this thing ready and complete it. I finished the track and sent it up there but they said, 'No, there's not enough of Otis's voice.' I thought, God, I've got to go back and redo this thing – it was really like torture. Anyway, we got it finished, and it's the record 'Dock Of The Bay' as you know it. The last time I saw Otis I was putting on the horns for the song. Everybody was getting tuned up, I was getting the tape up, and Otis said, 'Well, I'll see you guys on Monday,' because he was just going out for the weekend and coming right back. That's the last we saw of him. He never heard the horns, or the waves and the seagulls ... " Steve Cropper

"Few could touch Otis Redding. He was not only writing his own songs, but if he took someone else's song, he would reinterpret it until it became pure Otis. He'd listen to Bobby Darin records, The Rolling Stones – not what your typical black performer would be listening to. He was just a wonderful person, with this really engaging personality, terrific smile, and when he hit a room, he'd just eat that room up. He loved the South and was very much a Southerner. I think he is a great example of a person, who, through his presence and success, and by remaining in the South, did so much for the civil rights movement. He made it terribly difficult for young whites to hate him because, I mean – he was so loveable!" George Treadwell

Aretha Franklin TL: 60s

"Aretha is a one hundred per cent inspirationally motivated person. The Aretha who sits down and accompanies herself singing the song is the Aretha Franklin that you get on 'I Never Loved A Man', the Aretha Franklin that you get on 'Respect'. When she sits down to do one of those numbers, she is not with us, she's in a different world. Leave her alone. She's out there as a different human being. Then the Aretha Franklin who comes in when you've recorded a song and says, 'I want to re-sing that song,' and stands up in front of the microphone and sings, is an entirely different human being – an entirely different artist. The artist that stands up in front of the microphone is more related to the artist that made the historic Columbia albums. You can't say anything bad about her singing; it is spirited, it is incredible artistry and control of an instrument. The spiritual motivation that comes when she plays the piano, closes her eyes, and is doing a number, rocking back and forth, is different from the artist standing up there, wide-eyed and trying to sing. And they're both great artists. There are not too many people who, when they hear something, will say, 'I want to repair that.' And if they do, usually you say, 'I haven't got room,' or, 'If we repair it we might risk losing the whole thing.' And you argue about it, and then you try it; and then you lose it. Now you're frustrated, because you've just wasted something that you'll never be able to recapture again. But if Aretha looked at me and said that she wanted to do that line again, I could never say no to her. Because when she wanted to try it again, I didn't know if she was going to do as well as what we had, but I knew she was going to do something that was so unusual, so unique and so tasty, I didn't give a damn what she did. Go ahead. I'll hit the button, you tell me when. I'll go. She couldn't sing a bad note, she doesn't know what they are." Tom Dowd

Aretha Franklin in the recording studio

Opposite: Aretha Franklin

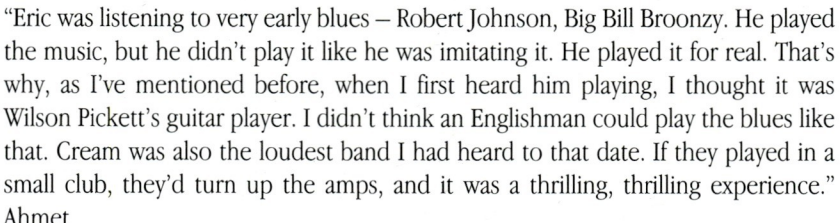

Above and below: Eric Clapton TL: 60s

"Eric used to dress in this weird way at that time. Aretha Franklin was recording in our studios on Broadway and Jerry was producing. I told Jerry I was going to bring Clapton in and maybe he'd play – nothing was decided. So Clapton and I went in and he was dressed in one of these crazy outfits and had all kinds of strange make-up on his face. The moment we walked in the studio, even before I could introduce him to Aretha, she looked at him and went into this roaring bout of laughter. So I said, 'Well, when he starts playing you're not going to laugh.'

"At that time, the British Invasion had already hit. It would have been difficult not to be aware that it was going to be an extremely big influence on American music. The Beatles, The Rolling Stones were getting all this adulation, even more than had been given to Elvis Presley. All the kids had their pictures all over their walls. I wanted to get into that area of music. Jerry, in those days, felt that it was derivative and not as musically valid as the original American music. I agreed that some of the groups that were popular at that time were not musically great, but I thought that some of them were terrific.

"Eric was listening to very early blues – Robert Johnson, Big Bill Broonzy. He played the music, but he didn't play it like he was imitating it. He played it for real. That's why, as I've mentioned before, when I first heard him playing, I thought it was Wilson Pickett's guitar player. I didn't think an Englishman could play the blues like that. Cream was also the loudest band I had heard to that date. If they played in a small club, they'd turn up the amps, and it was a thrilling, thrilling experience."
Ahmet

"*Disraeli Gears* was a four-day album. Ahmet walked into the studio one day and said to me, 'There's this English group who've been on tour here – they belong to Robert Stigwood, and we're releasing them in the United States – and we're going to record them. They'll be here on Thursday night, but remember they have to be out of the country by Sunday on the seven o'clock flight, because their visas expire.' That was when I met Cream, and we did *Disraeli Gears* on Thursday, Friday, Saturday and Sunday. When the limousine driver came in at five o'clock on the Sunday, he said, 'I'm looking for a group.' I said, 'They're ready.' The three guys got in the car, and they were gone. The equipment was still sitting in the studio smoking when they were on the plane! So that started my association with Eric Clapton."
Tom Dowd

"First of all, I wanted a vehicle for my songwriting – that was the most exciting thing for me, the chance to have these songs played. You don't, however, immediately have a repertoire overnight, so Eric was very useful – not least because he had a great

Clockwise from above, Cream:, from left: Jack Bruce, Ginger Baker, Eric Clapton; Ginger Baker; Eric Clapton, Felix Pappalardi, Ginger Baker and Ahmet. TL: 60s

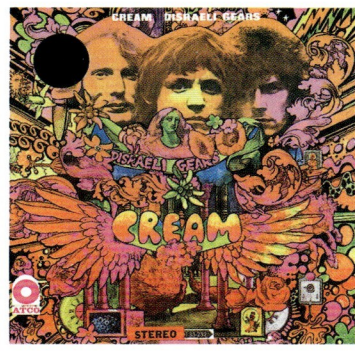

knowledge of the blues, a great knowledge of country blues, the Delta blues in particular – Robert Johnson, Skip James, people like this. So it was decided that we would start with a basic blues repertoire, which, although new to a lot of people at the time was, of course, built up of non-original songs. Then we would gradually begin to develop our own original material." Jack Bruce

"I wanted to keep the blues alive, but put it into some kind of new, contemporary setting – instead of playing exactly like the original records all the time, or being that true to the code. Then I met Ginger Baker and felt this kind of fire from him and Jack Bruce, and experienced their jazz improvisation, the vibration which they could set up, and discovered that they were such forward-thinking musicians. It really just swept me off my feet. There was this dynamic, extraordinary bass playing and drumming, and I realized that there was more than just doing it by the book. There was taking it somewhere else and being totally creative with it." Eric Clapton

"When I was present at Cream's *Disraeli Gears* recording session, taking my photographs, I have to say I was utterly amazed at the degree of input that I witnessed Ahmet to be having – in terms of choice of song, tempo, arrangement. I remember thinking whether any other head of a record company would or could be this influential and this much involved with any band, let alone these songwriters and musicians, who clearly had so much talent but who were equally so genuinely looking to him for guidance." Don Paulsen

Above and below: Roberta Flack TL: 60s

"The person who told me about Roberta Flack was Les McCann. Les and I were really good friends. He'd been playing in Washington, and when he came to New York, he told me, 'There's this marvellous piano player/singer in a little club in Georgetown. She teaches music at school by day and plays in this club at night – you should check it out,' as the saying goes in the jazz world. 'Check it out.' So I said, 'Okay,' and put Joel Dorn on the case. Joel went to hear her and came back raving!" Nesuhi Ertegun

"I had no idea that Roberta would ever become that big. I knew she would be that good, because she could really sing and play. She received a standing ovation after practically every number, and you just wanted to cry – each song was a gem." Joel Dorn

"Roberta has a sound all her own. She's really, in my mind, like a jazz singer. And I believe that all her manager wanted her to be was a huge pop singer. She had a string of massive hits, but in the long run, I believe that if she had been a jazz singer, she would be the greatest jazz singer of today. It's a little difficult for her now to be accepted by the jazz people, but that's what I believe she should do. Maybe she will. I hope she does it for us." Ahmet

Dusty Springfield TL: 60s

"In preparation for that first session in Memphis, I got together maybe 40 or 50 songs because I had no idea what the interaction would be between Dusty and me when I presented material. She came over to my house in Great Neck, and by the time we got through, we were wading in albums, acetates, and tapes – which had become far more than 60 songs, maybe a hundred – out of which Dusty gave approval to exactly none. So we were nil out of a hundred. I don't think that's particularly weird or strange, however, because the sensibility of an artist as fragile as Dusty – and she was such a fragile person in so many ways – is that to say yes to even one song was almost like a lifetime commitment. To me it was another job, doing another album. To her, the next album was a milestone in her career. She truly was the great white lady." Jerry Wexler

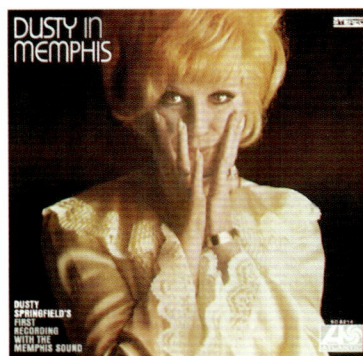

"I was just an English singer, and I felt an enormous responsibility – I was very intimidated, but they were wonderful with me. Jerry has gone into print saying I was the most insecure singer he had ever come across, and at that time he was absolutely right. What he didn't realize, I think, was just how over-awed I was. They were telling stories and talking about Aretha and I'm thinking, what am I doing on this label? Why are they recording me? Those thoughts were manifested in the time it took to get vocal performances out of me, because if there's one thing that inhibits good singing, it's fear. I was also allowing the natural critic in me, which at that time was well over the top, to criticize a vocal performance or to criticize a note before it had left my throat – which can, of course, destroy the flow of anything. I don't know if they understood what was happening with me, because it probably came out in scowls and grumbling and all sorts of things – which was a tendency of mine: let's cover the fear by being the pain in the ass. They may have read it that way – I don't know if they know by now that it was just plain, unadulterated fear. The fact that *Dusty In Memphis* came out of it is a supreme credit to their patience and understanding. If they ever read this, I hope they know by now how intimidated I was and that it had nothing to do with them. They were terribly patient with me, and I know I drove them crazy, but we got it." Dusty Springfield

The Rascals, from left: Felix Cavaliere, Eddie Brigati, Gene Cornish and Dino Danelli TL: 60s

The Rascals

"We had been working for Robert Kennedy at the time, and I was vacationing in Jamaica when I heard on my short-wave radio that he had been assassinated. I also remember being in the Atlantic studios the night that Martin Luther King was killed. We were the only white guys in the building – there was a particular kind of remorse in the air, which I guess must have been similar to when we lost President John F. Kennedy. You lose a leader, and it's almost like a family member has gone. That's really what inspired 'People Got To Be Free'.

"We ran into difficulty with the record label because they didn't really want the song. 'Why are you getting involved in politics? Why don't you just mind your business and keep making your records?' We really thought that we were here for a purpose, not just to go out and buy Mercedes cars, have swimming pools and fun with nice-looking ladies. We really thought we had to do something through our music. Teach people love, if they weren't fortunate enough to have it in their lives. Teach people that your neighbour's colour and race does not mean anything, it's his soul and heart – stop this war! From a record company point of view, I think Atlantic was probably not interested in those kinds of issues. I think they were out for one purpose, which was fine, just to sell records and to make music. They felt it would be detrimental to our career. I mean, Jerry told me that right to my face. Jerry, in those days, was a very hot-tempered guy. When he wanted to say something to you, you got the point, real quick. He used to have these pills for his heart, so he'd be yelling at you and popping these pills into his mouth at the same time. We had a relationship with Atlantic, however, where I always just felt this tremendous respect for these guys. I mean, look at the records that came out of the place! So I always held back just a little bit, and I'm sure they did too, because they were doing so well with us." Felix Cavaliere

Dr. John TL: 60s 70s

"It's kind of an historical thing in New Orleans. It's not an original idea, it's a tradition. There's always been a Dr. Ya Ya, a Dr. Mighty, and a Dr. John. At first, I had not intended it to be myself, but to get somebody else to do it. Then I just went ahead and said, well, I'll do it and that was that. We had started playing a few love-ins and be-ins and whatever kind of ins were popular in those days. It kind of fitted in with the acid or hippie culture and what was going on out there in California at the time – even though they were looking at us as being something totally different to what we were. They didn't have any kind of clue that this was something to do with New Orleans. They thought this was about Timothy Leary or dropping out."
Dr. John (Mac Rebennack)

"I don't even remember how I met Dr. John. It seems like I've known him forever. I guess I first met him when he was a young kid playing New Orleans style R & B music and blues, and trying to be like a hip black guy. I saw him as an appreciator or a fan of this kind of music, and he was a good player. He can play a little Professor Longhair, but that's not his natural style. Longhair couldn't play any other way but Longhair. Dr. John can play like a lot of people. I enjoy listening to him a great deal." Ahmet

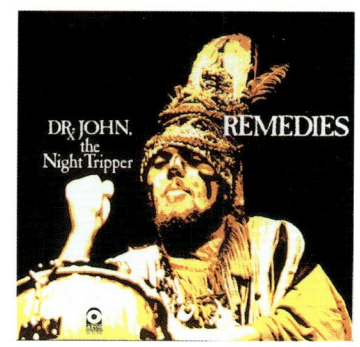

Yes, from left: Bill Bruford, Chris Squire, Peter Banks, Jon Anderson and Tony Kaye TL: 60s

"I auditioned Yes live one afternoon at a club called the Speakeasy, which was the hot club in London. The band had an extremely avant-garde approach that produced a classical music sound coupled with blues-based British music. It was a different thing. I was struck by the beautiful and kind of eerie vocal sound of Jon Anderson. There was a tremendous amount of British emotion in his singing: he had a really poetic voice, reminiscent of some of the Irish tenors, with a mixture of Welsh and Northern English sensitivity. Hard to put your finger on, but it had all of that, along with some jazz and some blues feeling. It was something very special – he had a very powerful sound and was an exceptional-looking person. He had the eyes of a poet and a dreamer. Their first couple of records didn't sell very well, but we stuck with them, and they eventually became a great stadium group and are still one of the best rock'n'roll bands in the world to this day." Ahmet

"The idea of the band was simply to have an extremely musical but also very vocal group. At that time, there was a band in England called The Nice, with a great instrumentalist, Keith Emerson, and a band in America called The Fifth Dimension, which had wonderful vocals – so we tried to marry those ideas together. We also wanted to become a bit jazzier, Frank Zappa-like – with free-form ideas plus very strong harmonies. My voice is just above tenor, alto tenor, and that is one of the sounds that actually comes through, even if you have a lot of noise going on. So I was lucky over the years, in that I developed this silvery voice that really creates a sort of dome-like shape to the sound of the band." Jon Anderson

Boz Scaggs TL: 60s

Arif Mardin and Atlantic staffers, late 1960s

"There are two things that go into making a great record. First, there's understanding an artist — what is appealing about them and where their fire comes from, and then letting that artist flourish. That's perception. The other essential thing in producing a record is to bring to that artist all of those things out of which you hope the magic will evolve — the material, the setting, the instrumental accompaniment, and so forth. In the end, you have to move the listener to such an extent that he or she has to get up out of bed, walk ten blocks, borrow 20 dollars from a friend and run to an all-night shop to buy the record to hear it again."
Ahmet

Above and below: Archie Bell & The Drells, including: Lee Bell, James Wise, Joe Cross and Archie Bell TL: 60s

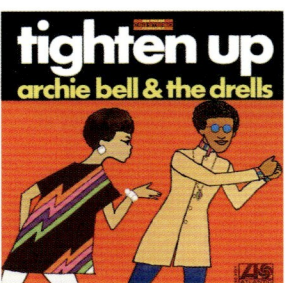

"Archie Bell & The Drells were a fabulous in-person act. Unfortunately, Archie Bell was suddenly drafted, and when 'Tighten Up' reached number one on the charts, he was serving in the army." Jerry Wexler

"There were a lot of rock'n'roll bands playing at clubs on the Sunset Strip. So one day I asked Dewey Martin, the drummer with Buffalo Springfield, which, in his view, was the really hot new band. Dewey told me, 'There's a band called Iron Butterfly which I think is great. They've got a fantastic guitar player.' That guitarist, Danny Weis, was creating a big buzz. So I went to see the band and they were terrific. I said to them, 'Look, I'm gonna have two of my people come and talk to you.' And I called up the managers of Buffalo Springfield, Charlie Greene and Brian Stone, and said, 'There's a band I want to sign up, come down and see them. They don't have a manager as far as I know.' So I signed up the band and Greene and Stone signed on as their management.

"The first record they made was quite good, but we didn't think it was great. So we delayed it for a long time and kept saying, 'We'll put it out next month.' In the meantime, the leader of the band, keyboard player/singer Doug Ingle kept calling me and saying, 'Listen man, when are you going to put out the record? I can't keep the guys together. Please put out the record so we can work.' So we finally released the album. It didn't hit right away, but little by little it started to sell quite a lot in the Los Angeles area. We ended up selling maybe 100,000 or 150,000 copies. So I said, 'There's something here, we'll cut another album.'

"So I went to Los Angeles to hear their new songs. But when I got to the rehearsal, it was a totally different band. So I said, 'What happened to the guitar player?' And they said, 'Oh, he quit right after we made the first record.' They ran through the songs

Iron Butterfly TL: 60s

and I said, 'This is terrible, I mean the new guitarist … ' And Doug said to me, 'Well, of course, he's only been playing three months.' I said, 'You mean he's been with the band for three months?' He said, 'No, he's only been playing the guitar for three months.' And I thought, 'Jesus!' But we had sold enough that there was a demand for another album, so we had no option really other than to record the band that was there. At one session I looked down at an acetate across which someone had scrawled 'In-A-Gadda-Da-Vida'. So I asked the new guitarist, 'What does that mean?' He said, 'Oh, that's a misspelling – it should read 'In A Garden of Eden'. Somebody must have got drunk or something and rearranged a few letters.' That was around the time that The Beatles and The Stones were going to India, so I said, 'You know, we should leave it as it is. It's a good title, it conjures up the feeling of some kind of Eastern spirituality.' So the final track was very long, and it had on it what sounded like a Gene Krupa drum solo. But I tell you, this record came out and man, it seemed like every college student, like the whole country went out and bought it. It became the biggest record that we'd ever had up to that time — with a band that was just learning their instruments. It was incredible." Ahmet

Ahmet and Jerry Wexler with Iron Butterfly, including: Ron Bushy, Doug Ingle, Lee Dorman, Erik Brann TL: 60s

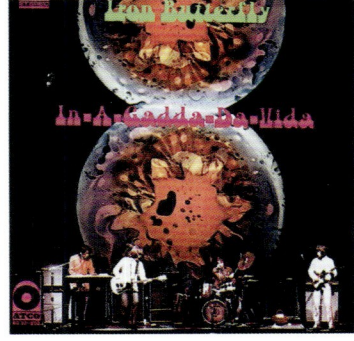

Maurice and Robin Gibb

"I knew that they were going to be a huge group. I remember sitting in hotel rooms with them, and each one would be writing a different song – one in one corner and another in another corner. They were just writing song after song after song. I tell you, they are so brilliant with harmony – their voices just blend together so beautifully." Ahmet

The Bee Gees TL: 60s

Barry, Maurice, and Robin Gibb: The Bee Gees

Robin Gibb

Opposite: Julie Driscoll of the Brian Auger Trinity TL: 60s

Vanilla Fudge TL: 60s

"When we supported Vanilla Fudge on our first American tour in '68, Bonzo used to sit and watch Carmine Appice playing. Carmine used to show him tricks, Bonzo used to show Carmine stuff, and each of them pretended he was king – but really, of course, none of us was. They were so good to us, though, so nice, and really the epitome of everything I'd hoped for in music. They were absolutely sensational." Robert Plant

"I was the first drummer to pound the living daylights out of the drum set. I mean, guys who were around at the time – Keith Moon, Ginger Baker, Mitch Mitchell – were all incredible players, but they didn't beat the living hell out of their drums like I did. I had the sticks turned round, I'd break things, I was hitting real hard and heavy. A lot of the frequencies we used together sounded really heavy, so we were considered one of the first 'heavy' bands. Then heavy translated into 'heavy metal' later on. We were pioneers of heavy progressive rock, which in essence, with that vocal style, that heavy vibrato, has I think translated into heavy metal music.

"We took an idea from The Vagrants, who actually started making songs longer, more epic-sounding – big production numbers we called them. They would take a Rolling Stones song and do their production number on it. So we used to take the black R & B songs and do our production number on those – that's what made us different. It was a fad going around New York, a lot of bands were doing it. The Vagrants only had one singer, but we had four good vocalists and that's also what made us different. We were all around at the same time, and we were all doing the same kinds of things. We were called The Pigeons at that time. Finally, our manager hooked up with Shadow Morton, who became our producer, and we went into the studio and made a dub, a demo of 'You Keep Me Hangin' On'. We had been playing that in the clubs, and it was always a big favourite with everyone. The producer loved it, wanted to cut it, and I believe we did it in one take on a mono machine. We had a friend, Scott Muni, who was on WOR-FM, one of the first 'underground' stations, as they called them. He played the demo, and WOR put it in a contest with The Beatles and The Beach Boys, and we won! Then they did it two or three nights in a row, and we won every time. Someone from Atlantic heard it on the radio and said, 'Wow! Who is this group?! Let's sign them!' We finished the rest of the album, 'You Keep Me Hangin' On' came out as a single, and two weeks later, it was on the charts. It was like, 'Wow, we're really happening now.'" Carmine Appice

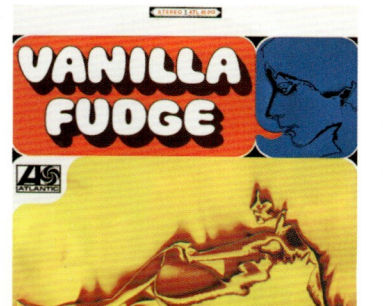

"Vanilla Fudge was a different kind of group. They really got the spirit of some of the black music, and they made a sensational recording of 'You Keep Me Hangin' On', the old Motown song, which became a big hit for them." Ahmet

Vanilla Fudge, above, from left: Vince Martell, Tim Bogert, Carmine Appice and Mark Stein TL: 60s

Jimmy Page and Robert Plant

"As the late sixties arrived, the West Coast scene was still developing in America and the British Invasion was still taking place. We were pretty naive altogether at the time, but I had a real big lean toward Buffalo Springfield, to the work of Steve Stills and Neil Young. We knew that Atlantic had this wonderful thoroughbred catalogue and consistently seemed to be able to deliver the credible side of popular music. They were always able, by whatever means, from what I can glean, to capture some of the hottest stuff around. Even if they were doing a deal with Stax, or had a little thing here and there, for us in England, their label meant it was going to be good – you didn't get any crap. So the whole idea of our first efforts being taken over there and viewed and listened to by such moguls, although quite a daunting thought, was also great. I was really proud. The fact that we were signed up by them was amazing, and the fact that I got £8,000 was even more astounding. It was the beginning of an incredible relationship." Robert Plant

"Perhaps the best deal I made in the late sixties involved Jimmy Page and Led Zeppelin. I had known they were forming in England and had already been speaking with other labels, but it was a tip from the British singer Dusty Springfield that really encouraged me to go after the group. I was familiar with Page's work through Bert Berns, who'd brought him over from London to do session work for us back when he was known as 'Little' Jimmy Page. I remembered he'd played his ass off. I also knew John Bonham was a hell of a drummer, but I'd never heard Robert Plant sing. It didn't matter. Dusty's endorsement was so enthusiastic and her taste in music so impeccable, I went on the hunch. Clive Davis and Mo Ostin were also in the horse race, but I prevailed by offering Zep a five-year contract with a $75,000 advance for the first year, and four one-year options. Their lawyer, my friend Steve Weiss, said that for another $35,000 we could have world rights. I called Polydor, our English distributors, and suggested they chip in $20,000, but they passed. That meant it would cost Atlantic the full $110,000. We paid up – and even if the advance had been $11 million, it wouldn't have made any difference; any up-front money would have been recouped, since Zep was the biggest seller of the seventies. I was proud of the signing but, as it turned out, didn't really hang out with the group. Ahmet got along famously with them and their manager, Peter Grant, and soon took over their care and nurturing." Jerry Wexler

"Of course, I knew that Led Zeppelin would be a huge, huge hit. I really did. I mean, they were the best players all put together. We'd used them previously on sessions. Originally we were going to call them the New Yardbirds. Then they thought of Led Zeppelin." Ahmet

From left: Robert Plant, John Paul Jones, Jimmy Page, and John Bonham of Led Zeppelin

220 THE ATLANTIC STORY

Ahmet

"King Crimson was a revolutionary band."
Ahmet

King Crimson, from left: Greg Lake, Charles Giles, Robert Fripp and Gordon Haskell TL: 60s 70s

"Nesuhi and I produced *Swiss Movement* by remote control. Nesuhi wasn't going to the Montreux Jazz Festival that year, and there was no budget for me to go. Eddie Harris and Les McCann got over there, and they did this one set which they had rehearsed maybe once or twice, or maybe not even at all. The tapes came back and we couldn't believe it. I mean, the reason we put them together had nothing to do with what was on the tapes. With this record it really happened by itself, it was a gift from God. The album and the single, 'Compared To What', each sold in excess of a million, which for jazz music was very rare in those days. Gene McDaniels wrote the single's lyrics, which were not casual, but were really riding the crest of the whole civil rights movement in America at that time. The whole thing struck at middle class values – black or white at that point, it didn't make a lot of difference. It really hit a chord." Joel Dorn

Above, Les McCann and top, Eddie Harris TL: 60s

Roland Kirk TL:70s

"I guess you could say that I was on a 'mystical trip' when I realized I was part of an 'inflated tear'. I went back into myself to find out how that 'tear' began. When I was one or two, a nurse came into work, drunk or high or mad at somebody, and she slipped and put too much medicine in my eyes. I think that's when the 'tear' began, because I went through years where my eyes used to run and hurt and be nothing but tears." Roland Kirk

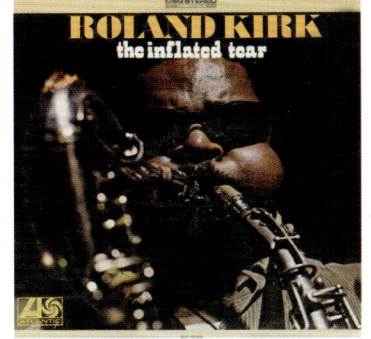

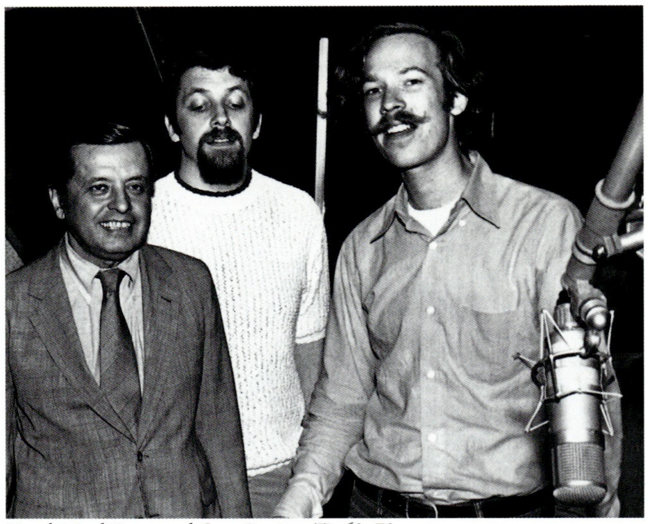

"I was brought up in this little town in the suburbs of Philadelphia. I was into music, but I was also into sports. So one day, I'm walking up to bat and I'm singing 'Ruby Baby'. This tiny kid Tony, from downtown, throws down his catcher's mitt and says, 'I can't take this, why are you singing that nigger shit all the time?' So real quick I said, 'I wasn't singing The Drifters' version of 'Ruby Baby', I was singing the one by Dion and the Belmonts.' So he says, 'Oh that's all right, I'm sorry man.' I mean, how could you make a story like that up? When I graduated from college, I became a disc jockey in Philly, and I pestered Nesuhi every other week to let me join Atlantic. He would send me records, call me in for interviews and ask my opinion on new releases. One day he asked me in, and I figured I'd get my refusal number two hundred, but he offered me the job. I nearly fell off the chair! But I came in as Nesuhi's assistant, so I did what I was told. He was a fascinating character, a brilliant guy, an art collector who really knew what he was collecting, a guy who could translate Turkish poetry of the 14th century, and he spoke a bunch of languages. I'm a street guy from Philly; I'd never met anyone like him. So I got an education – I was exposed to things I never would have encountered if I hadn't been fortunate enough to have met him. Here's the way he produced: he was a documentarian, in the strictest and loosest sense of the term simultaneously. He invested in talent. He wasn't a producer the way my generation were producers, where we had all kinds of magic tricks and concepts. He was a man of phenomenal taste. So he bet on artistry, and he signed all of these great artists at the right time. He was also ego-less enough, so that when he assumed other duties, and other responsibilities were coming his way, he brought me in. I was his guy, I was tested, but I'd like to be tested like that again. I always worked for him, he was always running it, but I was doing the day-to-day work, and, at a certain point, I could sign pretty much whomever I wanted. He trusted me, and I delivered. After the first year or so, I brought Roland Kirk and Yusef Lateef to the label, I took over Eddie Harris – whom he had signed, and we both brought Les McCann in. For seven or eight years there, we had another golden age of jazz at Atlantic." Joel Dorn

Nesuhi, Joel Dorn and Gary Burton TL: 60s 70s

Yusef Lateef: TL: 60s 70s 80s

"Yusef was from Chattanooga originally, but he grew up in Detroit. So I said, 'I want to do an album called *Yusef Lateef's Detroit*. I want you to draw on your memories of growing up in Detroit and just paint me pictures of Detroit musically.' I rented this little studio, called Yusef up, and said, 'There are some guys I want you to record with. Why don't we do some sides with them and some sides with your guys?' So he said, 'No, we'll record everybody together.' So we crammed into this tiny studio, and those Jazz and R & B studio musicians just went in there and really jammed. It was just a matter of two separate parts of the same culture meeting, and it just melted, and you heard these sounds and colours. Yusef's guys were playing African drums and bells, and the other guys were doing licks that they had just played on an Aretha or a King Curtis or some other pop / R & B session. That was a key cut." Joel Dorn

"I've known Herbie Mann since 1952/'53. One day, he came bursting in on me and said, 'What do you think of me going down to Memphis with you and making a record?' I said, 'Okay, that's cool.' He said, 'Okay, let's go.' So we went down there and cut the album *Memphis Underground*. When it became a big hit, Herbie said, 'You know what, once every five years you and I make a record that's kind of wild.'" Tom Dowd

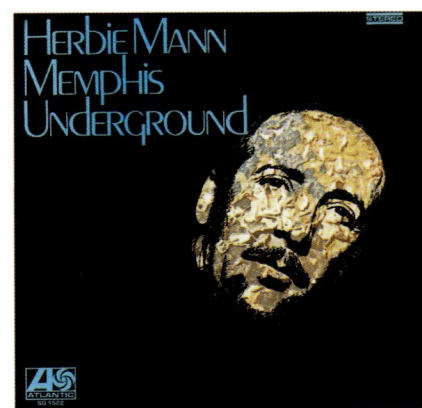

Herbie Mann TL: 60s 70s

"For the album *Shirley Scott And The Soul Saxes*, it was my idea to put King Curtis, Hank Crawford and David Newman together, but I'll be honest, I was a little disappointed with the result. I think if the arrangements had been better, it would have helped, but I wish that I'd known more about what I was doing then, because I would have made a better record. The idea was great, but it just didn't come off right, and it was such a great opportunity because it was the only time those three guys were on the same record. It was early in my career, I was 26 years old, I'd had a great idea, but I didn't set it up to work properly. Shirley and her sax-playing husband, Stanley Turrentine, were going through their divorce at the time. I knew Shirley from my days as a DJ in Philly. She was very intelligent, but soft spoken, very sweet, and low-key. She was a pianist originally, but moved into the organ because that provided work in the clubs, on what used to be called the 'chitlin circuit'. The organ's like an orchestra in a box, and organ/tenor trios or quartets were really in demand. It was a genre that was looked down on by the orthodox jazz crowd, but if you like to have fun, it's incredible music." Joel Dorn

Shirley Scott TL: 60s

Joe Zawinul TL: 60s

"Through the years, Joe Zawinul has been a major influence on many musicians. His way of blending colourful melodies, intricate changes, and beautiful lines has always sounded like unfinished pieces of music that merge into one song." Raymond Silva, former Atlantic A & R man

"I didn't have the formal background that Nesuhi did. I graduated from the only college I could get into, because I'd been thrown out of school 800 times for being a bad kid. Nesuhi didn't get thrown out of the Sorbonne for starting a fire in the gym, and Arif came from a well-to-do, prominent Turkish family. So Nesuhi and I never really socialized. When we went to Europe or to places in this country together, I was always his boy, but I used to disappoint him sometimes, because I was basically a street guy, and I didn't always have great judgement. In those days, I had long hair, but I was in a certain kind of shape. The first time we went to California, Nesuhi said to me, 'Stay in your hotel room 'til I call you.' I didn't know that was going to be for a day and a half. So I'm sitting at the Sunset Hotel, I'm in L.A. for the first time, I'm looking to find Marilyn Monroe. Finally I get the call, he gives me an address, and he tells me, 'Now look, I want you to come over here, but I don't want you to say a word to anyone.' So I get to this palatial house, and I'm shown into a large room and confront what is clearly a long-running poker game – which Nesuhi is losing. I picked up on what was required of me pretty quick – I sat in a chair to the side of the game, arms folded, looking as tough and as mean as possible. Eventually, Nesuhi started winning. When I guess he kind of broke even, we got up to leave. He bade everyone an excellent night, and when we got outside, he thanked me very much and dropped me back at the hotel." Joel Dorn

Sonny Sharrock (left) with Livingston Taylor (right) TL: 70s

Jimmy Scott TL: 70s

"You know what? King Curtis was a real street-smart guy. As a musician he had everybody's respect. When I came to New York, I was really a brash kid. One night, he said, 'You working tonight at the studio? I'm gonna pick you up later.' So I knew we were going to smoke some reefer, we were going to do some drinking, and we were going to end up in a good club. Curtis always had a Cadillac with a leather roof, and it was fun; we'd go uptown and hang. So he came up this night and took me in the car and said, 'I'm gonna take you someplace.' I'd been to the Apollo and to the clubs up in Harlem, but I'd never been on this scary street. It was pitch black; there wasn't a light on in any window, and it almost looked abandoned. He took me into this place, and down a hallway, there was a guy guarding the door who was as big as the door. I knew we were in a new place. The guy said, 'Hey, Curtis,' opened the door and let us in. It was a cut house where all these old Cuban ladies were smoking cigars – some of them cutting coke, some cutting heroin. There were guns all over the place and I mean, it was far out. So Curtis went over to one of the tables, and he put his finger in this white powder. He said, 'Stick your tongue out.' It was the tiniest little bit of something. He said, 'Can you taste it?' I said, 'Yeah.' He said, 'Remember that taste.' It was so tiny, I didn't catch a buzz off it, but I know now, unfortunately, it was coke. He waited about fifteen minutes, he's talking with these guys. I was standing there watching these old Cuban ladies – they used to work with screens, the kind of screen you use as a cover if you're frying something and you don't want grease to splash out. They had screens with handles, and they were jabbering in Spanish. I had never seen a woman smoke a cigar! All of a sudden: boom, boom! They would flip and then the cut would be in. Well, they could lose $100,000 worth of heroin in one flick of a wrist if they didn't know what they were doing. So I got this coke taste in my mouth, Curtis waited about fifteen minutes, and we took a drink of soda or water. We went over to another part of the place, and there was more white powder, more Cuban women, more flipping of this stuff. He said, 'Stick your tongue out again.' Again, a tiny bit. He said, 'You got that taste?' I said, 'Yeah.' He said, 'Rinse your mouth real quick.' After a few more minutes, he said, 'You remember that taste of the first one? You remember that taste of the second one?' I said, 'Yeah.' We waited a few more minutes and left. He looked at me – Curtis was a funny character, but he was serious this time – and he said, 'That first thing you tasted was cocaine, the second thing you tasted was heroin. Stay away from all this shit, but if you ever do it, look for that taste first. I don't want you to die.'" Joel Dorn

King Curtis TL: 60s 70s

Keith Jarrett TL: 60s 70s

Steve Winwood of Blind Faith TL: 60s

"I wanted to be making music. I had an impulse to create the music at the moment, and jazz was the only form of music that allowed you to do that." Keith Jarrett

"The great thing for me about Blind Faith was that we were able to work with Stevie Winwood. When I first heard his records all those years earlier, I couldn't believe that an English kid could sing such good blues and sound so completely like black music. He's a great, great artist." Ahmet

The original cover for Blind Faith's only album and, above right, the alternative version TL: 60s

Blind Faith: Eric Clapton, Steve Winwood, Ginger Baker and Rick Grech on tour

Ginger Baker TL: 60s 70s

"Ginger Baker had this red hair and, appropriately, he could be a very hot-headed person. When I first met him, he said, 'Listen, if there are some things that you don't understand about me, keep one thing in mind.' I said, 'What's that?' He said, 'I'm a communist. You understand? I'm a communist. You keep that in mind, and you'll understand a lot about the way I behave.'

"At the end of a Blind Faith tour, Robert Stigwood, who managed them, called me up and said, 'Ginger's very tired. It's been a very gruelling tour, so he's going to Jamaica for a month.' After Ginger got to the island, Robert called me and said, 'Listen, you have connections. He'd like to rent an Aston Martin.' Ginger had a similar sports car in England. Anyway, in Jamaica at that time, no one particularly knew what an Aston Martin was. So I said, 'Rent one! You can't rent that anywhere. I mean, you can't rent that in New York. How are you going to rent that in Jamaica?'

"I called up Chris Blackwell [founder of Island Records], who told me he had a cousin named Pringle who was a Minister of Tourism in Jamaica. So I called up Mr. Pringle and told him that we'd like to rent a sports car. He called me back and said, 'Listen, there's no sports car here for rent. But I have a friend who has a Ferrari who's a very big music fan and he told me that he would loan Ginger Baker his car for the month he's going to be here, as long as you guarantee the repair of any damage that might be done to the car.' So I said, 'Well, that's no problem.' I called Stigwood up and said, 'Look, I couldn't get him what he wanted, but an English guy is able to loan him a Ferrari.'

"A couple nights later I got a call in the middle of the night from Ginger Baker, who was ranting and raving, screaming down the 'phone at me. 'Who the fuck told you? I don't want a fucking wop car!' So I said, 'I'm terribly sorry, but there are no other cars in Jamaica.' That didn't seem to appease him, he just kept yelling and screaming at me down the 'phone. So I called up Stigwood and said, 'Stiggie, we might as well ship him his car, because there is no car there which he wants to drive.' So they put the car on the plane and sent it to Jamaica, but somehow the shipment got lost and then we had to trace it. It landed in Atlanta instead of Jamaica … and finally the car got to Ginger Baker two days before he was leaving. He was furious.

"Anyway, next time he saw me he apologized. We were going up in an elevator. I said, 'Well, that's okay. I kept one thing in mind that you told me some time ago and I didn't get angry.' So he said, 'What was that?' I said, 'Remember you told me you were a communist? I just kept that in mind.'" Ahmet

Opposite: Freddie King TL: 60s

Cher and others during the making of 3614 Jackson Highway TL: 60s

Lulu with Tom Dowd TL: 70s

"The hot sun, the warm winter, the fresh fish, the boat in the backyard ... I bought the whole bit; I'd loved Miami Beach since I was stationed at the White House Hotel during the war. If ever I were to relax – and I never would – it would have to be in a subtropical climate. Moreover, I was convinced I could create a musical climate of my own. Not only did I want a boat in the backyard, I wanted a band as well – at least a band at my disposal – in a studio down the street.

"My first choice was the Muscle Shoals group. By then the rhythm section was fixed at Barry Beckett, David Hood, Roger Hawkins, and Jimmy Johnson. I loved these guys and wanted them on a permanent basis. They had long since left Rick Hall and opened a studio of their own with my backing, a little down-home ex-funeral parlour immortalized by the title of Cher's 1969 solo album, *3614 Jackson Highway*. In fact, I went down to produce that record. The next Muscle Shoals sessions during that summer were with Lulu – whose 'To Sir With Love' had been huge – but they yielded only a mini-hit in 'Oh Me, Oh My (I'm A Fool For You Baby)', which later was covered by Aretha. Since Cher's record produced no hits, for the most part I was striking out." Jerry Wexler

Jerry Jeff Walker TL: 60s

"It was on WBAI, the voice of the 'radical' underground culture of New York City, that I heard Jerry Jeff Walker's 'Mr. Bojangles'. I jumped on it. Acquired the master rights for Atlantic and half the publishing. I also signed Jerry Jeff, commending him to the tender ministrations of Pasha Arif Mardin. They made some great albums together." Jerry Wexler

"We'd been toiling away in the new studio Jerry had helped set up, and all of a sudden we're cold as ice. We're dying for a smash, dying to prove ourselves, but nothing's happening. We're frustrated, Wexler's frustrated — and then out of nowhere Ahmet Ertegun slides into town. Naturally we'd heard of him — he was our pal Jerry's legendary partner — but we'd never worked with him before. He shows up with a singer, R. B. Greaves, and a song, 'Take A Letter, Maria'. While the band puts the arrangement together, Ahmet's riding around town in his big rent-a-car buying cowboy boots. He gets back to the studio, sits behind the board, doodles pictures on a yellow pad, and gabs on the 'phone. Unlike Jerry, there's nothing scary about Ahmet. He's relaxed. He casually nods his head after the second take. A few weeks later the record rockets to number one. The whole thing was so easy, I think it kind of bugged Jerry." David Hood

Above left, Ahmet, and above, with R. B. Greaves TL: 60s

"As Atlantic became larger, a lot of people wooed us with the idea of buying us. Personally, if you're asking about how a woman felt, I felt that it was wrong. I felt that if we were absorbed into a large company my job, which was on an individual level, would be over. I mean, I thought it was a very bad idea because I thought the company was just going to get bigger and bigger. I never believed it was going to fail, but it was bought, and for what today is a ridiculous amount of money. I still think it was a mistake and probably the people who were then in favour of the purchase also now think that it was a mistake." Miriam Beinstock

"At the time we decided to sell Atlantic, Miriam had already been bought out, so there were only three of us: Jerry Wexler, Nesuhi, and I. We were all getting along, but it wasn't the happiest of moments for anybody. Jerry felt a need to consolidate what he was doing; he was concerned about the future and about getting enough money so that he didn't have to worry in the future. Nesuhi, I think, just wanted to get out and do something else. I didn't want to sell the company – the company was my idea, it was my brainchild, and we were doing well. I saw no reason to think that disaster was imminent.

Mr. and Mrs. Steven Ross

However, they were so insistent on selling, I really didn't have an option. There was one possibility, which was that I would buy them out, but I really didn't want to do that because I needed them. I needed Nesuhi and Jerry, because they produced a lot of things, and Jerry was really more involved in the day-to-day administration of the company. He was more the business end of it and he was great at it, heavily into promotion and sales and all of that. The music business is not just music, it's also business. Anyway, I couldn't come up with any other option. What I did do was raise the price a great deal. When we sold we had to sign a three-year employment contract. By the end of those three years, Warner-Seven Arts, the company to which we had sold, had in turn sold the entire business to Steve Ross's company, Kinney. Kinney was in various businesses, but mostly funeral homes and parking lots. They'd just completed a merger with Ted Ashley, who was an entertainment agent, because that was the field they wanted to move into. Steve Ross thought that he could move into music as well as films, but our first three-year contract was running out at the time they bought the company. So we had meetings with Steve Ross, who brought in his own business adviser, Felix Rohatyn, whom I already knew, and who later became the American ambassador in Paris.

"So Felix said to me in French, 'This is a very good opportunity for you.' And I said, 'Listen, I'm not staying. I don't care how good the deal is with Steve Ross, I for one am not going to stay.' But then Steve said, 'If you stay, I guarantee you'll be very happy, because we're not going to interfere in anything. We'll give you whatever you want.' So he talked us into staying and in order to do that, he really gave us a whole new deal, which involved getting paid all over again. Steve was a gambler, very generous. He was one of a kind. I must say I've no complaints about having stayed with the company. We did very well out of it and managed to accomplish a lot of things, which we may not have done had we owned the company. For example, I signed up The Rolling Stones. The deal we made was probably the richest one in the history of the music business up to that point. I don't know how many millions of dollars I would have given out of my own pocket to any band or any artist. But suddenly it was no longer my money, it was the company's money – it's a different take. The company grew to the point where we became the number one record label in America. In a way, Steve Ross had the same kind of ethos as we did, to let people get on with what they do well, which was very unusual to come across in a business setting at that time." Ahmet

"It was Ahmet's foresight and his vision of what this music could bring that really took Atlantic from being a little Tiffany speciality company doing interesting jazz, funk, rhythm and blues into being a global giant. I have to say that if my then partner had not exploited other areas, I don't know if the label could have continued to exist." Jerry Wexler

Ahmet

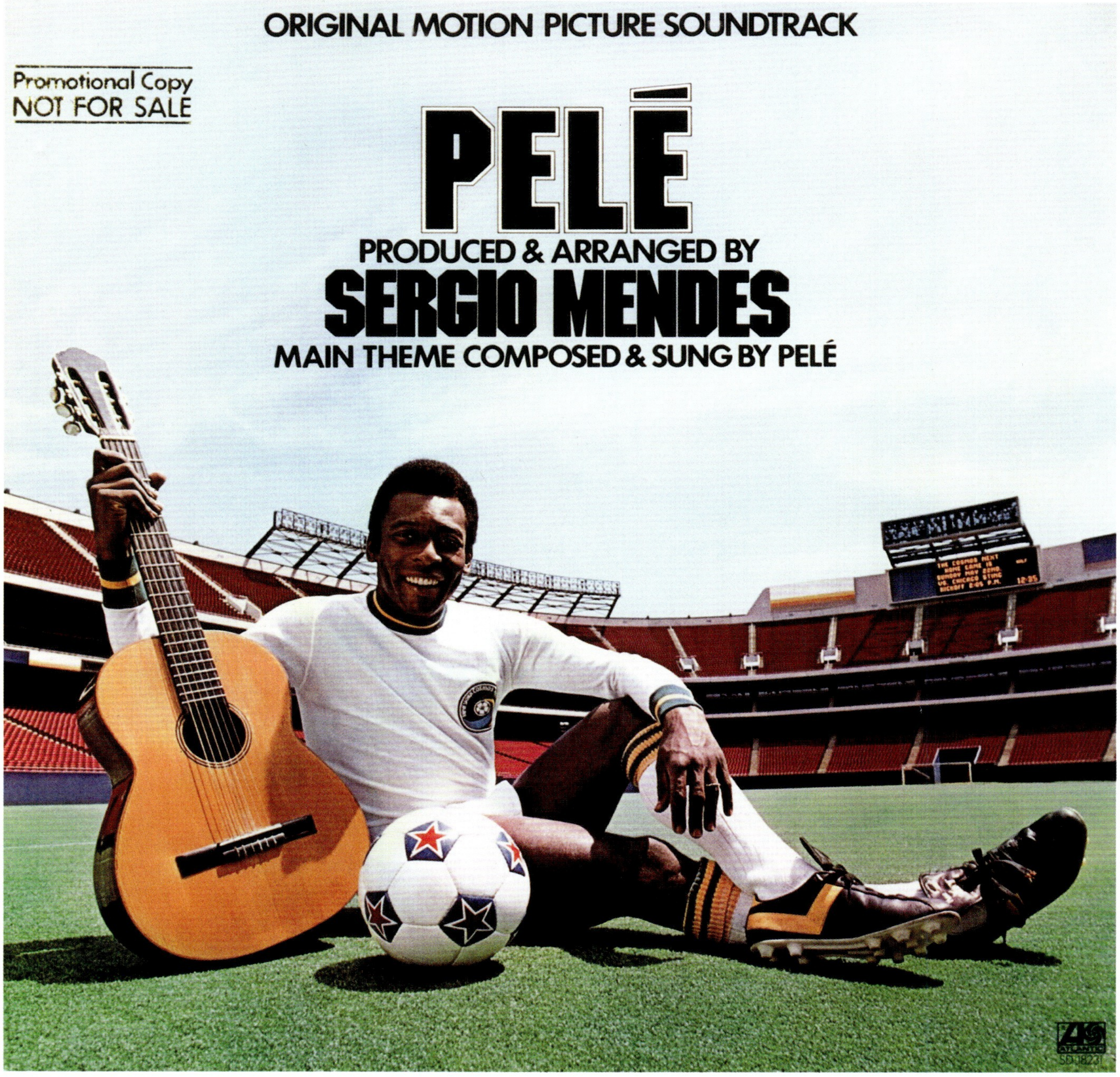

ORIGINAL MOTION PICTURE SOUNDTRACK
PELÉ
PRODUCED & ARRANGED BY
SERGIO MENDES
MAIN THEME COMPOSED & SUNG BY PELÉ

Promotional Copy NOT FOR SALE

"Then came the next step, where Steve wanted Nesuhi to set up an international company. Nesuhi wasn't quite so sure, so Steve said, 'Well, what would you like?' Nesuhi said, 'I'd like to have a football team, a New York soccer team.' So Nesuhi started a team called the Cosmos, which joined the North American Soccer League. Nesuhi was a great savant of soccer. He probably knew more about it than anyone except a couple of British football critics. We wanted to be able to include some of the greatest players in the world on our team. So Nesuhi flew down to South America to try to talk Pelé out of retirement and into joining our club. Part of the deal with Pelé coming to play for the Cosmos was that he got to make an album. Pelé is a giant of a man, probably the most popular sports figure of this century, apart perhaps, from Muhammad Ali. Although there are probably 20 times as many soccer fans as there are boxing fans. Soccer is the most popular sport in the world and Pelé is not only a great player, he is such a gentleman. He comports himself so well and is an extremely loveable personality. We were lucky to have two of the world's all-time greatest players on the team – Pelé and Franz Beckenbauer, who was also a true gentleman. I'll never forget we were in the changing room one practice day when a reporter came in, went up to Pelé, and asked him, 'Where's Beckenbauer?' So Pelé said, 'Beckenbauer, back-in-hour.' We had sell-out crowds – 76,000 on several occasions – and a team of players from every country. We had South Americans, Britons, Germans, Italians, French, Belgians, Yugoslavs, Turks … the only problem was that none of them could understand one another. Eventually though, if they couldn't speak it already, they all learned a little English.

"So, in 1971, the same year we started the Cosmos, Nesuhi took on a huge job when he created WEA International [now known as Warner Music International], the umbrella company formed to oversee the gobal operations of the three record labels owned by what was then known as Warner Communications [now Time Warner] – Warner Bros., Elektra, and Atlantic. He got very, very good music people to work with him, and initially, since it was the youngest of the international companies, it was the smallest. He travelled constantly, and under his great leadership more and more countries were added. As a result, Nesuhi left us this legacy of a huge network of companies and licensees around the world.

"He was also the head of IFPI, the International Federation of Phonogram and Videogram Producers, through which he devoted his last few years to fighting piracy around the world and fervently supporting the protection of intellectual rights. He succeeded in many places including Turkey, Indonesia and Taiwan." Ahmet

Ahmet, Oscar de la Renta and the cheerleading 'Cosmos Girls'

"Jack Nitzsche was an arranger/producer, and one of the reasons that Buffalo Springfield broke up was that Neil Young wanted to make solo records with Jack, who was working at the time for Warner Bros. Records. So, as Buffalo Springfield was breaking up anyway, I told Neil to go ahead and do the thing with Jack, and that I would keep the other guys – the other guys being Stephen Stills and Richie Furay. Then Richie wanted to go with Poco, who were with another company, and so I let that go. At about the same time, a young agent from William Morris, David Geffen, came to see Jerry Wexler. He had heard some music that was being done by Stephen Stills, Graham Nash and David Crosby, who were friends and were just making tentative demos together. He had been blown away by them and came to see if he could get us to release Stephen Stills from his contract, so that he could sell this group to Columbia, where he had some friends. Jerry Wexler threw him out of his office. He then came to see me and I said, 'Look, that's not going to happen, we're not going to let Stephen Stills go. However, I love the group and we could place them here.' Well, we became great friends, David and I, and we're still very great friends. He and I worked together in developing Crosby, Stills & Nash, whose first album was such an incredible success. Then we got Neil Young back for the second record, Déjà Vu. So that's how that went." Ahmet

"One day in early '67, David said to me that he wanted me to meet a friend of his. So we take off in David's Porsche down the lower canyon, bang on this door, which opens. Smoke pours out and no one can see, there's only tiny red and green lights in the corner, and there's this guy playing the piano, thumping the hell out of it, but it's making a wonderful sound. The guy stops, David takes me over and says, 'This is my friend Stephen Stills, we're going to have to start making music together. I know what you sound like with The Hollies, I know what I sound like with The Byrds, I know what Stephen does with the Springfield, and we've got to make music together.' Crosby, Stills & Nash have no claim to notes – anyone can sing the same notes that we sing – but nobody sounds like we do. There's something that happens when we physically blend our voices, something about the movement of the air that creates a certain wave form which is totally unique, and which is why I

left The Hollies in the first place. I heard David, Stephen and me sing and I went, 'What in the hell is this?!' It shocked me. We sang two verses and had to stop and just started laughing because it was ridiculous how good it sounded. I don't really know how that works, I can only put it down to the combination of our voices." Graham Nash

"We rehearsed the very first Crosby, Stills & Nash record out on Long Island, at Sag Harbour. We were very close to John Sebastian from The Lovin' Spoonful, and he rented us a house about five minutes away from his place. We went there in the middle of winter with six feet of snow all around, moved our stuff into this big house, and started to rehearse. I had a song that I'd started to write at

From left: Stephen Stills, Graham Nash and David Crosby TL: 60s 70s
Above: David Crosby

Stephen Stills

a funny club in the north of England, a workingman's club. So I had the title and idea for the song 'Teach Your Children', and then I wrote this set of words down, together with a melody, and that was what I played for Stephen. It must have sounded to him like something that Henry VIII had written. I mean, it was English country, not American country, English folk country, kind of slowish stuff. He said, 'That's a really pretty tune, let me show you what I'd do to it.' Then he totally turned it into what it is – he didn't change any of the melody, the chords, or the words, but he put the musical influence into it which gave it the American country beat that it has." Graham Nash

"David Crosby was a great friend of Steve Stills as well as of Graham Nash. As a matter of fact, when I first met Steve, he kept telling me that I should record David Crosby as a jazz singer, and David does have a bit of that, there's no doubt about it. His father was a famous Hollywood photographer and cameraman, so David met a lot of celebrities and was exposed to a great deal more than the usual child growing up in California at the time. He's a very sensitive and complex personality – he's had a tumultuous life with many ups and downs, and has survived the whole thing and remained a terrific songwriter. I think one of the greatest songs by Crosby, Stills & Nash is 'Guinnevere'. *'Guinnevere had green eyes like yours, baby, like yours …'* Crosby, Stills & Nash are a phenomenal vocal group, because not only are they great singers who can sing in beautiful harmony, but each of them has a totally different, distinct voice. Yet, no matter who is singing lead on a particular song, it nevertheless always has that unique CSN sound. I don't think there's ever been an album that has had so many great songs on it as the first CSN album. They wrote some better songs after that, but as a complete group of songs, that album is unbeatable." Ahmet

"Paul Marshall represented the promoters of Woodstock, which was going to be this big outdoor rock festival – but, of course, nobody could have predicted what happened. Anyway, we expected to have three or four of our groups perform, so through Paul I bought the recording rights to the concert for $75,000. He asked me if I would also be interested in acquiring the movie rights. I had little interest in a documentary of another rock'n'roll show and furthermore, we were not in the movie business, so I turned him down. But he couldn't get a deal, so he came back to me and said that I could have both the record and the movie for $100,000. So I thought, why not? – especially since there were a great many stars who were scheduled to appear. Meanwhile, some of our groups dropped out, so the only Atlantic artists who ended up performing at Woodstock were Crosby, Stills, Nash & Young – and it was only their second gig! Personally, I thought that I wouldn't do too well out there in the field and the mud. Of course, it turned out to be a monumental, historic event. Less than two years before, we had sold Atlantic to Warner-Seven Arts, and when that company in turn was acquired by Steve Ross's Kinney group, he suddenly discovered he had the film of Woodstock – which is probably worth what he paid for our entire record company." Ahmet

"Woodstock was an experience. I didn't go to the concert but I did do all the accounting for it, the royalties – that was another experience!" Fran Wakschal

Woodstock TL: 60s
Top, Jefferson Airplane; above right, Sly Stone; and right, the Woodstock audience
Opposite, clockwise from top: Joe Cocker; Arlo Guthrie; Janis Joplin; Joni Mitchell

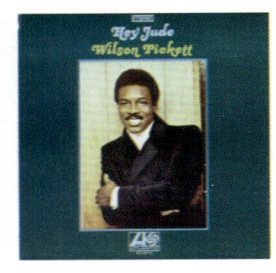

"Duane Allman had the ability very pleasantly to get his way with people. He was convinced that Wilson Pickett should record a cover version of The Beatles' song 'Hey Jude'. Wilson said, 'Are you crazy? The Beatles have released it, it's in the 20s, it'll be #1 in two weeks.' Duane replied, 'That's the whole point. I mean, it shows we've got balls. We'll cover The Beatles, the biggest thing in the world. This is going to get the world's attention that you, as a black act, have the guts to cut the same record which The Beatles have got out and that you think you can have a hit record with it.' Which is, of course, exactly what happened. That's how Duane thought, which was an incredible attitude to have towards our business and our world."
Rick Hall

"Duane's whole career spun off that Pickett session. It's amazing how one incident, one session, can change a person's life. Duane did that great solo on the end of the record, Atlantic heard it, and that was that."
Jimmy Johnson

Wilson Pickett above, below, with King Curtis and right with Duane Allman TL: 60s 70s

"I was in New York; Rick Hall was there also and called me down to his room to hear a new track from a Wilson Pickett session. He was *en route* to play it for Jerry Wexler and Ahmet. It was Pickett's cover of The Beatles' song 'Hey Jude'. As I listened, I mentioned to Rick, 'That's not your guitar player – who the hell is this guy, he's great?' Rick said, 'One of those long-haired old hippie boys, hair hanging down his back, but boy, he can play the guitar.' I said, 'What's his name?' He said, 'Duane Allman.' I said, 'Hell, I'm going down there to sign him and put a group together,' which is exactly what I did. I put together a band, which we initially tried to record with Rick, but they weren't what Duane was looking for, thank goodness. I ended up paying $10,000 for those tapes, and Duane just disappeared on the road for several months. He would call from time to time from this place or that, and I'd send him a little money. Finally, he called me from Jacksonville, Florida and said, 'I've got it.' I said, 'You've got what?' He said, 'I've got the band.'" Phil Walden

Above and below: Duane Allman TL: 60s 70s

"We were all influenced by Robert Johnson, of course, who goes back to the thirties. Elmore James was Duane's great influence on the electric slide guitar. Albert King was another, and especially for Duane and me, it was B. B. King. We listened to all the great blues players and did everything possible against being commercial, which is not really the thing to do if you're trying to have a successful album. Luckily we got away with it.

"Those long instrumentals and drawn-out pieces were not really commercial at that time. In fact, if it hadn't been for FM radio, which was like a real underground radio system that would play these extended pieces of music, we would never have been successful. In the late sixties and early seventies, it was a very free period for musicians. The Allman Brothers Band would also never have made it without that particular attitude of the audience, who wanted to hear the improvisation and the individual expression of each different band member. If you listen to the records, I was on the left and Duane was on the right in the stereo mix. You could hear it go back and forth, but I guess it would not be easy to pick that up if you hadn't seen the group live. We always made a point to mix it that same way, instead of mixing it together and having it come out of the middle. There was really a certain degree of telepathy, because we created a lot of things right on the stage. When you listen to it you may think, well, that had to be rehearsed, since the bass guitar with Duane and myself playing the harmony line sounds like we must have spent a month writing it. If you listen closely, though, you can hear that one person would come up with an improvisation – a nice line that had come into his mind – stay with it, play it alone a couple of times, and then Oakley, myself, or Duane would pick up on it. It would happen so quickly, however, that you'd think, 'Wow, that has to be a written passage.' Three hours was the normal set then, but we'd play five, sometimes six hours." Dickey Betts

"The Allman Brothers really founded their own community within the South. They became the people's band, going out into these parks, playing for hours for free, and the word just travelled. They represented the regional pride of the South. A lot of other great players were Southern by birth, but with success moved to San Francisco, New York, L.A., or wherever. These were Southern guys, they were living in the South, they were playing Southern music. They didn't really care if they got paid $1.80 or $10,000 to play. The music was the most important thing in their life. They lived in this big house together, and the music reflected their entire lifestyle, their communal sense of living." Phil Walden

"John is a terrific talent, and made several albums with us including, *Southern Fried* with Duane Allman." Ahmet

John Hammond Jr. TL: 60s 70s

240 THE ATLANTIC STORY

Allman Brothers Band, clockwise from left: Dickey Betts, Jai Johanny Johanson, Gregg Allman, Berry Oakley, Butch Trucks and Duane Allman TL: 60s 70s

Gregg Allman

"I can recall when we proposed to Jerry Wexler that *Fillmore East* was going to be a double album and contain some songs 15 or 16 minutes long, he said, 'No way! We're going to have a single album and you've got to edit it. It's not all art, Phil, it's not all art. Every note is not essential to our heritage.' I said, 'You don't understand, this is a people's band and this is the way it's done with them. Plus we're going to sell it for $6.98.' He said, 'That's impossible, economically impossible!' Well, because we controlled the publishing rights, we were able to do that – they didn't have to pay out as much and we gave a rate on that." Phil Walden

"As far as the Allman Brothers are concerned, I think that the most important person was really Duane Allman, who was one of the all-time greatest guitar players. His death was a terrible tragedy. They were very much in that Southern tradition, and, of course, stayed in the South, and so contributed a considerable amount to the change in attitudes and perceptions in that part of the world." Ahmet

"They represent the essence of the Southern rock band, which is very blues-related. They're just a great bunch of kick-ass good ol' boys that have a great feel for blues-orientated rock. Duane Allman was a genius – I mean, he's absolutely my favourite rock guitarist, and I shouldn't say rock guitarist because that's almost a put-down. He could play blues as unbelievably well as rock and jazz – and he was a great session man, and a great feel man. He really knew how to back a vocalist." Jerry Wexler

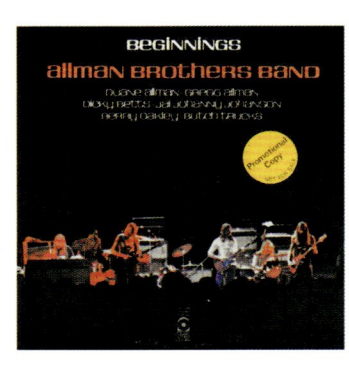

Clockwise from right: Duane Allman; Allman Brothers Band; Duane Allman and Berry Oakley; Duane Allman

Front line from left: King Curtis, Delaney Bramlett, Duane Allman

"The Southern whites, the music they played, was organically the same as the blacks', because they were from the same culture, there was no difference. Certainly there was Jim Crow and separatism in the South, segregation and so on. At the bottom end of the agrarian ladder, however, which was where these musicians lived, black and white, they came from the same place. There were many things they shared: they did the same things and squished the same red mud between their toes. There's something about playing that music as it exists and learning it *in situ*, as it were, that beats learning it off phonograph records. It just does. There had to be a reason why Delaney and Bonnie's music was so attractive to people like Eric Clapton and George Harrison. They sensed a certain nourishment there that they couldn't find elsewhere. When Delaney and Bonnie first hit, they were so exciting – there was nothing more exciting out there." Jerry Wexler

"I've always been so blessed with great musicians. There were four guitar players: Dave Mason, Eric Clapton, George Harrison, and myself. The way that happened was that Blind Faith wanted us to open up their show for them, which we did, but we also broke the group up in the process. I mean, we were hot, we had some great musicians, and we just actually broke that group up. Eric started riding with us on the bus and playing with us on stage. They couldn't figure that out. Here was a guy whose group is getting ready to follow us, and he's on the stage with me. Pretty soon, he just joined the band. Then George saw what was happening and said, 'Well, can I join too?' I said, 'Sure.' He said, 'Well, pick me up at my house.' So I picked him up and he was on the tour. Then Dave said, 'Mate, I'm here too. Can I go as well?' 'Okay, you're coming as well.' Unbelievable, but all those guitars worked together on stage. It sounded great, nobody getting in anybody's way, nobody had a fight with a guitar.

"'Coming Home' was a hit in England before anybody had even heard of it in America. That's the main reason I went to England, because people liked us there. In America, people would still be saying, Delaney and Bonnie who? What's a Delaney and Bonnie? People would say to my brother, who was our manager then, 'Where's Delaney and how is she?' 'Oh, she's fine!' I don't know what they thought a Bonnie was! We had some really crazy times, though, unbelievable! I mean, we really got to rocking. We'd do a show and the owners would holler, 'Please get off! Curfew time! Please!' We'd play a three-hour show without stopping, and if we were in some place where they had a curfew, they just almost had to pull the plug on us because I didn't like to quit! We were having a ball, y'all!" Delaney Bramlett

Bonnie and Delaney Bramlett with Duane Allman TL: 60s 70s

Derek and the Dominos, from left: Duane Allman, Jim Gordon, Eric Clapton, Carl Radle and Bobby Whitlock TL: 60s 70s

"I introduced Eric and Duane to each other. I mean, here's Duane, who is Jerry's input from America, and here's Eric, who is Ahmet's input. I knew Duane from one side and Eric from the other. Working in the studio with Eric and the band, I said, 'Eric, d'you know Duane Allman?' He said, 'D'you mean that guy who plays all those new licks? How does he do that?' I said, 'He's going to be here on Saturday and he's playing a concert.' Eric said, 'I want to see him!' So we went down to this open-air concert, which was a benefit that the Allman Brothers were doing, and Eric just kind of sat there watching Duane. Duane was in the middle of a solo and all of a sudden he opened his eyes, looked down, and stopped dead on stage. He just froze, he just stopped, and he looked. The two of them were just staring at each other. Dickey Betts is playing, the band is going crazy, and here's Duane and Eric somehow locked into each other. Duane had to kind of turn around and close his eyes and get back to playing – he wouldn't look in our direction again!

"That night, Derek and the Dominos and the Allman Brothers are in the studio and they're trading licks. Bobby Whitlock and Gregg Allman are playing piano and organ, Jim Gordon and the percussionist are there going 90 miles an hour, everybody is just having an all-out jam. Over in the corner, Duane is saying to Eric, 'How do you play such and such?' while he's trying to play something on his guitar, and when Eric says, 'No, man, no, I did it this way,' Duane is saying, 'Why didn't I think of that?' Now Duane's playing 'right, and all of a sudden Eric is asking him, 'How did you do this?' to which Duane says, 'No, you've got it on the wrong finger, put it on this finger,' and then Eric is there. By six or seven o'clock in the morning, they're still talking to each other at a hundred miles an hour; they've got each other's guitars now, I mean they're trading everything. That's when it started.

"When we had finished *Layla*, it had been about a two-week project. I called up New York and said, 'This is the best damn record we've made since *The Genius Of Ray Charles*.' Jerry said, 'Tom, you're making an extremely weighty statement, you know.' For a year it didn't sell. One whole year. I was embarrassed. I thought this was insane – we'd spent that much money, and I'd had such a good time doing it, and the guys were playing so incredibly well – it's pitiful that with all that love and energy and everything that went into creating it, it wasn't getting the recognition that it deserved. Then a year later, it was like a national anthem – it was another huge thing, but it took a whole year to break." Tom Dowd

Derek and the Dominos TL: 60s 70s

244 THE ATLANTIC STORY

Above from left: Rick Hall and Clarence Carter TL: 60s 70s

Clarence Carter

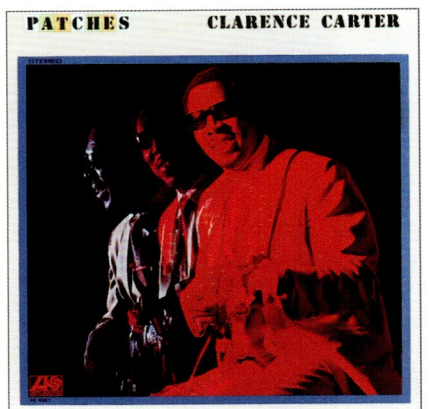

"I heard 'Patches' on an album by Chairmen of the Board and I thought, 'God, it's me, it's my life, me and my father. I've got to do this – it's a movie, it's a soundtrack for a movie, I mean, it's everything.' I could hear Clarence Carter performing on the finished record, I could hear the wind, I could hear the rain, and I could see the father's face when he died. I could create all of this … I'd always wanted to be a movie producer anyhow, and I could see this tobacco road approach to life that I knew so well.

"Clarence Carter was less impressed. He said, 'Black people don't relate to that kind of lyric … *My papa was a fine old man, I can see him with a shovel in his hand* … That's slave days, those days are over. I won't cut that – it's too, it's too white! It'd be degrading my race, Rick, you've got to understand that.' I said, 'Oh, c'mon, Clarence, it's a song, it's an era, it's truth, it's history, it's not you, it's the past … Clarence, look, do me a favour, let me cut the track with you. If we get halfway through the track and you're not happy, we'll throw it in the garbage – but give me one shot, let's just try it. If you don't start getting enthusiastic about it like I am, then we'll just ditch it.' He said, 'Okay, fair enough, I'll do that.'

"We started in on it, but he hadn't had time to learn the lyrics. Clarence is blind, and we didn't have time to write the Braille lyrics down, which would have taken a couple of hours. So Sonny Limbo, my engineer and assistant, took the lyrics and read them to him in his ear. How a man can sing with any conviction with someone else whispering the next line in his ear while he's singing the previous one, and having to think, I'll never know, but it came off. I said, 'Clarence, you know the trouble with this is that you sing it too straight.' He said, 'What d'you mean?' I said, 'It won't make it.' He said, 'How come?' I said, 'Look, you've got to listen to the writer – it's got to be more dramatic, you've got to live the part. It's death here, it's history. I mean, this is the end of the line with black people.' That's the difference in the record. We had a heck of a time getting that out, because he wanted to sing it straight, very round-mouthed and very expected. I said, 'You've got to get emotional, and you've got to live the song,' which eventually is what he did, and I think that is what brought the song around." Rick Hall

Brook Benton with Arif Mardin TL: 70s

"Jerry Wexler said, 'Look, we've signed Brook Benton. I want you to go to Miami. Here's a great song by Tony Joe White, why don't you record that?' I listened to it and it was beautiful. So I went down to Miami, and Brook Benton said, 'I don't want to sing about Georgia.' At this time, the civil rights problems were clearly mounting. I said, 'No, this man is trying to get out of Georgia, it's a good song.' Anyway, we recorded it, brought it back to New York, and added all the sweetening. Sometimes a hit record is there but one doesn't realize it. I worked feverishly to make something great out of it; I was really enjoying it, and when Ahmet and Jerry heard it, they said, 'Wow! This is a Top Five record – fantastic!' I said, 'Is it? A Top Five record, great!'"
Arif Mardin

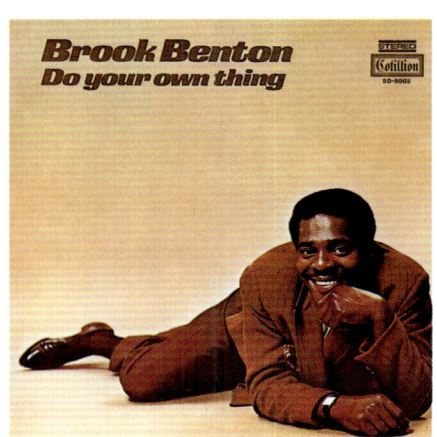

From left: Neil Young, Stephen Stills, David Crosby and Graham Nash TL: 60s 70s

"David and I are not good enough musicians in the lead guitar department to spark Stephen and to get him off. With Stephen, when he's excited, he's a monster; when he's bored, he's as bad as everybody else. So one day he came to me and said, 'Listen, I've been talking to Ahmet about going out live and about who's going to be in the band, and Ahmet's suggestion was that we get Neil.' I said, 'Neil who?' He said, 'Neil Young.' Now I knew Neil's music through Buffalo Springfield, and I mean, 'Expecting To Fly' was, I thought, one of the nicest pieces of music I'd ever heard. So we got Neil. To be able to stand between Steve and Neil when they're like two stags getting at each other, conversing and talking with lead guitars, is really a thrill. It was just one of the best things that we ever did.

"Neil saw the Kent State atrocity on TV, and he wrote 'Ohio' that night. He and David had been staying with friends up north, and they came down to Los Angeles. We went into the studio that night and recorded it. Ahmet was there, so we recorded a B-side too, and gave him the masters. He took them back with him to New York, and it was out eight days later. In fact we killed our own single that we'd just released, 'Teach Your Children', because we were so outraged that this massacre had taken place, that the National Guard had murdered four unarmed students who were demonstrating against the Vietnam War. Ahmet delighted in the fact that we did that, and that we all went against every rule that you can have." Graham Nash

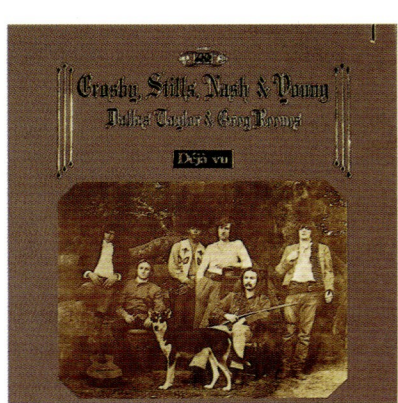

David Crosby

Aretha Franklin TL: 60s 70s

"When Aretha was having emotional and personal problems, it was difficult to get her to come into the studio. Let's say, if she was living in Detroit, she might come into New York, but then find it impossible to leave the hotel. I might have to go and beg and plead and cajole just to get her into the studio." Jerry Wexler

"At the time of the sessions for 'Spirit In The Dark', Aretha had left Ted White or Ted White had left her, and apparently, as long as Ted was with her, it was a lot easier to record her. So no one knew if she was going to show up or not, especially not for a bunch of white boys. I was out on the boat with Wexler – we were out on the Big A, his yacht. He would take me out on that damn yacht whenever he wanted me to agree to something he knew I didn't want to do, because he knew I was scared out there. For a year or more, I didn't realize that he was actually taking me out into the Bermuda Triangle – I mean, that's where we were going. So we were out there again when we got the call on the radio that Aretha had actually turned up. Boy, he took that boat back as fast as it could possibly go – it was like *Miami Vice*. He beached it, we leapt out, and were in the studio – still in our Bermuda shorts – inside of 45 minutes. We cut 'Spirit In The Dark', 'Don't Play That Song' and a few others." Jim Dickinson

Eric Clapton TL: 70s

"I'd always encouraged Eric to sing, because I thought he had a great voice and could have a wonderful solo career. He had something of a block when it came to being able to sing – something which he overcame, I believe, through his first solo album." Ahmet

Lou Reed TL: 70s

"This record with Lou Reed and the Velvet Underground was a great moment." *Ahmet*

Duke Ellington TL: 70s

"It beats me why African-American music is played and loved all over the world. People may say it's the rhythm, it's sexy, makes you feel good, helps you to think, you can dance to it – but you're still left with the question: Why? There's a story Milt Gabler used to tell of how he was recording Louis Armstrong in 1942/'43, redoing Louis's theme song, 'Dear Old Southland'. There's a line in it that runs, *darkies singing soft and low*. Gabler stopped the recording and told Louis, 'You can't say "darkies" anymore.' Louis replied, 'Well, if you're not going to call them "darkies", what are you going to call them?' There are so many levels to this art form, from the home cooking of Muddy Waters to the dicty, fine cuisine of the Duke or Louis Armstrong. But the point is that all of this music is rooted in the blues, and for me, that's what really counts." Ahmet

"There's clearly a certain unmistakable vibrancy about African-American music. I remember, for example, when Dizzy Gillespie's orchestra first came to Istanbul. My father was suspicious by then of my intentions. I still hadn't told him whether I was going to be working in his company, but he knew I had a lot of jazz records at home, and was writing a lot of arrangements for local bands, so he wanted to check this orchestra out. So he went to the theatre with the intention of not liking the music, but found that he loved the rhythm, energy, and precision. He came back so inspired, he said, 'Son, these people are playing with such energy, they're so wonderful. They even played the national anthem in such a fantastic way.' Usually it was played at lento tempo, but these guys didn't know that, so they swung it, and my father was raving, 'It was so great – I wanted to get up and march!' To make the second point, we have to go back to history. Ravel heard jazz and put jazz elements into his music. Stravinsky heard jazz and then wrote a jazz concerto, which he entitled *The Ebony Concerto*, for the Woody Herman Orchestra. Then he used jazz elements in other pieces. It was fashionable to work with jazz in the thirties, to add a little bit of that flavour, especially for composers who were living in Paris at that time. Ragtime fascinated them – the originals, Jelly Roll Morton, 'Maple Leaf Rag', for example. That music originally came from Europe, from the quadrilles and other types of European dance forms. They have a bridge section called the 'trio', which is an exact European dance, music and song form. This then became transformed by black New Orleans musicians based in the blues, with the history of African field-shouts and hollering, and then came back again to Europe. Just as later the white rock bands in England took this European music – now completely transformed and rooted in the blues – and reinterpreted it again to become European-sounding music, but with a lot of energy. Again, they kept that certain vibrancy, they kept that particular energy." Arif Mardin

Noreen Woods and Ahmet

"I came to Atlantic in 1957 – I was 12. No, I'm kidding! I started by relieving the switchboard operator, typing orders, doing copyrights – I mean, I did everything! Then I became Jerry Wexler's secretary. There were about 15 employees then. It was small and everyone did everything. Miriam Beinstock, who at the time was married to Herb Abramson, ran the office until she retired. She was a partner and very much involved. Ahmet, Jerry, and Miriam all have strong personalities, but they worked well together. The Label was well-run. When Herb came back from his military service, he was given Atco to run, but he left because he and Miriam got divorced. In the beginning it was just a job – I needed a job. I had been working in the Bronx for a record company called ABC-Paramount, which made copies of popular hits and sold them for half the price. I was a secretary to five people there – it was just too much, so I quit the job. You know, it was 24 hours a day, seven days a week – you never caught up and were always behind. It was totally different at Atlantic. I got more involved. I went to sessions and hired musicians – so it was much more exciting for me. It was a different business, there was much more interaction with the artists – I mean, everyone did everything. When Ahmet and Jerry had decided whom they wanted to record, I hired the musicians, fixed dates and did the paperwork. Tom Dowd, at that point, was doing most of the recording and producing the masters. Ahmet and Jerry brought in outside producers to work on the sessions, but they weren't called producers, they were arrangers, A & R men. It wasn't that organized then, but they knew what they were doing. And they loved what they were doing, so that made a big difference. The office was such fun to be in – I mean, I worked there for 25 years! Oh, I did like it. After Jerry left, I became Ahmet's assistant. They have totally different personalities, they are totally different, but I will always love them both." Noreen Woods

Noreen Woods and Arif Mardin

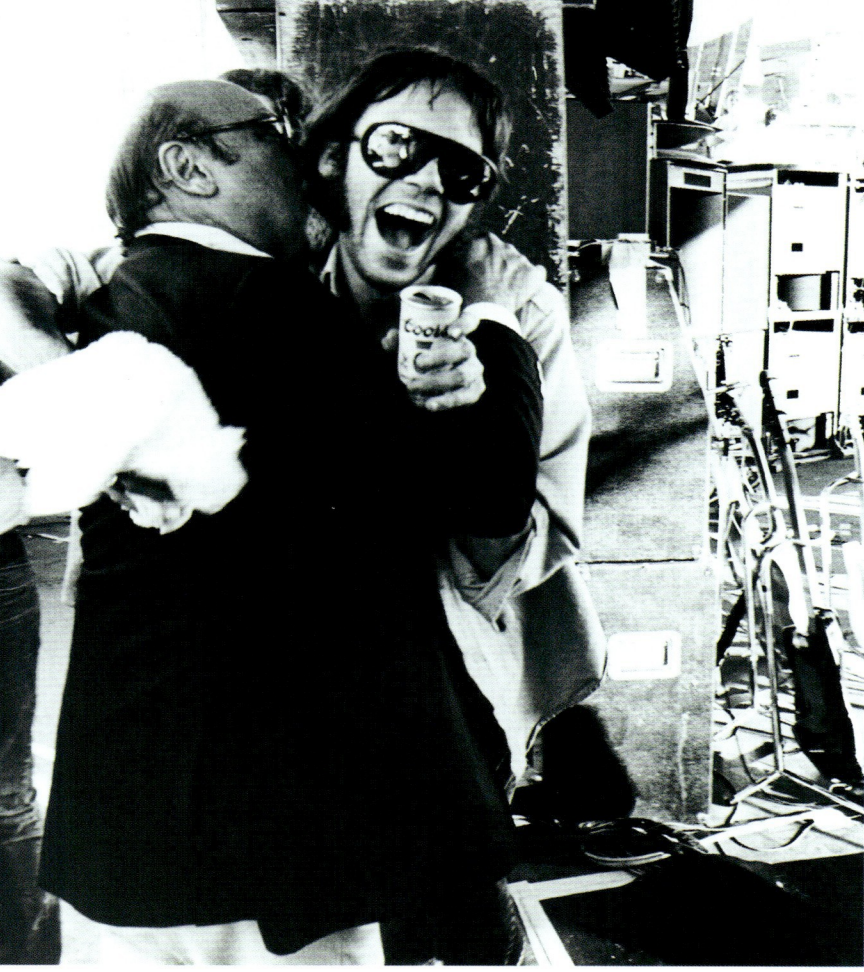

"I credit us for really caring about each other. We all loved each other very much and these were not very possessive relationships. When I went with Joan I loved her and it was a wonderful time, but I didn't expect to stay there, and neither did she. When she went to Graham, my feeling was, 'How could I feel unhappy about two people I really loved being together?' I couldn't see anything wrong with that. I didn't feel I owned her in the first place and we avoided most of the pitfalls there."
David Crosby

"'Skin on skin', Mongo Santamaria once said, 'is what makes the sound that can move you.' Mongo makes that sound every time his tough, but flexible hands hit the skins of the conga drum or the bongos. The sound can move you and thrill you and, when it reaches a particular pitch of excitement, it can spread through your own skin, unseen, heavy with its strength, irresistible in its impact, but invisible. Latin rhythms have always had the power to move, as Gene Krupa noted years ago in the preface to his drum book. But Mongo has given the Latin rhythms the real salt and pepper of the native Cuban culture – the close ties to blood, sweat, tears, love, life, and nature that mark that exceptional people. When he gets it on, the smile spreads slowly around his face as his great hands rap out the rhythms, skin on skin, and you can watch the warmth seep slowly through the band and out into the audience." Ralph J. Gleason

Opposite: Mongo Santamaria TL: 70s Above, clockwise from left: Steve Stills, David Crosby, Graham Nash, Joni Mitchell, Neil Young; Ahmet with David Crosby, and Neil Young TL: 70s 80s 90s

Jerry Wexler, Tom Dowd and Ronnie Hawkins TL: 70s

"Ronnie Hawkins owned a couple of farms and nightclubs outside Toronto, but he was still stone Arkansas swamp. You never heard a bitter breath or bad vibe from the guy who lost his band [The Hawks, later known as The Band] to Dylan, and his guitarist, John Till, to Janis Joplin.

"My good buddy Stanley Booth, the writer, and Jim Dickinson put together The Dixie Flyers – a name out of Flannery O'Connor, who wrote, referring to William Faulkner, *but when the Dixie Flyer comes down the track you better get out of the way*. Thus was born the only rock band named after Mr. Bill. Aside from Jim, the Flyers were Tommy McClure on bass, Sammy (Beaver) Creason on drums, Mike Utley on keyboards and, on guitar, the legendary Charlie Freeman – Steve Cropper's mentor in Memphis and a full-blooded Indian, who once referred to me as a 'full-blooded New York Jew'. According to Tom Dowd, 'Essentially The Dixie Flyers would go on to become Kris Kristofferson's band. But while they were in Miami, they were a red-hot funk outfit.'" Jerry Wexler

Tom Dowd and Jerry Wexler (centre) with The Dixie Flyers: (from left) Tommy McClure, Mike Utley, Sammy Creason, Charlie Freeman and Jim Dickinson TL: 70s

Jerry Wexler with Aretha Franklin TL: 70s

"Aretha has made a fantastic impact on American culture. She has always had absolute integrity, stayed true to her roots, and her raw vitality and honesty have won her universal acceptance. The songs she's chosen or written are loosely but significantly autobiographical. If she couldn't feel it, forget it; if she didn't live it, she can't give it. She would never play the part of the scorned woman: she wouldn't beg her man to come back, no matter what. Her middle name is 'Respect'. She devoted an enormous piece of her life to Martin Luther King, yet she never became merely a sloganeer or polemicist. She acted out of the purest wellsprings of faith and belief. To hear her sing 'Precious Lord', the hymn she recorded as a teenager, at King's funeral service in 1968, was to witness what Yeats called 'a terrible beauty', a holy blend of truth and unspeakable tragedy. In the years we recorded together, I never heard Aretha utter a racist remark. She could enjoy and identify with modern rock, show tunes and pop ballads. She was always culling albums for songs that might suit her. She didn't think in terms of white or black tunes, or white or black rhythms. Her taste, like her genius, has always transcended categories." Jerry Wexler

"Aretha's background vocalists could be her sisters, or they could be the Sweet Inspirations, or they could be her group, which she called the Sweethearts of Soul. In any case, they would be at home, relaxing, watching TV, maybe eating some soul food, talking about shopping and this and that. And then they'd say, 'Let's rehearse this passage.' So while they're sitting around, they would go, *together, forever, da da da da* … And they would do that over and over. Then they'd watch a little more TV, have a good time, and then they would rehearse again and again. It was sort of a communal affair, and then all of a sudden the background arrangement was done – and it was so solid that there were no mistakes. So when they came to the studio, it was ready. So Aretha works with backgrounds, in a relaxed atmosphere at home, everything fun and musical. Then you just bring that in and put it on record." Arif Mardin

The Sweet Inspirations, from left: Cissy Houston, Myrna Smith, Sylvia Shemwell and Estelle Brown TL: 60s 70s

256 THE ATLANTIC STORY

From left: Carl Palmer, Greg Lake and Keith Emerson TL: 70s

Below: Emerson, Lake & Palmer on stage TL: 70s

"ELP were a very avant-garde group. The first things I heard by them sounded extremely way out, but it turned out they had a growing audience for that music and they did very well. Keith Emerson is an especially talented keyboard player and was very, very far ahead of his contemporaries at that time, particularly in playing electronic instruments." Ahmet

"Actually, what surprised us was that Atlantic, which we knew as a soul label, was willing to risk taking on a white European band which was, I suppose, quite critically categorized as playing pseudo-classical-jazz-rock. Atlantic desperately wanted to label our music before the critics did. However, the media finally had their go, and in frustration, I guess, they gave up – choosing the easy way by just about damning everything we did. To our surprise, Atlantic released 'Lucky Man' as the first single. That put us on the spot, because Greg had over-dubbed all the vocal harmonies and people probably expected another Crosby, Stills & Nash. But we sang it so badly together on stage, deaf people refused to read our lips. Actually, we got off lightly when Greg sang it solo and accompanied himself on acoustic guitar and carpet." Keith Emerson

Above and below: Stephen Stills TL: 70s

"Stephen Stills made a lot of records on his own. He's an artist who really should still be making solo records today, because he's a very special kind of guitar player. As opposed to the British guitar players, who play in the style of black musicians they listened to, Stephen has his own original style of playing. He's also very much into black music and he can play the blues, but his blues have got a bit of a country tinge to them. He's a natural musician, a great singer, and a very good songwriter. He wrote 'Love The One You're With' in his hotel room when we were both staying at the Plaza Athene Hotel in Paris. He later married a very famous French singer, Veronique Sanson. In the late nineties we signed their son, Chris Stills, to Atlantic.

"Once, when Stephen was recording in London, the night before one of the sessions, I think he'd gotten drunk in a West Indian bar and he ended up hiring the drummer and the bass player from the band that was playing in the club. Jimi Hendrix was also a great friend of Stephen's, so the next night he had Hendrix and Eric Clapton playing with him in the studio. They had already laid down the rhythm track with the drummer and the bass player from the club, and the three guitarists were doing overdubs. I was sitting in the control room with these two cats that Steve Stills had picked up the night before. One of them looked at me and said, 'Are you with the record company?' I said, 'Yeah.' He said, 'Who are those guys?' I figured maybe they'd heard of them, so I said, 'That's Jimi Hendrix.' They had no idea who that was, and they certainly did not know Clapton or Stephen Stills. He pointed to Steve and said, 'Well, that cat was in the club last night.' Then they looked at me and one of them said, 'Are we going to get paid?' I said, 'Yeah, you're going to get paid.' You can imagine how great the music was. Those are unforgettable moments." Ahmet

"Roberta Flack is a fantastic jazz singer. 'The First Time Ever I Saw Your Face' is a seven-minute piece and a great song. Due to its being featured in the Clint Eastwood movie, *Play Misty For Me*, she had a hit, and immediately stepped into pop music – so great! Instead of only playing in clubs all her life, she has hit records and obviously, for her, that's wonderful. That's what we want – for her to enjoy her art and her music.

"Joel Dorn and I co-produced an album by Roberta Flack and Donny Hathaway. The day of that last session, the percussionist Ralph McDonald and his partner gave us a song called 'Where Is The Love?' – interesting title. We cut the track with the minimum number of people – bass, drums, and piano – and then Roberta and Donny forgot about it. Right at the end of the session, Joel and I said, 'Aren't you going to do this song?' So they sang their parts, I added the orchestra, and it became like a stepchild, that song." Arif Mardin

Donny Hathaway TL: 70s

"I remember after we finished recording 'Where Is The Love?', we were playing it in the office. And this is what a fantastic record man I am – I was trying to get this song off the record because I just did not like it, but all the secretaries kept saying, 'Boy, that's a smash!' I'm saying, 'What's a smash?!' They're all telling me that 'Where Is The Love?' is gonna be a smash. Well, when you get to your ninth secretary saying the same thing, you know your market testing programme is over. They're jumping up and down saying, 'Boy – if my boyfriend only knew …' That record really struck a chord. There's not an elevator or a dentist's office where you don't hear that song." Joel Dorn

Roberta Flack TL: 70s

Above: Aretha Franklin and, below, with Ray Charles TL: 70s

"I thought that the musical taste of the kids was very limited and watered down, but I was wrong, and two occasions in particular proved that to be the case. One was the way they responded to Otis Redding at Monterey, and the other was the way they responded to Aretha Franklin live at the Fillmore West. These kids were hot, they picked up on every shade and nuance. They were among the best audiences I've ever seen." Jerry Wexler

"Somebody told me that Aretha was singing at this club. Of course I love Aretha, so I thought, well, maybe I'll drift by there. My intention was to go by there, be inconspicuous and sit way in the back. I didn't want to bother nobody, I just wanted to hear the music, maybe stay for half an hour, and then leave. Well, it didn't work that way – somebody spotted me and told her, and Aretha came down into the audience and got me. Well, if Aretha Franklin comes to you, what are you going to do? If she says, come on, you're going to go, I mean, it's not likely that I'm not going to go! So I went up there and I said, 'Now what are we going to do?' She said, 'Well, you just follow me.' That's all it was, really, just follow me and get with this. I'm very happy that it worked out good, because we got a nice record out of it, but believe me, it was very, very far away from my intentions, and had it not been Aretha Franklin, it wouldn't have happened at all, because I wouldn't have done it. But I love her so much." Ray Charles

"The Fillmore West was certainly a high point in my career, and it was absolutely one night to remember. The building itself I guess held about 5,000 people, but there must have been about ten thousand people in there. They were screaming and they were quite an enthusiastic audience!" Aretha Franklin

Joni Mitchell

David Geffen

"I really owe everything to Ahmet. He is, for me, quite simply the greatest music man of all time, and I'll always love him." David Geffen

"I suggested to David Geffen that he start his own label and Atlantic would be his partner. We put up the money, and in quick succession he signed up The Eagles, Jackson Browne, Joni Mitchell and J.D. Souther, among others. The Asylum label, as we called it, became the hot new boutique label – very special, with very, very good taste, and lots of hits. By this time, we'd sold our company to Warners which had recently bought Elektra Records, which did well under its founder, Jac Holzman. Then Jac decided to retire and I suggested to Steve Ross, who was then chairman of Warners, that David would be the ideal person to run Elektra. So we gave David and Asylum to Elektra, and they, of course, had one tremendous success after another." Ahmet

The Eagles, from left: Bernie Leadon, Randy Meisner, Don Henley and Glenn Frey

Jackson Browne

MC5, from left: Fred 'Sonic' Smith, Dennis Thompson, Wayne Kramer, Rob Tyner and Michael Davis TL: 70s

"Fred Smith and I started playing guitars together, must have been in the tenth grade – in '64 we played in a lot of rival bands. Then we ended up in the same band together and we met Rob Tyner, Dennis Thompson and Michael Davis and we all moved away from home together. We were all getting to be 16, 17. We moved to the beatnik neighbourhood. That's where we met John Sinclair – the archetypal beatnik poet. John was a little older, a little better educated than we were, and seemed to be able to relate to everybody. We decided he should manage the MC5.

"When we started out me and Fred used to say I was the lead player and I played all the solos. And Fred Smith was a genius rhythm guitar player. But after a while, Fred's technique developed so well that we didn't draw the distinction anymore. He was a one-of-a-kind original. Later, the more we started writing, and when he started writing his own songs and guitar breaks, he had his own whole musical vocabulary." Wayne Kramer

"The extent of our relation to politics was the high-energy intensity of it. And when we were 18 or 19, we wanted to take over the world. We wanted the world to be the way we saw it. We didn't relate to convention." Fred "Sonic" Smith

Led Zeppelin, TL: 70s; from left: Jimmy Page, John Paul Jones and Robert Plant receiving gold discs from Mr. Anthony Grant MP

"'Immigrant Song': that's a voice at the beginning, incidentally, which somebody said was a wailing guitar. On stage this number has already developed into a much longer thing, with full instrumental passages. The hiss at the beginning is a tape build-up, then John Bonham comes in. It's not really tape hiss, it's echo feed-back. Robert wrote the lyrics to this one.

"'Friends': again Robert wrote the words. He did them all except 'Tangerine'. The idea was to get an Indian style with the strings. The string players were not Indian, however, and we had to make on-the-spot changes. John Paul Jones wrote an incredible string arrangement for this and Robert shows his great range – incredibly high. He's got a lot of different sides to his voice which come across here. It has a menacing atmosphere. A friend came into the studio during the recording and it was bloody loud and he had to leave. He said: 'You've really done something evil!' Moog synthesizer at the end, and that's bottle-neck string bass with John Paul playing.

Robert Plant, Jimmy Page and John Bonham

"'Celebration Day': the reason his voice is alone is the tape got crinkled in the studio and wouldn't go through the heads so the ends got ruined, but it worked out all right by using the idea of bringing the synthesizer down in pitch to the voice. It was either that or leave the track out altogether. Why 'Celebration'? It's saying, 'Im happy,' that's all.

"'Since I've Been Loving You': this was a 'live' track. John Paul plays organ and foot bass pedals at the same time. My guitar solo? It could have been better, but, y'know. You are never satisfied with a performance, although of course there are those lucky musicians who can play it perfect every time. On these type of numbers, John decided his own drum beat to play. We might occasionally suggest the use of conga drums on a particular number, but he always fixes his own beat.

"'Out On The Tiles': this is Bonzo's riff. Originally we had a set of lyrics to go with this relating to a night out on the tiles.

"'Gallows': a traditional song which stems from Leadbelly. I first found it by Fred Gerlac. He was one of the first white people on Folkways Records to get involved with Leadbelly. We have completely rearranged it and changed the verse. Robert wrote a set of new lyrics. That's John Paul on mandolin and bass and I'm playing the banjo, six-string acoustic, 12-string and electric guitar. The bloke swinging on the gallows is saying wait for his relatives to arrive. The drumming builds nicely.

"'Tangerine': that's commonly known as a false start. It was a tempo guide, and it seemed like a good idea to leave it in at the time. I was trying to keep the tempo down a bit. I'm not so sure now if it was a good idea. Everybody asks what the hell is going on. I did the pedal steel guitar and Robert did the harmonies as well as lead.

"'That's The Way': this was written in Wales, where Robert and I stayed at a cottage. It was one of those days after a long walk and we were heading back to the cottage. We had a guitar with us. It was a tiring walk coming down a ravine, and we stopped and sat down. I played the tune and Robert sang a verse straight off. We had a tape recorder with us (that sounds a bit strange, but it was part of the kit) and we got the tune down. This wasn't recorded in Wales, if I gave that impression. The 'Los Paraguyos' bit is the mandolin.

Robert Plant

"'Bron-Y-Aur Stomp': that's an acoustic bass. It's like an acoustic guitar with a reasonable body. John Paul took the frets out and he plays it acoustically. This has got the rattling of the kitchen sink – we've got everything on it! We over-dubbed Bonham on castanets, and spoons.

"'Hats Off To (Roy) Harper': there's that freaky echo. The voice sounds like that because it went through a vibrato amp. This came out of a jam Robert and I had one night. There's a whole tape of us bashing different blues things. Robert had been playing harmonica through the amp then he used it to sing through. It's supposed to be a sincere hats off to Roy because he's really a talented bloke, who's had a lot of problems.

"I like the song 'Gallows Pole'. But there are others – the point is we had 17 tracks to choose from to put on the album. Some were written out at the cottage. Some show different stages of development.

"There was a lot that was pretty powerful. John Paul Jones wrote a piece which was all piano, which would have related to what's coming up in the future. This album was to get across more versatility and use more combinations of instruments.The next one will be just one long track on one side with these combinations of instruments, mandolin, banjo and so on. It will last about 25 minutes with instrumental sections. It's still in the planning stages.

"We'll never stop doing the heavy things, because that comes out naturally when we play. But there is another side to us. The new album is totally different from the others and I see that it's obviously a new direction.

"The fourth album should be our best, and if it isn't, well, we might as well give up and retire with red faces. I haven't read any more of the reviews but people have to give the LP a reasonable listening.

"Everybody in the band is going through some changes. There are changes in the playing and in the lyrics. Robert is really getting involved in his lyric writing.

"It was my idea to have a revolving wheel as part of the cover on Led Zeppelin III. I remembered those old gardening catalogues. You'd turn it to 'roses' and find out what kind of manure to use. There's a lot more to see on the wheel. When you get fed up with the LP there is the added pleasure of ripping the cover apart to find out what's on the rest of the sleeve." Jimmy Page

Robert Plant and Jimmy Page TL 70s

The Rolling Stones signing party at the Canto Club House, Cannes TL: 70s From left: Mick Taylor, Eddie Barclay, Mick Jagger, Ahmet, Keith Richards, Charlie Watts, Bill Wyman.

"I'd met Ahmet in the sixties with Phil Spector, and he already was a semi-legendary figure. I always liked him, but we had this long-running contract with Decca Records. So when we were shopping around for a new Rolling Stones record deal, he was one of the people who wanted to sign the band." Mick Jagger

"I arrived in L.A. early one morning, attended many meetings and, late in the day, was informed that Mick Jagger wanted to talk to me. We arranged to rendezvous that night at the Whiskey, where Chuck Berry was playing. After several drinks, jet lag was taking its toll, and by the time Mick showed up I was slowing down. Chuck was blaring away and Mick was sitting next to me saying, 'The reason I wanted to see you, Ahmet, is because our contract is up, and … ' – but by then I had dozed off. Someone kept shaking me – 'This is important, Ahmet, wake up, wake up' – but I'm afraid I kept nodding off while Mick was saying how interested The Stones were in Atlantic, a label they had long admired. My insouciance served me well, you see, because Mick loathes pushy people. He loved the fact that I fell asleep in his face. He finds indifference intoxicating. The next day he came to my hotel and put it simply: 'We don't want to shop around. We want to be on Atlantic.'" Ahmet

From left: Eddie Barclay, Mick Jagger, Ahmet, Keith Richards, Bill Wyman and Mick Taylor

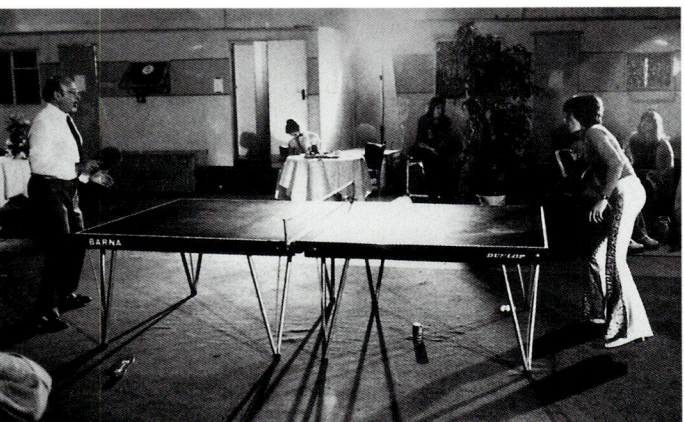

Ahmet and Bill Wyman

"I never went on a whole tour with the Stones, but I'd arrive for various dates. I introduced them to The J. Geils Band who supported them on one of those U.S. tours. Then J. Geils became a huge band in their own right. I'd known the Stones since the sixties, from those first years when there was this great feeling in the air, that seemed to come especially from that early British renaissance crowd – The Beatles, The Stones, The Who – I mean so many wonderful artists and characters. Keith Moon was a great friend of mine, he was a fabulous drummer, and one of the most charming and fun people I've ever known. He, Jimi Hendrix and I used to ride around London and hang out a lot together – those were great times." Ahmet

"*Exile On Main Street* is a very important album for us. We'd had to leave England, we were at a bit of a low point and had a lot of tax problems. So certainly as much as ever, a good album was an absolute must for us. We figured the best way to make it would be to hole up somewhere and just do it. So we found this great house on Cap Ferrat near Ville Franche, rented it for a couple of months and set up a recording studio in the basement. We had to put huge commercial electric cables across the patios and in through the windows – somewhat unsightly for a posh Riviera villa. Villefranche was a little pirate harbour – one of the deepest in the Mediterranean – so there were all these Russian, American and French warships anchored there on manoeuvres. Then on the other hand we also had Onassis, Agnelli, and their kind of yachts in the bay as well. I bought a speedboat and started zooming around, buzzing the destroyers in particular. A lot of people came to visit, there was a fair share of mayhem going on most of the time, but in amongst it all we managed to come up with the goods." Keith Richards

Clockwise from top left: Anita Pallenberg and Ahmet; the album Exile On Main Street*; Ian Stewart (the piano-playing "sixth Stone"); Mick Jagger, Keith Richards and Charlie Watts on stage in Paris TL: 70s*

"We recorded the Soul To Soul Festival in Ghana, which Wilson Pickett headlined with Ike and Tina Turner, Roberta Flack, Eddie Harris, Les McCann, The Staples Singers and Santana.

I remember once Ike and Tina Turner were playing at Ciro's on Sunset Boulevard in L.A. and I walked in during the middle of the show. Tina was performing with these beautiful girl back-up singers. When I walked down the steps towards the stage, she stopped singing and said, 'Here comes my boyfriend!' After the show Ike and Tina came over and sat with me and Tina turned to me and said, 'You know, this is not the Ike and Tina Turner Revue, this is a travelling bordello.'"
Ahmet

Ike Turner and top, Tina Turner TL: 70s

Wilson Pickett TL: 70s

The Persuaders, including: Charles Stodghill, James B.J.Barnes, Douglas 'Smokey' Scott, Willie Holland TL: 70s

"I didn't really want 'Clean Up Woman' to come out, because it wasn't finished. I never did get the middle verse from Clarence Reid, because Clarence behaved like a true Aquarian – he wrote the song, did part of it, then left and never came back to give us the middle verse. So you hear me just going *do-do-do-do* while the guitar is running – that's probably the secret to the success of the song, because it made the guitar so important. All three guitar parts were played by Willie 'Little Beaver' Hale, and the bass guitar was played by Ron Bogdon. They were like an in-house rhythm section that played on just about everything that came out of the TK studio at the time. Ron Bogdon was another little white guy who was too soulful, and Little Beaver kept coming up with one guitar part after another and we left them all on there. It was like the only thing to fill up the eight tracks. I never got to learn the song. If you listen real well, you'll hear the paper rattling in the background. I was reading the words and I just read what was on there. I talked the whole record, it's not even singing – there's not even a melody! I tell everybody, I get more hits when I don't sing!" Betty Wright

Clarence Reid

Betty Wright TL: 70s

King Curtis TL: 70s

"King Curtis was one of the finest people I have ever known in my life. He was just as sweet and kind as a man can be. He was also a great artist. The first time I heard him play was in a little club on 8th Avenue, and he just sounded so great, his tone was so big, and he played so beautifully. I said, 'My God! This is the man we need for our records, we've got to get him!' He was really just superior to anyone else around in playing rhythm and blues. He'd come up to New York from Texas with his band The King Pins, which Jimi Hendrix joined at one point for a short spell. Of course, Hendrix soon went off on his own to England and started recording and breaking it up there. King Curtis was like a father figure to all of the other musicians. They all respected him not just for his playing and musical direction, but because he was a monumental person – when he walked into a room, it was like joy had walked into the room. Then the tragedy occurred – he became the victim of one of these absolutely insane killings. He'd bought a house on West 72nd Street, in what was a very expensive, supposedly safe, area. He was just standing in front of the stoop of his house when this complete stranger came up to him, started arguing and shouting at him, then pulled out a gun and shot him. It was a terrible tragedy for all of us. Noreen Woods was very close to him, as was Aretha. Everybody was a great friend of his; you can see something of how wonderful he was in his pictures – his smile – and in his music. We miss him, we really miss him." Ahmet

Aretha Franklin, with above from left: Brenda Corbett, Carolyn Franklin and Margaret Branch, and below with Reverand James Cleveland on piano and backing from the Southern California Community Choir TL: 70s

"My dad was there that night, Clara Ward was there as well. Of course, I had sung in church when I'd come back home to Detroit, but I hadn't recorded anything of that magnitude in church for, I guess, about eight or nine years. There's just a feeling you get there that you don't get anywhere else. Having gone to Europe and all the way around the world, to come home and to be in church is just a feeling that I really can't describe to you."
Aretha Franklin

Mr and Mrs John Prine TL: 70s

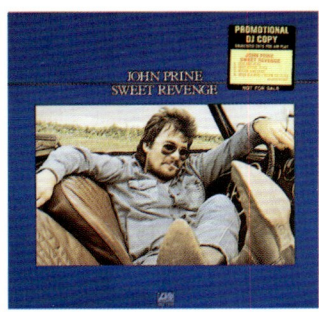

"John Prine is a very, very important folk artist. We released his debut album in 1971, and he made several other wonderful records for us." Ahmet

"A tree had fallen on the sign outside the concert hall and my name was kinda dangling there, so poetic. The sound man had walked off because a tree had fallen on his house, so I guess he had decided it wasn't worth doing a sound check. And literally the first two rows were filled and that was it. I was angry and depressed, but there was this large, fat woman, who must have been 65 years old, in the middle of the front row, and it was like God had put her there. I played the whole show for her, and the other 25 people joined in – it was a great show, because she was willing. This was her night out, and goddamn it, she was going to have a good time." Loudon Wainwright III

Loudon Wainwright III TL: 70s

"Manassas was actually supposed to have gone back to more of a Buffalo Springfield sound, but to me it's all been kind of seamless. Manassas had a pedal steel guitar player, as well as Chris Hillman, who could play the fuck out of a mandolin – so the band did have a bit more of a traditional country approach. But the pedal steel guy could also play rock'n'roll on his instrument, which scared me to death!" Stephen Stills

Stephen Stills and Manassas TL: 70s

Manassas, from left: Dallas Taylor, Joe Lala, Steve Stills, Calvin 'Fuzzy' Samuels, Chris Hillman, Al Perkins and Paul Harris TL: 70s

"'Roundabout' was a song that we wrote in Scotland. Travelling from Aberdeen to Glasgow, you go through this beautiful valley with the mountains rising sheer from the road right up into the sky, but we couldn't see the top because it was all cloudy, so the mountains seemed to come out of the sky. That was the idea of the lyric. Then we went past Loch Lomond and the lakes, and within 24 hours we were home in London – so that was the basic premise of 'Roundabout'." Jon Anderson

Yes, from left: Steve Howe, Patrick Moraz, Jon Anderson, Chris Squire and Alan White TL: 70s

"The Art Ensemble of Chicago is an historic jazz group."
Ahmet

Art Ensemble of Chicago, from left: Roscoe Mitchell, Don Moye, Lester Bowie, Malachi Favors Magoustous and Joseph Jarman TL: 70s

Atlantic In Paris — PICTURES FROM THE 1973 25TH ANNIVERSARY SALES MEET

JAC HOLZMAN, left, president of Elektra, who attended the convention, with Atlantic president Ahmet Ertegun, and executive vice president, Jerry Wexler.

ATLANTIC EXECUTIVES, Nesuhi and Ahmet Ertegun, and Jerry Wexler, with, second from right, Joel Friedman, WEA president who received two awards.

JERRY GREENBERG, second from left, senior vice president, general manager and Dave Glew, vice president marketng, present awards to Don England WEA-NY, left, and Vic Faraci, WEA-Chicago.

LEFT TO RIGHT Paul Johnson, r&b promotion, Dick Klein, popular promotion and Rick Willard, merchandising.

AHMET ERTEGUN and Wexler congratulate jazz saxophonist Johnny Griffin, one of the first artists to record for the label.

GREENBERG, taking time out as one of the Atlantic All Stars, playing for listening and dancing pleasure.

TOM DOWD, vice president engineering, left, and Wexler at the opening session.

LEFT TO RIGHT, Joel Dorn, vice president, Bob Rolontz, vice president, advertising, Dave Glew.

LEFT TO RIGHT Sheldon Vogel, vice president, Henry Allen, promotion vice president and Bob Kornheiser, vice president tape and one of the organizers of the convention.

ROBERT STIGWOOD, president RSO Records, congratulates the three Atlantic executives.

APRIL 28, 1973, BILLBOARD

Atlantic's 25th anniversary celebrations in Paris

"Our 25th anniversary was a very special event because we celebrated by taking everybody in the company to Paris for a four-day visit. One evening we had a wonderful concert with Johnny Griffin and Stephane Grappelli. We were 200 or so for the whole four days, and it was a great time." Ahmet

"I'd heard a lot about Bette Midler, this girl who was breaking it up at the Continental Baths and various other gay spots. So I decided I'd better hear her, check her out right away. The same week as I'd heard about her, she was having one of her first engagements in a club which was called Upstairs Downstairs, Downstairs at the Upstairs, or whatever. I'd gone to some charity dinner at the Plaza Hotel with my wife, Mica, and I said, 'I've got to go hear this girl and she goes on around 11 o'clock.' So we left the dinner and went a few blocks downtown to Upstairs Downstairs, and the place was jammed.

"She had this little trio – Barry Manilow was her piano player – and they were definitely swinging. She was singing a lot of the old Ronettes songs, early rock'n'roll standards, and really breaking it up. She had everybody in stitches and got an incredible reaction. I've never seen people scream and yell and jump up and down in a little club like that. So I turned to my wife and said, 'Listen, if anybody gets this kind of reaction, there's no way she can't make it.' It was unbelievable. So after the show was over, we went back to Bette's dressing room and I told her if she wanted to she could sign with Atlantic straightaway. I had a contract ready the next morning and we signed her up that day. She'd already done some theatre. She'd been in a couple of shows on Broadway, but it's as a singer in nightclubs that she really came into her own. The first record she made was produced by Joel Dorn, but Barry Manilow and I had a lot to do with it as well, and we had a tremendous success with that album. We shared over 20 years of her great career with her." Ahmet

Above: Bette Midler with her piano player, Barry Manilow (left) and her manager, Aaron Russo (right)

Opposite, above and top right: Bette Midler TL: 70s

John Lee Hooker TL: 60s 70s

"I learned it all from my stepfather, Will Moore. He'd sing and play guitar for hours on end. When I was 11, 12, 13, I loved to listen to his music. He sounded like no one else. He took me one day and said, 'Look, son, this is the real, real blues. I want you to know that.' I always watched his tunings – open A, regular tunings, and I played them in all keys. I used to watch another guy called Tony Holland play, and Wes Montgomery. I sued to sit and watch him. Wes Montgomery, he says, 'John Lee Hooker, you my idol in the blues.' I go, 'You's my idol in jazz.'

"I don't know how songs come to me. I just get an idea and then all of a sudden I've got a song. I remember back in Detroit, I used to go to the Apex Bar every night after I got off work. The bartender there used to call me Boom Boom. I don't know why, but he did. One night, I walked in and he said, 'Boom Boom, you're late.' I said to myself, 'That sounds like a song.' I left Mississippi when I was 14 years old. I didn't want to be a farmer. I wanted to be a musician. I set out to go north, went to Memphis and then to Detroit. I was playing house parties and stuff like that. I had a day job to survive. I was an usher in a theatre showing people to their seats, and I worked in steel mills, places like that. Then I got discovered by Elmer Barbee playing at night and on weekends. Blues definitely come from the country. People think the blues is the dollar but it's not, the blues is a feeling. You gotta be able to produce and deliver it with heart and soul. You can't write it on a piece of paper. I know that for me it was a born gifted talent. You talk about people, life experience. People hear the song they can relate to it, know what you're saying, what you're talking about. People think to play the blues you got to be livin' hard, starvin' to death. No, you ain't, that's ridiculous.

"If you can feel the blues, you can do it right. You got to feel the blues. I got everything: money, cars. I'm a happy man in every way. But when I play the blues, I play dirty and sad. I haven't had any money all my life. I was a poor kid with nothin', but I was happy 'cause I played my music – happy I could do it and deliver it to people." John Lee Hooker

Buddy Guy and Junior Wells TL: 70s

"Buddy Guy and Junior Wells. Eric Clapton, Tom Dowd, and I produced an album for them in the early seventies called *Buddy Guy And Junior Wells Play The Blues*. They're great players, and I love them both." Ahmet

Dr. John (a.k.a. Mac Rebennack) TL: 70s

"Shuffle rhythms are a straightforward rhythm changed to an eighth-note rhythm. That's what rock music is today. The difference between that and New Orleans rock is that instead of a bass drum going along with that, it becomes more syncopated. So that pattern going along with the eighth notes delivers the basic feel of New Orleans rhythm. In olden days, New Orleans rhythm was second line. You can turn that rhythm and play against it, add in the eighth-notes, a little syncopation, and you have up-to-date funk rhythms. Then by syncopating that, you've got any one of the Professor Longhair rhythms, or any one of the Meters rhythms, or you've got 'Iko, Iko' and the rhythms on *Gumbo*." Dr. John

Doug Sahm TL: 70s

"What Mac Rebennack is to New Orleans, Doug Sahm is to Texas. From Western swing to Lightnin' Hopkins's Houston Blues, from Tex-Mex ditties to polkas, Doug integrated it all and came out with something similar: his own sound on guitar, his own voice, his own songs. I also loved the irony of his calling his great sixties group The Sir Douglas Quintet – the Texan passing as a Brit to entice American ears. I was proud to produce an album documenting Sahm's soul, embracing everything from T-Bone Walker to Bob Wills. We recruited an eclectic bunch of sidemen – Dr. John, Bob Dylan, Arif Mardin on electric piano, conjunto accordionist Flaco Jiminez, and Fort Worth tenorman Fathead Newman, formerly with Ray Charles and long a star in his own right. The album, *Doug Sahm And Band*, didn't sell but I was defiant, proud of it, and determined to follow my bliss." Jerry Wexler

Jerry Wexler, Arif Mardin, Doug Sahm, Bob Dylan, Dr. John and other muscians at Muscle Shoals

Doug Sahm

"Willie's one of my heroes. He exudes love, and he also shares with Sinatra a gift for incredible vocal rubato – prolonging one note, cutting short another, swinging with an elastic sense of time that only the finest jazz singers understand. *Shotgun Willie*, his first album for us, included the title cut, Johnny Bush's 'Whiskey River' and 'Sad Songs And Waltzes' – all of which have become Nelson classics. For his second album, his blues were brilliantly conceptualized in a cohesive suite of songs. He called it *Phases And Stages* and – set against the rhythm section of Barry Beckett, David Hood, Roger Hawkins and Pete Carr – the album flowed from start to finish. We cut it in two days – the first side taking a woman's point of view on the highs and hurts of romance, the second seen through the eyes of a man. The album is a milestone, at least in my mind, of solid American music." Jerry Wexler

Top: Willie Nelson, and above, with Jerry Wexler TL: 70s

Eric Clapton and Tom Dowd

"We were recording Crosby, Stills & Nash in Miami, and Stephen bought a 52 ft sports boat. Somebody said, 'Eric's over in Nassau, let's break the boat in and go and see him.' So David is at the helm, they get through to Clapton on the ship-to-shore, and his lover Patti Boyd says she'll go out and wave a sheet to guide them in. Each of them trains his binoculars on the beaches, the ship-to-shore crackles and then explodes into life as Stephen yells, 'It's okay, Eric, we've spotted her, we'll be right there!' Then they hang up, and a few minutes later, they've gone right into the beach. I wouldn't say they were high, but they had burned the wheels right off a brand new 52 ft sports boat." Tom Dowd

Graham Nash, Stephen Stills and David Crosby TL: 70s

"Many of the English rock'n'rollers who began to emerge in the early sixties had been turned on to the blues by such fellow countrymen as Lonnie Donegan and Alexis Korner. A lot of American blues records were reissued in England, and there were a lot of collectors' music shops there. So these young guys grew up not only loving the blues, but learning to play the blues. They had, and still have, great blues collections. When I used to go to Keith Richards's house, that's all you'd hear all day long, the blues. Go to Eric Clapton's house, all you hear is the blues. It was a much more conscious effort to digest that music than Americans seem to have made, because Americans took it for granted and figured, 'Well, the blues is here, it's part of our country.' In the U.S., hillbillies were playing the blues, sometimes in a very corny way, but few young musicians have studied it in the way they did in England, and they really got it.

"What I think really upsets a lot of these bands is that, even though they think they're playing black music, they look out into the audience and there are almost no black faces. How come? Part of the reason is that, at least vocally, the music they're playing doesn't come out the way black music would; it's reinterpreted. The guitar players could go to Mississippi and hide their faces and play, and people would think they're black. But the singers, by definition, have to interpret what it is they're doing. But the main reason there are few black faces out there is that even in the early sixties black music had gone somewhere else, and in the black community the blues was a music which, even in those days, was a music of the parents and the grandparents." Ahmet

Top: Mick Jagger and above, Magic Dick of The J. Geils Band TL: 70s

Left: Led Zeppelin and above: Robert Plant and Jimmy Page. TL: 70s

"Ahmet and Jerry started to get more white bands and singers at that time. That's when we got Led Zeppelin, and they never stopped selling. There was just some kind of intrigue. Zeppelin just kept going on and on and on." Fran Wakschal

Robert Plant

John Paul Jones and Jimmy Page

"There was a great mystique around Led Zeppelin that was created in part by the members of the group, especially Jimmy Page. But it was also created, in large part, by their manager Peter Grant. He was a man who was around six foot three, weighed 550 pounds, and had been a wrestler and strong man in circuses, and a fighter at carnivals who would take on all comers. He was an incredible character himself. And he kept this shroud of 'the unknown' around the group. He wouldn't let anybody get close to them for fear that they'd talk and disturb this huge aura of mystery. The band wouldn't do interviews and they wouldn't do television. As a result, when they got involved in all kinds of escapades, their antics were magnified by the press. They used to tear up hotel rooms, throw television sets out of the windows, have motorcycles in the hallway. There was a lot of other nonsense – for instance the Plaster Casters, these girls who came rolling in around the group. One girl would go down on the musician, 'til he got really wrecked, then another one would slap on the plaster, and they would make these plaster moulds of their favourite rock star. The band would order cases of Dom Perignon like there was no tomorrow and pop the corks into all kinds of weird places – it was just madness.

Robert Plant and Peter Grant

"They became legendary right away and they carried on that mystique throughout their existence. When they first appeared, there was an awful lot of resistance to them from the press. *Rolling Stone* dismissed them, whereas now their music is probably the most influential on young groups, on emerging bands. They're still the idols of young rock'n'rollers today. Songs like 'Kashmir' and 'Stairway To Heaven' are anthems. You know there's nothing like time to really bring out the truth of whether a song is good enough. You go back and play a record when there's no hype and it's either good or it isn't. They were the first band to want to approach a kind of no-name identity. They put out albums without any title or without their name on the cover or the spine. Of course, the more I told them that it was going to hurt record sales, the more records they sold." Ahmet

John Bonham

Jimmy Page TL: 70s

Bad Company below, and above from left: Boz Burrell, Paul Rogers, Simon Kirke and Mick Ralphs TL: 70s

"Bad Company came to us through Peter Grant, Led Zeppelin's manager. Right from the start they were obviously an incredible band, a phenomenal combination of talent. I'll never forget hearing that first record. It went platinum, it went big, it took off like gangbusters." Joel Dorn

"The guitarist said, 'How about calling it the James Gang?' and we said, 'Okay!' Of course, we lied about that over the years because that wasn't a very good story. We'd say Jesse James was our uncle to make it interesting." Jim Fox, Drummer

"Elvis Presley told me I should record LaVern Baker's R & B hit 'Jim Dandy', and you don't say no to the King of Rock and Roll." Jim 'Dandy' Mangrum TL: 70s

The James Gang TL: 70s

Chick Corea TL: 70s

"Since the tune had a soft quality, it reminded me of my wife, Joan. I wanted to dedicate it to her, but I didn't want a mushy title. I tend to veer away from the romantic in words. So I drove around all night trying to find a title, and 'Tones For Joan's Bones' is what finally emerged ... The more I listen, the more I find it difficult to confine what I enjoy to any kind of list. And I'd add that the more I listen to all kinds of musicians, the more I enjoy what I hear." Chick Corea

"I knew the Ertegun brothers, Nesuhi and Ahmet, even before they started their record business, operating from one small room in Manhattan. They loved and nurtured American music, and, in the dark days of the seventies when very little attention was being paid to jazz, Atlantic Records gave many of us a home base. Through Nesuhi's urging and support, I recorded the first two albums with my sons, and albums with Gerry Mulligan, Paul Desmond, Alan Dawson, Anthony Braxton, Jack Six and Roy Haynes, and, most incredibly, recorded 'Truth Is Fallen', my cantata for rock group, chorus and symphony orchestra. In other words, at Atlantic, one was free to follow the muse wherever it might lead." Dave Brubeck

Dave Brubeck TL: 70s

Carmen McRae TL: 70s

"Please believe me when I tell you that this session was one of the most gratifying of my musical experiences. I was surrounded by 'giants'. Not only can they 'play their ass off', but nicer cats are hard to find. It was a last-minute decision, on my part, to record with these guys. And for once in my life, I think I made a good one. Joe Pass, without a doubt, is the greatest living jazz guitarist. His accompaniment on 'What Are You Doing With The Rest Of Your Life?' completely wiped me out. Along with Jimmy Rowles, the guy every girl singer in her right mind would love to work with is Chuck Flores, a very competent drummer, and Chuck Domanico, who is a phenomenal bassist. I couldn't let that moment pass by without sharing it. I sincerely hope that jazz lovers agree with me. Whether you do or not, I love you all anyway." Carmen McRae

Billy Cobham TL: 70s

"What is life but a *Spectrum,* and what is music but life itself?" Billy Cobham

Genesis, clockwise from top left: Steve Hackett, Peter Gabriel, Tony Banks, Mike Rutherford and Phil Collins TL: 70s

"When we signed them, Genesis was a band which had a very small but very fervent following in America. With every release, we expected them to break bigger and bigger, and finally they did." *Ahmet*

Above and below: Genesis, with Peter Gabriel in costume

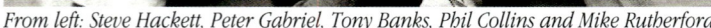

From left: Steve Hackett, Peter Gabriel, Tony Banks, Phil Collins and Mike Rutherford

THE ATLANTIC STORY 289

King Crimson, from left: David Cross, John Wetton, Bill Bruford and Robert Fripp TL: 70s

"In 1974 with King Crimson I wrote 'melodic music'. I wrote the ballad part in *Starless And Bible Black*. It was the fact that the track became longer and longer which made it a progressive piece but if you take that ballad part out of it, you get a song in its own right." John Wetton

David Cross

Robert Fripp

ELP, from left: Greg Lake, Carl Palmer and Keith Emerson TL: 70s

The Move Into Rock
By Robert Christgau

If Atlantic's standing as the greatest indie label of the fifties is unassailable, at least you can poke holes in it. Maybe, one could argue, the R & B canon isn't quite as lopsided as the Rock and Roll Hall of Fame says it is; perhaps, one might venture, the power and spontaneity of the Chess or Sun catalogues means more in the end than the scope and sophistication of Atlantic. What is beyond question, however, is that alone among its rivals, Atlantic negotiated the transition that the fifties imposed. Sun and Chess, King and Imperial, Duke and Vee-Jay, Speciality and Aladdin, Morris Levy's fronts and George Goldner's brainchildren – not one of these companies knew what to make of the black music of the sixties, much less the white. By contrast, Atlantic (and its subsidiaries – an essential codicil, as we'll see) was as crucial to Southern soul as Motown was to its Northern variant. And when we look back at white rock, its only real competition comes from Clive Davis's CBS group and Joe Smith and Mo Ostin's Warner-Reprise. Despite Beatles and Who one-offs, Atlantic missed out on Beatlemania, which meant no Kinks or Animals or Hollies – or Rolling Stones, yet. Despite a Boz Scaggs one-off, it skipped the Haight-Ashbury action as well. A little later, its attempts to cash in on singer-songwriterdom, unlike those of the briefly allied David Geffen, were not richly rewarded. Yet it was Atlantic's Cream who established Britain's long-term viability in the U.S. market, and Atlantic's Buffalo Springfield who foreshadowed the true future of California rock. The company also kick-started two vocally challenged guitar-strummers who sold sporadically but ended up writing more good songs than any New Dylan this side of Joni Mitchell herself: John Prine and Loudon Wainwright III. Atlantic's Southern loyalties netted it the seminal boogie of the Allman Brothers and the connubial roots-rock of Delaney & Bonnie. And Atlantic concealed among famously atrocious best sellers by Iron Butterfly and Vanilla Fudge a number of brilliant oddities that charted weakly or not at all, by Dusty Springfield and the Velvet Underground and Dr. John and the MC5 and the Insect Trust. There's a sense in which Atlantic's sixties achievement is more significant commercially than aesthetically. Whether or not Eric Clapton was God, Cream was at the forefront of many dubiously profitable pop trends: the power trio, the endless jam, the bad poet as worse lyricist, and, via the underdiagnosed Jack Bruce virus, the strained, melodramatic art-song vocals appropriated by so many arena-rock bands who lacked a Robert Plant. And the future of California rock is embodied by the real *Buffalo Springfield Again* (and Again), Crosby, Stills & Nash, whose postfolkie perfectionism sold better as its arrogance decayed into complacency and was still going platinum in 1982 – not to mention such relentless pickers and grinners as Poco, Loggins & Messina, and Atlantic's own Firefall, or the antiseptic studio-rock conventions defined by Linda Ronstadt.

But not only is this to insult the bottom-line stalwarts who have shored up thousands of honourably unprofitable pop ventures since the sixties turned every young jerk with a guitar into an artist-with-a-capital-A. It's also to put the worst possible face on Buffalo Springfield and Cream, both excellent bands, and overlook some even better ones. Second-generation Anglophilia ends up giving us *Layla* and *ZOSO* and *Exile On Main Street*, which you would not be astonished to hear a guitar maven of a certain age call the three greatest albums ever made. Whatever the ultimate importance of Steve Stills, Richie Furay, and Jim Messina, Buffalo Springfield gives us Neil Young, who turned CSN into CSNY at Atlantic before stretching into fecund unpredictability at Reprise. Working down from its guitar bands, Atlantic's early rock catalogue is not only a triumph of capitalism but a treasure house of durable music – so much so that you have to ask yourself how it came to be that the label of Aretha and Otis also put out as much good white rock in the hippie era as any other.

The obvious answer is one that reverberates through this book: Ahmet and Jerry, Ahmet and Jerry, Ahmet and Jerry. With all respect to hustling intermediaries from Ralph Peer and John Hammond to Berry Gordy and Seymour Stein, this was a combination like no other record company of any size or prominence has put on the floor. Over and above their individual gifts, their willingness to work as a team, while merely strengthening their label in the R & B days, was essential to their rock success. The indie world of the forties and fifties was a fraternity of wise guys who enjoyed each other's company even as they stabbed each other in the back. They entered occasional alliances, but except for a few brother combos, preferred to act alone. For *bon vivant* record collector Ahmet Ertegun to make the equally quick and charismatic trade-reporter-turned-song-plugger Jerry Wexler his partner, especially in a label already up and running, evinced a rare confidence that Wexler turned out to share. These men never felt threatened by intelligence, talent, or taste. In addition to assembling a loyal staff of the highest quality, they regularly collaborated with such brilliant and often volatile characters as Jerry Leiber and Mike Stoller, Bert Berns and Phil Spector, Stax's Jim Stewart and Fame's Rick Hall, and Alston's Henry Stone. In rock, crucial outsiders include Brian Epstein crony Robert Stigwood, Ahmet's connection to Cream and the Bee Gees, Otis Redding's manager Phil Walden, Jerry's conduit to the Allmans; and the notorious partnership of Charlie Greene and Brian Stone, who brought the label first Sonny and Cher, then Buffalo Springfield, and finally Dr. John and Iron Butterfly.

Ahmet and Jerry weren't the only record men with smarts, ears, and a passion for music, although none of those virtues is a biz-given and Atlantic's principals were exceptionally well-endowed. But their aptitudes transcended the basics. Both were cultured men whose far-reaching appetite for music was complemented by interests in painting and literature and (in Ahmet's case) philosophy that extended well beyond it. So when they began courting hirsute artists-with-a-capital-A, they were neither taken aback nor doomed to offend. Relative to the music business if not the priesthood, they were known for integrity. It was the rare guitar-slinger who didn't fondly recall one or another of their R & B protégés. And classwise they could split the room with Jerry's street salt made to order for those mistrustful of Ahmet's aristocratic attentions and vice versa. As their act evolved, Jerry became more the music guy and Ahmet more the biz guy, Jerry the go-getter and Ahmet the charmer, but each could don the other hat at the drop of one. Jerry's role as the emotional roots guy and Ahmet's as the playful pop guy were more permanent. But both shared an active interest in making good records and good money. And so they did. Starting with the classiest of the Italian teen idols, Bobby Darin, whose shifting artistic requirements brought Ahmet into the Los Angeles studio world, and working through various pre-Beatle Brits who made nowhere near as big a splash, Atlantic had recognized that white teenagers would never limit themselves to the black pop that was its lifeblood. But only in 1965, after losing the Who, did they make their breakthrough – when genuine teenager Cher and her 30-year-old husband Sonny Bono, a dogged hustler with what Atlantic's Bon Rolontz calls "an incredible ability to grab nothing and turn it into something real," somehow convinced folk-besotted American teenyboppers they were its ideal couple, a masquerade good for seven Top 20 singles in under two years. Not long after, Jerry located and Ahmet landed deeply gifted Italian-Irish R & B group The (Young) Rascals, whose memorable skein of pop-soul *tour de force* would finally bog down in psychedelica in late 1968. But by then everything else had changed anyway, and Atlantic was in the middle of it. As crucial as any strictly musical development was a corporate cataclysm that had the long-term effect of rigidifying a productive yin-and-yang. It was Jerry who pushed to sell the label to Warners in 1967 for $17.5 million, which wasn't enough by half if they should have sold at all. But it was Ahmet who thrived among the captains of finance. It's as if Ahmet's relationship to music was like Duchamp's to art – he was so good at it that he got a little bored, preferring high-stakes games of boardroom chess instead. Jerry, on the other hand, stuck more and more stubbornly with the more and more Southern music he knew and loved, which had its own downside; as roots genres slowed to a crawl, his tastes stopped growing, so that Chic, Atlantic's most significant post-soul black-music act, was Ahmet's project. During the hippie era, however, these tendencies were only starting to surface, as the challenge of outsiders looking over their shoulders energized both men. The 1967-1972 period was as rich musically as any six years in the company's history except perhaps 1954-1959. And in 1967-1972 the achievement ranged from Aretha to Led Zep.

So many years on, it's hard to remember, much less imagine, what it was like to encounter this stuff without benefit of hindsight. The records are encrusted in legend and nostalgia,

their historical context and raw sonic identity obscured by layers of accrued status. So try to project what it might have been like for what are now clichés to be so new that they seemed thrilling or perilous, intrinsically progressive or hopelessly misconceived or, even more confusing, sometimes one and sometimes the other – sometimes revolutionary, sometimes just plain fucked up. Like, for instance, the idea that songs on the radio could be couched in darkly poetic language and address social or spiritual issues. Or the idea that people would pay to hear pop musicians improvise on their instruments. Or the idea that rock'n'roll spearheaded a cultural vanguard destined to change the world – for the better.

Ahmet and Jerry mainly worried about whether Cream and the Bee Gees, Led Zeppelin and Iron Butterfly, Dr. John and Delaney & Bonnie, Steve Stills and John Prine, Mott the Hoople and Emerson, Lake & Palmer would make good records, with quality defined in more abstruse technical terms than many artists or almost any consumer would accept, and whether the records would turn a profit. But for those on the receiving end, every release was fraught with cultural unknowns and ideological imponderables. Were the Bee Gees pop poets like The Beatles? Like Donovan? Like the Strawberry Alarm Clock? Was it possible they had more to say than Jack Bruce's buddy Peter Brown? Were Buffalo Springfield's missteps and disjunctures artistic strategies? Was Iron Butterfly heavy? Was Vanilla Fudge even heavier? Did heavy actually mean ponderous? Dull-witted? Did Led Zeppelin's Nordic mysticism prefigure the rise of a ponderous barbarism? A dull-witted barbarism? Were endless drum solos forever? Was CSNY's commitment to song form put on earth to save us from said solos? Had ex-Yardbird/Mayall/Cream Eric Clapton found his place in life as Delaney Bramlett's sideman? And just exactly what race did Dr. John belong to anyway? On and on the conundrums went, and because they were good for business, Atlantic felt no obligation to clear them up for us. But certain facts did emerge at the time, and certain judgements crystallized early and evolved. Despite 1967's haunting 'For What It's Worth', remarkable as a hit single about police brutality however murky its meaning and self-regarding its vision of oppressed "young people speaking their minds", Buffalo Springfield never achieved the commercial recognition of Quicksilver Messenger Service, much less Jefferson Airplane. With the third album scattered and the debut hoisted on Greene and Stone's belief that Richie Furay was the band's most saleable vocalist (he sings three of Young's five compositions), the grandiose, songful, band-produced *Buffalo Springfield Again* is the consensus masterpiece, although it's a little too ungainly for that. Ahmet co-produced two tracks by Stills, for whom he clearly harbours special affection. (Even now he regrets never recording the band during their long 1966 residency at New York's Ondine.) Despite Stills's Al Kooper-Mike Bloomfield supersessions and creditable solo debut, *Buffalo Springfield Again* is certainly the best use of his moody, blues-tinged vocal intensity and quick, strong guitar. Song form made a comeback soon enough, but we can see now that the comeback was inevitable without them. The Bee Gees had already proved it with pseudo-meaningful hit singles, and after descending into their own psychedelic morass would prove it again with the candidly meaningless froth of *Main Ingredient*, produced by Atlantic's Arif Mardin before Robert Stigwood took his stable and John Travolta to Polydor. And the Velvet Underground would prove it in their radically distinct, equally prescient way on 1970's *Loaded*, an Ahmet sign-off recorded at Atlantic's historic 1861 Broadway studio.

Cream retired in premature disarray and some disrepute in 1968. Eric Clapton, Jack Bruce and Ginger Baker, who had never gotten along to begin with, were among the first to discover how wearying the hard-touring superstar life could be. Scathing reviews in *Rolling Stone* of a Boston concert written by Jon Landau in May, and of the half-live double-LP *Wheels Of Fire* by Jann Wenner in July, blamed rock's premier concert virtuosos for the long-winded showmanship of a musical concept that had barely existed two years before, and rarely has Clapton soloed so freely or vacuously since. But the band's flaws seem totally forgivable now that they're recognized as such. Once you accept Bruce's renderings of the 'White Room' and 'Tales Of Brave Ulysses' as the opaque wordsound clusters they are and cherry-pick the posthumous live solos, you can hone in on a fierce three-man shoot-out that blistered in the studio (at its purest on *Fresh Cream*) and could rock out live (as in *Wheels Of Fire*'s 'Crossroads', *Goodbye*'s 'I'm So Glad'). Sure, Hendrix was really God, but he never conjoined a trinity like this. Even later with Blood Ulmer or Living Colour you won't find such explosive chemistry, roiling all the more violently under the pressure of the pop formulas Cream was obliged to respect.

Cream

Baker and especially Bruce remained active, often in far more jazz-like or avantish contexts than Cream fans would have tolerated, as Bruce's art-rock and Baker's big band showed Atlantic quickly enough. But all that freedom spooked Clapton into permanent neotraditionalism, and up against love trauma and drug struggles he soon made the strongest music of his life out of the reaction. Between the summer of 1969 and the summer of 1970 he found his legs surviving the abortive Blind Faith supergroup, backing Delaney & Bonnie on a tour that soon spawned a live album, and venturing a Bramlett-produced solo debut, the first test of the J.J. Cale/Don Williams whisper that cured his fear of singing. The triumph of this technique came with 1974's *461 Ocean Boulevard*, where a rueful, tender sensuality permeated some of the subtlest blues derivatives ever recorded. But well before that Clapton poured everything he'd learned (including some stuff he'd later forget) into 1970's *Layla*, where he and a rhythm section that had jilted Delaney & Bonnie for their famous sideman were joined by none other than Jerry's prize discovery, the chord-busting slide-master Duane Allman. Allman had already strutted his stuff with Wilson Pickett, Aretha Franklin, and the crowning moment ('Loan Me A Dime') of that Boz Scaggs one-off, as well as arraying his blues-plus against Dickey Betts's bluegrass-plus on the Allman Brother's debut (to be followed before year's end by *Idlewild South* and then the defection of Walden's Capricorn to Warners proper). But Derek and the Dominos would see the Allmans and double them. In two weeks of inspired excess, this makeshift band (which would tour with Bramlett taking Allman's parts) did nothing less than hammer out a rock'n'roll monument. Fusing the following ease of Southern boogie with the contained chaotic tension of Cream, *Layla* showcases the first and best rock singing of Clapton's career as it achieves a joyful twin-guitar transcendence that has never been equalled. In company terms, it's the union of Jerry's gumbo and grit with Ahmet's flair and flash, with the two principals, Allman the redneck virtuoso and Clapton the blues-crazy English fop, confounding such schematic dichotomies as naturally as Ahmet and Jerry themselves. Yet for all that it could be argued that Derek and the Dominos weren't Cream's greatest progeny – nor Atlantic's most quintessential coup. For if any power trio vies with Cream, it's the guitar-bass-and-drums of the colossal Yardbirds spin-off Led Zeppelin. Zep was Jerry's signing. Dusty Springfield had raved about them in the Memphis studio where the two battled to be the greatest pure pop production of Wexler's career and soon he had closed a worldwide deal for $110,000 with the appropriate lawyer, a neighbour of his in Great Neck – without hearing the band. It was Cream who made this risk plausible, and though Jerry never really got the music, he had no regrets.

Like Cream only more so, because they worked as a unit and never fetishized improvisation, Led Zeppelin were sonic architects. From the start there was clearly something humongous in that sound that, whether inhuman or superhuman, couldn't be pigeonholed with Iron Butterfly's *In-A-Gadda-Da-Vida* and Blue Cheer. Some say Jimmy Page ruled in the studio, some say fat-bottomed bassist John Paul Jones was master of the maelstrom, some say Robert Plant's vocal guitaristics transformed trio into true quartet, some say

John Bonham's Pantagruelian beats trampled everything before them. Doesn't matter – all four understood gestalt, and given the collective ego-mania of their sound, it proved miraculously cohesive. Unlike The Who, they had the self-knowledge to pack it in when their drummer died. But before they did, they redefined the sixties in the image of all teenagers for whom hippiedom was a cultural given rather than a historical inevitability – all the kids forced by economic reality and personal limitation to escape from rather than into, to settle for representation of power because the real power their older siblings pretended to was so obviously a hallucination. Its broad strokes configured more subtly than your average free-former, folkie, or blues adept could hear, with fantastic lyricism and savvy dynamics tempering rhythms and tempos more varied than its sludgy distortions led a new generation of old farts to believe, Led Zeppelin's music seems at least as likely to remain fresh as any rock in the Atlantic (or any other) catalogue. No matter how little it may mean in the lives of those who didn't grow up with it, it's only gotten more evocative and more itself with age.

Buffalo Springfield

Although Jerry was proud to have bagged Led Zeppelin, he was more than pleased to leave their care and feeding to Ahmet, by then clearly the label's chief head-hunter and Don Juan. Having established his art-rock bona fides with his 1969 acquisition of Robert Fripp's King Crimson, who wouldn't shake off the pretensions their fans admired them for until 1975's *Red*, Ahmet was in pursuit of the schlockier Yes and Emerson, Lake & Palmer by 1970. But his most dangerous quarry and sexiest love object was The Rolling Stones. Signing battles in this saga go back to The Rascals and The Who, and before that Ahmet had known what it was to lose Ray Charles to ABC-Paramount, Bobby Darin to Capitol. But his Stones quest signalled a new era of music-biz infighting, as the contracts of the first generation of rock stars drew to a close. Both Ahmet and Jerry had long since noted the Stones' command of R & B, and with The Beatles kaput and the Stones coming off the superb *Beggars Banquet* and *Let It Bleed* as well as a notorious U.S. tour, there was only one World's Greatest Rock'n'Roll Band. Ahmet was buying quality, status, credibility, and he was ready to pay the cost – whatever the profit-and-loss, the promotion value-added was incalculable. The Stones repaid this gamble with the scarily good *Sticky Fingers* and the even better *Exile On Main Street*, a dark and risky double-LP that took a while to sink in and is now regarded as their pinnacle. After that they became a grade-A product machine, freshening their sales face with triennial tours in a relationship that lasted 15 years and still satisfies Ahmet: "For me, the all-time great group is The Rolling Stones. Such songs, such beautiful ballads. 'Angie' is such a record – I still hear it, it runs through my mind." By this time Wexler was a self-described "studio wonk", pursuing his muse in Muscle Shoals and Miami, opening a Nashville office as the label's only certifiable country fan. Yet though he credits Ahmet with "finding the bodies", his weakness for the good and the beautiful served the world well and did his label proud. His buddy Kris Kristofferson tipped him to John Prine, who proceeded to give Atlantic four laconically sung, eloquently observed post-folk albums, the last and weirdest of which topped out at #66, Prine's chart peak. Although it took 20 years for him to hit such a groove again (on a label he owned himself), it's a measure of his immense gift that after 20 years he still could. In 1975 Jerry shepherded Willie Nelson to Muscle Shoals for the artistic turning point of *Phases And Stages*. He also supported two seminal albums by Detroit's high-timing protopunks, the MC5. And it was Jerry who signed off on the Insect Trust's wacky bohemian-blues excursion *Hoboken Saturday Night*, sure to inspire a cult craze immediately upon its long overdue re-release. But even as Ahmet tended the corporate coffers, his musicality told. Mott the Hoople and Loudon Wainwright III were quality signings who soon came into their own with Columbia. And although Dr. John made his mark with 1972's Wexler-produced *Gumbo*, which did nothing less than revitalize New Orleans piano, Mac Rebennack was an Ahmet discovery whose good music began earlier (try the first side of 1970's *Remedies*). Out in L.A. Ertegun went so far as to unearth his own Insect Trust, in the form of a now forgotten bunch of studio rats led by sideman-to-the-stars Danny Kortchmar and vocalist Abigale Haness. In 1971, Jo Mama (get it?) released their second and final album, *J Is For Jump*, sexy loungecore a quarter of a century ahead of its time – a droll testament to the obscurer passions of the rock era's most urbane record man.

In many respects the rock of the sixties was a theatre of illusion. Smart people with more staked on it than Ahmet and Jerry made fools of themselves espousing values they had no feel for and hyping fatuous hippie kitsch. Ahmet and Jerry certainly partook of the time's intoxications – they would have been fools, and prudes, if they hadn't. But Jerry's dedication to the American roots so many counter-culturalists thought they were celebrating and Ahmet's metier as an elegant Titan of the new showbiz saved them from the era's dumbest excesses and led them to music that summed it up – in one way at the time, when they certainly sold their share of the crap the record business has always run on, in another now that we can hear the music both as music pure and not so simple and as the signal that a whole phalanx of popular artists was never going to submit to the formulaic again.

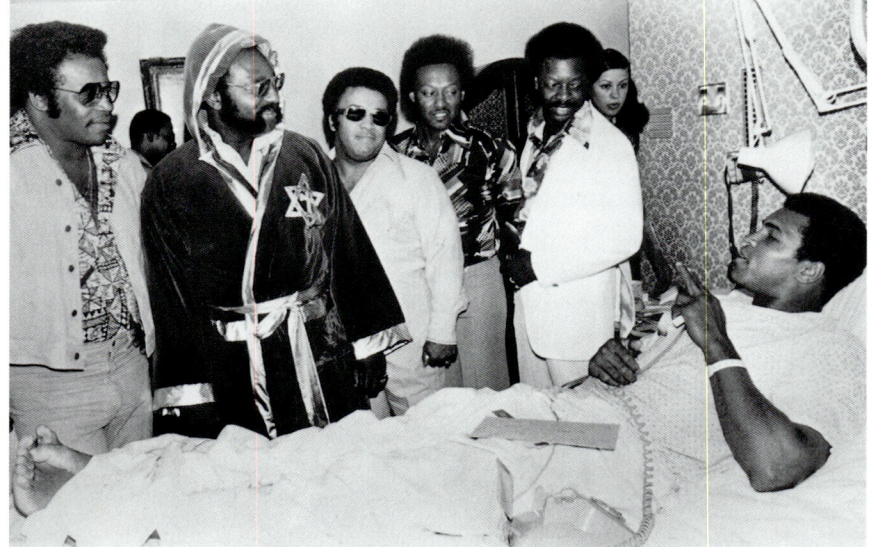

The Spinners below, and above from left: Henry Fambrough, Billy Henderson, Bobby Smith, Philippe Wynne and Pervis Jackson TL: 70s

"I was there because the fight was to be preceded by a gigantic music festival featuring James Brown. I was Brown's music director, and along with his band, I had flown to Kinshasa, Zaire, on the same overloaded DC-8 as Muhammad Ali and his crew. The plane was so overloaded because the organizers had tried to get all the people who participated in the music festival on the same aeroplane. I don't think they had properly anticipated the amount of equipment the performers carried with them. I bet the wardrobe for The Pointer Sisters alone took up an entire bin. Along with Brown and The Pointer Sisters, the cast included B. B. King, the Fanya All-Stars, The Spinners, Bill Withers and Sister Sledge. The plane barely got off the ground." Fred Wesley

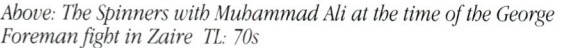

"It's lack of faith that makes people afraid of meeting challenges, and I believed in myself." Muhammad Ali

Above: The Spinners with Muhammad Ali at the time of the George Foreman fight in Zaire TL: 70s

Roberta Flack TL: 70s

"Roberta Flack is on a plane travelling from New York to L.A., and if you travel much, you know that each month you have a different selection of music on most of the major American airlines. So she's just dialling around, listening to different things, when all of a sudden she hears 'Killing Me Softly' by Lori Lieberman. As soon as she lands, she calls me and says, 'I got it! This is the song I've been looking for!' She had to stay in Los Angeles for a couple of days, so I put the rhythm section together, just 'phoned around and said, 'Roberta's called, says she's got one, and I believe her.' We did the session in about an hour and a half, two hours, it was just one of those things – it just came out of her, there was no thinking. It was one of those Zen kind of things that happens once or twice in three or four lifetimes. That song seemed to have its own momentum. It was as if God had delivered it to us and said, 'Here children, it'll just float through – do what you're told.'" Joel Dorn

"I first heard about Hall and Oates from Earl McGrath, who had a little label with us that Robert Stigwood and I financed. At the same time, Tommy Mottola, who was their manager and who had discussed them with Earl in California, came to New York. So, as it turned out, one of our A & R people actually signed them directly to Atlantic. They ended up making three albums with us, and then Jerry Greenberg gave them their release from their contract, for which Tommy Mottola must have been very grateful – since they then made an even bigger deal with RCA and became hugely successful. Ironically, their biggest hit for us, 'She's Gone,' hit the Top Ten after they had already left the label." Ahmet

Daryl Hall and John Oates TL: 70s

Above: Yusef Lateef TL: 70s 80s; and below, The Modern Jazz Quartet TL: 70s

Above and below, from left: Joel Dorn and Rahsaan Roland Kirk, and above with Kirk's wife, Dorthaan TL: 70s

"Listen, black music is this country's gift to the world. I'm not telling you anything you don't know, but black artists really went through a tremendous amount of turmoil. It was not easy for black artists to express themselves in terms of their own culture. They always had to 'adapt themselves to the business'. So in retrospect, when you look back now you may think: what was the big deal? But in those days what they were doing was ground-breaking work, and the jazz artists were always at the forefront. They were trying to make a statement."
Joel Dorn

Average White Band, from left: Onnie McIntyre, Steve Ferrone, Hamish Stuart, Molly Duncan and Alan Gorrie TL: 70s

"We got along immediately because I was an arranger, knew chords, and was able to help them. Their strength, I think, was reverence for R & B and black music, rather than copying it. Reverence and development. They loved the music and the stars so much, to the point of calling themselves Average White Band – which I thought was a very nice gesture, and which had a very positive reaction from black radio and amongst black musicians. Ahmet called me in Miami and said,

'Look, we've signed this new group called Average White Band. Why don't you give it a try? We have rights to use their old material from MCA, so why don't you cut a few of their new songs and we'll add them to the album?' The chemistry was so great that these three new songs became like gems so they said, 'Let's scrap the old material and recut the whole thing.' MCA was very upset, but when they looked in the fine print of their contract, they discovered that there was a stipulation which enabled us to use those titles and recut them – so they couldn't sue us. That was the way the first record, and also a friendship, was born. I wasn't sure about 'Pick Up The Pieces' as a single, since it's mostly an instrumental. But then from the field, reports came in that everybody wanted that song, they were dancing to it – so it was the first song we released as a single, and it became a number one hit."
Arif Mardin

"It was wonderful for us being on Atlantic during that period. We met a lot of musicians and artists on the label who all loved the band, and that was really encouraging. When our first album was doing really well, we went up to the Apollo to see The Spinners, and they introduced us from the stage. We were just flabbergasted by all of that. Atlantic wasn't our first label, however. We did do one album previously with MCA, but they weren't too interested in us, put it that way. At that point we managed, through a friend of a friend, to hook up with Jerry Wexler. We played him what we'd been working on and he loved it! He wanted to sign us up right away. The first step was going to Criteria in Miami. At that point, Tommy Dowd, Jerry and Arif Mardin were all producing Aretha Franklin together. The idea was to take us down there and see which of the three might really want to produce us. That was very exciting for us, working with these legends all of a sudden. After a few days, Arif really started to come into the picture much more, and I think he'd really decided that he wanted to do it. As 'Pick Up The Pieces' began to happen, we wondered where exactly it was going to go, but it just kept rolling. People were telling us it was going to be a number one record, and we were saying, 'Oh sure – course it is!' Sure enough, though, it was." Hamish Stuart

"Average White Band were one hell of a band, but they had a tragedy, which was that their drummer died in Los Angeles before they really came into any prominence. They somehow managed to get over that and carry on as a great group. I loved going to their gigs because their music was so soulful and so right." Ahmet

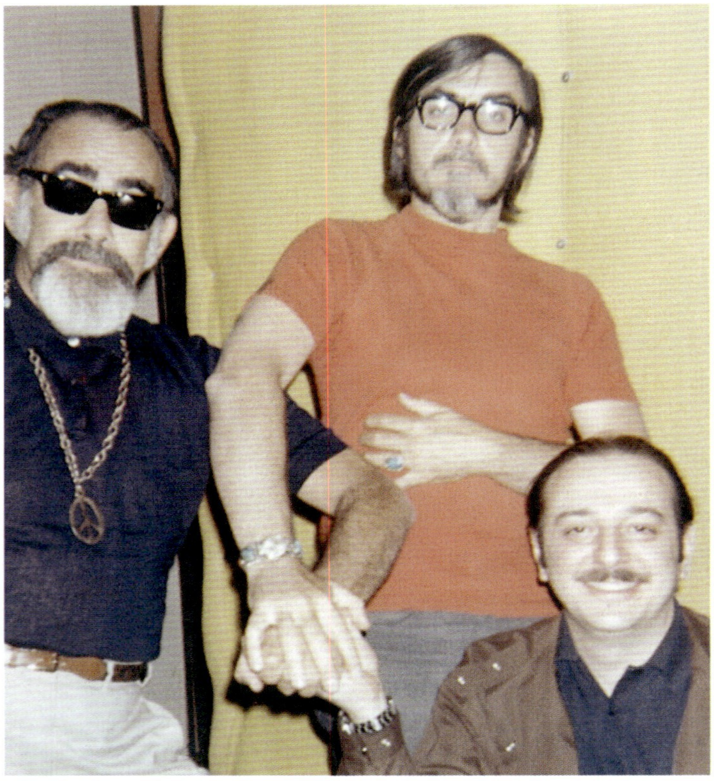

Left: Jerry Wexler, Tom Dowd and Arif Mardin; and above left, Jerry Wexler and Arif Mardin with Average White Band, including fourth from left, the late Robbie McIntosh

THE ATLANTIC STORY

"I remember on one occasion Roxy Music had been in the studio for ten or 12 hours, and we'd just got stuck on this particular song – we could not get it right. We were getting annoyed with each other, the producer, the engineer; it just wasn't happening. It was about three o'clock in the morning when, 'bang', the doors to the studio flew open and Ahmet breezed in, complete with black tie, dinner suit, white scarf around his shoulders, flanked by quite a few people, including several women decked out in furs, ball gowns, and dripping with jewels. I remember a couple of the introductions as being to people with triple-barrelled surnames from some long-since-forgotten, once-aristocratic American family. There was a kind of aura of faded glamour about the whole thing that I loved and which was very romantic. The point is that Ahmet was having a great time, he was on a roll, and no one was going to stop him – certainly not some band in a recording studio. So he cracked a few jokes, brought all of us lot along with him, and I swear to God, hey presto, the block was suddenly gone, the engine had been greased and we were away. We had such a great time and we finished the track, the harmonies, all the over-dubbing that night." Bryan Ferry

Bryan Ferry TL: 70s

Roxy Music, fom left: John Gustafson, Paul Thompson, Phil Manzanera, Eddie Jobson, Bryan Ferry and Andy Mackay TL: 70s

Below: Jerry Wexler; and above, with Maggie Bell TL:70s

"I had lived and breathed Atlantic Records for a good part of my adult life, but it was the end of the road … In an odd way, I was glad to be leaving. The industry was going big time, entering an era in which middle executives ran companies with perfunctory approval from above, and top executives had become too involved with mega-million-dollar deals to spend much time thinking about … what, music? I'm a man who lives by and for his enthusiasms. I listen to music all day, every day – except on the golf course. Music plays all night in my bedroom. I thrive in the studio. I belong there. Hands-on is what I want." Jerry Wexler

Black Oak Arkansas, from left: Stanley Knight, Harvey Jett, Wayne Evans, Jim Mangrum, Pat Daugherty and Rick Reynolds TL: 70s

"People in Arkansas think that we're pretty well up there now, and they can't conceive of us goin' much higher because they ain't conceived of anybody gettin' where we got, but really, it's just started. We're just findin' the road. Just to succeed at somethin' is really amazin' to those people 'cause nobody's ever come from around here and ever done anything. That we done it just really freaks 'em out, 'cause they thought that we was the worst bums in the world." Pat 'Dirty' Daugherty

Yes, from left: Jon Anderson, Chris Squire, Steve Howe, unidentified friend, Patrick Moraz, and Alan White TL: 70s

The Manhattan Transfer below, and above, from left: Janis Siegel, Tim Hauser, Laurel Masse and Alan Paul TL: 70s

"There is so much space in The Manhattan Transfer between the highest voice and the lowest, much more than in an all-male group. There is much more room in between to do things. That was my idea – that there would be a much larger playing field for chords and stuff, even though our close harmony at the time was based on the Count Basie sax section, two altos and two tenor saxophones. Bette Midler used to play the Continental Baths, which was a gay bathhouse. She loved, and went down really well with, that whole kind of drag, transvestite thing, which was just exploding back then. That kind of theatre was very much in vogue. We were playing a lesbian bar, Trudy Heller's, which had been the big twist bar in the sixties. They also had a disco there and a cabaret. Our first audience was mostly gays – they were the first people really to get behind our scene and support us." Tim Hauser

"The Manhattan Transfer's manager, Aaron Russo, played me a demo tape, which had an incredible melange of thirties and forties music on it. The girl sounded just like Ella Fitzgerald on one cut, then like a gospel singer on another. The male singers did everything from old big band-type arrangements of vocal sound to sounding like rock'n'roll punk the next minute. So I said, 'This is incredible!' Aaron said, 'Listen, they're playing in Philadelphia. Do you want to go down and hear them?' I said, 'Let's go down.' So we walked into this small club and it was just astonishing. The reaction to the group from the crowd there was just tremendous, and the band sounded even better live than they had on tape. I went into the dressing room afterwards and right away got on so easily with everybody, it was great. We made this fabulous first record, which was an international hit. I worked very closely with them, but right from the beginning they really had their whole range already defined – they just did everything that they'd been doing on stage." Ahmet

"We all agreed that if we had our first choice, Atlantic would be the one. We were playing that weekend at a place called the Bijou Cafe in Philadelphia, sharing the bill with Martin Mull. Our manager had told us that he was bringing Ahmet down, and then he telephoned and told us that they'd gotten stuck in traffic and would be late. So we held up the show and the owner of the club, who was very appreciative of us and understood how much this meant to us, put on an Amos 'n' Andy movie – which the audience, under the circumstances, applauded and were quite pleased with. Then Ahmet walked in, and I mean, my God – we were so excited! It was just too much! I mean, he'd come – he's in the audience, and it's like, 'Ahmet!' So we do this show and afterwards he comes upstairs and says, 'I'm not supposed to do this in front of the group's manager – it's not good business, but I can't help it. I want to ask you formally if you would like to record for Atlantic Records?' Well, I mean, 'We'll have to think about it … ' It was like, 'Yesssssss!'" Tim Hauser

Abba the day after winning the Eurovision Song Contest TL: 70s

"We got Abba for the United States. They were already quite successful by the time we got the American rights. I went to London to hear them after we signed them, and I was amazed to see a lot of family groups in the audience. I went backstage and saw the same crew that had been working for The Stones, except now they were all very neatly decked out with neckties and little jackets. I asked one of the roadies, 'Jesus! What's happening here?' He said, 'Well, this is very different, we don't have to use the broomstick.' I said, 'What broomstick?' He said, 'We always had to use a broomstick to poke Keith Richards to tell him his solo was coming up.' The same guys who were smoking joints and all dishevelled with The Stones were now neatly dressed up and very sober." Ahmet

From left: Bjorn Ulvaeus, Agnetha Faltskog, Anni-Frid Lyngstad and Benny Andersson

Ahmet with The Bee Gees, from left: Robin, Barry and Maurice Gibb TL: 70s

Below: Arif Mardin

"In the early seventies I was bringing home these rough mixes of what I was working on, and I remember my wife saying, 'You know this stuff you're doing now, it's nothing like what I hear at the hairdressers!' That's because what I was working with then was disco! She tried so hard to warn me that I was doing wrong!

"I was working with Average White Band and The Bee Gees about the same time. We'd give dinner parties for them and their wives and a lot of alcohol was consumed, but we had some great times. They were the closest I came to working in dance tempo at that time – especially, I suppose, with The Bee Gees' 'Nights On Broadway' and 'Jive Talkin''. We had an electric metronome that the drummer would see, and no click track. We made the album and we loved it – it was so exciting, and there was so much interplay in the studio. Barry says that I asked him to try taking his voice up an octave and he said, 'Sure, I'll try!' We were very pleased with what we were doing, we loved the music, but we didn't think of the songs as particularly being hits. Then Ahmet came down and said, 'This is a dance record! This is a huge hit!'" Arif Mardin

Left and above: The Bee Gees TL: 70s

"It was really Henry Allen who pushed for me to join Atlantic. I was working in Hartford, Connecticut as a local promotion man for Atlantic, Chess, Mercury – about 25 different labels – and Henry Allen wanted me to come and work for Atlantic directly. I was supposed to be meeting with Jerry, Ahmet and Henry, but Jerry couldn't make it, so Ahmet and Henry drove up to Connecticut. The three of us had dinner, because even though the job was supposed to be working for Jerry Wexler, Henry wanted me to meet Ahmet. He was dressed impeccably, we talked about music, and I have to say I was very, very impressed. About six months after that, in 1967, I joined Atlantic. They sold the company around the same time, and eventually Jerry went to Florida, so he wasn't around that much. That's when I became very close with Ahmet. When he signed The Stones, he took me to France for the signing party and told me, 'You're the only person I trust Mick talking with when I'm not there!' That was a great compliment, and that's when I started making my rise. Ahmet was the most incredible 'boss', but I don't even want to use that word because it's the wrong expression. Working with him just made you feel that this was your company, too, and even though it was a Warner company, it still felt like a family – like Ahmet was my father, I was the son, and he was bringing me up through the business. He would teach me, but I can never remember him yelling at me, getting mad or anything – I could have made a deal where we lost a million dollars, but Ahmet would just say, 'Okay – we tried.' He was always only encouraging. He brought me up through the ranks and he introduced me to his family. There was a circle of friends, which not only included close business associates like Robert Stigwood and Chris Blackwell, but he'd invite me to dinner with Earl McGrath, the Zipkins, his closest friends. In fact, he and his wife Mica treated me just like I was a member of the family. It was the most incredible time.

"In the seventies, the company had it all – we had the biggest bands in the world, from both England and America: Crosby, Stills & Nash, Iron Butterfly, Led Zeppelin, ELP, The Stones, Genesis, Foreigner. And then on the black side we had Aretha, we had Chic, Sister Sledge – it went on and on and on. There was not one company – not Columbia, not Warner Bros., not A & M – there was nobody even close to Atlantic Records during the seventies going on into the eighties. I'm not saying they've done badly at any time, they've always done pretty good, but there was nothing like Atlantic in those days. That range came from Ahmet, because he's always understood music and he understands people. I don't think you'll find anyone who has a bad word to say about him. He gives credit where credit is due and he always acknowledges the people he works with. He's built a four or six billion dollar company from practically nothing! With the exception of The Stones, and a few things that maybe didn't work so well, we signed everything pretty much from scratch. We found Bette Midler and Roberta Flack; we found The Manhattan Transfer in the Village and Yes in England; I found Genesis through Tony Stratton-Smith; Ahmet heard through some groupie about Emerson, Lake & Palmer and followed up the lead. He didn't go out and buy record companies. We went out and found it from the street, from knowing music, and being smart enough to recognize great talent. That's what Ahmet did and we all tried to do. If I had to put something next to Ahmet Ertegun, I would write, 'It's all about music.' Because it wasn't about money – the money came – it was about his love and passion for music, which he shared with everyone who worked with him. We'd often all sit around until God knows what hour of the night listening to songs, talking about what we were going to do. It was that kind of an atmosphere where it wasn't a job, it was really all about the love of the music and the artists. When I first joined Atlantic there was never any pressure like, how much money did we make this week, how were sales? Sales were the afterthought. The first thoughts were: 'Is the record good?' and 'How many radio stations are playing it?' It was not corporate or run by numbers. No rushing records out, or not setting them up properly – never just trying to make those quarterly numbers. No hurrying bands out of the studio instead of maybe going back in and recording a few more songs – it was never all about making numbers every year. Talent doesn't work that way at all.

"At the first big budget meeting that Ahmet and I went to when Warner Communications had taken over the company, they congratulated us on a great year, on being the number one company for them – better than Warner Bros., better than Elektra. Warners used to do more gross, but we did better bottom line. So they were singing our praises saying, 'Oh my God, you guys are great. We don't know how you do it.' And then they gave us our budget and told us, 'This is what you've got to do next year.' They had about 30

Ahmet, Henry Allen and Jerry Greenberg

accountants there, so Ahmet asked them, 'How did you get these numbers?' And they replied, 'Well, there'll be a new Rolling Stones, a new Bette Midler, a new this and that … ' So Ahmet looked at me and said, 'Jerry, let me ask you a question. Do you think we're going to get a Rolling Stones record next year?' And I said, 'No, I don't think so.' 'A Bette Midler record next year?' And I said, 'No, I don't think so – she just gave us a record.' So he looked at all of these people and he said, 'Listen, it kind of doesn't work that way, so I'll tell you what: you write in any numbers you want and we'll do the best we can.' There was nothing else to talk about, so Steve Ross said, 'Okay, Ahmet, congratulations again, I guess the meeting's over!' At least Steve knew enough to leave us alone, no question about it. Ordinarily, the accountants would watch the numbers and point out if too many pencils were ordered. But Ahmet could always do pretty much whatever he wanted, not least because Atlantic was always the most profitable company. If you think about the catalogue, even if we didn't break a new act one year, the amount that was always still selling was incredible.

"You could make a movie about Ahmet that no one would believe – because the guy hardly ever sleeps, he's always doing something, he's always travelling, he's always just stumbling on shit that ends up turning great. But seriously, it's all about relationships – believe me, if Ahmet, Wexler, and other people at the label had bad reputations, all of these great artists would never have joined Atlantic." Jerry Greenberg, (former President of Atlantic Records)

Overleaf: The Rolling Stones playing on board a flat-bed truck travelling down Fifth Avenue, New York, to announce the launch of their '75 Tour to a surprised but substantial gathering of the world's press

Ben E. King TL: 70s

"I wasn't with Atlantic at that point, but I was on tour down in Florida, and Ahmet was vacationing there at the same time. So he came to see me at one of the clubs I was working in. Most of my songs are baritone, which was really the only range that Ahmet had heard me in up until then. On stage I can switch about, though, and I was singing much higher, way up in the tenor range. Ahmet said, 'You sound great! Why haven't you called me? Your voice is too good. We've got to do something!' I said, 'Really?' He said, 'Absolutely – we've got to go back in the studio. As soon as you get finished with this tour and get home, come by the office.' So, sure enough, when I got back to New York, we set up a meeting. Right away, Ahmet said, 'We've got to do an album.' So I went in and we did *Supernatural Thing*. That was great, because Bert de Coteaux is a wonderful producer and working with him was a treat. He was very familiar with the things I'd done, and – very much like Jerry Leiber and Mike Stoller – was totally prepared to take a chance and bring me into a completely different area, to do something on Ben E. King that had never been done before. I was a bit nervous when he said, 'Forget all that other old stuff you've done, we're going to do some new things.' I said, 'Really?' But then they came up with all of these funky tracks. It was great and it worked. It came off pretty well, and I was very proud of myself!" Ben E. King

"Ben E. King is a really great friend and such a wonderful person. He's idolized by a lot of rock'n'roll singers – people like Robert Plant – and he has something of the presence that King Curtis had, that Otis Redding had. He had a terrific resurgence in the seventies with *Supernatural Thing*, which everyone was so happy about. Then, in the eighties, 'Stand By Me' – which has been covered so many times – became a hit all over again through its use in the film of the same title, as well as in a Levi's commercial in England. I would say that to this day, Ben E. King remains one of the great artists and performers of the last 40 years." Ahmet

The Spinners, from left: Henry Fambrough, Bobby Smith, Phillippe Wynne, Billy Henderson and Pervis Jackson TL: 70s

"Among our biggest successes in the R & B field in the seventies were The Spinners. They began in Detroit in the early sixties, and had already had a number of hits before they came to us. When we signed them in the early seventies, they started working with producer Thom Bell in Philadelphia, and their career really exploded. They gave us a lot of terrific records, many of which hit number one on the charts, and all of which still sound marvellous to me today." Ahmet

Above from left: Henry Allen, Ahmet, Pervis Jackson, Aretha Franklin, Billy Henderson, Henry Fambrough, Bobby Smith and Philippe Wynne TL: 70s

Hot Chocolate from left: Larry Ferguson, Patrick Olive, Erroll Brown, Tony Connor, Tony Wilson and Harvey Hinsley TL 70s

Abba, TL 70s

"I really don't know where it comes from or why it ends up as a ballad or a rock'n'roll song. That's why we spend so much time with it because you never know what's going to happen. I spend a lot of time alone playing the piano or synthesizers and it's more like therapy, just to be prepared."
Benny Andersson

Opposite: The Trammps, from left: Earl Young, Harold Wade, Jimmy Ellis, Stanley Wade and Robert Upchurch TL: 70s

Roxy Music, from left: Paul Thompson, Phil Manzanera, Andy Mackay, Bryan Ferry and Eddie Jobson TL: 70s

"People think that because I attend premières and go to parties, I do nothing else. But I am the son of a Newcastle miner - I get bored when I'm not working" Bryan Ferry

The J. Geils Band, from left: Seth Justman, J. Geils, Stephen Jo Bladd, Danny Klein, Magic Dick and Peter Wolf TL: 70s

"I think our main objective is just to give people a good time without being pretentious, and just keep a certain type of funky music alive."   Peter Wolf, The J. Geils Band

314 THE ATLANTIC STORY

Led Zeppelin: clockwise from above left, Robert Plant and Jimmy Page. Below right; Robert Plant with John Paul Jones, above right John Bonham and above from right, John Bonham, Jimmy Page, Robert Plant and John Paul Jones

"'Stairway to Heaven' crystallized the essence of the band." Jimmy Page

Atlantic's signing party for Ringo Starr TL: 70s

"Working with Ringo Starr was great – he's such a natural guy. We had a lot of fun, but I also suffered a lot of heartburn! While we were making the album I would be up early, working with the musicians and so on. Then Ringo would come into the studio around 5p.m. and order these massive spreads of hot Chinese food. After the session, I'd go to his home, drink Cognac, watch him and his friends play pool, and leave there at five o'clock in the morning. Then I'd get up again at nine. Between that schedule and the food, I actually developed some kind of hiatus hernia from doing this for a few weeks – I wasn't built for that!" Arif Mardin

Dave Edmunds TL: 70s

"The gifted Welsh guitarist/singer/producer Dave Edmunds was one of the artists who came to Atlantic through Led Zeppelin's Swan Song label. He released a series of acclaimed albums for us in the late seventies and early eighties." Ahmet

Alice Cooper TL: 70s

"Alice Cooper would be my favourite band if I were a kid, because I would react to the visual stuff – giant spiders, the nine-foot cyclops, the big snake. That's great, especially with the rock music behind it. I've got a Barnum & Bailey attitude to rock'n'roll. I think it should really be a circus all the time. I work real spontaneously on stage. Just follow me with a spot, you know?" Alice Cooper

The Small Faces TL: 70s

"In the middle to late seventies, we happened to become involved with a number of great British musicians whom we had never had on Atlantic before, but who were all interconnected in various ways. We released a couple of albums by a reformed version of that terrific sixties pop group, The Small Faces, which featured Steve Marriott – whom I had previously tried to sign with the group Humble Pie. Meanwhile, Ronnie Wood – who had been in the line-up of The Faces with Rod Stewart – joined The Rolling Stones, who had by then been with us for five or six years. Around the same time, we released a soundtrack, *Mahoney's Last Stand*, which was a collaboration between Wood and Ronnie Lane, who had been an original member of The Small Faces, but was not part of the reunion. When the new Small Faces broke up, Rick Wills – who had filled Lane's bass spot in the band and who had toured with another Atlantic group, Roxy Music – replaced the original bass player in Foreigner. Wills, incidentally, had also played for several years with Peter Frampton, who had also been in Humble Pie, and who went on to make a couple of albums for us in the late eighties. Small Faces' keyboard player Ian McLagan went on to tour with The Stones, and drummer Kenny Jones replaced Keith Moon in The Who. And although The Who didn't record for Atlantic, we did sign Pete Townshend to a solo deal shortly after that. It was all very incestuous." Ahmet

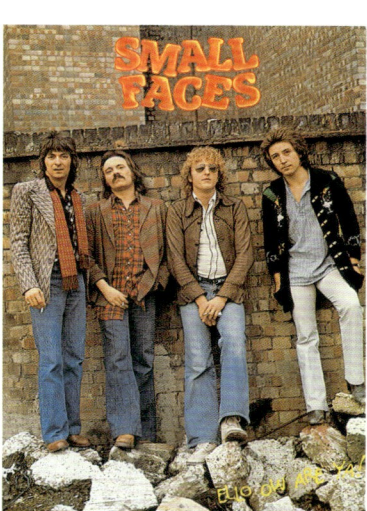

From left: Ian McLagan, Steve Marriott, Rick Wills and Kenney Jones TL: 70s

Ronnie Lane TL: 70s

Ronnie Wood TL: 70s

Above: Bad Company and below, from left; Paul Rodgers, Boz Burrell, Simon Kirke and Mick Ralphs TL: 70s 80s 90s

"I always thought it was important for Bad Company to have more than one writer. There was quite a bit of pressure on us being the first artists signed to the Zep's Swan Song label. Behind the scenes, we did take the mickey out of each other mercilessly. We would stand on the side of the stage and yell, 'Rubbish!' And do things like that to them. We never did shows together, but we did jam quite a bit. There was a real rapport between the bands and if there was any competition between us, it was always friendly." Paul Rodgers

"We made two terrific solo albums with Peter, but then he delivered an album which some people were not that crazy about. So Jerry Greenberg decided to let him go and we released him from his contract. In retrospect, that was a big mistake. Peter is a great, visionary artist." Ahmet

Above, Peter Gabriel; and below, Roy Buchanan TL: 70s

"Roy Buchanan was a legend. Everyone talked about him. We signed him up because so many guitar players had told me how great he was. We made some very good records with him and we did have some success, but nothing incredibly commercial." Ahmet

Esther Phillips TL: 70s

Jean-Luc Ponty TL: 70s

opposite, Bryan Ferry TL: 70s

"Jean-Luc Ponty is a phenomenal modern jazz player. He's the second world-famous French jazz violinist, following the legendary Stephane Grappelli. Jean-Luc can play jazz, rock, funk, abstract music – such an inventive and exciting musician."
Ahmet

Bon Scott

"When I used to come home from school, I'd grab the guitar and run out of the door with it to go and play with a few mates, always trying to get together little bands. My sister always used to be saying, 'He's nuts! You won't see him until dinnertime.' So when my older brother Malcolm said that he wanted me to be in the band – apart from anything else, he thought my being so young would look good – it was my sister who suggested that I perform in my school uniform. It would give people something to look at, on top of my just being a guitarist. My other brother, George, played with The Easybeats. He also used to get Malcolm and me to play on records here and there. He was like a sixth member of our band.

"Then George teamed up again with Harry Vanda, who had also been in The Easybeats, and the two of them started a full-scale production company. From then on, it was as if they were as much a part of the band as we were. The reason, I think, why people compared us to the heavy metal thing is that if you listen to a lot of the early Easybeat stuff, it has a lot of that hard, gritty edge and is very much, I think, more Led Zeppelin than Led Zeppelin. The chords we played on the guitar were practically always A-C-D-C, hence the name – which we thought if anyone was clever enough they would suss out. We had written this song called 'High Voltage' using the chords A-C-D-C; George heard it, thought it was great, and so we immediately went into the studio and put it straight down. Certainly, in Australia, that was the song that helped push us through." Angus Young

"I used to go with Seymour Stein [Sire Records founder] to CBGB's, the club downtown in New York, and listen to bands such as The Ramones. At Atlantic, we were more into powerful rock-'n'roll like AC/DC, however, who really came up very strong and are still going very strong. AC/DC was signed to Atlantic by Phil Carson in our London office, and it took a little time to break them. The first time I heard them, they were playing at CBGB's; we had just signed them and I think it was their first American tour. I went backstage, and they were cocky little kids. They kinda put me through the ropes. They didn't have any respect for older people. When they'd finished their show, they were all crumpled and sweaty, and when I walked into the room they all started laughing, and I thought they were laughing at me. I was thinking, 'Jesus, they must think I'm an old jerk.' I didn't realize that hiding behind one of the band members, the lead singer was peeing into an empty beer can, since there was no bathroom back there. We became great friends, and they are one of the all-time great rock'n'roll groups." Ahmet

"'Whole Lotta Rosie' is about a big girl from Tasmania. We were fortunate in having Bon Scott, not least because he was a natural storyteller and could put those stories into words for songs. We were in Melbourne, Australia, staying in a motel where all the local bands used to stay. Two girls lived in a house just up the street, right before the first bar you came to. Bon was walking from the hotel up to the bar when these two girls saw him and pulled him over to come inside. So he went in and had a drink with them. They kept bringing out more drinks and this one girl, who I have to say was pretty big, kept telling him about all the famous people she had slept with and how she really was a bad girl. Slowly but surely, as he kept drinking she began to look more and more beautiful, so he ended up spending the night. In the morning he said, 'You know, what impressed me about the girl was that she told me how that month she had slept with 28 famous people, and in the morning she turned to her friend and said, 'Twenty-nine'.

"When I first met Bon, he was very wild. One night, I watched him just down a couple of bottles of bourbon, and I said to Malcolm, 'This I've got to see – if he can walk on that stage and sing, it's going to be good.' He was fine, and funnily enough, he did that for the first week he was with us and then one night he just said, 'I don't need this,' and stopped. I think where people got the idea that he was a bit of a partygoer was because if we had a bit of free time, he liked to go out and see a lot of his friends. And everywhere we went, there were people who knew him, so that's when he just usually let rip and would have a good time. Not only was Bon a singer and a lyricist, he was also a complete character in everything he did, from his attitude to his lifestyle." Angus Young

AC/DC, opposite: Angus Young; and above, with Bon Scott and Mark Evans TL: 70s

Firefall, from left: Rick Roberts, Larry Burnett, Mark Andes, Jock Bartley and Michael Clarke TL: 70s 80s

"Firefall was formed in Colorado by a group of accomplished musicians who had come from a number of well-known bands, including The Flying Burrito Brothers, The Byrds, Spirit and others. They wrote some great songs and made some really wonderful records for us. Their first few albums went gold and platinum but, unfortunately, they went through a series of personnel changes and eventually broke up." Ahmet

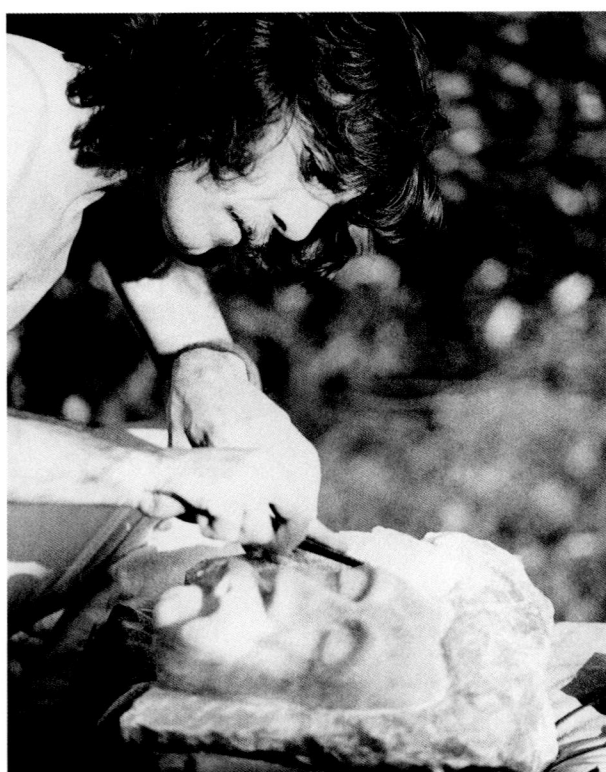

Graham Nash carving a sculpture of David Crosby TL: 70s 80s

Jimmy Webb TL: 70s

"Jimmy Webb is, of course, a major talent. We were very fortunate to make the *El Mirage* album with him, which George Martin produced. I think it will always stand as a great record." Ahmet

"As a result of Peter Gabriel leaving Genesis, the band auditioned a whole bunch of singers. They finally decided that their drummer, Phil Collins, would be the new lead vocalist. He became incredibly masterful onstage, as well as a phenomenal songwriter." Ahmet

Phil Collins and Tony Banks

Phil Collins

Genesis and friends TL: 70s

"Yes were always phenomenal musicians – concert jazz mixed with rock – unbelievable! Ahmet, of course, first recognized their talent and capabilities. They knew I played drums, so one Christmas in New York, they bought me a brand new drum set. I told them that this meant I'd have to sit in with them. They thought I was joking, but for their next concert at the Coliseum, I had their roadies take the kit and set it up at the side of the stage, ready to be wheeled on during the gig. So then at the end of the show, they called me out and I played with them on their encore. About a quarter of the way through the song, I knew that I was in deep shit. This was not like playing with a club blues band and I mean, by this point in their show, they were really blazing. Anyhow, I went at it like crazy, and somehow we all got through it – and then they told me that they were recording the show for a live album!"
Jerry Greenberg

Yes: above, from left: Chris Squire, Jon Anderson, Steve Howe, Alan White, Rick Wakeman; right, Steve Howe and Jon Anderson; top, Yes; and opposite, Steve Howe TL: 70s 80s

Foreigner below, and above from left; Dennis Elliott, Mick Jones, Lou Gramm, Eg Gagliardi and Ian McDonald TL: 70s

"I think that the period I went through prior to forming Foreigner helped toughen me up a bit and let's say, prepare me for something. I felt that I had gone down so far, there was only one way to go, and that was to come back up. At that point I started writing again, which I had sort of abandoned for a few years. I didn't feel that creative during my associations with Spooky Tooth and Leslie West, which preceded Foreigner. At first I had no idea what I was going to do with what I was writing, but gradually the songs started coming. Funnily enough, 'Feels Like The First Time' was the first song I wrote during this period. It pointed me in the direction of forming a group. I knew the musicians that I wanted to involve, and it kind of hit me immediately that the singer should be Lou Gramm, whose last group, Black Sheep, had disbanded a few months earlier. So I called Lou up and he was carrying a hod up the ladder of a building site, I think, at the time. He had kind of given up in a way – his group had broken up and he had resigned himself to not singing with a band again. Within a couple of days we had all met up. It clicked immediately, and from that point on, it worked beautifully. The other funny thing was that it happened for us at a time when punk was taking over in England. Of course, I wanted to be successful in England, but at that time, there wasn't much chance of getting through. Any group that sold millions of records was totally out in England, didn't have a chance."
Mick Jones

Lou Gramm and Ed Gagliardi

From left: Ed Gagliardi, Mick Jones and Ian McDonald

"Foreigner was a group that we signed and worked closely with from the very beginning. As a matter of fact, I took Jerome Robbins down to one of the rehearsals. He was fascinated, and the band loved having him there. They were playing loud, but Jerome had been to a couple of discotheques, so he was not surprised. I was going to ask him to do some choreography for them, but I don't think we ever got around to that. I also wanted to get some of my designer friends to create their wardrobe. I was convinced that they were going to be a very big band and in those early days, Mick Jones and I became good friends very quickly. Mick had spent part of his adult life playing with the French rock'n'roll idol Johnny Halliday and, as a result, had become partly Frenchified. He loves France and spent many years there. When he formed his band, Foreigner, he had a very clear idea of where he wanted it to go. The first album sold four million, and there were hits right from the start. Mick is a great songwriter and producer and 'Waiting For A Girl Like You' and 'I Want To Know What Love Is' are great, great ballads." Ahmet

Above top, Al Greenwood and Lou Gramm, and above Mick Jones signing autographs

Claude Nobs

Charles Mingus TL: 70s

Don Cherry (seated) and fellow musicians at Montreux

"In 1977 Charles Mingus came to Montreux for the second time, and he told me he only wanted two things – a big steak and a big Cuban cigar. Some artists are easier to please than others! In 1973 I became, thanks to Ahmet and Nesuhi, the Director of WEA [Warner/Elektra/Atlantic] in Switzerland. So from then on, even more artists would come to Montreux: other jazz giants such as Rollins, Quincy and Ella, Basie and Miles; as well as Bobby Dylan, Frank Zappa, the Pretenders, Stephan Eicher ... Brazilian enchanters João Gilberto, Jobim Nascimento, Gilberto Gil, as well as Leonard Cohen, Piazzola, Camaron's heart-rending flamenco, African drums, and the strings of the Orchestre National de Lille – to name but a few. Montreux is a place of blends, a place of contrasts: the lake and the mountains, the pleasures of life and decibels, blue notes and electric frenzies, superstars and undiscovered talent ... transcending musical barriers. I certainly believe that we're very fortunate and blessed to be able to continue to share so many outstanding moments."
Claude Nobs

Arif Mardin with Herbie Mann, Average White Band and fellow musicians TL: 70s

"Jay McShann is a legendary Kansas City big band leader and pianist. Charlie Parker played in his band. He had a big hit record in 1938 or '39 called 'Hootie Blues'. He was a very great jazz pianist and he made a few recordings for us. I saw him last when he played at a Rhythm & Blues Foundation dinner where he was being honoured, and he is certainly still a great player." Ahmet

Jay McShann TL: 70s

Lenny White TL: 70s

Sonny Sharrock TL: 70s

Emerson, Lake & Palmer, from left: Keith Emerson, Greg Lake, Carl Palmer TL: 70s

Carl Palmer

"When we started recording *Works Volume 1,* the first thing we did was set up a stereo microphone in the studio in Switzerland, heat up the Yamaha GX-1, and dish out the chord chart for 'Fanfare' to Greg and Carl. The only instructions were: give it a shuffle. Literally, it was born right in one take, complete with solos and everything else. Then I forgot all about it. The next thing I know is that Ahmet is over in Switzerland and Greg is playing 'Fanfare' to Ahmet and they're raving about it. I'm saying, 'Now, hang on a second, that's just one take. I think I can do better than that!' But no, that's the way it stayed.

"Copland is like a teenager at heart, and he loved to hear something different done to his music. He got to hear our version of 'Fanfare For The Common Man' and gave his approval. In fact, in interviews he's very complimentary about my arrangement. So much so, that several other people approached him with ideas of doing a disco version of the piece. He turned each one of them down, apparently saying, 'Everyone thinks that Emerson wrote it anyway – in any event, it's the definitive version and that's as far as I go with it.'"
Keith Emerson

Nesuhi

Aretha Franklin, with from left: Brenda Corbett, Carolyn Framklin and Margaret Branch TL: 70s

"There's the metaphysical Aretha and there's also the down-home, pots-and-pans, cooking-up-a-storm Aretha – arriving in the studio with baskets of homemade chicken, ribs and ham hocks. Or Aretha leaving the presidential suite of the Fontainebleau in Miami to hang out in the neighbourhood with my R & B DJ pal Fat Daddy, who hipped her to the best pig's feet joint back of town. Back at the hotel, walking through the opulent lobby, the damp pig's feet went through the take-out bag and spilled all over the carpet. Aretha didn't miss a beat. She kept on walking, straight into the elevator and into her room.

"She's regal and she's also Mother Earth. I'd be waiting for her at the studio and she'd keep a group of musicians waiting an entire day; but the moment she walked through the door with a mountain of food for the boys, all was well. Joy was everywhere. Magic was about to be made. Aretha was about to sing.

"To my way of thinking, there are three qualities that make a great singer: head, heart and throat. The head is the intelligence, the phrasing. The heart is the emotion that feeds the flames. The throat is the chops, the voice. Aretha, like Sam Cooke, has all three qualities. Her gift seems to have sprung like Minerva, full-fledged from Jupiter's head." Jerry Wexler

"Ray Charles had this record for which he and Ahmet made some kind of a deal, but I think it was really Ahmet wanting to stay associated with Ray. It isn't a cliché in this context, it really is like a family situation that keeps on rolling – whether people are on the label or not, they still remain friends." Jerry Greenberg

Above: Ray Charles, and right, signing again for Atlantic with Ahmet TL:70s

"When I first started in Jamaica, I was quite unusual for a white kid because I was into what was happening in black music there. It was entirely from the root culture of Jamaica – people like Sir Coxsone Dodd, King Edwards, Buster Smith – and the whole thing was based on the sound system. Depending on how good and big it was, people would book them. So there was the money at the gate and then the band would also carry in the liquor – the most popular sound system would sell the most liquor. Everyone was, of course, always very keen to get the hottest records. So I would go to New York and raid the record stores all along 6th Avenue. I would be paying 43¢ for these great 78s and some 45s. I'd scratch off the labels, bring them back, and sell them for £40 or even £50. What I discovered in doing this was that if I took a record with the Atlantic label on it, played it and didn't like it, then I would doubt my own taste. So that was a great inspiration for me to establish a label with that kind of breadth of quality. They had the artists and also the producers and the musicians to work with those artists. When I first went to Atlantic, I met with Miriam Beinstock because I wanted to get the Jamaican rights for Atlantic's artists. She was very civil and polite, but I didn't get the rights. Then I met Ahmet in the early sixties, but our first deals didn't really work too well. Then, as Island got going, various bands wanted to sign with us in the U.K. and Atlantic in the States – King Crimson and ELP, for example. Then we opened up our own offices in the U.S.

I think that the only people who should feel threatened by innovations in production and distribution are those in the middle echelons of the record industry. I mean, when an artist signs with Ahmet, they sign with extra value added – that's to say, part of the deal is who and what they're signing with – the character, the quality, the attitude, the cultural range. I think that the independents, the characters, will always come through – people who are doing it because they love it, because they have a passion for it and because it's fun. Ahmet really has always been my hero in the record business, always was, and still is today." Chris Blackwell

Ahmet with Chris Blackwell

Average White Band with Ben E. King, from left: Molly Duncan, Alan Gorrie, Ben E. King, Hamish Stuart, Onnie McIntyre, Roger Ball and Steve Ferrone TL: 70s 80s

"'Queen Of My Soul' was really something I wanted to say about the way I felt about music in general. It took quite a while to get it all in there. I was listening to a lot of Brazilian music at the time, so we played around with that a bit. It's not what you'd call a Brazilian piece, but there's a bit of that influence in there – and we had some fun cutting that! We had a great conga player on it, and also David and Eddie Brigati did background vocals. It was a real funny session. Crazy people. Then a few months later we were able to work with the great Ben E. King, making the album *Benny & Us*. That was another wonderful experience because Benny really is a terrific character and a phenomenal artist." Hamish Stuart

"It's such a joke with us, people say, 'Can you do 'Chanson D'Amour'?' and we all go aaaahhhhhhhh! It associated us with something we never thought we were. It was just a straighter, much more clean-cut song and that's how we were, but there was this image that was created, and we got turned off by the image because that's not what we were into. But in a way we succumbed to it with our show and a lot of the marketing stuff; I don't think we were just tough enough at the time to say, no, no, no." Tim Hauser

The Manhattan Transfer TL: 70s

The Spinners, from left: Henry Fambrough, Billy Henderson, Bobby Smith, Pervis Jackson and Phillippe Wynne TL: 70s 80s

The Spinners with Mike Douglas (second from left) on The Mike Douglas Televison Show TL: 70s 80s

Sister Sledge. TL: 70s

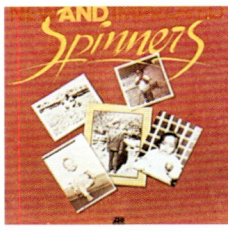

The entire travelling party of Atlantic's Super Soul On Tour: Ben E. King, The Spinners, Sister Sledge, The Jimmy Castor Bunch, Arif Mardin and 60 musicians, roadies, logistics crew and Atlantic coordinating and executive personnel

Chic below, and above from left: Nile Rodgers, Alfa Anderson, Bernard Edwards and Norma Jean Wright TL: 70s

"Nile Rodgers was something of a genius producer, as was his partner, Bernard Edwards in the band named Chic. They had a series of fantastic disco hits." Ahmet

"We just played whatever was on the Top 40, and in those days, it was very much integrated. One song would be 'Lowdown' by Boz Scaggs and the next would be a Funkadelic song, and then the next would be a Lynyrd Skynyrd song. That was the repertoire we had – we just thought that was what music was all about and figured why can't one band do all of that. Why can't I play a song that sounds like 'Sweet Home Alabama' and then turn around and play 'Cosmic Slop'? That's just how we grew up and it was very innocent. When we put all of these different forces together, it came out as Chic. Then we heard this record called 'Sunny' made over in a disco style, and all of these other more middle-of-the-road artists were getting on pop radio with disco – so now we thought, 'Here's the ticket, this is great.' Several record companies turned down our early demo tapes, so we sold all of our instruments to finance a full-scale master recording of 'Dance, Dance, Dance (Yowsah, Yowsah, Yowsah)' – which Buddha Records picked up and released as a single. Now we were going round with our chests poked out. We were beaming. We're artists now, we're recording artists – we've made it. In fact, our record wasn't even going to come out, because they couldn't get the records pressed. Finally, the guy who was our sort of manager played the record for an old buddy of his named Jerry Greenberg, who happened to be the President of Atlantic Records at the time." Nile Rodgers

"The manager called me and said, 'Listen, I'm in New York for a disco convention. I had a deal for a record by this group, Chic, called 'Dance, Dance, Dance (Yowsah, Yowsah, Yowsah)'. The guy was supposed to get the record out in thirty days. The contract ended today, and he still hasn't got the record out. Can I come up and play it for you; are you interested?' I said, 'Absolutely.' He came up to my office, played me the song and I said, 'I want the record, let's make a deal.' He said, 'How quickly can you get this out, because the disco convention is going on right now and I want to give it to all the guys?' I said, 'You got the master tape now?' He said, 'Yeah.' I said, 'Watch this.' I sent it right over to the Atlantic studio at 1 p.m., Friday afternoon. They cut the master disc and it was then driven out to our plant in Pennsylvania. That night, it was put in what they call 'the bath'. I kept the plant open, and they pressed five hundred records Saturday morning. I had those flown in from Philadelphia on a helicopter Saturday afternoon, and by Saturday evening, these 12-inch records were being handed out to all the guys at the disco convention. We signed a deal memo on Monday, and that's how Chic became a reality on Atlantic Records." Jerry Greenberg

Lost In Music: Atlantic's Disco Years
By Vince Aletti

Though it had been gestating underground for a few years – mutating relentlessly in a score of crowded, darkened rooms – disco was still unformed and unnamed when it slipped briefly into the mainstream in 1973. That spring, a record named 'Soul Makossa' shot out of New York's tight-knit network of juice bars, gay private clubs, floating parties, and after-hours dives, and landed in heavy rotation on the city's hippest, hottest radio station, the black-owned WBLS. DJ-programmer Frankie Crocker, already legendary for his pillow-talk patter, had always been quick to pick up on club records, but never one quite so unlikely or so infectious. 'Soul Makossa', whose only English lyric was contained in its title, was an almost impossible-to-find French import 45 recorded the previous year by the Cameroonian musician-composer Manu Dibango and his group of Paris-based West Africans. Since most of the original pressing had disappeared before it hit the airwaves, once Crocker started banging it, 'Soul Makossa' quickly went from being the most sought-after unavailable record in town to the most pirated and illegally covered one.

Enter, with stunning decisiveness, Atlantic Records. Literally within days of the label's locking in on the Dibango buzz, Atlantic had snapped up US rights and had its own single-pressing on the street, effectively closing down the competition and opening up the record's legitimate market beyond New York. The underground sensation flared memorably, peaking in the pop chart's Top 40 only a month later, but fizzled fast, a fluke out of water. Without clubland's tribal hordes – or New York's international hothouse – to sustain it, 'Soul Makossa' was a novelty without context. But the context not only remained, it thrived. Though the dance crowd was exhilarated by Dibango's success and the flash of recognition 'Soul Makossa' brought to the scene, most club DJs were content to remain cult leaders. After all, DJs on the New York circuit had been discovering and breaking records for years, driven not by the desire to create pop hits but by the determination to find an alternative to pop mediocrity. They were comfortable underground, where they didn't have to please anyone but themselves and their immediate audience; where there was no playlist, no format, no hype, no dead air; where listener response was immediate and unequivocal. Before disco became disco! and its tastemakers found themselves hitmakers, DJs were happiest playing records no one had ever heard before – fusion jazz LP tracks, obscure R & B singles, instrumental flip sides, Italian imports – but everyone (or at least everyone they cared about: an elite group of perhaps 400) would be screaming for the next two months. So 'Soul Makossa' was business as usual for New York's club jocks, a shot of mellow exotica perfectly calibrated for their jungle gyms. But it was something of a revolution for Atlantic and for the other major labels following the action from the sidelines. Though none of these companies could have been entirely unaware of the early boost the club crowd gave to hits like 'Papa Was a Rolling Stone', 'Yes We Can Can', 'I'll Take You There', or 'Theme From Shaft', few had any sense of its growing power as an alternative market. Because discos thrived on obscurity, they were the ideal indie launching pads, and small New York labels were the first to notice and feed their appetite for eccentric grooves. When Manu Dibango broke, he illuminated this market for the majors but it didn't divert them for long. Disco was marginal, freakish, too unpredictable; even the R & B departments couldn't be bothered. "I don't think that it was really a serious commitment at that time," says Jerry Wexler about Atlantic's 'Soul Makossa' moment. "It was just a spasm, just a random thing." All that changed, of course, in 1974 when first, 'Love's Theme', Barry White's ultralush Love Unlimited Orchestra instrumental, then the Hues Corporation's 'Rock The Boat' and George McCrae's 'Rock Your Baby' hit the top of the pop charts in the first half of the year. For most industry observers, these records came out of nowhere, but 'Love's Theme' had been the ruling club anthem for nearly six months before radio discovered it and, perhaps because they were beginning to see themselves as potential music biz movers and shakers, club DJs were now eager to take credit for playing the hits first. But there was ambivalence and confusion on both sides. Club jocks who had always prided themselves on their instincts and their openness to idiosyncratic grooves from all points of the musical spectrum were suddenly under pressure to define and shape a new genre: disco.

To DJs, labels meant limits. To the record companies, they meant sales – not just a voracious new niche market but a vital pipeline to radio. Perversely, however, most DJs preferred underground exclusivity to mainstream popularity. Neither record execs nor radio programmers could ignore the massive number of disco singles selling without radio play; more than one company claimed to have sold upwards of 100,000 copies of a disco single before it crossed over to radio. But once a disco hit appeared in the Top 40, it was usually dead with the club crowd, which had long since moved on to a newer cult jam. The marketer's dream was also a bit of a nightmare, and the club crowd was happy to keep it that way. "Discos are going great," an unnamed 'Atlantic Records executive' told *Billboard* in the spring of 1975. "We don't know how long it'll last, but we'll be deeply involved as long as they're around – be it for six months or six years." The statement's guarded optimism was typical. Discos were going great that year, but they hadn't become any more predictable and, especially for the major labels, they'd proved to be a difficult market to crack. Jerry Wexler left Atlantic that year, but he remembers its disco successes as being mostly "accidental and peripheral – things that just happened to fit". That was true for most established companies, but Atlantic had had more accidental club hits than most because its sophisticated brand of contemporary R & B was – along with Motown and Sly Stone and James Brown and Philadelphia soul and Phil Spector – the key to the evolution of disco's ever-mutating sound. Disco in its earliest stages was simply a collage of unselfconscious dance music, and Atlantic's great neoclassic soul groups, the Spinners (with 'Could It Be I'm Falling In Love?', 'One Of A Kind', 'Love Affair' and 'Mighty Love') and Blue Magic (with 'Look Me Up' and 'Welcome To The Club') were club favourites long before they started deliberately making disco records. Another record that "just happened to fit" in the clubs: the flukey, funky 'Pick Up The Pieces' by the Scottish fusion-soul group Average White Band, which topped the American charts early in 1975.

But two of Atlantic's biggest hits that year were anything but accidents. Both Herbie Mann's 'Hijack' and Consumer Rapport's 'Ease On Down The Road' were designed as disco records, and their self-consciousness almost defeats them. 'Hijack' was a faithful cover of an import record by the Spanish sextet Barrabas, whose earlier singles, 'Wild Safari' and 'Woman', had turned them into a club cult group. Mann, the pop jazz flautist with a long history at Atlantic, had been recording a disco-themed album and was searching for a kick-off single. The Barrabas song, unreleased in America but already picking up a serious club buzz, has been slipped to Atlantic's head of A & R, Jim Delehant, and it fitted the bill perfectly. Mann's version, featuring Ray Barretto on congas and the Sweet Inspirations with Cissy Houston, was rush-released, giving him first shot at one of the year's quirkiest, most atmospheric songs. With its feathery chorus change threaded through a series of instrumental breaks, 'Hijack' was an early Eurodisco template of radiant minimalism and the best-selling single of Mann's career. In an unusual move, Atlantic also picked up the Barrabas original, which trounced Mann in the discos but couldn't compete on the pop charts. Though Mann followed through with his promised *Discotheque* album (which included jazzy covers of 'Pick Up The Pieces' and 'Lady Marmalade'), that didn't stop him from bad mouthing the genre. "Disco is like a great porno film," he told *Rolling Stone* later that year. "If the characters and filming technique are interesting, it's great for five minutes. That's what disco music is, good for five minutes. If that's all you want to hear, fantastic, but it bores the shit out of me." 'Ease On Down The Road' was an airy, punched-up version of Charlie Smalls' already disco-styled centrepiece song from *The Wiz*, the all-black Wizard of Oz just kicking off its successful Broadway run. It sounds over-calculated and not a little corny today, and even then it represented the kind of formulaic disco commercialization that hardcore club freaks found repugnant. Though it would be a few years before Atlantic released an album of disco orchestrations of Led Zeppelin tunes, other labels were turning out cookie-cutter disco versions of everything from 'Tubular Bells' to the *I Love Lucy* theme song. Still, 'Ease On Down The Road' had real verve, plenty of soaring instrumental breaks in the Philadelphia-patented MFSB vein, and it captured one of disco's defining moods: blissed-out optimism. Atlantic was excited by the success of these records but even more psyched by the extraordinary growth of the dance music market; by the end of 1976, *Newsweek*'s cover story on "one of the biggest entertainment phenomena of the seventies" reported that there were "an estimated 10,000" discos in the U.S. compared with 1,500 just two years before. Virtually alone among the majors but along with nearly every other record label anxious to be in on what was clearly the Next Big Thing, Atlantic plunged further into disco.

Abba

Because old-guard promo men and A & R departments steeped in R & B and rock were ill-equipped to handle or relate to the proliferating legions of after-hours tastemakers – most of them young, gay, black, Latin, or any combination of the above – labels began hiring a new wave of company freaks. Like the hippies who preceded them these upstart experts were valued both for their ears and their entrée to a scene that was beginning to be a gold mine. Because many of the newly hired DJs and other biz-savvy disco devotees were also young, gay, black, Latin, etc., their presence helped subvert a corporate culture that had begun to get stale and self-satisfied. At Atlantic, of course, some of the corporate types were known to hit the occasional dance floor. Ahmet and Mica Ertegun were frequently spotted at clubs both funky and chic, but the label's president, Jerry Greenberg, became a self-described "disco freak" after his friend Steve Rubell opened the decade's most celebrated ballroom, Studio 54. "Discos are a great way to sell records," Greenberg told *Forbes* magazine in 1976. "We used to have our hands tied because if the radio stations wouldn't play our records, no one knew they existed. Discotheques are giving us an extra shot at getting our records known, and then getting them on the radio stations." But it wasn't strictly business. Greenberg, who says he "personally signed" The Trammps, Cerrone, Sister Sledge and Chic – all the acts that made Atlantic a major player in the disco-to-pop market – also remembers the electric rush of a new record churning up Studio's dance floor. "You didn't have to be a rocket scientist with this stuff because the street told you where the hits were," Greenberg says today. "When they liked a record – bingo! The reaction was amazing." But in an increasingly competitive market, making that record happen required specialized expertise on both the production and promotion end. Disco's most successful producers learned quickly that a hit record needed more than a relentlessly driving beat. The best ones appreciated disco as a musical experience: a song amplified by dancing; music felt at once physically and emotionally. Ideally, such a song had movement, scope, expression, surprise – in short, breaks to die for: moments when the dance floor would erupt in pure, tribal joy. Though many of disco's first hits were songs of standard length, longer tracks meant more and longer breaks, and the record companies that provided them had an edge. Encouraged by its in-house disco advisers, Atlantic was one of the first labels to press up longer versions exclusively for disco DJs. Their initial series of five "disco discs" was announced in Billboard's May 1975 Discomania Special (the first of two that year), and included a typically mixed bag of hits and misses, from Consumer Rapport's 'Ease On Down the Road' and Hot Chocolate's 'Disco Queen' to 'Clap Your Hands' by The Manhattan Transfer and 'Mad Love' by Barrabas. "It All Started Here And It's Not Stopping", the ad's tag line promised.

That early format – a seven-inch, 33 ⅓ disc – was almost immediately upgraded to a 12-inch version, a major improvement in sound quality that also allowed for the inevitable: much longer tracks. If the mini-disc experiment had flopped, Atlantic's latest innovation caught on immediately; the 12-inch disco disc became the industry's standard promo tool and, early in 1976 (with Salsoul's release of 'Ten Per Cent' by Double Exposure), its first new commercial format since the introduction of the 45. Disco went from being a special-interest sideline to a driving force in the music business. Unfortunately, savvy marketing was often wasted on sappy product. Disco's earliest formulas were thoroughly exhausted by the middle of 1975, leaving the bandwagon open to a flood of frantic, clueless performers and producers determined to ride it to glory. A surprising number of them actually did. Like much pop music, disco was fickle, prey to one-shots and studio groups, Eurotrash and has-beens, mercenaries, geniuses, and eccentrics. Over the next few years, before disco crashed and burned in 1980, Atlantic had its share of them all. The label's Europop quartets, Abba from Sweden and Boney M from Germany, had only marginal success in US clubs, where the soul melting pot was more open to Barrabas. But among its successes was brilliant oddball Jimmy Castor, the writer-performer-producer and sax player whose songs (including 'E-Man Boogie' and 'Bertha Butt Boogie') were like funky Saturday-morning cartoons, full of bounce and crude wit. Two of the label's big neofunk bands, Mass Production and Slave, managed a few respectable disco hits each – particularly during the period when singer Steve Arrington was handling Slave's lead vocals. Still, great studio-group one-shots like Kleeer's 'Keep Your Body Workin'' and Phreek's 'Weekend' actually had more explosive and memorable club impact. Atlantic's signature disco group was the Philadelphia-based Trammps, a solid, old-school R & B band whose previous hits, 'Zing Went The Strings of My Heart', 'Where Do We Go From Here?' and 'Love Epidemic', had made them underground club legends. Philly soul was one of disco's seminal sounds, and The Trammps production team – Norman Harris, Ronald Baker, and one of the group's lead singers, Earl Young – had been involved as producers and musicians with a slew of disco's most influential records. Like Motown, Philadelphia was rooted in traditional, hook-driven songwriting and an utterly contemporary blend of the raw and the cooked: a percussion-spiked rhythm section floating on a gorgeous cushion of strings. Baker, Harris and Young didn't need to retool their sound for disco; they'd already defined it with their pumping grooves. But when The Trammps joined Atlantic in 1975 they were quick to style themselves as a disco band, and their first big single, 'That's Where The Happy People Go', became one of the genre's anthems – propaganda that perfectly embodied the joyous release it was designed to sell. 'Disco Inferno', the record that set them firmly in disco's pantheon, is a darker sort of celebration, inserting Black Power's most provocative slogan, 'Burn, baby, burn,' in a chorus urging the ultimate conflagration of the senses. 'Disco Inferno' captures the gospel fervour of the club experience – a yearning for transcendence and rapture. "I'm not talking about burning down a building," singer Jimmy Ellis assures us in a raspy spoken break. 'Soul Fire' was the subject of this inspired sermon, and disco's true believers knew just what he meant when he sang, "Let my spirit burn free". Though The Trammps grounded Atlantic in disco's bedrock soul, the label couldn't ignore the Eurodisco revolution. When Donna Summer and Giorgio Moroder redefined the genre with 'Love To Love You Baby' late in 1975 – asserting the primacy of the synthesizer, the (over)extended track and the pulsating thump-thump beat – the pulse of dance music quickened and the orgasm metaphor took over. Though disco continued in its idiosyncratic ways – offering up strange brews as various as Dr. Buzzard's Original Savannah Band, Grace Jones, Sylvester and the Village People – the Summer sound became both the ruling disco formula and the one to beat. Jean-Marc Cerrone, a 24-year-old French composer-producer and studio drummer who recorded under his last name only, became Summer's most conspicuous challenger early in 1977 with 'Love In C Minor', a 15-minute orgasmic symphony that first swept American clubs as an import album track. Atlantic snapped it up just about the time Casablanca jumped on the similarly frantic 'I Found Love' by Cerrone's Paris-based collaborator, Alec Costandinos, and the Eurobattle was joined. With its panting *ménage à trois* fantasy revolving around Cerrone himself, 'Love In C Minor' is outrageously camp and astonishingly effective, building rush upon rush, climax upon climax, until the dance floor is as exhausted as it is exhilarated. Cerrone's more pop-oriented follow-up, 'Supernature', was, like 'Disco Inferno', another dark vision. In this sci-fi scenario, Cerrone imagines a toxic Island of Lost Souls where mutant creatures revolt in the night; even at the peak of their mainstream acceptance, disco freaks could empathize. Though Cerrone insisted he wasn't particularly taken with disco, he knew what made it tick. "A disco producer doesn't have to be a conductor like some people think," he told *The Los Angeles Times* in 1979. "Arranging is the major thing. You have to know how to put together an album people will love to dance to. You have to know and feel the rhythm. It's very subtle." If that subtlety was lost on disco's detractors, it was also overlooked by many of the music's most active producers At the height of its popularity, disco was a magnet for kitsch sentimentality and a target for rocker animosity. The turning point was 1978, which began with Debby Boone's 'You Light Up My Life' at the top of the pop singles chart and ended with Chic's 'Le Freak' in the same spot. In between was the *Saturday Night Fever* juggernaut. But how could the ultimate triumph of disco's musical multiculturalism mean the

The Spinners

Bee Gees ruled the charts? Though it surely benefited from the Bee Gee's pop reinterpretation of the genre, Chic brought the focus back to the dance floor by crafting a glossy new disco sound. Streamlined but intricately worked, sophisticated but funky, Chic's style was a clean machine, a shrewd-merger of form and function. Their debut, the commanding 'Dance, Dance, Dance (Yowsah, Yowsah, Yowsah)', was aimed directly at the clubs, where its sweep of real violins was especially welcome after seasons of buzzing synths. As Jerry Greenberg points out, Chic was when "disco became big-time pop" and record after record exploded on the singles charts; 'Le Freak' was certified platinum even before it hit number one pop and remained there for six weeks, becoming Atlantic's best-selling single to date. Though studio built, Chic's sound was no vinyl-only concoction, and co-creators Bernard Edwards (bass) and Nile Rodgers (guitars) knew that Chic's bright leanness was crucial. Whittled down to rhythmic basics, their 'Good Times' is definitive – at once a smart bomb of pop cool and the secret seed of hip-hop to come. That record's insistence that "these are the good times" sounded a note of wilful self-delusion even then; disco's early optimism had been badly bruised by 1979, and only a die-hard escapist could fail to see that the good times were elsewhere. Still, Edwards and Rodgers, as the Chic Organization, Ltd., were able to sustain and extend the celebration. Their glamour makeover on labelmates Sister Sledge – Philadelphia-born siblings Kathy, Debbie, Joni and Kim – was perhaps the most successful. Again, they targeted the aspirations of the disco crowd but discovered that a much wider audience shared its vision. All bold strokes and savvy syncopation, 'We Are Family' spoke directly to disco's ecstatic community – an extended family drawn closer by their identification with the music – but it endures as a sing-along pop standard. 'Lost In Music' took a harder look at club life and its ambivalence was very much of the moment. Crisp and lovely, 'Lost In Music' is a song about enthralment, immersion, stepping off the edge of the workaday world: "Feel so alive/I quit my nine to five". The singer could be a dancer caught up in the nightlife or a musician focusing her energies, but there's an all-or-nothing tone here that feels almost desperate. "No turning back", indeed. Within the year, disco was unceremoniously buried. Tell that to Madonna, the Pet Shop Boys, Michael Jackson, Culture Club, Janet Jackson, Erasure ... Long live disco.

The Trammps TL: 70s

Slave, including: Steve Arrington, Starleana Young, Steve Washington, Danny Webster, Orion Wilhoite and Tim Dozier TL: 70s

"People think you have to be pieces of the same cloth to be able to work successfully together. Not so! As people, we are really very different couples. Bjorn and I are what I would call 'morning people'. Benny and Frida prefer to sleep late. We don't like to hang about much, eating fancy food in late night restaurants for example. When we are on tour, Benny and Frida almost always disappear after the show until the small hours of the morning." Agnetha Faltskog

Above and below: Abba TL: 70s

This page clockwise from top: Pele, Ahmet and Steve Ross; Ahmet with Walter Yetnikoff; Jimmy Page with Ahmet; Alice Cooper and Bette Midler; Ahmet at a sales conference with (from his right) Dave Glew, Sal Uterano, Henry Allen and Bob Greenberg; Ahmet with Bette Midler and her husband, Martin von Haselberg; Doug Morris with Jerry Greenberg

Clockwise from top left: Party time at Studio 54; Steve Rubell and Ian Schrager; logo designed by Gilbert Lesser; Jerry Greenberg; guests arriving at the Hookers Ball.

"The people who opened Studio 54 were friends of ours. Steve Rubell was a great friend of Jerry Greenberg's, so we were there from the beginning. We were not only going to Studio 54 but also to places like Xenon, which was a very up club. The club scene at that time was a great phenomenon. When we put out 'Miss You' by The Rolling Stones, I sent a copy to Steve Rubell and he called me up the next day and said, 'You've got a smash! This is the biggest hit The Rolling Stones ever had.' He could tell by the crowd's reaction." Ahmet

The Rolling Stones, from left: Keith Richards, Mick Jagger and Bill Wyman TL: 70s

"One time I was in Washington, staying at the Watergate Hotel, and I ran into the great Russian dancer Baryshnikov in the hallway. He asked me what I was doing, and I told him I was going to see The Stones that night and asked him to join me. From the side of the stage he watched Mick dancing and said, 'You know, that's the best dancer I've ever seen, he's incredible. I think there are two people who can dance like that. Him and me.' After the show I introduced them and they got along very well." Ahmet

"'Mick – the thing is, Mick, you gotta finish this record. This record's gonna be great, it's gonna be a great record, Mick. We're gonna put all our resources behind the record. But listen, Mick, the promotion – forget the promotion – we don't wanna spend money on the promotion, Mick. We'll just have a big fuckin' party and promote the shit out of the party, and that'll sell a million.'" Mick Jagger quoting Ahmet

"When The Stones were doing the song 'Some Girls', I asked Mick to please change the lyrics. He said, 'No, no, no, you don't understand, this is supposed to be a stupid guy talking, it's an ironic song. Obviously it's not true that French women don't bathe, it's not true that Italian women are this way, or English girls are cold, or whatever. All these generalities are stupidities, which is why we're talking these things up. Some girls do this, some girls do that – it's supposed to be satire.' I said, 'I don't think people are going to understand that when they hear *black girls like to fuck all night*.' It came to a point where I couldn't get him to change the lyrics, so I knew that trouble was going to come. But if I hadn't put out the record the way it was, The Stones could have left the label. Our contract was set so that he had the right to put whatever he wanted in the records, as long as it wasn't illegal – and it wasn't illegal to say that.

"So the record came out, and for several months I was amazed. I thought, Jesus, we've gotten away with this. Nobody was calling, until one day Harold Jackson 'phoned. Harold was one of my oldest friends, a Washingtonian and one of the first people to play Atlantic's records on the radio. He owned a professional basketball team in Washington; I used to go to the games with him. Now Harold was a terrific guy, so he called me up and said, 'Ahmet, I hate to tell you this, I've been deluged with complaints about this record. You've got to take it off the market.' I said, 'I can't, I'm not allowed to take it off the market.' The long and the short of it was that there were 15 associations of Baptist ladies, and Harold had received a letter representing all of them.

"Then Jesse Jackson called me up and said, 'Ahmet, you're in a world of trouble.' I said, 'I know.' So he said, 'They're coming from all over, all of these different associations. They've written to me insisting that you do something.' So I tried to explain to Jesse that Mick was not racist; quite the contrary, that this was supposed to be an ironic comment about

From left: Mick Jagger, Keith Richards and Bill Wyman

From left: Ron Wood, Charlie Watts and Mick Jagger

people who actually say things like that. And I said, 'Well, what can we do?' He said, 'Well, they're going to organize a massive boycott of all of your records. You know what you do, you come here, come by yourself, and we'll work it out.' So I said, 'Well, I'm going to come with Noreen.' Noreen Woods was my assistant and she was like my guardian angel. Noreen was a great friend of Jesse Jackson's. He would always call her when he came to New York and go by to see her.

"So Noreen and I went to Chicago, and Jesse said to us, 'Look, I'm going to talk. Don't get upset, Ahmet, because I'm really going to light into you. I'm going to curse you and say horrible things. But you just go ahead and calmly explain what this is about.' I was scared to death when I walked in. I mean, it was a sea of black faces – there must have been a hundred people there, all filled up with anger. But we went through this whole thing, explaining: this is on The Rolling Stones' label and we have no control over what goes on that and furthermore, Mick Jagger is not a racist. Quite the contrary: he has a black child. In the meantime, Jesse Jackson is saying, 'Oh man, are you kidding?' He starts to curse me and says, 'You go there, take advantage of black people, and on top of that, you take their money selling records … then you do this, then you do that, then you turn around and insult them like this. This is black womanhood you're insulting.' But then he started to insult me irrationally, and to such an extent that the crowd suddenly began to react against him – because I was calmly continuing on, while he was ranting and raving. So suddenly I felt this turn in the audience, and right then, Jesse said, 'On the other hand, Ahmet, you've done so much for so many black artists: you've done this, you've done that, you can't control what this musician has done. I guess Jagger didn't mean to say that, he meant to say something else. It might not be clear on the record, because you can hardly understand the lyrics … '

Above and below: Mick Jagger and Keith Richards

"And suddenly this whole thing had come to an end. Then we all went and had lunch, which of course Jesse had organized. And everybody came over and asked me questions about LaVern Baker or Wilson Pickett. And we all left as happy and contented as can be. Jesse is a genius, you know, because he had orchestrated this whole thing, knowing that I had tried not to put the record out with that lyric." Ahmet

350 THE ATLANTIC STORY

Ahmet playing backgammon with Samuel Reed, watched by Oscar de la Renta

"I signed Cerrone in '77 and we put out 'Love In C Minor', which he co-wrote with Alex R. Costandinos. It made the Top Three slot of the *Billboard* disco chart for two solid months, as well as the R & B bestseller charts, and it was really a tremendous hit on the dance floors. Cerrone was always very talented. Next he made the album *Cerrone's Paradise,* a terrific fantasy about the Garden of Eden. Then he made *Supernature,* a disco fairytale, warning man not to play God. *Billboard* named Cerrone Disco Artist of the Year, Disco Music Arranger of the Year, Best Producer of a Disco Record, Male Disco Artist of the Year, and Disco Instrumentalist of the Year. Quite an achievement." Jerry Greenberg

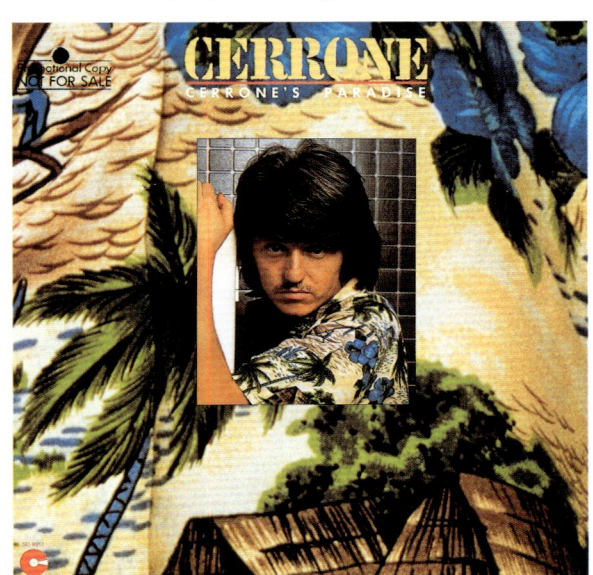

Cerrone TL: 70s

Ahmet (centre) dancing with Oscar and Francoise de la Renta

Roberta Flack TL: 70s

Above: Mick Ralphs and Simon Kirke of Bad Company TL: 70s 80s

Earl McGrath

"On one occasion when I was with The Rolling Stones on tour, I received an invitation from Bad Company inviting me to a party they were throwing in New York. So I replied, thanking them very much for the invitation, explaining that I would of course have loved to attend, but that unfortunately I was with worse company." Earl McGrath

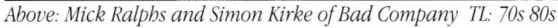

From left: Bad Company's Simon Kirke and Boz Burrell with Mick Jagger and Ahmet

Bon Scott with AC/DC TL: 70s

"I've been on the road for nearly 15 years and have no intention of stopping. We meet a lot of people, we drink lots of stuff and have lots of fun." Bon Scott

"We enjoy what we do. It's the kick we still get out of being on stage and playing. I enjoy just the feeling of it, you know? The only image we've ever had is what we really are. We never cover up anything. I mean if Bon's kissin' a film star's wife down the room and someone spots him, well tough shit. Nobody can blackmail him." Angus Young

Bon Scott

Angus Young

Above and below: Blackfoot TL: 70s 80s

Above from left: Jakson Spires, Rickey Medlocke, Greg T. Walker and Charlie Hargrett

"Look, when a guy says to me that he has 'made it', man, I think he's a lying son of a bitch. You never make it until you're dead, man. Only then have you made the ultimate step in life, because what have you really 'made' when you think you've reached the top? You've just made another step, that's all. All those bucks you have coming in, that beautiful house and the shiny new car, hey man, those things can be taken away from you in a day. Cos when you've 'made it', buddy, you've still got the blues, still payin' dues. You never quit payin' dues.

"The South is basically a poor section of the country and the people are looking for something to bring them out of that. I did, and music was a way of making myself heard, of showing people that I am somebody, not just some dumb Southerner sitting down there who's poor, and is going to stay that way all his life. I've got feelings, I've got emotions and basically, I'm as good as anybody else and I just think that, for people in the South, music is a great tradition.

"I was legally pronounced dead on the operating table when I was small, but it wasn't my time to go, that's all. I knew I was sick and didn't stand the best chance in the world, but I also knew I wanted to play music and be a great entertainer, and it was music that kept me going – that and those kids out there who're starved of entertainment and shell out their hard-earned bucks just to see us. 'Cos if I can stand out there and just one of those kids looks up at me and thinks, 'Yeah, I want to do that.' If I can give that kid the kind of incentive to really work at it, then I'm gonna stand up there every night I can and play as long as I can. People say I almost take on the role of preacher in my own way, that's why some call me 'Deacon' Rick, what with the hat and the long coat that I wear ... maybe that's what I should have been, man. Still, I suppose I am a preacher in rock'n'roll, I don't think the music's very sinful, like some people say. I honestly believe that everyone makes their own heaven and hell right here on earth. I just try to do the best I can." Rickey Medlocke

Opposite: Lou Gramm of Foreigner TL: 70s 80s

Ahmet with Bryan Ferry TL: 70s 80s

"Bryan Ferry is one of the great people in the history of rock'n'roll. He can throw you off a little bit, because he's always dressed extremely well and in the old-fashioned style. You may think you're talking to a very successful stockbroker, because he doesn't look like the stereotype of a rock'n'roller. He's extremely intelligent, very elegant, and cultivated. We have long discussions about the Bloomsbury school; he's very knowledgeable about art as well as literature. He's a wonderful person." Ahmet

Jean-Luc Ponty TL: 70s 80s

Donny Hathaway TL: 70s

"Before his tragic death, I think Donny was really showing the way he wanted his music to develop. For instance, he experimented with time signatures, like having a 5/4 time in a funk tune; with different instrumentations; with grandiose ballads with symphonic backgrounds. I hope that young black musicians never forget who Donny Hathaway was. I mean, I don't want these geniuses to be forgotten. These heroes should really be kept alive." Arif Mardin

"I think Donny Hathaway's untimely death leaves a huge void in American and maybe world music. This man was a genius – not only a great instrumentalist and piano player, but a terrific vocalist. It's such a shame that this happened, because I believe he would have shown the way to a lot of people. I was really privileged to work with him, because after a long day in the studio – where you work hard, you hear tedious things, you hear the same song over and over, the same passage again and again just to fix something or put a part on – your payoff really comes when you hear a good vocal. When you hear Aretha sing, or Chaka Khan … with Donny it was the same thing. When he sang, you just forgot about the daily grind and all your problems, and you'd know why you were doing what you were doing. I'd be listening to a vocal that nobody had heard before, which the artist may better – or not even use – but I'd have this memory of a wonderful evening, which is one of the privileges of working with great people." Joel Dorn

"Donny Hathaway is certainly one of the great singers in the history of American music. The recordings he did on his own, as well as those he did with Roberta Flack, are among the most beautiful ever made. His untimely death was a great, great tragedy. He never really got to do all of the things he could have done. He had certain personal problems, health problems, which eventually dragged him down." Ahmet

Above and opposite: Charles Mingus TL: 70s

"Charles Mingus was one of the great jazz band leaders, and he left a trove of treasures. He is sorely missed. However, there are several groups that regularly get together to play his music, and I'm sure that his name will live on as one of the most brilliant and influential jazz musicians of the century."
Ahmet

Larry Coryell TL: 70s

Charles Mingus (far right) with musicians and Atlantic staff members. TL 70s

"As an inspired musician and inspired singer, I travel the garden of music, through inspiration. I see so many different ways of interpreting reggae. Reggae is a spiritual music, with spiritual ingredients."
Peter Tosh

Peter Tosh TL: 70 80s

Below right, Jim Carroll; and above, with backing from Keith Richards TL: 80s

"We went into Wally Heider's studio and started recording *Catholic Boy*. Earl McGrath had brought a hot young engineer named Bob Clearmountain to record us. This was long before Bob had become hugely successful with Bryan Adams and others. He had just done some remixes for the Stones. Years later, after I had become an engineer, I ran into him at an Audio Engineers Society show, and he told me that he had gotten hired by Bryan Adams because of the *Catholic Boy* album." Steve Linsley, bass player on *Catholic Boy*

Chic TL: 80s

The Spinners and Ahmet with Jerry Greenberg and radio pioneer Hal Jackson (seated left and right)

Sister Sledge, Kim, Debbie, Joni and Kathy Sledge, with Bernard Edwards and Nile Rodgers TL: 80s

"Ironically, we wrote the song 'Good Times' in the midst of a very bad financial and political period in America. It was our kind of ironic lyric – we were trying to point out that things weren't so good, but that music, film, dance, or any kind of performing art allows you the space where you can get lost for the moment … where you can forget everything that is going on outside of your life and get into this fantasy or escapist type of art form. That's what it was all about. We enjoyed going up there on stage and just losing ourselves for an hour or two. That's what we were saying—that in the midst of all this tragedy and hard financial times, we can just dance, party and have a good time. That's what the disco thing was about to me – if you'd just gotten fired, you didn't go out and kill somebody. You really could go into a club, start dancing, meet somebody, and go hang out. People were very sexually active in those days and it was fun. I mean, it was great. Very different times.

"I remember when I went into a club and heard 'Rapper's Delight' for the first time. It was the best record I thought I had ever heard. Why? Because the rhythm track was my rhythm track and somebody had come up with lyrics that were cleverer than mine. I thought, 'This is great, why didn't I write that?' It's funny when I think about it now, but it seems like that was the beginning of a whole movement. Now it's incredibly common to sample a record, make a little tape loop using exactly the same rhythm track, and just start rapping over it. The first time that was done really effectively on a large scale was with 'Rapper's Delight' and 'Good Times'. Now it's an industry standard." Nile Rodgers

The Brides Of Funkenstein, Lynn Mabry and Dawn Silva TL: 70s 80s

Above and below: Sister Sledge, Kim, Debbie, Joni, Kathy Sledge TL: 70s 80s

SISTER SLEDGE

"I had signed Chic, which led to the success of Sister Sledge, whom Henry Allen had signed. Nile Rodgers was in my office after we'd hit with Chic and he said, 'What I like is Sister Sledge.' So I said to him, 'You know, we're family, we're like a family.' And he went out and wrote the song 'We Are Family'. I should have gotten a writer's credit!" Jerry Greenberg

"'We Are Family' is a blessing to me because the lyrics were really written about my sisters and me. That makes it special to me." Kathy Sledge

"When we go on the road, we need about 40 people plus a whole mass of equipment to ensure that we get the results on stage that we want. We've relied on films to boost our record sales, rather than undertake the high cost and problems involved in doing a tour. Touring can make you mad. It's the most anti-social life you can lead. You don't live like normal people and it's difficult to get both feet back on the ground after a tour has finished."
Bjorn Ulvaeus

Agnetha Faltskog and Anni-Frid Lyngstad

Abba: Bjorn Ulvaeus, Agnetha Faltskog, Anni-Frid Lyngstad and Benny Andersson TL: 70s 80s

Abba

Boney M, from left: Maizie Williams, Marcia Barrett, Liz Mitchell and Bobby Farrell TL: 70s

"The Spinners came to Atlantic through Henry Allen and me. They've always been just the most fabulous artists, and wonderful characters. Once we put them together with Thom Bell, I knew that we had a group with a really strong black base but that could also cross over massively into pop. And from 'Rubberband Man' and those other early records on down, that's exactly what they did. They kept that balance and they just had one huge hit record after another. And they toured, they'd play 450 dates a year, I mean phenomenal, and the records they made throughout that time are still classics." Jerry Greenberg

The Spinners, from left: Henry Farnborough, Billy Henderson, John Edwards, Bobby Smith and Pervis Jackson TL: 70s 80s

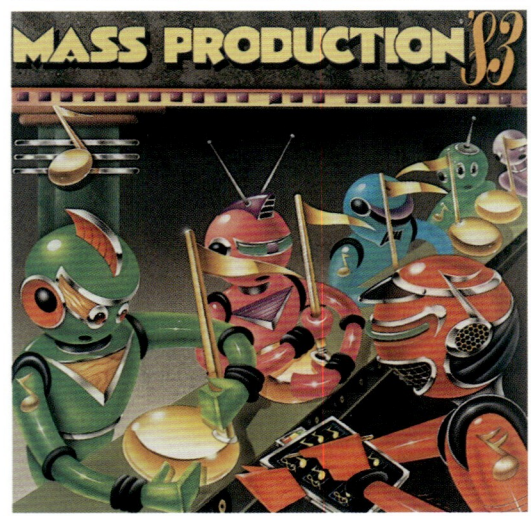

Ahmet M. Ertegün
requests the pleasure of your company
at a supper dance
in honor of
the Spinners
on Tuesday, February tenth
at eight o'clock
in the Crystal Room
at the Beverly Hills Hotel

R.S.V.P.
(213) 278-9243
Ms. Ayer

This invitation
is not transferable.
Please present at door.

"Initially I wanted the record *The Bride Stripped Bare* to have an East side and a West side. In a sense it was a risky album. It was done during the Punk explosion and I was aware that if I made a record like my first records from six years before, which were sort of rough-edged, it would have been just right for the time. But instead I endeavoured to make an album that was smooth on the surface, but jagged underneath – on its emotional side.

"I had the idea for Manifesto for simply ages. That's happened with every album we've made. I always have the title down first. I saw it as the perfect statement of intent if you like – a very strong word which conjured up cross-references with the Futurists … not that I'd be so immodest as to align myself with them." Bryan Ferry

Bryan Ferry TL: 70s

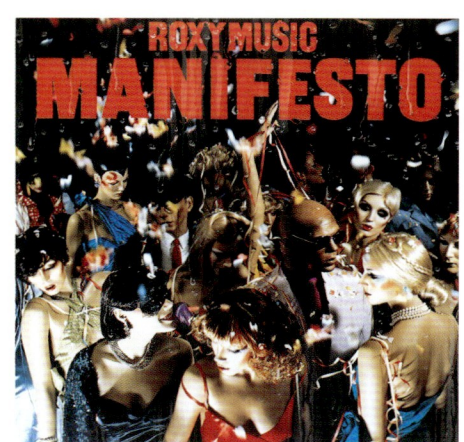

Roxy Music TL: 70s

Roxy Music, from left: Phil Manzanera, Gary Tibbs, Paul Thompson and Bryan Ferry TL: 70s

Robert Plant and fan

"We'd been on the road since '68, and even though we hadn't toured for a couple of years, we knew that the music would always speak for itself. It wasn't a question of 'are we heroes any more?' We always knew that we were what we were when we walked out on stage and played." Robert Plant

Jimmy Page

Led Zeppelin, from left: Robert Plant, John Paul Jones, John Bonham and Jimmy Page; and opposite: Led Zeppelin TL: 70s 80s

Pete Townshend TL: 80s

"Pete Townshend is, I would say, the philosopher of rock'n'roll and one of the most intelligent people that I have ever met. He is a charming man with a great sense of humour. He is also a person of extreme dedication to his friends: I remember when Eric Clapton had some personal problems, how hard Pete fought and how much he tried to help straighten things out for Eric. He has a very strong personal ethic and has written some of the most moving moments in music history. There aren't many epic tales like *Tommy* in rock'n'roll. Pete has the vision and the ability to create large bodies of work." Ahmet

"I think when Keith Moon died I gave myself permission to do a proper solo deal. I had a small record label and I'd spent a lot of money on a book publishing company, among other things – a mini-empire. The Who were never really big money-earners in any shape or form. Our first managers were on 40%, and we'd insisted on remaining English residents right the way through the most pernicious, socialist tax reign of 98% – 'We're Londoners, and we are not going to Lichtenstein or wherever.' We had a couple of tax schemes that worked okay, but as we didn't really make any money, we couldn't really use the tax schemes. We did okay, but I think I was something like a couple of million dollars in the hole. So doing my solo deal when I did it was part of a bigger picture – of getting out of the hole that I was in. The other element involved, though, for me at that time, and entirely separate to the money, was that I wanted to become an artist again – the way that I had been an artist during the early days of The Who.

"My agent, Ina Meibach, kept pressing me towards CBS, which of course is a great label – Bob Dylan, Paul Simon, various singer-songwriters – but I couldn't get an emotional fix on it. The label that I favoured, just purely for romantic reasons, was Atlantic. Ina rang me up and said, 'Listen, I know that you love Atlantic, but I think you need a company that's truly international.' She said, 'As a reflection of what CBS thinks they can do with you as an international artist, they have offered you a million dollars non-recoupable on top of your deal.' I asked her what that meant and she said, 'It means they're going to give you a million dollars to sign with the label.' So I said, 'Thanks very much,' went away, thought about it, and somehow that offer made the decision for me. It was so obvious to me at that moment that I didn't care about the money. I just knew then that there was no choice. I rang up Ina and told her that I'd decided to go with Atlantic. She told me that I was insane, that nobody ever got offered a million dollars. I told her I understood and, looking back, it was kind of insane because, in actual fact, being on Atlantic didn't increase my collateral with Ahmet, didn't mean that I saw him any more or less than before. It didn't change my relationship with him whatsoever really but it was important for me and I don't regret it.

"I love it when *Guitar Player* magazine asks young guys who play in the latest hot band, 'And who are your influences?' And they reply, 'Oh, Jimi Hendrix, Segovia and Brahms.' What they see is a direct line from Brahms to Segovia to Jimi Hendrix to Freddie Philipot of the Wandering Jam Pots! – as it was for me when I wanted to be in a direct line with some of these great Atlantic artists. So, when I came to make my first record for Atlantic, I worked much harder on *Empty Glass* – which was my first serious solo album – than on any of the solo records that I had made before, because I wanted it to be a part of the classic Atlantic repertoire.

"For me it's about the label. It's the fact that when I go to my collection of vinyl records and pull them out, I remember. For me pop music is interesting. People seem to want to demean it and say, 'Why not just get it down to size and say, it's just an aide-mémoire: I danced to Jimi Hendrix, I can remember The Beatles but compared to Bartok, it's nothing.' Some people think, 'Who's going to remember this in 20 years' time?' The fact of it is, this business of calling it pop is demeaning to R & B and to jazz, because the perception that we have of the word 'pop' is that it is just a pop, like a bubble bursting. Any kind of cultural relativism is wrong, of course, in this respect, but if you accept that I'm generalizing when using the word 'pop' to mean all of this stuff which is quintessentially good, then when I pull out one of these records, I am pulling out a chapter – not just of my life at art college when I first heard it, but a whole building block. It's part of my foundation so that today, when I look back through my life, I suddenly realize that this is more than just a brick in who I am, it's actually a signpost to everything that I'm made of. Once you've got a true line between yourself and your history, you'll know who you're going to be. Better than that, you'll know who your children are going to be, and even better than that, you'll know who they probably are today. It really roots you and lands you. The great thing is that I think if I had gone and signed with CBS I would have become a New York artist, and I don't think that, for example, I would ever have been able to take *Tommy* to Broadway.

"I remember thinking it so strange when Ina said to me, 'You want an international label.' While it may be true that CBS has offices all over the world, when you look at Atlantic and consider that Ahmet is Turkish, has always led an extremely cosmopolitan life, speaks so many different languages and has accomplished so much, then, of course, Atlantic is the crucible – it's like the Mecca of this music. There are so many other great labels, other centres, so many other great people in American musical history, that one doesn't want to pretend that there was only one label. If I had to fix it, I would hate to lose Wes Montgomery, Sinatra, Ella – I would hate to lose a number of people who have never recorded for Atlantic – but if you had to strip my little collection down, I'd just hold on to the Atlantic records. If I was just going to pick one record as a *Desert Island Disc*, it would be a single recording that somebody made by accident of a Ray Charles concert. That's the one I would want to live with, or maybe an Aretha album. It wouldn't be *Sgt. Pepper*, *Pet Sounds*, *The Wall*, *Tommy*, *Aftermath* – it wouldn't be white music, I can tell you that.

"My friend Dick Seaman and I were standing in a doorway at college, we were only about 17, when another friend of ours, Vince, came walking down the corridor towards us. Vince had been out the night before to the Roaring Twenties Club and, as usual, he's pretending to be a Caribbean. This is 1961/62, he's wearing a three-quarter mac with a short brimmed hat, trying to walk in a reggae style, and as he passes by us Dick says, 'Nigger,' and Vince replies, 'Thanks.' That's what it's about, a sense of knowing what it is that you should really uphold. That's what the label meant to me and you know, strangely enough, what I did with *Empty Glass* goes straight back into that.

"It seems to me that the indignity and hypocrisy of foul deeds being committed in the name of God were often brought about by the chain of command that had been set up, namely: God – Pope – King – Priest – People. When people say they are going to sing directly to the source, what you then have is where this music began." Pete Townshend

Pete Townshend

From left: Donald 'Duck' Dunn, Elwood Blues (Dan Aykroyd), Matt Murphy and Jake Blues (John Belushi) – The Blues Brothers TL: 70s 80s

"I was woken up very late one night by a telephone call, with a voice on the other end of the line telling me he was John Belushi. I said, 'All right now, it's too late and I'm tired,' and hung up the 'phone. He called back and said, 'Do you know Tom Malone?' I thought, 'Uh-oh,' and said, 'Yeah, I know Tom Malone.' Tom was playing trombone on the *Saturday Night Live* show. He said, 'This is John Belushi.' I thought, 'Oh shit, I done hang up on John Belushi.' So anyway, he said, 'I know you played with Otis Redding, you happen to be one of my favourite bass players, and I want you in this band I'm starting. Can you come to New York?' So then I got scared and a little bit intimidated by the calibre of those musicians, including Malone, Paul Shaffer and Steve Jordan – they were an incredible band and I didn't know whether I could play with those guys or not. When I got there, however, I came to find out that if a song didn't work, well, John just said, 'Goodbye – we'll go to another song.' That's the way it was. There were a lot of critics who said it was a joke, that it shouldn't be done and that he was maybe hurting the blues. But what he actually did, I think, was help to rejuvenate the blues. When they got into those characters, they were as sincere as anyone. They may not have had the talent of John Lee Hooker or anyone like that, but there was a sincere love of what they were doing and it wasn't a joke to them. What a band, too, what a band!" Donald 'Duck' Dunn

From left: Dan Aykroyd, Steve Cropper and John Belushi

"John Belushi became a good friend to me. He came to my house with Lorne Michaels, the executive producer of *Saturday Night Live*, who was also a friend of Johnny Pigozzi who was staying with me at the time. I had the whole

group out to dinner one night in Southampton, all of those now-famous people. John Belushi used to come to the Cosmos games, and he and a couple of the other guys used to do a comedy routine at half-time. They bought a bar downtown which they didn't allow anybody into except their friends. Needless to say, the place was always full and everything went on in there. John was a great blues fan and we used to listen to records together at his house in New York. He had a walk-up apartment. It was such a natural idea, this Blues Brothers thing, so I said, 'Well, man, let's record it.' For people who are not professional musicians, he and Dan Aykroyd made some incredible records and were very successful. Then out of all that came the great movie.

"They got Duck Dunn and Steve Cropper involved. They picked whoever they wanted to play – Dan Aykroyd knows all those people. I tell you, John Belushi was one of the most wonderful people I knew. He was of Albanian origin and we liked a lot of the same things. His death was a bitter blow to many of us. Dan Aykroyd still keeps up the Blues Brothers tradition, and he's such a brilliant actor – I love Dan." Ahmet

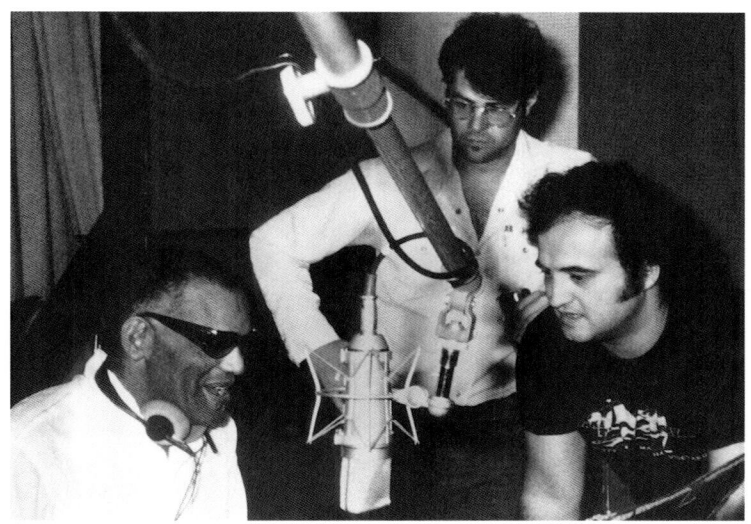

Clockwise from top: John Belushi with Bill Graham; Steve Cropper; Donald 'Duck' Dunn; and Dan Aykroyd and John Belushi with Ray Charles

The Rolling Stones' Mick Jagger and Charlie Watts TL: 80s

"My father had a small department store, so I began working there and eventually became controller of the store, which turned over about a million dollars a year. Then the malls opened up and I got a job at Barney's Clothes. The owner of the store, Barney Pressman, was at that time in his seventies and paid me the fabulous salary of $15,000 per annum. This was 1960, '61. Barney, however, was really uncouth and very rude. One day he came into the office where a few of us worked and started screaming, 'Who the hell needs any of you – I don't need bookkeepers!!' So I thought, 'Well, maybe I'd better start looking for a different line of work.' My uncle, William Gottlieb, heard about this and suggested that I go and see the people who were running this small record company, Atlantic. Bill had been friends with the Erteguns for years and at that time the partners at Atlantic were Ahmet, Nesuhi, Jerry and Miriam. So Bill fixed up an appointment for me to meet Miriam. I had no idea at the time what an album was - I pictured an album to be four or five 78s put together in a kind of book, but this didn't seem to worry Miriam. She said to me, 'You seem intelligent and accounting's accounting.' So I got the job as controller. Then over the years I became Vice President, Senior Vice President, and eventually Vice Chairman.

"An interesting feature to me of the whole situation was that although Ahmet and Nesuhi had been brought up to enjoy all of the luxuries surrounding the embassy life, they had never actually had much money of their own. When they chose to stay in America they really pretty much had to fend for themselves. There's a lovely story of how one night, Jerry and Miriam had arranged to meet Ahmet for dinner and he didn't show up. So they waited and waited, and as they'd received no word from him either, they began to get a little bit worried, and went up to his apartment. There they found Ahmet sitting around on his own, stripped to the waist. So Miriam enquired what the hell was going on, and Ahmet told them that he was sorry, but he didn't have a shirt to wear. So Miriam went snooping through his closets and discovered 20 or 30 scrunched-up shirts waiting to be cleaned. So she asked him, 'Why don't you have these laundered?' And he replied, 'Well, who would do that?'

"Nesuhi's great love was jazz. He also became very involved with producing wonderful covers for the records. He would commission and work with the artists completing these covers, then he'd also spend hours and hours with the printer getting the shades of colour and the details absolutely right.

Top, from left: Foreigner's manager, Bud Prager, and Atlantic's, Tunc Erim and Sheldon Vogel; and above, from left, Sheldon Vogel, Fran Wakschal, Nesuhi and Ahmet

"By the time I joined them in 1962 they had enjoyed and continued to enjoy a tremendous amount of success, but Atlantic still really remained a small company. The majors were no more interested in them at that time than they were in, for example, the record company Roulette. Then one day three or four years later, Ahmet came in with a recording he had made of a duo called Sonny & Cher, explaining them as being 'people he'd met on the West Coast.' Well, that record, 'I Got You Babe', was an international, worldwide smash hit. For the first time we'd sold over two million copies of a record. It came as a shock to us. As well as Ahmet and Nesuhi's circumstances, Jerry and Miriam had certainly never had substantial amounts of money of their own, but here we were suddenly selling records on a truly grand scale, and we began to get offers from outside. We nearly sold the company to Paramount because, can you imagine, the four partners being offered $2.7 million to share just between themselves? That was incredible! Unbelievable! So the guy from Paramount started calling me every day. I was speaking with him more than I was with Ahmet and Jerry! Then he'd ask me how his company was doing, how were his artists. So I'd say, 'Well, hold on, you haven't bought the company yet!' Then they tried to make us responsible for any claim any artist might have made in the future. So I told them that we were completely up-to-date, we'd always paid the royalties due, and we'd paid all of our taxes - that they were welcome to come and audit all of our books, but we could not sign a deal where we were responsible for a claim that might be made four or six years down the line. So because of that one stipulation they backed out. They could have bought Atlantic for $2.7 million! Then right after they walked out on the deal we really exploded. Out sales and profits went through the roof, so that a year or so later, we sold to Warner for 17-18 million. Maybe in retrospect it wasn't enough, but that was a lot of money back then. Also, for people who'd been earning $1,200 a month, to pay $60,000 or $70,000 for an artist was unthinkable. I don't think we'd have paid that much if it had been our own money, but suddenly we were free to deal in those kind of sums – it was phenomenal!

"Then of course, Steve Ross got involved, bought out Warner and really paid each of the principals all over again and provided Atlantic with complete autonomy. His attitude was: anything you want to spend, spend. We could make a $10 million deal without talking to anyone at the corporate level. Steve's attitude was: who in my company is going to know more about music and making records than Ahmet and the people at Atlantic? So through the seventies we became more and more successful. We were constantly growing and growing, doing super-well just on catalogue, never mind new artists. The real upsurge in sales came about, I think, through the development of new technology. The first example of this was cassette tapes. As well as the new music, a lot of people bought all of their favourite music all over again, but on cassette, so that they could listen to it in the car, on a Walkman, in the street or whatever. The next example of this was of course CDs – better sound quality, no scratches, etc., so the whole catalogue got bought all over again. So all of this brought about an enormous increase in unit sales. The record companies appeared to be extremely profitable and artists asked for and were paid huge advances. Now, this is the age of online delivery, music in digital form. These are very exciting times, similar in a way to how it was in the forties when there were also really just four major record companies, and a lot of independents coming through. I think that this new technology should be embraced as quickly as possible, but of course I hope that fair dealing will also be applied.

"Even in the beginning, when he really had no money whatsoever, Ahmet always behaved like a millionaire. It was more than that though that led people like the management team Greene & Stone, Robert Stigwood, and a lot of others to bring their artists to Ahmet. He was their hero. They would want their artists to sign with Ahmet for 'X' amount rather than Joe Blo for twice that, because they knew that Ahmet knew the music. That he understood how to work and have a great time with the artists. Also, how many executives stay out 'til three o'clock in the morning every night? I could do that maybe on Saturday night, but the rest of the week I'd want to get to bed! Ahmet would be out every night. In fact, he had to have a series of relief drivers because he'd wear each of them out, they'd get too tired to drive! And he's exactly the same today! He has great ears for talent, but he's also always been able to read very well the trends and moods of the times. He's a very good friend and an exceptional man – he's still out partying all night, travelling all over the world, discovering and developing great artists. Ahmet, I would say, has always been in at the time, all the time." Sheldon Vogel

AC/DC with lead vocalist Bon Scott

Bon Scott

"I think after Bon died so tragically, I felt horribly grown up in a way; that time really spun me around. But whenever I'd think of Bon I'd remember his great sense of humour. He was such a wonderful character, and we had to be strong, we had to carry on." Angus Young

Angus Young

"Bon Scott had supported Geordie, the band I was in, and later mentioned my name to the boys in AC/DC. He must have said something nice to them. Anyway, he saw me the night I either had appendicitis or acute diarrhoea. It was one of the two, but I was writhing around on the floor and Bon was on the side of the stage going, 'Wow – what a guy!' About six years later I was thinking to myself, 'Oh well, Brian, at least you have had the chance where other people haven't. At least you were in the charts once.' It had got to the stage, though, where people used to say, 'Didn't you use to be Brian Johnson out of Geordie?' I still thought I had a little bit more to give, that I wasn't finished yet, not by a long chalk. When the chance came along for AC/DC, it was just sent from heaven. I'd gone down to London to do the singing on a Hoover advert: 'The cleaner from Hoover, it's a beautiful mover.' Something like that. I got three hundred quid and thought that was a fortune. It was 1980 and this was the first work I had done since 1974 with Geordie. The same day, somebody asked if I would like to go and audition for AC/DC. It was a great jam, and I think everybody enjoyed themselves because, as the boys said, everyone else who came in for the audition were doing versions of heavy metal stuff and I just came in and said, 'Do ya know 'Nutbush City Limits', lads?'" Brian Johnson

Brian Johnson and Angus Young TL: 80s

"As soon as he opened his mouth and started singing we were all totally impressed and knew that he'd be the guy best suited for the job. From then on me, my brother and Brian sat down and worked out the rest of the new album. Then we recorded it in the Bahamas with Mutt Lange at the helm." Angus Young

Phil Collins

"I remember going with our manager Tony Smith to visit Ahmet at his house in London to play him the tapes of *Duke*, the Genesis album we had just finished. By this point, he was very into the band and all of us were friends of his. It was almost like going along and saying, 'Hey, Dad, what do you think of this?' So we played him the tapes and he said, 'Oh, that's great, great – it's a big album.'

"Then Tony said, 'Phil's been doing some solo demos, you know.' So Ahmet said, 'Oh, so what have you been doing?' It just so happened I'd brought my demos along so I took out the cassette, played it, and he was genuinely very excited by it. He said, 'I want to be involved in this, I want to be involved – if only just to be there when you mix it.' So we just kept sending Ahmet tracks as we were finishing the record. We mixed it and took it to New York to master it. When Ahmet came down to the cutting room, I was playing the record through. 'In The Air Tonight' came on and I said, 'This is what we have just done, what do you think?' He was walking around the studio as the song played and he said, 'Where's the backbeat?' I said, 'The backbeat's there, Ahmet, the drum pattern is implied.' He said, 'Yeah, it's implied for you and for me, but not for the public. You know it's there and I know it, but the kids won't know that – you've got to have the drums in there.' I said, 'Yeah, but if you listen just a minute, the drums come in at the end of the song.' As he quite rightly said, 'That's three minutes into the song – they may not even live that long. They may want to change stations before then so you've got to get them hooked, you've got to bring the drums in earlier.' I said, 'Well, I can't do that because the drums come in at the end, and I can't face going back and remixing this thing because it's taken us so long to get it the way we want it.' To which he replied, 'Well, you're going to have to do it, otherwise it's not going to be a hit.'

"So Hugh Padgham and I took the tape back to 10cc's studio and I set my drums up in the maintenance room – which was built of brick, down the corridor from the control room. They put on the tape and I played the drums along to it so that we got a big sound, but quite a quiet sound that wouldn't take the steam away from the end. Then they recorded that mix with the new drums onto another tape. So we did it, and Ahmet was right. I mean, we will never know whether the record would have been a hit without it, but I don't think it would have been because this new version spelt out where the rhythm was straight away. Who knows how many countless times he has done that with other artists? He has definitely got a great ear for what works and what doesn't."
Phil Collins

Ahmet with Phil Collins TL: 70s 80s

"When I first heard the demo Foreigner had made for us, I said on the way over to their audition, 'I'm going to sign this band.' The two songs on that demo were 'Cold As Ice' and 'Feels Like The First Time'. Someone said, 'Have you seen them?' But I said, 'I don't need to.' I just had a gut feeling, I knew that this man and his band were ready to happen. Mick Jones was mostly the creative force, he would write the songs, but then Lou Gramm would add bits and they'd work and write together in that way. But I knew right from the start, and they became the fastest-breaking act in the history of Atlantic up to that time. Then they kept coming up with a flood of wonderful songs and music, one great hit record after another. They were also fantastic live. We became and remain great friends, even at that first audition I played drums with them on a few songs. I said, 'If I sign you, you're going to have to let me play drums with you sometimes!' – again I was really joking but after we'd become friends and they'd discovered that I could actually play, and loved music so much, they always had a second drum set on tour for me to play if I wanted to. So I'd get up when I was free to and play with them on their encores – it was great. We had such a terrific time and the songs – they have stood the test of time and they remain absolute classics. Foreigner is a band that without a doubt totally and utterly deserve all of their phenomenal success." Jerry Greenberg

Foreigner, above: Mick Jones and top, with Lou Gramm Lou Gramm

Mick Jones and Rick Wills

Bette Midler TL: 80s

Abba TL: 80s

The Manhattan Transfer, from left: Janis Siegel, Alan Paul, Cheryl Bentyne and Tim Hauser TL: 70s 80s

"The Manhattan Transfer do whatever occurs to them, which can be anything you can think of, because they have a great volume of references. They've all listened to a vast range of music from just about every country and they will always come up with something special, I'm sure. Their biggest hit so far was something atypical, 'Boy From New York City', but what they really love to do is sing jazz – that's their first love." Ahmet

Leon Redbone TL: 80s

Genesis, from left: Mike Rutherford, Phil Collins and Tony Banks TL: 80s

"We still have it. We still mean it. It's not for the money. It never was. It's for the music." Graham Nash

Crosby, Stills and Nash, below from left: David Crosby, Stephen Stills and Graham Nash TL: 80s

Above, below, and below right: Stevie Nicks TL: 80s

"At one point we had a Rolling Stones album, a Foreigner album and a Stevie Nicks album 1-2-3 in the album charts. So I wanted to take an ad that said: 'Two Micks and a Nicks'. Stevie Nicks has a fabulously special sound in her voice which combines pathos, joy, and sexuality – she's just a tremendous singer and performer. She was brought in by Doug Morris, who became a close friend of hers." Ahmet

Ahmet, Stevie Nicks and Doug Morris

Robert Plant and Ahmet TL: 80s

"When John Bonham died so tragically in 1980, obviously Led Zeppelin exploded as well. It was like staggering away from a massive blast. Standing there on the street corner clutching 12 or 16 years of your life of knowing Bonzo, holding it close to your chest with a lump in your throat and a tear in your eye, and not knowing which way to go, was a most peculiar experience. Apart from anything else I knew that all of that dream was over, just like that. Gone – everything gone, because if it isn't current then it doesn't matter, really. If you can't do it tomorrow, then it's of no relevance to your life, it's just a memory. So setting off to create a new musical environment was a little confusing, because I'd never written with anyone else and I felt quite intimidated at the idea of baring my limited talents to people who could quite easily be cynical or take advantage of me ... here's this guy, 30 or 31 years old, a sort of retired 'rock god' – all those sorts of ideas were going through my mind. Basically, when I put my first solo single out, Atlantic thought that it was going to be another super-group-individual-artist-puts-a-record-out-type of thing, and that it wouldn't do much. I had the strangest feeling that at the back of everyone's mind was the conviction that, after a few months, Led Zeppelin would re-form and we could go back to how it was before. They didn't realize how serious I was about it: I knew that without Bonzo, I was going to have to keep going, for better or worse. Atlantic soon came to realize that I was serious, particularly when 'Big Log' was a hit. The song which they chose, 'Other Arms', was a top-requested record for four weeks, but I flatly refused to put it out as a single. I said, 'No – I'm not a hard rock artist, I can sing from anywhere. People's expectancy shouldn't be for me to be prancing around with my shirt open to my belly. I insisted on 'Big Log' as the single and, fortunately, a lot of people liked it." Robert Plant

"After Led Zeppelin, Robert Plant made some great solo records which were adventurous and very avant-garde musically. Robert has a mystical side to him and is very knowledgeable about world cultures and philosophies, travels extensively, and is extremely well-read. In addition, he has an encyclopedic knowledge of rock'n'roll and rhythm and blues." Ahmet

"Ahmet asked to hear me sing at his brother Nesuhi's house. I brought my piano player and sang one song, and then Ahmet stood up and announced, 'Okay – audition over.' So I thought, 'Oh well, another one bites the dust!' But then he said, 'I would love you to be with Atlantic Records!' I really very nearly fell over, I was so excited. Then he continued, 'I'd like to work with you every step of the way and be really involved.' Then he asked me to sing another song just for the sake of it all. I remember it was the first time I took a cab home instead of a bus! I was just so excited.

"Doug Morris, then President of Atlantic, introduced me to a German producer named Jack White. Doug thought that Jack would be perfect for me, and he turned out to be right because he brought me a song called 'Gloria'. I thought it was very European-sounding and had a kind of magic to it. We took it and he rewrote the lyrics, although I was involved in that process too. Originally 'Gloria' was a love story: *You're the Sun, and the Moon, and the Earth*. I couldn't really sing that, so we changed it around and made it into a bit more of a hard-edged story about a girl who's running too fast for her own steps. We gave it a sort of American kick, so that it became half-American and half-European, which is really what my sound is – and off she went!" Laura Branigan

"Laura Branigan was brought to me by her manager, Sid Bernstein, who said, 'You've got to hear this girl.' I didn't have a piano in my house at that time, but Nesuhi did. So Sid brought her up to Nesuhi's apartment, where this beautiful Irish-American girl got up, and she had a wonderful, strong voice. I had her under contract for at least a year before we started making any records, because we couldn't find the right material, the right thing. Finally, Doug Morris found some good songs for her and her first record was 'Gloria', which was an instant international smash." Ahmet

Above and below: Laura Branigan TL: 80s 90s

"Billie Joe Royal was an established artist who came to us through Jerry Wexler's country music connections. He made several albums with Atlantic and enjoyed tremendous success in the country, and a little later, in the national charts.

"Tangerine Dream came to us through Virgin. They struck me as being an avant-garde, underground kind of 'head' band. They always had a comparitively small but loyal following and I guess they probably still do." Jerry Greenberg

"We were sitting around an uptown New Orleans bar called the Boot trying to come up with a name. After a few pitchers of beer, we saw a picture on the wall of a lady riding a zebra, liked the image and decided that was it." Randy Jackson

Above, Felix Hendman and below, Randy Jackson of Zebra TL: 80s

Above, Billy Joe Royal TL: 80s and below, Tangerine Dream, including: Chris Franke, Johannes Schmoelling, Edgar Froese TL: 80s

The Great Age of Excess, 1972-1986
By David Fricke

It was almost as if the album had never been released at all. It was not reviewed in *Rolling Stone*. There was no major advertising campaign, no heavy commercial-FM airplay. Drummer Hank Ransome recalls a photo that appeared in *Billboard* of his band actually signing to Atlantic Records: "I'm standing there with Ahmet Ertegun, putting my name on the contract. That was a big time for a little band from Philadelphia."

But it was short-lived glory. The self-titled Atlantic debut album by Good God – a sharp, swinging quintet playing edgy, electric jazz-rock fusion long before the genre even had a name – was like most of the hundreds of new rock albums issued in 1972, the ones that didn't go on to become hits. It was recorded, released and, for the most part, forgotten. But in rock'n'roll as in everything else, all politics is local. In Philadelphia, where Good God was an institution on the club, college and free-show-in-the-park circuit, the arrival of their one (and, as it transpired, only) album in local stores was an event. I know; I come from Philly. When *Good God* was released in late '72, I dutifully bought a copy and played it so much the grooves turned green. It was a remarkable record for its time and place. In a city known worldwide for its contributions to R & B and jazz, where *American Bandstand* was born and Sun Ra was in residence, no one else was playing the kind of punked-up, freaked-out, bent-riff smart rock that was Good God's peculiar, dynamic specialty. The band – Hank Ransome, saxophonist Greg Scott, keyboard player Cotton Kent, guitarist Zeno Sparkles (aka Larry Cardarelli) and bassist John Ransome, Hank's twin brother – did not go entirely unnoticed outside of Philly. Good God's manager, William Eib, recalls that shortly after *Good God*'s release, the band met Frank Zappa and laid a couple of copies on him. The record included what was, for that time, a rare Zappa cover: a nine-minute wigout on 'King Kong'. "Years later," Eib says, "Skip Drinkwater, one of the guys who produced our record, was at a party at [producer] Jack Nitzsche's house and they were comparing notes on who they worked with. Our guy brought up Good God. Nitzsche then takes him into his record library, pulls our record out and says, 'Frank Zappa gave me this record and said, "You should listen to this. This is one of the best covers of one of my songs that anyone has ever done."'" Back in Philly, it was impressive enough – to mere fans like myself – that one of our own had put out a record on Atlantic, on a label where they shared history, cachet and glory with Aretha Franklin, Cream, Ornette Coleman, Ray Charles, Buffalo Springfield, John Coltrane and Led Zeppelin. The standard line about Atlantic in the mid-seventies, among the old school disciples who swore by the old red and black label and the streetwise, missionary A & R aesthetic that defined the label's independent origins and original R & B identity, was that money changed everything – for the worse. It was like the line from Joni Mitchell's 1970 hit 'Big Yellow Taxi': *They paved paradise /And put up a parking lot*. Except in this case, the parking lot bought a piece of music paradise and turned it into a profit centre. First sold in 1967 to the Warner-Seven Arts film and music combine, then sold again a year later as part of Warner-Seven Arts to Kinney Services, Inc. – which actually operated parking lots nationwide and, under the late, legendary Steve Ross, eventually morphed into Warner Communications, Inc. – Atlantic was now a major cog in an even bigger machine. But success has its privileges, not all of them apparent from the net-income columns in annual financial reports. The combination of unusual executive largesse (Ross believed that dyed-in-the-wool record men were the only ones capable of running great record companies) and the big early-and-mid-seventies payback of Ahmet Ertegun's hot streak of late sixties rock signings – The Rolling Stones, Led Zeppelin, Yes, Crosby, Stills & Nash and Emerson, Lake & Palmer – meant that Atlantic was awash in capital and possibility. In fact, for a company that now answered to a higher boardroom authority, Atlantic continued to act more like an independent label than a corporate subsidiary. The accountants at Kinney would never have signed Good God; Atlantic did. Good God is actually part of the secret history of Atlantic Records. Some of the bravest, strangest, commercially improbable records of the 1970's classic-rock era came out on Atlantic and family imprints such as Atco, Cotillion and Embryo – most of those releases financed by the gold and platinum profits of megahits like *Led Zeppelin II*, Crosby, Stills, Nash & Young's *Déjà Vu*, *Close To The Edge* by Yes and The Rolling Stone's post-*Sticky Fingers* catalogue. In 1972 and '73 alone, the company issued *Good God; Keyboard Tales*, a collection of lavish baroque-rock fantasias by Michael Perlitch, who played and overdubbed all of the instruments; *Guns and Butter*, the sole release by a post-psych, art-jazz-folk sextet from Boston; *Cosmic Furnace*, an album of florid synth-rock instrumentals (sample title: *Tensegrity: A Dymaxion Triptych*) by Roger Powell, future keyboard player with Todd Rundgren's Utopia. In Japan, Atlantic's local office signed a bizarre hard-rock outfit called the Flower Travelling Band (a kind of Zen-samurai variant on Black Sabbath) which issued at least two albums there as well as one U.S. single. And that's only the non-hits. Black Oak Arkansas was a brass-nuts boogie band fresh out of the small mountain town of the same name in 1971, with a debut album on Atco about which *Rolling Stone* critic Jon Mendelsohn gushed in no uncertain terms ("a rousing and rowdy rave whose grooves virtually ooze $1.98-a-gallon Chablis"). Within two years, BOA were headlining arenas on the strength of their Top 30 cover of LaVern Baker's 1956 Atlantic hit 'Jim Dandy'. In 1973, Atlantic picked up an English baby imprint, Virgin, for distribution and went Top Five with the label's flagship release, Mike Oldfield's one-man overdub symphony *Tubular Bells*.

Then there was Abba – two singing, songwriting couples (Agnetha Faltskog and Bjorn Ulvaeus, Benny Andersson and Anni-Frid Lyngstad) who were beautiful, Swedish, financially astute (licensed to Atlantic through their own Polar label) and unashamedly pop at a time when Atlantic was top-loaded with black funk and so-called "progressive" rock. Between 1974 and the quartet's break-up in the early eighties, 12 of Abba's 20 Atlantic singles – fresh, bite-size radio candy like 'Waterloo', 'Fernando', 'Dancing Queen' and 'Take A Chance

On Me' – went Top 30. Genius or formula? Who cared? Sometimes glitz, tune and rhythmic buoyancy are their own simple reward. Besides, as the group's manager, Stig Anderson, said to *Rolling Stone* in 1977, "If it's a formula, why don't you go out and find it?" Good God did not sell in Abba, Mike Oldfield or Black Oak Arkansas numbers. William Eib estimates that Atlantic pressed only 5,000 copies of *Good God* during the band's brief tenure on the label. The signing of Good God had been an example of the A & R nerve and verve that still existed at Atlantic, the willingness to take a flyer on an unknown quantity. But in the 1970s, Atlantic – like any other major company with an extensive, in some ways exhausting, product line – prioritized its releases, allocating marketing budgets, media campaigns and tour support on a most-favoured-nation basis. If you were The Rolling Stones, for example, you got the personal touch. "Atlantic, the business in general, was becoming very corporate," the Stones' Keith Richards says now. "But we weren't so much aware of that – especially in the vital years of our association – because of Ahmet. We didn't go beyond any other powers-that-be. Ahmet would be the guy who came down to the sessions, hung out. He'd call up and say, 'About that other track ... ' He was an inveterate record maker. He never stopped interfering. But it was the kind of interference that was helpful. Basically," Richards claims, "in working for Atlantic, we were really working for Ahmet."

Good God weren't so lucky. Hank Ransome suggests that the band's big mistake was deciding to record at home, in Philly, instead of in New York, at Atlantic's own legendary studio: "Because all the creative energy that went into the album was happening away from the Atlantic office, without any oversight or any exposure to the movers and shakers. We could have had more people there, swinging by, seeing what's going on – 'What are these guys about?' Instead, we just went, 'Here's the product.'" "Atlantic was a very special label for us," Eib insists. He still remembers, quite vividly, the day the finished copies of *Good God* arrived at his office: "The first thing I did was slide the record out of the jacket and look at the Atlantic label. Atlantic had been a source of an incredible amount of music for me. To look at the Atlantic label and see 'Good God' printed on it – it was a real honour."

In 1972, Atlantic in England issued a budget-priced sampler LP of music by new and established acts on the label. The artists included Led Zeppelin, Buffalo Springfield, The J. Geils Band, Dr. John, the young singer-songwriters John Prine and Loudon Wainwright III, the overheated arena-blooz band Cactus and Gordon Haskell, a British songwriter who sang with King Crimson for about ten minutes in 1971 (check the fine print on Crimson's *Lizard* album). The most notable track on the record, otherwise comprised of recently released material, was Yes's impressively florid ten-minute cover of Simon and Garfunkel's 'America' – blown wide open in art-rock technicolour with billowing mellotron, ingeniously subdivided rhythms and breathless guitar arpeggios. The album was called *The New Age of Atlantic*. It could just as well have been called *The Great Age of Excess*. Atlantic was good to the seventies; Zeppelin, Yes, ELP, Bad Company, the Stones and Australian proto-punkers AC/DC were the heavy-rotation stars on eight-track car tape players throughout America's Stoner Years. But the seventies were also very good to Atlantic. Great ambitions begat big money; big money begat confidence and grand opportunities, which in turn begat even bigger money. In 1977, combined record and concert-ticket sales in America reached nearly $4 billion. Maybe that doesn't look so impressive now, in the wake of astonishing end-of-the-century record deals like Aerosmith's recent $50 million contract with Columbia and the $80 million package that R.E.M. got in 1995 for resigning with Warner Brothers. But that $4 billion was a stupefying figure in mid-seventies dollars – especially when you consider that it was nearly twice the gross income of the American movie industry in that same year.

The trick for a company like Atlantic – with a stalwart artistic reputation, embodied in the rock'n'roll sector by the continued, active stewardship of Ahmet Ertegun, and continually rising commercial expectations – was to maintain a good business sense in a time of rampant egomania. With the runaway growth of record sales and concert grosses came the rise of a *nouveau riche* pop aristocracy, comprised in great part of young, once-disenfranchised, middle- and working-class musicians who now lived like country squires and believed, many of them in earnest, that size – of the audiences, the venues, the pay cheques, the road crews and lighting rigs – did matter. The global, cross-generation explosion of the music was supposed to be a good thing, evidence that the youth revolt of the 1960s had not fizzled in vain and that the music could still be as inspiring as it was profitable. But bigger crowds meant a wider chasm between the stage and the kids in the back rows; the stars became more remote than ever, simply in terms of enforced physical distance. When Yes made their U.S. tour debut in 1971, hot in the wake of *The Yes Album*, you could see the band in small clubs or warming up intimate-theatre crowds for Jethro Tull. By the time I – and 130,000 other people – saw Yes at John F. Kennedy Stadium in the summer of 1976, just five years and four studio albums later, the closest I got was the third balcony at the 50-yard line. It wasn't that I didn't have a great time. I did. I just wondered, even worried a little, if this kind of mass-communion rock extravaganza was as good as it was ever gonna get. (20 years later, while interviewing Atlantic alt-rock kings Stone Temple Pilots, I found out that the band's guitarist, Dean DeLeo, had been at the exact same show.)

It was an era of bonafide musical adventure and harebrained rock-god chutzpah – and some of Atlantic's biggest artists of the day personified both extremes: artist-run labels (Rolling Stones Records, Zeppelin's Swan Song and Emerson, Lake & Palmer's Manticore imprints); extravagant album covers (Zeppelin's die-cut tenement sleeve for 1975's *Physical Graffiti*, ELP's H. R. Giger-designed, fold-out package for 1973's *Brain Salad Surgery*); double-LP operas (Genesis' *The Lamb Lies Down On Broadway* in 1974, Yes's 80-minute oratorio *Tales Of Topographic Oceans* that very same year); and triple disc live albums (*Yessongs* in 1973 and ELP's *Welcome Back, My Friends, To The Show That Never Ends – Ladies And Gentlemen*, released a scant 15 months later). Then there was the Solo Album Syndrome. At once exhausted by six years of non-stop recording and touring and emboldened by the success of their breakthrough albums *Fragile* and *Close To The Edge*, Yes went on extended hiatus in 1975 and '76 – and presented Atlantic with individual records by every member of the band for release. Emerson, Lake & Palmer took a slightly more conservative approach to the solo-record issue; singer-bassist Greg Lake, keyboard player Keith Emerson and drummer Carl Palmer crammed their respective busman's holiday recordings on to the ELP-billed collections *Works Volume 1* and *Volume 2*. This was not just a matter of English prog-rock hubris. Crosby, Stills & Nash were the undisputed supergroup jewel of the Atlantic roster, an Anglo-American alliance of impeccable sixties pedigree (The Byrds, Buffalo Springfield, The Hollies), crystalline guitar jangle, luminous heaven's-radio harmonies and poetic, mature hippie optimism. But after issuing their self-titled debut and *Déjà Vu*, made with sometime member Neil Young, in rapid succession in 1969 and '70, the original trio made only one other studio album during the whole of the seventies, the fine, underrated *CSN*. Atlantic otherwise marked time with the double-live album *4 Way Street*, a greatest-hits package and a virtual blizzard of solo and side-project releases: a David Crosby record, two Graham Nash albums, a Crosby and Nash LP, two Stephen Stills albums and a further two albums (one of them a double) by Stills' short-lived band Manassas. Good records, most of them; sometimes great; many of them hits, to varying degrees – but the sum of the parts was not what was really under contract; it was the band.

"I don't know what the wisdom in all that is. Too much ego. Too much self-indulgence," Lake suggests today. "You're either in a band – and that's the priority and the band has a spirit – or you're not. But nobody wants to see Band X, the money machine, the meal ticket, just disintegrate. You have to keep it together at all costs. To be honest, it was very difficult for the label," Lake says of Atlantic's precarious place in that logic. "They didn't want to put out all those solo albums. It was supposed to be very cosy – the band makes an album, goes on tour, sells two million records. Hey, send round the limo. But then the buggers want to make six different albums. And they, the label, didn't know which one, if any of them, would suddenly leap out and be the one. Whoops, Phil Collins! They didn't want to indulge us, but they had to. Until they really put their thinking caps on and learned, by bitter experience, that these things were, by and large, not working."

By the turn of the 1980s, the coincidental squeeze of an increased severity in major-label economic policy and the brute, impolite arrival of punk – a small but inexorable, culturally defining teenage mutiny against bloat and bullshit in rock'n'roll – put an end to such whimsy and virtually wiped art rock off the playboard. "The media was responsible for shutting down progressive music, *per se*, by making it *musica non grata*," says Lake, who was also a founding member of King Crimson. "On the other hand, it did get very self-centred and pretentious. We were pissing in our own idealism."

Nevertheless, one of my own, fondest memories of seventies gig-going was seeing the electrifying *Larks' Tongues In Aspic/Starless And Bible Black* line-up of Atlantic's own King Crimson at the Spectrum in Philadelphia in 1974. It was the kind of music that you expected to find on arthouse record labels, played in lofts and storefront galleries to 50 guys with glasses and big brains. Instead, Crimson, with indomitable guitarist Robert Fripp at the helm, made dense, agitated instrumental magic in that arena for 15,000 weedheads – and connected. Atlantic saw something special in the English music of those years," Lake says.

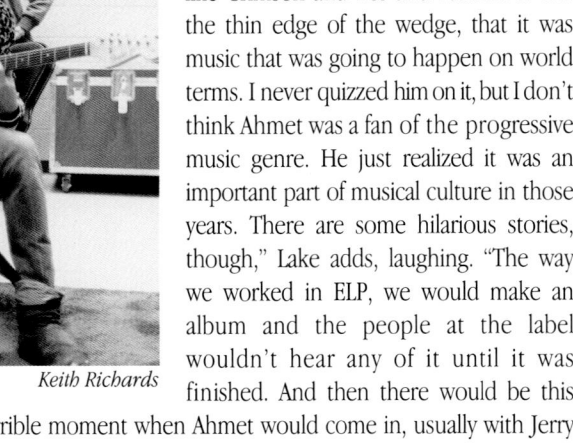

Keith Richards

He still remembers, with great fondness, the first time he met Ahmet Ertegun at Crimson's Atlantic audition in London in 1969. "The company looked into things like Crimson and Yes and realized it was the thin edge of the wedge, that it was music that was going to happen on world terms. I never quizzed him on it, but I don't think Ahmet was a fan of the progressive music genre. He just realized it was an important part of musical culture in those years. There are some hilarious stories, though," Lake adds, laughing. "The way we worked in ELP, we would make an album and the people at the label wouldn't hear any of it until it was finished. And then there would be this terrible moment when Ahmet would come in, usually with Jerry Greenberg, and sit down. And although they were emitting confidence, you could see it in their faces: 'Oh God, they've spent $350,000 on *this*.'"

In the record business, nobody is right 100 per cent of the time. Everybody screws up. And Atlantic nearly screwed up, in a very big way, in 1976, when a demo tape of a new band called Foreigner arrived in the A & R department at the company's New York office. The company took a pass. "We got a form letter that basically said, 'Thanks but no thanks. Keep us abreast of what you're doing,'" recalls the band's founder, guitarist Mick Jones, with bemusement. "It was politely worded. But firm." Fortunately, an Atlantic staffer, John David Kalodner, recently promoted to A & R from the press department, heard the tape and discovered a few interesting things about the band's lineage – Jones had been in a late version of the British hard-rock band Spooky Tooth, instrumentalist Ian McDonald had been in the founding line-up of King Crimson and drummer Dennis Elliott played with Mott The Hoople's Ian Hunter. "It piqued John's interest," says Jones, "and the demo got to Jerry Greenberg." Foreigner would go on to become one of the biggest acts of Atlantic's fourth decade, indeed of the label's entire history – selling over 22 million records and racking up ten Top 20 singles over the next eight years. The common wisdom about rock'n'roll's middle age is that corporatization crushed the life out of the music that mega-platinum bands like Foreigner, Boston, Styx and Journey were board-room constructs, playing immaculately groomed, bloodlessly executed, mass-consumption music that was rock only by association. In fact, Foreigner had been formed by Jones in New York in virtual anonymity, as a result of a long, hard series of auditions and rehearsals and the fortuitous recruiting of then-unknown vocalist from Rochester, New York, Lou Gramm. True, the music was meticulously designed for broad appeal – hard and melodic – but by musicians, not A & R committee. It was Jones, for example, who picked 'Urgent', a stylish, uncharacteristically funky romp with a steamy Junior Walker sax break, as the leadoff single from the 4 album in 1981. ("It was quirky, but it was still us.") And Foreigner had been signed the old-fashioned way – by a demo tape that happened to land on the right desk. "People drew their own conclusions," Jones says. "I think there was resentment in the press in that they hadn't discovered us, which was the normal way bands emerged, building a reputation and slogging away. But collectively, we had slogged away. And we had a genuine feeling of support from the label, which meant a lot to us. I'd been in bands where the people who worked at the company were treated like peons by musicians: 'Let's see what we can get out of them, how much we can spend at dinner.' I think we were the first band who took local promotion people out to dinner, instead of the other way around." Mick Jones's spiritual connection with Atlantic Records stretched back to the label's R & B salad days. As a teenager in England, working in a record store in the town of Woking, he always zeroed in on the new releases bearing the trademark red and black label. He had a band, too, that learned Ray Charles and Solomon Burke songs like homework. But Foreigner's instant chart coronation in 1977 marked a dramatic change of seasons at Atlantic, and in the music industry at large. For one thing, for the rest of the seventies and well into the 1980s, the numbers were simply insane. The demographic sprawl of the rock audience – from 40-year-old baby boomers to pre-teens who, as the old gag goes, thought Paul McCartney's first band was Wings – meant that records which sold in seven and eight figures were no longer an anomaly. They were becoming part of a label's annual sales projections. And there were new means to achieve those numbers. The nationwide launch in 1981 of MTV – a 24-hour music-video cable channel partial to youth, good looks, slick graphics and playful irony – and the cross-marketing possibilities presented by movie soundtracks forever transformed (and specifically in the case of MTV, dramatically accelerated) the process of artist development. Genesis singer-drummer Phil Collins was already established as a solo star by 1984; his first two albums, *Face Value* and *Hello, I Must Be Going!*, records of slightly arty, R & B-juiced pop, had sold a combined six million copies. But it was a sumptuous ballad, 'Against All Odds (Take A Look At Me Now)', written and recorded by Collins for the Hollywood weeper *Against All Odds*, then pounded into the public consciousness by MTV, that made him a superstar, a ladies' man of George Michael proportions if not features. Collins was hardly a new artist. He'd come to Atlantic in the early seventies when the company picked up Genesis through a distribution pact with the band's original U.K. label Charisma.

Yet Atlantic continued to have great success, sometimes improbably so, with the old reliables. Led Zeppelin disbanded in 1980 after the tragic death by alcoholic misadventure of drummer John Bonham, but vocalist Robert Plant had effectively reinvented himself as a smart-metal singer and writer on the albums *Pictures At Eleven* (1982) and *The Principle Of Moments* (1983). Yes enjoyed a surprise resurgence in 1983, scoring their first-ever #1 single with 'Owner Of A Lonely Heart', a striking combo of up-to-date synth-pop precision and the old rosy boy-angel vocal harmonies. And AC/DC, who couldn't get arrested on radio or in the press during their first five years at Atlantic in spite of their relentless touring and grade-A guitar crunch, paid off on the company's investment – big time – in 1980 with *Back In Black*, a Godzilla-rock classic rapidly cut with new singer Brian Johnson in fond memory of the band's late, brilliant, mad-dog frontman Bon Scott.

Pete Townshend

Still, a generational shift was at work at Atlantic, not only in who was making records but in who was having hits. In 1982, the same year that Who guitarist Pete Townshend, hitched to Atlantic as a solo act, issued the highly regarded but moderately successful album *All The Best Cowboys Have Chinese Eyes*, Atlantic held the #2 slot on the *Billboard* singles chart for three weeks running with 'Gloria', a lavish, galloping disco-pop hit by a fresh, young Ertegun protégé, Laura Branigan. Pillars of the label like Plant, Collins and even Foreigner found themselves jockeying for chart positions and sharing label resources with the upstart likes of Twisted Sister and Ratt.

For someone like Foreigner's Mick Jones, caught between his love for the old Atlantic and his success in the New Platinum Order, it was the best of times and the hardest of times. At one point in the late seventies, Jones claims, sales of Foreigner's *Double Vision* and The Rolling Stones' *Some Girls* accounted for between 80 and 90 per cent of Atlantic's gross annual income. But eventually the hits stopped coming, friends and supporters at the label moved on, the company's promotional enthusiasms shifted. In 1994 Jones finally went to Ahmet Ertegun and personally asked him to release Foreigner from the label. "That was not a very happy day for me," he concedes. "And I don't think it was very happy for him either.

"Mind you," Jones adds, laughing, "they didn't offer to give us our masters back. But I remember the good years. And I did think that we changed the shape of the label, just from the fact that this was a band started from the ground floor in America, not just imported from England. We mirrored their beginnings with our own." And because there is no sense in wasting a good Ahmet Ertegun anecdote, here's one more: When Jones met Ertegun for the first time, at a Foreigner rehearsal in New York after the first album was completed, the executive showed up with a friend – the great Broadway choreographer Jerome Robbins. "I think he brought Jerome Robbins down to see if we needed any help with stage presentation," Jones recalls, still with some amazement. "We did this small set for them, about six or seven songs, really loud, and the poor guy was sitting there, being blasted by this music. I don't think Robbins really understood quite why he was there. It was just one of Ahmet's whims – 'This is my new band, do you have any ideas for them?' Right away, I saw the zany side of Ahmet."

"Sippie Wallace was one of the early blues singers and was in her eighties when she recorded the album *Sippie* for us. It's a record that I love."

Ahmet TL: 80s

"The Rolling Stones really are the greatest rock'n'roll band still playing today. We had 14 great years with them, and we still have the honour of recording Mick as a solo artist." Ahmet

The Rolling Stones, clockwise from far left: Charlie Watts, Mick Jagger and Keith Richards, opposite and below right, Keith Richards, Bill Wyman, and Ronnie Wood TL: 80s

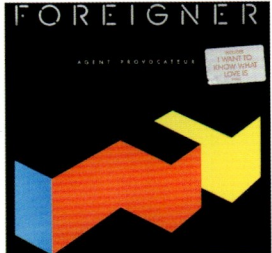

Mick Jones with Nile Rodgers

Foreigner TL: 80s

Foreigner and The New Jersey Mass Choir

"The gospel singer Jennifer Holliday brought them in, but The New Jersey Mass Choir had never been in a recording studio before. They were still getting used to the surroundings, so I just sat down at the piano with all the choir around me and we just worked on the song. We started off, and things were a little shaky because I think they felt a little bit intimidated by all of the equipment in the studio. Just before the first take we did of 'I Want To Know What Love Is', they formed a big circle, held hands, and prayed. It was really quite moving. Jennifer produced some wonderful standout bits here and there and it was just an incredible experience. My mother and father were in the room, too. Then Ahmet came by, as he always did, to listen to the rough mixes of what we had. So we sat and listened to the album and I saved 'I Want To Know What Love Is' for last. Halfway through the song, I looked over and there was a tear rolling down Ahmet's cheek. At that point I thought, 'Wow, I've done it, I've finally gotten through to him, to that heart inside there,' and I started crying. We were looking at each other, with tears streaming, and in that moment I felt, 'Oh my God – the thing I wanted to do, all through this association with him, has been to have some sort of reward like that.' It meant so much to me." Mick Jones

From left: Jeff Beck, Ahmet and Robert Plant TL: 80s

"One of the most fun things Robert Plant and I did was when we decided to make a record of old rhythm and blues songs without putting his name or the names of any of the musicians on it. We called the group "The Honeydrippers" after an old R & B group that Robert and I both love – Joe Liggins and the Honeydrippers. Liggins's song, 'The Honeydripper', is a killer and was a huge hit in the forties. The Honeydripper was originally the nickname of a singer and piano player named Roosevelt Sykes who was a very sweet-singing bluesman. We had a really hot band for the album. We got Jeff Beck, Jimmy Page and Nile Rodgers on guitars. We did things like 'Rockin' At Midnight' by Roy Brown – Jeff Beck played some incredible blues guitar on our version of that. Then we went to London and did some recording with Jimmy and a string section. For the producer's credit, I used my old songwriting pseudonym, Nugetre. The album had one huge hit single, 'Sea Of Love' and went platinum. We called the album *The Honeydrippers Volume One*. We're still talking about making *Volume Two*." Ahmet

"We were really flying, doing 'Rockin' At Midnight' at Atlantic's studios – live. It was so exciting. Beck's amp was set on a table just feet from the drums. So we couldn't push the drums up because if we did, his guitar would come searing out onto the track since he was being picked up in the overhead mikes. As we were playing, the doors were open and people from the other studios were coming down the corridor. I looked in the control room and it was full of beaming black faces. We were playing their music back to them, well and truly! Harry Belafonte – who was there working on a film soundtrack – was dancing up and down, clicking his fingers and I said, 'Good Lord! I don't know, what has it come to?' Great." Robert Plant

"I'm in the studio when I get a 'phone call from Ahmet, and he says, 'Hey, Nile, you wanna come over here and work with Robert Plant on something?' Ahmet is extremely eloquent, and he explained what they were doing in a really nice way and it totally captured me. I mean, my mouth started watering because I'm a huge Led Zeppelin fan and for me to work with Robert Plant – believe me, I would have done anything!" Nile Rodgers

"In black music, there have always been so many different cross-currents of influence and so many different things happening, that it is difficult to identify one development as being directly related to something else. However, the important thing is that through the blues other forms have developed. I met two young Frenchmen who wrote a book called *The Road To The Blues*. They had made a trip from New Orleans travelling up the Mississippi – hitting all sorts of juke joints and looking for blues players. So I said, 'How did you get to this? To decide to study the blues?' They told me that they had gotten to it from Led Zeppelin. They were great Zeppelin fans and so they researched where their inspiration came from, where those types of songs were originally played – and they got to the blues and became blues scholars." Ahmet

Ahmet producing The Honeydrippers Volume One

Above and below, Ratt, including: Stephen Pearcy, Bobby Blotzer, Juan Croucier, Warren DeMartini and Robbin Crosby TL: 80s

"We considered ourselves from the birth of Ratt to be the ultimate hippie-pirate-cowboys in Hollywood and looking more, well, just fashionable. One magazine called us 'fashion metal' or something really dumb, but it made sense in a way because we were looking totally different. We had our own identity. I had my hair over one eye. We weren't into the studs and leather, we were just into being ourselves, wearing what we had to wear because we had no money to buy clothes. We would be constantly ransacking friends' houses for clothes and belts and pants and shoes, so it just came about that way. We didn't like to follow trends or fads. It's always good to know what's going on around you, which I always try to do, but a lot of bands looked the same, as if they went to 'the rock store' to get their 'rock clothes'. I'd rather dig in the closet or have something made that's totally out of the ordinary, with 100 mirrors on my legs or something." Stephen Pearcy

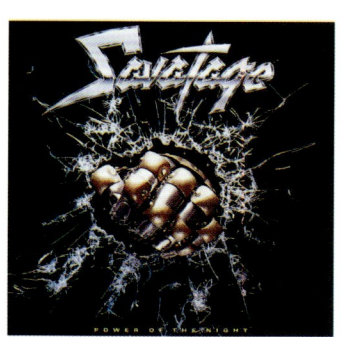

Savatage, from left: Jon Oliva, Steve 'Dock' Wacholz, Johnny Lee Middleton TL: 80s 90s

"We were essentially a heavy metal band, but we were combining the make-up and theatrical influences of the glam era with the attitude and sound of bands like AC/DC and Black Sabbath. We were really one of the first bands carrying the banner over from the glam days, literally battling our way through the pubs in an effort to keep that shock-rock-flash-look going. I guess the combination that we put together was a little bit different from the T. Rex and David Bowie-type bands and a little more accessible to the headbangers. It seemed that with 'We're Not Gonna Take It', which was the big single for us, we really had found the music and the words to go with the image and the attitude that Twisted Sister always had. In trying to look for the one song which really expresses what you're all about and hits that chord with your audience, 'We're Not Gonna Take It', with its rebellious nature and its sort of sing along Slade style, was what did that for us.

"A lot of us fell foul of the 'Washington wives', so we attended the committee hearings in order to prevent our rights from being completely trampled on. John Denver came in and, I mean, who can be more American and Mom's apple pie than John Denver? He actually stunned the room when he said, 'My children can survive a poster of Ozzy Osbourne. I'll explain to them that this is just fantasy, not reality, and I'll take the poster down if I don't like it. I don't need the government to pass some regulation to prevent my children from seeing these things.' I think the 'Washington wives' were proved beyond a shadow of a doubt to be totally off base with regard to our lyrics – that they had actually lied and creatively edited a number of them to misrepresent what our music was about. Our songs essentially are about rebellion and standing up for your rights and your beliefs, which is a practice as old as all the countries in the world and all the governments in the world. I told them, 'Isn't that what the United States is all about? We fought for our rights and if there's now something wrong with that, then there's something wrong with our government, and I'm not going to stand here while you badmouth the United States of America.'" Dee Snider

Twisted Sister, above from left: Dee Snider, Mark 'The Animal' Mendoza, J.J. French TL: 80s

"I just want people to judge the music without prejudice."
Julian Lennon

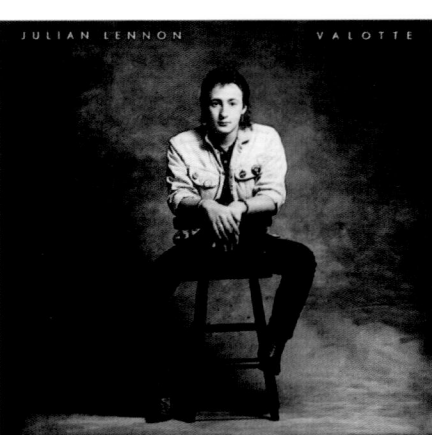

"Ahmet's the biggest star around, the boss. I think he is a wonderful character. Maybe one day I'll be as wise as he is."
Julian Lennon

"Julian Lennon came to us like a bit of British fresh air. He had beautiful songs. As the saying goes, 'The apple doesn't fall far…'" Ahmet

Top and above: Ahmet with Julian Lennon TL: 80s

Roger Daltrey TL: 80s

"Along with Pete Townshend, we also recorded Roger Daltrey as a solo artist. The Who still performs as a group today. Like the Stones they have survived inner conflicts and whatever else happens to a group over a period of so many years. They are a monumental band in the history of rock'n'roll." Ahmet

"Paul Rodgers had left Bad Company, and I encouraged Paul and Jimmy Page to form a band together, which they called The Firm." Ahmet

The Firm, from left: Paul Rodgers and Jimmy Page TL: 80s

The Firm's drummer, Chris Slade

Ahmad Jamal TL: 80s 90s

"I believe in improvisation. Even Bach, Mozart and Beethoven improvised. Improvisation and freedom are synonymous. I'm a wordless storyteller, somone who cares about the dynamics of music ... musical dynamics are human dynamics." Ahmad Jamal

From left: Ahmet, Tony Smith (Phil Collins's manager), Phil Collins and Doug Morris

Yes, from left: Chris Squire, Trevor Rabin, Tony Kaye, Alan White and Jon Anderson

"'Owner Of A Lonely Heart' was a breakthrough to the band's being alive again. We were still interested in creating a very strong group of musicians. We were going to go on tour, play well and we were going to put on a good show. At the back of our minds we were hoping the album 90125 was going to do well, because we'd been out of the picture for three or four years. When we had the hit single obviously everything changed, we were returning heroes sort of thing." Jon Anderson

Mike + the Mechanics, from left: Paul Young, Paul Carrack, Peter Van Hooke and Mike Rutherford TL: 80s 90s

"Mike + the Mechanics sort of fell off the shelf, so to speak. Genesis' studio was being rebuilt, so I went to record in Montserrat with Adrian Lee, the keyboard player and Peter Van Hooke, the drummer, whom I hadn't worked with before. We recorded the tracks and then thought, 'Who the hell's going to do the vocals?' When we came back from Montserrat and someone recommended Paul Young from Sad Cafe, the songwriter B. A. Robertson brought him down, they started singing, and it was great. You know, it's wonderful that just so much of what happens is luck. I had started working over 'Silent Running' with B. A. Robertson. It was one of those funny songs – when I first wrote it, I thought, 'This is really good.' Then, during the course of the album, as so often happens, I went off it. It wasn't sounding very good until we finally finished the lyrics. Paul came in and sang it, we put the backing on it, remixed it and it suddenly took off. Within a week, it went from being my least to my most favourite track on the album." Mike Rutherford

Doug Morris, John Parr and Ahmet

"There I was with David Foster, this world-famous producer, who played me this really naff song and said, 'I would like you to sing this.' I was faced with the devil and the deep blue sea and I thought, how do I tell this *numero uno* that this session is just not happening? In general, I hate soundtracks because so often they use the eleventh-best song from some artist's album. So I said, 'Well, I'm sorry, but I think this sounds like a second-rate American soundtrack song.' He said, 'What do you mean?' I replied, 'Well, give me a shot, give me two hours writing with you.' So he did, and we wrote 'St. Elmo's Fire' in two hours. The greatest feeling of all is to have the number one record. It's difficult to describe, but in 1983, I booked a really cheap flight to New York and I remember feeling like a little boy as we came in to land, looking down to see New York from the air for the first time. It's one of the greatest sights for anybody who's never seen it. This immense, what looks like an amusement arcade, so large, beautiful and fascinating. Then two years later I was flying above New York again, this time during the day - and I was number one - and I thought, 'In my own field for this one or two weeks, I'm in the position so many people are striving to reach.'" John Parr

Genesis, from left: Tony Banks, Mike Rutherford and Phil Collins TL: 80s

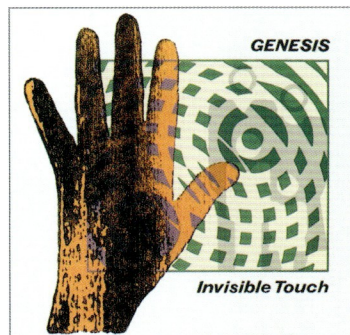

"As soon as they saw me with my instrument, drummers who were used to playing with Grappelli would take out their brushes to play softly. But as soon as they felt my energy, they'd switch back to sticks and let go. I realized that the sound coming out of the amp. was not a traditional violin sound at all, but that the roundness of the low notes – that amplitude which was like a saxophone – gave me the punch I needed to play this style of music, and so I stayed with it." Jean-Luc Ponty

Stevie Nicks TL: 80s

Jean-Luc Ponty TL: 80s

"We were in Paris, in a big rehearsal room, and me and my brother were playing the riff to 'For Those About To Rock' when in the background there was this firing of cannon salutes. Each salute seemed to happen on the breaks, so that's how all of that part of our stage show came about. I remember once we were playing, in Leeds I think, with our cannons going off left, right and centre, and plaster and stuff pouring off the roof. I mean, it was a bit Monty Python in a way, because in some cities there were structural engineers going round the building while we were playing. I think it was probably the first time some of those people had bothered to do that, so I guess a concert by us is a good way of getting the structure of a building checked out." Angus Young

AC/DC: top left, Angus Young; top right, Brian Johnson and above from left, Malcolm Young, Brian Johnson, Phil Rudd, Angus Young and Cliff Williams TL: 80s

Pete Townshend TL: 80s

"*White City* was slightly fictionalized. What was interesting about that for me was that I was trying to work out where I had come from, and I think maybe my pathway was rather littered at the time. I think, however, it was a good record; I'm very proud of it. It was supposed to try to look at, if you like, the West London experience – the fact that, for me, that was what I believed had created my audience. Henry Purcell's boss was Charles II – he was the guy who paid, or didn't in this case, his wages. In my case it was the audience at a West London club. It wasn't my mates at art college, it wasn't anybody who was around me at the time. I found myself playing a few R & B tunes, writing a couple of songs, and realizing that there were kids there from Ireland, Trinidad, Jamaica, from all over the world, but certainly a lot of ordinary London kids as well. They were gathered together in the melting pot of that bit of West London, responding to what I was writing by saying, 'You're expressing things we can't say ourselves,' and I was thinking, 'This is what I've always wanted, someone to commission me, and they're doing it.' So that was what *White City* was supposed to be about. I remember taking it and explaining it to Doug Morris and he knew what I was talking about.

"What had actually got that inarticulate misogyny out of our audience was admitting that we couldn't say what it was we wanted to say. You look at the person you are angry with, and you're angry with them because you love them, and they think you're behaving like a shit, and they're telling you that you're a shit because you're behaving like a shit. You say, 'Just because I'm behaving like a shit, doesn't mean I am a shit,' and they say, 'Yes you are,' and you don't know what to say back, so what you do is punch. What you needed was a few more months at school, you needed to read some Jane Austen, some George Eliot or something, and know what the human experience was about. But you didn't and so, suddenly, a little pop group comes along and starts to tell you that it's okay not to be inarticulate, that you can learn to speak." Pete Townshend

Above: Michael Hutchence; and opposite, with Ahmet

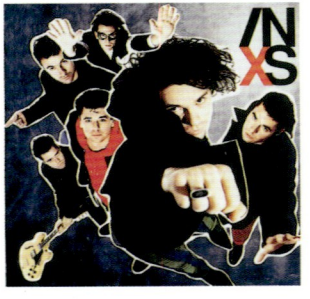 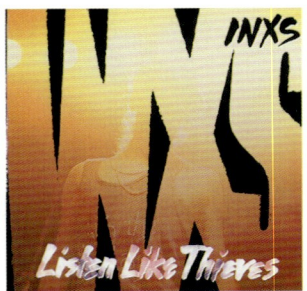

"I knew INXS was going to be a hit band because so many young people, so many children of my friends, were coming to me and asking about them. It took a while, but gradually their success grew. They were a great band, probably one of the best bands ever to come out of Australia. Michael Hutchence was not only a talented singer, but a really great-looking guy and the girls were really crazy about him." Ahmet

INXS, from left: Kirk Pengilly, Tim Farriss, Andrew Farriss, Michael Hutchence, Jon Farriss and Gary Beers TL: 80s

"I guess seeing Genesis on the label, Phil Collins and all, I said, 'Well, that seems great.' What I like about Atlantic is that it's not an idolmaker situation – they have a lot of strong talent and they give their artists creative control. I mean, you can tell that nobody picked Genesis' songs for them, you can tell that it's them, which is what I like the most.

"'Only In My Dreams' was a song which I wrote when I was 13. At the time I had a four-track studio, so I demo'd it in there, and it was my first attempt at a dance/pop song. Later on, when I got my 12-track studio I was listening to an old demo tape and I heard 'Only In My Dreams' and I said, 'You know, this song still sounds up-to-date and it's two years later. I'm going to demo it again and kind of flip it onto the tape of my new stuff,' which I was about to give to Atlantic. It was actually the song we decided was going to be the first single. It was released first as a 12-inch, and whether or not it was going to be sold as a 7-inch single was dependent on how the 12-inch did – and it went very well. It turned out to be the number one-selling 12-inch of the year in America, so Atlantic had no complaints. They put it out as a single and then released the album." Debbie Gibson

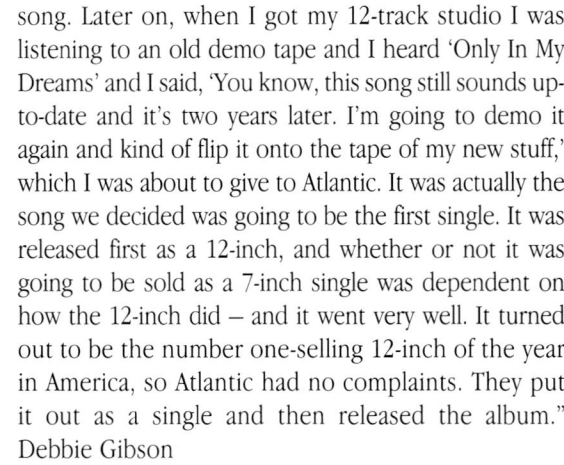

"Debbie Gibson was an extremely talented teenager – very bright, with a good read on what was happening with the kids. She built an incredible following with her first couple of albums and went on to great success on Broadway as her singing style matured." Ahmet

Top, Ahmet with Jann Wenner (left) and Mick Jones (right); Ahmet, Mica and clowns; above, Debbie Gibson and Ahmet; and opposite, Debbie Gibson TL: 80s

"When I grew up and even when I was playing, the music I was into then was the early rock'n'roll thing. Chuck Berry, Little Richard and also a lot of blues music. It was never music that was popular with the mass audiences. That's what I was listening to then and I'm still the same now. I'm very much a big fan of Buddy Guy and Muddy Waters. That's the music that I always tune in on. In the beginning, the major thing we learnt from listening to these people was that they didn't work things out note by note. They played how they felt the tune should go.

"For us we get on stage and music is why we're doing it, that's what we concentrate on first. Especially for myself, I follow the guitar. If the guitar says left, I go left. I'm a little guy, 5' 2" tall, but if you're a big guy and you've got big fingers, your fingers bend the strings. With me, 'cause I'm little my whole body's got to bend the string." Angus Young

Top and above: AC/DC TL: 80s

"Mike Rutherford, a founding member of Genesis, decided to make some recordings on his own. So now he's made some wonderful, wonderful records, including an especially moving song about the death of his father, 'In The Living Years', which was a huge hit. Mike is one of those extremely intelligent Englishmen, a polo player, terrific songwriter, a person for whom I have a very deep affection." Ahmet

Brian Johnson and Angus Young

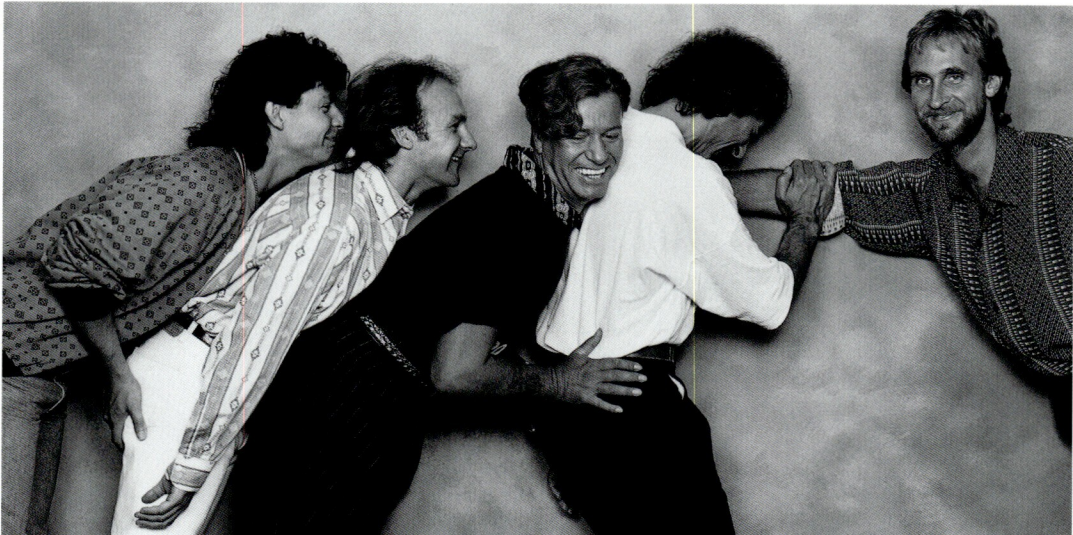

Above: Mike + the Mechanics, from left: Paul Young, Paul Carrack, Adrian Lee, Peter Van Hooke and Mike Rutherford TL: 80s 90s

Robert Plant TL: 80s

"In my solo capacity, a lot of realism had to come into the game. I could have fallen on my face and be down to selling 200,000 albums at a push and be really flagging. My determination and what I've written has not been the easiest job for Atlantic to market. However, they've stuck with me and I've learnt more, and more, and more, and I've even learnt what a chorus is. I think Atlantic is so pleased, as especially Ahmet has let me go into all of these meandering little things and has kept on tapping me on the back and saying, 'Well, anytime you want to come back into the fold, into the straight and narrow, see your name on the chart sheets, give us a chorus.' He must have said that to a lot of other artists over the years, it's that chorus. So thanks to the new band, we now have choruses. I don't make any bones about it, I thought when Jimmy played on a couple of tracks on *Now and Zen*, if the whole kind of expectancy is the way it had been, then I was going to play up to it this time around. I have to say we had the Zoso symbol on the inner bag and all that sort of thing, and it was like, 'Okay, we'll have a little bit of this and let's all think about it again.' I find it kind of fun. 'Tall, Cool One' was certainly tongue-in-cheek Led Zeppelin." Robert Plant

Foreigner, from left: Lou Gramm, Bob Mayo and Mick Jones TL: 80s

The Coasters

The Manhattan Transfer, Ahmet, LaVern Baker, and Ruth Brown

Bob Geldof

Ruth Brown

Wilson Pickett

Bobby Short

Rufus Thomas

Laura Brannigan

40TH ANNIVERSARY CELEBRATION OF

Graham Nash, David Crosby and Stephen Stills

The Spinners

Led Zeppelin reunion

The Manhattan Transfer

Debbie Gibson

Herbie Mann

All-Star Jam

The Bee Gees

The Rascals

Roberta Flack

Sam Moore and Dan Aykroyd

From left: Dizzy Gillespie, Arif Mardin, Quincy Jones III, Ahmet and Quincy Jones

"I met Quincy Jones in 1955. He was playing trumpet and arranging for Dizzy Gillespie's big band. They were on a worldwide tour sponsored by the U.S. State Department, so they came to play in two cities in Turkey – Istanbul and Ankara. I was a big band groupie – at every concert and backstage whenever I could be. So when Dizzy and his band came to Turkey I got to meet them and I became friends straightaway with Quincy. Then, a year later, I sent some compositions of mine to the radio broadcast *Voice of America*, where I had a friend, who called Quincy and gave these pieces to him. Quincy then put together this fantastic, small New York band: Art Farmer, Lee Konitz, Hank Jones ... I mean a great, great ten-piece band. They recorded my three compositions for *Voice of America*, and they were used on the air. The wonderful disc jockey Willis Conover, who did *Voice of America*'s 'Jazz Hour', liked it very much, as well as the aspect of its being a cultural exchange between the U.S. and Turkey. So Quincy then took that tape and sent it to Berklee College of Music in Boston. He knew that they were looking for a candidate for the scholarship which had been set up there under his name, and he told them that he had found one. So I got a letter from Berklee offering me this scholarship. I went to my father, whose reaction was, 'Son – what do you want to be?' I replied, 'I want to be a big band arranger.' To him, it was like I was saying, 'I want to go to Mars.' He said, 'But how are you going to make a living?' And the poor man was right! At the time, though, I just said, 'Don't worry about it – I'll do some arrangements!' So I flew to Boston, six months later my wife joined me and we were living in a tiny one-bedroom apartment with a shared bathroom, hoping beyond hope for what really is an American success story to happen. I graduated, started to teach and then we moved to New York. Throughout all of this Quincy had a lot to do with my career, and so in fact did Diz – he had encouraged me to move to the States as well and he also recorded some of my pieces. I mean, when you have people as good as those people around you, it certainly helps!" Arif Mardin

From left: Nesuhi, Ahmet, and friends Emilio Gioie and Julio Mario Santo Domingo

"The Atlantic Story could not be scripted. It really is too incredible for that!" Julio Mario Santo Domingo

"We started off our album with seven songs that me and Marc Gordon produced and wrote. We went to the company and they loved the songs and said, 'Great! Great!' Then they said, 'But we need some uptempo stuff,' and we were, like, kind of ooohhhhhkay. When they mentioned Reggie Calloway we thought, 'Fine, he's got hits, okay, cool.' So we went to Reggie, and at first he came up with two songs that we really didn't care for, that we didn't think were us and weren't strong enough. Then he called me back and said, 'I've got a song, it's called 'Casanova'.' I said, 'Well, okay.' He said, 'Listen to this melody,' and started singing, *'I ain't much on Casanova, me and Romeo ain't never been friends.'* So when I heard that part, I said, 'Me and Romeo – that's a killer, we've got to do that, that's a smash, we've got to do it.' He said, 'You really think it's a smash?' I guess he didn't quite believe it himself but we did it, and look what came out of it."
Gerald Levert

Levert, from left: Marc Gordon and Gerald Levert TL: 80s

Levert, from left: Gerald Levert, Sean Levert and Marc Gordon TL: 80s

The Modern Jazz Quartet, from left: John Lewis, Percy Heath, Connie Kay and Milt Jackson TL: 80s

"For me, Muddy Waters and all the blues songsters are the bottom-rock source, the mother lode for the music. If it doesn't have that, then it might be interesting but it won't have the uniqueness and depth that music can achieve. The great challenge in improvisation is to take material that wasn't invented for improvisation and use it to define the blues. That's what I'm trying to do and the great people that I admire, that's what they do – whether consciously or subconsciously. So the way we use this particular means of expression, the blues, and the way we jazz it up, is born in America, not Africa or Europe. I think you'll also find something similar to this musical culture in some Spanish, Romanian and Hungarian gypsy music, as well as in the music of the Middle East and North Africa – but it's quite a distance away and they developed independently.

"So the basic ingredients of this music were invented in the United States. Like all music, it has its influences, and care surely has to be taken not to let it be gobbled up by fads. Before the war, communication took much longer and travelling around took a longer time than it does now, which means that we were isolated enough to develop something that had an identity of its own, and it continues to have that." John Lewis

MJQ with Nesuhi

THE ERTEGUNS' NEW YORK
NEW YORK CABARET MUSIC

MAE BARNES · JOE BUSHKIN · BARBARA CARROLL · EDDIE CONDON
CHRIS CONNOR · JIMMY DANIELS · GOLDIE HAWKINS · GRETA KELLER
JIMMY LYON · CARMEN McRAE · MABEL MERCER · JOE MOONEY
HUGH SHANNON · BOBBY SHORT · TED STRAETER · SYLVIA SYMS
BILLY TAYLOR · MEL TORME · CY WALTER

Mabel Mercer with Bobby Short

"What a thrill it was to drive into the environs of New York, the approach to the big city, and get the first glimpse of the skyline. I lived in Washington D.C. in the thirties and New York was a place I regarded with wonder and awe. New York, to me, was glamour, elegance and modernity. As a teenager, the thought of spending a few days there filled me with excited anticipation of sophisticated, romantic experiences, urbane city life and, most of all, jazz, 52nd Street and Harlem. In those days and into the forties, my brother Nesuhi and I went to all the jazz clubs and heard and met virtually all the jazz performers. We also had a parallel interest – great performers such as Astaire and Rogers, Bing Crosby, Josephine Baker, Marlene Dietrich, Maurice Chevalier. Then there was the music of Cole Porter, Kurt Weill, Rodgers and Hart, Gershwin, and on and on.

"I had some very special friends in those years, who understood this music as it was happening and understood its particular character and importance. They were New Yorkers as much at home at El Morocco and at the Stork as they were in the Village and in Harlem. Among them were George Frazier Jr., Bob and Jean Bach, Jimmy and Marjorie Downey, Rogers Whittaker, the great singers Lee Wiley and Blossom Dearie, Harper and Lu Soules, Billy and Fay Harbach, Eddie Collins, Dwight and Joyce Hemion, Tom Rees and the composers Vernon Duke, Frank Loesser, Johnny Mercer and Cy Coleman.

"In the late eighties, we put together a boxed set of the cabaret music which Nesuhi and I recorded for Atlantic through the years. Of course, we were not able to include everything but I hope that it conveys a feeling for the music – the music of Harlem, the Village, the East Side and Broadway, and the influence of Paris, London and Berlin and, of course, jazz." Ahmet

Jazz
By Will Friedwald

"Jazz has never moved in so many directions all at once as it [does] now. From basic blues to atonality, from rediscoveries of traditional roots – for some that means Basie, for others Jelly Roll Morton, for others still, Bach – to experimentations so daring they might shock the most confirmed modernists, from total improvization to fully arranged compositions which leave no room for improving, jazz has never before been so thoroughly adventurous."

The year is 1956, the venue is the jazz magazine *Down Beat* and the speaker is Nesuhi Ertegun. This description is astute enough to apply to virtually any era of jazz: indeed, if Charles Dickens were to abandon fiction to review CDs for *Jazz Times*, he could label almost any era as being at once "the best of times" and "the worst of times" for jazz. Yet there's one technological point of reference which directly links the 1950s to today, and that's the way in which new mediums open up the music to new audiences. In the last ten years, the compact disc has been doing for jazz what the 12-inch long-playing disc began achieving for the music in 1955. The new medium of LP provided the only McGuffin necessary for Nesuhi Ertegun and his brother, Ahmet, to rekindle their professional commitment to jazz as well as to each other. "We always recorded jazz," Ahmet Ertegun, younger of the two brothers, says today, "from the beginning." Ahmet had, in fact, done his first session with the "progressive jazz" orchestra (as it was then known) of Boyd Raeburn back in 1946. For the next seven years, Atlantic paid the most attention to the sub-genres of jazz that grew out of the label's primary areas of activity, such as the R & B-rooted jazz guitarist Tiny Grimes and the cabaret-oriented jazz of pianists Erroll Garner and Joe Bushkin.

With the onset of the 12-inch LP, Ahmet decided to launch a more aggressive, straight-down-the-middle jazz line, and it was a foregone conclusion that his older brother, Nesuhi, would return to New York to run it. Since moving to Los Angeles in 1944, he'd been one of the key architects of the New Orleans jazz revival on the West Coast: he'd helped re-launch the careers of such legendary figures as Jimmie Noone and Kid Ory, and had started two independent labels, Jazzman and Crescent, to record this music. When Nesuhi helped Les Koenig found the Contemporary Records label, he branched out, as a producer, into more modern areas of jazz. Using his Californian connections as a starting point, Nesuhi managed to lure one of the biggest stars of the entire jazz scene, trumpeter Shorty Rogers, to inaugurate the new Atlantic jazz line. This debut effort was, highly appropriately, numbered Atlantic 1212, *The Swinging Mr. Rogers* by Shorty Rogers and His Giants.

While this equally well-titled LP led to many subsequent projects both by Rogers and other West Coast jazz groups, the rock and foundation of Atlantic's jazz division would not arrive until ten months and 20 releases later with *Fontessa*, Atlantic 1231, by The Modern Jazz Quartet. "The MJQ," says Ahmet, without hesitation, "was the most important group we had." Although the group's earliest recordings had been for the Prestige label, the quartet switched affiliations just around the same time it switched drummers (its only personnel change in 40 years), and the double-move wasn't a coincidence. "I put Atlantic in business," drummer Connie Kay told me in a 1984 interview. "I made all the records – Ruth Brown, LaVern Baker, Ray Charles, The Coasters. Then, when I joined The Quartet, Panama (Francis) took over. In fact it was through me that The Quartet recorded for Atlantic. Nesuhi and Ahmet asked me if I would talk to the guys. They were getting interested in putting out some jazz records."

As Atlantic partner Jerry Wexler put it, "The most important collaboration was with The Modern Jazz Quartet." Nesuhi himself elaborated, "Their two dominant personalities were in marked contrast to one another. John Lewis, the musical director (and pianist), was the consummate professional, always controlled, with a strong sense of classical music, a man who could play Bach as well as anyone. Milt Jackson, the vibist, was certainly one of the most fluid improvisers and essentially a blues player." The group's remarkable energy came from the contrast of Lewis's tightly laced baroque backgrounds against Jackson's hell for leather wailing. What we could call the "unified duplicity" of the group extended also to its compositional underpinnings, from Lewis's intricate, though rarely fussy, fugal pieces to Jackson's hard-blowing blues, like 'Bags Groove'. Nesuhi continued, "Without question, the MJQ became the backbone of our jazz catalogue." To start with, there were the 28 or so albums by the full Quartet on Atlantic, almost all of them taped before the group's temporary retirement in 1974. Then there were the non-MJQ projects by Lewis and Jackson. One hesitates to describe these "solo" outings because, like so much of the best jazz, Lewis's and Jackson's extracurricular efforts both, coincidentally, were predicated on the theme of encounters. In a series of teamings with bop giants, Jackson re-established that his good vibes could more than hold their own against such heavyweight sparring partners as Coleman Hawkins (*Bean Bags*), Frank Wess (*Bags & Flutes*), John Coltrane (*Bags & Trane*) and even Ray Charles (*Milt Jackson & Ray Charles*). Where Jackson's teamings came primarily from the bop and blues mainstreams, Lewis liked to "lock horns" as it were, with artists who appealed to his penchant for things European. Lewis introduced American listeners to any number of remarkable international jazzmen, such as French guitarist Sacha Distel (*Afternoon In Paris*), violinist Svend Asmussen (*European Encounter*) – the titles of both of which qualify as triumphs of truth in labelling – and German trombonist Albert Manglesdorf and The Zagreb Jazz Quartet (*Animal Dance*). Perhaps inspired by Lewis's example, Ertegun also imported a number of masters by the leading Euro-jazzmen, such as British tenor Ronnie Ross, Stockholm big band leader Harry Arnold and the remarkable Swedish baritonist-composer Lars Gullin. Atlantic also released two albums by the finest of all continental jazz orchestras, the Clarke-Boland Big Band, co-led by The MJQ's original drummer, Kenny Clarke. Lewis also helmed any number of experimental, large-scale projects in these years, both with (*Third Stream Music, The Modern Jazz Quartet and Orchestra*) and without (*The Golden Striker, Jazz Abstractions, Original Sin*) the rest of The MJQ. Further, Lewis brought the talented singer Nancy Harrow to Atlantic, and more importantly, the connection between the label and Quartet's manager, Monte Kay (no relation to The Q's drummer, Connie Kay) led to the signing of two major mainstays of the company's catalogue, Chris Connor and Charles Mingus. In fact, both the singer and bassist-iconoclast cut their first albums for Nesuhi within a few weeks of The MJQ (Connor's debut set featuring both Lewis and Kay).

Because of their classical component, The MJQ's music was occasionally labelled "cool" jazz, a description which flew in the face of its unmistakable bop basis (and the members' upbringing in the Dizzy Gillespie band). However, the white and West Coast musicians whom the label also recorded had less ammunition to dispute the charges. The Swinging Mr. (Shorty) Rogers had launched the Atlantic jazz line, and this lyrical yet hard-driving trumpeter-composer would record six albums for the company. Like all of the best West Coasters, Rogers was undoubtedly perturbed by the stigma of words like "limp" and "subdued" that some territorially minded listeners applied to his work. Rogers could swing as hard as any East Coast brassman, and his original blues lines (as he had proved as an arranger for both Woody Herman and Stan Kenton) were every bit as earthy. Plus, as Rogers established with a series of album and tune titles à la *Martians, Stay Home* as well as covers that depicted the diminutive dynamo in tree houses and outerspace gear, Rogers also had a sense of humour. The Dave Pell Octet – who made two excellent albums under Rogers's supervision – were even more listener-friendly than Rogers, and created a brand of western bop that was every bit as danceable as Dixieland. Other westerners, like the pianist Lou Levy, who co-led the excellent *West Coast Wailers* LP (supervised by Ahmet in Los Angeles), were primarily interested in doing exactly that. So was tenor saxist Jack

Montrose, who starred on a self-titled set that remains one of the only albums to feature the brilliant baritonist Bob Gordon, only three months before the latter died in a car crash at the age of 27. *The Swinging Mr. Rogers* spawned a further series of Atlantic LPs in that the other half of that pivotal album's front line was another masterful horn-player, composer and arranger out of The Herman Herd, the multi-reedist Jimmy Giuffre. Giuffre's albums for the label included his quirky, idiosyncratic treatment of the score to Broadway's *The Music Man*, such extended works as *The Western Suite* (this being after the Dallas-born composer had come East), and *The Four Brothers Sound*, in which he recreated the four-tenor sound he helped pioneer for Woody Herman's band a decade earlier (and his famous composition of that title), this time playing four multi-tracked tenors all by himself. But by far Giuffre's best remembered recordings spotlighted *The Jimmy Giuffre 3*, a remarkably democratic trio in which he played all the reeds, with guitarist Jim Hall and either bassist Ralph Pena or valve-trombonist Bon Brookmeyer. "The important thing was I found two men who thought my way," the saxist-leader recalled, "each of us had to play a part all by himself and not depend on the rhythm section, we had to constantly listen for balance, and we each had to find a part that went with the other parts."

Atlantic continued recording "cool" and West Coast musicians for many years to come; doing several sets with Shelly Manne and the fortuitous teaming of Gerry Mulligan and Dave Brubeck (as well as the puzzling *All The Things We Are*, which teamed the pianist with Lee Konitz and Anthony Braxton) into the seventies. Still, the most remarkable "cool" sub-school of musicians were those who gathered around the amazing pianist-pedagogue and demagogue Lennie Tristano, and his two most prodigious prodigies, altoist Lee Konitz and tenorist Warne Marsh. When Ertegun spoke of jazzmen who regarded Bach as the roots of their music, he not only had John Lewis in mind but also Tristano and his clique. However, Tristano was also probably the first major musical instructor to make sure his students learned as much from Louis Armstrong as they did Beethoven, and to work out a comprehensive pedagogical method for jazz performance. Konitz had already achieved a reputation as a rapidly rising post-Parker player (with Claude Thornhill and Miles Davis) when he began studying and playing with fellow Chicagoan Tristano, and with the addition of Los Angelian Marsh, the three men formed the core of one of the most formidable ensembles in jazz. Though they had recorded for other companies, most notably Tristano's self-produced Jazz label, Ertegun was the first big-time producer to give the Tristano-ites full vent. "My brother decided he wanted to record Lennie, so he called him up, but Lennie was not too receptive," as Ahmet puts it – and rather mildly. "We went over to Lennie's place, and since Lennie was blind he didn't have any lights. He had to lead us around. Then he played us a bunch of records, and wanted to see if we could identify them. I don't think Lennie would have recorded for us if Nesuhi hadn't known so much and was able to name him everything he played." Albums like *Lennie Tristano*, *The Lennie Tristano Quartet*, *The New Tristano*, *Requiem* (under Tristano's name), *Inside Hi Fi*, *Lee Konitz with Warne Marsh*, *Worthwhile Konitz*, *The Real Lee Konitz* (by Konitz) and *Warne Marsh* make it clear that the most significant body of work by the Tristano-ites is on Atlantic. Here the endless invention of the saxes, particularly Konitz, finds a perfect context in the contrapuntal chords of the leader. Although Tristano was accused – mainly by those who never listened to his music – of over-intellectualizing jazz, most of his sounds are amazingly accessible even to uninitiated ears. Despite its foreboding title, for instance, 'Requiem' turns out to be as straightforward a blues line as anything Joe Turner might have recorded. Konitz, the only member of the threesome alive today, remains one of the most compelling improvisers that music has ever known.

It's a lesser-known fact that although the Erteguns devoted their lives to "black music", i.e. the blues and jazz, both brothers were equally committed to celebrating the "standard" songs of Tin Pan Alley. However, unlike the "white"-oriented major labels, Atlantic had no straight-down-the-middle mainstream pop singers. What they did have, on one hand, were cabaret style singers who sang Cole Porter and Richard Rodgers with a healthy respect that bordered on reverence. And on the other side of the coin, the Erteguns recorded many out-and-out jazz vocalists who took all manner of liberties with the canon of American composers.

Dizzy Gillespie

Ahmet Ertegun had been recording cabaret artists since the early fifties, recognizing that, as with jazz, there was another valid and vital American artform that too was being overlooked by the major labels. It was, however, far from exclusively a "white" medium, in that both of cabaret's leading exponents, Bobby Short and Mabel Mercer, were Afro-Americans. Naturally enough, Short and Mercer became the flagship artists of the label's cabaret line. Mercer started her Atlantic association with three classic ten-inch volumes of *Songs by Mabel Mercer* in 1953, and climaxed her recording career with the masterful *Mabel Mercer Sings Cole Porter*. Long admired by Frank Sinatra for her ability to tell a story in song, Ms. Mercer's Atlantic career climaxed in 1968 with a live album from New York's Town Hall. Her colleague on that double-disc collection, Bobby Short, had been the label's major male cabaret star since 1955's *Songs By Bobby Short* (Atlantic 1214). Short – who had four albums in the 1200 series alone – continually sought to introduce jazz elements into the East Side piano-singer tradition. He used all manner of "hot" musicians on *Sing Me A Swing Song* and *The Mad Twenties*, and would himself later record a definitive songbook series for the label.

From 1955 to 1962, Chris Connor reigned as the Queen of jazz singers on the label. "Chris was a great singer, in the June Christy-Anita O'Day school," says Ahmet today, "and for a while she was very, very popular." Connor's Kansas City-bred tone may have been "cool" (that word again), which was a prerequisite for singing with Stan Kenton's Orchestra, but her approach was warm and earthy. Using all manner of brilliant New York musicians and arrangers (as opposed to her Kentonian predecessors O'Day and Christy, who were part of the West Coast scene), Connor's emphasis was on strong performances of both classic (as on her double-length *George Gershwin Almanac of Song*) and unjustly-neglected songs. (Her final Atlantic album, *Free Spirits*, included melodies by both John Lewis and Ornette Coleman.) Whether swinging or cooing a love song, Connor had and has a knack for cutting to the emotional core of her material. Connor's Atlantic releases constitute the most essential output of her nearly 50-year career. Yet many other crucial jazz singers stopped in at the label to put forth some of their most significant statements, such as Carmen McRae, whose *Bittersweet* (released on the Focus subsidiary) ranks as one of the great lady's most powerful releases of the sixties. Mel Tormé made three brilliant albums for Atlantic, most notably *Comin' Home Baby*, an album inspired by a hit single, in which he and fellow West Coaster Shorty Rogers come to hard-swinging grips with such East Coast writers as Benny Golson and Bobby Timmons.

In the fifties in particular, Atlantic specialized in finding the most unique talents around, and their vocal department was no exception, as their albums by such cult favourites as the soulful Jackie Paris. "Joe Mooney, who sang and played organ (and accordion) was a particular favourite of mine," says Ahmet. "He was a great, neglected talent, and I'm glad we could do an album with him, late in his life." In fact, both Atlantic's most celebrated practitioners of the Great American Songbook (after Short and Mercer), came to the standards tradition from completely different, equally unforeseen directions: Ray Charles and Bobby Darin.

Still, even in a roster comprised entirely of die-hard individuals, Mose

Allison stood out. The Mississippi-born, Delta-blues-enriched pianist first attracted attention with modernists like Stan Getz and the Zoot Sims-Al Cohn Quintet. (One early supporter was George Wallington, who heavily featured Allison's compositions on his fine album *The Prestidigitator*, released on Atlantic's East-West imprint). However, when Allison began recording on his own, he favoured a simpler, more traditionally flavoured brand of playing and singing. Allison's first Atlantic album, *I Don't Worry About A Thing* led to ten more releases for the label between '62 and '76. It also yielded the typically anthemic 'Your Mind Is On Vacation (But Your Mouth Is Working Overtime)' which perfectly matches Jerry Wexler's description of "Father Mose ... carrying on in his spare, flame-under-a-bushel style".

If there was a "house-style" at Atlantic in the fifties and early sixties, it almost certainly was bebop, in its East Coast, "hard bop" permutation. Virtually every major modernist turned up at the label for at least one album, from Dizzy Gillespie (the father, as it were, of the Modern Jazz Quartet) on down. Sonny Stitt recorded a definitive sample of straight-down-the-middle bop of *Stitt Plays Bird*, and Atlantic was also the only label of note to document Buster Smith, the legendary Kansas City alto giant who was himself a major influence on Charlie Parker.

Indeed, it would be difficult to think of an important bop player who didn't come to Atlantic at some point: *Thelonious Monk With Art Blakey And The Jazz Messengers* was triply unique being the only Atlantic appearance of either Monk or the Messengers, and their only waxing together (although Monk had worked with most of the band individually, most frequently with Blakey himself). "That was a very difficult record," Ahmet explains, "the other musicians were hanging around waiting for Monk to show up, and it turned out he was sitting outside in a car. We tried for hours and hours, but we couldn't persuade Monk to come in. I was afraid that Art and the guys would get fed up and leave." Further tribulations stemmed from the Messengers' inability to comprehend Monk's thorny compositions on the first night (bassist Spanky DeBrest fainted from the effort). However, they more than rallied on the final two sessions, producing a Monkian masterpiece. Then too, Monk's custom of dancing in between his solos never failed to take his producers by surprise. In addition to Monk, Atlantic would document all manner of major pianists, like the swingingly mainstream Sir Roland Hanna (who shone on the album of music, Harold Rome's *Destry Rides Again*, among others) and the amazingly fleet-of-finger Phineas Newborn (on the early winner *This Is Phineas*). On an appropriately appellated set called *Max Roach Presents The Legendary Hassan*, the great bop drummer spotlighted an obscure keyboard wiz who helped bridge the gap between Monk and "outside" pianists like Cecil Taylor. (The great pioneer bop drummer Roach made other fascinating albums for the company, particularly *Lift Every Voice And Sing*, which combined his quintet with a gospel choir. Other masters of the bop *batterie* on the label included Philly Joe Jones and Elvin Jones.)

Altoist Phil Woods and trumpeter Art Farmer rate as two of the most recorded of all modern jazzmen, who appeared on thousands of sessions between them. Yet their Atlantic albums rate as some of their most challenging performances. Typically, trumpet players work in units of five or larger and hire a saxophonist to play off. Yet in Farmer's three great quartet sets of 1963-64, the veteran not only eschewed the use of a second horn, he further exposed himself by employing Jim Hall's guitar instead of a piano. Another important trumpeter of the era, Freddie Hubbard, recorded several LPs for the label, introducing his classic composition 'Up Jumped Spring' on the 1966 album *Backlash*. (Not content to stop there, they also recorded such great sixties trumpet stars as Ted Curson and Jimmy Owens.)

Nesuhi Ertegun's schedule of jazz projects for the Atlantic label kept true to the definition of jazz that he outlined in *Down Beat*, ranging from "back to the roots" efforts to "futuristic" works. The trouble with the future was that it kept changing – in 1955, a third-stream opus like Bill Russo's ambitious ballet *The World Of Alcina* seemed to point towards the next step in jazz, yet by 1960 Ornette Coleman had established a different idea of *The Shape Of Jazz To Come*. Jazz is such a vital music that even the past was "unpredictable". Traditional jazz was almost as important to the brothers as blues and bop. "We love that music," says Ahmet. "Don't forget that Nesuhi taught the first college course for credit on the history of jazz." In the fifties, the label's classic jazz roster was dominated by trombonist Wilbur De Paris, who led a phenomenally entertaining unit usually spotlighting Omer Simeon's clarinet and the trumpets of both Doc Cheatham and De Paris's younger brother Sidney. Here was no group of funny hat Dixielanders grinding out tired rehashes of 'Tiger Rag'; here was an exciting, polished ensemble, under the thumb of a leader and producer who had the intelligence to create such unusual packages as an album of Cole Porter songs and a full-length collaboration with blues singer Jimmy Witherspoon. Then, after ten uniformly excellent De Paris albums on Atlantic, the past suddenly changed. "We started going down to New Orleans," says Ahmet. "We would send a production crew or go ourselves." The highpoint of this activity was an outstanding series entitled *Jazz At Preservation Hall* (partially inspired by *Riverside New Orleans: The Living Legends* series). These releases focused on less "urbane" units than De Paris's, such as the rugged-sounding Eureka Brass Band and the earthily eloquent clarinet of George Lewis. Indeed, the Young Tuxedo Brass Band, recorded by Ahmet and Tom Dowd in 1958, sounded so "far out" that listeners on a blindfold test (informally administered by critic Gary Giddins) assumed that they were some kind of avant-garde collective. In his own way, George Lewis was as graceful and sophisticated as the MJQ, and that confluence of jazz genres, where the very old sounds like the very new, is precisely what Atlantic Records was always about.

While Atlantic continued to record bop, cool and traditional jazz, the sixties were dominated by soulful saxes. In this, the jazz division was perfectly in step with the rest of the company which, through Ray Charles and then Aretha Franklin, can be said to have served as the cradle of the soul movement. In fact, Charles's band became a nucleus of jazz activity much like the MJQ. Both David "Fathead" Newman and Hank Crawford, who would become two of the company's biggest-selling talents, had initially tested their mettle in the company of "The Genius". "Nesuhi was really crazy about Hank and Fathead," says Ahmet. "He was the first to recognize that they would be major stars, even apart from Ray." Newman and Crawford quickly established a four-way connection between each other, Charles and Atlantic Records, resulting in no less than 22 albums. The two saxists (and even Charles himself) would frequently guest star on each other's dates, and, like Charles, who played and sang, they also doubled, Newman on alto and tenor, Crawford on alto, baritone and arrangements. Together, they set the standard for Atlantic's jazz stars of the sixties, who were to a man players equally at home in the language of bop, ballads and the blues. This was a direction encouraged by Joel Dorn, who gradually established himself as the label's most important producer after Nesuhi, beginning in the mid-sixties.

Atlantic's popular instrumentalist was undoubtedly Herbie Mann, a multi-reed player who paraded his flamboyant flautistry through all manner of funky contexts. In April 1970, when Mann's biggest hit, *Memphis Underground*, had been on the charts for just a year, Leonard Feather noted that one out of four records on the selfsame jazz charts was a Herbie Mann release. His association with Atlantic was longer and far more prolific than any other musician, tallying up by 1980 at 20 years and 50 albums. In 1970, Atlantic and Mann founded Embryo Records, for which Mann produced his own albums as well as those of other artists (most notably Phil Woods and Ron Carter). In 1976, Mann was appointed head of jazz A & R for the entire Atlantic label, at which time he was quoted as saying, "I'm still playing popular music as musically as possible." The diversity of Eddie Harris's accomplishments have caused more than one critic to wonder aloud if there might not be more than one Eddie Harris.

It does seem hard to believe that the Eddie Harris who composed 'Freedom Jazz Dance' (recorded by Harris on his label debut, *The In Sound* and the most "avant" vehicle of Miles Davis's sixties band), could be the same Eddie Harris who created hit singles and later became jazz's foremost experimentalist in the area of electronic horns. Surprisingly, Harris's most celebrated Atlantic performance would occur in a spontaneous and acoustic setting. It occurred when Harris and funky pianomeister Les McCann (along with the gifted expatriate trumpeter Benny Bailey) decided to join forces for an impromptu concert at the 1969 Montreux Jazz Festival, which resulted in the blockbuster 'Compared To What'.

Philly Jo Jones

The ideas of Yusef Lateef (as expressed on his seven Atlantic LPs) have always seemed so contemporary that it's difficult to keep in mind that the saxophonist was working with Roy Eldridge even before he joined Dizzy Gillespie during the first wave of the bebop movement. Lateef pioneered many trends now commonplace in jazz, such as the use of certain African elements as well as a multi-instrumental technique that utilizes an encyclopaedic storehold of instruments gathered from the four corners of the third world, and that's in addition to such Western influences as forms from medieval and baroque traditions. His 1987 return to Atlantic, *Yusef Lateef's Little Symphony* won the somewhat surprised Lateef a Grammy in the New Age Category.

Yet Atlantic's supreme accomplishment in these years was the ten-year (1966-76), 12-album output of Rahsaan Roland Kirk, who first came to the label via Charles Mingus (on the 1961 *Oh Yeah!*). Kirk's skills as a simultaneous multi-instrumentalist parallel the extent of his appeal, which combined the accessibility of Mann and Harris with the soulfulness of Newman and Crawford and a capacity for eclecticism even stronger than Lateef's. The most striking feature of Kirk's technique was his ability to play harmonic and even contrapuntal lines on several saxophones simultaneously, yet for all his showmanship, Kirk was far more than a novelty act. He was a remarkable composer, bandleader and one of the most engaging personalities that the music has ever known. Starting from a solidly hardbop foundation, Kirk explored the entire length and breadth of what he called "Black Classical Music", from New Orleans-style pieces as authentic as Preservation Hall to Free Jazz as outside as Ornette and Don Cherry. (Kirk also served as a producer for Atlantic, supervising an album by Chicago tenor colossus Von Freeman. Both Freeman and long-time cohort Clifford Jordan did some of their best work for the label, Jordan excelling on a marvellous collection of songs by Leadbelly, entitled *These Are My Roots.*)

In a very real way, the infusion of soulful sounds (like the R & B saxophone of King Curtis) and devices like the electric organ (as on altoist Leo Wright's wailing 'Soul Talk') led to the development of fusion. The phenomenally successful Atlantic recordings of Charles Lloyd (like the 1966 *Forest Flower*) are another early example of the genre. The musicians who used the form at Atlantic defined fusion very broadly indeed, implying any mixture of jazz and rock elements. As demonstrated by its most celebrated practitioner, Miles Davis, "fusion" generally implied the juxtaposition of rock-style guitars and electric keyboards with "jazzy" acoustic horns. Two of Davis's sidemen, Billy Cobham and Joe Zawinal, used Atlantic to extend the experimentation in the developing style that they'd begun with the trumpeter. Zawinal, a very gifted Viennese composer-keyboardist, had actually made several acoustic releases for the company (including a 1967 Vortex that contemplated *The Rise And Fall Of The Third Stream*), before plugging in a rhythm section and adding several of his Milesian cohorts on *Concerto Retitled*. Cobham, also known for his drumming with the Mahavishnu Orchestra, put the fusion genre solidly on the map with his hit 1973 album *Spectrum* and its key composition 'Stratus'. He would cut seven further sets for Atlantic over the next five years. Nesuhi himself signed up Atlantic's biggest jazz-rock star of the years 1975-86, electric violinist Jean-Luc Ponty. Like Cobham he was a former Mahavishnite, and like Zawinal he was European (a Parisian, specifically), having grown up studying classical violin and later turning to jazz. Upon arriving in America, Ponty plunged straight into hard rock with Frank Zappa and Elton John. Ponty's 12 Atlantic albums reflect the culmination of his mastery of all these musics, never more successfully than on 1978's *Cosmic Messenger*. Other fusionists prove that one can sustain a fusion mentality even without the aid of high-tech implements. Keyboardists Keith Jarrett and Chick Corea had also come out of Miles Davis's early electric bands, Jarrett being a veteran too of Lloyd's *Forest Flower* group. Individually, they're each accumulating a following that combines the quality (in terms of dedication) of the jazz audience with the quantity of the pop market. Corea and Jarrett are, essentially, jazz's biggest rock stars. It's hardly a surprise that they make their leader debuts — and some of their most enduring music — on Atlantic (or rather, its Vortex subsidiary).

Atlantic's jazz output was so rich and so diverse that it would be difficult to name a genre of the music that the label didn't excel in. For instance, although the Erteguns rarely delved into big band swing, they did produce such outstanding sets as Jess Stacy's *Tribute To Benny Goodman* and the 1960 Woody Herman and his Big New Herd at the Monterey Jazz Festival, as well as the similarly themed Newport Jazz Festival All-Stars with Buck Clayton and Pee Wee Russell. There were also several outstanding packages by the more modern Kenny Clarke-Francy Boland Big Band.

After creating a sensation with Ornette Coleman and some of John Coltrane's further out explorations, Atlantic continued to explore the outer reaches of free jazz, most successfully with the Art Ensemble of Chicago, in two sets produced by Michael Cuscuna. Like the Modern Jazz Quartet before it, this was an all-star collective (each of its members, particularly Lester Bowie and Roscoe Mitchell, recorded extensively on their own) who pooled their talents and egos into an ensemble that was greater than the sum of its parts. And like Charles Mingus, for all of their flakiness, they managed to rally and put out some of their most together music on Atlantic, the first American major to record the group. The Art Ensemble's motto, "ancient to the future", is a slogan that applied to the entire scope of jazz on Atlantic. Although the AEC may well qualify as the furthest-out group ever to appear on the label, they hardly signify the end of jazz on Atlantic. The label continued working in the fusion and avant-garde forms in the seventies and eighties, while the nineties, remarkably, saw a return to more straight ahead bop-based stylings spearheaded by James Carter and Cyrus Chestnut.

A comprehensive history of jazz on Atlantic (and Atco, and Cortex, and EastWest, and Focus ...) Records would probably require several books. Nearly every record produced by Atlantic's jazz division would qualify as, at the very least, an artistic endeavour. Yet Nesuhi Ertegun also never forgot that he was, in the end, also part of a commercial enterprise. As such, the producer was obliged to seek out sounds he hoped would be — in the words of Atlantic artist Ahmad Jamal — "grabbed up by a certain number of people". But when Nesuhi went into a recording studio, he was after something greater than a merely marketable product. "Because of the peculiar nature of jazz," Nesuhi said back in that 1956 *Down Beat*, "you hear a musician say something during a solo you never heard him say before; you hear a rhythm section suddenly take on fire; as the session progresses, an infinite amount of things come into being that nobody could foresee. It is this element of surprise which is the greatest fascination of jazz. When it occurs, the A & R man sitting in the booth forgets sometimes he is a record producer and becomes a fervent jazz listener."

NESUHI ERTEGUN BY JOHN LEWIS

It was 1954, and the Modern Jazz Quartet was playing to a wonderfully receptive crowd at a club called Ciro's. Among the celebratory activities was a big party, thrown by a famous photographer, in our honour. It was attended by a lot of people, many of whom were from the jazz community — that's where I met Nesuhi for the first time. We saw each other after that because he came by the club a number of times to hear us play, but our relationship really blossomed when he joined Atlantic Records and signed the group. From that moment on, throughout the entire history of the MJQ, there were only six key people involved in the development of the group: the four musicians; Monte Kay, our manager; and Nesuhi, our producer.

Nesuhi had phenomenal taste in music in general, and particularly in jazz. In those days, producers not only gave the artists little leeway in the production end of the recording, but also liked to act as A & R men. Nesuhi, on the other hand, let us decide what we wanted to play. His thing was to make sure that what we did was well-recorded, well-packaged and properly promoted. As musical director of the Quartet, I prepared the material that we planned to record, and we performed it for at least six months before we went into the studio. By then, we knew the music fairly well, and it never took much time at all to record it. Once it was on tape, Nesuhi and I would edit the whole thing.

Some producers would do a record and that would be the end of it. But Nesuhi genuinely cared for the music, and it showed. Not only was it obvious in the way he produced it, but in the way it was ultimately packaged. He made sure that the package matched the quality of the contents. He had great taste in art and a real feel for what an album cover should look like. Many of those covers have become classics in their own right.

Nesuhi sensed what the MJQ was about early on. He realized that we were attracting a more sophisticated audience than most groups at the time and he capitalized on that. As we were looking for some direction in those early years, his foresight gave us the incentive we needed. But nothing between us was forced. It all happened quite naturally, as a total creative fusion. We understood what we were about and what we wanted to achieve.

Today, with many of our albums being reissued on compact disc, I marvel at the things we did at that time — he had a most definite input. Of all these albums, two particularly stand out for me: *The European Concert* album, because it was a two-record set, which was very unusual in those days; and *The Last Concert*. I think they were important recordings because they show the development of the group, as well as that of its producer.

I have fond memories of Nesuhi, but the trip that we made to France is one that remains most vivid because of an amusing incident. I forget which city it was, but we had to make a fast train connection. Due to the lack of time, we started throwing our suitcases out the window of the train we were riding in and into our connecting train, which was on the track right next to us. Nesuhi had just bought a set of nice Louis Vuitton suitcases and was throwing them as gleefully as we did our battered ones. Somehow, it was characteristic of him. Even though he was a very powerful man, he never lost a very endearing down-to-earth quality and he saw nothing wrong with doing the job himself if he had to.

He was also one of the most generous people I have known. If you needed something and it was within his power to get it, he would go out of his way to give it to you. This quality extended to his business deals as well. One day I went in, out of the blue, and suggested that he record a certain controversial young musician I'd heard of – Ornette Coleman. Nesuhi took the suggestion, paid for Ornette and Don Cherry to come to the Music Inn in Lenox, where the MJQ was in residence, and agreed to record them. That was the start of their careers.

"This is a painting by Abidin Dino, a great friend of Nesuhi's. The memorial service for Nesuhi was very moving. Many of his close friends were there. We played, as a musical prelude, some of Nesuhi's favourite records. Roberta Flack sang a wonderful version of the song 'Always', by Irving Berlin, which brought the house down. It was an incredible concert with Sergio Mendes, The Manhattan Transfer, Nino Tempo, Sylvia Syms, Bobby Short, Phil Collins, the Modern Jazz Quartet, and Claude Nobs with George Wein. I had the great fortune of having Nesuhi as my older brother. He was my mentor, not only in music, but in the fine arts and literature, guiding me toward a sound education in the classics of the Western world. He was a great man and my greatest influence. I owe everything to Nesuhi." Ahmet

His life was gentle, and the elements
So mix'd in him that Nature might stand up
And say to all the world, 'This was a man!'

William Shakespeare

His dedication to the music went beyond recording the notes that were played. He even recorded round-table discussions that we had at the Inn. They were dialogues, bringing together old and young musicians, that lasted for hours and covered all facets of music. You'd be hard-pressed to find someone to put up the money and the equipment to record anything of that kind today.

In fact, Nesuhi has left a track record that will be very hard for anyone to match. Not only did he have respect for music, his dedication also extended to the musicians themselves. As President of IFPI (the International Federation of the Phonographic Industry), he fought very hard against record piracy on behalf of us all. And through his work at WEA International, he made sure that our music was heard all over the world. With the passing of Nesuhi Ertegun, the music world has lost one of its champions, and jazz has lost one of its best producers.

I have lost a very dear friend.

Illinois Jacquet TL: 80s

"Illinois Jacquet is one of my favourite musicians; he is a great saxophone player. He's from the New Orleans area, home of some of the greatest reed players of all time. Illinois first came to national attention for his great solo on Lionel Hampton's version of 'Flying Home'. He was a star of Norman Granz's *Jazz At The Philharmonic* series. He plays in many styles and he has a wonderful warm tone. Illinois is a terrific person. He's one of the few people from his generation still playing, and playing beautifully." Ahmet

Stevie Nicks TL: 80s
"All the characters in my songs – the Gypsies, the Saras, Alice and Juliet – they're all me. But they're all different sides of me. What I really need is to love the music that goes out. I have everything I need on a living basis, so whatever the sales I want the music to be true to me and my songs. The desire to do what I do, to sit at the piano and write some words that I love, is still as strong as it ever was. I would say I'm a very romantic person and very intense, I don't write real happy songs, but I don't ever write a song that leaves people with no hope." Stevie Nicks

Sebastian Bach, lead singer of Skid Row TL: 80s 90s

"Skid Row was a band that was found by Jason Flom [then Atlantic VP of A & R, now President of Atlantic's Lava label], but in the final analysis it took me and Doug Morris to sign them. I went to hear them in Allentown, Pennsylvania, and I must say that the lead singer struck me as being an incredibly good-looking young man, with long blond hair. And even though they only had something like 30 or 40 people who'd come to hear them in that small town, we thought they put on a great show and were convinced they were going to become a big group. Of course, it didn't take them very long to become very successful. The lead singer had a great line of gab, on stage and off – he said some revolutionary things which the kids wanted to hear, and they went to see them as much for that as for the music. They had an impact not only in America, but all over the world." Ahmet

Winger, from left: Paul Taylor, Kip Winger, Reb Beach and Rod Morgenstein TL: 80s 90s

"You know, when I was trying to sign Skid Row, I was following them around to every show that they did. I'd been to about ten of their shows in a row in New Jersey and Staten Island, and then I had to go to Chicago to a friend's Bar Mitzvah. Meanwhile, I'd been talking to Ahmet about the group; he hadn't seen them yet. So I got to Chicago only to have a message from Ahmet to come home: he wanted me to go with him that night to see Skid Row in Allentown, Pennsylvania. So I gave my nephew a hundred bucks and some CDs and immediately after the ceremony I ran to the airport and got on a 'plane back to New York. I met Ahmet and we took a helicopter to Allentown. When we landed at the heliport there was a limo waiting for us, which was kind of ridiculous because the club was across the street from the heliport. And, as it turned out, the driver had travelled an hour and a half from Philadelphia to meet us. Later, on the way home, when we were coming in to land in New York, Ahmet said, 'Hey, I've got a great idea, why don't we call Cincinnati and ask them to send a car for us?'

"Anyhow, we walked into the club in Allentown. I didn't know what Ahmet would think of the band because they were still very young and had only played about a dozen gigs. After the first song he said, 'Hey man, this motherfucker is better looking than most of the girls I know.' So I guessed he liked it and I figured I was safe. Ahmet made a big impression on the band but even after that, it was a long process getting them to sign. But he persisted – he would call the manager and he would track them down. I mean, no one ever refuses a call from Ahmet. So we wound up signing them and we sold ten million albums." Jason Flom

White Lion, from left: Greg D'Angelo, James Lomenzo, Vito Bratta and Mike Tramp TL: 80s 90s

Mr. Big, from left: Billy Sheehan, Eric Martin, Pat Torpey, Paul Gilbert, with Doug Morris (centre) and their manager Sandy Einstein (kneeling) TL: 80s 90s

"In the early seventies, I had a record by a group called the Magic Lanterns on my own little label, which was called Big Tree Records. I had found this record and purchased the rights to it from a lawyer, and it came on the *Billboard* charts somewhere around #80. All of a sudden, I got a call from Ahmet and his people at Atlantic saying, 'What are you doing putting out our record?' I said, 'What do you mean?' and they told me that they'd put the same record out several years previously. That lawyer had sold me a record that they already owned – that's how I met Atlantic. Then they started distributing Big Tree and after it had done very well for quite a few years, Ahmet bought the label. Quite soon after that, I became the President of Atco Records, where I signed Stevie Nicks, Pete Townshend and INXS, among others. In 1980, when Jerry Greenberg started his own label, Ahmet asked me to become the President of Atlantic. He and I had an affinity for the same music, we had very similar tastes and we shared a certain kind of logic. I have always liked Ahmet very much. We had adjoining offices, and when I'd hear something great in his room, I'd bang on the wall; or if he heard me play something, I'd hear him coming in with his cane – clop, clop, clop – or banging on the wall … we were always in sync. It was a wonderful experience. We worked together for close on 20 years without ever having a bad word between us and we were always very supportive of each other. He's a wonderful man, and I learned a lot from him.

"In 1990, Ahmet told me to try to really expand the company – so we started the country division with Rick Blackburn, bought half of Rhino records, began EastWest America with Sylvia Rhone, and started Interscope with Jimmy Iovine. Ahmet's and my primary focus has always been on making the artistry come through. Both of us have written songs and both of us understand the dream of the artist. So we both have always made an endeavour to do everything we can for our artists. Ahmet started his own company, and I started my own company, and what happens when you own a company is that you learn to do everything because you can't afford to hire a lot of people. You learn to be the chief cook and bottle washer! When people are hired straight into these big companies, they have a job as a publicist or a production person or whatever and they don't really get a chance to see the entire spectrum of the business. Today, there are a lot of new independent record companies and the people who are starting them will, I'm sure, be one source of great executives for the future. With new technology, you can make a recording very inexpensively, press a CD and put it out on your own label. So I think it's a wonderful time for the record business – all sorts of music sells, and you can reach people by a lot of different means. It's really an interesting moment. I think that there will always be new independents started by people who love music. We all share the same disease. If you don't have it, you're just pushing a pencil. Music really is what runs the whole thing. That's the grease – there's nothing else that matters in a record company other than the music and the people who are talented and intelligent enough to understand the people who make the music. That's the whole thing. It's quite simple. Ahmet, of course, has always had that tremendous love of music. There are many facets to Ahmet Ertegun, and he truly is an incredibly interesting, intelligent and talented person."
Doug Morris

Fran Wakschal and Doug Morris

From left: Doug Morris, Bette Midler, Mica Ertegun, Ahmet and Phil Collins

Opposite: Bette Midler TL: 80s 90s

"Individually, we are an ass; but together, we are genius."

One of the inspirational slogans on the walls of the Rush studio.

Top and above: Rush, and above from left: Alex Lifesome, Geddy Lee, Neil Peart TL: 80s 90s

"I'm sort of an outsider. I don't feel I'm cool enough to fit into the alternative-rock community. I'm too much of a geek." Juliana Hatfield TL: 90s

En Vogue above, and below from left: Terry Ellis, Dawn Robinson, Maxine Jones and Cindy Herron TL: 90s

"Sylvia Rhone signed En Vogue, and they became one of the top new vocal groups of the nineties. When we started a new division at Atlantic, called EastWest America, Sylvia was named President and En Vogue moved to the new label. Later, when Sylvia took over Elektra Records, one of our sister companies, the EastWest roster went with her. But En Vogue started off on Atlantic, and they were a tremendous success for us." Ahmet

Phil Collins TL: 90s

"Not only did Phil Collins have a lot of big hits with Genesis but, as a solo artist, he has become one of the greatest stars in the world. The scale of his success came gradually. And he eventually turned out to be not only an incredible drummer, but a marvellous singer, a brilliant songwriter and a great showman. Like so many British rock artists, Phil is a great lover of American R & B, which is reflected in a lot of his music. Phil is one of my dearest friends. He's a very sweet, wonderful person and he's had a lot of ups and downs in his life. He really is the most considerate person of all the artists I know. He won't take a drink until everyone in the band has had a drink. He's more concerned about the well-being of the other musicians in his group than he is of himself, to such an extent that they all love him. He's not putting on a show, he really is like that. He wants to make sure that everyone else is taken care of before he's taken care of, which is the opposite of what can happen with some other artists. So as a result, when Phil goes out on stage, the band kills for him. There's nobody yawning. They want him to make it more than anything, and that's a wonderful thing to see. And that atmosphere carries on into his recordings." Ahmet

Alannah Myles TL: 90s

Marc Cohn TL: 90s

Anita Baker with Roberta Flack TL: 90s

"Anita Baker and Roberta Flack are both grand ladies. In a way they're both half pop, half jazz singers. You've got to be a great singer to do either – to do both, you've got to be even greater. To have found one person, let alone two people, who can actually achieve that is very rare." Ahmet

Tori Amos TL: 90s

"Tori Amos is a young lady who was signed by Jason Flom. We put out her first album, called *Y Kant Tori Read*, but it did not really happen – there was no strong reaction to it. So Doug Morris had the idea of taking her to England and letting her work there, to see if something would come out of it. We played her music for Max Hole, who ran our English company, and we said, 'Look, just let her live here a few months, and let's see if we can generate some interest.' I'll never forget one particular night when Doug and I had invited Tori to join us for dinner at a restaurant in London. It had a piano in the entrance hall and at the end of our meal the guy playing the piano had taken a break. So Tori got up and went and sat at the piano. We asked the restaurant owner if he minded if she played, and he said, 'Of course not.' Tori launched into a song she'd written called 'China'. At that moment, we felt certain that she was going to be a big winner. She developed and hit first in England, just as we had planned. Then she broke in America. Tori is a very, very special artist. She writes songs that have great meaning to the large following of young people who idolize her. She's a forthright human being with great poetic sense, depth of soul and brilliant musicality; I love her." Ahmet

Stone Temple Pilots, above from left: Scott Weiland, Dean DeLeo, and below from left: Robert DeLeo, Dean DeLeo, Scott Weiland and Eric Kretz TL: 90s

"Doug Morris and I had adjoining offices, so whenever one of us heard something that felt good, we'd bang on the wall and turn it up loud. That was how he first played me Stone Temple Pilots, who blew my mind. The first demos that we heard were so powerful. Actually, I wanted them to play on the Mick Jagger solo album we were about to record, but Mick and Doug wanted to use the producer Rick Rubin, who had a different point of view. Stone Temple Pilots really came through anyway, and became a huge success." Ahmet

"I think we all know we have something very special between us. There is a lot of love there, and we still appreciate making music together – and that outweighs all the negative shit and gives us a reason to work through our personal problems." Scott Weiland

"It's really beautiful when we write a song and then give it to Scott. What he adds is so satisfying that it just brings it all to another level." Dean DeLeo

Above and below left: Evan Dando TL: 90s

"I really enjoy performing and I like it when people hear our music. I always thought all of that promotion stuff was funny. I didn't expect it, but I was up for it – I never thought that it could actually detract from people's perceptions of me as a serious musician. I never thought that things like getting my picture taken by Bruce Weber could make people think, 'He must not be a good musician if he does that.' I don't regret it; it was just a funny period in my life. I had my fun and then it got really ugly, and I split for a while." Evan Dando

The Lemonheads TL: 90s

THE MODERN JAZZ QUARTET

The Modern Jazz Quartet with Ahmet and New York City Mayor, David Dinkins (third from right)

"In 1992, The Modern Jazz Quartet celebrated their 40th anniversary. We released a four-CD boxed set of their entire recording career, which I put together with John Lewis and Didier Deutsch. To mark the occasion, the group played a special concert at New York's Cafe Carlyle and the Mayor of New York declared the 14th of January 'Modern Jazz Quartet Day'." Ahmet

"It's been a long and enjoyable association with Nino, starting off nearly 40 years ago, when he worked with me as a session musician. Then, of course, along with his sister, April Stevens, we had the massive hit 'Deep Purple' in 1963. Recently, we've made another couple of records with him, including a live album at the Cicada in L.A. I must say, it's always a pleasure working with Nino." Ahmet

Nino Tempo TL: 90s

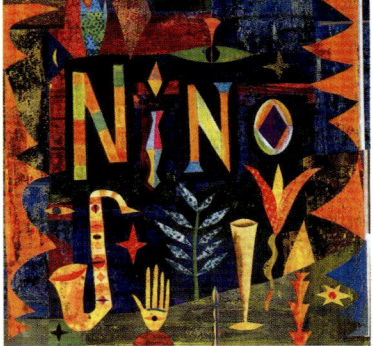

Genesis TL: 90s

"We weren't going to be shy of trying anything with this album. I think *We Can't Dance* is the best thing we've ever done." Phil Collins
"First and foremost, we get on very well. Secondly, there aren't any ego problems in the group. We do it because there's something we see in Genesis that is special, that we can't produce on our own." Mike Rutherford
"When you've been together a long time, you know the kinds of things that work and until you've exhausted the whole supply, there's no reason to stop. Whole new areas of music open up to us and that keeps it fresh." Tony Banks

Ray Charles with Michael Hutchence of INXS TL: 90s

"I am what I am. It's not as if I sat around with choreographers and stylists and said, 'Okay, let's make me this way.' It is hard to find people you can work with. We have all worked solo, and we realize how good you have it when you have a connection to people." Michael Hutchence

INXS TL: 90s

Above: Mick Jagger (TL: 90s), and below with Doug Morris and Ahmet

"Mick is influenced by modern R & B. He was the first one really to recognize Prince as a great artist and had him open for the Stones on one of their tours before he was famous. Mick gets all the new records and keeps up with the current music scene.

"You can tell two things by the accent in England: where the person is from geographically, and where they are in the class system. Mick, in the beginning, was putting on more of an accent than he actually had. He had formal training and his father was a university professor, although they were never, I believe, a rich family and I'm sure they suffered from the war. Mick is very well aware of his beginnings and is not swayed that easily. He's anything but *noveau riche*. He is very real and treats everyone with the same amount of respect, no matter how apparently important or unimportant they may be. He's actually very humble, but he's proud of his achievements – as well he should be. He is also very sophisticated. He's very well-read, is aware of what's going on in the world, has strong political opinions, is a charming conversationalist and knows an awful lot about what makes life pleasant. Mick has elegance, style and grace – not only on stage, but in private life as well. His wit, intelligence and zest for life are a joy to all who know him. He's tasted all the good things in life, and he's tasted a lot of the bitter things as well. We've been through a tremendous amount together and he's somebody with whom I always have a very good time. I love him." Ahmet

"I feel excited every time I do a new project; I look forward to doing something different, meeting new people, making new music. I don't just make up stories and turn them into songs. They are all about something I feel or someone I know. I've always looked at my albums as little movies.

"You know, sometimes I'll be sitting in an airport or someplace, waiting, absolutely exhausted, maybe I'm late for a rehearsal or something, and all I really want to do is be alone at home reading in a bubble bath. I'll be just about to lose it completely when some shy person will carefully approach me and tell me about how much a certain song of mine helped them through a crisis or a time in their own life. That's exactly what makes it all worth it. What I get back from those who listen to my music cannot ever be measured. It's all about love, and trust, and acceptance, and it is completely priceless."
Stevie Nicks

Stevie Nicks TL: 90s

"I grew up as a girl unheard by the boys. I felt it at school as I got to a certain age. The guys would be like, 'You don't know anything, you're a stupid girl,' because my interests were different. When I got to college, then it was all, 'You don't know anything about music.' I made that whole album *Exile in Guyville* because they thought I knew nothing about music and I was like, 'You don't have to fucking know the genealogy of a band to know something about music.'" Liz Phair

"Something happens when you put our three voices together, a unique thing. And once you've tasted it, it's hard to let go of it in your mind. We were individuals who came together to make music and could make music with whomever and in whatever form we wanted. Consequently, when people say, 'They broke up, they reformed, they re-broke up, they re-reformed,' it's all bullshit. We've never looked upon ourselves as a thing that could break up. It was designed to fractionate." Graham Nash

Liz Phair TL: 90s

Crosby, Stills & Nash TL: 90s

Jewel TL: 90s

"I felt a lot of social pressure to figure out what I was gonna do with the rest of my life. I had no desire to go to college, but I also felt no peace in travelling or just bumming around. I got a number of dead-end jobs … got fired a couple of times. I was frightened and a little depressed. The idea of spending my life in a nine-to-five job made me feel trapped and hopeless." Jewel

"It's only the birth of the modern song that made rock'n'roll possible. Blues and gospel music are an element, but the modern song is made up of lots of different things. For me, it's just as important that black church music is one of the pillars of the modern rock song as is the sophistication of a man like Cole Porter. The other pillar that is in rock'n'roll is the force, the angst, the mindlessness of unchallenged military and mechanical power – the fact that those wheels are going to keep turning and if you get in the way, they're going to trample on you. This is the modern world that we live in. There are lots of elements in it and it's the balance of those elements that makes it exciting.

"When I delivered *Psychoderelict* to Atlantic, both Ahmet and Doug reckoned it was going to sell at least five million, they were so thrilled with it. They hyped it up as much as they could and they told me, 'This is going to be the biggest record you've ever made!' When I first started to get sales figures in for the album, they were pretty lean. So Val Azzoli came to see me, just to tell me that, as a label, they didn't quite know what to do. He insisted that it was a great piece of work, that they were proud to have it and if it didn't sell, it was entirely their fault. It eventually turned out to be the smallest-selling record that I've ever done. It was a creative success for me, though, because it actually achieved something of what I wanted to say in 1993. Then I decided to take time out, but I owed one record to Atlantic. So I went back and asked if they

Pete Townshend TL: 90s

would release me from my contract. They didn't even stutter. All they would have had to do was give me $80,000 and they could have held me. My experience with Atlantic has always been divine.

Without Ahmet and Atlantic, we would have had to live without so much great music we take for granted. Without the early Atlantic recordings, jazz and R & B would not have developed with such exact direction, and with the benefit of such vital beneficence and freedom. Atlantic has also released some of the pop records we know today will stand the test of time as examples of the real art of our time. My advice? Sell de Kooning and Pollock – buy LaVern Baker and Aretha!"
Pete Townshend

Bad Religion, from left clockwise: Jay Bentley, Brett Gurewitz, Bobby Schayer and Greg Graffin TL: 90s

The Melvins: Buzz Osborne (centre) with Dale Crover and Mark Deutrom TL: 90s

"Whether or not punk is the flavour of the month is not important for us. Bad Religion has been popular through many different climates. When heavy metal was popular, when new wave was popular, Bad Religion was still there underneath the main stream selling more and more records. Next thing is this dance craze happens and we don't even pay attention to it. We just continue to do what we do, and more and more people buy our records every year. That's what we focus on. Punk was never a fashion trend and treating it as one cheapens the whole movement. Bad Religion existed for so many years under the mainstream and even when punk goes away, which I don't think it will, we'll still have our desire to provoke people. The genre punk itself, for me, has always been around. It has never gone away and it's becoming - especially in America - a new form of folk music, because there's always a new generation of people who feel that they don't fit in society and people who are skeptical about the world they live in. Because of that, it's going to be around for a long, long time." Greg Graffin

"*Rolling Stone* magazine called *Houdini* the best heavy metal release of the decade. But they called it that in 1993, so go figure. Last time I checked, there were a few more years left in the decade. One person's heavy metal is another person's power pop. We take it all with a grain of salt." Mark Deutrom

Hootie & The Blowfish, from left: Mark Bryan, Dean Felber, Jim 'Soni' Sonefield and Darius Rucker TL: 90s

Darius Rucker

"In retrospect I get credit for things that a lot of other people have done. I mean, there is a difference between taking credit for being with the label which signed up Brandy and Jewel, and taking credit for signing up Joe Turner and Ray Charles. In those days there were three of us and we did just about everything together. Now, there's around 400 of us here. So you can give me credit for being with the company that signed up Hootie & The Blowfish, but you know who really found Hootie & The Blowfish? Our research department, which finds out what's selling in various areas around the country. But the important thing is that they are a phenomenal group, a very determined bunch of talented singers and players and we are very happy to have been able to sign them to Atlantic. Their first album was a record that [Atlantic Co-Chairman/Co-CEO] Val Azzoli worked very hard and stayed with. Even when we had reached three or four million copies sold he said, 'I'm going to get at least six out of it.' And it just kept going – he got 16 million out of it in America alone. Of course, it's impossible to repeat that kind of success and we didn't expect to. They are a fabulous band and they write great songs. And that's all we can ask for." Ahmet

"To be the introverted person I tend to be, and then to write the kind of personal songs I do, has put me in an unusual position. It's wild to think that because of what I sang in a song, there's somebody in South Dakota who knows something about me that I've never told anybody. Still, I'd rather not talk about some stuff, and if someone wants to come away with their own idea, that's okay." Darius Rucker

The Soul in the Machine, 1986-2000
By Barney Hoskyns

"Unfortunately, we're running a big business here now," Ahmet Ertegun confessed to author Gerri Hirshey in 1982. "And it sort of . . . well, it drives you away from the kind of music you like, which, you know, is not gonna sell very much but should be recorded just for the musical value of it." Atlantic, said Ertegun, now had its hands full with "the important artists who are selling four million albums, and you can't let them down". These artists included Foreigner, Genesis, and other bands who had precious little in common with Ruth Brown or Ray Charles or any of the label's other early R & B stars. Foreigner's Mick Jones might have sung with LaVern Baker at a party Ahmet threw for Manhattan gadfly Jerry Zipkin, but the group – which had sold millions more albums for Atlantic than The Rolling Stones ever had – was far removed from the D.I.Y. spirit of the records Baker had made with Ertegun and Jerry Wexler in the office on West 56th Street. Mick Jagger, having jumped ship to Columbia for a cool $28 million, dismissed Foreigner as "corporate rock, music for beer ads".

The music industry was indeed a very different place now. Ertegun may have regretted the passing of the R & B and soul eras, not to mention the dropping of several black music veterans from the label, but he had little time now for anything other than the business of survival in a viciously competitive marketplace. "As you grow, the whole machinery of releasing and promoting records becomes bigger and more complicated," he reflected in 1997. "We have to feed the machine that we've built." The man who had always remained one unsentimental step ahead of the game – all the way back to the signing of Bobby Darin in 1958 – was dealing with a business in which the goalposts shifted every day and you couldn't afford to take your eye off the ball for a second. This was especially true in the early-to-mid-eighties, when the recession hit the industry hard and Atlantic found itself struggling. Never mind defending Mick Jones and Phil Collins to critics who saw the label betraying the legacy of Jerry Wexler; Ertegun's job was now to reinvent the label and to make sure his executives were astute enough to carry the company into the next era. "There's a natural thread that runs through this business," says Doug Morris, whom Ertegun had named the label's president in 1979. "If you look at it from the perspective of how the music changed from what it was in the fifties to what it is in the nineties, then it becomes very daunting. But if you've been part of the thread of the business for a long time, it just seems to be another day in its life." By the mid-eighties, concedes Morris, Atlantic was doing poorly – above all in the area of black music. "The black division was in very bad shape," he says. "After Jerry Wexler left, the division really languished, and they had very few artists of any consequence. It was a concern, because the company had started as a black company, and Ahmet and Jerry were very responsible for changing 'race music' into pop music. They had had such an enormous reputation." Since the disco heyday of Chic and The Trammps in the late seventies, Atlantic had all but lost its way in black music. Aretha Franklin's final album for the label, the lacklustre 1979 set *La Diva*, seemed to mark the end of a golden age. "I think the saddest thing I've ever seen happen is the black music section of Atlantic disappear almost completely," said Ben E. King, who'd re-signed with the label as a solo artist in 1975. "Somewhere along the way, someone stopped paying attention." Ertegun himself acknowledged that the label had lost touch with its roots: "It's true, we did decline from being one of the top two or three R & B labels. It's part of our tradition, but somehow, for one reason or another, we've had a serious decline over the last 12 years or so." Some people blamed Ertegun himself – for not being around, for spending too much time jetting around the globe. He countered by pointing out the brutal reality of the market: that when Atlantic released a seven-album set of its greatest R & B recordings in 1985 – to rapturous reviews – it sold only about 15,000 copies in the U.S. Genesis' *Invisible Touch*, meanwhile, was released to indifferent reviews and sold millions. Morris took his first steps to reversing the downward trend by elevating Sylvia Rhone from the label's promotion department and making her head of its black division. Rhone signed LeVert, who included two of O'Jay Eddie LeVert's sons, and promptly hit with the R & B #1 '(Pop, Pop, Pop) Goes My Mind' (1986) and the Top Five pop smash 'Casanova' (1987).

Another big problem in the second half of the eighties seemed to be breaking new pop acts and helping them go the distance. The label had plenty of heavyweights on its roster – Foreigner, Genesis (and the solo Phil Collins), AC/DC, Pete Townshend, Stevie Nicks, Robert Plant, Bad Company, Roger Daltrey and more – but it was having trouble competing in the new field of videogenic synth-pop. Dance-pop diva Laura Branigan had hit big with 'Gloria' in 1982, but by the end of the decade, not even the presence of Doug Morris himself as executive producer could propel the *Laura Branigan* album into the Top 100. One female star who did achieve massive success in the late eighties was Debbie Gibson, a precociously talented Long Island teenager whom Morris signed before she'd even left school. Gibson's peppy, infectious pop songs provided a kind of girl-next-door contrast to Madonna and led to huge hits with 'Only In My Dreams', 'Shake Your Love', and the #1 smash 'Foolish Beat'. The albums *Out Of The Blue* and *Electric Youth* were no less successful. Atlantic had slightly more to boast about in the domain of hard rock – a strong area for the label ever since the signings of Cream and Led Zeppelin in the late sixties. In the wake of Twisted Sister, a new wave of big-hair metal groups was epitomized by the raucous Hollywood band Ratt, whose Atlantic debut *Out Of The Cellar* went Top Ten in 1984, and by the New York-based White Lion. Other tattooed combos on the label included Kix, Winger, Saigon Kick, all in their different ways pretenders to the Guns N'Roses throne. The most promising by far of these bands was Skid Row, formed in New Jersey by bassist Rachel Bolan and Dave 'The Snake' Sabo and considerably strengthened by the arrival in 1987 of poutingly pretty singer Sebastian Bach. Their eponymously-titled debut album was released in January 1989 and included the harrowing '18 And Life', about a teenager facing a life behind bars. There was less testosterone in the post-punk, new-wave-Rolling Stones sound of INXS, who came from Australia and went platinum with the 1985 album *Listen Like Thieves*. On the even more successful *Kick* (1987), the band perfected a sinuous funk-rock style that made frontman Michael Hutchence a giant sex symbol in America. Of course, some of the Atlantic veterans did some of their best work – and scored some of their biggest hits – in this period. Phil Collins chalked up five Top Five hits from 1989's *But Seriously* . . . , including 'Another Day In Paradise' while another Genesis spin-off, Mike + the Mechanics, hit the top with 1988's 'In The Living Years'. On Paul Fishkin's Modern Records subsidiary, Stevie Nicks' *The Other Side Of The Mirror* continued her run of strong solo albums. Pete Townshend recorded a spirited live album with *Deep End Live!* (1986), together with a fascinating adaptation of Ted Hughes's *Iron*

Man (1989) and a second collection of unreleased tracks and solo demos of Who songs, *Scoop* (1987). Canadian prog-rock legends Rush defected from Mercury and signed to Atlantic in 1989. And Robert Plant brought the Atlantic story full circle with *The Honeydrippers, Volume One*, which included such Atlantic R & B staples as Ray Charles's 'I Got a Woman'. The ex-Zeppelin frontman went on to record some of his most inventive, muscular music on *Now And Zen* (1988) and *Manic Nirvana* (1990), the latter including the thrilling 'Tie Die On The Highway'.

Tori Amos

Nonetheless, when Atlantic's 40th anniversary bash took place at Madison Square Garden in 1988 – a night climaxing in the reunion of Led Zeppelin's three surviving members – all was not exactly well with the company. "The second half of the decade was very difficult, because it was a rebuilding process and we didn't really hit our stride till 1990," admits Doug Morris. "That's when things were really put together." In 1990, Morris appointed Rick Blackburn to head Atlantic's first country division since Jerry Wexler had signed Willie Nelson back in the mid-seventies. Morris also signed a deal to distribute the hugely-successful Curb label, whose artists include the multi-platinum superstars LeAnn Rimes and Tim McGraw. With Tracy Lawrence, Neal McCoy, John Michael Montgomery and the rowdy, Lynyrd Skynyrd-ish band Confederate Railroad signed to Atlantic Nashville, the company was at last able to claim a very strong presence in country.

Added to this was the formidable rise of Sylvia Rhone, who had been put in charge of the new EastWest America label. "The idea of having a very brilliant black woman ghettoized into running just a black division seemed unfair," says Morris. "It seemed like it would be good to give her the opportunity to deal with a multi-racial label. So that was the genesis of EastWest." What Rhone had started with Atlantic's black division was symptomatic of the company's general revitalization. "Clearly there was a time when Atlantic was not regarded as a front-runner artist-development label," says Ron Shapiro, the company's general manager. "I think that what Doug was doing was attempting to change that. When I started at the company in the summer of 1993, Doug was in the process of making Atlantic a much bigger and more diverse music company." "The point is that in the late-eighties and early-nineties, the label did reinvent itself," says Roy Trakin, Senior Editor at industry weekly *Hits*. "It went from the hoary land of the eighties hair bands into a more alternative and street identity. The paradox is that Doug Morris presided over the company when it stultified into the ultimate corporate eighties label, but he also brought about the changes that made the label what it is today. I mean, they were always sustained by the legendary aspect of the label – the catalogue that had kept them afloat during the years when they couldn't break new stuff – but you have to credit Doug with recognizing that there was a degree of inertia there and bringing in the Danny Goldbergs and Val Azzolis and overseeing the turnabout."

Foremost among the changes that Morris – through Goldberg, initially Senior V-P on the West Coast and then President of the company – brought about were the hiring of hungry young executives like Craig Kallman, whose independent label Big Beat was acquired by Atlantic in 1991 and who subsequently oversaw much of the company's growth in R & B. Another black music imprint brought into the Atlantic fold was Tim O'Brien's Blitzz label, which promptly hit with the ginormous vocal group All-4-One: their 'I Swear' remained at #1 for an astonishing 11 weeks. "Obviously there have been some dark days in the past decade with regard to black music," says Ron Shapiro. "Clearly the black division has become much more of a priority, and it's something that Craig Kallman has been very instrumental in. I myself came to Atlantic after four years at MCA when that label was number one in black music. So, ironically, Craig and I, being two young white Jewish men, have actually had a great passion for and understanding of R & B." Following Atlantic's acquisition of Big Beat, Kallman spent three years "really trying to gear the label towards hip hop and cutting-edge R & B". The label had big hits with records like Robin S's 'Show Me Love' and Changing Faces' 'Stroke You Up', successes that Kallman built on by signing artists like Brandy, Junior M.A.F.I.A., Lil' Kim, Quad City DJs, Timbaland, and Aaliyah. Brandy and Aaliyah were both just 15-years-old when they hit the Top Ten in 1994; Aaliyah, who came to Atlantic as part of the L.A.-based subsidiary label Blackground, followed up with 1996's double platinum *One In A Million* and became one of the company's biggest R & B stars. "R & B was certainly an area where I thought I could help Atlantic, and quickly, because R & B artists tend to break faster than rock artists," says Kallman. "The original spirit of Atlantic was always entrepreneurial: Ahmet started the label out of his one-room office, and I started Big Beat out of my bedroom as a one-man operation. Once I was acquired, I felt that if I kept a real close presence on the street for Atlantic, we could really build up a cutting-edge division again." On top of this, Kallman assembled the *High School* and *Space Jam* soundtrack albums, the latter the best-selling U.S. album of the first half of 1997. Atlantic also scored big dance-pop hits with Donna Lewis's 'I Love You Always Forever' and the superb Todd Terry remix of Everything But The Girl's 'Missing'. (EBTG had signed to the label in 1989, debuting with the Tommy LiPuma-produced *The Language Of Life*. 'Missing' gave the duo a new lease of life, preparing the ground for 1996's *Walking Wounded*.) For three years the label was also home to the brilliant British duo Pet Shop Boys, prime exponents of intelligent dance pop. *Bilingual* was another riveting chapter in Neil Tennant's and Chris Lowe's long career. Giant hits like Changing Faces' 'G.H.E.T.T.O.U.T.' and Brit star Mark Morrison's old-skool 'Return Of The Mack' helped to make Atlantic the number one R & B label of 1997. Since then, the label has become a bastion of hip-hop superstars from pint-sized Lil' Kim to pimpadelic Motor City rock-'n'rapper Kid Rock. The latter's *Devil Without A Cause* shifted a stupendous nine million copies, a feat its follow-up, *The History Of Rock*, looks like topping. "I've been keeping Ahmet in the loop with all of this," says Kallman. "He has often gotten involved with some of the artists. To this day he'll come in and join some of the pitch meetings. He's still amazingly active, and I know he's very proud. This is a key area for the heritage of Atlantic."

As important as the revitalization of black music at Atlantic were new developments in alternative and hard rock in the early nineties. When the label hit with the Lemonheads' *It's A Shame About Ray*, it announced to the industry that Atlantic was a place where alternative music could flourish. "That was such a major step for a label that on an almost institutional level had missed out entirely on alternative rock," says West Coast A & R man Tim Sommer. "It was such a significant thing when the Lemonheads went gold and scored the first true success at alternative radio that Atlantic had ever had. That opened up a lot of doors for bands and led the industry to take the label a good deal more seriously." Lemonheads frontman Evan Dando recalls that growing up as a Led Zeppelin and AC/DC fan played a big part in the decision to sign to Atlantic. "I was well past my idealistic 16-year-old days and listening more to the Atlantic jazz stuff," he admits. "But when I actually signed I just wanted my album to look like a Led Zeppelin record!" With 'Ballarat', the noisy opening track on 1990's *Lovey*, the band announced unequivocally that it wouldn't be compromising. "We wanted to make it clear that we weren't going to change for a major label," says Dando. With the guidance of Danny Goldberg, the "bubble-grunge" classic *It's A Shame About Ray* went gold in 1992. No less significant than the Lemonheads was the rise of Stone Temple Pilots as a credible hard rock band – a kind of amalgam of Metallica and Pearl Jam whose debut album *Core* climbed into the Top 20 in the summer of 1993. Four million copies of that record later, the group's superior sophomore release *Purple* (1994) lodged itself at the top of the album chart for three weeks. "Atlantic had had a lot of bands like Skid Row and Saigon Kick," says Tim Sommer, "but Stone Temple Pilots were the first true long-term successful rock band the label had signed in ages. That turned things around in a very significant way, and there was a much more positive work ethic at the label as a result. I'd say 60-80% of that was because of the spirit that Danny Goldberg brought here. Stone Temple Pilots returned the label to what had made it famous, and the Lemonheads opened up a door to what this label could sell." Among the acts who came through the door were L.A. punk veterans Bad Religion, who made their Atlantic debut with 1993's *Recipe For Hate*, grunge godfathers The Melvins, whose *Houdini* (1993) was co-produced by Kurt Cobain; Collective Soul, an alternative band from Atlanta whose 1994 debut *hints, allegations & things left unsaid* was essentially a demo tape by lead singer Ed Roland; Canadians The Tragically Hip, signed from MCA; and Evan Dando's erstwhile companion Juliana Hatfield, whose *Hey Babe* (1992) and *Become What You Are* (1993) brought the Mammoth label into the Atlantic fold. Mammoth was home, too, of Seven Mary Three, whose darkly brooding *American Standard* was a huge alternative-rock hit in 1995. Other subsidiary alternative labels include Matador, Tag, Seed, and Lava, the latter headed up by former Skid Row A & R man Jason Flom and enjoying considerable success with new bands like Sugar Ray and matchbox twenty. (By the close of 2000, the latter's *Yourself Or Someone Like You* had sold over eleven million copies in America.) One of the most lauded American debuts of 1996, the self-titled album by retro-power-poppers Fountains Of Wayne, was on Scratchie, a label formed by the band's Adam Schlesinger with members of Smashing Pumpkins but distributed in a one-off deal by Atlantic. "The thing I've always appreciated with Atlantic," says Schlesinger, "is that no matter what else has happened, they've always respected our artistic decisions. We've never had any fights with them about creative decisions – even if we've had disagreements, they always give up in the end!" 1999's follow-up, *Utopia Parkway*, was even better – and featured on numerous year-end Best Of lists.

The biggest Atlantic success story of the nineties was also the most unlikely one. Take a hard-working South Carolina bar band and make a warm, friendly, post-R.E.M. record that you hope will sell about 150,000; then sit back and watch as the album slowly climbs into the Top Ten and proceeds to dominate the charts for over a year, selling over 16 million copies in the process. "I never underestimate the value of karma in the success of Hootie & the Blowfish," says Tim Sommer, who signed the band in late 1993 and oversaw the recording of *Cracked Rear View* the following year. "They never expected to be a famous band or even to be signed. They would still be playing regardless of whether they'd signed to Atlantic or were doing it for $200 and a case of beer. They were an interesting turning point, too, because Atlantic had never had a blockbuster. Obviously something like *Back In Black* had over the years accumulated millions of sales, but they'd never had anything like a Michael Jackson record. Hootie was the first time Atlantic had been able to do one of those." With *Cracked Rear View* carrying the company through a rather turbulent period – one that saw the departures of both Doug Morris and Danny Goldberg – Atlantic emerged in the mid-nineties as a label once again ready to do battle. After the soullessly corporate eighties, the company rediscovered the human touch that had distinguished it back in the fifties and sixties. "I think we have really begun to establish ourselves as an artist-driven, artist-developing company," says Ron Shapiro. "We can find quick hits and chase them as well as anybody, but we have all worked very hard here to make Atlantic a place that is once again thought of first as somewhere to bring fresh talent. I'll quote Jewel here, who says that hard wood grows slow. We are trying, in an industry that wants everything to go faster and faster, to remember Jewel's words and apply them at least a healthy amount of the time."

Jewel

The citing of Jewel is pertinent, since nowhere is Atlantic's new commitment to its artists more evident than in the area of its singer-songwriters. True, Atlantic had broken Julian Lennon in the mid-eighties, but the label had never been renowned for nurturing solo artists in the way Warner-Reprise on the West Coast had been. Things began to change with Doug Morris's signing of Tori Amos, a prodigiously gifted singer-pianist who sounded a little like an American version of Kate Bush. Albums like *Little Earthquakes* (1991) and *Under*

The Pink (1994) established Amos as a key voice for the nineties, opening the door for other female artists like Jill Sobule and Melissa Ferrick. (A recent Atlantic signing was legendary Irish chanteuse Sinéad O'Connor, whose first album on the label is the beautiful *Faith and Courage*.) No one, however, could have anticipated the extraordinary success of Jewel, a young folk singer from Alaska whose debut album *Pieces Of You* was produced by sometime Neil Young sideman Ben Keith at Young's ranch near San Francisco. Thanks to an unstoppable promotional department, Jewel was worked relentlessly for a year until the album – trailed by its first single 'Who Will Save Your Soul?' – at last began to take off. After the noisy gnashings of grunge, Jewel's artless post-Joni sincerity and semi-yodelling vocal style came to the American marketplace as a breath of pure mountain air. By 2000, *Pieces Of You* had sold a phenomenal eleven million copies, with the tremblingly pretty 'You Were Meant For Me' clocking up an astounding 35 weeks in the Hot 100 Singles chart. Coincidentally, Duncan Sheik's 'Barely Breathing' was in the Hot 100 for exactly the same amount of time. Here was another singer-songwriter whose arrival was barely noticed, and who on another label might well have been lost in the shuffle. "Atlantic have definitely changed their outlook," says Adam Schlesinger. "They're more patient, and they give a record more time to develop. With the first Fountains album, everyone seemed to genuinely like it and really tried hard with it for a good period of time."

Perhaps one of the most significant deals Atlantic has done in the nineties is the one that entrusted a good chunk of its illustrious back catalogue to Rhino Records in Los Angeles. Deciding that it was too hard to combine the business of running a day-to-day record company with the marketing of a major catalogue, Doug Morris and Yves Beauvais masterminded an agreement with a company which had more than made its mark as a classy repackager. "Yves had already started the Atlantic/Atco Remasters series, so it's important to give him credit," remembers Rhino's Gary Stewart. "But we were able to put out more product, because it was our sole focus. Atlantic came to us for our marketing savvy: we'd had relationships with press and with retail that were about our archival abilities, and about people trusting us. As far as I know, Atlantic have been very happy and complimentary. We're very fortunate to be involved with them, and we never want them to regret getting involved with us." Among the achievements that make Rhino proudest are the three boxed sets dedicated to Atlantic's three jazz giants: *John Coltrane: The Heavyweight Champion*; *Ornette Coleman: Beauty Is A Rare Thing*; and *Charles Mingus: Passions Of A Man*. "I think it's so important to keep the catalogue alive," says Ahmet Ertegun. "The jazz roster that my brother developed has been a terrific backbone for Atlantic." In addition, Rhino has released exemplary compilations by everyone from Mose Allison to Ben E. King, as well as reissuing classic albums by Otis Redding, Aretha Franklin, Dusty Springfield and MC5.

Precious few other labels even warrant such deluxe treatment, let alone receive it. As Ertegun looks back over all this extraordinary music – remembering in particular how his late brother built up the label's formidable jazz roster in the fifties and sixties – he must feel an enormous sense of accomplishment. One wonders if he isn't also prey to a certain *nostalgie de la blues*. (His involvement in the Rock and Roll Hall of Fame and his pioneering efforts to recalculate and make payment of back royalties to R & B artists would suggest as much.) "Ahmet and I took different roads," mused Jerry Wexler in 1982, seven years after departing Atlantic. "I stayed with the music … and he stopped making records. He does administration, having to travel and attend meetings and all [...] I still don't know that much about what goes on inside him." Significantly, though, Ertegun was present when, in December 1995, the Blues Foundation honoured Jerry Wexler with a bash at the House of Blues in L.A. Five years earlier, after reading Wexler's liner notes for a Charles Brown album, Ertegun had written to his old friend, "How moved I was by your incisive recollection of times that we will never live through again".

Rob Thomas of matchbox twenty

Some people would like Atlantic to have stood still while the music business changed around it: they would prefer Ahmet Ertegun not to have taken the company into the corporate era. This is what perhaps Ertegun meant when he said that, "I think Mick Jagger would have liked to be on [tiny Southern blues label] Excello – we were the closest he could get to Excello and still get five million dollars." (Significantly, Jagger returned to Atlantic as a solo artist with 1992's more than credible *Wandering Spirit*.) The fallacy here is that if Atlantic hadn't grown in the way it did, it probably wouldn't exist at all. "Atlantic's history will never go away, will it?" says Tim Sommer. "We don't hold Elektra to the same standards that signed Phil Ochs and Love, or Reprise to the standards that signed Joni Mitchell and Randy Newman, yet for some reason Atlantic is a bigger thing, and people do hold it to those standards. At least the label is healthy and successful enough that the imprint still exists. Because the imprint still exists, the past still exists." The hankering for an Atlantic Records that's somehow friendlier and more "authentic" is also based on a fallacy. The label's early hits were, in their way, no less sophisticated or urbanized than any of their later music; certainly they weren't field recordings, and were as much a part of translating black music into white pop culture as any R & B record of the period. The admixture of urban and rural, as of commerce and soul, remains a constant the whole way through the Atlantic story. As Ahmet Ertegun points out, "We went pop with Bobby Darin, but we also went pop with Ray Charles and Aretha Franklin." That story always comes back to the Ertegun brothers' original apprehension of America in the thirties and forties as a land of gangsters and cowboys and (as Ertegun put it in a famous *New Yorker* profile of 1978) "big glowing men … with gleaming brass instruments". The Turkish kid with his big American dreams is still there behind the hooded eyes and the patrician aura of the corporate mogul and socialite. "When Ahmet goes, the charisma, the love, will change," says Tom Dowd. "And people will say, 'It's not like it was'."

"I'm still the same person," Ertegun says. "I still look for songs and artists, and for new ways of selling records. But the whole thing now is about being on the cutting edge. Back in the forties we knew a lot of things our competitors did not know. Today there is no such animal."

"I don't think there's another label in the industry that could speak of a 54-year history where they started on fire and are still on fire today," says Craig Kallman. "It's a pretty astounding thing that Atlantic has continued to remain at the top for over half a century. It's an incredible accomplishment for Ahmet and all the people he's hired and signed."

The Three Tenors, from left: Placido Domingo, Jose Carreras and Luciano Pavarotti TL: 90s

The Three Tenors

"The Three Tenors first performed together in Rome in 1990. The World Cup was being played there that year and they are all soccer fans, so they decided to do a concert. It was recorded and, of course, became a big success. We didn't release that album, but before the next World Cup took place in Los Angeles in 1994, I got a call from a lawyer friend of mine who had some dealings with Tibor Rudas, an impresario of Hungarian origin. I was told that Tibor had made arrangements for The Three Tenors to sing together again in Los Angeles, as they had in Rome, and that he wanted to have top distribution. He had been told about the WEA [Warner-Elektra-Atlantic] system in America and he wanted to go through that network. So I met with Tibor and his charming wife on several occasions and we made a worldwide deal for the tenors' concert in L.A. The performance at Dodger Stadium was a tremendous, sold-out event, and the album and the video combined sold upwards of ten million copies." Ahmet

"There had been a lot of stuff flying around between us, Jimmy and me, and most of it was coming from my determination not to have anything to do with a Led Zeppelin rerun. I'd seen so many artists from way back who had come together again, and the outcome was so pedestrian, almost just an excuse for leaving the house. Whatever we were to do had to be very positive and full of intention. I'd missed Jimmy's playing so much that as soon as we started working, I realized that we'd wasted quite a bit of time. Working in that old room down in King's Cross, it really started sparkling again. But it took until halfway through the *No Quarter* world tour to realize that we were really happening, and if we wanted totally to enjoy ourselves musically, we had to put our backs into what we were doing." Robert Plant

Top and left, Robert Plant and Jimmy Page; and above, Jimmy Page TL: 90s

John Michael Montgomery TL: 90s

"I really didn't know Ahmet very well at all until he hired me in 1989. He's like an idol, you know. I had run the country division at CBS until the company was sold to Sony, and Ahmet wanted me to put together a country music operation for Atlantic. Some years before I had asked each of my artists at CBS, if they had their choice of singing a duet or making an album with anybody in the world – they didn't have to be country – who would that artist be? And they all said: Ray Charles. Long story short, I signed Ray Charles to our Nashville division and we made four albums with him – including an album of duets. He would always speak of Ahmet Ertegun, so I kind of felt that I knew Ahmet through Ray. He spoke so fondly of him and he kept saying, 'You ought to know this guy, because you'd like him and he'd like you.' Somewhere along the line, I think Ray mentioned my name to Ahmet.

"Anyway, I had a year off between CBS and Atlantic, during which I had started my own music publishing company. I found a couple of writers, bought a few songs and was actually having a lot of fun just dabbling around in publishing. One day, the 'phone rings and my secretary says, 'There's a fellow with a strange name on the 'phone – it's like "Urlygen" or something, but I think it's Norro Wilson disguising his voice.' Norro is a songwriter around Nashville and we worked together for years at CBS. He does voice imitations, so I thought it was him and said, 'Norro, I don't have time for you today,' but the voice said, 'Oh – you must have picked up the wrong line. This is Ahmet Ertegun here, and I want to talk to Rick Blackburn.' I said, 'Well, you've got him.' I don't know if he remembers that story, but I was totally embarrassed and I said, 'I thought you were Norro!' So that was my first introduction, but then he and Doug Morris flew down, we met, and then I flew up to New York. We kicked around some ideas and they wanted my thoughts on how to go about starting something like they had in mind. In the seventies, Atlantic had had an existing operation here in Nashville, but it was more of a production company and it only lasted six to eight months – not very long. But when I was over at CBS, that's how we got Willie Nelson. Willie, at that time, recorded in Austin and he had done two albums for Atlantic. So when Atlantic folded their country division, they released Willie. He had already recorded his demo of 'Red Headed Stranger', and we signed him.

Confederate Railroad, clockwise from left: Wayne Secrest, Chris McDaniel, Gates Nichols, Michael Lamb, Danny Shirle and Mark DuFresne   TL: 90s

"Ahmet's probably the best person I have ever worked for and I've worked for a lot of interesting people in my life. Ahmet's management style is very much one of a counsellor. He's not a slave driver, he doesn't yell and scream – he has more of a counsellor-type of style, which motivates me. His personal favourite music is blues and jazz — and I don't claim much appreciation for jazz — but he likes country okay. We have a good time. We laugh a lot. I can't drink as much vodka as he can, although I try. I ask him to come down to Nashville and give talks from time to time — he's done about four or five — and the funny thing is that the town loves Ahmet. He doesn't pander to Nashville and his love for music is legendary. He writes everything out on a legal pad and rehearses what he's going to say. But the really good part is when he puts that away and we start doing questions and answers, and the audience is just captivated. He's kind of shy when it comes to giving his talks and yet he gets a standing ovation.

"From 1990 to '95, country had phenomenal growth — from a $700 million a year business to two and a half billion. Country music is a lifestyle form of music — it's no longer just about drinking and cheating, now it's about a complex lifestyle. There are 2,500 country radio stations, and you also have country music television which is in 50 million homes. Throw in some really great songs, add it all up, and you've got an amazing upswing. I've been here in Nashville for 25 years and I've seen a lot of the peaks, and the valleys too. Country music is what it is, and every time we stray from the roots of country, we hurt. Down here in this division I started out in 1990 with 15 people and today I still have 15 people on the payroll. I don't want any more, don't want any less. I only have eight artists, and you know what, there's no correlation between head count and platinum. Platinum's about songs. So I keep it small and we spoil our artists to death. I sit them down every three months like a board of directors, and they sit there and ask questions about anything to do with the business that they want to know, be it chart methodology or distribution. It's just me and the artists and they're allowed to talk about anything except how much royalty the other one gets, although they go off and have lunch together and I'm giving them all the same deal anyway.

Tracy Lawrence TL: 90s

"There's nothing hard about it. I mean, it could be made very complicated, but basically it's a very simple business. The real effort is trying to find what we call a career song and, you know, we'll go through 600 songs to get ten. You've just got to keep hunting and that's the way it works – we listen to a lot of music. I don't have any magic formula. The press asks me all the time – what do you look for when you sign an artist? I don't know what I look for – you listen for a style; you want something that when the voice comes on the radio, in the first five seconds you know who it is. You look for that charisma, that persona. It helps if they write fairly well, that's a plus, but you know there's a lot of things that go into it. I guess subconsciously you make these evaluations, at least I do, but the bottom line is that I'm terribly attracted to that person. And if it works, they're attracted to me. The artists I deal with are people, not companies. I am real select – but when I find one, I've got to have them. I mean, it's not a question of price or money, it's just that I've got to have that person. I can't give anyone a formula for it. I've worked for several companies, but one thing that's important about Atlantic is that there's no corporate feel. There's very little paperwork – I mean, I've never got a memo from Ahmet in my life and I've never sent one. We pick up the 'phone and we talk – I know that sounds like a little thing, but there's no hit songs coming out of a memo. Ahmet has set the tone and Atlantic is real communication-heavy, but it's by voice; or I'll get on an aeroplane and go and see them, or he'll come back down here. Ahmet doesn't see any walls in his house as far as music's concerned. I know I'm the country guy but when I go up to his office, we send out for egg salad sandwiches and hell, he plays me jazz music, or he'll play me rock, and I mean, I'm not *just* a country guy. One thing Ahmet drove into my head – it's not about distribution, it's not about publicity, it's not about this, it's not about that – I mean, all that's a part of it, but the artist and the song are everything. If you think about that, that just kind of sums it all up. There's always a challenge with Atlantic, because you're not describing a very corporate environment at all, you're describing an entrepreneurial environment, and Time Warner has to be up to meeting the challenge of harnessing that. It's what I call a 'bottom up' process, not a 'top down' process. With a public company you have windows of 90 days, with quarterly reports, and it does have a major impact on the stock on Wall Street. If you miss your forecast by a cent, it puts tremendous pressures on the financial side of the corporation. There has to be a balance there, and Ahmet has always seemed to be able to temper that pretty well, at least at Atlantic, but at corporate level, those pressures, I understand, have got to be enormous. But this is not a 90-day business, and it never will be, so I try not to address it; it just doesn't make any kind of sense. It's like playing a football game where you've got four quarters and saying, 'Okay, let's leave after the first quarter.' Now, most people would probably understand that, but when I have this conversation at a conference or with our finance department, they look at me cross-eyed, because their outlook is totally different. But somewhere, creativity has got to win, and as long as there's an Ahmet Ertegun in there, I think it will." Rick Blackburn

Opposite: Neal McCoy TL: 90s

Above: Wessell Anderson; and below, Cyrus Chestnut TL: 90s

"Wessell Anderson is a great jazz alto player. Wynton Marsalis and James Carter are two of his greatest fans." Ahmet

"I think the blues is the foundation of any black music. Listening to early gospel records by artists like Clara Ward, Professor Charles Taylor, early Shirley Caesar – there's a great degree of blues in what they're doing. Thomas Dorsey, when he wrote 'Precious Lord', that was a blues, in a sense. The blues is something which touches all aspects of black life." Cyrus Chestnut

"Cyrus Chestnut is one of the great young jazz pianists of our time." Ahmet

"James Carter is probably the greatest technician on the saxophone today. He plays all saxophones, from soprano to bass. His main instrument is the tenor saxophone of which he is one of the most outstanding players today. He is young but he has a very full and deep knowledge of jazz and he appreciates the playing of Coleman Hawkins and Lester Young, all the great tenor men who preceded him, and, he plays some of that music as well as very contemporary and avant-garde music. He is, for me, best when he plays some of those lovely ballads that he plays with such a beautiful tone." Ahmet

James Carter TL: 90s

"I like watching old cartoons with orchestra music, especially the Warner Bros. cartoons with music by Carl Stalling, and even the Flintstones. I'm always interested in what instruments are being played, how the sounds they make are applied, cross-referencing those sounds to what I can do on my horns. I mean, the saxophone is an inanimate object. You're pretty much breathing life into it, so why not breathe the best life into it that you can?" James Carter

"We had to grow somewhere, so we grew vocally. We tried to do neat things, stretch ourselves. Lots of little tricks. I'd rather All-4-One be known as a singing group – not a pop group, a doo-wop group, or an R & B group. We plan to be together for a long time, making great music." Jamie Jones

All-4-One top, and above from left: Jamie Jones, Tony Borowiak, Delious and Alfred Nevarez TL: 90s

Brandy TL: 90s

"Brandy is a gifted young singer and a terrific actress. She's not only one of the top female R & B vocalists, but she has crossed over to the pop market because – like all of the truly great artists – her appeal is universal. She has genuine charisma and enormous talent and I think she will only get better as the years go by. I am sure that she will be a major star for a very long time to come." Ahmet

Tracey Thorn and Ben Watt: Everything But The Girl TL: 90s

"We were bored with our own music in the early nineties and wanted a change. Dance music had deepened and lost some of its hedonistic edge and seemed like a great place to explore new ideas. On a recommendation, we worked with John Coxon on *Amplified Heart*. We liked a lot of his approaches to making music. We wrote 'Missing' at his studio to be remixed – at that particular tempo, simple minor chords. I don't consider EBTG a 'dance outfit', just a band moving with the times.

"I always think 'Missing' sounds like a classic. I am very proud of it. There are very few people who can say they hit the charts with one of their best songs. So often for bands their hit record ends up being a compromise or just a piece of candy floss." Ben Watt

"Seven Mary Three came to Atlantic through our deal with Mammoth Records, which was started by Jay Faires. He took me somewhere down South to hear them when we'd first signed them up. They were very impressive." Ahmet

Seven Mary Three with Arif Mardin, from left: Jason Pollock, Arif Mardin, Ghita Khalsa, Casey Daniel and Jason Ross TL: 90s

Collective Soul below, and above from left: Ed Roland, Will Turpin, Shane Evans, Dean Roland and Ross Childress TL: 90s

"We're grateful for what *hints allegations and things left unsaid* did. We were really shocked, because essentially it was a collection of songwriting demos. I'd been hoping to sell just enough to make a real Collective Soul album. When I start feeling down, I feel like I'm being selfish because there are so many people out there who wish they could be doing what we're doing. I worked hard for many years to be in this position, and I'm very thankful to be here. I won't take it for granted."
Ed Roland

"It's kind of funny how our growing up together has made it so we even think alike. There are times when we'll all show up to dinner wearing the same shirt. We're individuals, but we communicate on this weird unspoken level. Musically, it makes for the ideal situation. Our strength is our chemistry."
Will Turpin

Donna Lewis TL: 90s

"I didn't really want to go into a commercial studio to record. Before I got signed, I used to write my songs and record them myself at home. Often the first time you record a new idea, it's magical. That was my intention this time around. I made sure that I had a great studio setup so that I could keep the first takes if I wanted to." Donna Lewis

Jill Sobule TL: 90s

"On a pop album, you're supposed to write about love, sex and violence … but the biological clock? It seems almost taboo. At this time in my life, I have no real responsibilities to anybody. I can fuck up and the only one it hurts is me. Right now that's okay, but there's a certain emptiness and innate selfishness to it, too." Jill Sobule

"Sugar Ray is one of our great emerging bands; they were also a group signed by Jason Flom and are surely going to continue to be big stars." Ahmet

"We started the band for fun and it's a totally collaborative effort. Someone will write a verse, someone will write a chorus – it's amazing because we each take our influences, what we were raised on, and then we throw it in the mix, and it just seems to come together." Mark McGrath

Sugar Ray, from left: Rodney Sheppard, Mark McGrath, Matthew Carges and Charles Frazier TL: 90s

matchbox twenty, from left: Paul Doucette, Brian Yale, Rob Thomas, Adam Gaynor and Kyle Cook TL: 90s

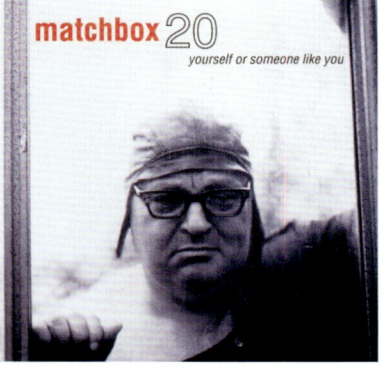

"I think we get up there and try to convey the songs in as energetic and heartfelt a way as we can. These are our songs, and we really feel good about 'em. I don't think we try to put any dramatics into it but after a show, when we're just talking to people, they'll tell us, 'You know, you were so into it, that was so intense to watch.' To us, we were just playing the songs and losing ourselves in them. If you come to a rehearsal, you're gonna see the same thing. It's not something that we can help, really.

"We giggle and say, 'Wow, we're huge.' But it's really like a comic-book world. Little pieces of it are what you thought it might be, but you never consider that everything is still going on in your daily life. So now I'll be 'Famous Rob', but really Rob still has to keep going through his day, getting things accomplished, just like always." Rob Thomas

Stone Temple Pilots, from left: Robert DeLeo, Dean DeLeo, Eric Kretz and Scott Weiland TL: 90s

"I can't really give you the potion or concoction that we have, but I can tell you that the four of us share something really, really special when we're writing songs, and it's a beautiful thing. Aside from anything else outside or personal, when we get down and write songs, it's a wonderful experience."
Dean DeLeo

"The Corrs opened a few stadium shows for us, and they were on the verge of blowing us – The Rolling Stones – off our own stage!"
Mick Jagger

The Corrs, from left: Jim, Caroline, Andrea and Sharon Corr TL: 90s

Ahmet with John Michael Montgomery TL: 90s

"Janis Roeg and her partner Joe Boyland took Doug Morris and me down to Nashville to meet with the manager of the group Alabama, because their contract was coming up. Although we didn't sign them, the trip was worth it because their manager introduced us to Rick Blackburn, whom we eventually decided to make head of our new Nashville operation. He has been just sensational. Rick has the top batting average of any recordman I've ever known. He has the smallest stable and the highest percentage of platinum artists. He built a stellar roster of country artists, including people like John Michael Montgomery and Tracy Lawrence. We also are very lucky to have a deal with Mike Curb of Curb Records who has, among others, one of the hottest young artists in the country field, LeAnn Rimes. So we have our share of chart-making country artists, which is a particular pleasure to me, having tried so many times previously to break into the Nashville thing." Ahmet

"My dad said the song 'Blue' was too old for me. I loved it, though, and I kept bugging him about it. Then I got the idea to put the yodel thing to it. I want to continue singing and writing songs. I'd like to act. College is also an option for me. I've always wanted to help children, and I've thought about studying speech pathology." LeAnn Rimes

LeAnn Rimes TL: 90s

"When 'Then You Can Tell Me Goodbye' won the Video of the Year award, I think a lot of people were happy for me – the other artists, the executives, everybody. You could tell they really meant it. I think they know that I'm in this for the long haul, that I care about the music and that I want to contribute. I don't know what it is. I just know that once the music gets in me and I see the fans out there, I just can't keep still. The people who come out to see us know they're going to get everything we've got every night. We built that trust one night at a time over a period of years." Neal McCoy

Above: Neal McCoy and, left, with Ahmet and Rick Blackburn TL: 90s

Above and right: Tim Mcgraw TL: 90s

"It's kind of funny, we're into the year 2000, the space age. What does that say for cowboys? Does it seem practical any more to wear a cowboy hat when you're into the year 2000?" Tim McGraw

"The punk rock thing – that was the fuel that got us playing. You're listening to stuff on the big rock radio and you pick up a guitar and you can't play like that. Then you see the Ramones on TV and you go, 'Wait a minute…' We couldn't figure out how to learn songs well enough to be a cover band, so we just made our own stuff up. We weren't trying to stay in that college music scene or whatever. We were like, 'Man, we want to be on the big radio! Let's go all the way!' Of course, we're too ugly to get too far." Brian Henneman

The Bottle Rockets above, and right from left: Tom Parr, Mart Ortman, Tom Ray and Brian Henneman TL: 90s

"It's a double-edged sword. Being the 'Friend of Hootie' gave me the exposure that turned people on to us. In that respect, I feel like it was amazingly helpful. But in the longer run it started hamstringing us. We all decided that it was probably better to create some distance between us. I would like to think the stuff I do can stand on its own. Still, the second question that I get asked every time I go to a radio station is, 'Hey Edwin, so how do you know Hootie?'" Edwin McCain

"With the second album, *Fairweather Johnson*, we didn't want to sit around and overthink the whole thing. We just went straight in to record, and it happened for us. Don Gehman was key in helping us introduce some new elements and instrumentation into the mix. We had grown as songwriters and we wanted the production to reflect that. We weren't after *Cracked Rear View*. We didn't want to go down the exact same musical road again." Jim Sonefeld of Hootie & the Blowfish

Edwin McCain, above from left: Larry Chaney, Dave Harrison, Edwin McCain, Scott Bannevich and Craig Shields TL: 90s

From left: Mark Bryan, Darius Rucker, Jim 'Soni' Sonefield and Dean Felber TL: 90s

Left and above: Hootie & the Blowfish TL: 90s

Duncan Sheik TL: 90s

Fountains of Wayne, from left: Jody Porter, Adam Schlesinger, Brian Young and Chris Collingwood TL: 90s

"I'm just into fresh sounds. I want to combine an adventurous sonic palette with songs that people can sink their teeth into. One of the songs on the first album, 'November', is about coming to grips with a relationship from my past. And when I sing it now, I realize that I was writing about something deeper and darker, and probably subconscious – it's like some tragedy that happened to me in another life. If there are demons like that lurking in all the other songs, I don't know. Yet." Duncan Sheik

"I think it's funny, our audience is pretty divided up. It's a lot of young girls, then there are, like, older boys and then these sort of 45-year-old men from Hoboken, who know too much about pop music. They come up to us and ask us these obscure questions about whether we know these old albums." Chris Collingwood

THE ATLANTIC STORY 475

Above: Tori Amos; and below, Poe TL: 90s

"I crossed the River Styx with *Boys For Pele*." Tori Amos

"I'm interested in combining different parts of different cultures, because I saw so many different cultures as a kid. And the one thing that tied every culture together was music. I prefer this, as opposed to 'I AM a folk singer' or 'I AM an alternative rock singer' or 'I AM' whatever, because I am evolving – I am and have been affected by and inspired by the things I've come into contact with, both creatively and personally." Poe

Everything But The Girl; Ben Watt, and Tracey Thorn TL: 90s

"Drum'n'bass is the most exciting thing to happen to music in a long time. To me, it often sounds like 21st century bossa nova, which is where we have so often naturally written and felt music. People have responded so strongly to our recent records and collaborations that it has opened up new areas to us in rhythm and melody." Ben Watt

"Half of the album *Walking Wounded* was written in London, half in New York. We wanted to make an album that could be played in the city as much as in the house. London and New York gave us the inspiration and the beats, whilst the success of 'Missing' gave us the courage." Tracey Thorn

Clannad, from left: Padraig Duggan, Máire Brennan, Noel Duggan and Ciarán Brennan TL: 80s 90s

"We paint pictures with our songs. It's not so much telling a story with verses and choruses. Instead, it's done through emotions and feelings." Maire Brennan

Rick Braun TL: 90s

"I really couldn't do anything else. Mine was a career by default. I always had this love of music and it always came fairly easy to me. It hasn't been a real struggle for me. From an early age, I was playing along with all the Herb Alpert records." Rick Braun

"I wanted to make *Give and Take* different- sounding. I've got eight records now on Atlantic Records and six of them are more electric-sounding. A lot of what I do is more straight-ahead bebop with a contemporary edge to it. I think all my records have a live quality, but this one probably more so. So we had one rehearsal, and really did the record in a couple of days." Mike Stern

"I saw an interview with Wynton Marsalis, and he said that he feels the true path of jazz today is the fusion of different classical forms – and that's what we did on the *Swing* album. We combined things that you ordinarily wouldn't hear combined. We took urban styles of swing and we took rural styles of swing and we brought them together. For instance, on Charlie Barnet's 'Skyliner', we have the vibes, the piano and the guitar playing underneath us when we're singing, and they're playing what is considered the George Shearing sound – but we have that happening along with Buddy Emmons, who is the premier steel guitar player in Nashville. It's all happening at once, and it works!" Tim Hauser

Mike Stern TL: 90s

The Manhattan Transfer, from left: Tim Hauser, Janis Siegel, Cheryl Bentyne and Alan Paul TL: 90s

Timbaland (right) and Magoo (left) TL: 90s

"*Welcome To Our World* is a great rap record. It has great emotion and terrific funky tracks." Ahmet

"We're not into the 'keep it real' thing. If you listen to 'Up Jumps Da' Boogie' or any other track on the album, that's just how we are – straight up. We're being ourselves. Of course, we've been through some bad things, but we choose not to talk about it. We choose to enjoy life. There are enough brothers and sisters out there already talking about the negatives that've happened to them. There's nothing wrong with that, but we've taken a different route. We're making music for the people. That's something a lot of people in hip-hop have forgotten to do recently. Guys back in the day – people like Afrika Bambaataa – didn't worry about keeping it real. They made music for the people. That's how they made a difference. Even when they were getting political, it was also about having a good time. It was never, 'If you not like this, then you not down.' We need to get away from that crap. We've chosen to take it back to the old school, to the way rap music started. Music is for the soul. Shit, I'll listen to Mozart if it hits me on that emotional level. I'm always checking out new things. You never know what will spark your mind and give you an idea." Magoo

"We're firm believers that it doesn't matter if you have a demo or not, because we got our deal singing live on Fifth Avenue and 25th Street." Cassandra Lucas

Changing Faces right, and above from left: Charisse Rose and Cassandra Lucas TL: 90s

Junior M.A.F.I.A. featuring MC Lil' Kim, Little Ceasar, Chico, Nino Brown, Larceny, Trife and MC Kelpto TL: 90s

"I think that to make a great rap song you have to be a great rapper! If the song is a social protest about the inner city, people may not even understand the language, but they still like it. Now, we have French rap, German rap, and because of the Turkish workers in Germany, we now have Turkish - German rap! Personally, I think the best rap content that I've heard is when it's an urban protest song - it can be so incredible, so beautiful." Arif Mardin

Quad City DJs featuring C.C. Lemonhead and Jay Ski TL: 90s

"I think jazz originated with the Indian. If you listen to the music, there's a basic swing beat, on top of which they put all these ornate melodies, which are highly syncopated and very jazzy. Especially with the Plains Indians, like the Sioux, Cheyenne and Blackfoot – they all use those highly syncopated melody lines. In 1948, when I visited the Blackfoot tribe in Idaho, I realized I was one of them at heart. I would sit down at the big sundance tom-tom, and we'd play together. I felt a community of spirit. When I came to New York, I was very classical-minded. I got to meet the great conductor Arthur Rodzinski and he let me come to all the rehearsals of the New York Philharmonic. I was always taught that the model was Bach, but the more I studied Bach's scores, the more I found he violated the basic rules. About half the time he did it right and half the time he made terrible mistakes. I think he didn't analyse his work; he wrote so many pieces and had so many children to support, he just didn't have the time." Moondog

Above, Moondog TL: 90s, and below, Paul O'Neill of Trans Siberian Orchestra TL: 90s

"With the Trans-Siberian Orchestra, there's an ideal. The basic notion is that we have to make the best music possible. Whatever has to be done to get the best song, the best lyric, the best arrangement, and then find the person who can best pull it off, that's what's done. At one point, we had five studios going at once. We were auditioning singers in the studio, juggling horn and string sections, and then the mix engineer would come up to me saying, 'Okay, what else do you have for me?' It was an insane pace, but we were intent on having the album ready for that Christmas." Paul O'Neill

"I started out just wanting to get out of the house. So I took my guitar and learned some music. Songs I learned from different friends will always be associated with those street musicians I met in Paris. With a song like 'Walkin' After Midnight', there's more to it because you've lived it. And if you're playing a blues song on the street, you have more to sing the blues about than if you were sitting at home trying to make sense of a piece of sheet music. It's a whole other world." Madeleine Peyroux

Above: Madeleine Peyroux; and below from left: Jason Ross, Gitti Khalsa, Casey Daniel and Jason Pollock of Seven Mary Three TL: 90s

"I question everything and after a while I am so busy with the questions that I am all thought and no feeling. For me, the only way to start living was to stop asking so many damn questions. In the end, you've just got to go on your nerve.

"Orange Ave. is the fourth record we have made in our six years together as a band. And like my head, it's full of questions. But like any form of expression, Orange Ave. was a means to get out of a very tired way of thinking. The record echoes the feelings I get walking down Orange Avenue in Orlando on any given night. It's more than just a slice of reality. It's a lot of different people doing a lot of different things. And when the street's lit up, the lovers and has-beens and comers and kingpins are all there together asking the same questions and maybe giving up a haphazard answer or two. And always there is music bleeding out into the traffic, bleeding into our consciousness. It may be shit or it may be brilliant, but regardless it reminds me that someone, somewhere, has got the nerve. I now get the feeling that hope is on the way, a notion that is, in fact, refreshing to me. But it promises nothing. And like an idea, it was born to stand alone on swagger and attitude. So I hang on, listening for the person that will be the anthem for the end of suffering, loneliness, and dissatisfaction. Find the truth behind the questions." Jason Ross

"Gerald Albright, he sure can play!" Ahmet

"I wanted to make a record that had a combination of the styles that people are used to hearing me do, but on a new tip, to add some more of an R & B element into the music. The urban sound of today is reminiscent of the seventies era – it's an R & B sound where you hear live strings and heavily orchestrated productions of real songs. With that, I was also adding flavours from traditional artists like Cannonball Adderley and Stanley Turrentine and John Coltrane. So here you have a project that has a distinct R & B base and yet there's an improvisational flavour on top. I think of *Live To Love* as 'Genuine Gerald'. It's the way I'm hearing music today." Gerald Albright

"You could say it's just the right time. I never had the desire to make a record before. I was just in show business. In my home town along the Mississippi we never talked about making records, we just played music. The guys on *In The World* come from all over the world and from all different musical schools. The guitarist is Ghanain, the percussionist is Congolese, the organ player is from the Islands, the trap drummer and saxophone player are from Cleveland and the bass player's from Long Island. This way, nobody's going to take over with any particular style. It's going to be about the music." Olu Dara

Above: Gerald Albright TL: 90s; and below, Olu Dara TL: 90s

"It's my hope to be an interpreter of life. I love classical music. And I want to be able to perform and compose pieces of my own that reflect different periods. Instead of playing Bach or Beethoven I'd rather do something of my own, so my roots come into it and it's a more personalized statement – like the music of Jelly Roll Morton or Fats Waller. I was watching one of Waller's early clips one day, and he was doing some real hip harmonic manoeuvring which I thought was reminiscent of the sixties but here he was, in the twenties and thirties, doing the same thing. Fats was a showman, but when he would focus in and just think about playing, it was something to behold. And I always loved Fats's joyous spirit; it's just something I would like to be able to do – develop a joyous spirit of my own in performance and in the music that I write and play." Cyrus Chestnut

Opposite: Cyrus Chestnut TL: 90s

Rush: above, from left, Alex Lifeson and Geddy Lee; and below, Neil Peart

Big Wreck, from left: Dave Henning, Ian Thornley, Forrest Williams and Brian Doherty TL: 90s

"Being for years an opening act for other bands turned us into what we are. I think we're something apart from trends. We're neither a trendy nor a fashionable band; none of us feels that music is threatening us. Playing is the most fun we have out there on the road. That's the best time of the entire night. The whole day leads up to the performance. We've always done at least a two-hour show, and you really can't enjoy your beer after the show unless you've gotten a good workout." Geddy Lee

"Everybody borrows, but not everybody can create something new. You've gotta go back and actually live some of it yourself — not because Ry Cooder said so, but because you want to find out for yourself why Ry Cooder got to be as good as he is. And that means going back to Son House, not Soundgarden. As for us, we don't want to regurgitate whatever the last trend was. Everyone in Big Wreck has a particular musical vision about where they want this band to go: forward." Ian Thornley

"I jumped on every stage that would have me. My thirst for performing was insatiable. When I first started to play with people it was like getting to kiss everybody that I wanted to kiss in the whole world. I remember my mother calling me a 'jam slut', and it was true. My mother, Lotus Weinstock, was a performance artist and comedienne and her music and humour have actually had the biggest impact on me. That, and the classical music I've played throughout my life, is what's really brought me to where I am." Lili Haydn

Lili Haydn TL: 90s

"Aaliyah is a sensational singer and a grand young lady. She's going to be around a long time." Ahmet

Aaliyah TL: 90s

Scott Weiland TL: 90s

Davíd Garza TL: 90s

"Grunge is dead and I shed no tears at the funeral. Dirty jeans, pavement T-shirts and dreadlocks are boring. Rock stars used to be alluring! We're like magicians, ya know? We get to project love and positive energy. We get to create magic! The thing is, I don't really give a shit what's cool and what's not cool, because I've never been regarded as cool." Scott Weiland

"Rock'n'roll is my religion. There's some blood and there's some sweat and there's speaking in tongues. I just think of the stage as the altar, and the music as the offering." Davíd Garza

"I'm out in the middle of Lake Powell in Utah, all alone, and lying on the bottom of this boat … and I fall asleep. When I wake up, right over the boat is this image of what appears to be an eagle in the cloud. Instinctively, I put my hand to my side, pick up my camera and … click I've got it. From that moment, I knew this album would be called *On Eagle's Wings*. For me, the album is about love – the love for God, love of life, and of the world around us." Michael Crawford

"*Dance Into The Light* is a turnaround in that it's really up and optimistic, which is the way I feel at the moment. This time, it all started from a basis of guitars, and because I'm playing all the drums myself, rather than using machines like I did the last time, it's a lot more rhythmic – almost tribal. Also – and this is good news for anyone who listened to *Both Sides* and wondered what on earth was wrong with me – I think it shows I've rediscovered my sense of humour. Not that I was writing 'issue' songs out of sheer bloodymindedness: again it was just a question of the album reflecting what I was going through personally. But that was then and this is now." Phil Collins

Above: Michael Crawford; and below, Phil Collins TL: 90s

Mark Morrison TL: 90s

"Nobody sings the way I do, because it's not 100 per cent singing. What I do is more of a blend of vocal tones, street talking and rapping all at once. When I wrote 'Return Of The Mack', it was all about my moving from the negative into the positive. And that's how it turned out. Within the space of a year I went from the lowest point of my life to return as 'The Mack' and move forward to what's become the highest point of my life." Mark Morrison

"There is no match for the experience of singing with a band. It's nourishment for every singer. After all, you can't feel the funk of a computer-generated guitar. I now look at myself as a messenger of hope … of love … and as a messenger of the fact that perseverance and faith will win out in the end. I've got work to do and it will get done." Robin S

"I'm a very sexual person and what I'm revealing on my album is my personality and experiences. I used to associate a lot with girls, but they were always talkin' a whole lotta 'he-say-she-say,' getting into trouble and taking me along. Now I hang with my niggas, especially Biggie Smalls, whom I owe 85 percent of my career to; he's the one that gave me and the rest of Junior M.A.F.I.A. our shot at stardom. I'm gonna keep doin', what I'm doin', 'cos it's workin'." Lil' Kim

Robin S TL: 90s

Opposite: Lil' Kim TL: 90s

Regina Carter TL: 90s

Martin Sexton TL: 90s

"I think a lot of people look at the violin and they get a little bit nervous. They have a stereotype of what the violin is – very high, kind of shrill sounding, with long notes and a lot of vibrato. It doesn't have to be that at all, it can be a very fiery percussive instrument and that's how I like to use it.

"I don't think of the music trying to fit the violin, or how to make the violin work in this music. For me, it just does. I'm not approaching the instrument from a violinistic point of view, I'm not playing it as a violin. Instead of being so melodic, which I can be, I tend to use the instrument in more of a rhythmic way, using vamp rhythms or a lot of syncopated rhythms, approaching it more like a horn player does. So I don't feel that I have a lot of limitations – I feel I can do anything.

"I followed a more non-traditional route. I initially learned by ear, then later learned to read music, then learned theory. I think that kind of experience has freed my playing up a lot more, so I'm not stuck on the page. A lot of people are afraid not to have a piece of music in front of them." Regina Carter

"Whether it's boogie-woogie, jazz, the blues, soul, rock'n'roll, or folk, it's all American music. Because of where I've been travelling, I am constantly living and breathing American things. At first I thought, 'I can't just call it, *The American*,' but really, everything about it is American. It's about the diners and the music, the places and the people.

"I go into a different world on a good night, which is most nights. It's almost like I get high. My manager refers to it as 'getting my heaven on'. But you can see it in my eyes by the middle of a show if I'm really into it. It's kind of a blank state, but yet very much in the present as well. It's totally based on energy, like the energy coming out of me to the audience and vice versa. When I'm getting that energy back from them, it's almost like sex. It's these two parties engaged in this dance, and one reaction creates another, which creates another, which creates another, and it becomes this whirling dervish of activity." Martin Sexton

James Carter TL: 90s

"The organ sound has been a pervasive part of the black experience throughout history, from spirituals all the way up to seventies' funk and everything in between. The organ has pretty much run the gamut. It's got that downhome resonance. *In Carterian Fashion* is designed to serve as a microcosm of the instrument's contributions to that heritage. The first time I ran the idea past Cyrus [Chestnut], he was kind of reluctant. Once I'd convinced him to come aboard, he was on the money. I knew he was up to it. I've always dug Cyrus. I like the soulfulness of the cat." James Carter

"This album, *Every Kind Of Mood: Randy, Randi, Randee*, is filled with many different kinds of adult music. It's good to drive with, it's good to make love with. I always want to associate myself with any piece of music that feels good and sounds good – and a good song can come from anywhere. I hope I will always sing. I don't want to do anything else." Randy Crawford

Randy Crawford TL: 90s

The Three Tenors in rehearsal at the Eiffel Tower, Paris. From left: Placido Domingo, Jose Carreras and Luciano Pavarotti TL: 90s

"As we had done in 1994, we made a deal with Tibor Rudas to record the 1998 World Cup concert with The Three Tenors. As the matches were being played in France, the concert took place in Paris and what a wonderful programme it was. The stage was built under the Eiffel Tower which allowed the public gardens and streets of Paris to be filled with people, stretching away from the stage. It was a magnificent event. The combination of the voices of Carreras, Domingo and Pavarotti is unmatchable. Everybody was surprised that I was involved with bringing The Three Tenors to Atlantic because it's not my usual kind of music, but I've been friends with Placido for many years and both Carreras and Pavarotti are friends of mine today." Ahmet

Above and opposite: The Three Tenors in concert at the Eiffel Tower, Paris

"For me, blues has always been more than pleasure, it's always been an absolute necessity - an outlet for expression that has never been arbitrary. There's always simply been no other way. I believe that Ahmet is very much aware of the cultural ramifications of what he does. He's also very shrewd, however, and would make the opposite of any claims which would dilute the beneficial effects of what he might be able to help bring about. I think also that he is a genuinely modest person, which I believe to be a great human quality. Both Ahmet and Nesuhi, for me, have always exemplified what being civilized means." John Lewis

"We at Time Warner are proud of Atlantic Records' status as one of the world's most successful recording companies. But Atlantic is also much more than that. For half a century, Atlantic and its artists have helped nurture and define our culture. The innovative and seminal music it has produced has given voice and significance to some of the world's greatest musicians and artists. Atlantic's success – a paradigm of how to mix business with creative expression – is inextricably linked with its founder, Ahmet Ertegun. Ahmet's vision, energy and compassion have shaped and propelled Atlantic. Though many will continue to try to emulate Atlantic's success, they will never surpass the impact it has had on our country and our world." Gerald M. Levin, Chairman and CEO, Time Warner Inc.

"Claude Nobs has helped many of our artists by allowing them to take part in his festival at Montreux. He's documented all of those performances, and literally has millions of recordings and videos; he archives everything. Nesuhi supported him from the very beginning and was one of his great champions. Claude's a great character, full of enthusiasm, and loves the music and what he is doing." Ahmet

"In 1960, Ahmet Ertegun walked into my life and left footprints on my heart, after which I was never the same. I treasure his friendship and can only hope he lives forever, for I prefer a world with Ahmet in it. As the writer of the song, I feel I can quote from it, connect it with Ahmet and say, without reservation, 'To Know Him Is To Love Him'." Phil Spector

clockwise from top; John Lewis, and Ahmet with; Claude Nobs, Phil Spector, and Gerald M. Levin

From left: Ahmet, Mark Bryan and Darius Rucker of Hootie & The Blowfish, and Val Azzoli

"You know, when I began this partnership with Val, I don't think many people in other record companies outside of Atlantic and Time Warner really gave it much of a chance for success. They wrote us off out of hand and figured it would last maybe a few months at most. Well, they've been proved very wrong." Ahmet

"The company has changed; we're more sophisticated, we're bigger, we're more profitable, we're more this, we're more that. But the essence of Atlantic Records today is the same as it was when there were five people here running the whole thing. It's basically Ahmet and me, like Ahmet and Jerry, or Ahmet and whoever it was; it's the two of us. Ahmet still flies around the world and does all the things he used to - he doesn't get involved in the day-to-day stuff, but he never did. That's why he's always had a partner. It's a perfect balance. Ahmet and I never argue about the music. Sometimes he'll want to sign someone and I won't and vice versa. So we sign them. We never look at each other and say, 'Well, you can't sign that artist.' We just sign them. Why not? We agree on most of the things we don't want to sign. We talk and we do what we do. The important thing about it is that we have mutual respect for one another and we have a lot of respect for the artists who in turn, I think, have respect for us.

"I think the other important thing is that nobody here has ever been a businessman first. I came up through the music, Ahmet came up through the music. Unfortunately, as you come up to the top of the ranks, then you have more responsibilities to deal with. But I never came to do this because I wanted power, I came to do this because I liked the music. See, the other thing that's interesting is that our egos aren't big, and certainly not Ahmet's. Ahmet will admit that there are a lot of successful records he thought were shit. Not many people will admit that. I mean, readily, not even sheepishly, he will say, 'Oh man, I thought that was shit! I can't believe anybody's buying that record, that's the biggest piece of crap I ever heard in my life!' Ahmet was once asked if he was aware of the cultural impact Atlantic was having when he was making all those records in the early years of the company. He said, 'Are you kidding? I was just trying to survive.' He was just making music and selling records. But, he has always had this great ability to be what I call a bullshit detector. Take Buffalo Springfield. There were a hundred other bands like them, but Buffalo Springfield was the band who had that particular magic which happened between them. Ahmet recognized that quality in them just as he had done earlier with Ray Charles, and so on down the line. And all of these artists have always wanted to be with Ahmet because of what and who he is. He's the same today; he doesn't change like a chameleon. He'll be sitting with Kissinger and later the same day he'll be sitting with the rapper Lil' Kim. He's entirely himself with each of them, and I'm sure that everyone he deals with appreciates that fact. Ahmet is an ambassador, the ultimate diplomat with a passion for music. He has never been clouded in his way of running a record company. He has thought closely, about what people want, about the mood of the times. I mean very serious thinking about what people want and how the moods are shifting, how the climate is shifting in the creative world. Ahmet's very aware of how music is a reflection of what's going on. He consistently gets involved with the artists that represent the movement of the time, because he's a music man … because he's truly a great music man.

"Atlantic is Ahmet's company – it always has been, and it will be after he's gone. It will always be Ahmet's company. And I'm really proud to say that I hope I can keep it his company for another 50 years. It's all about the artists and that's something that he has really taught me … don't get too full of yourself – help the artists. A corporate guy said to Ahmet, 'Well, what are you going to do next year with these profits?' Ahmet said, 'Make more hits.' He didn't even think of anything else. As long as you have hits, everything else will come." Val Azzoli

From left: Jewel, Ron Shapiro, Atlantic's Executive Vice President and General Manager, Brandy and Val Azzoli, Co-Chairman and Co-CEO of Atlantic

Val Azzoli

"I grew up in Toronto, in a very poor, but very typical Italian household – extremely emotional, a lot of yelling, a lot of food and a lot of wine. My parents worked their asses off and that's where I learnt my work ethic. I never did well in school. I was always interested in things other than algebra. I didn't actually finish high school, but I ended up taking an entrance exam to get into a small college in Toronto because I realized I was just messing around doing a lot of stupid jobs and not making anything. So I graduated from this college and worked for a meat packing company. I was a salesman, on the road all the time. I shared an apartment with a guy I went to high school with who was in a rock band and so was also on the road all the time. Once in a while we would run into each other and he'd bitch about how his manager was stealing money from him and so on. Of course, at that age I thought I knew everything, so I would give him all this great advice to the point where he said, 'Well, why don't you manage me?' And I said, 'Yes.' It took me about 13 seconds to decide. The band was called Charity Brown. I wasn't really a manager; I was a glorified roadie. I drove the truck, loaded the equipment, fought with club owners. Those were gruelling years. We used to play literally every club in Canada. We'd go from the Atlantic coast all the way across the country and back again, never eating properly and so always be fighting some kind of flu or cold. I remember coming back from British Columbia, driving the truck through the Rockies, and in the back of my mind I was thinking, 'Should I go back to school?' At that point something came over me, and I decided, 'I want to stay in the music business no matter what. This is now my career.' And it was like a 16-ton weight off my shoulders. 'Yeah! That's it, that's who I am.' And I felt fantastic once I had accepted that. But with Charity Brown we never made any money, none of us did. So when I was offered a job at the publishing company ATV and the guy said, 'I'll give you $175.' I said, 'A week?' He said, 'Yeah.' 'Every week?' He said, 'Yeah, you get paid every week.' I said, 'I'm in.' What a concept! And I kept saying, 'So, every week I get paid?' And he kept looking at me like I was from Mars. So here I was, this 22-year-old schmuck running ATV in Canada, and we had The Beatles catalogue. And I'm telling you, I had no idea what I was doing. I was such a bad publisher at the beginning, because I had no idea what a publisher did. I was the first publisher in Canada to sign bands to production deals, because in my naiveté, I thought, 'This is great. I'll sign the band, we'll make a record, I'll take them over to a label, I'll take two or three points for being the production company, plus we get all the publishing.' No one was doing that. There are probably many reasons why you shouldn't do that, but none of us knew what we were doing, so we became a successful company.

"I used to go to BMI to get the performance money for The Beatles. Again, not knowing anything, I'd say, 'How have you come to this number?' And it was a big number. So they'd explain this and that but I didn't know what they were talking about. So I said to myself that we'd better get another catalogue on ASCAP, BMI's competition, so we got John Denver's publishing for Canada. I used to take whatever I got for The Beatles from BMI, say $100,000 a year for argument's sake, and then I'd ask them, 'How big are The Beatles?' They'd reply, 'Well, they're the biggest band in the world!' So I'd say, 'Well, John Denver at ASCAP earns us $90,000, so something's not right here.' And every time, they gave me more money. It was a successful publishing company, but I was young, and when you're young in the music business, the most unglamorous part of it is publishing. I mean, I learned about the importance of the song, but when you're 22 years old you want to party. I was getting bored of it all. The manager Ray Danniels had a partner at the time whom he wasn't getting along with. I guess I was the hot kid in town – Toronto's not that big a town – and we would all run across each other at clubs. He'd worked out an arrangement to end his partnership, and had gotten wind that I was ready to make a move. So

From left: Craig Kallman, Vice President/Office of the Chairman, Val Azzoli, Tori Amos, Ahmet, Ron Shapiro, Executive Vice President and General Manager, Andrea Gannis, Executive Vice President, and Arthur Spivak, Tori Amos' Manager

one night when we were talking over beers he said, 'Have you ever tried management?' and he asked me if I'd come work with him. I said, 'Yeah,' and I never regretted a day of it. I've been fortunate that I've worked with great people, and I learned a lot from Ray Danniels. His whole thing was that he was the best deal-maker I'd ever, ever seen in my life. Ray would go every which way but loose. He knew how to squeeze the most amount of money from a promoter, from a record company, from merchandising. Then after almost ten years with Ray, I joined the management company Q-Prime because its principals, Cliff Burnstein and Peter Mensch, had been friends of mine for a long time. We used to go to watch baseball spring training together every year, and one year while we were there they asked me if I would like to come and work for them in New York. The thought of moving to New York had never even crossed my mind, but I went back home and it wasn't a hard decision. I talked to my wife, she was very supportive, so we packed up and moved. It felt right from the beginning. Even though I started to worry a little bit, I figured, what the hell. I'm working with two of the smartest people in the industry, and we were friends and we still are friends. It was a great experience. As a manager, I also learned a lot from them, and again I thought I knew it all.

"When I was working with Ray Danniels, I spent most of my time with Rush. I was so fortunate to work with three really intelligent, respectful musicians who put a lot of care into what they did, cared a lot for other people, and were perfectionists - and I mean that in a complimentary way. Everything had to be great. Those were terrific years because they were a rite of passage, not only professionally but personally. The world opened up to me. We went through everything together: marriages, births, and we're still friends. It's interesting, because they almost came to Atlantic in 1982, and that's how I got to know Doug Morris. But back then they decided to re-sign with Mercury. Later, when their deal was up with Mercury, Doug came back into the picture. I wasn't working at Atlantic at the time, but one of the reasons I came here was that Rush was here, and I thought, 'It's nice to be back on familiar stomping grounds.'

"Having been a manager, one of the hardest things about it is that you realize that you can't do everything on your own. What makes a good manager is that he or she has to recognize what tools they have to work with and get the highest level of performance from everybody. I try to do that at Atlantic and fortunately it's working. It is about a team, and I've really, really spent a lot of time and effort building what I'm happy to say is probably the best team of executives in the industry right now, and no one individual is stronger than the team. We only sign and develop acts we think are great – not sounds, not flavours-of-the-month, but great acts that we feel could hit a nerve. I sit with the team and say, 'This is terrific. I don't know if it's going to take a month, two months, three months, 12 months, three years, but if we all believe it's great we're all going to have to keep going and going and going, literally one brick at a time.' Sometimes we flatline, sometimes we drop and sometimes we drop some more. But if you stick it out long enough and it truly is good, it will come back around. So then I'm portrayed as a marketing whiz, which is really funny because as an ex-manager I simply did all of the things that when I was managing bands I couldn't believe record companies didn't do. It was a no-brainer. I did these things, and they all worked. When I was a manager I used to think, 'Why am I going around checking stores, why is it so difficult?' I used to tell the record company: 'I'm landing in Chicago at ten o'clock and my hotel is the Hyatt down the road. I'm going to be at this Tower store at 10.30, and at 10.45 I'm going to be at Rose's store, and at three o'clock I'm going to this other store.' Well, you'd think they'd put posters in all these stores, but for the longest time they never did and I would raise so much hell. So all this fundamental grass-roots marketing I did as a manager I applied to Atlantic and it worked. One of the things we've done dramatically over the last couple of years is to put out fewer releases. If you do that you have to work what you have longer because there's nothing coming behind you. It's do or die because you need to break a record. I figure my job is to build the catalogue of the future, for Atlantic, for Ahmet's company.

Ahmet is truly a legend, but I was never intimidated by him because he's such a warm guy, and he reassured me. After I'd been given the gig, he called me from the Hamptons one Sunday and said, 'You know, I'm proud that you're my partner.' Well, that blew my mind. That's the highlight of my career. He said, 'It's going to be great having you as my partner,' and I'm thinking, 'I shouldn't be washing this guy's cars, let alone be his partner!' But we have a great relationship, I have a lot of respect for him and I get the same respect back. It's been great, and I hope we keep doing it for another 20 years." Val Azzoli

Val Azzoli with Atlantic executives, and third from right, Jason Flom, president of Lava Records, matchbox twenty, and fifth from right, their manager, Michael Lippman

Noreen Woods

"Ahmet has always cared about artists and been in every facet of their lives. It was never just, 'Come in and record and get your royalty and bye.' Ahmet is my best friend. I made some life-long friends and met people I would never have gotten close to if it had not been for him. I'd like to do it all over again."
Noreen Woods

"It was as if God had sent me an angel to look after me. She appeared from nowhere 41 years ago and became a most important part of my life. And she was an enigma. Noreen had a radiantly beautiful face that lit up any room she walked into – a face that combined innocence and wisdom, tragedy and humour. She had the light in her eye that only comes from intelligence and perception and goodness. And, of course, she had the depth of sorrow and the carefree lifestyle and the elegance of the hip attitude that only comes with the black experience in America. She knew. She understood. Whatever it was, she understood. She was truly a cool lady. And she was childlike and she was a wizened elder – and most of all she was good. She served her family and she served her friends, and sometimes she even served those she didn't like. And to those she did like she brought joy and laughter and happiness. And she had style. She was meticulously manicured, always simply and elegantly turned out, with the ease, freshness and taste of the truly fashionable. She was clean!

"I was in London last weekend just after having heard of Noreen's death. It was like a miracle. It seemed as if so many of Noreen's friends were there – the ones she really loved: Lord Hesketh, whom she called Sonny Boy; Earl McGrath, whom she called names I can't repeat in this holy chapel; Julio Mario Santo Domingo, whom she always favoured; Chris Blackwell, Johnny Pigozzi, Mick Jagger, Rupert Lowenstein, Reinaldo Herrera, Kenny Lane were all there – and it was a tearful gathering of the Noreen Woods Fan Club. And I guess that's a club to which we all belong. She was shy and reticent about going to social events but once she got there, she was the hit of the party. She made us all feel good. It never failed. Her life was about love and loneliness. She was a lady in the highest sense of the word, proud and humble, never complained and never explained. She had invincible character. She had compassion and love for her friends. She helped and guided so many artists through their careers. She was always there for them. They trusted her.

"Noreen was a member of my family. She was at home at all our houses. A sister to Mica, the Selmas, Nesuhi and myself . . . an aunt to my nieces and nephews. A confidante to most of her friends. She was the model of discretion. The keeper of secrets. Noreen was neither classifiable, nor categorizable. She was a person unto herself – an original. Mica said to me, upon hearing of her death, 'You have lost your best friend.' It was as if God had sent an angel to look after me, and now my angel is no longer here." Ahmet's eulogy for Noreen Woods, 29th of September, 1998

Chris Stills TL: 90s

"My Dad, quoting Wordsworth: 'Art is the expression of passion through acquired skills'. I believe in that, and I think that Ahmet is someone who actually recognizes that and defends it. Ahmet brings an integrity to his work that is amazing and I am in complete admiration of the guy. I saw him tonight at a party – he's dancing with girls, I'm not dancing with girls. I'm 23 years old and I don't have half the panache that this guy has. Ahmet and his brother Nesuhi were into jazz and blues records. They had this crazy idea that they believed in. They picked it up, made it from thin air, and made it happen. It transcends all borders, it crosses every line, and it does so no matter what – no one can stop it. I think Ahmet and all of those guys read between the lines. They see right through that piece of paper that tells them they can't do what they want and they see exactly what's on the other side. They just go right through it, and they do that with the music. That, to me, is the most respectful way to be. We're so set up to take a fall in so many different ways for the most meaningless things. It should be possible to grow up and understand that concept. It's not taught to you in school, university, anywhere. It's taught through experience. Some people are afraid to be alone and some people only want to be alone, but these huge billion-dollar businesses are governing more than the government. People call me an activist; I think that's ridiculous, I'm just a participant." Chris Stills

"Whatever music comes to me, I'll just do it. At the time when we're recording, if I think of this song or that song, I just kinda trust that it's the right thing. It's very free." Victoria Williams

Victoria Williams TL: 90s

Above: Members of The Afro-Cuban All Stars, including in front from left: Eliades Ochoa, Juan de Marcos González, Ibrahim Ferrer, Compay Segundo and rear centre Ry Cooder TL: 90s

Compay Segundo with Ry Cooder

"At the *Buena Vista Social Club* sessions, the younger musicians revelled in playing with living legends and the older players were inspired by the energy of youth. The atmosphere was electric. There was an incredible spark. The musicians spent the first day jamming together. They all knew each other, but hadn't necessarily played together before. They played all the time, not just when the tape was running. It was a totally organic thing, everyone sitting close together in the studio with ambient mikes. I collected Ry Cooder from the airport and he asked for the pianist Rubén González and the guitarist/singer Compay Segundo. We had Rubén, but we couldn't find Compay. Eventually, we tracked him down, only to find he had just signed a new exclusive recording deal – not bad at 89 years old. But after some contractual negotiations, we managed to get him, too. Ry would sit with Compay and record him on a small tape recorder. He would listen overnight to the tape and then go back and tell Compay which tunes he liked. He is a genius at finding repertoire and putting things together in a very unusual way." Nick Gold, World Circuit Records

Kid Rock TL: 90s

"I can pick up a guitar and play a Hank Williams song, then pick up the turntables and rock a basement apart. I can get on the drums and bust beats. And I can put it all together in a studio. You know my motto, man: If it looks good, you'll see it. If it sounds good, you'll hear it. If it's marketed right, you'll buy it. But if it's real, you'll feel it." Kid Rock

LeAnn Rimes TL: 90s

"I don't let it all go to my head. It could disappear overnight. So I keep reminding myself of that and of how hard I've worked to get here." LeAnn Rimes

"I write from how I feel, and on *Disciplined Breakdown* I was dealing with more emotional things than I'd ever dealt with in my life. It was painful to write these songs, to be honest. But, in the end, it felt more like therapy. These songs allow themselves to be read in many different contexts. They can be experienced as angry and disappointed, or liberated and free, or hurt and just generally sad." Ed Roland

Collective Soul, from left: Dean Roland, Shane Evans, Ed Roland, Ross Childress and Will Turpin TL: 90s

Tori Amos TL: 90s

"I developed *from the choirgirl hotel* around rhythm. I wanted to use rhythm in a way that I hadn't used it before; I wanted to integrate the piano with it. The whole record has piano and vocal cut live with a drummer and a programmer. I didn't want to be isolated this time round. I've done the 'girl-with-the-piano' thing. I wanted to be a player with the other musicians – with guitar, bass and drums. The piano player knew her head was on the chopping block with this one. She really had to practise hard to be able to play with these guys! Each song, to me, is complete. They're not as interconnected; they're not dependent on each other to work. They get to hang out together and you get to know them together, but they exist quite happily without each other. This is not a victim's record. It deals with sadness, but it's a passionate record – for life, for the life force. And a respect for the miracle of life. This record got me through a real bad patch. But I can laugh with this record and I can move my hips to this record, which is really good for me. It's very sensual – that's the rhythm." Tori Amos

Sinéad O'Connor TL: 90s

"On stage, you find something that will make you feel it's a different thing each night. You can tune into the music or tune into yourself. It's about having a relationship with yourself in the moment.

"I think religion and God are very separate. I like the idea of trying to rescue God from religion. I'm a part-time priest, and I love the idea of working as a priest for two hours every night. Why not everybody be a priest? All people are priests anyway – it says that in the bible." Sinéad O'Connor

matchbox twenty, from left: Brian Yale, Adam Gaynor, Kyle Cook, Paul Doucette and Rob Thomas TL: 90s

"Your career is just one aspect of who you are. Most of the things I write about are still basic emotions. If you sell a billion records and the only thing you can come up with to write about is selling a billion records, then you're probably a pretty shallow person. There has to be something else in your life that you can draw on other than, 'I'm rich and famous'." Rob Thomas

"matchbox twenty is currently our hottest band to emerge very recently, and I'm sure will continue to be a fabulous, great group in the future as well." Ahmet

"I think the reason for our popularity is that our music is very melodic. Also, there's something about the traditional Irish music element that, all around the world, seems to capture everybody's heart. Each song is different. There's love, life, tragedy, hope, dreams, fantasy. It's whatever the music inspires." Andrea Corr

The Corrs, from left: Caroline, Andrea, Sharon and Jim Corr TL: 90s

"We have a young, wonderful group from Ireland called The Corrs – three sisters and their brother. They are not only some of the finest singers I have ever heard, but they are the most beautiful-looking group, I think, anywhere in the world. They are so refreshing and were clearly always bound for great stardom." Ahmet

"Jimmy Page and Robert Plant are once again making musical history with the incredible music they're producing, both on record and on tour. They are part of the soul of Atlantic Records and I am very proud that they are still with us." Ahmet

"When we first got back together, it was so immediately apparent that the two of us were just channelling the music. That's what we had always had and it was so apparent that it was there. It was almost effortless. It was undeniable, and it was something not to be abused." Jimmy Page

"I think what distinguishes Atlantic today is the same as what distinguished it 50 years ago – we really don't mess with the music. We keep that raw talent and just kind of let the artist do what they do. We have enough respect for the artists to realize that what they do is unique. And we leave that alone. What distinguishes one artist from the next is that raw talent, and our philosophy has always been: don't mess with it. How do you mess with Jimmy Page and Robert Plant? They've been making great music for 30 years. How do you mess with Tori Amos? You don't mess with her. She's just such a rock talent. Tori comes in and she does what she wants. We facilitate when they want facilitation. But only that. In the old times, it was the same rhythm section on everybody's records. Now it's different. There are so many accessible, good players. But what has always distinguished great music is that raw talent and the song. It's all about the song." Val Azzoli

Robert Plant and Jimmy Page; and top, with Val Azzoli TL: 90s

Brandy TL: 90s

"If I can't feel it, then I won't sing it. And many of the songs I heard were not 'me'. They didn't express what I wanted to say at this point in my career. And I critiqued myself. I'm not the little girl I was when I made my first record. My voice is a stronger instrument now and my vocals come from both my heart and my diaphragm. My heart, because I've matured in the four years since the last album and I'm more emotionally there. The diaphragm, because I've been practising, doing more scales with my father, just strengthening my sound. I feel like my whole career has been a proving ground. But that's what I like. It makes things interesting and makes me work harder on my projects." Brandy

Sugar Ray, from left: Charles Frazier, Matthew Karges, Mark McGrath, Rodney Sheppard and DJ Homicide
TL: 90s

"This band started out at a party. Anyone who has ever put a band together has a fantasy of becoming a rock star larger than life. Anybody would love to make a lot of albums, so we kept on playing and it kept snowballing and snowballing. Our manager got us to Doug Morris and Ahmet. I met Ahmet one night at a show, and we were drinking whiskey. For a small band like us – not really responsible for the history of Atlantic Records – you can feel like you are crashing the party. You can tell why Ahmet is a success: he can hang with the premier class and with a rock'n'roll band like us and carry on the same conversation and still be so in his element. He's a businessman with such an artist's sensibility. He's written songs, he's produced records. It's hard for me to put into words what it means for us to be involved with Atlantic Records – that grand history. Our first record sold 35,000 copies in the United States, which could mean you'd be dropped, but Atlantic made a commitment to us – which is rare in this industry. They said, 'We're here for the long haul with you guys, we're going to develop you and do everything that we can to put you where we want you to be.' You hear those words and you're like a kid in a candy store and try to steal as much candy as you can before you get kicked out of the store. But they did what they said: they stuck with us, they developed us. You can see Ahmet in the hall or at a meeting and you just get the word from him … very inspiring for a group like us. They stood by us and now here we are with multi-platinum records. He still loves it. You see his eyes light up, he has such a passion for the music. I mean, you're talking about a guy who gets medals for being the Man of the Year in France, but he still cares about what the fifth song on a Sugar Ray record's gonna be. He's just indefatigable – he did about a million interviews today and a million interviews yesterday. I do three and I start complaining and crying, sort of. So he's an inspiration, he really is. To be able to work for someone like that, it's incredible. It's a really amazing, hands-on operation – very intimate even though it's such a huge operation. You just feel so secure. We wanted to have our own artistic control and while a guy might come into the studio and say, 'Hello,' they don't impede your progress. They have full faith in you to create the music, but will absolutely assist you in any way with producers, collaborators in songwriting – they will make them available to you. They will do everything in their power to make that happen, but by no means would they go, 'You need to have a hit or you need to do this, you should sound like this.' So you're getting back to the feeling of being on an independent label. Atlantic is so intuitive about how it works that they are sort of acting as an independent, in spite of the huge offices and stuff like that. These guys said, 'We've gotta give artists freedom and carry on that tradition,' and that's where we're at. They left us to our own devices, and luckily it's paid off for us. It's really good being validated and looking at Ahmet and being able to say, 'Well, we did it! We did it, man! It's another flag you can dust off in your basement someday but we did it and it means everything in the world to me.' It's incredible." Mark McGrath

Sugar Ray, with Ahmet and to his left, Jason Flom (President of Atlantic's Lava label), and second from right, their manager Chip Quigley, and friends

Jewel TL: 90s

"I knew exactly what I wanted to do with my songs and what I wanted them to do to people. I wanted to write a record that was the antidote to all the things which made me worry in the world – so that it's comforting somehow." Jewel

"Jewel is a phenomenon, and a very happy phenomenon for Atlantic Records. She is an incredibly good singer – I love the meaning in her phrasing, and she imparts great depth to her material. She's a great poet as well and she writes songs that have substance. The beauty of her soul is reflected in her voice and in her eyes." Ahmet

Above, below and opposite: Ahmet

"In 1947, if someone had told me that Atlantic would still be around in half a century, I wouldn't have believed them. I thought we would make records for two or three years, and then I'd have to figure out what to do with the rest of my life. I honestly never imagined I would be able to make a living from doing something that was so much fun. I am very glad I was wrong ... especially since it meant I never had to get a real job. I'm very fortunate to have always worked with so many terrific characters. Arif Mardin is an incredibly talented artist, arranger and producer; a great friend, like family, and remains a cornerstone of Atlantic. Tom Dowd also remains a great friend to this day. He is such an incredible talent, a legendary producer, an innovator in the recording and arranging of music and was always vital to the success of Atlantic. There are two things: there's understanding an artist and where his or her fire comes from, and then there is providing the circumstances for that talent to develop. I also recognized very early on that there are then a further two things: there is coming up with a good record and then there is getting that record played as widely as possible. If you can do that then the rest will all fall into place. I am very lucky to have had so many great collaborators working with me since I started Atlantic. To begin with, Herb Abramson, who knew all the aspects of the music business which I didn't know: how to get a lawyer, how to write a contract, what the going rate of pay was, how to sell records. The actual business of selling records is taking orders, because you can ship as many records as you want but when they don't sell they come right back home and you have to pay for them. Miriam Abramson, now Miriam Beinstock, was an important person in keeping discipline at Atlantic, keeping everything on the up and up. She's unheralded, unrecognized, but she ran the office and if we hadn't had her in those developing years, the company would have folded. She also, of course, has always had extremely good taste in music. Then there's Jerry Wexler, who became such a great friend as well as a partner, who has always been extremely honest and has such impeccable ethics. My brother, Nesuhi, who joined Atlantic a couple of years after Jerry Wexler, and who not only built our great jazz catalogue, but created our first album department and oversaw the design of our covers which gave the company a great new image. Later, he was responsible for developing our foreign presence and that of all the Warner-owned record labels. There was Sheldon Vogel, who kept us together on the business side for many, many years. Then I had Jerry Greenberg, who was always so enthusiastic, such a great personality, a fabulous promotion man, so good with the lawyers and managers of artists and such a terrific character. Then I had the great good fortune to work with Doug Morris, who is also one of the most important people in the history of Atlantic. Doug and I always agreed on what's a good song, what isn't a good song, who can sing and who can't. I was the first person that Doug always played a thing for and he was the first person I always played something for, whenever we thought we'd found anything. Now, in Val Azzoli, we have someone who has exactly the same values and priorities that all of my partners have had, shares the same love and passion for music and who is also extremely honest, intelligent and is another exceptional character. So I've always had nothing but terrific partners and am extremely happy and fortunate to have worked with all of them and count them amongst my closest friends. Val has put together a great team to lead this company into its second half century. On the creative side, we have a couple of real music men who are signing and developing a whole new generation of Atlantic artists – Jason Flom, who runs our Lava label and Craig Kallman, who oversees our A & R department. Since I started Atlantic, I've had so many thrills, and thank God they don't stop. Music has gone through a series of incredible changes. Styles have come and gone, merged and evolved, become transfigured and transformed. Today we can talk of an endless variety of musical forms, from rap to alternative, from house to metal, fusion to new age, from pure pop to jazz purism. The majority of American music is inspired by black American music, by African-American music. It's not African music, and it's not American music – it's African-American specifically. We have blues strains and blues phrasing in today's hip-hop music. Rap is not just a thing that appeared out of nowhere, it's an out-growth of the blues, blues phrasing, and jazz phrasing, as invented by Louis Armstrong, which continues to be a part of what everybody does. That's going to stay with us. That's what makes rhythm & blues, hip-hop music, the dance music of today and rock'n'roll the most popular music in the world. There's no other music which has been that strong, it's everywhere – and that's what counts" Ahmet

Index

Note: Page references in italics refer to illustrations only

Aaliyah 451, 487
Abba 303, *311, 341,* 342, 344, 365, *381,* 388
Abramson, Herb 11, 22, *24,* 25, 29, *45, 62, 63,* 64, 65, 67, 75, 113, 514
Abramson, Miriam *see* Beinstock, Miriam
AC/DC 322–3, 376–7, 391, 404, 410
Acadians 11
Acea, Johnny 86
Adams, Bryan 361
Adderley, Nat 142
'Adorable': The Drifters 78
Aerosmith 389
Afro-Cuban All Stars *502*
Against All Odds: Collins, Phil 391
Aladdin Records 290
Albright, Gerald 485
Aletti, Vince *Lost In Music: Atlantic's Disco Years* 340–3
Alexander, Arthur 192
Ali, Muhammad *294*
All-4-One 451, 462,
All-Star Jam *413*
All The Best Cowboys Have Chinese Eyes: Townshend, Pete 391
Allen, Henry 'Red' *13,* 305, *309, 346,* 366
Allen, William B. 44
'Alley Cat': Fabric, Bent 125, 139
Allison, Mose 143, 420, 453
Allman Brothers 238–41, 240, *242,* 243, 290, 292
'America': Yes 389
Ammons, Albert 11
Amos, Tori 437, 452–3, *475, 499,* 505
Ampex 75, 113
Anderson, Benny 303, 365
Anderson, Ernie 42
Anderson, Jon 212, 272, *326,* 401
Anderson, Stig 389
Anderson, Wessell 87, 460
'Angie': The Rolling Stones 293
Annapolis, Maryland 7
Apex studios 26
Apollo Theatre, Harlem 28, 29, *29,* 56, 65, 70
Appice, Carmine 218
Applebaum, Stanley 110
Archie Bell and The Drells 193, 214
Arlington National Cemetary 20
Armstrong, Lil 6
Armstrong, Louis 7, 8, 9, 11, 22, 39, 126, 202, 250
Arnold, Harry 418
Arnold, Joe *170*
Arrington, Steve 342
Art Ensemble of Chicago 272, 421

Ashley, Ted 232
Asmussen, Svend 418
Astors, The *162*
Asylum label 260
Ataturk 4, 7
Atco Records 113, 125, 251, 388, 428, 453
Atlantic Records: *Atlantic Records 1947-54* by Greil Marcus 64–7; *The Jazz Heritage of Atlantic Records* by Nat Hentoff 84–7; *The Second Taste 1954-1962* by Lenny Kaye 122–5; *Southern Soul* by Robert Gordon 190–3; *The Move Into Rock* by Robert Christgau 290–3; *Lost In Music: Atlantic's Disco Years* by Vince Aletti 340–3; *The Great Age of Excess, 1972-1986* by David Fricke 388–91; *Jazz* by Will Friedwald 418–21; *The Soul in the Machine, 1986-1999* by Barney Hoskyns 450–3
Atlas, Abe 44
Auerbach, Gene 70
Avakian, George 10
Average White Band 298, *330, 336,* 341
Axton, Estelle 130, 132, 190
Axton, Packy *130,* 191
Ayers, Roy 184
Aykroyd, Dan (Elwood Blues) *372,* 373, *413*
Azzoli, Val 449, 497–9, 510, 514

Baby Jane *169*
Bach, Sebastian 426, 450
Back In Black: AC/DC 391
Backlash: Hubbard, Freddie 185
Bad Company 285, 318, 352
Bad Religion *448,* 452
Baker, Anita 436
Baker, Ginger *182,* 207, 228, 292
Baker, LaVern 61, 93, *103,* 114, *123, 412*
Baker, McHouston 'Mickey' 141
Baker, Mickey 'Guitar' 59, 64
Baker, Ronald 342
Ballard, Hank 138
Band, The 254
Banks, Tony *288, 325, 383, 403,* 441
Bar-Kays, The 193, 194, *195*
Barbee, Elmer 276
Barclay, Eddie 171, *264*
Barge, Gene 123
Barker, Danny 8
Barnes, George 128
Barrabas 341, 342
Barrelhouse Sammy *see* McTell, Blind Willie
Barretto, Ray 341
Baryshnikov (dancer) 348
Basie, Count 11, 56, 65, 85, 118
Battiste, Harold 200

Bauduc, Ray *11*
Bayar, Celal 7
Beatles, The 180, 182, 206, 238, 265, 290, 498
Beauty Is A Rare Thing: Coleman, Ornette 453
Beauvais, Yves 453
Bechet, Sidney 8, 12, 65, 86–7
Beck, Jeff 395
Beckenbauer, Franz 233
Beckett, Barry 230, 279
Bee Gees, The 200, 216, 290, 292, 304, 343, *413*
Beers, Gary *406*
'A Beggar For Your Kisses': The Diamonds 55
Beinstock, Freddie 70
Beinstock, Miriam (was Abramson) *45, 62,* 64, 67, *70, 88, 89,* 113, *121,* 232, 251, 335, 375, 514
Belafonte, Harry 395
Bell, Al *170,* 193
Bell, Thom 309, 366
Bell, William 132, 190
Belushi, John (Jake Blues) 372–3
Benton, Brook 245
Berklee College of Music, Boston 414
Berns, Bert 132, 160, 219, 290
Bernstein, Cliff 499
Bernstein, Sid 180, 386
Betts, Dickey 239, 292
'Beyond The Sea': Darin, Bobby 125
Big Beat Records 451
'Big Log': Plant, Robert 385
Big Tree Records 428
Big Wreck 486
Bigard, Barney *6*
Biggs, Howard 29, 59
Bilk, Acker 125, 139
Bill Haley and His Comets 66, 69
Billy Ward and The Dominoes 66
'Black And Tan Fantasy': Ellington, Duke 11
Black Oak Arkansas 388
Blackburn, Rick 428, 451, 456, 458, 470, *471*
Blackfoot 354
Blackwell, Chris 228, 335
Blackwell, Ed *134*
Bladd, Stephen Jo *313*
Blaine, Jerry 22, 25
Blakey, Art 105, 420
Blanshard, Terence 87
Blesh, Rudi *17*
Blind Faith 227–8, 242, 292
Blue Moon Boys 65
Blue Note Records 86
'Blue Velvet': The Clovers 123
Blues Brothers, The 372–3
Blues Kings, The 64
Bobbettes, The *103*
'Body And Soul': Hawkins, Coleman 21

Bogdon, Ron 267
Bogert, Tim *218*
Boney M 342, *366*
Bonham, John 219, 262–3, *284*, *314*, 385, 391
Bono, Sonny 155, 168–9
Boogie Woogie Boys 11
'Boogie Woogie Roll': McPhatter, Clyde 62
Booker T. & the MGs 149, *158,* 190
Boone, Debby 343
Booth, Stanley 254
Both Sides: Collins, Phil 489
Bottle Rockets, The 472
Bowie, Lester 87, 421
Bradshaw, Tiny 137
Bramlett, Bonnie *242*
Bramlett, Delaney *242*
Brandy 451, 463, *497*, 511
Branigan, Laura 386, 391, *412,* 450
Braud, Wellman 8
Braun, Rick 478
Braxton, Anthony 286, 419
Brennan, Maire 477
Brides of Funkenstein, The *363*
Brigati, Eddie 180, *210,* 336
'Bron-Y-Aur Stomp': Led Zeppelin 263
Brookmeyer 419
Broonzy, Big Bill 206
Brown, Clifford 86
Brown, Lawrence 6
Brown, Ruth 42–3, 59, 64, 66, 74, *103, 110, 412*
Browne, Jackson *260*
Brubeck, Dave 286, 419
Bruce, Jack *182,* 207, 290, 292
Bruce, Lenny 155
Bruford, Bill *289*
Bryan, Mark *497*
Bryant, Willie 28
Buchanan, Roy 319
Buffalo Springfield 182–3, 215, 219, 234, 246, 290, 389
Buffalo Springfield Again 291
Burke, Solomon 133, *150,* 164, 190, 194
Burrell, Boz *318*
Bushkin, Joe 50, 418
Buster Williams Plastic Products 190
Butler, Billy *25*
Butler, Michael 200
Butler, Robin *120*
Byas, Don *197*
Byrd, Roeland *see* Longhair, Professor
Byrds, The 234

Cactus 389
Caesar and Cleo *see* Sonny and Cher
Calloway, Blanche 42
Calloway, Reggie 415
Calvert, Rosalie *101*
Campbell, Glen 152
Capitol Theatre, Washington 11
Cardarelli, Larry *see* Sparkles, Zeno

Cardinals, The (Mellotones) 55, 66
Carey, Mutt 18–19
Carmichael, Stokely 171
Carney, Harry 6
Carr, Linda *174*
Carr, Pete 279
Carrack, Paul *402*
Carreras, José *454,* 494–5
Carroll, Jim *361*
Carroll, Ray 28
Carson, Phil 323
Carter, Benny 7, 11
Carter, Betty *147*
Carter, Clarence 190, 193, 244
Carter, James 87, 421, 460–1, 493
Carter, Regina 492
Carter, Ron 420
Cary, Dick 42
'Casanova': Levert 415
Casey, Al 8
Cash, Dave 171
Castor, Jimmy 342
Cat Records 122
Catlett, Big Sid 8
''Cause I Love You': Carla and Rufus Thomas 130, 190
Cavaliere, Felix 180, 210
CBGB's Club 323
CBS Group 290, 371, 456
'C.C. Rider': Willis, Chuck 93, 123
'Celebration Day': Led Zeppelin 262
Cerrone (Jean-Marc) 343, 350
'Chains Of Love': Turner, Joe 57, 65
Chairmen Of The Board 244
Changing Faces 451, 480
'Chanson D'Amour': Manhattan Transfer 336
Charity Brown 498
Charles, Ray 21, 58, 66, 79, 84–5, *108,* 118–19, *123,* 125, 161, 190, 259, 335, 418, 420, 456
Cheatham, Doc 90, 420
Checker, Chubby 138
Cher 168–9, 230
Cherry, Don 117, *134,* 423
Chess Records 22, 31, 64, 290
Chestnut, Cyrus 87, 421, 460, 484–5, 493
Chic 291, 339, 343, 364
children, stories for 64, 74
Chords, The 72, 122
Christgau, Robert: *The Move Into Rock* 290–3
Chudd, Lew 77
Cincinnati Records 44
'Clap Your Hands': Manhattan Transfer 342
Clapton, Eric 182, 193, 206, 242, 243, 248, 257, *280,* 290, 292
Clark, Bob 15
Clark, Dick *101*
Clarke, Kenny 418
Clarke-Boland Big Band 418
'Clean Up Woman': Wright, Betty 267
Clearmountain, Bob 361
Close To The Edge: Yes 388, 390

Clovers, The 52–4, 64, 66, *101,* 123
Clown, The: Mingus, Charles 85
Coasters, The 100–1, *111,* 124, 125, *128,* 412
Cobham, Billy 287, 421
Cocker, Joe *237*
Cohn, Al 86
Cohn, Marc *435*
Colbert, Melrose 26, 31
'Cold As Ice': Foreigner 379
Coleman, Ornette 84–7, 117, 134, 184, 419, 420, 423
Collective Soul 452, 465, 504
Collingwood, Chris 474
Collins, Phil *288,* 325, 378, *383,* 391, *401, 403, 428, 433,* 441, 450, 489
Coltrane, Alice 84
Coltrane, John 84–5, 116, 135, 418
Columbia Records 21, 64, 188, 189, 193, 204, 234, 293, 389, 450
'Coming Home': Delaney and Bonnie 242
Commodore Music Store 9
Commodore Records 86
Condon, Eddie 42, 86
Confederate Railroad 457
Congress, Library of 8
Conley, Arthur *170, 171, 172,* 176, 193
Connor, Chris 95, 418, 419
Conover, Willis 42, 414
Consumer Rapport 341, 342
Contemporary Records 77, 86, 418
Cooder, Ry 502
Cookies, The *102,* 103
Cooley, Eddie 52
Cooper, Alice 316, *346*
Cordoba, Diana de *120*
Corea, Chick 286, 421
'Corinne Corinna': Turner, Joe 91
Cornish, Gene *210*
Cornshucks, Little Miss 14–15, 42, 61
Corr, Andrea 508
Corrs, The *469,* 508–9
Coryell, Larry *358*
Cosimo's Studio 63
Cosmos, The (soccer team) 233
Cotillion Records 388
Covay, Don 162
Coxon, John 464
Crawford, Hank 143, 161, 224, 420
Crawford, Michael 489
Crawford, Randy 493
Cream 182, 206, 207, 290, 292
Creason, Sammy 254
Crescent Records 77, 84, 418
Crew Cuts, The 72, 122
Crocker, Frankie 340
Cropper, Steve 130, 149, 165, 167, *170,* 178, 191, 202, 203, *372, 373*
Crosby, Bob 11
Crosby, David 234–5, 253, *324, 383*
Crosby, Israel 49
Crosby, Stills & Nash 234–6, 235, 246, 280, 290, 292,

390, *413,* 445; & Young 234, 236
Cross, David *289*
Crystal, Billy 9
Crystal, Jack 9
Crystal Caverns Club 42
CSN: Crosby, Stills & Nash 390
Culley, Frank 'Coleslaw' *34*
Culley, Frank 'Floorshow' 54, 65
Curb Records 451
Curtis, King 141, 179, 193, 224, 226, *238, 242,* 268, 421

Dahl, John 75
Daltrey, Roger 399
'Dance, Dance, Dance (Yowsah, Yowsah, Yowsah)':
    Chic 339, 343
Dance Into The Light: Collins, Phil 489
Dando, Evan 439
Danelli, Dino *210*
Daniels, Ray 499
Dara, Olu 485
Darin, Bobby 112–13, 124–6, 154–5, 181, 291
Daugherty, Pat 'Dirty' 301
Dave Pell Octet, The 418
Davenport, Cow Cow 58
Davenport, John 52
Davis, Clive 290
Davis, Michael 261
Davis, Miles 86, 421
Davis, Richard 180
Davis, Steve 499
Dawson, Alan 286
de Coteaux, Bert 308
de la Renta, Oscar *233, 350, 351*
De Paris, Sidney 8, 90, *139,* 420
De Paris, Wilbur 64, 90, *91, 96, 120,* 420
'Dear Old Southland': Armstrong, Louis 250
Decca Records 9, 21, 69, 176, 264
Dee, Joey 138
Dee, Sandra *124, 154*
Deep Purple: Nino Tempo and April Stevens 125, 153, 441
Déjà Vu: Crosby, Stills, Nash & Young 234, 388, 390
Delaney and Bonnie 242, 290, 292
Delehant, Jim 341
DeLeo, Dean 438
Delta Rhythm Boys, The *39,* 64
Denver, John 397, 498
Derek & the Dominos 292
Desmond, Paul 286
Deutrom, Mark 448
'Devil Or Angel': The Clovers 123
Diamonds, The 55
Dibango, Manu 340
Dickenson, Vic *139*
Dickinson, Jim 254
Dinkins, David *440*
Dino, Abidin 423
'Disco Inferno': The Trammps 342
'Disco Queen': Hot Chocolate 342

Discotheque: Mann, Herbie 341
Disraeli Gears: Cream 206
Distel, Sacha 418
Dixie Flyers, The 254
Dixieland music 8, 87
Dixon, Willie 196
'Do Right Woman': Franklin, Aretha 188, 193
'Dock Of The Bay': Redding, Otis 203
Dodds, Baby *9*
dog, the (dance) 151, 190
Domanico, Chuck 287
Domingo, Placido *454,* 494–5
Domino, Fats 77
Dominoes, The (Billy Ward) 63, 66,
'Don't You Know I Love You': The Clovers 54
Dorn, Joel 275, *297,* 420; on Bad Company 285; on
    black music 297; on Donny Hathaway 357;
    161; on King Curtis 226; on Nesuhi Ertegun
    222, 225; on Roberta Flack 208, 258, 295; on
    Shirley Scott 224; on *Swiss Movement* 221; on
    Yusef Lateef 223
Dorsey, Jimmy 29
Dorsey, Lee *174*
Dorsey, Tommy 7
Dominos, (Derek &) The 243
Dot Records 21
Double Vision: Foreigner 391
Doug Sahm And Band 278
Douglas, Mike *337*
Dowd, Tom 64, 119, *136,* 158, *159,* 180, 190, 193, *230, 254, 298, 453,* 514; on Ampex 113; on Aretha
    Franklin 204. on Crosby, Stills & Nash 280; on
    Danny 'Rum Joe' Taylor 103; on *Disraeli
    Gears* 206; on Eddie Barclay 171; on Herbie
    Mann 224; on Jim Stewart 132; on John
    Coltrane 135; on *Layla* 243; on Leiber &
    Stoller 128; on the Stax tour 170; on studios
    74; on 234 West 56th Street 89, 118; on
    young songwriters 101
Dr. John (Mac Rebennack) 211, 277, 278, 290, 293, 389
'Dream Lover': Darin, Bobby 112
Drifters, The 63, 66, 67, 78, *78,* 110, 123, 124, 125, 127, 147, 160
'Drinkin' Wine Spo-Dee-O-Dee': McGhee, Stick 44–5, 64, 190
Drinkwater, Skip 388
Driscoll, Julie *217*
Duke: Genesis 378
Duke, Vernon 75
Duke Records 290
Dunn, Donald 'Duck' *130,* 149, *149,* 171, 178, 191, 372–3
Dupree, Champion Jack *106*
Dupree, Cornell 179
Dylan, Bob 11, 200, 278

Eagles, The *260*
'Ease On Down The Road': Consumer Rapport 341, 342

Easton, Mack 64
EastWest America 87, 428, 432, 451
Easybeats, The 323
The Ebony Concerto: Stravinsky 251
Eckstine, Billy 22
Edmunds, Dave 316
Edwards, Bernard 339, 343, *362*
Eib, William 388, 389
Einstein, Sandy *428*
El Mirage: Webb, Jimmy 324
El Morocco Club *120,* 121, 138
Eldridge, Roy 22
Elektra Records 233, 260, 305, 432, 453
Ellington, Duke 6, 7, 8, 9, 11, 12, *20,* 38, 39, *39,* 42, 65, 84, 85, 118, *250*
Elliott, Dennis *328*
Ellis, Jimmy 342
Embryo Records 388, 420
Emerson, Keith 212, 256, 332, 390
Emerson, Lake & Palmer 256, *289,* 332, 390
Empty Glass: Townshend, Pete 371
En Vogue 432
Epstein, Brian 180, 200
Erin, June *375*
Erlewine, Stephen Thomas 85
Ertegun, Ahmet *4, 5, 7, 10, 45, 52, 57, 76–7, 87, 220, 231, 232, 251, 346, 395,497, 514, 515*; early life
    4–10; education 20–1; on starting the busi-
    ness 23–6, 36–7, 44; on the sale of Atlantic
    232; on Atlantic's half century 514; on the
    blues 281, 395, 481; on making great records
    213; on Nesuhi 233, 423; on New York 417;
    on songwriting 52, 54; on Noreen Woods 500
Ertegun, Ambassador Munir (Ahmet's father) 4, 7, 20
Ertegun, Hayrunisa (Ahmet's mother) 4, *4,* 7
Ertegun, Marili (Nesuhi's wife) 18
Ertegun, Mica (Ahmet's wife) *120,* 153, 169, *408, 428*
Ertegun, Nesuhi 4–13, 18–21, 25, 76–8, 105, 117–18, *121, 136, 139,* 196, 222, 225, 232–3, *333,* 375, *375, 414, 416,* 514; and jazz 84–8, 418–22; *Nesuhi Ertegun* by John Lewis 423
Ertegun, Selma (Ahmet's sister) 7
Eureka Brass Band 420
Evans, Herschel *11*
'Every Time': Green, Lil 57
Everything But The Girl 451, 464, 476
Excello label 453
Exclusive Records 21
Exile On Main Street: The Rolling Stones 290, 293
'Expecting To Fly': Buffalo Springfield 246

Fabric (Fabricius-Bjerre), Bent 125, 139
Face Value: Collins, Phil 391
Falcons, The *149,* 167
Faltskog, Agnetha 303, 345, 365
Fame Music 190, 192, 193
'Fanfare For The Common Man': Emerson, Lake & Palmer 332
Farmer, Art 414, 420

Farriss, Andrew, Jon & Tim *406*
'Feels Like The First Time': Foreigner 328, 379
Ferbie, Willie 67
Ferrick, Melissa 453
Ferry, Bryan 299, *321*, 356, 367
Fields, Ernie *21, 22*
Fifth Dimension, The 212
Fillmore East: Allman Brothers 240
Firefall 290, 324
Firm, The 399
'The First Time Ever I Saw Your Face': Flack, Roberta 258
Fitzgerald, Ella 10
Five Crowns, The 110, 125
Flack, Roberta 85, 208, 258, 295, *351, 413*, 423, 436
Flom, Jason 426, 427, 437, 452, 467, *499, 512*, 514
Flores, Chuck 287
Flower Travelling Band 388
Floyd, Eddie *170*, 178
Fontessa: The Modern Jazz Quartet 82
'Fool, Fool, Fool': The Clovers 54
For Those About To Rock: AC/DC 404
'For What It's Worth': Buffalo Springfield 291
Foreigner 328–9, 379, 384, 390–1, 394, *411*, 450
Foreman, George *294*
Forrest Hotel, New York 15
Foster, David 402
Foster, Pops 8
Fountains of Wayne 452, 474
461 Ocean Boulevard: Clapton, Eric 292
4 Way Street: Crosby, Stills & Nash 390
Frampton, Peter 317
Frank (Ahmet's chauffer) *98*
Franklin, Aretha 11, 188–9, 190, 193, 204–5, 247, 255, 259, 269, *309*, 334, 453
Freed, Alan 28, 65, *89*
Freeman, Bud *139*
Freeman, Charlie 191, 254
Freeman, Von 421
Fresh Cream: Cream 292
Fricke, David *The Great Age of Excess, 1972-1986* 388–91
Friedwald, Will 90, 185; *Jazz* 418–21
'Friends': Led Zeppelin 262
Fripp, Robert *289*, 390
'Funky Broadway': Pickett, Wilson 193
Furay, Richie 183, 234, 290, 291

Gabler, Milt 9, 250
Gabriel, Peter *288*, 319
Gagliardi, Ed *328*–9
Galkin, Joe 149, 190, 191–2, 192
'Gallows': Led Zeppelin 262
Gannis, Andrea *499*
Gant, Private Cecil 21
Garland, Ed *18, 19*
Garner, Erroll 31, 64, 418
Garza, David 488
'Gee Whiz': Thomas, Carla 125, 130

Geffen, David 234, 260, 290
J. Geils Band, The *313*
Geldof, Bob *412*
Genesis 288, 325, *383, 403, 441*
George Lewis Band, The *21*
Georgetown University 20, 21
Gerlac, Fred 262
Giant Steps: Coltrane, John 85, 116, 135
Gibb, Barry, Maurice and Robin *see* The Bee Gees
Gibbs, Georgia 93
Gibson, Debbie 408–9, *413*, 450
Gillespie, Dizzy 17, 82, *110*, 251, *414*
Ginsberg, Allen *168*
Gioie, Emilio *414*
Girard, Adele *6, 7*
Giuffre, Jimmy 85, *121*, 419
Gleason, Ralph J. 253
Glew, Dave *346*
'Gloria': Branigan, Laura 386, 391, 450
Goffin, Gerry 101
Gold, Nick 502
Gold Star Studios 183
Goldberg, Danny 452
Goldner, George 290
Golson, Benny 419
'Gone': McPhatter, Clyde 62
González, Rubén 502
Good God 388
'Good Times': Chic 343, 362
Goodman, Benny 7, 11
Gordon, Bob 419
Gordon, Jim 243
Gordon, Marc 415
Gordon, Robert *Southern Soul* 190–3
Gordy, Berry 290
Gottlieb, Bill *4, 7*, 11, *16*
Gottlieb, Delia *4*
Gottlieb, William *4*
Graffin, Greg 448
Gramm, Lou 328–9, *355, 379*, 391
Grant, Peter 219, 284
Granz, Norman *17*, 45
Grappelli, Stephane 145, 273
Greaves, R.B. 193, 231
Green, Charlie 215, 375
Green, Lil 57
'Green Onions': Booker T. & the MGs 149, 191
Greenberg, Bob *346*
Greenberg, Jerry 295, 305, 326, 339, 341, 343, *346, 347*, 350, *362*, 366, 379, 514
Greene, Charlie 168, 182, 290
Greenfield, Howie 101
Greenwood, Al *329*
Griffin, Johnny 26, *37*, 58, 273
Grimes, Tiny *22*, 26, *44*, 418
'Groovin'': The Rascals 180
Guinle, Mr. and Mrs. Jorge *17*
'Guinnevere': Crosby, Stills & Nash 235
Gullin, Lars 418
Gumbo: Dr. John 293

Guthrie, Arlo 237
Guy, Buddy 277

Hackett, Bobby 42
Hackett, Steve *288*
Haden, Charlie 117
Haggart, Bob *11*
Hair (show) 200
Hale, Willie 'Little Beaver' 267
Hall, Daryl 295
Hall, Edmund *139*
Hall, Jim 419, 420
Hall, Rick 173, 174, 192, 193, 238–9, 244, 290
Hall, Tony 176
Hall & Oates 295
Hammond, John (Jr.) *239*
Hammond, John (Sr.) 10–11, 15, 65, 188, 290
Hamp-Tone Records 23
Hampton, Gladys 23
Hampton, Lionel 10, 16, 23, *26*, 496
Haness, Abigale 293
'Hang Up My Rock And Roll Shoes': Willis, Chuck 114, 123
Hanna, Sir Roland 420
Hardee, John 26
Hardin, Tim 181
Harlem 7, 28–9, 39
Harlem Records 44
Harlemaires, The *25*, 29
Harris, Eddie 221, 222, 420–1
Harris, Norman 342
Harrison, Donald 87
Harrison, George 242
Harrow, Nancy 418
Haskell, Gordon 389
Hatfield, Juliana 431, 452
Hathaway, Donny 258, 357
'Hats Off To Harper': Led Zeppelin 263
Hauser, Tim 302, 336, 479
Hawkins, Coleman 21, 184, 418
Hawkins, Ralph *6*
Hawkins, Roger 230, 279
Hawkins, Ronnie 254, *254*
Haydn, Lili 487
Hayes, Ernie 59
Hayes, Isaac 156
Haynes, Roy 286
'Heartbreaker': Charles, Ray 58
Heath, Percy 82, 117, 134, *416*
Heavyweight Champion, The: Coltrane, John 453
Heavyweight Champion: The Complete Atlantic Recordings 85
Hello, I Must Be Going: Collins, Phil 391
Henderson, Fletcher 9
Hendman, Felix 387
Hendricks, Jon 87
Hendrix, Jimi 179, 257, 265, 268
Henneman, Brian 472
Hentoff, Nat *The Jazz Heritage of Atlantic Records*

84–7
Herman, Woody 421
'Hey Jude': Pickett, Wilson 238, 239
Hi Records 193
Hibbler, Al 38
Higginbotham, J.C. *6, 13*
Higgins, Billy 117
High Voltage: AC/DC 323
'Hijack': Mann, Herbie 341
Hill, Teddy *22*
Hillman, Chris 271
Hines, Earl 31
Hoboken Saturday Night: Insect Trust 293
Hodes, Art *6, 13*
Hodges, Johnny *6, 7*
'Hold On, I'm Comin'': Sam and Dave 177, 192
Hole, Max 437
Holiday, Billie 10, 28, 86
Holland, Tony 276
Holliday, Jennifer 394
Hollies, The 234
'Honey Hush': Turner, Joe 64
'Honey Love': McPhatter, Clyde 66, 73, 124
Honeydrippers, The 395
Hood, David 230, 231, 279
Hooke, Peter Van *402*
Hooker, John Lee 64, 276
Hootie & the Blowfish 449, 452, 473
'Hootie Blues': McShann, Jay 331
Horne, Lena 12
Hoskyns, Barney *The Soul in the Machine, 1986-1999* 450–3
Hot Chocolate *311*, 342
Hot Discography, The 21
Hot Record Society (HRS) 9
Houston, Cissy 341
Hovak, Blackie 37
Hovakimian, Mrs 37
Howard Theatre, Washington 11, 82, 84
Howe, Steve *272, 326, 327*
HRS *see* Hot Record Society
Hubbard, Freddie 185, 420
Hues Corporation 340
Hughes, Jimmy 192
Hunter, Ivory Joe 79, 123
Hutchence, Michael *406–7*, 442, 450, *453*

'I Can't Stop Dancing': Archie Bell & The Drells 193
'I Got A Woman': Charles, Ray 79, 125
'I Got You Babe': Sonny and Cher 168, 169, 375
'I Love You Always Forever': Lewis, Donna 451
'I Never Loved A Man': Franklin, Aretha 188, 189, 193, 204
'I Want To Know What Love Is': Foreigner 329, 394
'I Wonder': Gant, Private Cecil 21
'If I Were A Carpenter': Darin, Bobby 181
'If You Need Me': Pickett, Wilson 192
IFPI (International Federation of the Phonographic Industry) 233, 423

'Immigrant Song': Led Zeppelin 262
Imperial Records 77, 290
In-A-Gadda-Da-Vida: Iron Butterfly 215
'In The Midnight Hour': Pickett, Wilson 167, 178, 192
Ingle, Doug 215
Insect Trust 290, 293
Interscope 428
INXS 406, 442, 450
Iovine, Jimmy 428
Iron Butterfly 215, 290
Island Records 335
Isley Brothers 132
'I've Got That Feeling': Green, Lil 57
Ivy, Quin 173
Izmir Restaurant 37

J. Geils Band 265, *281*, 313, 389
J Is For Jump: Jo Mama 293
Jackson, Al 149, 165, *170*, 178, 191
Jackson, Chubby 75
Jackson, Hal *362*
Jackson, Harold 348
Jackson, Jesse 349
Jackson, Mahalia 28
Jackson, Milt 82, 119, *416*, 418
Jackson, Randy 387
Jackson, Wayne *130, 170*
Jackson, Willis 'Gator Tail' *59*
Jacquet, Illinois 424
Jagger, Mick 264–5, *281*, 348–9, *352, 374, 392*, 443, 450, *453*, 469
Jamal, Ahmad 400, 421
James, Elmore 239
James, Skip 207
James Gang, The 285
Jarrett, Keith 227, 421
jazz: course at UCLA 77, 84; at Music Inn, Lenox 115
Jazz by Will Friedwald 418–21
Jazz Festival, Montreux 196, 221, 330, 421, 496
The Jazz Heritage of Atlantic Records, Nat Hentoff 84–7
Jazz Messengers, The 420
Jazzman Record Shop 18, 84
Jazzman Records 77, 418
Jefferson, Blind Lemon 41
Jefferson Airplane *236*
Jefferson Hotel 26, 37
Jenkins, Johnny 149
jerk, the (dance) 167, 192
Jewel 446, 452–3, *497*, 513
'Jim Dandy': Black Oak Arkansas 388
Jiminez, Flaco 278
Jimmy Castor Bunch, The *338*
'Jive Talkin'': The Bee Gees 304
Jo Mama 293
Joey Dee and The Starlighters 190
Johnny Jenkins and the Pinetoppers 191
Johnson, Blind Willie 41
Johnson, Brian 377, 391, *410*

Johnson, Budd 59
Johnson, Buddy *89*
Johnson, Bunk *9, 13*, 22
Johnson, Ella *89*
Johnson, Jimmy 193, 230, 238
Johnson, Pete *6*, 11, 12, 64, *91*
Johnson, Robert 206, 207, 239
Johnson, Terry *130*
Jones, Booker T. 149, *170, 176*, 191, 202
Jones, Elvin 187, 420
Jones, Hank 414
Jones, Jamie 462
Jones, Jo *11*
Jones, John Paul *219*, 262–3, *284, 292, 314*
Jones, Kenny 317
Jones, Mick 328–9, *379*, 390–1, 394, *408*
Jones, Philly Joe 58, 420
Jones, Quincy 85, 118, 414
Joplin, Janis *237*
Jordan, Clifford 421
Jubilee Records 22, 25
Junior M.A.F.I.A. 451, *481*
'Just Out Of Reach': Burke, Solomon 190
Justman, Seth *313*

Kallman, Craig 451, 453, *499*, 514
Kalodner, John David 390
'Kansas City': Little Miss Cornshucks 15; Robinson, Bobby 70
'Kashmir': Led Zeppelin 284
Kay, Connie 50, 59, 64, 82, 117, *416*, 418
Kay, Monte 82, 418, 423
Kaye, Lenny *The Second Taste 1954-1962* 122–5
Kaye, Tony *401*
'Keep Your Body Workin'': Kleeer 342
Keith, Ben 453
Kennedy, Robert 210
Kent, Cotton 388
Kenton, Stan 26, 184
Keske, Lee 86
Kid Ory Band *18*
Killen, Buddy 163, 175
'Killing Me Softly': Flack, Roberta 295
King, Albert *198*, 239
King, B.B. 239
King, Ben E. 100, 110, 124, 125, *127*, 129, *160*, 193, 308, *336, 338*, 450, 453
King, Carole 101
King, Freddie 229
King, Martin Luther 193, 210, 255
King Crimson 220, 289, 293, 390
King Curtis 226
King Pins, The 268
King Records 21, 138, 290
Kinney Group 232, 236, 388
Kirby, Steve 87
Kirk, Roland 186, 222, *297*, 421
Kirke, Simon *318, 352*
Kleer 342

Klein, Allen 265
Klein, Danny *313*
Koenig, Lester 77, 418
Konitz, Lee 81, 136, 414, 419
Kortchmar, Danny 293
Koylan, Sadi (Ahmet's cousin) *4, 7*, 26
Kramer, Wayne 261
Krefetz, Lou 52, *128*
Kristofferson, Kris 254
Kutlu, Vesamet 7

La Gallienne, Eva 75
Lake, Greg 256, 390
Lamond, Don 126
'Land Of 1,000 Dances': Pickett, Wilson 193
Lane, Ronnie *317*
'Last Night': Mar-Keys, The 191
Lateef, Yusef 222–3, *296*, 421
Lauderdale, Jack 21, 58
Laws, Hubert 180
Layla: Cream 243, 290, 292
'Le Freak': Chic 343
Leadbelly 12, *13*, 64, 262, 421
Led Zeppelin 219, 262, 283–4, 284, 292–3, *314–15*, 368, 385, 388, 389, 391, *413*, 451
Lee, Geddy 486
Leiber, Jerry 78, 100, 110, 124–5, 127, 128, 129, 290
Lemonheads, The *439*, 452
Lennon, Julian 398, 452
Lenya, Lotte 126
Lesser, Gilbert *347*
Let It Bleed: The Rolling Stones 293
'Let The Boogie Woogie Roll': McPhatter, Clyde 66
Levert 415, 450
Levin, Gerald M. 496
Levy, Lou 418
Levy, Morris 67, 290
Lewerke, Jack 168, 169
Lewis, Barbara 156, *157*
Lewis, Donna 451, 466
Lewis, George *21*, 22, 420
Lewis, John 82, 86, 115, 134, 136, 416, 418, 419, 496; *Nesuhi Ertegun* 423
Lewis, Meade Lux 7, 11, 49, *49*
Lewis, Rudy 124
Library of Congress 8
Lieber, Jerry *496*
Lifeson, Alex *486*
Lift Every Voice And Sing: Roach, Max 185
Liggins, Joe 395
Lil' Kim 451, 490–1
Limbo, Sonny 244
Lincoln Center Jazz Orchestra 87
Linsley, Steve 361
Lippman, Michael *499*
Little Miss Sharecropper *see* Baker, LaVern
Little Richard 158
Lloyd, Charles 187, 421
Loaded: Velvet Underground 292

Loggins & Messina 290
London 4, 6
Longhair, Professor 41, 64, 211, 277
'Losin' Hand': Stone, Jesse 67
'Lost In Music': Sister Sledge 343
Lost In Music: Atlantic's Disco Years by Vince Aletti 340–3
Lou Reed 249
'Love In C Minor': Cerrone 343, 350
'Love The One You're With': Stills, Stephen 257
Love Unlimited Orchestra 340
'A Lover's Question': McPhatter, Clyde 123
'Love's Theme': Love Unlimited Orchestra 340
Lovett, Baby 65
Lovett, Leroy 29
'Lovey Dovey': Otis Redding and Carla Thomas 203
Lowe, Chris 451
Lowe, Jackson 26
'Lowe Groovin'' 26
Lucas, Cassandra 480
Lucas, Ray 179
'Lucky Man': Emerson, Lake & Palmer 256
Lulu 193, 230
Lunceford, Jimmie 7
Lyngstad, Anni-Frid 303, 365

'Mack The Knife': Darin, Bobby 125, 126
Mad Lads, The 156
'Mad Love': Barrabas 342
Magic Children's Album, A 74
Magic Dick *281, 313*
Magoo 480
Mahoney's Last Stand: Ronnie Wood and Ronnie Lane 317
Main Ingredient: The Bee Gees 292
Malachi, Johnny 15
'Mama, He Treats Your Daughter Mean': Brown, Ruth 59, 74
Mammoth Records 452, 464
Manassas 271, 390
Manglesdorf, Albert 418
Mangrum, Jim 'Dandy' 285
Manhattan Transfer, The 302, *336*, 342, 382, *412, 413*, 479
Manilow, Barry 275
Mann, Herbie *144*, 145, 184, 224, *330*, 341, *413*, 420
Manne, Shelly 184, 419
Mar-Keys, The *130, 173*, 191
March of Time, The (news movies) 42
Marcus, Greil *Atlantic Records 1947-54* 64–7
Mardin, Arif 136, 141, *160*, 213, 231, 278, *298*, *330*, *338*, *414, 464*, 514; on African-American music 251; on Aretha Franklin 255; on Average White Band 298; on The Bee Gees 304; on Brook Benton 245; on David Newman 161; on Donny Hathaway 357; on Elvin Jones 187; on King Curtis 179; on Quincy Jones 414; on Rap 481; on Ringo Starr 316; on Roberta Flack 258; on The Young Rascals 180

Marriott, Steve 317
Marsala, Joe 6, 7
Marsalis, Wynton 87, 479
Marsh, Warne 94, 419
Martell, Vince *218*
Martin, Dewey *183*, 215
Martin, George 324
Maryland 7
Mason, Dave 242
Mass Production 342
matchbox twenty 452, 468, *499*, 507
Mayfair Theatre, London 170
MC5 261, 290, 293, 453
McCain, Edwin 473
McCann, Les 208, 221, 222, 421
McClure, Tommy 254
McCoy, Neal 471
McCrae, George 340
McDaniels, Gene 221
McDonald, Ian *328–9*
McDonald, Ralph 258
McDowell, Fred *48*, 49
McGarity, Lou 6
McGhee, Brownie 44, *46*
McGhee, Howard *22*
McGhee, Stick 44, *46*, 64
McGrath, Earl 295, 352, 361
McGrath, Mark 467, 512
McGraw, Tim 472
McLagan, Ian 317
McLemore, Leon 190
McPhatter, Clyde 62, 63, 65, 66–7, *71*, 73, *103*, *111*, 123
McRae, Carmen 142, 287, 419
McShann, Jay 331
McTell, Blind Willie *40*, 41, 64
Medlocke, Rickey 354
Meibach, Ina 371
Mellotones, The *see* Cardinals, The
Melvins, The *448*, 452
Memphis 158, 170, 190, 193
Memphis Underground: Mann, Herbie 224
Mendelsohn, John 388
Mensch, Peter 499
Mercer, Mabel 98, *99*, *417*, 419
Mercury Records 15, 41, 86, 499
Merit Distributors 168
'Mess Around': Charles, Ray 58
Messina, Jim 290
Meyer, Eugene 20
Mezzrow, Mezz *13*, 16
MGM 29
Midler, Bette 275, 302, *346*, *380*, *428, 429*
'Midnight Cannonball' 63
'Midnight Special Train': Turner, Joe 91
Mike + the Mechanics 402, *410*, 450
Milburn, Amos *35*
Miller, Mitch 15
Mingus, Charles 82, *83*, 84–5, 87, 137, *330*, 358–9, 418, 453

Minton's Playhouse, Harlem 22
'Miss You': The Rolling Stones 347
'Missing': Everything But The Girl 451, 464
Mitchell, Joni *237*, 260
Mitchell, Roscoe 421
Mizner, Wilson 63
Modern Jazz Quartet, The 50, 82, 84, 87, *115*, *296*, 416, 418, 423, 440
Moman, Chips 132, 149, 189
'Money Honey': The Drifters 62, 63, 66, 67, 122
Monk, Thelonious *22*, 86, *104*, 105, 420
Montgomery, Eurreal 'Little Brother' 49
Montgomery, John Michael 456, *470*
Montgomery, Wes 276
Montreux Jazz Festival 196, 221, 421, 496
Montrose, Jack 419
Moon, Keith 265
Moondog 482
Mooney, Joe *80*, 81, 419
Moonglow label 155
Moore, Johnny 124
Moore, Sam *170*, *413*
Moore, Will 276
Moraz, Patrick *272*
Morden, Marili *18 see* Ertegun, Marili
Morgenstern, Dan 85
Moroder, Giorgio 343
Morris, Doug *346*, 384, 386, *401*, *402*, 426, 428, 438, *443*, 450, 451, 452, 453, 499, 514
Morris, Joe 26, *36*, 58
Morrison, Mark 451, 491
Morton, Jelly Roll 8, 9, 10, 11, 12, 39, 96, 251
Mott The Hoople 293
Mottola, Tommy 295
Mountain 190
The Move Into Rock by Robert Christgau 290–3
Mr. Big *428*
'Mr. Bojangles': Walker, Jerry Jeff 231
'Mr. Pitiful': Redding, Otis 165
Mulligan, Gerry 286, 419
Murphy, Matt *372*
Muscle Shoals 189, 192–3, 230
Music Inn, Lenox 115, 136
'Mustang Sally': Pickett, Wilson 193
'My Girl': Redding, Otis 176
Myles, Alannah *434*

Nash, Graham 234–5, 246, *324*, *383*, 445
Nathan, Syd 21
National Press Club, Washington 12
National Records 22, 29, 56, 65
Nelson, Willie 279, 293, 456
Nesuhi Ertegun by John Lewis 423
The New Age of Atlantic 389
New Jersey Mass Choir, The 394
New York: 52nd Street *32*
Newborn, Phineas 11, 97, 420
Newman, David 'Fathead' 161, 224, 278, 420
Nice, The 212

Nicholas, Albert 8
Nicks, Stevie 384, *403*, *425*, 444, 450
Nick's Jazz Club, New York 8
'Nights On Broadway': The Bee Gees 304
Nitzsche, Jack *168*, 234, 388
Nix, Don *130*
Nobs, Claude 196, 330, 496
Noone, Jimmie 18–19, 418
Nugetre 395

Oakley, Berry *241*
Oates, John 295
O'Connor, Sinéad 453, 506
'Oh Me, Oh My': Lulu 230
'Ohio': Young, Neil 246
Oldfield, Mike 388
Oldham, Spooner 189
Olympia, Paris 200
'On Broadway': The Drifters 147
One In A Million: Aaliyah 451
'One Mint Julep': The Clovers 54
O'Neill, Paul 482
'Only In My Dreams': Gibson, Debbie 408
Orlein, Norman 89
Ory, Kid 18, 84, 418
Osbourne, Ozzy 397
Ostin, Mo 168, 290
'Out On The Tiles': Led Zeppelin 262
'Owner Of A Lonely Heart': Yes 391, 401

Pacific Jazz 25
Page, Jimmy 219, 262–3, *283*, *284*, 292, *314*, 315, *346*, 368, 395, 399, *455*, 510
Pallenberg, Anita *264*
Palmer, Bruce *183*
Palmer, Carl 256, *332*, 390
Panassie, Hugues 16
Paris, Jackie 419
Parker, Charlie *17*, 105, 137, 141
Parker, Colonel 70
Parr, John 402
Pass, Joe 287
Passions Of A Man: Mingus, Charles 453
'Patches': Carter, Clarence 193, 244
Patti LaBelle & the Bluebelles *194*
Paul, Les 113
Pavarotti, Luciano *454*, 494–5
Payne, Cecil 58
Payne, Cleo 6
Peacock Club, Atlanta 79
Peacock Records 21
Pearcy, Stephen 396
Pearls, The 132
Peart, Neil *486*
Peer, Ralph 290
Pelé (soccer player) 233, *346*
Pena, Ralph 419
Pengilly, Kirk *406*

Penn, Dan 188–9, *189*
'People Got To Be Free': Rascals, The 210
Pepper, Art 64
Peppermint Lounge 138
Perlitch, Michael 388
Persuaders, The *267*
Pet Shop Boys 451
Peterson, Oscar 31
Petrillo, Caesar 25
Pettiford, Oscar *22*
Peyroux, Madeleine 483
Phair, Liz 445
Phases And Stages: Nelson, Willie 279
Phillips, (Little) Esther 61, 161, *202*, 203, *320*
Phillips, Sam 70, 122
Phreek 342
'Pick Up The Pieces': Average White Band 298, 341
Pickett, Wilson 167, 174, 182, 190, 192, 238–9, *266*, *412*
Pictures At Eleven: Plant, Robert 391
Pigeons, The (Vanilla Fudge) 218
Pinetoppers, The 149
Pinkney, Bill 63, 67
Pithecanthropus Erectus: Mingus, Charles 84–5, 87
Plant, Robert 218, 219, 262–3, *283*, *284*, 290, 292, *314*, 368, 385, 391, 395, 411, 451, 455, 510
Plaster Casters 284
Poco 234, 290
Poe 475
Poitier, Sidney 28
Poll Cats, The 26, 64
Polydor 219, 292
Pomus, Doc 26, *39*, 57, 124, 127
Ponty, Jean-Luc 320, *356*, 403, 421
Porter, Cole 64, 420
Porter, David 156, 177, 192
Powell, Ginnie 15
Powell, Roger 388
Prager, Bud *375*
Prater, Dave *170*
'Precious Lord': Franklin, Aretha 255
Presley, Elvis 65, 70, 123, 158, 190
Prestige Records 86, 418
Price, Lloyd 158
The Principle Of Movements: Plant, Robert 391
Prine, John 270, 290, 293, 389
Prysock, Red *22*, 26
Psychoderelict: Townshend, Pete 447
Purdie, Bernard 179

Quad City DJs 451, *481*
Quality Music Shop 21, 26
Quality Radio Repair Shop 21
Quality Records 22
'Queen Of My Soul': Average White Band 336
'Queen Of The Hop': Darin, Bobby 112, 113, 125

Rabin, Trevor *401*

Radio 1 (BBC) 176
Radio London 176
Raeburn, Boyd 15, *418*
Raeletts, The *118,* 125
Ragovoy, Jerry 160
'Rainbow Mist': Hawkins, Coleman 21
Rainbow Music Store 21
Rainey, Chuck 179
Rainey, Ma 93
Ralphs, Mick *318, 352*
Ransome, Hank 388, 389
Ransome, John 388
Rascals, The 210, 291, *413*
Ratt 391, 396, 450
Ravens, The 22, 67
RCA 21, 29, 41, 70, 190, 295
Ready, Steady, Go (TV show) 171
Rebennack, Mac 293 *see* Dr John
Red: King Crimson 293
Redbone, Leon *382*
Redding, Otis *148,* 149, 165, *170,* 171, 176, 190, 192, 193, 197, 202, 203, 453
Reed, Samuel *350*
Reich, Howard 87
Reid, Clarence 267
R.E.M. 389
Rene, Otis and Leon 21
Reprise Records 290
'Respect': Franklin, Aretha 193, 204
Rhino Records 428, 453
Rhone, Sylvia 428, 432, 450, 451
Rice, Sir Mack *195*
Rich, Buddy 42
Richards, Keith 264–5, 303, 348–9, *361,* 389, *392, 393*
Righteous Brothers, The 155, 168
Riley, Billy Lee 191
Rimes, LeAnn 470, 471, 504
'Riot In Cell Block No. 9': The Robins 100
Roach, Max 136, 185, 420
Robbins, Jerome 329, 391
Robertson, B.A. 402
Robin S 451, 491
Robins, The 100, 124
Robinson, Bobby 70, *71*
Rock, Kid 451, 503
Rock, The Move Into by Robert Christgau 290–3
'Rock The Boat': Hues Corporation 340
'Rock Your Baby': McCrae, George 340
Rockin' Highlanders, The *44*
Rock'n'Soul: Burke, Solomon 133
Rodgers, Nile 339, 343, 362, 364, 394, 395
Rodgers, Paul 318, 399
Rogers, Shorty 81, *418*
Rohatyn, Felix 232
Roland, Ed *465,* 504
'Roll 'Em Pete': Turner, Joe 65
Rolling Stones, The 182, 193, 206, 232, 264–5, 293, 305, 348–9, *374,* 389, 392
Rollins, Sonny 86
Romeo and Juliet 64, 75

Ronstadt, Linda 290
Rooney, Mickey 169
Roscoe 171
'The Rose Of The Rio Grande': The Harlemaires *25,* 29
Ross, Ronnie *418*
Ross, Steve 232–3, 236, 305, *346,* 375, 388
Rothschild, Baroness 105
Roulette Records 138
'Roundabout': Yes 272
Rowe, Dick 176
Rowles, Jimmy 287
Roxy Music 299, *312,* 367
Royal, Billy Joe *387*
'Rubberband Man': The Spinners 366
Rubell, Steve *347*
'Ruby Baby': The Drifters 78, 222
Rucker, Darius 449, *497*
Rudas, Tibor 454, 494–5
Rundgren, Todd 388
Rush 430, 451, 486, 499
Rush, Otis *199*
Rushing, Jimmy 56
Russell, Paul 87
Russell, Pee Wee 12
Russo, Aaron *275,* 302
Russo, Bill 420
Rutherford, Mike *288, 383,* 402, *403,* 410, 441

Sabit, Dr Vahdi *7,* 25, 64, 67, 113
'Sad Songs And Waltzes': Nelson, Willie 279
Safranski, Eddie 26, *27,* 184
Sahm, Doug 278
sale to Warner-Seven Arts 232, 291, 375, 388
Sam and Dave 166, *170, 177,* 190, 192
Sanson, Veronique 257
'Santa Fe Blues': Hunter, Ivory Joe 123
Santamaria, Mongo *252,* 253
Santo Domingo, Julio Mario *120,* 414, *500*
Satellite Record Shop 132
Satellite Records 190 *see also* Stax
Saturday Night Fever: The Bee Gees 343
Savatage *396*
'Save The Last Dance For Me': The Drifters 127
Scaggs, Boz 190, *213,* 290, 292
Schlesinger, Adam 452, 453
Schrager, Ian *347*
Scotch of St James' Club, London 182
Scott, Bon 323, 353, 376–7, 391
Scott, Bud *18*
Scott, Greg 388
Scott, Jimmy *226*
Scott, Shirley 224
Scratchie label 452
'Sea Of Love': The Honeydrippers 395
'Searchin'': Leiber, Jerry 110
Sebastian, John 234
The Second Taste 1954-1962 by Lenny Kaye 122–5
Sedaka, Neil 101
Segundo, Compay 502

Sensations, The *111*
Seven Mary Three 452, 464, 483
Sexton, Martin 492
'Sh-Boom': Chords, The 72, 122
'Shake, Rattle and Roll': Turner, Joe 65, 69, 122, 141
The Shape Of Jazz To Come: Coleman, Ornette 86, 87, 420
Shapiro, Ron 451, 452, *497,* 499
Sharrock, Sonny *225, 331*
Shaw, Billy 58
Sheik, Duncan 453, 474
'She's Gone': Hall and Oates 295
Short, Bobby 64, 98, *417,* 419
Shotgun Willie: Nelson, Willie 279
Shuman, Mort 124, 127
sideways pony, the (dance) 190
'Silent Running': Mike + the Mechanics 402
Sill, Lester *110, 128*
Silva, Raymond 225
Silverman, Max (Waxie Maxie) 20, 21, 22, 26, 42, 52, 75, *121*
Simeon, Omer 90, 420
Simon, Paul 190
'Since I Left You Baby': Hunter, Ivory Joe 123
'Since I've Been Loving You': Led Zeppelin 262
Sinclair, John 261
Singleton, Zutty 7, *18,* 19
Sir Douglas Quintet, The 278
Sister Sledge *338,* 343, *362,* 364
Six, Jack 286
'634-5789': Pickett, Wilson 192
Skid Row 426–7, 450
Slade, Chris 399
Slave 342, *344*
Sledge, Percy *172,* 173, 190, 192
Slim, Guitar 109
'Slip Away': Carter, Clarence 193
Small, Charlie 341
Small Faces, The 317
Smashing Pumpkins 452
Smith, Bessie 9, 10
Smith, Buster *140,* 141, 420
Smith, Fred 'Sonic' 261
Smith, Joe 290
Smith, Steve 9
Smith, Tony 378, *401*
'Smokey Joe's Cafe': The Robins 100
Snider, Dee 397
'So Long': Brown, Ruth 42, 43, 64; Little Miss Cornshucks 15
Sobule, Jill 453, 467
'Some Girls': The Rolling Stones 348–9
Some Girls: The Rolling Stones 391
Sommer, Tim 452, 453
Sonefeld, Jim 473
Sonny and Cher 168–9, 200, 290, 291, 375
'Sorghum Switch': Stone, Jesse 29, 65
Soul Clan, The 193
'Soul Finger': The Bar-Kays 194
The Soul in the Machine, 1986-1999 by Barney

Hoskins 450–3
'Soul Makossa' 340
'Soul Man': Sam and Dave 192
Soul Meeting: Soul Clan 193
Southern Soul Robert Gordon 190–3
'Spanish Harlem': King, Ben E. 125, 129, 193
Spark Records 100, 124
Sparkles, Zeno (Larry Cardarelli) 388
Speakeasy Club, London 212
Speciality Records 290
Spector, Phil 125, 129, 132, 147, 154–5, 168, 180, 203, 290, 496
Spinners, The *294*, 309, *337, 338*, 340–1, *362*, *366*, *413*
Spirit In The Dark: Franklin, Aretha 247
Spirituals to Swing (concert) 11, 65
Spivak, Arthur *499*
'Splish Splash': Darin, Bobby 112, 113, 125, 126
Springfield, Dusty 193, 209, 219, 290, 453
Squire, Chris *272, 326, 401*
Stacy, Jess *421*
'Stairway To Heaven': Led Zeppelin 284, 315
'Stand By Me': King, Ben E. 129
Starless And Bible Black: King Crimson 289
Starliters, The 138
Starr, Kay 66
Starr, Ringo 316
'Starvation Blues' 64
Stax 125, 130, 132, 149, 156, 190–3; on tour *170, 174*
'Steal Away': Hughes, Jimmy 192
Stein, Mark *218*
Stein, Seymour 290
Steinberg, Lewis 191
Stern, Mike *479*
Stevens, April 125, *152, 153*, 168, *441*
Stewart, Ian *265*
Stewart, Jim 130, 132, *158*, 190, 193, 290
Stewart, Rex *6, 7*
Sticky Fingers: The Rolling Stones 193, 293, 388
Stigwood, Robert 200, 206, 228, 290, 292, 295, *304*, 375
Stills, Chris 257, *501*
Stills, Stephen 183, 219, 234–5, 246, 257, 271, 290, 292, *383*
Stitt, Sonny 137, 420
Stoller, Mike 78, 100, 110, 124–5, 128, 147, 290, *496*
Stone, Brian 168, 182, 215, 290, *375*
Stone, Henry 290
Stone, Jesse 29, *30*, 42, 54, 57, 58, 59, 63, 64, 65, 67, 69, 74
Stone, Sly *236*
Stone Temple Pilots 438, 452, *469*
stories for children 64, 74
'Stranger On The Shore': Acker Bilk 125, 139
Stravinsky 251
Stuart, Hamish 298, 336
Studio 54 *347*
'Such A Night': McPhatter, Clyde 66
Sugar Ray 452, 467, 512
Summer, Donna 343
Sun Records 70, 122, 190, 191, 290

Supernatural Thing: King, Ben E. 308
Supernature: Cerrone 343
Swan Song label 316, 318
Sweet Inspirations, The 255, 341
'Sweet Soul Music': Conley, Arthur 176, 193
Swingin' Medallions 65
The Swinging Mr. Rogers: Shorty Rogers and His Giants 418, 419
Swingtime Records 21, 58
Symphony Sid 28
Syms, Sylvia *16*

'Take A Letter Maria': Greaves, R.B. 193, 231
'Tales Of Brave Ulysses': Cream 292
'Tangerine': Led Zeppelin 262
Tangerine Dream *387*
Tather, M.S. *89*
Taylor, Billy *16*
Taylor, Danny 'Rum Joe' 103
Taylor, Johnnie *195*
Taylor, Livingstone *225*
Taylor, Mick *264*
Taylor, Sam 'The Man' 50, *51*, 59, 64, 67
Tea Roller's Rub 10
Teach Your Children: Nash, Graham 235, 246
A Tear Fell: Hunter, Ivory Joe 79
Teardrops From My Eyes: Brown, Ruth 42
Tempo, Nino 125, 152–3, 168, 189, *441*
Tennant, Neil 451
Terry, Sonny 44
Tex, Joe 163, *163*, 175
That Old Black Magic: Grimes, Tony 26
That's The Way: Led Zeppelin 262
That's Where The Happy People Go: The Trammps 342
Thelonius Monk With Art Blakey And The Jazz Messengers 420
There Goes My Baby: The Drifters 125; Leiber, Jerry 110; Stoller, Mike 110, 129
These Arms Of Mine: Redding, Otis 192
This Is My Beloved 75
Thomas, Carla 125, 130–1, *173, 177*, 190–1, 203
Thomas, Rob 468, *507*
Thomas, Rufus 130, 151, 158, 190, 191, 192, *412*
Thompson, Dennis 261
Thompson, Sir Charles *26*
Thorn, Tracey *464, 476*
Thornley, Ian 486
Thrasher, Andrew 'Bubba' 63, 67
Thrasher, Gerhart 63, 67
3614 Jackson Highway: Cher 230
Three Tenors, The 454; 1998 World Cup concert 494–5
'Tighten Up': Archie Bell & The Drells 214
Till, John 254
Tillman, Floyd 123
Timbaland 451, *480*
Time Warner 233, 496 *see also* Warner Communications

Times Square 52
Timmons, Bobby 419
To Sir With Love: Lulu 230
Tommy: The Who 370, 371
Tones For Joan's Bones: Corea, Chick 286
Toombs, Rudy 26, 42, 52, 54
Tormé, Mel 139, 419
Tosh, Peter 360
Townshend, Pete 317, 370–1, 391, 405, 447, 450–1
Tragically Hip, The 452
Trakin, Roy 451
Trammps, The *310*, 342, *344*
Trans-Siberian Orchestra 483
Travolta, John 292
Treadwell, George 110, 127, 203
'The Treasure Of Love': McPhatter, Clyde 123
Tristano, Lennie 81, 86, 94, 419
Trotman, Lloyd 59, 64
Troy, Doris *150*
Truman, Harry 20
'Truth Is Fallen': Brubeck, Dave 286
Tubular Bells: Oldfield, Mike 388
Turner, Ike 266
Turner, Joe 11, 12, 22, 56–7, 63, 64–5, *68*, 69, *89*, 91, *91*
Turner, Tina 266
Turner, Titus 163
Turpin, Will *465*
Turrentine, Stanley 224
'Tweedlee Dee': Baker, LaVern 93, 123
25th Anniversary of Atlantic 273
twist, the (dance) 138
'Twist And Shout' 132
Twist With Bobby Darin 138
Twisted Sister 391, 397
234 West 56th Street 75, 89, 118
Tyner, Rob 261

UCLA 77; jazz course at 84
Ulvaeus, Bjorn 303, 365
Umar, Leyla 20
'Under The Boardwalk': The Drifters 160
Union Restaurant, New York 11
'Up Jumped Spring': Hubbard, Freddie 185, 420
Upstairs Downstairs Club 275
'Urgent': Foreigner 391
USS Missouri 20
Uterano, Sal *346*
Utley, Mike 254
Utopia 388

Vagrants, The 218
Vanda, Harry 323
Vanilla Fudge 190, 218, 290
Vaughan, Sarah 37, 64, 86, *110*
Vee-Jay Records 21, 290
Velvet Underground 249, 290, 292
Ventura, Charlie 184

Virgin Records 388
Vogel, Sheldon 375, 514
von Haselberg, Martin *346*
Vreeland, Diana 169

Wailey, Wade 19
Wainwright III, Louden 270, 290, 293, 389
'Waiting For A Girl Like You': Foreigner 329
Wakeman, Rick *326*
Wakschall, Fran 52, 74–5, 236, 283, *375, 428*
Walden, Phil 171, 176, 239, 240, 290
Walker, Jerry Jeff 231
Walker, Johnny 171
Walker, 'Jumbo' Jack 28, *29*
Walker, T-Bone *106*
'Walkin' The Dog': Thomas, Rufus 158, 192, 200
Wallace, Sippie 392
Waller, Fats 9, 87, 485
Wallington, George 420
Walls, Harry Van 'Piano Man' 54, 57, 59, 69
Ward, Clara 189, 269
Warhol, Andy *169*
Warner Brothers 168, 233, 234, 389
Warner Communications (Time Warner) 233, 305, 388
Warner Music International 233
Warner-Reprise 290
Warner-Seven Arts 193, 232, 236, 291, 388; sale to 232, 291, 375, 388
Washington, Dinah 11, 28, 61, 66, 86
Washington, Sister Ernestine 22
'Watcha Gonna Do': McPhatter, Clyde 62
Waters, Ethel 28
Waters, Muddy 39
Watt, Ben 464, 476
Watts, Charlie *264, 265, 349, 374, 392*
Waxie Maxie *see* Silverman, Max
WBLS radio 340
'We Are Family': Sister Sledge 343, 364
We Can't Dance: Genesis 441
WEA International 87, 233, 330, 423, 454, 499
Webb, Chick 7
Webb, Jimmy 324
Weber, Bruce 439
'Weekend': Phreek 342
Weiland, Scott 438, 469, 488
Weill, Kurt 125, 126
Wein, George 139
Weis, Danny 215
Weiss, Steve 219
Welles, Orson 18–19
Wells, Junior 277
Wells, Mary 179
Wenner, Jann *408*
'We're Not Gonna Take It': Twisted Sister 397
Wesley, Fred 294
Wess, Frank 418
Wess, Richard 126
West Coast Wailers 418
Weston, Randy 54

Wetton, John 289
Wexler, Jerry (Partner in Atlantic) 64–7, 73, *89, 91,* 121, *153, 162,* 173, *188, 189, 254,* 293, *298,* 450, 453, 514; on Acker Bilk 139; on The Allman Brothers 240; on Aretha Franklin 188, 247, 255, 334; on Atlantic Records 62–3, 113, 124, 232, 290–3, 301; on black music 70; on Delaney and Bonnie 242; on The Dixie Flyers 254; on Doug Sahm 278; on The Drifters 160; on Dusty Springfield 209; on Hank Crawford 143; on 'Honey Love' 73; on Jerry Jeff Walker 231; and LaVerne Baker 123; on Miami 230; on Otis Redding 197; on Ray Charles 79, 85–6; on 'Sh-boom' 72; Stax 130, 132, 191; on 'the jerk' 167; on 'There Goes My Baby' 110; on Willie Nelson 279
WGST radio studio 79
'What Are You Doing With The Rest Of Your Life?': McRae, Carmen 287
'What'd I Say': Charles, Ray 58, 118, 125
'Wheel of Fortune': The Cardinals 55, 66
Wheels Of Fire: Cream 292
'When A Man Loves A Woman': Sledge, Percy 173, 192
'When Something Is Wrong With My Baby': Sam and Dave 192
'When The Swallows Come Back To Capistrano': The Dominoes 67
'Where Is The Love?': Flack, Roberta and Hathaway, Donny 258
'Whiskey River': Nelson, Willie 279
White, Alan *272, 326, 401*
White, Barry 340
White, Jack 386
White, Lenny *331*
White, Ted *188,* 247
'White Christmas': McPhatter, Clyde 66, 67
White City: Townshend, Pete 405
White Lion *427*
'White Room': Cream 292
Whitlock, Bobby 243
Who, The 182, 265, 290, 317, 370, 399
'Whole Lotta Rosie': AC/DC 323
Wickham, Vicky 171
Wilkins, Ernie 86
Williams, Buster 130
Williams, Cootie 4, 127
Williams, John Gary 156
Williams, Louise 188
Williams, Mayo 44
Williams, Victoria 501
Willie and Ray 28
Willie Bryant Band *28*
Willis, Chuck *92, 93,* 114, 123
Wills, Rick 317, *379*
Wilson, Buster *18*
Wilson, Norro 456
Wilson, Teddy *7,* 10
Winger *427*
Winwood, Stevie 227
Witherspoon, Jimmy 90, 420

Wolf, Peter 313
Womack, Bobby 193
Wood, Ronnie 317, *349, 392*
Woods, Noreen 251, 268, 349, 500
Woods, Phil 420
Woods, Randy 21
Woodstock Festival 236
Woody Herman Orchestra 75, 251
WOR studios 26
Works Volume 1: Emerson, Lake & Palmer 332
Wright, Betty 267
Wyman, Bill *264, 392*

Yaged, Sol 127
Yalman, Ahmet Emin 7
Yancey, Jimmy and Estelle (Mama) *48,* 49
Yes 212, 272, *301,* 326, 389, 391, 401
Yetnikoff, Walter *346*
'You Better Move On': Alexander, Arthur 192
'You Keep Me Hangin' On': Vanilla Fudge 218
Young, Angus 323, 353, 376–7, 404, 410
Young, Earl 342
Young, Lester *7, 17*
Young, Neil 183, 219, 234, 246, 290, 390
Young, Paul *402*
Young Rascals, The 180
Young Tuxedo Brass Band 420

Zagreb Jazz Quartet 418
Zappa, Frank 388
Zawinul, Joe 225, 421
Zebra 387

Timeline

1947 **Ahmet Ertegun** and **Herb Abramson** found Atlantic Records in September 1947 with a $10,000 loan from Dr. Vahdi Sabit, Ertegun's dentist. Atlantic is officially incorporated in October 1947. Label founders Ahmet Ertegun and Herb Abramson record feverishly through the final months of 1947 creating a stockpile of recordings to be released through 1948 before the proposed recording ban by the American Federation of Musicians scheduled for 1st January 1948. The first master recording by Atlantic Records is **The Harlemaires**' 'Rose Of The Rio Grande'. Other recordings in this year include further tracks by The Harlemaires, 'If You Mean What You Say', 'Oo Dot En Pow' and 'Pretty Eyes', as well as **Boyd Raeburn** and his Orchestra's 'How High The Moon', 'The Lady Is A Tramp' and 'St. Louis Blues'.

1948 **Eddie Safranski**, double bassist with Stan Kenton's big band, records for Atlantic as leader in December, 1947. Atlantic's first release in 1948 is Safranski's 'Sa Frantic' backed with 'Base Mood'. He also releases 'Turmoil' backed with 'Jumpin' For Jane'. Atlantic's other early releases in this year are by **Joe Morris**, **Lloyd 'Tiny' Grimes**, and **Melrose Colbert**. Atlantic releases Joe Morris' 'Lowe Groovin'' in March featuring Johnny Griffin on tenor sax. Morris is a trumpet-playing bandleader/vocalist from Alabama who is a prime force in Atlantic's early days. 'Lowe Groovin'' becomes the theme song for Jackson Lowe, a Washington DJ, and according to sources at that time it "was a new sound, not fitting into any jazz, bop or race categories and represented the first step toward an easily identifiable R&B sound". 'The Applejack', featuring Philly Joe Jones on drums, is also released by Morris in 1948. Singer/guitarist Lloyd 'Tiny' Grimes records 'Annie Laurie' and 'Midnight Special' in Cleveland in August. The group on this session becomes the core of the kilt-adorned Rockin' Highlanders. Produced by Ahmet, 'Midnight Special' reaches #12 on the *Billboard* Juke Box chart in November 1948. Vocalist, Melrose Colbert, releases 'Blues In The Dark' backed with 'Heart And Soul' on Atlantic. In December, **Frank Culley** – who pioneered the school of 'hard-honking' R&B sax solos – is one of the first artists to be signed to Atlantic.

1949 In January, **Frank Culley**, accompanied by **Harry Van 'Piano Man' Walls** and his Little Blues Band, records 'Floor Show', which he adopts as part of his stage name. Culley and his band, with Van Walls on piano, records 'Rhumboogie Jive' in September. 'Coleslaw', written by Atlantic's legendary arranger and musical director **Jesse Stone**, provides a showcase for Frank Culley's signature 'honking' tenor sax style that becomes an integral part of rock'n'roll. It hits the charts in May 1949, making it up to #12 on the Best Sellers in Stores and #11 on the Juke Box charts. Based on its success, Culley changes his middle name from 'Floor Show' to 'Coleslaw'. In April, Atlantic scores its first major hit with **Granville 'Stick' McGhee**'s 'Drinkin' Wine Spo-Dee-O-Dee', which goes to #2 Juke Box and #26 Pop. The record enters the Best Sellers chart on 16th April and stays for 23 weeks. 'Tall Pretty Woman' is recorded at the same session on St. Valentine's Day and features a piano solo by 'Big Chief' Ellis.

Vocalist **Ruth Brown** is taken to the Apex Studio where Ahmet and Herb Abramson are cutting a session which includes 'After Hours' with R&B pianist **Amos Milburn**. She sings 'Rain Is A Bring Down' and this leads to a test recording which takes place at the end of an **Eddie Condon** session at the WOR Studio on May 25th. Featured is Condon's band, which consists of Bobby Hackett, Will Bradley, 'Peanuts' Hucko, Joe Bushkin and Big Sid Catlett. Brown records 'So Long' (written by bandleader Russ Morgan in 1940), at this session and the song peaks at #4 on the R&B chart during a 9-week run. **Texas Johnny Brown**, a sideman with Amos Milburn, records a session with Atlantic in New York on April 6th. The session produces 'There Goes The Blues' and 'The Blues Rock', with Amos Milburn on piano. **Joe Morris** records 'Beans And Corn Bread' in May. It sells 70,000 copies by December. Ahmet and Herb Abramson record jazz pianist **Erroll Garner** in a series of sessions between 1949 and 1950. He is accompanied variously by Leonard Gaskin or John Simmons on bass and Charlie Smith or Harold Wing on drums. Originally from Oklahoma, then New Orleans, **The Delta Rhythm Boys** recordings for Atlantic include 'Don't Ask Me Why', 'Sweetheart of Mine' and 'If You See Tears In My Eyes', as well as later providing the backing for various Ruth Brown tracks including, 'I'll Come Back Someday', 'Why' and 'Sentimental Journey'. **Vernon Duke** writes the score for Atlantic's first 10-inch disc, *This Is My Beloved*, based on a popular poem of the time narrated by the actor, John Dall.

Professor Longhair, a.k.a. Henry Roeland Byrd, records 'Mardi Gras In New Orleans' in October. Produced by Ahmet and Herb Abramson during a long session at J&M Studios, the record is released in January. Bluesman **Blind Willie McTell** records under a variety of names for different labels. 'Barrelhouse Sammy The Country Boy' is one of the 15 tracks he records in Atlanta with Ahmet and Herb Abramson, eventually released in January 1950. These tracks are later released as an LP entitled *Atlanta Twelve String*.

1950 **Ruth Brown** records the Rudy Toombs composition 'Teardrops From My Eyes', her first major hit, which reaches #1 R&B within seven weeks of its October release. It stays on the charts for 11 weeks, the Best Seller chart for 25 and the Juke Box chart for 19. In 1950, Brown also records 'I'll Get Along Somehow' and 'I'll Wait For You' (#3 R&B).

The talented pianist **Joe Bushkin** records *I Love A Piano*, one of Atlantic's first 10-inch discs. **Harry Van Walls** records Joe Turner's 'Chains Of Love' in late February at Apex Studios. An exceptional blues player, Walls' instantly recognizable style is distinguished by his frenetic pounding of keys in the upper register. Walls records with Frank Culley, Brownie and Stick McGhee, The Clovers and Joe Turner. A true eccentric, Walls often showed up for sessions dressed in a Sherlock Holmes outfit complete with cape, deerstalker cap and calabash pipe.

Al Hibbler, the blind vocalist whose style combined jazz, pop and R&B, worked with Jay McShann and Duke Ellington before recording for Atlantic. One of his cuts is a smooth, stylish rethink of 'Danny Boy' with bandleader Billy Kyle which goes to #9 on the R&B charts. **Joe Morris** records 'Anytime, Anyplace, Anywhere' with Little Laurie Tate on vocals. Fuelled by Tate's plaintive, high-pitched style, the song simultaneously charts on the R&B, Most Played On Juke Boxes and Best Seller In Stores charts in October, staying there for 22 weeks and peaking at #1 R&B. A leading R&B sax stylist, **Sam 'The Man' Taylor** is featured on many tracks for Atlantic. His muscular tenor can be heard later on Big Joe Turner's immortal 'Shake, Rattle And Roll', as well as backing The Drifters and LaVern Baker.

1951 On January 1st, Atlantic announces it will be pressing records in the new 45 rpm format. Introduced by RCA-Victor in 1949, the 45 represents a more compact, efficient and better-sounding alternative to its predecessor, the 78. For their first two 45s, Atlantic re-releases two 1950 hits, Joe Morris's 'Anytime, Anyplace, Anywhere' and 'Teardrops From My Eyes' by Ruth Brown. 'Jump Everybody Jump/Yeah, Yeah, Yeah' by **Joe Morris** is Atlantic's first new release on 45 rpm. Morris records 'Don't Take Your Love From Me', a #3 R&B hit also pressed in the new 45 format.

Considered the first modern R&B/rock'n'roll group on the label, **The Clovers** ultimately record 13 Top Ten R&B hits for Atlantic, most written and produced by Ahmet. Their 'Don't You Know I Love You', written under the pseudonym Nugetre (Ertegun spelled backwards), and featuring Frank Culley on tenor sax and Randy Weston on piano, crests at #1 on the R&B chart in September. 'Fool, Fool, Fool' stays on the R&B charts for 22 weeks, six of them at #1. In December, they cut 'One Mint Julep' with Harry Van Walls, which is released in 1952 and goes to #2 R&B. A seminally important vocal group that bridged the gap between popular black and white musical styles, The Clovers were an important foundation stone in Atlantic's early history.

Kansas blues legend **Big Joe Turner** debuts on Atlantic with 'Bump Miss Susie' accompanied by Harry Van Walls and his Orchestra. Turner's 'Chains Of Love' hits the R&B charts and goes to #2 during a 25-week run. Turner also records 'Oke-She-Moke-She-Pop' and 'The Chill Is On' later in the year. The latter spends eight weeks on the charts, peaking at #3.

Material recorded by boogie-woogie pianist **Jimmy Yancey** for Atlantic in July, shortly before his death, is released later in the LPs *Pure Blues* and *Yancey Special*. His wife, singer **'Mama' Estella Yancey**, appears on this last session of his. Songs recorded by Atlantic with **Fred McDowell** are released several years later on the LPs *Sounds Of The South*, *Roots Of The Blues*, and *Blues Roll On*. The great boogie-woogie pianist **Meade "Lux" Lewis** records, among other tracks, his classic 1927 song 'Honky Tonk Train Blues' for Atlantic, which is included on Lewis's *Boogie-Woogie Interpretations*. **Eurreal Wilford Montgomery** cuts several sides for Atlantic, including 'Vicksburg Blue', 'Bluebird', 'Shreveport', 'Farish Street' and 'Jive'.

Professor Longhair, records 'Hey Little Girl' for Atlantic in September. The fountainhead of New Orleans blues/R&B piano who influences countless players to come, the Professor stays too close to home for national success at this time.

One of the most popular blues vocalists of the forties, **Lil Green**'s career is tragically cut short at the age of 34 after a long illness. Her vibrant vocal style is in full form when she cuts 'Every Time' and Doc Pomus' 'I've Got The Feeling' for Atlantic.

The Cardinals, originally The Mellotones, are signed after an audition for Ahmet and Herb Abramson at the Super Music Record Store in Baltimore, the group's hometown. Sam Azrael, owner and manager of the store, had told Atlantic's founders about the group. The Cardinals are Ernie Warren (lead tenor), Meredith 'Prince' Brothers (tenor), Donald 'Jack' Johnson (baritone) and Leon 'Tree Top' Hardy (bass) and are later joined by Jack 'Sam' Aydelotte (tenor and guitar). Jesse Stone, who helps fashion the Cardinals' R&B sound, supervises their first session at Apex Studio in March. This produces the track 'Shouldn't I Know'(#7 R&B). The Cardinals go on to release two more Top Ten singles, a cover of Kay Starr's 'Wheel of Fortune' (#6 R&B) and 'The Door Is Still Open' (#4 R&B).

Willis 'Gator Tail' Jackson, a tenor sax player with a big sound who'd earned his nickname on a jazz hit of the same name with Cootie Williams, is brought to Atlantic by vocalist **Ruth Brown**, whom he later marries. He later solos on Brown's '5-10-15 Hours'. He also releases his own songs 'Wine-O-Wine' (with the Four Gators) and 'Gator's Groove' a year later.

Jazz pianist **Billy Taylor** records the *Piano Panorama* album featuring John Collins on guitar, Albert Hall on bass and Shadow Wilson on drums. Cabaret singer **Barbara Carroll** releases two Atlantic discs, *The Barbara Carroll Trio* and *Piano Panorama*, the latter with Joe Shulman (bass) and Herb Wasserman (drums).

1952 **Ray Charles** signs to Atlantic and releases 'The Midnight Hour' in September. Born in Georgia and raised in Florida, the gifted instrumentalist and singer comes from the Swing Time label and goes on to become a dominant creative force in R&B, jazz, country and virtually every modern genre.
Dizzy Gillespie, the trumpet virtuoso whose musical and visual style helped define modern jazz in the bop era, records four tracks for Atlantic when the company buys four of his masters from the French Blue Star label. Most of these tracks come out on the *Dizzy At Home And Abroad* album in 1957. Featured on the sessions are Don Byas on saxophone, Milt Jackson on vibes and piano and Percy Heath on bass. Herb Abramson supervises the New York sessions.

The Clovers release another R&B classic written by Ahmet Ertegun, 'Ting-A-Ling', in July. It charts for 17 weeks before going to #1, staying there for 14 weeks. This is The Clovers and Ahmet's third #1 record. R&B vocal group, **The Diamonds** (not to be confused with the white group of the same name), featuring Harold "Sonny" Wright, Ernest "Rocky" Ward, Daniel Stevens and Myles "Mousey" Hardy, cut three singles with Atlantic including 'A Beggar For Your Kisses'.

Rudy Toombs writes two hits for **Ruth Brown** in 1952. 'I Know' reaches #7 and '5-10-15 Hours' goes to #1 for seven weeks. **Odelle Turner** with Jessie Stone's Orchestra record 'Alarm Clock Boogie' with Harry Van Walls on piano.

Clarinettist **Wilbur De Paris** releases *Wilbur De Paris And His Rampart Street Ramblers*; *Wilbur De Paris, Vol. 2*; and *Marchin' and Swingin'*. Vocalist **Sylvia Syms**, not to be confused with the British actress of the same name, signs with Atlantic. Called the 'world's greatest saloon singer' by no less than Frank Sinatra, she releases *Songs By Sylvia Syms* and records more albums for Atlantic later in 1954.

1953 **Jerry Wexler**, former *Billboard* staffer and now a writer and aspiring producer joins Atlantic as a partner.
Ray Charles records the Memphis Curtis song 'It Should've Been Me' in May of 1953 with Sam 'The Man' Taylor (tenor sax), McHouston 'Mickey' Baker (guitar) and Connie Kay (drums). Arranged by Jesse Stone and produced by Ahmet and Herb Abramson, it reaches #5 R&B in 1954. Charles also records a song that marks a stylistic departure, 'Mess Around', written by Ahmet under the name Nugetre. He also records 'Don't You Know' at Radio Station WDSU in New Orleans which becomes a #10 R&B hit in 1954.

'Daddy, Daddy', written by Rudy Toombs for **Ruth Brown** reaches #3 R&B. 'Mama, He Treats Your Daughter Mean', by Herb Lance and Johnny Wallace, is released in mid-February and becomes Brown's biggest hit. It goes to #1 R&B three weeks later and stays at the top for five weeks. Ray Charles leads her backing band on the record. Ahmet writes the #3 R&B hit, 'Wild, Wild Young Men' for Brown. Bandleaders claim the tempo on this song is so fast that no vocalist can be understood at this speed, but Ruth Brown succeeds nonetheless. On the B-side, 'Mend Your Ways', she duets with herself in the first session where Atlantic employs the new recording technique pioneered by guitarist Les Paul called 'overdubbing', where vocal and instrumental tracks are recorded separately and mixed together later. Brown releases 'Oh What A Dream', a Chuck Willis song, on Valentine's Day which breaks into the R&B charts in August 1954 and stays at #1 for eight weeks.

Vocal powerhouse **LaVern Baker**, Chicago-born niece of the great blues singer Memphis Minnie, began her career in the forties performing as 'Little Miss Sharecropper'. Having a different style to Ruth Brown, Atlantic's other R&B 'diva', Baker is signed to Atlantic in 1953 and debuts with 'Soul On Fire'.

The virtuoso singer and performer, **Clyde McPhatter**, releases the solo single 'Seven Days', a #2 R&B and #44 Pop hit in June. **The Drifters** enjoy their first hit with 'Money Honey' featuring **Clyde McPhatter** as lead singer, Bill Pinkney (bass and tenor), Andrew Thrasher (tenor), Gerhart Thrasher (baritone) and Willie Ferbie (bass). It stays on the *Billboard* R&B chart for 21 weeks, 11 at #1. The B-side, 'The Way I Feel', is actually the first recording made by McPhatter and The Drifters. 'Such A Night', written by Lincoln Chase and featuring Sam 'The Man' Taylor on tenor, peaks at #2 R&B. That session also produces two more Jesse Stone songs, 'Bim Bam' (#7 R&B) and 'Don't Dog Me'. Bill

Pinkney takes over the bass from Willie Ferbie.

Atlantic releases **Big Joe Turner**'s classic 'Honey Hush' which reaches #1 after 12 weeks and stays there for eight more. **Charles Norris**, a regular session player for Atlantic, records 'Let Me Know'.

Sarah Vaughan releases four songs on Atlantic: 'It Might As Well Be Spring', 'You Go To My Head', 'I Can Make You Love Me' and 'I'm Scared'. One of the great cabaret vocalists, **Mabel Mercer** first records for the label in November 1951 and releases three classic 10-inch volumes, *Songs By Mabel Mercer*, in 1953. A collection of almost all her early fifties tracks, *The Art Of Mabel Mercer* is released over a decade later. Ahmet and Herb Abramson supervise this exceptional collection, which is engineered by Tom Dowd, with backing from Cy Coleman and other leading players. **Mae Barnes**, singer and former Ziegfeld Follies dancer, records *Fun With Mae Barnes*.

The Clovers, backed by Atlantic's house band, record 'Good Lovin'', a song by Danny Taylor, Jesse Stone, Leroy Kirkland and Ahmet, which charts for 18 weeks, peaking at #2 R&B.

Professor Longhair records classics like 'Tipitina', 'In The Night' and 'Ball The Wall' in 1953. Bluesman **John Lee Hooker** records material later released on the Atlantic albums *Don't Turn Me From Your Door* (1963) and *Detroit Special* (1972).

1954 **Big Joe Turner**'s timeless interpretation of **Jesse Stone**'s transcendent 'Shake, Rattle And Roll' charts for 27 weeks, peaking at #1 R&B. In 1955, the song is still selling well enough to make *Billboard*'s Most Played By DJs chart. Despite more successful covers by Bill Haley and Elvis Presley that followed the original, Turner's version is still credited as the foundation stone for rock'n'roll.

The Drifters record 'Honey Love', written by Clyde McPhatter and Jerry Wexler. The song is banned on several radio stations for "suggestive" lyrics, but still stays on the R&B chart for five months, spending eight weeks at #1. The same session also produces two songs made famous by Bing Crosby, 'The Bells Of St. Mary's' and 'White Christmas'. The latter becomes the second most popular version of the seasonal favourite after Crosby's. They also record 'What'cha Gonna Do', written by Ahmet, a #2 R&B hit and, later, 'Your Promise To Be Mine', with rare lead vocals by group member Gerhart Thrasher. The track is recorded by Jerry Wexler in New York with **Nesuhi Ertegun**, Ahmet's older brother, supervising the vocal overdubs in Los Angeles. **Clyde McPhatter** cuts his last session with The Drifters in October before being drafted into the Army.

Ray Charles produces the first of his 11 #1 R&B hits with 'I Got A Woman', recorded in November at WGST, Georgia Tech's radio station, and released in January of 1955. The propulsive track features Joe Bridgewater and Charles 'Clanky' Whitley (trumpets), Donald Wilkerson (tenor sax) and David 'Fathead' Newman (baritone sax). Arranged by Ray Charles, it is produced by Ahmet and Jerry Wexler. Other singles from the session include 'Come Back Baby' (#4 R&B) and 'Greenbacks' (#5 R&B), backed with 'Blackjack' (#8 R&B).

The Clovers get several Top Ten R&B hits in 1954. These include 'Lovey Dovey' written by Ahmet (#2 R&B), 'Little Mama' (#4 R&B), 'I've Got My Eyes On You' (#7 R&B), and the irresistible 'Your Cash Ain't Nothing But Trash' (#6 R&B).

Jerry Wexler, having coined the term 'Rhythm & Blues' whilst at *Billboard* magazine, now determines to call the newest departure in music 'Cat' music and Atlantic promptly starts a label under that name. Rock'n'roll is of course the phrase that catches on like wildfire throughout the US and the rest of the world. Singer/pianist **Floyd 'Mr. Magnificent' Dixon** records his best-known song, 'Hey Bartender', for Atlantic's Cat label. **The Chords**' seminal hit, 'Sh-Boom', is released on the Cat label in July. Sales are badly affected when a white cover version by the Crew Cuts comes out. Atlantic releases 'Mambo Baby', **Ruth Brown**'s fifth #1 R&B hit for the label. **LaVern Baker** records 'Tomorrow Night' with Sam 'The Man' Taylor on tenor sax.

Mabel Mercer Sings Cole Porter is recorded by **Mabel Mercer** at Atlantic's Studios on 56th St., with Cy Walter and Stan Freeman accompanying Mercer on twin simultaneous pianos.

1955 Atlantic offers Colonel Tom Parker $25,000 for singer **Elvis Presley**, but RCA-Victor eventually signs him for $45,000

Nesuhi Ertegun, having joined Atlantic, starts and continues to create the Atlantic jazz catalogue which, through his enlightened guidance, grows and evolves into one of the great jazz lines of all time. One of Atlantic's first jazz albums, *The Swinging Mr. Rogers*, features **Shorty Rogers And His Giants**, which include Jimmy Giuffre, Shelly Manne and Pete Jolly. Rogers, an accomplished musician, composer, arranger and bandleader, eventually becomes Artistic Director for the label. Rogers also releases *Way Up There*, *Martians, Stay Home!*, *Martians, Come Back!* and *Rogers In Stereo* in 1955. Other jazz releases in this year also include, **Bill Russo**'s ballet *The World of Alcina* and **Wilbur De Paris**' *New New Orleans Jazz*. The gifted pianist **Lennie Tristano**, along with saxophonists **Lee Konitz** (alto) and **Warne Marsh** (tenor), create an important body of work for Atlantic in 1955. Their impressive output includes *Lennie Tristano*, *The Lennie Tristano Quartet* (featuring Konitz, Gene Rainey and Art Taylor), *The New Tristano*, *Requiem* (featuring Tristano with Konitz and Art Taylor), *Inside Hi-Fi* by Lee Konitz, *Lee Konitz With Warne Marsh* (featuring Oscar Pettiford and Kenny Clarke), *Worthwhile Konitz* and *The Real Lee Konitz*. **Bobby Short**, a unique vocal stylist in the cabaret tradition, records *Songs By Bobby Short* in 1955, as well as another LP, *Bobby Short*, and goes on to enjoy a long and successful career at Atlantic spanning 40 years.

Ray Charles records the single 'A Fool For You' with his band at radio station WMAQ in Miami in April, 1955. As usual, the song is arranged by Charles and produced by Ahmet and Jerry Wexler. 'A Fool For You' goes to #1 R&B. 'This Little Girl Of Mine', based on a gospel song, featuring Mary Ann Fisher and band members David 'Fathead' Newman and Donald Wilkerson on backing vocals, is recorded during the same session and climbs to #9 R&B.

Put together by **Jesse Stone** a year earlier, **The Cookies** record 'In Paradise', which peaks at #9 R&B. The vocal group features variously Marjorie 'Margie' Hendrix, Ethel 'Earl-Jean' McRea, Dorothy Jones, Pat Lyles and Margaret Ross in the line-up. Big Joe Turner, Chuck Willis and Ray Charles use them as backing on some of their recordings. Charles eventually renames the group The Raeletts and makes them a fixture in his music.

LaVern Baker releases 'Tweedlee Dee' which is hit-bound on the R&B chart but soon has to contend with a white Pop cover version by **Georgia Gibbs**. Baker's record enters the R&B chart in January, stays there for 14 weeks and eventually goes to #4 and #14 Pop. Gibbs' version lingers on the Pop charts for 19 weeks and reaches #2 Pop. Baker records 'Play It Fair' in mid-July with Sam 'The Man' Taylor on tenor (#2 R&B). One of the most popular female R&B vocalists, LaVern Baker also appears in two Alan Freed movies, *Rock, Rock, Rock* and *Mr. Rock & Roll*, the latter also featuring fellow Atlantic artist **Clyde McPhatter**. She also stars in a popular R&B revue on *The Ed Sullivan Show*.

Following Clyde McPhatter's departure into the Army, **The Drifters** try out several new lead singers including David Baughan and Bobby Hendricks. The group records 'Adorable' in Los Angeles with Johnny Moore on lead and Nesuhi Ertegun producing. A #1 R&B hit, the song's B-side is entitled 'Steamboat' (#5 R&B), which features a rare lead by group member Bill Pinkney. **Ruth Brown**'s 'I Can See Everybody's Baby' reaches #7 on the Disc Jockey and Juke Box charts and 'As Long As I'm Moving' goes to #4 on the Best Sellers charts. 'It's Love Baby (24 Hours A Day)' battles it out on the R&B charts with two other covers. At this point, Ahmet decides to record Ruth and **Clyde McPhatter** together while McPhatter is on leave from the Army. A uniformed McPhatter joins Brown at the Brooklyn Paramount for three days on the *Dr. Jive Show*. The first result of their studio collaboration, 'Love Has Joined Us Together', goes to #8 on the Disc Jockey chart. Penned by **Big Joe Turner** and Jesse Stone, Turner's 'Flip, Flop, Fly' hits the R&B chart in March, climbing to #2. Johnnie Ray cuts a cover version. Turner also records 'Chicken And The Hawk' by future songwriting legends Jerry Leiber and Mike Stoller later that year. **The Clovers** record the classic 'Devil or Angel', which goes to #3 R&B. The record marks their 18th appearance on the charts and includes 'Hey, Doll Baby' on the flip side.

1956 Atlantic sign a vocal group on the West Coast formerly called **The Robins**. They quickly go on to become sensationally successful as **The Coasters**. As well as the group, Atlantic also sign their songwriters, arrangers and producers **Jerry Leiber** and **Mike Stoller**. It's the first time that an independent production team has been signed by a record label. The phenomenally talented duo go on to become one of the great songwriting and production teams of all time. **The Coasters** record 'Down In Mexico', a typically erudite short story by Leiber and Stoller that goes to #8 R&B. The group includes original members Carl Gardner (lead tenor) and Bobby Nunn (bass) from The Robins, plus Leon Hughes (second tenor), Billy Guy (baritone) and Adolph Jacobs (guitar).

A cornerstone of the Atlantic jazz tradition, the **Modern Jazz Quartet** release their groundbreaking *Fontessa* in 1956. Later that year they record a live album, *Modern Jazz Quartet At The Music Inn, Volume One* with **Jimmy Giuffre**. Founded in 1950 by Philip and Stephanie Barber, the Music Inn at Lenox, Massachusetts, was more than a concert venue, it was a place where critics and musicians could discuss and develop blues and jazz. Two years later, MJQ release the live recording *Modern Jazz Quartet At The Music Inn, Volume Two* featuring **Sonny Rollins**. MJQ's gifted pianist, **John Lewis**, records *John Lewis Piano* and *Afternoon In Paris* with French guitarist and vocalist Sacha Distel. Another major force in the Atlantic jazz tradition, visionary bassist and composer **Charles Mingus** records the album *Pithecanthropus Erectus*. The landmark recording also features Jackie McLean (alto), J.R. Monterose (tenor), Willie Johns (drums) and Mal Waldron (piano).

Ray Charles climbs to #1 on *Billboard*'s R&B chart with his soulful single, 'Drown In My Own Tears'. 'Hallelujah! I Love Her So', recorded at the same session, reaches #5 R&B. 'Lonely Avenue', written by the legendary Jerome 'Doc' Pomus and recorded in May, goes to #6 R&B. The classic track features Ray Charles sidemen Joe Bridgewater and John Hunt (trumpets), David 'Fathead' Newman (tenor sax), Emmett Dennis (baritone sax), Roosevelt 'Whiskey' Sheffield (bass), William Peeples (drums) and The Cookies on backing vocals. Arranged by Charles and produced by Ahmet and Jerry Wexler, 'Lonely Avenue' stays at the top of the R&B chart for four weeks. Atlantic also releases *The Great Ray Charles*. Mississippi-born **Eddie 'Guitar Slim' Jones**, a disciple of the great bluesmen Clarence 'Gatemouth' Brown and Albert Collins, debuts on Atlantic with 'Down Through The Years' in March. A born showman with a flamboyant guitar style, Jones went on to record 'It Hurts To Love Someone' and 'If I Had My Life To Live Over' on Atlantic.

Nesuhi Ertegun produces **The Drifters**' 'Ruby Baby', written by Leiber and Stoller and featuring Johnny Moore on lead. It reaches #10 on the R&B chart. In November, The Drifters record the Top Ten hit 'Fools Fall In Love', another Leiber and Stoller song, with Moore as lead vocalist which goes to #10 R&B in 1957. Other Drifters hits in 1956 include a reissue of their classic version of the chestnut 'White Christmas' (#12 R&B) and 'I Gotta Get Myself A Woman' backed with 'Soldier Of Fortune' (#11 R&B). **Big Joe Turner**'s *Boss Of The Blues* album features the legendary Roll 'Em Pete Johnson on piano, Joe Newman (trumpet), Frank Wess (tenor) and Walter Page (bass). Turner's single 'Corinne, Corrina' (#2 R&B) is his first to cross over to the Pop chart where it goes to #41. It stays on the R&B chart for ten weeks. Turner records 'Midnight Special Train', a composite of old blues lyrics put together by Ahmet and Jerry Wexler. **Chuck Willis** records 'It's Too Late' with The Cookies on backing vocals, his first chart hit for Atlantic (#3 R&B) in April. Known initially as the 'Sheik Of The Shake' not least because of the turban he wore, Willis goes on to record several major hits for Atlantic with his trademark plaintive style. **Ivory Joe Hunter** records 'Since I Met You Baby', which goes to #1 R&B and #12 Pop, helped by his performing the song on *The Ed Sullivan Show*. He also releases 'A Tear Fell' which goes to #15 R&B. **Jimmy Witherspoon** records *New Orleans Blues* with the Wilbur De Paris band featuring Omer Simeon on clarinet and Doc Cheatham and Sidney De Paris on trumpets. Tracks from the LP include 'In The Evening' and 'Trouble In Mind'. Wilbur De Paris also releases *At Symphony Hall* that year.

The Clovers cross over for the first time with 'Love, Love, Love', which charts in June and spends 13 weeks on the Pop, R&B and Juke Box charts (#4 R&B, #30 Pop). **The Sensations**, a vocal group from Philadelphia originally known as the Cavaliers, enjoy chart success with 'Yes Sir, That's My Baby' (#15 R&B) and 'Please Mr. Disc Jockey' (#13 R&B) on Atco. The new Atco subsidiary, is initially run by label co-founder Herb Abramson upon his return from the Army. **The Tibbs Brothers** record '(Wake Up) Miss Rip Van Winkle' and 'I'm Going Crazy' for Atco in May. **LaVern Baker**'s 'Tra La La', the B-side for the classic 'Jim Dandy' and part of the soundtrack of the movie *Rock, Rock, Rock* starring Tuesday Weld, is released in November. 'Jim Dandy' charts in mid-December and goes to #1 R&B and #17 Pop. Baker is voted Best Female Vocalist of 1956 by *Cashbox* magazine and also releases the album *LaVern*. **Ruth Brown**'s first Pop hit, 'Lucky Lips', written by Leiber and Stoller, is recorded in 1956 and released a year later when it goes to #6 R&B and #25 Pop. **Clyde McPhatter**'s first Atlantic solo recording since returning from the Army, 'Treasure of Love', becomes a #1 R&B hit and climbs to #16 on the Pop chart. McPhatter also has a hit with 'Without Love (There Is Nothing)', which charts at #6 on the R&B charts and #19 Pop. Ruth Brown and Clyde McPhatter's 'I Want To Do More', written by Leiber and Stoller becomes a #3 R&B hit.

Kansas City jazz vocalist **Chris Connor** releases her self-titled debut for Atlantic, with John Lewis and drummer Connie Kay in January. She follows this up with *A Jazz Date With Chris Connor*, featuring Mongo Santamaria and Al Cohn and produced by Nesuhi Ertegun. Other Connor albums in 1956 include: *He Loves Me, He Loves Me Not*; *Miss You So*; and *Chris Connor Sings The George Gershwin Almanac Of Song*. Multi-reed artist **Jimmy Giuffre** debuts on the label with *The Song Is You* and *The Jimmy Giuffre 3*, the latter with a multifaceted jazz trio featuring guitarist Jim Hall and either Ralph Pena or Jim Atlas on bass. Atlantic releases the critically acclaimed album *The Piano Artistry Of Phineas Newborn*, featuring the fluent young jazz artist **Phineas Newborn** accompanied by Oscar Pettiford on bass and Kenny Clarke on drums. *Midnight At Mabel Mercer's* is recorded in June by **Mabel Mercer** at the Atlantic studios with George Cory and Sam Hamilton (pianos) and Milt Hinton on bass. The record is arranged by Cory, engineered by Tom Dowd and produced by Nesuhi Ertegun. **Bobby Short** releases the album *Speaking Of Love*. Jazz singer, organist and accordionist **Joe Mooney** releases *Joe Mooney's Song*.

1957 The **Coasters**' 'Searchin'', one of Leiber and Stoller's most seamless collaborations, becomes a hit three weeks after its flip-side, 'Young Blood', qualifying as a double chartbuster. 'Searchin'' stays on the Pop chart for 26 weeks and goes to #3, also peaking at #1 R&B. 'Young Blood', written by Leiber, Stoller and Doc Pomus, stays in the Pop chart for 24 weeks, peaking at #8 and reaches #1 in the R&B charts. 'C.C. Rider', **Chuck Willis**'s first big hit, goes to #12 in the Pop charts and peaks at #3 R&B. The record inspires a dance craze called The Stroll, earning Willis the title "King Of The Stroll" along with other nicknames like "The Sheik Of The Shake". Later in the year he releases 'Betty and Dupree', which rides the Pop charts for 11 weeks, rising to #33 (#15 R&B). **Ivory Joe Hunter**'s 'Empty Arms' enters the R&B chart and goes to #2. It's quickly followed by 'Love's A Hurting Game' (#7 R&B) with the Ray Ellis Orchestra. Hunter's self-titled LP is also released in this year.

Ray Charles records, 'Ain't That Love', in November, 1956, which reaches #9 R&B in 1957. Featured on the track are Joe Bridgewater and John Hunt (trumpets), David 'Fathead' Newman (tenor), Emmett Dennis (baritone), Roosevelt 'Whiskey' Sheffield (bass), William Peeples (drums), Jerry Wexler (tambourine) and The Raeletts on backing vocals. As with many of his recordings, the song is arranged by Charles and produced by Ahmet Ertegun and Jerry Wexler. Ray records 'Swanee River Rock' later that year which reaches #14 on the R&B chart and #34 on the Pop chart. A self-titled album is also released in 1957. Texas bluesman **Aaron 'T-Bone' Walker** records 'Two Bones And A Pick' in December, as part of his 1956-57 Los Angeles sessions for Atlantic. The song features Walker's nephew R.S. Rankin and guitarist Barney Kessel. Walker laid the foundation for a distinctive blues guitar style incorporating more sophisticated jazz chord voices along with passionate and musical solos that have influenced countless musicians over the years.

Clyde McPhatter enjoys another #1 R&B hit with 'Long Lonely Nights' after battling it out with a cover by Lee Andrews & The Hearts. **Don Covay**, also known as 'Pretty Boy', records the single 'Bip Bop Bip' in March. Covay goes on to write and record several classics for Atlantic, most notably 'Chain Of Fools'. Covay is nicknamed 'Pretty Boy' by the great Little Richard, who together with his backup band, the Upsetters, collaborated with Covay on 'Bip Bop Bip'. Richard gives Atlantic the masters from that session. **Obie Young Jessie** records the Atco single 'Shuffle In The Gravel' in L.A. with Leiber and Stoller producing. The song comes from Jessie's experience growing up in Dallas where the dance floors were covered with sand and people 'shuffle danced'. This record has now become a highly prized collector's item. **The Bobbettes** immortalize their least favourite fifth grade teacher with the irresistible Top Ten hit, 'Mr. Lee'. The precocious group members range in age from 11 to 13. The song is a 'sleeper' which gets off to a slow start, also features a distinctive sax solo by Jesse Powell and charts for 27 weeks, peaking at #6 Pop and #1 R&B.

The Drifters lose two members when lead singer Johnny Moore and baritone Charlie Hughes are drafted. With dwindling hits and morale at an all time low, manager George Treadwell dissolves the group. But with many contractual obligations still to meet, he finds a group called **The Five Crowns** at the Apollo and renames them The Drifters with featured singer Benjamin Nelson, better known as **Ben E. King**. The group is assigned to Jerry Leiber and Mike Stoller.

The only Atlantic recording featuring these two great jazz artists, ***Thelonious Monk With Art Blakey And The Jazz Messengers***, is released in May. Besides Blakey on drums and Monk on piano, the album includes Bill Hardman (trumpet), Johnny Griffin (tenor sax) and Spanky De Brest (bass). **Charles Mingus** creates another definitive album, *The Clown,* which includes 'Haitian Fight Song'. The album features Jimmy Knepper on trombone, Shafi Hadi on alto and tenor and Charlie 'Dannie' Richmond on drums and percussion. Jean Shepherd narrates an improvised story based on the title track. The **Modern Jazz Quartet** release *One Never Knows* and *No Sun In Venice* (for a French film of the same name). Working with the Jimmy Giuffre 3 and the Beaux Arts String Quartet, the MJQ bridges jazz and classical music with the album *Third Stream Music*. Atlantic also releases *The Modern Jazz Quartet* featuring tracks such as 'Night In Tunisia' and 'Bags Groove'. The album *Plenty, Plenty Soul* combines two sessions of **Milt Jackson** playing with **Cannonball Adderley**, and features Horace Silver and Lucky Thompson. Jazz drummer **Max Roach**, a major force in the bop movement and beyond, releases his first Atlantic album, *Drummin' The Blues*. Jazz trombonist and bandleader **Wilbur De Paris** releases *New Orleans Blues* and *Plays Cole Porter*. **Bobby Short** releases the LPs *Sing Me A Song* and *Nobody Else But Me.*

1958 Ahmet takes the talented **Bobby Darin** in a fruitful new musical direction with 'Splish, Splash', which sells over 100,000 in less than a month of its release in July, 1958 (#3 Pop, #1 R&B). 'Queen Of The Hop' is also released this year, achieving gold sales (#3 Pop, #6 R&B). The supple ballad 'Beyond the Sea' is recorded in December (#6 Pop, #15 R&B), Ahmet, Nesuhi Ertegun and Jerry Wexler sharing production credits. The album *Bobby Darin* is also released this year.

Ray Charles enjoys more chart success in 1958 with 'Rockhouse Parts 1 & 2', which peaks at #14 R&B. Charles records the propulsive 'I'm Movin' On' in June, which goes to #11 R&B and #40 Pop. The seminal *Ray Charles At Newport*, a live recording of his first appearance at the Newport Jazz Festival is released in October. Charles's deeply soulful '(Night Time Is) The Right Time', recorded at Atlantic's studios in New York in late October and released in 1959, stays in the R&B charts for five months, reaching #5. The epic LP collaboration with Milt Jackson, *Soul Brothers*, is also released this year, as is *Yes, Indeed!* Ray Charles's sideman, **David 'Fathead' Newman**, releases his debut album as leader, *Fathead: Ray Charles Presents David Newman*. It features Newman on both tenor and alto and backing from Ray Charles on piano and **Hank 'Bennie' Crawford** on baritone, among others.

'Yakety Yak' becomes a #1 Pop and #1 R&B hit for **The Coasters**. The group goes on to record Leiber and Stoller's parental masterpiece 'Charlie Brown' in December with **King Curtis** on tenor sax. Released in 1959, the song stays at #2 on the Pop chart for three weeks and also goes to #2 R&B. The immortal hit single 'What Am I Living For?' recorded by **Chuck Willis** as a B-side for 'Hang Up My Rock and Roll Shoes' (#9 R&B) charts for 19 weeks, climbing to #1 R&B. Willis dies two months later in April. Hard-living blues guitarist **Eddie 'Guitar Slim' Jones** records the prophetically entitled single 'If I Had My Life To Live Over' as one of his last sessions for Atco. Thirty years later, all of the tracks recorded during these sessions are released on *The Atco Sessions*. Jones dies in 1959 aged 32.

Clyde McPhatter gets a #1 R&B hit with his seductive 'A Lover's Question' written by Brook Benton and Jimmy Williams. The song also goes to #6 on *Billboard*'s Pop chart. McPhatter also has a #3 hit with 'Come What May'. The fabulous **LaVern Baker** cuts her biggest hit, the powerhouse 'I Cried A Tear', in New York with **King Curtis** on tenor saxophone. It climbs to #6 on the Pop chart and #2 R&B. Atlantic also releases the album *LaVern Baker Sings Bessie Smith* featuring arrangements by Ernie Wilkins, Phil Moore and Nat Pierce, and musicians Buck Clayton, Vic Dickenson and Wendell Marshall. **Ruth Brown**'s last big hit for Atlantic, 'This Little Girl's Gone Rockin'', written by Bobby Darin and featuring another powerful sax solo by **King Curtis**, reaches #7 on the R&B chart and #24 Pop. She releases two more recordings for Atlantic, Brook Benton's 'I Don't Know' and Chuck Willis's 'Don't Deceive Me'.

Ivory Joe Hunter records the singles 'Yes I Want You' and 'Shooty Booty' and releases the LP, *Sings The Old And The New (Black Label)*. **Big Joe Turner** releases *Rockin' The Blues*. **Champion Jack Dupree**, an orphan who grew up in the New Orleans Coloured Waifs Home For Boys where Louis Armstrong also spent his early years, releases *Blues From The Gutter*. The Atco album is produced by Jerry Wexler and features Pete Brown (sax), Larry Dale (guitar), Willie Jones (drums) and Wendell Marshall (bass). Tracks include 'Can't Kick The Habit', 'Junker's Blues' and 'Frankie And Johnny'.

Bean Bags teams **Milt 'Bags' Jackson** and **Coleman 'Bean' Hawkins** with Tommy Flanagan (piano), Kenny Burrell (guitar), Eddie Jones (bass) and Connie Kay (drums). Framed by *The Music Man* and *The Western Suite* albums released in January and December, **Jimmy Giuffre** releases two more albums, *The Four Brothers Sound* and *Trav'lin' Light*. Sax virtuoso **Warne Marsh** releases a self-titled album featuring Philly Joe Jones. The prolific **Wilbur De Paris** releases three discs in 1958: *Over And Over Again; Plays Something Old, Gay, Blue*; and *That's Aplenty*. **Mabel Mercer** records *Once In A Blue Moon*, with Nesuhi Ertegun producing and Tom Dowd engineering. George Cory arranges and conducts and Douglas Cross acts as musical consultant. **Bobby Short** releases *The Mad Twenties*. **Chris Connor** records the album *Chris Craft* with leading players Mundell Lowe, Ed Shaughnessy, Stan Free, Al Young and George Duvivier.

1959 The landmark **Ray Charles** recording, 'What'd I Say', is recorded on February 18th with Charles's band, featuring The Raeletts, David Newman and Hank Crawford. It becomes Charles's first Top Ten Pop hit, charting in July and reaching #6 during a 15-week run. It goes to #1 on the R&B chart. Charles records 'Just For A Thrill' in May with Ralph Burns as arranger/conductor, which is released in 1960 (#16 R&B). He also records 'Let The Good Times Roll' with his regular band and the Quincy Jones Orchestra, arranged by Jones and produced by Nesuhi Ertegun and Jerry Wexler. The track is backed by 'Don't Let The Sun Catch You Crying' (#17 R&B). In what is a spectacular year for the label, Bordeaux wines and electric guitars, Atlantic releases *The Genius Of Ray Charles*, an exceptional crossover LP years ahead of its time featuring a stellar array of great musicians brought in by Nesuhi. The album is generally considered to truly be a work of genius on the part of Ray Charles. It is produced by Nesuhi Ertegun. Atlantic also releases the album *What'd I Say*.

In May, Atlantic releases **Ornette Coleman**'s prophetic Atlantic debut, *The Shape Of Jazz To Come*, a revolutionary manifesto in Free Jazz. The album is produced by Nesuhi Ertegun and includes Don Cherry (trumpet), Charlie Haden (bass) and Billy Higgins (drums). *Change Of The Century*, featuring the same musicians and the second of six albums Coleman records for Atlantic, is released later in the year. Atlantic later releases *Twins* and *The Art Of Improvisers* featuring tracks from these sessions. While still playing with Miles Davis, **John Coltrane** releases the groundbreaking *Giant Steps* album on Atlantic this year. A landmark recording that brings Coltrane's passionate and spiritual music to the fore, the album features his signature title song along with Tommy Flanagan on piano, Art Taylor on drums and Paul Chambers on bass. *Coltrane Jazz* is released later in the year. **Charles Mingus** records the studio album *Blues And Roots* with Pepper Adams and Jimmy Knepper, among others.

Atlantic releases another exceptional jazz collaboration, *Bags And Trane*, featuring **Milt Jackson** and **John Coltrane** with Connie Kay, Hank Jones and Paul Chambers. **The Modern Jazz Quartet**'s *Pyramid* features John Lewis' 'Django' and the group's version of Ellington's 'It Don't Mean A Thing (If It Ain't Got That Swing)'. Pianist/composer **John Lewis** releases *Improvised Meditations And Excursions* featuring Connie Kay, George Duvivier and Percy Heath. Two of Lewis's compositions, 'Delauney's Dilemma' and 'Love Me', are included on the album. Jazzman **Buster Smith** records for Atlantic his only solo LP, *The Legendary Buster Smith*. **Chris Connor** records the bittersweet *Ballads At The Sad Cafe* with Phil Woods, Snooky Young and Harry 'Sweets' Edison, among others. She also releases the LPs *Chris In Person* and *Witchcraft*. *Bobby Short On The East Side*, another of the many Atlantic albums by the unique cabaret artist, **Bobby Short**, is recorded at sessions in March and December.

Produced by Ahmet and Jerry Wexler, **Bobby Darin**'s hit, 'Dream Lover', peaks at #2 Pop and #4 R&B, and was a gold #1 hit in the UK. He also records and releases a sensational version of Kurt Weill's 'Mack The Knife' which goes to #1 in the US and UK. It is produced by Ahmet, Nesuhi Ertegun and Jerry Wexler. It wins Grammy awards for 'Record of the Year' and for 'Best New Artist' in 1959. 'Clementine' is recorded in September (#21 Pop). The album *That's All* reaches the Top Ten in the US album chart.

With **Ben E. King** on lead vocals, **The Drifters**' new line-up chart with 'There Goes My Baby', which peaks at #2 Pop after a 19-week run starting in June. It reaches #1 R&B after another 19-week run. 'Dance With Me' spends 15 weeks on the Pop chart, going to #15 and 12 weeks on the R&B chart, peaking at #2. '(If You Cry) True Love, True Love', featuring Johnny Williams on lead vocals, climbs to #5 R&B and #33 Pop. 'Lonely Winds', written by **Doc Pomus** and **Mort Schuman**, also recorded during those sessions, reaches #9 on the R&B charts in 1960.

The Coasters release 'Poison Ivy', their fourth Top Ten hit in a row, which peaks at #1 R&B and #7 Pop. 'Along Came Jones' (#9 Pop, #14 R&B) is also recorded this year, on the same day and in the same studio in which John Coltrane records *Giant Steps*. Influential R&B sax stylist **King Curtis** releases *Have Tenor Will Blow* and *The Good Old Fifties* on Atco. **McHouston 'Mickey' Baker** releases his debut Atlantic LP, *Wildest Guitar*. Baker is a guitarist who's played on countless Atlantic sessions in the early- and mid-fifties including ones for The Drifters, Joe Turner and Ruth Brown. *Late Date With Ruth Brown* is released in 1959 along with the disc, *Miss Rhythm*, a compilation of **Ruth Brown**'s Atlantic recordings.

The landmark Atlantic blues album *T-Bone Blues* by **T-Bone Walker** is culled from three different sessions, the first in Chicago in 1955 with Junior Wells and Jimmy Rogers, then two sessions in L.A. in 1956 and 1957. Classic tracks include 'Two Bones And A Pick', 'Call It Stormy Monday' and 'Papa Ain't Salty'. **Big Joe Turner** releases *Big Joe Rides Again* featuring the legendary Coleman Hawkins (tenor), Vic Dickenson (trombone), Paul Ricard (trumpet) and Jerome Richardson (alto).

1960 **Ornette Coleman** releases *This Is Our Music* with Don Cherry, Charlie Haden and Ed Blackwell. He also records *Free Jazz (A Collective Improvisation)* with the Ornette Coleman Double Quartet, including visionary talents such as Freddie Hubbard, Don Cherry, Eric Dolphy (trumpets), Charlie Haden and Scott LaFaro (bass), and Ed Blackwell and Billy Higgins (drums). **John Coltrane** records his *My Favorite Things* album in October, his first complete album with the legendary Quartet featuring Elvin Jones (drums), McCoy Tyner (piano) and Steve Davis (bass). The Coltrane Quartet is an integral part of subsequent albums in 1960 such as *Coltrane Plays The Blues*, *The Avant Garde* (also with Don Cherry and Ed Blackwell) and *Coltrane's Sound*.

The Drifters, with Ben E. King singing lead, hit the top with 'Save The Last Dance For Me', written by Doc Pomus and Mort Schuman. It cruises up to #1 on both the Pop and R&B charts. The flip side, 'Nobody But Me', was originally supposed to be the A-side. In May, they record another Pomus-Schuman collaboration, 'I Count the Tears' (#6 R&B, #17 Pop). **Ben E. King** gets a #10 solo Pop hit with the beautiful song, 'Spanish Harlem', penned by Jerry Leiber and Phil Spector and arranged by Stan Appelbaum. Recorded in October, it goes to #15 on the R&B charts. King also releases his first solo album, *Amor*. The title track, another Leiber and Stoller composition, goes to #10 R&B and #18 Pop. The same session produces 'Stand By Me', co-written by King and 'Elmo Glick' (a pen name for Leiber-Stoller), which reaches #1 R&B and #4 Pop.

The father and daughter team of **Rufus and Carla Thomas** records "Cause I Love You', backed with 'Deep Down Inside' at the Satellite Studios in Memphis with a 16-year-old Booker T. Jones on sax and Rufus Thomas's son, Marvell, on piano. The record gets Atlantic's attention and leads to a vital new production and distribution relationship with the Memphis record label, later to be known as Stax, which flourishes until 1968. The precocious young Carla Thomas writes 'Gee Whiz (Look At His Eyes)' at the age of 16 and records it. Backed by the Veltones, the song climbs to #5 on the R&B chart and #10 Pop. Coincidentally, the Innocents release a different song entitled 'Gee Whiz' at the same time.

Nearing the end of his extraordinary Atlantic career, **Ray Charles** releases the bittersweet 'Come Rain Or Come Shine', recorded last year. He also releases 'Tell The Truth' (from the same session in Atlanta) which goes to #13 on the R&B chart and releases two albums, *Ray Charles Sextet* and *Ray Charles In Person*. **David 'Fathead' Newman** records the album *Straight Ahead*. **Solomon Burke**'s ground breaking hit 'Just Out Of Reach (Two Empty Arms)' is produced by Jerry Wexler and

Bert Berns and arranged by Ray Ellis. It goes to #7 R&B and #24 Pop.

Bobby Darin scores a series of chart hits in 1960 including 'Won't You Come Home Bill Bailey' (#19 Pop); 'Minnie The Moocher'; and 'Milord' (Pop #45). In August he records 'Lazy River' (#14 Pop) and 'Artificial Flowers' (#20 Pop). In the US album charts *This Is Darin* peaks at #6, and *Darin At The Copa* reaches #9. Recorded in December, **The Coasters** record and release their wonderful performance of 'Shopping For Clothes', written by Kent 'Boogaloo' Harris. **Nat Kendrick** (James Brown's drummer) & The Swans record 'Mashed Potatoes', another Atlantic dance classic which goes to #8 R&B and #84 Pop after weeks in the charts. **Clyde McPhatter**'s single 'Ta Ta' goes to #7 R&B and #23 Pop. **LaVern Baker** records Leiber and Stoller's 'Saved' in December, which reaches #17 R&B and #37 Pop on the *Billboard* charts in 1961.

Mingus At Antibes, an epic live album by the legendary bassist and composer, features **Charles Mingus**' 'piano-less' quartet with Eric Dolphy on alto sax, flute and bass clarinet, Dannie Richmond on drums, Ted Curson on trumpet, and guest appearances by Booker Ervin on tenor and Bud Powell on piano. *Wonderful World Of Jazz* by **John Lewis** is originally released in 1960 and reissued in 1988 for Atlantic's *Jazzlore Series*. It features Jim Hall on guitar, George Duvivier on bass and Connie Kay on drums with guest appearances by Paul Gonsalves (tenor sax), Herb Pomeroy (trumpet), Eric Dolphy (alto) and Jimmy Giuffre (baritone). Lewis also releases *The Golden Striker* in 1960 while another 'third stream' LP, *Jazz Abstraction*, also known as *John Lewis Presents Contemporary Music*, showcases Lewis even though his only appearance on the LP is via his composition 'Django'. **The Modern Jazz Quartet** release *The Comedy*, drawing static from jazz purists that the group, and Lewis in particular, is too influenced by classical music. Other albums by the MJQ in 1960 include *European Concert Volume One* and *Volume Two* and *The Modern Jazz Quartet And Orchestra*. Some of the last recordings by **Wilbur De Paris**, *The Wild Jazz Age* and *On the Riviera*, are released in the sixties. Both include his brother Sidney De Paris and Doc Cheatham (trumpet), Sonny White (piano), John Smith (guitar) and Hayes Alvis (bass). Wilbur De Paris continues on as a bandleader until his death in 1973. Flautist **Herbie Mann** releases his first Atlantic LP, *Common Ground*, marking the beginning of a very successful relationship with the label over the decades to come. **Mabel Mercer**'s *Merely Marvelous* features material recorded at sessions in 1959 and 1960. She's backed by the Jimmy Lyon trio with a production team of Nesuhi Ertegun, Tom Dowd and Douglas Cross.

1961 The **Mar-Keys**' instrumental smash 'Last Night' lays the groundwork for 'The Sound of Stax'. The band's line-up features Steve Cropper (guitar), Donald "Duck" Dunn (bass), Wayne Jackson (trumpet), Don Nix and Packy Axton (saxophones), Terry Johnson (drums) and Jerry Lee Smith (piano). Steve Cropper (featured here on piano instead of guitar) explains the song's success by describing it as the first instrumental 'you could twist to' (a fast-emerging dance craze). It is originally released on Satellite, reaching #2 R&B and #3 Pop. Brother and sister **Jim Stewart** and **Estelle Axton** (who run Satellite) discover there's another record label with the same name, so they reissue 'Last Night' on Stax, a name that combines the first two letters of their last names. The Mar-Keys release 'The Morning After', 'About Noon', and 'Foxy' as follow-ups to 'Last Night'. **Carla Thomas** is attending college in Nashville when 'Gee Whiz (Look At His Eyes)' breaks nationwide. Stax and Atlantic are eager to capitalize on the song's success, so they cut 'A Love of My Own' (#20 R&B, #56 Pop) and '(Mama Mama) Wish Me Good Luck', which doesn't chart. Her other release for the year is 'I Kinda Think He Does' (lyrics by Everette and Burch, music by Carla Thomas) which also fails to chart. Carla then duets with her father **Rufus Thomas** on the Atco single 'I Didn't Believe', credited to 'Rufus and Friend'. It's decided from this point on that Rufus Thomas will be on Stax and Carla on Atlantic, an arrangement that continues until 1965. **William Bell** debuts at Stax with the classic song, 'You Don't Miss Your Water'. Recorded in November at Stax with Marvell Thomas, Donald 'Duck' Dunn and Howard Grimes, the track has been called 'the first great country soul ballad'. It enters the Pop chart in April but only goes to #96. Memphis studio ace **Chips Moman** puts together a group called **The Triumphs**, inspired by his sports car, featuring Marvell Thomas, Howard Grimes and Lewis Steinberg. Their only release, the first on the subsidiary Volt label, is the single 'Burnt Biscuits'. **Barbara Stephens**' 'This Life I Live' is initially released on Satellite, then reissued on Stax in 1961. Written by Marvell Thomas and David Porter, it marks the first time Porter's name appears on a Stax record. He goes on to write many hits for the label.

In June, **Bobby Darin** records 'Things' (#3 Pop) and 'You Must Have Been a Beautiful Baby' (#5 Pop). In July he records a cover of Ray Charles' hit, 'What'd I Say' (#24 Pop). He records 'Irresistible You' (#15 Pop) and 'Baby Face' (#42 Pop) in October. 'Multiplication', a November recording reaches #30 in the Pop charts. His albums include *The Bobby Darin Story* (#18), *Twist With Bobby Darin* (#48), *Love Swings* and *Two of A Kind – Bobby Darin & Johnny Mercer*. 'Some Kind Of Wonderful' by Carole King and Gerry Goffin, with **Rudy Lewis** on lead vocals, is released by **The Drifters**. It goes to #6 R&B and #32 Pop. 'Please Stay', written by Burt Bacharach and Bob Hilliard, is also released this year and soars to #13 R&B and #14 Pop. The Drifters also record 'Sweets For My Sweet', by Doc Pomus and Mort Schuman (#10 R&B, #16 Pop), 'Loneliness Or Happiness', by Burt Bacharach and Hal David and 'Mexican Divorce' (Bacharach and Hilliard). The latter's A-side, 'When My Little Girl Is Smiling', by Goffin and King, is released in 1962 (#28 Pop). **The Coasters** record their last major hit single for Atlantic in February with the Leiber and Stoller burlesque number, 'Little Egypt', which goes to #16 R&B and #21 Pop. **LaVern Baker** cuts 'Hey Memphis', supervised by **Phil Spector** and written by Doc Pomus and Mort Schuman as a response to 'Little Sister', the hit they'd written for Elvis. **The Ikettes**, on their own without Ike and Tina Turner, record 'I'm Blue (The Gong-Gong Song)'. Recorded in L.A. in October, it goes to #3 R&B and #19 Pop.

Ornette Coleman follows up the hugely influential *Free Jazz* LP with *Ornette!*, accompanied by Don Cherry, Ed Blackwell and Scott LaFaro. *Ornette On Tenor* features Coleman exclusively on tenor sax joined by Cherry, Blackwell and Jimmy Garrison. *Oh Yeah!* by **Charles Mingus** features Booker Ervin (tenor), Roland Kirk (tenor, manzello, siren, stritch, flute), Jimmy Knepper (trombone), Dannie Richmond (drums) and Doug Watkins (bass). The album is produced by Nesuhi Ertegun and engineered by Tom Dowd. **John Lewis** releases the album *Original Sin*. **Herbie Mann**'s second LP for the label is *Family Of Mann*. He also releases *At The Village Gate* which features 'Comin' Home Baby' and a 20-minute version of 'It Ain't Necessarily So'. Produced by Nesuhi Ertegun, the album's line-up includes Hagood Hardy, Ahmed Abdul-Malik and Ray Mantilla. Mann releases *Herbie Mann Returns To The Village Gate* in the same year. *Nirvana*, featuring legendary pianist Bill Evans, is also released.

The 1961 album *Soul Meeting* features the only recording of **Milt Jackson** on guitar, 'Bag Of Blues', with **Ray Charles** playing alto sax on a couple of tracks. They're backed by Billy Mitchell (tenor), Skeeter Best (guitar), Oscar Pettiford (bass) and Connie Kay (drums). Atlantic releases *Do The Twist With Ray Charles* and *The Genius Sings The Blues*. A mainstay of Ray Charles' orchestra, saxophonist **Hank Crawford** records his first solo Atlantic LP, *More Soul*, produced by Nesuhi Ertegun. In 1961, he also releases *From The Heart* with Sonny Forrest and fellow Ray Charles sideman David 'Fathead' Newman along with *The Soul Clinic*, also with Newman. **Champion Jack Dupree** releases three LPs: *Champion Of The Blues*; *Natural* and *Soulful Blues*.

1962 **Solomon Burke**'s epic 'Cry To Me' enters the Pop chart in January 1962 for a ten-week stay culminating at #44. It enjoys more success on the R&B chart, peaking at #5 during a 12-week run. **The Drifters** record, with **Rudy Lewis** on lead vocals, the timeless hit 'Up On The Roof', written by Gerry Goffin and Carole King. It climbs to #4 R&B and #5 Pop. They also release a cover of Mr. Acker Bilk's 'Stranger On The Shore'. 'Don't Play That Song (You Lied)' co-written by Ahmet and **Ben E. King** and produced by Ahmet, is recorded in March and hits the Pop chart a month later, peaking at #11. King also releases the album *Ben E. King Sings For Soulful Lovers* on Atco. **The Falcons**, including lead singer **Wilson Pickett** (later signed to Atlantic as a solo artist in 1964) and **Sir Mack Rice** (author of 'Mustang Sally', later to be a major hit for Pickett), record the fervent 'I Found A Love' which stays on the R&B chart for 16 weeks, eventually going to #6. The track goes to #75 on the Pop chart.

'Stranger On The Shore' is a surprise instrumental hit for British clarinettist **Mr. Acker Bilk**, who'd written the song for his daughter Jenny. The single goes to #1 in the US and also hits the top of the UK Pop chart, enjoying a 55-week run on the British charts. It is awarded gold status by the RIAA and wins Top Instrumentalist and Top Instrumental Single awards in the 1962 *Billboard* DJ Poll. **Nesuhi Ertegun** brings pianist **Bent Fabric**'s novelty instrumental 'Alley Cat' to Atlantic and it becomes a Top 20 hit in 1962. Fabric's real name is Bent Fabricius-Bjerre and he is at the time head of the Danish record company Metronome.

The extraordinarily gifted jazz violinist **Stephane Grappelli** releases *Feeling + Finesse = Jazz* on Atlantic with a quintet that includes Pierre Cavalli on guitar. Southern jazz raconteur, wit and singer/songwriter **Mose Allison** cuts his debut for Atlantic, *I Don't Worry About A Thing*. It includes a classic title track, the inimitable 'I Don't Worry About A Thing (Because I Know Nothing Will Turn Out Right)' and the signature piece 'Your Mind Is On Vacation'. The album, produced by Nesuhi Ertegun, is Allison's breakthrough. He also releases *Swingin' Machine* with Jimmy Knepper (trombone), Frankie Dunlop (drums), Jimmy Reider (sax) and Addison Farmer

(bass). Incomparable vocal interpreter **Mel Tormé**'s 'Comin' Home, Baby', recorded with the Claus Ogermann Orchestra during Tormé's 1962-63 period with Atlantic, becomes one of his biggest hits (#36 Pop). He also releases the *Comin' Home, Baby* LP and *Mel Tormé At The Red Hill*. As the Bossa Nova craze peaks in popularity, **Herbie Mann** releases *Do The Bossa Nova With Herbie Mann*, recorded in Brazil with Sergio Mendes and Antonio Carlos Jobim, a gifted composer and performer considered by some the 'George Gershwin of Brazil'. Mann also releases *This Is My Beloved* and *Right Now*.

John Lewis releases *European Encounter* with violinist Svend Asmussen, bassist Jimmy Woode and drummer Sture Kallin. He also releases the *Essence* and *Animal Dance* LPs, and records *A Milanese Story* in 1962. **Chris Connor**'s 1962 *Free Spirits* album includes music from John Lewis and Ornette Coleman and features Joe Newman (trumpet) and Phil Woods (alto sax/clarinet). She also releases the LP *No Strings*. Alto saxophonist **Sonny Stitt** releases *Stitt And The Top Brass*.

Booker T. & the M.G.s, featuring Booker T. Jones (keyboards), Steve Cropper (guitar), Al Jackson Jr. (drums) and Lewis Steinberg (bass), release the classic instrumental song, 'Green Onions'. The track, a perfect mix of compelling organ riff, irresistible 'slightly-behind-the-beat' Memphis rhythmic feel, with a seminally powerful guitar solo from Cropper, goes to #1 on the R&B chart where it stays for four weeks and to #3 Pop. The original house band for Volt, the M.G.s hit full form when Donald 'Duck' Dunn replaces Steinberg on bass. The original record comes about by accident when a B-side is needed for a track called 'Behave Yourself'. 'Green Onions', the product of a spontaneous studio jam, quickly becomes the A-side. Atlantic recommends the release be switched from Volt to Stax. **William Bell** follows up 'You Don't Miss Your Water' with 'Any Other Way' on Stax. **The Mar-Keys** release 'The Popeye Stroll', which goes to #94 Pop. Booker T. Jones and Steve Cropper write the song. It is well received in Europe, but makes less of an

impression in the US. **Carla Thomas** releases 'I'll Bring It Home To You' in response to Sam Cooke's hit, 'Bring It On Home To Me'. The song goes to #9 R&B and #41 Pop. For her last two outings on Stax, **Barbara Stephens** releases the self-penned 'Wait A Minute' and 'That's The Way It Is', written by Nashville songwriter Jerry Crutchfield.

1963 **Otis Redding** is recorded during a session for Johnny Jenkins & The Pinetoppers. The result, in addition to the discovery of one of the world's greatest vocal artists, is Redding's first hit single, 'These Arms Of Mine', on Stax (#20 R&B). The track features Jenkins on guitar and Steve Cropper on piano. Other defining Otis Redding singles released in 1963 include 'Pain In My Heart' (#61 R&B) and 'That's What My Heart Needs' (#27 R&B). **Rufus Thomas**' 'The Dog' goes to #22 R&B and #87 Pop. He has an even bigger hit with his classic 'Walkin' The Dog' in October (#5 R&B, #10 Pop). **Carla Thomas**' 'What A Fool I've Been' makes it to #28 R&B and #93 Pop. She also releases 'Gee Whiz, It's Christmas' (written by Carla Thomas and Steve Cropper). **William Bell** releases his compositions, 'I Told You So', 'Just As I Thought' (Steve Cropper and Deanie Parker), 'Somebody Mentioned Your Name' (William Bell and Booker T. Jones) and 'I'll Show You'. **Booker T. & the M.G.s** write and record 'Jelly Bread', 'Home Grown', 'Chinese Checkers' and 'Mo' Onions' (#97 Pop). **The Mar-Keys** release 'Bo-Time' written by Steve Cropper.

Written by Barry Mann and Cynthia Weil with Leiber and Stoller, one of the most evocative hit songs about New York, **The Drifters**' 'On Broadway' climbs to #7 R&B and #9 Pop. A subject of much speculation over the years, the short but memorable guitar solo is indeed by Phil Spector. The B-side is Bacharach and David's 'Let The Music Play'. At this point, Dock Green leaves The Drifters to be replaced by Eugene Pearson. **Johnny Moore** returns to the group and sings lead on 'I'll Take You Home' (#24 R&B, #25 Pop), another Mann and Weil song, while Rudy Lewis takes the lead on 'Rat Race', written by Leiber and Stoller

with Van McCoy. 'Only In America', a four-way collaboration between Mann and Weil with Leiber and Stoller, was originally a 'protest' song recorded at the same time Martin Luther King was arrested and placed in solitary confinement in Birmingham, Alabama. Later that year, **Bert Berns** takes over as producer and his first session delivers 'Vaya Con Dios' (#43 R&B) and 'One Way Love' (#56 R&B), the latter written by Berns (under the pseudonym Bert Russell) and Jerry Ragavoy. Saxophonist **Nino Tempo** and his sister **April Stevens** rack up a #1 Pop hit with 'Deep Purple' which also wins a Grammy for 'Best Rock'n'Roll Record' of 1963.

Solomon Burke's 'You're Good For Me' reaches #8 R&B and #49 Pop. Burke gets into a chart duel with Wilson Pickett when both record versions of 'If You Need Me'. Burke's peaks at #2 on the R&B chart (Pickett peaks at #30) and #37 on the Pop chart. He also releases the LP *If You Need Me*. Some of the material recorded with bluesman **John Lee Hooker** in 1953 is released on the Atco disc *Don't Turn Me From Your Door*. **Ben E. King** records the dramatic hit 'I (Who Have Nothing)' (#16 R&B, #29 Pop). Artie Ripp supervises **Doris Troy**'s only hit 'Just One Look' which climbs to #3 R&B and #10 Pop in June. **Barbara Lewis** releases the eternally seductive 'Hello Stranger' on Atlantic and it quickly goes to #1 R&B and #11 Pop. Industry 'bible' **Billboard** magazine stops publishing their R&B chart in late November of 1963 because R&B records are crossing over into the Pop charts and it's no longer deemed necessary. This decision will be reversed in January 1965 when the R&B chart is reinstated.

Hank Crawford releases his *Soul Of The Ballad* and *True Blues* albums. **David 'Fathead' Newman** records *Fathead Comes On*. Flugelhorn virtuoso **Art Farmer** releases *Interaction*. The Art Farmer Quartet with Jim Hall records three albums for Atlantic, the first being *Live At The Half Note* in 1963. Last heard on Atlantic as one of Art Blakey's Jazz Messengers, tenor sax ace **Johnny Griffin** returns to the label with **Matthew Gee** on *Soul Groove*. **The Modern Jazz Quartet** release *Sheriff*. *Stitt Plays Bird* features **Sonny Stitt** (alto sax), John Lewis (piano), Connie Kay (drums), Richard Davis (bass) and Jim Hall (guitar). Produced by Ahmet Ertegun, it features ten Charlie Parker compositions. **Mel Tormé** records *Songs Of New York* in 1963. The album is arranged by Shorty Rogers, Dick Hazard and John Williams, and produced by Nesuhi Ertegun. **Bobby Short** releases *My Personal Property*. The multifaceted jazz artist **Betty Carter** debuts on Atlantic with *Round Midnight* in January. The album features arrangements by Claus Ogermann and Oliver Nelson and musicians Shelly Manne (drums), Joe Newman (trumpet), Ed Shaughnessy (drums), George Duvivier (bass) and Phil Woods (clarinet, alto and tenor sax).

1964

'Under The Boardwalk' is the last Top Ten hit for **The Drifters**. The song is written by Artie Resnick and Kenny Young from Bobby Darin's music publishing company. Lead singer **Rudy Lewis** dies the night before the session and because the musician's union refuses to cancel it, former lead **Johnny Moore** takes over the vocals. He sings in a lower register than usual because the arranger doesn't have time to change the key. You can hear the sadness that permeates the session. Nonetheless, it goes on the Pop chart for 14 weeks, peaking at #4 and remains a true classic. It's backed by 'I Don't Want To Go On Without You', written by Bert Berns and Jerry Wexler. The group also records 'Saturday Night at the Movies' (#18 Pop), 'At The Club' (#10 Pop), 'I've Got Sand In My Shoes' (#33 Pop) and 'The Christmas Song'. **Nino Tempo** and **April Stevens** enjoy their second hit on Atlantic, 'Whispering' (#11 Pop). **The Righteous Brothers** record *Some Blue Eyed Soul* on the Moonglow label, distributed by Atlantic. **Tami Lynn** records 533'I'm Gonna Run Away From You' on Atco with Ray Ellis arranging and Bert Berns producing. **Jimi Hendrix**, then known as Jimmy James, makes his first recordings with the **Isley Brothers** on Atlantic this year. He will appear on Atlantic later on as one of King Curtis's Kingpins and as the incandescent final act on the Woodstock Festival soundtrack LP.

Otis Redding releases 'Security' which reaches #97 on the Pop chart. Redding also releases 'Come To Me', written by himself and manager Phil Walden, which reaches #69 on the Hot 100 and 'Chained and Bound' (#70 on the Hot 100). **Rufus Thomas** releases 'Jump Back' with backing by the Drapels, which goes to #49 on the Hot 100. Thomas also releases the dance track 'Can Your Monkey Do The Dog?' and duets with daughter Carla on 'That's Really Good' backed with a cover of Ray Charles' '(Night Time Is) The Right Time'. Both tracks chart in the 90s on the Hot 100. **Carla Thomas** releases 'A Woman's Love' (written by Steve Cropper and Carla Thomas), which gets to #71 in the Hot 100 and is later re-cut as a reply to Wilson Pickett's 'It's A Man's Way'. She also releases 'I've Got No Time To Lose', written by Deanie Parker and Steve Cropper, which reaches #67 in the Pop charts. 'Soul Dressing', by **Booker T. & the MGs**, reaches #95 on the Pop charts. **David Porter** releases 'Can't See You When I Want To' on Stax. Although not a hit, it's the first time he and songwriting partner **Isaac Hayes** (using the pseudonym Ed Lee) write together. **Wendy Rene** (formerly Mary Frierson of the Drapels, a Stax group that backed William Bell and Rufus Thomas) records three singles for Stax: 'After Laughter (Comes Tears)', written by Rene and her brother Johnny Frierson, 'Bar-B-Q' (Steve Cropper and Larry Brown), both in 1964, and 'Give What You Got' (Johnny Frierson and Steve Cropper) in 1965. Stax vocal group **Barbara & the Browns** record the single 'Big Party' at Chips Moman's American Recording Studio. It sneaks into the Hot 100, reaching #97. Still in high school, singer/songwriter **Deanie Parker** records her first singles for Stax, the self-penned 'My Imaginary Guy' and 'Each Step I Take'. They enjoy a modest regional success and Parker enjoys success writing hits for Carla Thomas, Albert King, William Bell and The Mad Lads.

Nat Adderley, Cannonball Adderley's brother, releases *Autobiography*. **Mose Allison** records *The Word From Mose* with Ben Tucker on bass and Ron Lundberg on drums. Drummer, composer and leader **Max Roach** showcases the talented young pianist **Haasan Ibn Ali** on his LP, *Max Roach Trio, Featuring The Legendary Haasan*. Ali only ever appeared on this one recording. **The Art Farmer Quartet** with Art Farmer (flugelhorn and trumpet), Jim Hall (guitar), Steve Swallow (bass) and Pete LaRoca (drums) record *To Sweden With Love*, a brief 33-minute set consisting of Swedish folk tunes.

Don Covay's 'Mercy Mercy' enters the Pop chart for a ten-week run, peaking at #35. He also releases *Mercy! Don Covay*. **Solomon Burke** releases the album *Rock'n'Soul*. 'Wicked' **Wilson Pickett** signs with Atlantic as a solo artist, another fortuitous pairing. Singer **Titus Turner** records 'Baby Girl, Pt. 1-2' in May, which is later included in the 1986 collections *Atlantic Blues Box* and *Atlantic Blues: Vocalists* LPs. The powerful blues/R&B singer **Esther Phillips**' first Atlantic recordings, produced by Jerry Wexler and Bert Berns, are the singles 'Mo Jo Hannah', 'I Saw Me', 'Double Crossing Blues' (a remake of her Savoy hit) and 'Hello Walls', the great country ballad by Willie Nelson. Her interpretation of The Beatles' 'And I Love Him' is produced by Ahmet.

1965

Billboard's R&B chart is reinstated in January. **Otis Redding** has his first Top Ten R&B hit with 'Mr. Pitiful' (#10 R&B, #41 Pop). Steve Cropper is inspired to write the song when he hears Moohah, a local DJ at WDIA, refer to Redding as 'Mr. Pitiful' on his radio show. Cropper and Redding write the song on the way to Stax. Other hits for Redding this year include the powerful 'I've Been Loving You Too Long', written by Redding and Jerry Butler (#2 R&B, #21 Pop). He also comes out with his second LP, *The Great Otis Redding Sings Soul Ballads*. **Carla Thomas** releases 'How Do You Quit (Somebody You Love)' (#39 R&B) in February. She also puts out 'Stop! Look What You're Doing' which reaches #30 on the R&B chart and #92 Pop. She also releases the single 'Comfort Me'. **The Mar-Keys** reappear on Stax with 'Bush Bash', written by Booker T. Jones, Floyd Newman and Gilbert Caples. **Booker T. & the M.G.s** score with 'Boot-Leg' (#10 R&B, #58 Pop). Jones is away at college during the recording and replaced by Isaac Hayes at the session. **The Astors**, a Stax group named after the Astor Hotel in New York's Times Square, release 'Candy', by Steve Cropper and Isaac Hayes. It climbs to #12 R&B and #63 Pop and stands as their only hit. **The Admirals** record the Steve Cropper composition 'Got You On My Mind' and disband shortly after. **The Mar-Keys'** instrumental 'Philly Dog', originally intended for Rufus Thomas, goes to #19 R&B and #89 Pop. **Eddie Floyd** has a UK club hit with his first Stax release, 'Things Get Better', written by Floyd, Steve Cropper and Wayne Jackson. 'I Had A Dream' is **Johnnie Taylor**'s first *Billboard* chart hit this year, going to #19 on the R&B chart. The Stax artist becomes known as 'The Philosopher of Soul'. At the end of this year and into the start of next, **The Mad Lads** climb the charts with 'Don't Have To Shop Around', #11 R&B and #93 Pop. 'I Want Someone', written by Deanie Parker and Estelle Axton, goes to #10 R&B and #74 Pop.

In May, **Wilson Pickett** goes to Stax to record the triumphant 'In The Midnight Hour', written by Steve Cropper. It enters the R&B chart for a 23-week stay, climbing to #1. It also reaches #21 Pop. Pickett scores another #1 R&B hit with '634-5789' (#13 Pop), also written by Cropper. These sessions are produced by **Jerry Wexler** who demonstrates the rhythmic feel he's looking for with an improvised 'funky jerk' Pickett also records 'Don't Fight It'(#4 R&B, #53 Pop)) and 'Ninety-Nine And A Half (Won't Do)' (#13 R&B, #53 Pop). Pickett releases the album *In The Midnight Hour* (#3 R&B). Jerry Wexler arranges for the powerhouse R&B vocal twosome **Sam and Dave** to record at Stax, teaming them with songwriters Isaac Hayes and David Porter. They release two Stax singles before hitting pay dirt with 'You Don't Know Like I Know', based on a Gospel song. Their first hit, it gets to #7 on the R&B chart. **The Del-Rays** release 'Don't Let Her Be Your Baby' written by Motown founder and producer Berry Gordy Jr. **Joe Tex**'s 'Hold What You've Got', recorded a year earlier at Rick Hall's Fame Studios in Muscle Shoals, holds on the R&B chart for 7 weeks, reaching #2. It peaks at #5 Pop. 'A Sweet Woman Like You' goes to #1 R&B and #29 on the Pop chart. 'I Want To Do Everything With You' is another #1

R&B hit for Tex which eventually goes to #23 Pop. **Solomon Burke** records 'Got To Get You Off My Mind' in January. It goes to the very top of the R&B chart, Burke's first #1 hit (#22 Pop). He also enjoys chart success with 'Everybody Needs Somebody To Love' (#58 R&B).

Aside from appearing on John Coltrane's albums as an integral member of the Coltrane Quartet, drummer **Elvin Jones** records two LPs of his own for Atlantic. *And Then Again: Elvin Jones* features his brothers Thad and Hank Jones along with Frank Wess and Paul Chambers. Arif Mardin supervises the album. Other jazz albums this year include **Art Farmer**'s *Sing Me Softly Of The Blues*, **Mose Allison**'s *Wild Man On The Loose*, organist **Jackie Ivory**'s *Soul Discovery* on Atco, tenor saxophonist **Eddie Harris**' *The 'In' Sound* and **Carmen McRae**'s *Bittersweet* on the Focus subsidiary label. Beat poet **Allen Ginsberg** records *Kaddish,* one of his most important poems, for Atlantic.

Don Covay's 'Seesaw', recorded with his band, The Goodtimers, enters the R&B chart in November and eventually peaks at #5. It stays on the Pop chart for nine weeks. Atlantic releases **The Drifters**' 'Come On Over To My Place', a Top Ten UK hit. **The Righteous Brothers** record *This Is Now!* on the Moonglow imprint. **Willie Tee**'s 'Teasin' You' goes to #12 R&B and #97 Pop. He also records 'Walking Up A One Way Street', arranged by Wardell Quezerque. **Barbara Lewis**'s unforgettable 'Baby I'm Yours' gets to #5 on the R&B chart and #11 Pop. 'Make Me Your Baby' reaches #14 Pop in the US. She records both tracks in New York with Bert Berns and Jerry Wexler producing. **Mary Wells** records for Atco this year and next. Her album, *The Two Sides Of Mary Wells,* and four singles recorded during this period will later be repackaged as *Dear Lover: The Atco Sessions* in 1995. The singles are recorded in Chicago with Carl Davis producing some of the tracks.

Vocal duo **Sonny and Cher** score their first Atlantic hit with 'Just You' (#20 Pop). Their career smash 'I Got You Babe' goes to #1 in the US and UK and will become one of the biggest-selling hit singles of the sixties. Their album *Look At Us* also goes to #1 in the States. Sonny's solo recording, 'Laugh At Me' is a Top 20 US hit.

1966 **Cream**, the premier British super group featuring virtuoso instrumentalists Eric Clapton on guitar and vocals, Jack Bruce on bass and vocals and Ginger Baker on drums, release their first Atco album, *Fresh Cream* (#39 Pop). The album goes gold and features Cream's anthemic single 'I Feel Free'.

Long Island's own **Young Rascals**, featuring Felix Cavaliere (vocals, keyboards), Gene Cornish (guitar), Eddie Brigati (vocals) and the stylish Dino Danelli (drums), hit the charts with their first Atlantic album, *The Young Rascals* which goes gold based on their uptempo #1 Pop single 'Good Lovin''. **Bobby Darin** makes a successful return to Atlantic with his first Top Ten single since 1961, Tim Hardin's modern folk classic 'If I Were A Carpenter' (#8 Pop), produced by Charles Koppelman and Don Rubin. He also records 'We Didn't Ask To Be Brought Here' and 'Funny What Love Can Do' this year. *The Wondrous World of Sonny And Cher* is also released this year.

Otis Redding records a turbo-charged version of The Rolling Stones' 'Satisfaction' (#4 R&B, #31 Pop) on the album *Otis Blue*, without ever having heard the original. A truly amazing year for Redding, 1966 yields 'Respect' (#4 R&B, #35 Pop), 'I Can't Turn You Loose' (#11 R&B, #85 Pop), 'Just One More Day' (#15 R&B), 'My Lover's Prayer' (#10 R&B), 'Fa-Fa-Fa-Fa-Fa (Sad Song)' (#12 R&B, #29 Pop) and the soaring 'Try A Little Tenderness' (#4 R&B, #25 Pop). **William Bell**, newly discharged from the Army, has national chart success with Steve Cropper and David Porter's 'Share What You Got (But Keep What You Need)' (#27 R&B). He also releases 'Never Like This Before' by Hayes, Porter and Booker T. Jones (#29 R&B). **The Astors** release 'In The Twilight Zone' by Hayes, Porter and Bailey. **Carla Thomas** generates more action on the charts with 'Let Me Be Good To You' (#11 R&B, #62 Pop) and Isaac Hayes and David Porter's 'B-A-B-Y' with backing vocals from Porter and Carla's sister Vanese.

Later in the year, Thomas releases 'Something Good (Is Going To Happen To You)', which goes to #29 R&B and #74 Pop. Stax vocalist **Ruby Johnson** releases 'I'll Run Your Heart Away' (#31 R&B); 'I Want Someone' and 'When My Loves Come Down'. Singer **Mable John**, sister of bluesman Little Willie John, moves from Motown to Stax and her single, 'Your Good Thing Is About To End' (written by Isaac Hayes and David Porter) goes to #6 R&B and #95 Pop. **The Mad Lads** release 'Sugar Sugar' (not to be confused with the song of the same title by the Archies) written by Eddie Floyd and Al Bell, 'I Want A Girl' written by the group and 'Patch My Heart' written by Steve Cropper and Isaac Hayes. **Isaac Hayes** and **David Porter** write the dynamic 'Hold On, I'm Comin'', which becomes Sam and Dave's first #1 R&B hit (#21 Pop). They follow it up with 'Said I Wasn't Gonna Tell Nobody' (#8 R&B, #64 Pop). **Eddie Floyd** and Steve Cropper write 'Knock On Wood', a #1 R&B hit for Floyd (#28 Pop). The track features David Porter on backing vocals and Al Jackson, Jr. on drums. Blues singer/guitarist **Albert King** signs with Stax and releases the singles 'Laundromat Blues' (#29 R&B) and 'Crosscut Saw' (#34 R&B), where his raw, roadhouse style is perfectly complemented by Stax's house rhythm section, Booker T. & the M.G.s.

Joe Zawinul, the gifted keyboardist and composer who would play a major role with Miles Davis and his own Weather Report, releases *Money In My Pocket* and *The Rise And Fall Of The Third Stream*. Joel Dorn, another studio talent destined to have a successful Atlantic career, produces both. In September, saxophonist **Charles Lloyd** records the live LP *Forest Flower* at the Monterey Jazz Festival with the Keith Jarrett Trio. In October, he releases *Charles Lloyd Live In Europe*. Another emerging talent spotted by the discerning Nesuhi Ertegun, trumpeter **Freddie Hubbard** is signed to Atlantic and releases three albums during the sixties: *Backlash* (1966), where 'Little Sunflower' made its debut; *High Blues Pressure* (1967); and *The Black Angel* (1969). Organist **"Brother" Jack McDuff** releases *Change Is Gonna Come* and *Do It Now* featuring his group Leo Johnson, Ray Appleton, Danny Turner and Melvin Sparks. Chicago-born jazz pianist **Junior Mance** releases *Harlem Lullaby* and *I Believe To My Soul* on Atlantic. **The Modern Jazz Quartet** release live LP *Blues At Carnegie*. *Mr. Blues* is released by **Hank Crawford**. *You Name It* is released by drummer **Shelly Manne**. **Nat Adderley** releases *Live At Memory Lane* and *Sayin' Something*. *Tones For Joan's Bones*, an album by the gifted young instrumentalist and composer **Chick Corea**, is released and is dedicated to his wife.

Rick Hall's Fame Studios in Muscle Shoals, Alabama produce another hit: **Jimmy Hughes**' 'Neighbor, Neighbor' (#4 R&B, #65 Pop). A year later, he releases the Atco album, *Why Not Tonight*. **Esther Phillips** releases the albums *And I Love Him, Esther*, and *The Country Side Of Esther Phillips* in 1966. Atlantic re-releases the LP that Lelan Rogers had made following the success she had with 'Release Me'. The decision to re-release her country record is due to her hit of this same year 'When A Woman Loves A Man' (#26 R&B, #73 Pop), an answer to the Percy Sledge hit. **King Curtis** releases *Live At Small's Paradise* with bassist Chuck Rainey and guitarist Cornell Dupree and *That Lovin' Feelin'* featuring Melvin Lastie on trumpet.

Stax closes its studios to visiting artists, so Jerry Wexler takes **Wilson Pickett** further South to Muscle Shoals, Alabama. Pickett responds well to the move by cutting monster hits such as 'Mustang Sally' (#6 R&B, #23 Pop) and Chris Kenner-penned 'Land Of 1,000 Dances' (#1 R&B, #6 Pop) with Rick Hall. Pickett also records 'Three Time Loser' and releases the albums *The Exciting Wilson Pickett* (#3 R&B), and *The Wicked Pickett* (#5 R&B). Another dance sensation, **The Capitols**' 'Cool Jerk' cruises to #2 R&B Chart and #7 Pop. Atlantic unearths more gold with **Percy Sledge**'s immortal 'When A Man Loves A Woman'. Recorded in Muscle Shoals with Quin Ivy producing, the song blasts up to #1 on the R&B and Pop charts. Other big hits for Sledge include 'Warm And Tender Love' (#5 R&B, #17 Pop) and 'It Tears Me Up' (#7 R&B, #20

Pop).

1967 Atlantic is purchased for $17 million by the Warner-Seven Arts media conglomerate. New to Atlantic, this proves to be an epic year for **Aretha Franklin**. 'I Never Loved A Man (The Way I Love You)' reaches #1 R&B and #9 Pop after a 14-week run. Her version of Otis Redding's 'Respect' (which inspired Redding to declare, 'That little girl stole my song!') hits #1 on both the R&B and Pop charts. The song also wins Franklin and producer Jerry Wexler a Grammy for Best R&B Recording along with Best R&B Solo Vocal Performance for Franklin as well. Her album *I Never Loved A Man The Way I Love You*, featuring King Curtis, sister Carolyn Franklin, Chips Moman and Spooner Oldham, engineered by Tom Dowd and produced by Wexler, is certified gold by the RIAA. 1967 also witnesses the release of *Aretha Arrives* and a number of gold singles including 'Baby I Love You' (#1 R&B, #4 Pop), the inspired '(You Make Me Feel Like) A Natural Woman' (#2 R&B, #8 Pop), the Don Covay song, 'Chain Of Fools' (#1 R&B, #2 Pop), and 'Do Right Woman – Do Right Man', written by Dan Penn and Spooner Oldham (#37 R&B).

Buffalo Springfield have been signed to Atlantic's subsidiary Atco by Ahmet in 1966. Now the group release their debut album, *Buffalo Springfield*, which includes their Top Ten hit, the generational anthem, 'For What It's Worth' (#7 Pop), based on the Sunset Strip riots. The Stephen Stills-penned classic literally defines a state of mind for that tumultuous period of the sixties. The group is fronted by an extraordinarily talented trio of singer/songwriter/instrumentalists, Neil Young, Steve Stills and Richie Furay, together with Dewey Martin (drums) and Bruce Palmer (bass), later replaced by Jim Messina. Singles from the group's second LP *Buffalo Springfield Again*, also released in 1967, include the lyrical 'Bluebird' (#58 Pop) and 'Rock & Roll Woman' (#44 Pop). British supergroup **Cream** continue their phenomenal rise with their second Atco LP, *Disraeli Gears* (#4), a Top Five US album featuring the hypnotic #1 hit single, 'Sunshine Of Your Love'.

John Hammond, Jr. records the gritty *I Can Tell* album for Atlantic with help from Robbie Robertson and Duane Allman, among others. **Vanilla Fudge** release their debut self-titled Atco album of local New York 'psychedelic rock' legends Tim Bogert (bass), Carmine Appice (drums), Mark Stein (lead singer, keyboards) and Vinnie Martell (guitar) the album is certified RIAA Gold. The single 'You Keep Me Hangin' On', an intense cover of the Supremes classic, goes to #6 on the Pop chart.

The Young Rascals release 'Groovin'' (#1 Pop, #3 R&B). They also enjoy chart success with 'A Girl Like You' (#10 Pop) and 'How Can I Be Sure' (#4 Pop). Atlantic purchases the **Bee Gees**' contract for $250,000. The promising Australian vocal group are made up of brothers Barry, Maurice and Robin Gibb. Their Atco debut, *Bee Gees First* produces the first of their many chart hits with 'New York Mining Disaster 1941' (#14 Pop), 'To Love Somebody' (#17 Pop) and 'Holiday' (#16 Pop). **Sonny and Cher** release three more Atlantic LPs in 1967, *The Best of Sonny & Cher* (#23 Pop), *Good Times* (#73 Pop) and *In Case You're In Love* (#45 Pop). The single 'The Beat Goes On' is a #6 Pop hit. Sonny also releases a solo LP, *Inner Views*.

Reaching a solo career high point, **King Curtis** releases *King Curtis Plays Great Memphis Hits* on Atco. 'Memphis Stew', a primer on instrumental funk, goes to #6 R&B and #33 Pop. Curtis follows up with the *King Size Soul* LP and his interpretation of 'Ode To Billie Joe'. **Solomon Burke** releases the *King Solomon* album and scores with 'Keep A Light In The Window' (#15 R&B, #64 Pop) and 'Take Me (Just As I Am)' (#11 R&B, #49 Pop). **Wilson Pickett** breaks it wide open again with 'Funky Broadway' (#1 R&B, #8 Pop), one of his biggest hits. His interpretation of Bobby Womack's 'I'm in Love' goes to #4 R&B. **Joe Tex** steps out with 'Show Me' (#24 R&B, #35 Pop) and 'Skinny Legs And All' (#2 R&B, #10 Pop). **Patti LaBelle & the Bluebelles**, consisting of the talented Nona Hendryx, Sarah Dash and Cindy Birdsong, release *Dreamer*. The album produces two minor R&B chart hits, 'I'm Still Waiting' (#36 R&B) and 'Take Me For A Little While' (#36 R&B). The group also record the original version of 'Groovy Kind Of Love', a future hit for Wayne Fontana & The Mindbenders and Phil Collins.

David 'Fathead' Newman releases *House Of David*. **Eddie Harris**, Chicago-born jazz tenor saxophonist and vocalist known for his experimentation with electric reed instruments, releases the appropriately entitled *The Electrifying Eddie Harris*. **Elvin Jones** records the solo LP *Midnight Walk* accompanied by Thad Jones, Hank Mobley and Dollar Brand, with Arif Mardin supervising. **MJQ**'s *Live At The Lighthouse* LP showcases new material like John Lewis's 'The Spiritual' and Milt Jackson's 'Novamo' and 'For Someone I Love'. **Carmen McRae** releases *For Once In My Life*, which is arranged and conducted by Johnny Keating, supervised by Nesuhi Ertegun and recorded at London's Olympic Studios. *Double Barreled Soul* and *Brother Jack And David Newman*, two LPs from legendary organist **"Brother" Jack McDuff** with **David "Fathead" Newman**, Melvin Sparks, Danny Turner, Leo Johnson and Abe Blasingame are released this year. Jazz vibraphonist **Roy Ayers** releases *Virgo Vibes* with solid support from Joe Henderson (tenor), Reggie Workman (bass) and Herbie Hancock a.k.a. 'Ronnie Clark' (piano).

Sam and Dave chart with 'You Got Me Hummin'' (#7 R&B), a live cover of the Sims Twins' hit 'Soothe Me' (#16 R&B, #56 Pop), Isaac Hayes and David Porter's plaintive 'When Something Is Wrong With My Baby' (#2 R&B, 42 Pop) – the only ballad they ever recorded for Stax – and the timeless 'Soul Man', Stax's most successful record to date, which goes to #1 R&B and #2 Pop. The track also wins a Grammy for Best R&B Performance, Vocal Or Instrumental. The duo also release a second Stax LP, *Double Dynamite*. **The Bar-Kays**' irresistible 'Soul Finger' goes to #3 R&B and #17 Pop. Neighbourhood children are recruited to provide partying sounds while they chant the song's title. The flip side, 'Knucklehead', is a #28 R&B hit. Groomed as the second featured studio instrumental group for Stax/Volt following Booker T. & the MGs, the Bar-Kays score with their next Volt release, 'Give Everybody Some' (#36 R&B, #91 Pop). **Johnnie Taylor**'s 1967 single 'Ain't That Loving You (For More Reasons Than One)' is written by Allen Jones and Homer Banks. Although it receives significant airplay in the South, it never makes the national charts. **William Bell**'s *The Soul Of A Bell* LP produces the hit 'Everybody Loves A Winner' featuring the Memphis Symphony Orchestra (#18 R&B, #95 Pop). 'Everyday Will Be Like A Holiday' hits the chart in January and goes to #33 R&B. **The Astors** release the single 'Daddy Didn't Tell Me', which fails to chart and marks the end of their career. **Booker T. & the MGs** record the instrumental 'Hip Hug-Her' in New York (#6 R&B, Top 40 Pop). They also cover The Young Rascals' 'Groovin'' (#10 R&B, #21 Pop). The multi-talented Booker T. Jones plays piano, organ, baritone sax, trombone, harmonica, guitar and tuba as the mainstay of Stax's house band.

Albert King releases his signature piece, 'Born Under A Bad Sign', written by Booker T. Jones and William Bell. The song only reaches #49 on the R&B chart, but its roughhewn vocal style and stinging guitar lines make it a part of every blues player's repertoire. His album of the same name is also released this year. **Carla Thomas** and **Otis Redding** recorded a collection of duets in December 1966, which are now released as the LP *King And Queen*. Stand out tracks include their cover of Eddie Floyd's 'Knock On Wood', a # 8 R&B and #30 Pop hit, Lowell Fulson's humorous 'Tramp' (#2 R&B, #26 Pop) and a cover of the Clover's 'Lovey Dovey' (#21 R&B, 1968). An Otis Redding discovery, the young soul stylist **Arthur Conley** achieves RIAA Gold with the #2 Pop/R&B hit 'Sweet Soul Music'.

Sir Mack Rice records 'Mini-Skirt Minnie' and 'Love Sickness' for Stax. **Rufus Thomas** releases another dance-oriented single, 'Sophisticated Sissy', written by Sir Mack Rice, Joe Shamwell, Isaac Hayes and David Porter. The track also features Jeanne and the Darlings as a backup group and is Thomas' first chart entry in three years. The Sissy becomes a minor dance craze of that era. **Carla Thomas** earns a #11 R&B hit (#85

Pop) with Eddie Floyd and Al Bell's 'I'll Always Have Faith In You'. She also releases 'Pick Up The Pieces' (#16 R&B, #68 Pop). **Eddie Floyd** releases the song he wrote with Steve Cropper, 'Love Is A Doggone Good Thing' (#30 R&B, #97 Pop), 'Raise Your Hand' (#16 R&B, #79 Pop) and 'On A Saturday Night' (#22 R&B, #92 Pop). **Mabel John** records 'You're Taking Up Another Man's Place' and 'I'm A Big Girl Now', both written by Hayes and Porter. Neither makes it to the charts. The songs are backed by 'Wait You Dog', written by Floyd and Cropper, and 'Don't Hit Me No More', written by Joe Tex although it is credited to his wife. Mabel John also releases 'Same Time, Same Place'. **Ruby Johnson** releases the Hayes and Porter song 'If I Ever Needed Love (I Sure Do Need It Now)'.

Although **Otis Redding** is extremely popular in Europe, the mainstream American music audience doesn't really 'get it' until he performs at the 1967 Monterey Pop Festival and blows everyone away with a typically supercharged set. He releases the album *Live In Europe* and his cover of 'Glory Of Love' goes to #19 R&B and #60 Pop. Other Otis Redding hits in 1967 include 'I Love You More Than Words Can Say' (#30 R&B) and a live cover of Sam Cooke's 'Shake' (#16 R&B, #47 Pop). On December 6th, Otis records what many feel is his greatest single work, '(Sittin' On) The Dock Of The Bay'. Three days later, Otis Redding and four members of the Bar-Kays are killed when their plane crashes into a Wisconsin lake en route to a gig. Steve Cropper is left to complete tracks from these final sessions. Within weeks of the tragedy, '(Sittin' On) The Dock Of The Bay' becomes Otis' first #1 Pop hit, staying for four weeks at the top, and is also his first #1 R&B hit. It also wins two Grammies for Best R&B Song and Best Vocal Performance.

1968

Another track from **Otis Redding**'s last session, 'Happy Song (Dum-Dum-De-De-De-Dum)' is released. His *Dock Of The Bay* is a #1 album in the US and England. *Otis Blue* returns to the UK charts after a two-year hiatus. Other albums include *At The Whiskey A Go Go*, from his successful 1966 West Coast tour, and *The Immortal Otis Redding*. The two remaining members of the Bar-Kays, James Alexander (bass) and Ben Cowley (trumpet) re-form the group a year later. **William Bell** records 'Tribute To A King', originally intended as a personal testimonial for Otis, but released nationally at the urging of Redding's widow. Originally the B-side of 'Every Man Oughta Have A Woman', disc jockeys flip the disc and 'Tribute To A King' becomes a #16 R&B hit.

Led Zeppelin, consisting of ex-Yardbird and session mainstay Jimmy Page (guitar), Robert Plant (vocals), John Bonham (drums) and John Paul Jones (bass), is signed to Atlantic by Jerry Wexler. The band goes on to make musical history in the next decades and becomes the label's biggest-selling group of all time. *The Beat Goes On* and *Renaissance* are released by **Vanilla Fudge**. **Cream** release the epic *Wheels Of Fire*, which goes to #1 on the album chart before the group break up. Besides launching three exceptional solo careers, the band stand as probably the ultimate and most artful definition of the rock power trio. **Buffalo Springfield** record their third and final Atco LP, *Last Time Around*, essentially a collection of individual solo tracks dominated by Stephen Stills and Richie Furay. Neil Young left the band on the eve of the Monterey Pop Festival in 1967. The band finally breaks up in May this year. Stills and ex-Byrds singer/guitarist David Crosby, who sat in for Young at the Monterey Pop Festival, start playing together and are eventually joined by the Hollies' Graham Nash to make musical history as Crosby, Stills & Nash. Pianist and singer Mac Rebennack, professionally known as **Dr. John, The Night Tripper**, serves up a steaming brew of New Orleans funk with his *Gris Gris* album. Rebennack and Harold Battiste, arranger/pianist for Sonny and Cher, record the album at Gold Star studios. *Sooner Or Later* is released by **John Hammond, Jr**.

Another gold album from **Aretha Franklin**, *Lady Soul* is recorded in New York with Jerry Wexler producing and a guest appearance by guitarist Eric Clapton. *Aretha Now* also goes gold. Franklin also dominates the singles charts with '(Sweet, Sweet Baby) Since You've Been Gone' (#1 R&B, #5 Pop, RIAA Gold), 'Ain't No Way' (#9 R&B, #16 Pop), 'Think' (#1 R&B, #7 Pop, RIAA Gold, #46 UK), 'You Send Me, Sam' (#28 R&B, #56 Pop), 'The House That Jack Built' (#2 R&B, #6 Pop), 'I Say A Little Prayer' (#3 R&B, #10 Pop, RIAA Gold) and 'See Saw' (#9 R&B, #14 Pop). **The Sweet Inspirations** release a self-titled debut album on the label in 1968. This talented vocal foursome is originally made up of Cissy Houston, Estelle Brown, Sylvia Shemwell and Myrna Smith. Later, the group includes Dionne Warwick, Dee Dee Warwick and Judy Clay. The group releases several singles from the album including 'Sweet Inspiration' (#5 R&B, #18 Pop). They are considered the premier vocal back-up group working regularly with artists such as Aretha Franklin, Solomon Burke, Wilson Pickett and Elvis Presley. *Instant Groove* and *Sweet Soul* are released by **King Curtis** on Atco.

British pop diva **Dusty Springfield** creates a masterpiece working with Jerry Wexler in Memphis at Chips Moman's studio. The record, *Dusty In Memphis*, produces the Top Ten US and UK hit 'Son Of A Preacher Man', which eventually goes platinum in the nineties as a featured song on the *Pulp Fiction* soundtrack. Another single, 'The Windmills Of Your Mind' (#31 Pop), written by Alan and Marilyn Bergman and Michel Legrand, also shows up on the Oscar-winning soundtrack for the Steve McQueen film, *The Thomas Crown Affair*.

Australian sensations, the **Bee Gees** climb the charts with 'Massachusetts' (#11 Pop, #1 UK) from their Atco LP, *Horizontal*. The Gibb brothers also release their *Ideas* LP 1968, and enjoy chart success with 'I've Gotta Get A Message To You' (#8 Pop) and 'I Started A Joke' (#6 Pop). **The Rascals** eliminate the 'Young' in their name and pick up a #3 Pop hit with 'A Beautiful Morning' and a #1 gold Pop smash with 'People Got To Be Free'. **Jerry Jeff Walker** writes the modern folk standard 'Mr. Bojangles' featured on the album of the same name, which goes on to become a Top Ten hit single (#9 Pop) for the Nitty Gritty Dirt Band. Walker is backed on the album by guitarist David Bromberg, bassist Ron Carter and The Dixie Flyers. **Brian Auger & the Trinity**, featuring the stylish **Julie Driscoll** on vocals, just misses the Top Ten (#11 Pop) with their Atco LP, *Open*. They follow it up with *Definitely What!* recorded without Driscoll, but she returns for the double-LP *Streetnoise*, also released in the same year. UK artist, **The Crazy World of Arthur Brown**, scores gold with the single 'Fire'. Another monster success for Atlantic, **Iron Butterfly** debuts in 1968 with the appropriately entitled, *Heavy*. Their second album in 1968, *In-A-Gadda-Da-Vida* (#4 US), spends 140 weeks on the *Billboard* chart, 81 weeks in the Top Ten and is still regarded as a milestone album. Even at 17 minutes, the title track still goes to #1, while an edited version reaches #30. The album sells four million copies, the most of any Atlantic album up to that time.

Sam and Dave's 'I Thank You' (#4 R&B, #9 Pop) is their last major chart hit. They also release an album of the same name in 1968. The final Stax recording released by Atlantic, **Johnnie Taylor**'s 'I Ain't Particular' reaches #45 on the R&B chart. **Albert King** charts with 'I Love Lucy' (#46 R&B), written by William Bell and Booker T. Jones, dedicated to King's Gibson Flying V electric solid body guitar. King's song 'Cold Feet' is his highest Pop placing at #67 (#20 R&B). He also releases *King Of The Blues Guitar*, a collection of his Stax singles.

The irrepressible **Archie Bell & The Drells** strike gold with a double #1 R&B and Pop hit, 'Tighten Up'. A re-recording of an old B-side, it hits #1 while Archie is serving in the Army. 'I Can't Stop Dancing' peaks at #9 on the Pop chart. **Tyrone Davis** gets a #1 R&B hit with 'Turn Back The Hands Of Time' in March of 1968 on the Atlantic subsidiary, Dakar. A few months later he releases the million-seller, 'Can I Change My Mind' (#1 R&B, #5 Pop). Recorded at Fame Studios and produced by Rick Hall, **Otis Clay**'s cover of the Sir Douglas Quintet's 'She's About A Mover' marks the first release on the Cotillion imprint. **Percy Sledge** releases *Take Time To Know Her*, which includes the single 'Sudden Step' (#41 R&B) and the title track which peaks at #6 R&B and #11 Pop. More magic from Muscle

Shoals: *This Is Clarence Carter* and *The Dynamic Clarence Carter* are recorded at Rick Hall's Fame Studios. Gold hits from **Clarence Carter** include 'Slip Away' (#2 R&B, #6 Pop) and 'Too Weak To Fight' (#3 R&B, #13 Pop).

Carmen McRae's *Portrait Of Carmen* is arranged and conducted by Benny Carter and Shorty Rogers, among others, and produced by Nesuhi Ertegun. McRae also releases *The Sound Of Silence* album in 1968. Atlantic releases *Mabel Mercer And Bobby Short At Town Hall*, a double live set produced by Nesuhi Ertegun, which features individual performances from both artists, and duets on several tracks. Ahmet and Nesuhi Ertegun recommend **Bobby Short** as a replacement for pianist George Feyer at the Cafe Carlyle, beginning one of the most successful associations in the history of cabaret.

Instrumentalist **Yusef Lateef** debuts on Atlantic with *The Blue Yusef Lateef*. He's backed by an eclectic collection of talents including Sonny Red (alto), Buddy Lucas (harmonica), Kenny Burrell (guitar), Blue Mitchell (trumpet), a string quartet and The Sweet Inspirations. Pianist **Keith Jarrett** releases *Somewhere Before*, a live album recorded at Shelly Manne's Manne-Hole in L.A. with Charlie Haden on bass, Paul Motian on drums and George Avakian producing. Vibraphonist **Roy Ayers** releases *Stoned Soul Picnic*. **Mose Allison** releases *I've Been Doin' Some Thinkin'*. **Max Roach** releases *Members Don't Git Weary*. **Junior Mance** releases *Live At The Top*. *Keith Jarrett With Gary Burton* is also released this year.

Versatile multi-instrumentalist **Roland Kirk** debuts on the label with *The Inflated Tear*, an LP featuring him on tenor sax, clarinet, flute, flexafone, whistle, English horn, manzello and stritch. Kirk also releases *Left And Right* featuring Alice Coltrane on harp. An exceptional vocalist, **Roberta Flack**, signs with Atlantic and records her debut album *First Take* in less than ten hours with backing from Ron Carter (bass) and Joe Newman (trumpet), among others. The album includes her smouldering cover of Ewan MacColl's 'The First Time Ever I Saw Your Face', which is later prominently featured in the 1972 soundtrack for Clint Eastwood's film, *Play Misty For Me*.

1969 Led Zeppelin is released in January. **Led Zeppelin**'s phenomenal debut reaches #10 on the *Billboard* Pop album chart two months later and goes on to sell over eight million copies by the end of 1999. Their second album in 1969, *Led Zeppelin II*, is another multi-platinum success, eventually selling in excess of 12 million copies. In 1999, *Led Zeppelin II* is awarded coveted 'Diamond' status by the RIAA (one of four Zeppelin LPs to achieve this) for selling more than ten million copies. It reaches #1 in the UK and US. 'Whole Lotta Love' from *Led Zeppelin II* is their first gold single.

Blind Faith, featuring Eric Clapton, Steve Winwood, Ginger Baker and Rick Grech, release an album of the same name on Atco, which quickly goes gold. *Blind Faith* is originally released with a controversial cover shot of a naked young girl, soon changed to a group photo after US record stores threaten to boycott it. Their only album, it includes stand-out tracks such as 'Presence Of The Lord' and 'Can't Find My Way Home'. Blind Faith's first live appearance in London's Hyde Park draws an audience of over 150,000. They follow this appearance up with a sell-out US tour that kicks off at Madison Square Garden. **Cream** albums *Goodbye* (#2 Pop), featuring 'Badge' by Clapton and George Harrison, and *The Best Of Cream* (#3 Pop) are released in 1969. Both are certified gold.

Aretha Franklin continues her string of hit singles with 'The Weight' (#3 R&B, #19 Pop, backed by Duane Allman) and 'Eleanor Rigby' (#5 R&B, #17 Pop). 'Share Your Love With Me' (#1 R&B, #13 Pop) is also the first #1 on *Billboard*'s newly created Best Selling Soul Singles chart, which debuts in August. In addition to winning another Grammy for Best Vocal R&B Performance, she releases the LPs, *Aretha's Gold* (#1 R&B, #18 Pop) and *Aretha Franklin: Soul '69* (#1 R&B, #15 Pop). **The Sweet Inspirations** release *What The World Needs Now Is Love* and *Sweets For My Sweet* LPs and *Sweet, Sweet Soul* a year later.

Crosby, Stills & Nash, release their debut LP *Crosby, Stills & Nash* (#6 Pop). A commercial and critical success that redefines acoustic/electric rock, it offers an eclectic, stunning set of songs, including 'Suite: Judy Blue Eyes' (#21 Pop), 'Guinnevere' and 'Marrakesh Express' (#28 Pop). Steve Stills, David Crosby and Graham Nash earn a Best New Artist Grammy and the album will sell three million copies by 1999. Their second live appearance is in front of half a million people at the fabled Woodstock Festival. Neil Young also joins the band this year. **The Woodstock Music and Arts Fair** is held at Max Yasgur's farm in White Lake, New York. A seminal event in America's cultural history, it attracts close to half a million music fans. Atlantic finances Mike Wadleigh's documentary feature film of Woodstock and releases a best-selling double album of the event in June 1970 that goes to #1 Pop, selling over a million copies. The Fender Stratocaster guitar played by Jimi Hendrix during his historic closing appearance there earned a record price of $320,000 at auction in 1990.

Representing another new direction for Atlantic, the British 'art rock' band **Yes** is signed to the label. The original line-up consists of Jon Anderson (vocals), Chris Squire (bass), Tony Kaye (keyboards), Peter Banks (guitar) and Bill Bruford (drums). Their first single 'Sweetness' is followed by their debut LP, *Yes*, in November. **Iron Butterfly** rocks the charts again with their gold LP *Ball*, which reaches #3 on the Pop album chart. **The Rascals** release *Freedom Suite* (#17 Pop), which includes the previous year's #1 hit, 'People Got To Be Free'. Guest artists include King Curtis, David Newman and Chuck Rainey. The **Bee Gees** build on their success with the Atco LP *Odessa* (#20 Pop) and another Top 40 hit, 'First Of May' (#37 Pop). They also release the LP *2 Years On* (#32 Pop).

Chris Blackwell, the colourful and musically savvy founder of Island Records, negotiates with Atlantic for the US rights of seminal groups like Emerson, Lake & Palmer, King Crimson and Mott The Hoople. This marks the beginning of a long and fruitful association and friendship between Blackwell and Ahmet. One of the most committed and unique 'progressive rock' groups, **King Crimson** release *In The Court Of The Crimson King*. Crimson's original line-up includes leader Robert Fripp (guitars, keyboards), Greg Lake (vocals, guitar), Ian MacDonald (flute, Mellotron, vibes, keyboards, vocals) and Michael Giles (drums, percussion). Led by Ian Hunter (lead vocals) and Mick Ralphs (guitar), **Mott The Hoople** releases a self-titled US debut album with a blend of promising original songs and covers of Sonny Bono's 'Laugh At Me' and the Kinks' 'You Really Got Me'.

In June, **Les McCann** (piano, keyboards, vocals) and **Eddie Harris** (piano, trumpet, tenor sax, vocals) release the album *Swiss Movements* recorded live at the Montreux Jazz Festival. Featuring the track 'Compared To What', which goes to #35 R&B, the LP and single sell over a million copies. Produced by Nesuhi Ertegun and Joel Dorn, the album's line-up includes Benny Bailey (trumpet), Donald Dean (drums) and Leroy Vinnegar (bass).

Flautist **Herbie Mann** goes to Memphis to record *Memphis Underground* with Larry Coryell, Roy Ayers, Sonny Sharrock and a local rhythm section. The popular Mann wins *Down Beat*'s reader's poll every year between 1957 and 1970. **Roland Kirk**'s remarkable *Volunteered Slavery*, features the Roland Kirk Spirit Choir and a medley of John Coltrane compositions. **Roy Ayers** releases *Daddy's Back* with backing from Ron Carter (bass), Herbie Hancock (piano) and Freddie Waits (drums). **Yusef Lateef** releases *Yusef Lateef's Detroit*, produced by Joel Dorn. Vibraphonist **Gary Burton** releases *Throb*, a 14-track anthology of two albums, five tracks featuring pianist Keith Jarrett. Burton also releases *Good Vibes*. **Mose Allison** releases *Hello There, Universe* with Pepper Adams (baritone sax), Jerome Richardson (flute/alto sax), Joe Farrell (tenor sax), Jimmy Nottingham (trumpet), Bob Cranshaw (guitar), Joe Cocuzzo (drums) and John Williams (bass). Jazz organist **Shirley Scott** releases *Shirley Scott & The Soul Saxes* which showcases sax greats Hank Crawford, David 'Fathead' Newman and King Curtis. Joel Dorn produces it. **Hank Crawford** releases *Mister Blues Plays Lady Soul*. **Bobby Short** and **Mabel Mercer** release their *Second Town Hall Concert* live album.

Gifted bluesman **Otis Rush** records *Mourning In The Morning* at Muscle Shoals with support from Duane Allman and Roger Hawkins. Stand-out tracks include 'Gambler's Blues'. The Texas blues guitarist **Freddie King** (Eric Clapton credits him as a major influence) signs to the Atlantic subsidiary label Cotillion in 1968 and releases *Freddie King Is A Blues Master* in 1969. Produced by King Curtis, it includes the inimitable David 'Fathead' Newman on sax. **Dr. John** follows his *Gris Gris* LP with *Babylon* on Atco. The inimitable **Clarence Carter** releases *Testifyin'* (#35 R&B) which produces the hit singles, 'Snatching It Back' (#4 R&B), 'Feeling Is Right' (#9 R&B) and 'Doin' Our Thing' (#9 R&B). Another classic single, 'Patches', goes to #2 R&B and #4 Pop, earning gold status. The album *Patches* is released in 1970. **R.B. Greaves**, a nephew of vocalist Sam Cooke, writes and records 'Take A Letter Maria' at Muscle Shoals. Produced by Ahmet, the single goes to #2 Pop (RIAA Gold). Greaves' soft R&B style is showcased on the *R.B. Greaves* Atco LP also produced by Ahmet. **Brook Benton** produces two LPs, *Brook Benton Today* and *Home Style* on the Cotillion imprint. His evocative 'Rainy Night In Georgia' is released in January of the following year and goes to #1 R&B, #4 Pop and is certified gold.

Marking the emergence of a new offshoot style known as Southern Rock, *The Allman Brothers Band* is released on Phil Walden's Capricorn label, another Atlantic subsidiary. Formed by already legendary Macon slide and lead guitarist **Duane Allman** and his vocalist/keyboardist brother Gregg, **The Allman Brothers** also consist of Dickey Betts (guitar), Berry Oakley (bass), Jaimoe Johanny Johanson (drums, percussion) and Butch Trucks (drums). Born in the blues, their material blends powerful originals like 'In Memory Of Elizabeth Reed', 'Hot 'Lanta' and 'Whipping Post' with intuitive rethinks of classics like Blind Willie McTell's 'Statesboro Blues' and T-Bone Walker's 'Call It Stormy Monday'. Their tireless and inspired live performances are marked by Gregg Allman's powerhouse vocals and Hammond organ, the dual lead guitar lines and incandescent solos of brother Duane and Dickey Betts, Oakley's loping bass lines and the shifting, multifaceted rhythms of Johanson and Trucks.

Recorded in 1968, **Wilson Pickett**'s *Hey Jude* album is released in 1969. It features backup by The Sweet Inspirations and an all-star Muscle Shoals line-up including Duane Allman, Jimmy Johnson and Albert Lowe (guitars), Barry Beckett (keyboards), Roger Hawkins (drums) and David Hood and Gerald Jemmott (basses). The title song, an impassioned cover of the famous ballad by The Beatles, goes to #13 R&B and #23 Pop. Singer/guitarist **Boz Scaggs** records his self-titled debut LP, modern Southern roots music with backing from Duane Allman, the Muscle Shoals rhythm section and vocalist Tracy Nelson. Scaggs and *Rolling Stone* publisher Jann Wenner co-produce the album, which features stand-out tracks like 'Loan Me A Dime'. The legendary **Muscle Shoals Rhythm Section** of Barry Beckett, David Hood, Roger Hawkins and Jimmy Johnson leave Rick Hall's Fame studios and open their own studio in a former funeral parlour, the address of which is used as the title of **Cher**'s 1969 solo Atco LP, *3614 Jackson Highway*.

The legendary **Rolling Stones** arrive in Muscle Shoals on November 19th to record three classic tracks in as many nights: 'You've Got To Move', 'Brown Sugar' and 'Wild Horses'. All three later become hits from the band's classic *Sticky Fingers* album on Rolling Stones Records, distributed by Atlantic in 1971.

Warner-Seven Arts is bought by Kinney, which is later renamed Warner Communications.

1970 The newly augmented **Crosby, Stills, Nash & (Neil) Young** release *Déjà Vu* in January of 1970. It reaches #1 on the US album chart and goes on to sell over seven million copies. Singles from the album include 'Woodstock', a Joni Mitchell composition (#11 Pop), Nash's 'Teach Your Children' (#16 Pop), Crosby's 'Almost Cut My Hair' and 'Our House' (#30 Pop). Later, the band release Neil Young's outraged and direct response to the shooting of four students at Kent State University by the National Guard, 'Ohio/Find The Cost of Freedom' (#14 Pop). 1970 marks the release of **Stephen Stills**' self-titled Atlantic debut (#3 Pop), showcasing the hit 'Love The One You're With' (#4 Pop) and guest performances by Jimi Hendrix, Eric Clapton, Cass Elliot, David Crosby, Graham Nash and others.

Aretha Franklin continues her incredible run at Atlantic with *This Girl's In Love With You* (#2 R&B, #17 Pop) and a flood of hit singles including 'Call Me' (#1 R&B, #13 Pop) and 'Spirit In The Dark' (#1 R&B, #23 Pop). Franklin covers 'Don't Play That Song (You Lied)', written by Ahmet and Ben E. King (#1 R&B, #11 Pop). Recorded at Miami's Criteria studios with The Dixie Flyers, it wins her another Grammy for Best Female R&B Vocal Performance. Her incandescent album *Spirit In The Dark* (#2 R&B, #25 Pop) features backing by The Sweet Inspirations, Duane Allman and Cornell Dupree.

In February, **Led Zeppelin** performs in Copenhagen, Denmark as The Nobs (a name 'borrowed' from Claude Nobs, director of the Montreux Jazz Festival). This comes to pass after the family of airship creator Ferdinand von Zeppelin threatens the band with a lawsuit if they perform using the name. In October, the hugely popular group releases *Led Zeppelin III*, a #1 album in both the US and UK, which sells six million copies by the end of 1999.

Vocal (and married) duo **Delaney and Bonnie** Bramlett get the chance to open for Blind Faith on their US tour. Drawn to their music, **Eric Clapton** rides the Bramlett's tour bus, eventually sitting in with them on guitar after Blind Faith break up. Clapton brings the Bramletts to England and, together with George Harrison, Leon Russell and Dave Mason, the resulting stage shows provide the basis for 1970's *Delaney & Bonnie & Friends On Tour With Eric Clapton* (#29 Pop US). *To Bonnie From Delaney* is also released, with the singles 'Free The People' and 'Soul Shake' (#43 Pop). Featuring Eric 'Derek' Clapton (guitar, vocals), Bobby Whitlock (keyboards, vocals), Carl Radle (bass) and Jim Gordon (drums), **Derek & the Dominos** release what is generally acknowledged as one of rock's great albums, *Layla & Other Assorted Love Songs*. Recorded at Miami's Criteria Studios with Tom Dowd producing, the LP races up to #16 in the US charts and features the seven-minute title track which becomes a Top Ten hit two years later (#10 US, #4 UK). It is still a staple on FM radio stations everywhere. Another, more laid-back version of 'Layla' goes to #12 on the US Pop chart in 1993 as well. 'Brownie', the 1956 Tobacco Sunburst Fender Stratocaster used by Eric Clapton on the *Layla* album and single will later earn $497,500 at auction. **Eric Clapton** releases a self-titled album on Atco. Produced by Delaney Bramlett, it includes a #18 Pop hit, J.J. Cale's languid 'After Midnight'.

The Allman Brothers Band release the album, *Idlewild South*, which expands on their concept of modern electric blues with extensive and passionate soloing. Jerry Wexler and Tom Dowd produce a self-titled album by the veteran rock'n'roller **Ronnie Hawkins**, recorded in Muscle Shoals with sidemen Duane Allman and Donald 'Duck' Dunn, among others. **John Hammond Jr.** releases the roots-ey *Southern Fried* album featuring backing from Duane Allman, Jimmy Johnson and Eddie Hinton (guitars), David Hood and Marlin Greene (bass), Barry Beckett (keyboards) and Roger Hawkins (drums), with production by his father, recording legend John Hammond Sr. **Jerry Jeff Walker** releases *Bein' Free* on Atco. **Dr. John** releases *Remedies*.

The Velvet Underground records *Loaded* during a summer-long residency at Max's Kansas City in New York, featuring vocalist/guitarist/writer Lou Reed, violinist John Cale, bassist Sterling Morrison and Billy Yule replacing Maureen Tucker on drums due to her pregnancy. Atlantic signs the **MC5** (Motor City Five), musical front men for the politically conscious Detroit rock scene fostered by their manager John Sinclair and his White Panther Party. Produced by critic Jon

Landau, their high energy *Back In The U.S.A.* album is hailed as a definitive hard rock statement and an omen of the coming punk rock movement. **The J. Geils Band** is signed to Atlantic in 1970 and releases a self-titled album in their superb blues style. The Boston-based band consists of Peter Wolf (vocals, master of ceremonies), Jerome Geils (guitar), Magic Dick (harmonica), Seth Justman (keyboards), Danny Klein (bass) and Stephen Jo Bladd (drums). The Florida-based band **Blues Image**, featuring guitarist Mike Pinera, releases *Ride Captain Ride* on Atco. The title track goes to #4 on the *Billboard* Pop chart.

Wilson Pickett records *Right On* and *Wilson Pickett In Philadelphia*. Singles include 'Cole, Cooke & Redding' (#4 R&B, #25 Pop) and 'Engine Number 9' (#3 R&B, #14 Pop). **King Curtis** gets **Esther Phillips** to return to Atlantic, playing on and producing her album *Burnin'*. *Brand New Day* is recorded at Criteria with The Dixie Flyers and production by Tom Dowd and Dave Crawford, but is not released until 1986. The single 'Set Me Free' reaches #39 on the R&B chart. King Curtis also releases two LPs of his own, *Get Ready* and *Everybody's Talkin'*. Bluesman **Clarence Wheeler** releases *Doin' What We Wanna* and *Clarence Wheeler And The Enforcers*. **Freddie King**'s *My Feeling For The Blues* on Cotillion is produced by King Curtis and features arrangements by Donny Hathaway. **Otis Clay** records *Pouring Water On A Drowning Man* on Cotillion. **King Floyd**'s 'Groove Me', originally released on the Malaco Studio's Chimneyville Records, is picked up by Atlantic for national distribution and goes to #1 R&B and #6 Pop. **Jackie Moore** enjoys her biggest career hit, 'Precious, Precious', recorded at Miami's Criteria Studios with the Dixie Flyers. Written by Moore and her producer Dave Crawford, the single goes to #12 R&B and #30 Pop.

Cuban-born bandleader and percussionist **Mongo Santamaria**, a veteran of orchestras led by Perez Prado, Tito Puente and Cal Tjader, releases three albums: *Mongo '70*, *Feelin' Alright* and *Mongo's Way*. Saxophonist **Phil Woods** releases *Phil Woods And His European Rhythm Machine At The Frankfurt Jazz Festival*, recorded with Gordon Beck, Daniel Humair and Henri Texier. **Joe Zawinul** releases *Concerto Retitled*. **David 'Fathead' Newman** releases *Captain Buckles*. **Jimmy Scott** has one album on Atlantic, *The Source*, produced by Joel Dorn with a stellar cast of musicians including David 'Fathead' Newman, Junior Mance, Ron Carter, Eric Gale, Billy Butler and Cissy Houston. Arif Mardin provides arrangements for five of the tracks. **Carmen McRae** releases *Just A Little Lovin'*, an interesting collaboration with The Dixie Flyers, conducted, arranged and produced by Arif Mardin.

Recorded in October, **Emerson, Lake & Palmer**, release their self-titled Atlantic debut (#18 Pop US, #4 UK) it goes gold partly on the strength of Greg Lake's 'Lucky Man' (#48 Pop). **Iron Butterfly** release the aptly titled *Metamorphosis* before breaking up next year. **Mott The Hoople** release the album *Mad Shadows* produced by Guy Stevens. The phenomenal British band **Slade** release *Play It Loud*, their one album with Atlantic, on the subsidiary label Cotillion. Atlantic releases *Live Cream*, a powerful aural documentary of **Cream** on stage. Scottish singer **Lulu**, born Marie Lawrie, releases *Melody Fair* on Atco. The album features backup by The Dixie Flyers, The Sweet Inspirations and Memphis Horns. The album is produced by Tom Dowd, Jerry Wexler and Arif Mardin. The **Bee Gees**, minus Robin Gibb who is pursuing solo work, release *Cucumber Castle*. Singer-songwriter **Loudun Wainwright III** debuts on Atlantic with *Album 1*.

Yes release their second Atlantic LP, *Time And A Word*. At this point, guitarist Peter Banks is replaced by Steve Howe, who appears on the cover, though Banks plays on the album. **King Crimson**'s second album, *In the Wake of Poseidon*, marks the departure of Ian MacDonald and Michael Giles from the band. Crimson also release *Lizard*, which features Jon Anderson of Yes on vocals. **Ginger Baker's Air Force**, an offshoot of Blind Faith, release *Air Force* and *Air Force 2* on Atco featuring Steve Winwood and Rick Grech

Roberta Flack strikes gold with her *Chapter Two* LP (#4 R&B, #33 Pop), featuring former classmate Donny Hathaway along with King Curtis, Hubert Laws and bassist Chuck Rainey. A multi-talented artist who excels at singing, writing and arranging, **Donny Hathaway** releases his debut album, *Everything Is Everything*. His first hit single, 'The Ghetto', reaches #23 R&B and #87 Pop.

1971 By now the predominant rock group worldwide, **Led Zeppelin** release *Led Zeppelin IV*, also known as *The Runes*, *Four Symbols* or *ZOSO* based on different interpretations of the medieval symbols on the cover. The album resides in the *Billboard* Pop chart for 234 weeks and stands as Atlantic's all-time best-selling album up to that time. It is also the third of Zeppelin's eight successive British #1 LPs, five of which go straight to #1. By the end of 1999, the album will sell in excess of 21 million copies, earning the RIAA's Diamond award for sales of over ten million. Classic tracks include 'Black Dog'(#15 Pop), 'Going To California' and the rock staple, 'Stairway to Heaven', which remains the most played song on US rock stations even though it has never been officially released as a single.

The Rolling Stones are signed to Atlantic on April Fool's Day. The band celebrates the birth of its own imprint, Rolling Stones Records, at a signing party in Cannes, France. Later in the year, their superb *Sticky Fingers* album, featuring the notorious 'Zipper' cover by Andy Warhol, goes to #1 in the US and goes on to sell three million copies.

Aretha Franklin's 'Bridge Over Troubled Water/Brand New Me' goes #1 R&B and #5 Pop in the US and wins her another Grammy. On *Aretha Live At The Fillmore West*, (#1 R&B, #7 Pop), she receives inspired backup from King Curtis and the Sweethearts of Soul. At one point, Ray Charles steps up from the audience to join Franklin on 'Spirit In The Dark'. More singles include 'Spanish Harlem' (#1 R&B, #2 Pop) and 'Rock Steady' (#2 R&B, #9 Pop). Franklin also releases the LP *Young, Gifted And Black* (#2 R&B, #11 Pop) featuring Dr. John and Donny Hathaway. **King Curtis** steps out with his own *Live At The Fillmore West* LP featuring Billy Preston, Cornell Dupree, Bernard Purdie, The Memphis Horns and with Arif Mardin producing. Curtis also teams with bluesman Champion Jack Dupree on *Blues At Montreux*, produced by Nesuhi Ertegun and Joel Dorn. Curtis is named musical director for Aretha Franklin. Tragically, however, in August later this year he is the victim of an insane killing, on the steps of his New York townhouse.

Donny Hathaway releases his self-titled LP. His silky smooth duet with Roberta Flack, the Joel Dorn-produced 'You've Got A Friend', goes to #8 R&B and #29 Pop. **Roberta Flack** releases her *Quiet Fire* album (#4 R&B, #18 Pop) with backing from Ron Carter, Hubert Laws and Les McCann. Recorded at Criteria Studios in Miami, **Ronnie Hawkins**' *The Hawk* features backup by Duane Allman and The Dixie Flyers.

Betty Wright is only 18 when she breaks through to the top of the charts with her sassy hit single, the legendary Clarence Reid composition, 'Clean Up Woman' (#2 R&B, #6 Pop). **Wilson Pickett**'s 'Don't Knock My Love, Pt.1' (#1 R&B, #13 Pop) is certified gold. The album of the same name goes to #1 on the R&B chart. He charts with two other singles in 1971, 'Don't Let The Green Grass Fool You' (#2 R&B, #17 Pop) and 'Call My Name, I'll Be There' (#10 R&B, #52 Pop). Atlantic releases the *Soul To Soul* album recorded live in Accra, Ghana at the Soul To Soul Festival. It features inspired performances from headliner Wilson Pickett, **Ike and Tina Turner**, Roberta Flack, Eddie Harris and Les McCann, The Staple Singers and Santana. **The Persuaders** release 'Thin Line Between Love and Hate' on Atco. Produced by Richard and Robert Poindexter with a brilliantly subtle arrangement by Arif Mardin, the single goes to #1 R&B and #15 Pop. The Bahamian group **Beginning Of The End** signs with Atlantic and climbs the charts with the Junkanoo-flavoured 'Funky Nassau' (#7 R&B, #15 Pop).

Rahsaan Roland Kirk releases two LPs in 1971, *Natural Black Inventions: Root Strata* and *Blacknuss*. Founder of the influential Weather Report, keyboardist-composer **Joe Zawinul** releases *Zawinul*

featuring fellow jazz heavyweights Herbie Hancock, Wayne Shorter, Jack DeJohnette and Hubert Laws. The **Dave Brubeck**-Gerry Mulligan quartet record the live album *Last Set At Newport* just before a riot by the audience closes the festival. The album features the signature Brubeck piece, 'Take Five'. A perfect musical match, **Bobby Short** releases the *Bobby Short Loves Cole Porter* LP. **The Modern Jazz Quartet** release *Plastic Dreams*.

The Bee Gees' *Trafalgar* album is the launching pad for yet another gold single, 'How Can You Mend A Broken Heart' (#1 Pop). **Lulu**'s *New Routes* LP, produced by Jerry Wexler, Tom Dowd and Arif Mardin, features Duane Allman on guitar. It yields the Top 30 hit, 'Oh Me, Oh My (I'm A Fool For You Baby)' (#22 Pop), later covered by Aretha Franklin. *Search For Nearness* by **The Rascals** is their final recording for Atlantic, which also marks the departure of singer Eddie Brigati. A mini-riot during one of **Mott The Hoople**'s shows in July plays a role in the decision to ban rock concerts from London's Royal Albert Hall. Ironically, the group's 1971 album *Wildlife* signals a more laid-back musical style. Detroit's **MC5** refine their 'kick out the jams' approach with *High Time*. **The J. Geils Band**'s second LP, *The Morning After*, includes the Top 40 hit 'Looking For A Love' (#39 Pop). **Delaney & Bonnie**'s *Motel Shot* LP includes their Top 20 hit single, 'Never Ending Song of Love' (#13 Pop). **Dr. John**'s Atco release, *The Sun, The Moon And Herbs* includes guest performances from Eric Clapton and Mick Jagger.

The Allman Brothers Band release *Beginnings* on Capricorn, a repackaging of their first two LPs, *The Allman Brothers Band* (1969) and *Idlewild South* (1970). After their eponymous debut, Duane continues to play on sessions with Boz Scaggs, Otis Rush, Delaney and Bonnie, Ronnie Hawkins and John Hammond, Jr. The group achieves its peak with the definitive *The Allman Brothers Band At Fillmore East* double-LP recorded on March 12th and 13th, which goes to #13 Pop. Hailed as one of America's premier live bands, The Allman Brothers Band loses its musical and spiritual core when Duane is killed in a motorcycle accident less than three months after the release of the *At Fillmore East* album. Bassist Berry Oakley dies a year later. A tribute to the enduring spirit of the band, The Allman Brothers Band goes on to record many more albums, becoming American musical icons still touring in the new millennium.

Following the breakup of **Crosby, Stills, Nash & Young** after the #1 album *Déjà Vu*, their live double album, *4 Way Street*, is released and also goes to #1 on the Pop album chart. By 1992, the album has sold four million copies. **David Crosby**'s *If I Could Only Remember My Name* LP is certified gold by the RIAA. *Stephen Stills 2*, another solo LP from the talented musician and songwriter, **Stephen Stills**, features Dr. John, Eric Clapton and David Crosby. **Graham Nash**'s solo debut for the label, *Songs For Beginners* (#15 Pop), goes gold.

Singer/songwriter **John Prine** is signed to the label by Jerry Wexler. Prine's self-titled debut, produced by Arif Mardin, is quickly acclaimed by fellow songwriters and critics who respond to his understated style and powerful lyrics. **Loudon Wainwright III** pushes the traditional singer-songwriter envelope with *Album 2*, earning evermore critical recognition.

Produced by Eddie Orford, *The Yes Album* reaches #7 in the UK album chart and #40 in the US, eventually going platinum. The album's single, 'I've Seen All Good People', is the first US hit for **Yes**. Rick Wakeman replaces Tony Kaye on keyboards. In December, the band releases *Fragile* (2 million sales, #4 US, #7 UK), featuring the hit single 'Roundabout' (#13 Pop). Alan White replaces Bill Bruford on drums. **Emerson, Lake & Palmer** release a hugely popular concept album about a mythical techno-creature, *Tarkus*, on Cotillion (#1 UK, #9 US, RIAA Gold). They also benefit further from their classical roots with a unique interpretation of Mussorgsky's 'Pictures At An Exhibition'.

Mongo Santamaria releases *Mongo At Montreux (Live)*, featuring his cousin Armando Peraza. *Gary Burton With Keith Jarrett* teams the gifted vibraphonist **Gary Burton** with Keith Jarrett on piano, Steve Swallow on bass and Samantha Brown on guitar. Burton also releases *Alone At Last* and *Live In Tokyo*. *Turn Of The Century* is a collection of his work on Atlantic culled from five different sessions. **Keith Jarrett** continues his ascendance at Atlantic with *The Mourning Of A Star* and *Birth* featuring Charlie Haden (bass), Paul Motian (drums) and George Avakian producing.

Mose Allison's *Western Man* disc features Chuck Rainey on bass and Billy Cobham on drums. **Max Roach**'s unique album *Lift Every Voice And Sing* features arrangements by William Bell and is produced by Joel Dorn. **David "Fathead" Newman** records *Lonely Avenue*, featuring vibraphonist Roy Ayers. **Freddie Hubbard** releases the anti-Vietnam war statement *Sing Me A Song Of Songmy*, combining an orchestra, organist, choral group and his quintet featuring Kenny Barron, Junior Cook, Art Booth and Louis Hayes.

1972 The **Rolling Stones** tour the US to packed houses. 'Tumbling Dice' becomes their 11th Top Ten hit (#7 Pop) on both sides of the Atlantic. Recorded in the South of France, their *tour de force* double album *Exile On Main Street* also goes to #1 and goes on to sell over a million copies.

Aretha Franklin wins Grammy Awards for 'Young, Gifted And Black' (Best R&B Vocal Performance, Female) and 'Amazing Grace' (Best Soul Gospel Performance). Another hit single, 'Day Dreaming', peaks at #12 R&B and #5 Pop. She also records a transcendent live double gospel album, *Amazing Grace* (#2 R&B, #7 Pop), at the New Temple Missionary Baptist Church in Los Angeles with the Reverend James Cleveland and the Southern California Community Choir, which sells over two million copies and earns enduring critical acclaim.

Roberta Flack's 'The First Time Ever I Saw Your Face' is featured in Clint Eastwood's popular directorial film debut, *Play Misty For Me*. The renewed exposure takes the single to #1 Pop, #4 R&B and is awarded RIAA Gold. Her LP *First Take*, originally released in 1969, also goes to #1, is certified RIAA Gold and wins a Grammy for Record Of The Year. Also in 1972, the *Roberta Flack & Donny Hathaway* duet LP goes gold and produces the hit single, 'Where Is The Love' that wins a Grammy for Best Pop Vocal by a Duo, Group or Chorus. The *Donny Hathaway Live* LP goes gold and produces the hit singles 'Little Ghetto Boy' (#25 R&B), 'Giving Up' (#21 R&B) and 'I Love You More Than You'll Ever Know' (#20 R&B). Quincy Jones hires **Donny Hathaway** to score the movie soundtrack LP, *Come Back Charleston Blue*, released on Atco.

One of **Dr. John**'s finest Atco offerings, *Gumbo*, produced by Jerry Wexler, features the New Orleans classic, 'Tipitina'. An authentic documentary of modern Chicago blues, **Buddy Guy & Junior Wells Play The Blues** also includes inspired performances by Dr. John, Eric Clapton and The J. Geils Band. Originally recorded in 1953, **John Lee Hooker**'s Atco tracks are subsequently released on *Don't Turn Me From Your Door* (1963) and *Detroit Special* (1972). **Clarence Wheeler** releases *New Chicago Blues*, featuring blues greats Buddy Guy and Junior Wells, and *The Love I've Been Looking For* with Hank Crawford, Joe Newman and guitarist Eric Gale. One of the legendary guitarist's first successful anthology albums, *History Of Eric Clapton* (#6 Pop) easily earns **Eric Clapton** RIAA Gold status. In September, Atlantic releases the **Ann Arbor Blues And Jazz Festival** live album with inspired performances from Bobby 'Blue' Bland, J.B. Hutto, Luther 'Guitar J.R.' Johnson, Johnny Shines, Koko Taylor, Muddy Waters, Howlin' Wolf, Luther Allison, Miles Davis, Bonnie Raitt and others. The uncompromising **Art Ensemble of Chicago** release a live LP, *Bap-Tizum*, taken from their performance at the Ann Arbor Blues And Jazz Festival.

John Prine releases *Diamonds In The Rough*, produced by Arif Mardin. Among other classic songs, it features 'Yes, I Guess They Oughta Name A Drink After You', a tribute to Hank Williams. **Graham Nash** and **David Crosby** go Top Ten (#4 Pop, RIAA Gold) with *Graham Nash And David Crosby*. **Stephen Stills** produces another gold LP, the group-based effort *Manassas* (#4 Pop), featuring Chris Hillman, Joe Lala, Al Perkins, Calvin 'Fuzzy' Samuels and Dallas Taylor. *Whole Oats*, the folkishsounding Atlantic debut by Philadelphia R&B vocal-instrumental duo **Hall & Oates** is produced by Arif Mardin. Philly band **Good God** release a self-titled album. **Black Oak Arkansas** release the deep-fried Southern rock albums, *Keep The Faith* and *If An Angel Came To See You*. **The J. Geils Band**'s dynamic *Full House Live*, a showcase for their outstanding in-concert performance style, goes gold.

Dave Brubeck's *We're All Together Again (For The First Time)* features the contrasting sax styles of Gerry Mulligan and Paul Desmond. **David "Fathead" Newman** records *The Weapon* in 1972 and *Newmanism* is released the following year. Atlantic releases the **Modern Jazz Quartet**'s *Legendary Profile*. Atlantic releases *Ella Fitzgerald Loves Cole* by 'The First Lady Of Song', jazz singer **Ella Fitzgerald**. Recorded live at Donte's in Los Angeles, **Carmen McRae**'s *Great American Songbook* features musicians such as the gifted jazz guitarist Joe Pass. **Mongo Santamaria** releases *Up From The Roots*, a mix of Afro-Cuban and Conjunto styles. **Mose Allison** releases the live album *Mose In Your Ear* backed by Clyde Flowers (bass) and Eddie Charlton (drums). *A Meeting Of The Times* by **Rahsaan Roland Kirk**, features the vocal talents of Duke Ellington's former singer, **Al Hibbler**. Also recorded by Kirk this year is the album, *I, Eye, Aye: Live At The Montreux Jazz Festival, Switzerland 1972*.

The Spinners, known in the UK as The Detroit Spinners to avoid confusion with another group of the same name, strike gold with 'I'll Be Around' (#1 R&B, #3 Pop). They follow up with the equally successful 'Could It Be I'm Falling In Love' a #1 R&B, #4 Pop hit. Atlantic releases **Betty Wright**'s album *I Love The Way You Love*.

Robert John's single 'The Lion Sleeps Tonight' (based on the African folk song, 'Wimoweh') goes to #3 Pop and is certified gold. Irreverent comedian and actor **George Carlin** releases *FM & AM* (#13 US) on Little David, a subsidiary of Atlantic. He follows with several successful albums including *Class Clown* (#22 Pop), *Occupation: Foole* (#35 US), *Toledo Window Box* (#19 Pop) and more.

One of **Yes**' most popular offerings, the platinum album *Close To The Edge* is a Top Five transatlantic success (#4 UK, #3 US). An edited version of 'And You And I' goes to #42 Pop in the US. The band's *Close To The Edge* Tour is recorded and released virtually untouched on the platinum triple-LP, *Yessongs* (#7 UK, #12 US). *Trilogy*, another epic from **Emerson, Lake & Palmer**, yields more hits, the Greg Lake ballad, 'From The Beginning' (#39 Pop), and their cover of Aaron Copland's 'Hoedown'. **Mott The Hoople** release the album *Brain Capers*, produced by Guy Stevens. The **Bee Gees** release *To Whom It May Concern*.

Bette Midler, the incandescent singer and entertainer discovered by Ahmet Ertegun at New York's Continental Baths, releases *The Divine Miss M*, her first album for Atlantic. Featuring strong backing from Barry Manilow, Ron Carter, David Spinozza and Cissy Houston, it produced the Top 40 hits, 'Boogie Woogie Bugle Boy' (#8 Pop), 'Friends' (#40 Pop) and 'Do You Want To Dance?' (#17 Pop). The album wins Midler a Grammy for Best New Artist.

1973 **Led Zeppelin**'s *Houses Of The Holy* debuts at #1 in the US and UK. The LP goes on to sell 11 million copies, earning another of the megagroup's RIAA Diamond awards. Zeppelin's record-breaking tour of the US climaxes at Madison Square Garden with a spectacular series of dynamic appearances documented in the film *The Song Remains The Same*, released in 1976.

Aretha Franklin notches another Grammy for 'Master Of Eyes (The Deepness Of Your Eyes)'. She also earns another #1 R&B hit single with 'Until You Come Back To Me (That's What I'm Gonna Do)'. Aretha and Quincy Jones co-produce her 1973 album *Hey Now Hey (The Other Side Of The Sky)*.

Roberta Flack's evergreen, 'Killing Me Softly With His Song', stays on the R&B and Pop charts for 12 weeks, going to #1 and #2 respectively. It also wins Flack two Grammies for Best Pop Vocal Performance, Female and Record Of The Year. She also releases the gold LP, *Killing Me Softly*. **Donny Hathaway**'s *Extension Of A Man* album includes the hit single, 'Love, Love, Love' (#16 R&B).

The Spinners score double gold with 'One Of A Kind Love Affair' (#1 R&B) and the album *Spinners* (#1 R&B, #14 Pop). **Percy Mayfield**, known to some as the 'Poet Laureate of the Blues', releases *Nothing Stays The Same Forever*. Atlantic releases **Bette Midler**'s self-titled album, which is produced by **Arif Mardin** and has backing from premier New York session players like Chuck Rainey (bass) and Cornell Dupree (guitar), together with her long-time accompanist Barry Manilow. **Bryan Ferry** releases his first solo Atlantic LP, *These Foolish Things*, recorded at London's AIR Studios. **Emerson, Lake & Palmer** form their own label, Manticore, distributed by Atlantic. They release the gold LP, *Brain Salad Surgery* (#11 Pop), featuring the 30-minute opus, 'Karn Evil 9'. **King Crimson** release the progressive rock classic, *Larks' Tongues In Aspic*. The group's new line-up includes John Wetton (replacing Greg Lake), Bill Bruford (drums), Jamie Muir (percussion) and David Cross (violin, viola, Mellotron, keyboards).

Rahsaan Roland Kirk releases *Bright Moments*, a double-LP of Kirk's apperance at the Keystone Korner in San Francisco. He also releases *Prepare Thyself To Deal With A Miracle*, which features the 21-minute 'Saxophone Concerto', and *The Art Of Rahsaan Roland Kirk*. **Dave Brubeck** releases *All The Things We Are*, which showcases saxophonists Lee Konitz and Anthony Braxton. **The Art Ensemble of Chicago** record *Fanfare For The Warriors*. Drummer **Billy Cobham**'s explosive *Spectrum* album features rock-to-fusion guitarist Tommy Bolin along with Ray Barretto, Ron Carter and Joe Farrell. Incorporating a conscious return to classical influences, the **MJQ** release *Blues On Bach*. **Cornell Dupree** steps out on his own with *Teasin'*. The effervescent cabaret interpreter **Bobby Short** releases the albums, *Bobby Short Live At The Cafe Carlyle* and *Bobby Short Is K-R-A-Z-Y For Gershwin*. *The Art Of Carmen McRae* stands as a compilation of the gifted vocal interpreter's earlier Atlantic work.

Peaking at #1 in the UK and US, **The Rolling Stones**' three million-selling *Goat's Head Soup* album features singles 'Angie' and 'Star Star', formerly entitled 'Starfucker'. **The J. Geils Band**'s *Bloodshot* LP goes #10 in the US album chart. The **Bee Gees** record *Life In A Tin Can* in Los Angeles. **Black Oak Arkansas**'s gold LP *High On The Hog* features their energetic cover of LaVern Baker's 'Jim Dandy' (#25 Pop), which puts them on the map. They then release *Raunch And Roll*, which also goes gold. **Hall & Oates**, now firmly rooted in the 'Philly Soul' style of their hometown, release the gold LP *Abandoned Luncheonette* (#33 Pop) with the bittersweet #7 Pop single, 'She's Gone'. The newly re-formed **James Gang**, featuring Tommy Bolin on guitar, release *Bang*, originally entitled *James Gang Bang*.

Stephen Stills and **Manassas** release *Down The Road*, which peaks at #26 in the US Pop album chart. **Graham Nash** releases the solo album *Wild Tales*. Produced by Arif Mardin, **John Prine**'s *Sweet Revenge* expands his musical style and features backing vocals from Cissy Houston and Judy Clay of The Sweet Inspirations.

Jerry Wexler and country legend **Willie Nelson** collaborate on *Shotgun Willie*, recorded at Atlantic's studios in New York. Texas phenomenon **Doug Sahm**, former leader and guiding spirit of the Sir Douglas Quintet, records *Doug Sahm And Band*. The album, produced by Wexler, Arif Mardin and Sahm, features Dr. John, Bob Dylan, David Newman, the legendary Tex-Mex accordionist Flaco Jimenez, guitarist David Bromberg and others. The sessions produce enough material to yield another LP, *Texas Tornado*, which also includes four Sahm-produced tracks. **Dr. John**'s presciently titled *In The Right Place* (#24 Pop) yields the Top Ten hit, 'Right Place, Wrong Time' (#9 Pop), produced by Allen Toussaint with backing from local New Orleans legends, the Meters.

1974 This is a banner year for **The Spinners**. Their gold LP, *Mighty Love* (#1 R&B, #16 Pop) produces the hit singles 'Mighty Love, Part 1' (#1 R&B, #20 Pop) and 'I'm Coming Home' (#13 R&B, #18 Pop). They follow with *New And Improved*

Spinners that goes Top Ten and a duet hit single with Dionne Warwick, 'Then Came You', that crests at #1 Pop and #2 R&B (RIAA Gold). The Spinners also appear at a concert in Zaire dubbed the 'African Woodstock' preceding the epic Ali-Foreman 'Rumble In The Jungle' heavyweight championship bout. **Abba** notch up a total of 12 Top 30 singles. They are licensed to the label from their own Polar imprint. Consisting of two singer-songwriter couples, Benny Andersson and Anni-Frid Lyngstad and Bjorn Ulvaeus and Agnetha Faltskog, the band starts down the golden road with the catchy single 'Waterloo'. It goes to #1 in the UK, #6 in the US and wins the 1974 Eurovision Song Contest. They also release the album *Waterloo*. British group **Hot Chocolate**, fronted by singer Errol Brown, releases the LP *Cicero Park* on Big Tree, the label founded by hit-savvy Doug Morris, who sells it to Atlantic and later replaces Jerry Greenberg as Atlantic President.

Crosby, Stills, Nash & Young get back together and produce the album, *So Far*. Their third in a row to go to #1, it sells six million copies by 1992. **Roxy Music** release *Stranded* on Atco. This same year, *Country Life* goes to #37 in the album charts, Roxy Music's first significant chart success in the US. The UK album cover is banned in some record stores in the States because of its revealing artwork. Featuring a completely authentic R&B style, the Scottish group **Average White Band**'s debut album, *AWB*, is certified gold and goes to #1 in both the Pop and R&B charts. Produced by Arif Mardin with backing from David Newman and Sonny Fortune, it produces the #1 R&B and Pop single, 'Pick Up The Pieces'. The band consists of Hamish Stuart (vocals, guitar), Onnie McIntyre (vocals, guitar), Alan Gorrie (vocals, bass), Roger Ball (keyboards, saxophone), Malcolm Duncan (saxophone) and Robbie McIntosh (drums). Tragically, McIntosh dies this year and is replaced by Steve Ferrone. **Yes** win the Top Group award in the *NME* poll and all their Madison Square Garden shows sell out. Their first UK chart-topper, *Tales From Topographic Oceans* (#6 US, RIAA Gold), is a double-LP set with four tracks, each one side long. Patrick Moraz replaces Rick Wakeman on keyboards. In November, the group releases *Relayer* (#4 UK, #5 US) which goes platinum. **The James Gang**, minus guitarist Tommy Bolin and vocalist Roy Kenner, release *Miami* before finally disbanding. **Genesis**, with Peter Gabriel (vocals), Phil Collins (drums), Mike Rutherford (guitars), Steve Hackett (guitars) and Tony Banks (keyboards), release the gold LP, *The Lamb Lies Down On Broadway*. **Roberta Flack** gets a #1 Pop hit with 'Feel Like Makin' Love'. *War Babies*, produced by fellow Philadelphian Todd Rundgren, represents another stylistic departure for **Hall & Oates**.

Produced by Joel Dorn, **Yusef Lateef**'s *Gentle Giant* album features the versatile artist on flute, piano, oboe and tenor sax. **Herbie Mann**, always keenly aware of the latest musical trends, releases his *Discotheque* and *Reggae* albums. **Charles Mingus**, the prodigious bassist and composer, releases the live LP, *Mingus At Carnegie Hall*. **Billy Cobham** releases *Total Eclipse* and *Shabazz* with stellar support from talents like guitarist John Abercrombie. Following a final concert at Avery Fisher Hall, documented in a two-record set, the **Modern Jazz Quartet** disbands. Keyboardist **Chick Corea**'s 1974 album *Inner Space* is a reissue of *Tones For Joan's Bones* together with unreleased tracks from that session. He is backed by Hubert Laws and Herbie Mann.

Bad Company, Paul Rodgers (vocals) and Simon Kirke (drums) from Free, Mick Ralphs (guitars) from Mott The Hoople and Boz Burrell (drums) from King Crimson, release a self-titled album on Led Zeppelin's Swan Song label, which goes to #1 Pop in the US and sells five million copies. The powerhouse single 'Can't Get Enough' also goes to #1 Pop worldwide. **Dr. John** releases his last Atco album, *Desitively Bonaroo*. **The J. Geils Band** release *Nightmares … And Other Tales From The Vinyl Jungle*, featuring the #12 Pop single 'Must Of Got Lost'. **Black Oak Arkansas** release *Street Party*. **Willie Nelson** records *Phases And Stages* and duets with **Tracy Nelson** on 'After The Fire Is Gone', a featured track on her self-titled Atlantic LP. Another exponent of Scottish soul, singer **Maggie Bell** releases *Queen Of The Night*, produced by Jerry Wexler. The **Bee Gees** record *Mr. Natural* with producer Arif Mardin at the helm. **Mike Oldfield**'s instrumental concept LP *Tubular Bells* (#3 Pop) is one of the top-selling albums of 1974. It features Oldfield (bass, guitar, percussion, keyboards, multi-instruments), Jabula (percussion), Sally Oldfield (vocals), Viv Stanshall (vocals) and a host of other luminaries. The title track vaults to #7 Pop on the US charts. **Emerson, Lake & Palmer** score again in 1974 with the gold LP *Welcome Back, My Friends, To The Show That Never Ends – Ladies & Gentlemen* (#4 Pop) on Manticore. **King Crimson** disband after releasing the cult classic *Starless And Bible Black*. They re-form in 1981.

Blue Magic's 'Sideshow' is a #1 R&B and #8 Pop hit, while 'Three Ring Circus' climbs into the Top 40. The group continues to have R&B hits into the nineties, but no Pop hits. Late this year, virtuoso lead guitarist Mick Taylor leaves **The Rolling Stones** to be replaced by Ronnie Wood. The Stones have a Top 20 hit (#16 US) with the anthem 'It's Only Rock 'N Roll (But I Like It)'. **Aretha Franklin** releases *With Everything I Feel In Me* (#6 R&B). The title track is a Top 20 R&B hit and her single 'Without Love' is #6 R&B. She also releases the album *Let Me In Your Life* which goes to #1 R&B.

1975 The prodigiously brilliant jazz multi-instrumentalist **Rahsaan Roland Kirk** releases *The Case Of The 3 Sided Dream In Audio Color*. The superb musician **Billy Cobham** releases *A Funky Thide Sings*. **Herbie Mann** records the LP, *Water Bed*. Seamless vocal harmony quartet **Charles Mingus** records the encyclopedic *Changes One* album. It features pianist Don Pullen, George Adams (tenor sax), Dannie Richmond (drums), Jack Walrath (trumpets) and tongue-in-cheek vocals by Catmouth Brown on 'Devil's Blues'. Later in the year, Mingus releases *Changes Two*.

John Prine's 1975 album release, *Common Sense*, is produced by legendary Memphis guitarist Steve Cropper and bassist Donald 'Duck' Dunn. The title track from the **Average White Band**'s album *Cut The Cake* goes to #10 Pop and #7 R&B. 1975 marks the rebirth of another **James Gang** incarnation with the album *Newborn*. The **Yes** compilation, *Yesterdays*, goes to #27 in the UK and #17 in the US.

The Spinners keep it going in 1975 with the Top Ten LP, *Pick Of The Litter* and *Spinners Live*. 'They Just Can't Stop It (The Games People Play)' is a #1 R&B and #5 Pop hit while 'Sadie' goes to #5 R&B. **The Manhattan Transfer**, Tim Hauser, Alan Paul, Janis Siegel and Cheryl Bentyne (replaced by Laurel Masse in 1979), are signed to Atlantic. Their eponymous debut LP, produced by Ahmet and Arif Mardin, features covers of 'Java Jive' and 'Tuxedo Junction' and a #22 Pop hit, 'Operator'. Embodying a more soulful direction, the **Bee Gees**' *Main Course*, produced by Arif Mardin, includes the hit singles 'Jive Talkin'' (#1 US, Top Ten UK) and 'Nights On Broadway' (#7 Pop). **Abba**'s self-titled 1975 album includes the hit singles 'Mamma Mia' (#1 UK, #32 US), 'SOS' (Top Ten UK, #15 US) and 'I Do, I Do, I Do, I Do, I Do' (#15 US). **Hot Chocolate**'s self-titled Big Tree LP produces the hit singles 'Emma' (#3 UK, #8 US) and 'Disco Queen' (#28 US). Marking Atlantic's growing success in disco, the Philadelphia-based **Trammps** score with 'Hold Back The Night' (#10 R&B, #35 Pop). **Sister Sledge** release *Circle Of Love*. **The Jimmy Castor Bunch**, fronted by vocalist, saxophonist, composer, arranger and group founder Castor, release 'The Bertha Butt Boogie (Part 1)' which charts at #6 Pop and #22 R&B. Their single 'King Kong' charts at #23 R&B.

Bobby Short records *Bobby Short Celebrates Rodgers & Hart,* another tribute to one of America's great songwriting teams. Avant-garde guitarist **Sonny Sharrock**, previously heard on Atlantic as a member of Herbie Mann's group, releases *Paradise* (Atco) featuring Linda Sharrock on vocals. The album is produced by Ilhan Mimaroglu and engineered by rising studio star Phil Ramone. Jazz-fusion violinist **Jean-Luc Ponty** debuts a long and successful recording career on Atlantic with *Upon The Wings Of Music* while still a member of the Mahavishnu Orchestra. He also releases *Aurora*. One of fusion's leading drummers and a key component of the popular fusion group Return To Forever, **Lenny White** releases *Venusian Summer* on the Nemperor label distributed by Atlantic. White releases a second LP, *Big City*, two years later. **The Baker-Gurvitz Army**, featuring Ginger Baker and brothers Adrian and Paul Gurvitz of Gun, releases *Elysian Encounter* on Atco.

Ben E. King is again signed to Atlantic and quickly notches a #1 R&B, #5 Pop hit with 'Supernatural Thing Part 1' from the album of the same name. The LP *Ben E. King Story* is also successful. Virginia-born soul stylist **Roberta Flack**'s seductive *Feel Like Makin' Love* (#5 R&B, #24 Pop) is released. **Major Harris** scores big with the hit single 'Love Won't Let Me Wait', which reaches #1 R&B and #5 Pop. He also releases the album *My Way* in 1975.

1975 marks another epic year for **Led Zeppelin**. The first group in history to have six albums on the charts simultaneously, they formed their own label, Swan Song, last year and this year's *Physical Graffiti* is the band's first album offering. Not surprisingly, the LP goes to #1 on both sides of the Atlantic, eventually selling well over 15 million copies. The awesome total generated by tour and concert sales makes them the most popular rock group in the world. Their only setback is an auto accident involving Robert Plant that causes the cancellation of a US tour. **Bad Company**'s LP *Straight Shooter* (#3 Pop), on Swan Song, sells three million copies and includes the hit, 'Feel Like Makin' Love', (#10 Pop) not to be confused with the Roberta Flack hit of the same name. Also on Swan Song, **Maggie Bell**'s *Suicide Sal* LP features guitar solos from Jimmy Page on the tracks 'If You Don't Know' and 'Comin' On Strong'. Atlantic releases *Stephen Stills Live*. **Aretha Franklin** records the Top Ten album *You* (#9 R&B). **Roxy Music** records *Siren* in London. It includes the mesmerizing 'Love Is The Drug', which goes to #30 on the US Pop chart. Solo LPs from different Atlantic group members include Roxy Music guitarist **Phil Manzanera**'s *Diamond Head*; Yes guitarist **Steve Howe**'s *Beginnings* and Yes bassist Chris Squire's *Fish Out Of Water*. **Alice Cooper**, on a brief hiatus from Warner Brothers, signs with Atlantic and produces the platinum LP, *Welcome To My Nightmare* (#5 US), with the hit single 'Only Women Bleed' (#12 Pop). *A Trick Of The Tail* by **Genesis** goes gold (#3 UK, #31 US). Over 400 singers audition for the lead vocal spot after Peter Gabriel leaves the band. Drummer Phil Collins takes over.

1976 *Black And Blue*, the sixth chart topping Atlantic album for **The Rolling Stones** (#1 Pop), goes platinum. Their single 'Fool To Cry' goes to #10 Pop. **The J. Geils Band** release the album *Blow Your Face Out* as a follow-up to the previous year's *Hotline*. Powerhouse Aussie hard rockers **AC/DC**, featuring Bon Scott (vocals), Angus Young (guitar, schoolboy outfit and 'strut'), Malcolm Young (guitar), Mark Evans (bass) and Phil Rudd (drums), make their Atlantic debut with the aptly-titled *High Voltage*, which amps up to over two million copies sold. **Bad Company** score their third consecutive platinum album *Run With The Pack* (#5 Pop), which includes their hit cover of the Coasters' 'Young Blood' (#20 Pop). **Led Zeppelin**'s *Presence* debuts at #1 and sells over three million copies.

Atlantic releases **Esther Phillips**' *Confessin' The Blues* featuring material recorded in 1966 and 1970. **John Prine** releases *Prime Prine*, produced by Arif Mardin. **Bette Midler**'s *Songs For The New Depression* (#27 Pop) features an eclectic mix including a duet with Bob Dylan, 'Buckets Of Rain', Todd Rundgren on guitar and vocals and Luther Vandross on vocals. **Aretha Franklin** goes gold and to the top of the charts with the movie soundtrack LP *Sparkle* (#1 R&B, #18 Pop), produced by Curtis Mayfield. Guitar legend **Roy Buchanan** brings his fiery Fender Telecaster-style to the album *A Street Called Straight* with backing from Luther Vandross on vocals and Billy Cobham on drums. **Billy Cobham** records *Life And Times* and *Live On Tour* In Europe with keyboardist George Duke. **The Baker-Gurvitz Army** release *Hearts On Fire* (Atco). **Jean-Luc Ponty** releases his influential fusion album *Imaginary Voyage*. Keyboardist-vocalist **George Duke** records *Live In Europe* backed by Billy Cobham (drums), Alphonso Johnson (bass) and John Scofield (guitar). *Your Mind Is On Vacation*, **Mose Allison**'s last album for Atlantic, features his rhythm section of Jack Hannah (bass) and Jerry Granelli (drums), along with appearances by Al Cohn (tenor sax), Joe Farrell (tenor sax), Al Porcino (trumpet) and David Sanborn (alto sax). **Rahsaan Roland Kirk** releases *Other Folk's Music*, produced by Joel Dorn.

Bryan Ferry releases the solo LP *Let's Stick Together* (recorded between 1973 and 1976) and **Roxy Music** comes out with the live album *Viva! Roxy Music*, recorded at the Apollo, Glasgow (1973), City Hall, Newcastle (1974) and Empire Pool, Wembley (1975). *Roxy Music* (1972) and *For Your Pleasure* (1973, the last LP with Brian Eno) are re-released on Atco. **Ringo Starr** goes for a solo outing on Atlantic with the album *Ringo's Rotogravure* featuring guest appearances by John Lennon, Paul McCartney, Eric Clapton, Harry Nilsson, Dr. John and others. It produces the Top 40 hit, 'A Dose Of Rock 'n' Roll' (#26 Pop) featuring Peter Frampton on guitar and Melissa Manchester on backing vocals. Yes' lead singer **Jon Anderson** goes solo with *Olias Of Sunhillow*. **Average White Band** records the platinum LP *Soul Searching* (#9 Pop), produced by Arif Mardin. **Firefall** release their self-titled debut album which goes gold and includes the hit singles, 'You Are The Woman' (#9 Pop) and 'Cinderella' (#34 Pop).

The Spinners spin more gold with *Happiness Is Being With The Spinners*. 'The Rubberband Man' (#2 Pop), is a gold-selling hit for the group and 'Wake Up Susan' peaks at #1 R&B. Another seventies disco classic, **The Trammps**' 'That's Where All The Happy People Go' reaches #12 R&B and #37 Pop. Their masterwork, 'Disco Inferno', also charts high (#9 R&B #11 Pop). *It's About Time* by **The Impressions** is released on the Cotillion subsidiary. **Hot Chocolate** release *Man To Man* with the hit single 'You Sexy Thing', their biggest US hit (# 3 Pop) and 'Don't Stop It Now' (#42 Pop). European disco producer **Jean-Marc Cerrone**, known simply as Cerrone, releases the landmark dance album *Love In C Minor* on Cotillion. The title track is a monster hit in Europe and resides on *Billboard*'s Disco chart for two months at #3 before reaching #29 R&B and #36 Pop. **The Manhattan Transfer**'s *Coming Out* LP includes the single 'Chanson D'Amour'. A sampling of other 1976 albums includes: **Major Harris**'s *Jealousy*; **The James Gang**'s *Jesse Comes Home* (their last for the label), **Herbie Mann**'s *Surprise,* **Keith Jarrett**'s *El Juicio*, **Ray Barretto**'s *Tomorrow: Barretto Live*, **The Small Faces**' *Playmates* and **Ronnie Lane**'s *Mahoney's Last Stand* (featuring Ron Wood).

1977 **Foreigner** sign to Atlantic. Mick Jones puts the band together with Ian MacDonald, Dennis Elliott, Alan Greenwood, Ed Gagliardi and Lou Gramm. The band's debut LP, *Foreigner*, sells over four million copies and stays in the US Top 20 for 12 months and the national charts for two years. The group produces the first of 14 Top 20 US singles with 'Feels Like The First Time' (#4 Pop), 'Cold As Ice' (#6 Pop) and 'Long, Long Way From Home' (#20 Pop). Group awards for Foreigner include Best New Artist (*Rolling Stone*); #1 New Artist, #1 New Group (Pop Albums), #1 New Group (Pop Singles) in *Cashbox* and four #1 awards in *Billboard*.

Genesis strike gold with *Wind And Wuthering* (#26 Pop), which includes the singles 'Your Own Special Way' and 'Spot The Pigeon'. Guitarist Steve Hackett leaves the group and is replaced by Daryl Steurmer prior to the release of their live double-LP, *Seconds Out*. Embarking on his post-Genesis solo career, **Peter Gabriel** releases the first of four self-titled albums *Peter Gabriel (1)*. Also known as *Car*, it features Robert Fripp, Phil Collins, Kate Bush, Paul Weller (The Jam) and the London Symphony Orchestra. The album also contains the classic single 'Solsbury Hill', produced by Bob Ezrin.

Representing a creative new force in dance music, *Chic* quickly goes gold and produces a #6 R&B and #6 Pop single 'Dance, Dance, Dance (Yowsah, Yowsah, Yowsah)', which sells a million copies within the first month of its release. **Chic**, featuring Nile Rodgers, Bernard Edwards and Tony Thompson, also release the hit 'Everybody Dance' (#12 R&B, #38 Pop). Another gold album for the successful Swedish vocal quartet, **Abba**'s *Arrival* climbs the charts with their most successful single, 'Dancing Queen' (#1 UK, US), 'Knowing Me, Knowing You' (#14 Pop), 'Money, Money, Money' and 'The Name Of The Game' (#12 Pop). German disco group **Boney M** score a Top Ten single in the UK with 'Daddy Cool' which charts in the Top 70 in the US. Other singles released that year include 'Sunny', 'Ma Baker' (#2 UK) and 'Belfast' (Top Ten UK). Teen idol **Leif Garrett**'s self-titled gold LP produces a Top 20 hit with his cover of the Beach Boys' 'Surfin' USA' (#20 Pop) and Dion's 'Runaround Sue', which goes to #13 Pop in the US and the Top Ten in the UK. **Hot Chocolate**'s *10 Greatest Hits* features the chart single 'So You Win Again' (#31 Pop). **The Trammps** release *Trammps III* on Atlantic and earn nationwide recognition with the inclusion of 'Disco Inferno' on the *Saturday Night Fever* soundtrack. Taking a break from their successful tenure at Motown, **The Temptations** release *Hear To Tempt You* and *Bare Back* on Atlantic before returning to the Detroit-based label.

The Spinners offer up two albums this year, *Yesterday, Today and Tomorrow* and *Spinners/8*. They enjoy a Top Five R&B hit with 'You're Throwing A Good Love Away'. Philippe Wynne leaves the group and is replaced by John Edwards. **Slave**, the Dayton, Ohio-based funk outfit led by Steve Washington (trumpet), releases two albums on Cotillion/Atlantic this year. The first, *Slave*, features the #1 R&B smash hit, 'Slide' and the second, *The Hardness Of The World*, features 'The Party Song' (#22 R&B). **Roberta Flack** releases *Blue Lights In The Basement*, featuring the hit 'The Closer I Get To You' (#1 R&B, #2 Pop), a duet with Donny Hathaway. Produced by Ahmet, the album features a host of top session musicians and backing vocals from Deniece Williams and Gwen Guthrie. **Bette Midler** releases the double-LP *Broken Blossom* and *Live At Last* with Shelly Manne on drums and Chuck Rainey on bass. **Ray Charles** returns to Atlantic for the album *True To Life*, which includes covers of songs by Johnny Nash, Joe Cocker and The Beatles. **Charles Mingus**' *Three Or Four Shades Of Blues* features gifted musicians such as George Coleman, Ricky Ford, Philip Catherine, Ron Carter, Jack Walrath and Larry Coryell. Guitarist **Larry Coryell**'s fusion album *Back Together Again* also features French guitarist Philip Catherine, drummer Alphonse Mouzon and others. Jazz saxophonist **Sonny Fortune** records three LPs for Atlantic. His 1977 release is *Serengeti Minstrel* featuring Kenny Barron (piano), Woody Shaw (cornet) and Jack DeJohnette (drums). **Jean-Luc Ponty** explores new directions with *Enigmatic Ocean*.

Ringo Starr releases *Ringo The 4th* with appearances from Bette Midler, Luther Vandross, bassist Chuck Rainey and guitarist Cornell Dupree. It is produced by Arif Mardin. British singer-guitarist **Dave Edmunds** kicks off the return to roots rock'n'roll, also known as 'Pub Rock', with *Get It* (Swan Song). Edmunds is backed by bassist-singer-writer Nick Lowe and an early version of the group Rockpile. **AC/DC** release *Let There Be Rock*, which eventually goes multi-platinum, and the single, 'Whole Lotta Rosie'. **Pete Townshend** of The Who and The Faces' **Ronnie Lane** collaborate on *Rough Mix* (Atco) which features guest appearances by Eric Clapton, John Entwhistle and Charlie Watts. **Emerson, Lake & Palmer** release a collection of their solo pieces, *Works Vol.1* and *Vol. 2*. ELP earn further success and recognition for their version of Aaron Copland's 'Fanfare For The Common Man'. Their last album for Atlantic, **The J. Geils Band**'s *Monkey Island* with vocalists Luther Vandross and Cissy Houston, represents a dramatic departure from their roadhouse blues style. **Yes**' *Going For The One* (#8 US, #1 UK) goes platinum. The album includes 'Wondrous Stories' along with the title track. Rick Wakeman returns to the group, replacing Patrick Moraz. **Bad Company**'s *Burnin' Sky* is another transatlantic Top 20 (#15 Pop) album for Atlantic. **The Rolling Stones**' in-concert LP, *Love You Live* (#5 Pop), goes gold. **Firefall**'s second album *Luna Sea* is certified gold and produces the hit single 'Just Remember I Love You' (#11 Pop). **Crosby, Stills & Nash**'s *CSN* album is a multi-platinum-seller that goes to #2 in the US. Their single 'Just A Song Before I Go' goes to #7 Pop in the US. Produced, arranged and conducted by George Martin, songwriter **Jimmy Webb**'s *El Mirage* embodies another musical direction for Atlantic. **Alan O'Day** releases the single 'Undercover Angel' which climbs to #1 Pop and goes gold.

Bryan Ferry releases the solo album, *In Your Mind*. A collaboration between **Average White Band** and **Ben E. King**, *Benny & Us* produces two Top 30 singles, 'Get It Up' (#21 R&B) and 'A Star In The Ghetto' #25 R&B). AWB's *Person To Person*, a live double-LP recorded in Philadelphia, Pittsburgh and Cleveland (#9 R&B, #28 Pop), is also released in 1977. Other Atlantic releases this year includes **Billy Cobham**'s *Inner Conflicts*, **Hall & Oates**' *No Goodbyes*, **Ray Barretto**'s *Eye Of The Beholder*, **Herbie Mann**'s *Herbie Mann With Joao Gilberto & Carlos Jobim* and *Herbie Mann And Fire Island*, **Roy Buchanan**'s *Loading Zone*, **Sister Sledge**'s *Together* (Cotillion) and **Jean-Marc Cerrone**'s Cotillion release, *Cerrone's Paradise*.

1978 The Blues Brothers are born as a quasi-fictional creation of John Belushi and Dan Aykroyd as Jake and Elwood Blues on the American TV show *Saturday Night Live*. They recruit an all-star line-up including Steve Cropper, Donald 'Duck' Dunn and guitarist Matt Murphy and record a live debut LP, *Briefcase Full Of Blues*. It goes multi-platinum, containing the Top 40 hit covers 'Soul Man' and 'Rubber Biscuit'. **Slave** releases *The Concept* and the group is joined by vocalists Steve Arrington and Starleana Young. A multi-platinum, #1 Pop album, **The Rolling Stones**' *Some Girls* sells over six million copies with the title track creating controversy about the lyrics. The singles 'Miss You' (#1 Pop) and 'Beast Of Burden' (#13 Pop) also chart in 1978. Ex-member of Bob Marley & the Wailers, **Peter Tosh** releases *Bush Doctor* (#20 Pop) on Rolling Stones Records. It features a duet with Jagger, '(You Got To Walk And) Not Look Back'. Tosh and his band, Word, Sound and Power tour with the Stones this year. **AC/DC** record the platinum *Powerage* with Cliff Williams replacing Mark Evans on bass and the live platinum album *If You Want Blood You've Got It*, recorded during their world tour. **Average White Band** release *Warmer Communications* with instrumental support from Cornell Dupree and Ray Barretto. **Roy Buchanan** releases the album *You're Not Alone*. **Bryan Ferry** releases the solo LP, *The Bride Stripped Bare*, recorded at Mountain Studios and remixed at Atlantic. **The Small Faces** record *78 In The Shade*. **Dave Edmunds**' album on Swan Song, *Tracks On Wax 4* is the first official Rockpile collaboration between Edmunds and Nick Lowe. **Firefall** produce another platinum LP, *Elan*, which includes 'Strange Way' (#11 Pop) and 'Goodbye, I Love You'.

In March, **Foreigner** embark on an unprecedented tour for a new group, Around The World In 42 Days. Their second album *Double Vision* (#3 Pop) is released on the 20th of June, certified gold that same day and platinum the next. It stays in the Top Ten for six months and produces two huge hit singles, 'Hot Blooded' (#3 Pop) and 'Double Vision' (#2 Pop). **Genesis**, now a trio consisting of Phil Collins, Mike Rutherford and Tony Banks, produces a platinum LP, *And Then There Were Three* (#14 Pop) with the hit single, 'Follow You, Follow Me' (#23, Pop). **Emerson, Lake & Palmer** release *Love Beach* which goes gold. **Yes**' album *Tormato* (#10 Pop) goes platinum. **Peter Gabriel** records the album *Peter Gabriel (2)*, also known as *Scratch*.

Charles Mingus releases *Cumbria And Jazz Fusion*, featuring Jack Walrath, Ricky Ford, Dannie Richmond and Jimmy Knepper. These recordings are originally intended for film soundtracks. **Herbie Mann** returns to the land of the Bossa Nova after a 15-year absence to record *Brazil* and *Brazil: Once Again*. **Jean-Luc Ponty** records the album, *Cosmic Messenger*. Atlantic releases **Ray Barretto**'s album *Can You Feel It?*. **Sonny Fortune** records *Infinity*, produced by Raymond Silva.

Chic hits again with their Top Ten platinum LP, *C'est Chic* (#1 R&B, #4 Pop). The platinum single 'Le Freak' goes to #1 in the US and 'I Want Your Love' reaches #7. The album features backing vocals by Luther Vandross and is engineered by Bob Clearmountain. **Abba**'s 1978 outing, *The Album*, climbs to #1 in the UK while reaching #20 and platinum status in the US. The 'Name Of The Game' is a #1 single in the UK (#12 Pop, US) and 'Take A Chance On Me' goes to #3 Pop in the US (RIAA Gold). **Boney M**'s double hit 'Rivers Of Babylon/Brown Girl In The Ring' (#30 Pop) becomes their only entry into the US Top 40. They also release the *Night Flight To Venus* LP on Hansa/Atlantic. The single 'Rasputin' is Top Ten in the UK and 'Mary's Boy Child – Oh My Lord' goes to #1 in the UK. Atlantic releases *The Best Of The Trammps*. **The Brides Of Funkenstein** record for Atlantic from 1978 to 1980. The group's roster for the Atlantic sessions includes Lynn Mabry and Dawn Silva. They release a Top Ten hit single with 'Disco To Go' (#7 R&B). Disco superstar **Cerrone** releases *Cerrone IV: The Golden Touch* and *Supernature*. Having sold over ten million albums at this point in his career, Cerrone wins *Billboard's* Disco Artist Of The Year, Male Disco Artist Of The Year, Composer Of The Year, Disco Music Arranger Of The Year, Disco Instrumentalist Of The Year and Best Producer Of A Disco Record.

Legendary Kansas City pianist **Jay McShann** is featured on *Last Of The Blue Devils* with John Scofield (electric guitar), Milt Hinton (bass), Joe Newman (trumpet), Buddy Tate and Paul Quinichette (tenor sax) and Jack Williams (drums). Produced by Ahmet with Ilhan Mimaroglu. **Aretha Franklin** records the album *Almighty Fire* (#5 R&B). **The Manhattan Transfer**'s *Pastiche* LP is the last to include singer Laurel Masse (replaced by Cheryl Bentyne) and includes the song 'On A Little Street In Singapore'. It also features appearances by a roster of Atlantic all-stars including Jimmy Giuffre, Lee Konitz, Al Cohn, Booker T. Jones, Donald 'Duck' Dunn and Steve Cropper.

1979 **Sister Sledge** break through to the top with their phenomenally successful *We Are Family*, a platinum #1 R&B, #3 Pop album. Written and produced by Nile Rodgers and Bernard Edwards of Chic and engineered by Bob Clearmountain, it includes the title track (#1 R&B, #2 Pop), 'He's The Greatest Dancer' (#1 R&B, #9 Pop) and 'Lost In Music'. 'We Are Family' becomes the soundtrack for the Pittsburgh Pirates' World Series win and literally defines the era as a modern soul anthem. **Chic**'s platinum album *Risqué* produces another era-defining hit single, 'Good Times' (#1 Pop, RIAA Gold), later sampled by both Queen in 'Another One Bites The Dust' and the Sugar Hill Gang in 'Rapper's Delight'. The album also features the hits 'My Feet Keep Dancing' and 'My Forbidden Lover'. **The Spinners** release *Dancin' And Lovin'* with the classic hit 'Working My Way Back To You' (#6 R&B, #2 Pop, RIAA Gold). **Mass Production** goes to #4 R&B and #43 Pop with 'Firecracker', their best known single. **Abba**'s gold LP *Voulez Vous* yields singles like the title track, 'I Have A Dream', Angel Eyes', 'Does Your Mother Know' (#19 Pop), which are all Top Five in the UK. **Boney M** charts in the UK with Top Ten singles 'Painter Man' and 'Hooray, Hooray It's A Holi-Holiday'. **The Trammps** release *The Whole World's Dancing*. **The Brides Of Funkenstein** release *Funk Or Walk*, **Slave** release *Just A Touch Of Love* featuring the R&B Top Ten title track (Cotillion).

Roxy Music release the atmospheric *Manifesto* album, recorded at Ridge Farm and Basing Street Studios and remixed at Atlantic. It includes the singles 'Dance Away' and 'Angel Eyes' and is the group's highest charting album in the US (#23 Pop). **Foreigner**'s *Head Games* album (#5 Pop) sells two million copies. Rick Wills replaces Ed Gagliardi on bass. The album produces two chart singles, 'Dirty White Boy' and the title track. One of their finest recordings, **AC/DC**'s *Highway To Hell* (#17 Pop) sells over four million copies. Unfortunately, it's their last album before the untimely death of lead singer Bon Scott. **Chuck Berry**, the legendary songwriter, performer, musician, singer, guitarist and pivotal force in R&B and rock'n'roll, releases *Rock It* on Atco. Atco signs the Southern rock band **Blackfoot**, featuring lead singer Rick Medlocke. Their debut album, *Strikes* (#42 Pop), eventually goes platinum. They follow this LP with a series of albums including *Tomcattin'* (1980), *Marauder* (1981), *Highway Song 'Live'* (1982), *Siogo* (1983) and *Vertical Smiles* (1984). British folk-rock group **Lindisfarne** release *Back And Fourth* on Atco. Their single 'Run For Home' climbs to #33 on the US Pop chart. **Emerson, Lake & Palmer** document their live performances with *In Concert Live* (Manticore/Atlantic). **Steve Howe**, Yes' popular guitarist, releases a solo self-titled album. **Dave Edmunds** releases *Repeat When Necessary* featuring the tracks 'Queen Of Hearts' and 'Crawling From The Wreckage'. His single, 'Girls Talk', written by Elvis Costello, goes gold in the UK. **Peter Tosh** releases *Mystic Man* on the subsidiary label, Rolling Stones Records. **Bad Company**'s *Desolation Angels* (#3 Pop) goes to the Top Ten on both sides of the Atlantic and the album sells two million copies in the States. It includes 'Rock And Roll Fantasy' (#13 Pop) written by vocalist Paul Rodgers. In 1979, **Led Zeppelin** play live for the first time in four years. They score their eighth and last successive hit in the UK with the #1 LP *In Through The Out Door*. It also goes to #1 in the US, eventually selling six million copies.

Aretha Franklin caps her triumphant Atlantic career with *La Diva* featuring Van McCoy, Carolyn Franklin and Cornell Dupree. **Ray Charles** releases *Ain't It So*, featuring standards such as 'Some Enchanted Evening' and 'What'll I Do?' *Big Apple Bash* is pianist **Jay McShann**'s second LP for Atlantic. **Bette Midler** releases *Thighs And Whispers* and the popular soundtrack album for *The Rose* #12 Pop), which sells two million copies. **Jean-Luc Ponty** releases *Live* and *A Taste For Passion*, **Herbie Mann** releases *Sunbelt* and **Sonny Fortune** releases *With Sound Reason*. *Extensions* by **The Manhattan Transfer** yields their exceptional vocal interpretation of 'Birdland', earning them a Grammy for Best Jazz Fusion Performance, Vocal or Instrumental and becoming their signature piece. Although **Charles Mingus**' last studio sessions are released on Gateway, he supervises several sessions on Atlantic before he dies. These are released as the albums *Me, Myself An Eye* (1979) and *Something Like A Bird* (1980). Too ill to play, Mingus supervises and directs the sessions from a wheelchair. Musicians include Lee Konitz, Larry Coryell, Slide Hampton, Jimmy Knepper, Pepper Adams, Randy Brecker, George Coleman, Charles McPherson, Ricky Ford and Jack Walrath.

1980 **The Rolling Stones**' *Emotional Rescue* goes on to sell two million copies, hitting #1 on the US and British charts. The title track goes to #3 Pop in the US and #1 in the UK. **Pete Townshend** signs with Atco and releases his first album, *Empty Glass*. It goes to #5 Pop in the US (RIAA platinum) and includes the singles 'Rough Boys', 'Let My Love Open The Door' (#9 Pop US) and 'A Little Is Enough'. **The Blues Brothers** release their soundtrack album for the film of the same name. The film features heavyweights such as Ray Charles and Aretha Franklin, James Brown, John Lee Hooker and Cab Calloway. The soundtrack album goes platinum and includes **The Blues Brothers** cover of 'Gimme Some Lovin'' (#18 Pop). Their second album *Made In America*, also released in 1980, features the cover, 'Who's Making Love' (#39 Pop). In February, **AC/DC** vocalist Bon Scott tragically dies. Later that year, Brian Johnson, a former member of Geordie, becomes the group's new lead singer. AC/DC release *Back In Black* (#4 Pop), dedicated to Scott, which goes on to sell 16 million copies in the US. By the end of 1980, the group received 17 platinum and gold awards in eight countries. *Back In Black* includes one of their best known songs, 'You Shook Me All Night Long' (#35 Pop), and hard rock classics 'Hells Bells', 'Back In Black' (#37 Pop) and 'Rock And Roll Ain't Noise Pollution'. In May, **Led Zeppelin** tour Europe for the last time. On the September 25th, drummer John 'Bonzo' Bonham dies and unable to continue without the heart of the band, Zeppelin break up.

Abba's *Super Trouper* album becomes the group's sixth successive #1 in the UK. 'The Winner Takes It All' is another single (#8 US, #1 UK). 'Super Trouper' also reaches #1 on the British Pop chart. **The Spinners**' *Love Trippin'* (#16 R&B) includes successful singles like 'Cupid/I've Loved You For A Long Time' (#4 Pop, #5 R&B). They also get R&B action with 'Now That You're Mine Again' (#25 R&B). Atlantic releases **Sister Sledge**'s *Love Somebody Today* (#7 R&B, #31 Pop). The title track goes to #6 in the R&B singles. **Chic** release *Real People* (#8 R&B,

#30 Pop) this year and go on to release *Take It Off* (#36) in 1981, *Tongue In Chic* in 1982 and *Believer* in 1984. **The Trammps** release *Slipping Out*. **Ben E. King** keeps the hits coming with 'Music Trance' (#13 R&B). **Slave** move from hardcore to sophisticated funk with the gold album *Stone Jam*.

The gold LP *Roberta Flack Featuring Donny Hathaway* is released following **Donny Hathaway**'s tragic death in 1979. The title track from **Bette Midler**'s *The Rose* climbs to #3 in the US. She also wins the Grammy for Best Vocal Performance and the LP goes multi-platinum. Midler also releases *Divine Madness* (#34 Pop). **Ray Charles** releases *Brother Ray Is At It Again*. **Jean-Luc Ponty** releases *Civilised Evil*.

Average White Band release *Volume VIII*. On their *Drama* LP (#18 Pop), **Yes** debut a new line-up including Geoff Downes and Trevor Horn (formerly of the Buggles) replacing keyboardist Rick Wakeman and Jon Anderson. Anderson releases his second solo LP, *Song Of Seven*, which he writes, produces and arranges. **Genesis**' platinum *Duke* album (#11 US, #1 UK) features the hits 'Turn It On Again' and 'Misunderstanding' (#14 Pop). **Firefall** release *Undertow* and *Clouds Across The Sun* and the singles 'Headed For A Fall' (#35 Pop) and, in 1981, 'Staying With It' (#37 Pop). Poet and novelist **Jim Carroll** (*The Basketball Diaries*) releases his debut album, *Catholic Boy*, featuring the track 'People Who Died'. Produced by Rolling Stones label head Earl McGrath and co-produced and engineered by Bob Clearmountain.

1981 This year marks the beginning of **Phil Collins**' solo career on Atlantic with the album *Face Value*, which goes to #7 in the US. The LP sells over five million copies and produces an avalanche of hit singles including 'In The Air Tonight' (#1 UK, #19 US), 'I Missed Again' (#2 UK, #19 US) and 'If Leaving Me Is Easy' (#17 UK, not released in the US). Artists appearing on the album include Eric Clapton and jazzman Ronnie Scott, among others.

Foreigner's album *4* goes to #1 in the US (#5 UK), staying at the top for ten weeks. The group's biggest-selling album, it sells six million copies and includes the hits 'Urgent' (#4 Pop), which features a sax solo by Junior Walker, 'Waiting For A Girl Like You' (#2 Pop) and 'Juke Box Hero' (#26 Pop, 1982). Another US Top Ten album, **Genesis**' *Abacab* (#7 Pop) includes the hit singles 'No Reply At All' (#29 Pop), 'Abacab' (#26 Pop) and 'Man On The Corner' (#40 Pop). **AC/DC**'s *Dirty Deeds Done Cheap* (#3 US) sells over five million copies in the US, while *For Those About To Rock We Salute You* goes to #1 on the album chart and notches another three million in sales. **The Rolling Stones** tour this year earns $50 million with a total audience of over two million. *Tattoo You* is a #1 US album with sales of over four million copies. It includes singles 'Waiting On A Friend' (#13 Pop), which features Sonny Rollins on tenor and the classic 'Start Me Up' (#2 Pop). Reggae maestro **Peter Tosh** releases *Wanted Dread Or Alive* on Rolling Stones Records. **Stevie Nicks**, lead singer with Fleetwood Mac, releases her solo LP *Bella Donna* which goes platinum (#1 Pop) and stays on the *Billboard* Pop album chart for 145 weeks. The album features a duet with Tom Petty, 'Stop Draggin' My Heart Around' which goes to #3 Pop. **Dave Edmunds** releases *Twangin'* (#48 Pop) as his backing band Rockpile are breaking up. **Slave** release *Show Time*. **Kix** release a self-titled debut LP.

Originally formed in 1974, **Mink De Ville** is a product of New York's downtown punk scene and a showcase for front man Willy De Ville. The band signs with Atlantic and release *Coup De Grace*. Unique vocal interpreter **Leon Redbone** releases *From Branch To Branch*, produced by Joel Dorn and featuring Dr. John. In January, Atlantic releases *Yesshows*, a double-LP compilation of live material by **Yes** (#43 US, #22 UK). In April, the group announce they are breaking up. **Jean-Luc Ponty** releases *Mystical Adventures*.

Abba's *The Visitors* album goes Top Ten in the UK and to #29 in the US. The title track and 'When All Is Said And Done' (#27 Pop), released in 1982, also grace the charts. Mahavishnu Orchestra drummer, Narada Michael Walden, produces **Sister Sledge**'s Cotillion LP, *All-American Girls* (#13 Pop). **The Spinners** release *Labor Of Love* and *Can't Shake This Feeling*. Former Temptation lead singer **Eddie Kendricks** releases *Love Keys*. **The Manhattan Transfer**'s *Mecca For Moderns* LP (#22 Pop) produces their biggest hit single, 'Boy From New York City' (#7 Pop). The song also wins a Grammy for Best Pop Performance By A Duo Or Group while 'Until I Met You (Corner Pocket)' nets the Grammy For Best Jazz Vocal Performance, Duo Or Group. They are the first group to win Grammies in the Pop and Jazz category in the same year.

1982 *Pictures At Eleven* (#5 US), **Robert Plant**'s platinum debut solo album on Swan Song, features drummers Phil Collins and Cozy Powell, among others. Their first UK appearance in six years, **The Rolling Stones**' concert at Wembley Stadium draws 140,000 fans. Their album *Still Life* goes to #5 in the US. **Pete Townshend**'s 1982 album *All The Best Cowboys Have Chinese Eyes* climbs to #26 on the US Pop album charts. **Crosby, Stills & Nash** release the platinum LP *Daylight Again* (#8 US). Stills writes most of the songs for the album, which yields the hit singles 'Wasted On The Way' (#9 Pop) and 'Southern Cross' (#18 Pop). **Firefall** release *Break Of Dawn*. **Jim Carroll** follows up his debut LP with *Dry Dreams*, again produced by Earl McGrath. The album features an appearance by Patti Smith's guitarist, pre-eminent music writer Lenny Kaye, on the track 'Still Life'. **Bad Company** release *Rough Diamonds*, their last LP with the original line-up. **Led Zeppelin**'s *Coda*, a compilation of outtakes assembled by guitarist Jimmy Page, goes to #6 and earns RIAA platinum status.

Phil Collins releases *Hello, I Must Be Going* (#2 UK, #8 US), which sells three million in the States. His cover of the Supremes' 'You Can't Hurry Love' reaches #1 UK and #10 US. Featured artists on the album include Sting and Peter Gabriel. Featuring three sides of live material and one of studio material, **Abba** disband in 1982, putting an end to a seemingly nonstop stream of hit singles. Phil Collins produces Anni-Frid 'Frida' Lyngstad's debut solo album *Something's Going On* with the single 'I Know There's Something Going On', a British Top 20 hit. Abba's other diva, Agnetha Faltskog, also releases a solo album, *Wrap Your Arms Around Me* that reaches #29 in the UK. **Sister Sledge**'s self-produced *The Sisters* (#17 Pop) includes their hit cover of Mary Wells' 'My Guy' (#14 R&B, #23 Pop). **Gloria Gaynor** releases a self-titled album. Singer **Laura Branigan**'s gold-selling *Branigan* album (#34 US) features the platinum hit single 'Gloria' (#2 Pop). **Jon Anderson** releases *Animation*. Irish group **Clannad**, featuring Maire, Ciaran, Eithne and Paul Brennan, release the album *Fuaim*.

Ray Charles releases *A Life In Music*. Atlantic release **Professor Longhair**'s posthumous album *The Last Mardi Gras*. **Bobby Short** releases *Moments Like This*. The Manhattan Transfer lead vocalist **Janis Siegel**'s solo album *Experiment In White* wins a Grammy for her interpretation of the classic 'Route 66'. **Carole King** releases *One To One*. **Genesis**' *Three Sides Live* (#10 US) goes gold and produces the Top 40 hit 'Paperlate' (#32 Pop). A compilation of **Foreigner** tracks entitled *Foreigner Records* (#10 US) sells three million copies. Atlantic releases another **Yes** compilation album, the platinum-selling *Classic Yes*.

1983 The **Rock And Roll Hall Of Fame** is established by Ahmet, *Rolling Stone* publisher Jann Wenner, Seymour Stein, Bob Krasnow and Noreen Woods to honour artists who have made a significant contribution to the history of music. Over a decade later, the Rock And Roll Hall Of Fame Museum, designed by architect I.M. Pei, will open in Cleveland, Ohio.

Stevie Nicks' The Wild Heart (#5 Pop) is produced by Jimmy Iovine and features the hit singles 'Stand Back' (#5 Pop), 'Nightbird' (#33 Pop) and 'If Anyone Falls' (#14 Pop). *The Principle Of Moments* (#8 US) is the first release on Robert Plant's Es Paranza label and goes platinum by next year. The Atlantic single 'Big Log' reaches #20 in the US. AC/DC's Flick Of The Switch goes to #15 on the

Billboard Pop album chart. Bad Company lead vocalist Paul Rodgers releases the solo album Cut Loose. Pete Townshend's Scoop goes to #35 on the US album charts. Crosby, Stills & Nash release Allies. Firefall's last album for Atlantic is Mirror Of The World.

Known for exceptional songs, a solid instrumental sound and the sultry presence of lead singer Michael Hutchence, Australia's **INXS** are signed to Atco and release the gold LP, *Shabooh Shabooh* and *Dekadance* (four dance tracks from *Shabooh, Shabooh*). Chic mastermind Nile Rodgers guest produces the single 'Original Sin' (#58 Pop), which is included on *The Swing* next year. Long Island heavy metal kings **Twisted Sister** make their Atlantic debut with *You Can't Stop Rock 'N' Roll*, which is certified RIAA Gold. **Kix** release *Cool Kids*. **Zebra**, a heavy metal band featuring guitarist/vocalist Randy Jackson, release the gold album *Zebra* (#29 US). **Genesis** release a self-titled album (#1 UK, #9 US), which sells four million copies in the US and produces the hit singles 'That's All' (#6 Pop), 'Illegal Alien' (#44 Pop), 'Mama' and 'Taking It All Too Hard'. Tony Banks releases *The Wicked Lady*. **Laura Branigan**'s *Branigan 2* (#29 US) goes gold. It includes two hit singles, 'Solitaire' (#7 Pop) and 'How Am I Supposed To Live Without You' (#12 Pop), written by Michael Bolton. **Slave** release *Visions Of The Lite* and *Bad Enuff* on the Cotillion subsidiary. **Bette Midler** releases *No Frills*. **Jim Carroll**'s third and final Atlantic LP, *I Write Your Name*, is produced by Earl McGrath, engineered by Gene Paul and once again features Lenny Kaye on guitar. German synth band **Tangerine Dream** release a number of Atlantic albums in the eighties: *Wavelength* (1983), *Streethawk* (1985), *Three O'Clock High* (1987), *Shy People* (1987) and *Marrakesh* (1988).

Jean-Luc Ponty releases *Individual Choice*. **Freddie Hubbard**'s return to the label is marked by the album *Sweet Return*. *Bodies And Souls* by **The Manhattan Transfer** features appearances by Four Seasons legend Frankie Valli on vocals and Stevie Wonder on harmonica. They also release *Bop Doo-Wop*, an anthology culled from previous sessions. At the age of 83, blues legend **Sippie Wallace** records *Sippie* on Atlantic, her first album in 15 years. She's backed by her number one fan and a great artist in her own right, Bonnie Raitt, with Jim Dapogny's Chicago Band.

1984 *Agent Provocateur* (#4 US) stands tall as yet another multi-platinum album for **Foreigner**. It's capped off by the #1 gold single 'I Want To Know What Love Is', which features backing from the New Jersey Mass Choir and Jennifer Holiday. The flip side is 'Street Thunder', the marathon theme written for the 23rd Summer Olympics in Los Angeles. **Robert Plant** releases the platinum album *The Honeydrippers, Volume One* (#4 US) featuring successful covers of the classic 'Sea Of Love' (#3 Pop) and Roy Brown's R&B hit 'Rockin' At Midnight' (#25 Pop). Plant is backed by a formidable trio of guitarists in Jimmy Page, Nile Rodgers and Jeff Beck with production supervised by Ahmet. **Phil Collins**' 'Against All Odds (Take A Look At Me Now)' goes to #1 in the US and wins Collins a Grammy For Best Pop Vocal Performance, Male plus an Oscar nomination. It is taken from the *Against All Odds* soundtrack album which goes gold. **Julian Lennon**'s platinum album *Valotte* (#17 US) is produced by Phil Ramone and named after the French chateau where it was recorded. It features the hits 'Valotte' (#9 Pop) and 'Too Late For Goodbyes' (#5 Pop). **Roger Daltrey**'s *Parting Should Be Painless* is his first solo outing since the breakup of The Who. The title track from **Laura Branigan**'s 1984 platinum album, *Self Control* (#23 US) goes to the Top Ten in the UK and to #4 in the US. **Jean-Luc Ponty** releases *Open Mind*. A newly reconstituted **Yes** featuring Jon Anderson, Trevor Rabin, Chris Squire, Alan White, Trevor Horn and Tony Kaye release the successful three million-selling comeback album *90125* (#5 US), featuring the #1 single, 'Owner Of A Lonely Heart'.

AC/DC's gold EP *'74 Jailbreak* includes five Australian releases and a posthumous appearance by the late Bon Scott on vocals. **Zebra** release their second album *No Tellin' Lies*. **Twisted Sister**'s *Stay Hungry* features the heavy metal anthems 'We're Not Gonna To Take It' (#21 Pop) and 'I Wanna Rock'. It blasts into the Top 20 (#15 Pop) and sells over three million copies. L.A. 'hair' metal band **Ratt** make their Atlantic debut with *Out Of The Cellar* which sells three million copies, goes to #7 in the US and features the hit 'Round And Round' (#12 Pop).

1985 **Phil Collins**' landmark album *No Jacket Required* goes straight to #1 on the album charts in the UK and US. Its star-studded cast includes Sting, Peter Gabriel and others with production by Hugh Padgham. The LP stays on the US charts for 123 weeks and will go on to sell over 10 million copies by the end of 1998, earning one of the RIAA's rare Diamond Awards. Successful singles for this banner year in Collins' Atlantic career include: 'Sussudio' (#1 US, #12 UK); 'One More Night' (#1 US, #4 UK); 'Don't Lose My Number' (#4 US, not released in the UK); and 'Take Me Home', released in the US in 1986 (#7 US, #19 UK). **Bette Midler** releases the comedy LP *Mud Will Be Flung Tonight*.

Pete Townshend releases the gold concept album *White City: A Novel* (#26 US). **AC/DC** release the gold-selling album, *Fly On The Wall* (#32 US). **Robert Plant** releases *Shaken 'N' Stirred*. **INXS** break through in the US with the two million-selling, Top 20 album *Listen Like Thieves* (#11 US). It includes the #5 hit 'What You Need'.

The heavy metal group **Savatage** (formerly known as Avatar) release their Atlantic debut album, *The Power Of The Night*. The group are led by brothers Jon and Criss Oliva. **Twisted Sister** release *Come Out And Play*, which is certified gold by the RIAA. **Ratt** release the platinum-selling LP *Invasion Of Your Privacy*. **Kix** release *Midnight Dynamite*. *Sportin' Life* is released by **Mink De Ville**. Paul Rodgers and Jimmy Page form **The Firm** with Tony Franklin (keyboards) and Chris Slade (drums). Their debut, *The Firm* (#17 US), goes gold. The single 'Radioactive' peaks at #28 Pop.

Stevie Nicks releases the album *Rock A Little* (#12 US), featuring the single 'Talk To Me', which goes to #4 Pop. Guitarist Mike Rutherford of Genesis forms **Mike + the Mechanics**, including former Ace lead singer Paul Carrack, and strikes gold with the band's self-titled debut on Atlantic (#26 Pop). It features the hit singles 'Silent Running' (#6 Pop) and 'All I Need Is A Miracle' (#5 Pop). **John Parr**'s 'St. Elmo's Fire (Man In Motion)' from the *St. Elmo's Fire* soundtrack gold-selling album goes to #1 in the US and Top Ten in the UK. **Roger Daltrey** releases his second Atlantic album, *Under A Ragin' Moon*. **Laura Branigan** releases *Hold Me*.

The Manhattan Transfer release *Vocalese*, an album dedicated to the work of pioneering jazz lyricist and vocalist Jon Hendricks, with support from the Count Basie Orchestra, Dizzy Gillespie, Philly Joe Jones and Jon Hendricks himself. Jazz pianist **Ahmad Jamal** records *Digital Works* and double-LP, *Live At The Montreal Jazz Festival*. Jazz fusion violinist **Jean-Luc Ponty** releases *Fables*. Flautist **Herbie Mann** releases *See Through The Spirits*.

The gold soundtrack album *The Lost Boys* features contributions from Roger Daltrey, Echo & The Bunnymen, INXS and Foreigner's Lou Gramm. Atlantic releases the *White Nights* soundtrack album (#17 US), which goes gold and features tracks by Phil Collins, Robert Plant, Lou Reed, Roberta Flack and Chaka Kahn.

1986 A year after Live Aid, former Boomtown Rat lead singer **Bob Geldof** launches his solo debut, *Deep In The Heart of Nowhere* on Atlantic. The album features all-star performers including Eric Clapton, Midge Ure, Annie Lennox and Alison Moyet. **Genesis** release *Invisible Touch* (#3 US), which sells six million copies by 1996. It produces five Top Five hits: the title track (#1 Pop), 'Throwing It All Away' (#4 Pop), 'Land Of Confusion' (#4 Pop), 'In Too Deep' (#3 Pop) and 'Tonight, Tonight, Tonight' (#3 Pop). **Phil Collins**' #1 album *No Jacket Required* wins both Grammy and BRIT awards for Top Album, while Collins wins the BRIT award for Top Male Artist. **Julian Lennon** continues his Atlantic success with *The Secret Value Of Daydreaming* (#32 US) which goes gold and the hit single 'Stick Around' (#32 Pop), produced by Phil Ramone. **Billy Joe Royal** scores a Top Ten country hit with 'Burned Like A Rocket'.

AC/DC release *Who Made Who* (#33 US), the three million-selling soundtrack disc from the Stephen King movie *Maximum Overdrive*. **The Firm** release *Mean Business* (#22 US), produced by Jimmy Page, Paul Rodgers and Julian Mendelsohn. **Bad Company** releases the multi-platinum album *10 From 6*, ten tracks from six of their albums. Vocalist Brian Howe replaces Paul Rodgers, now in The Firm. **Savatage** release the album *Fight For The Rock*. **Ratt** goes platinum with *Dancing Undercover* (#26 US).

Guitarist **Mike Stern**, previously with Miles Davis, releases *Upside Downside* on Atlantic, his first album as a leader. Other Atlantic albums from Stern include *Time In Place* (1987) and *Jigsaw* (1989). **Ahmad Jamal** releases *Rossiter Road*. **David 'Fathead' Newman** returns to Atlantic and releases *Heads Up*. Atlantic releases **Bobby Short**'s *Guess Who's Back In Town, The Songs Of Andy Razaf*. Originally recorded in New York's Bearsville Studios and released on King Records, **Dizzy Gillespie**'s *Closer To The Source* is reissued on Atlantic. It features guest appearances by Stevie Wonder and Branford Marsalis.

The year after the death of **Big Joe Turner**, Atlantic releases the *Big Joe Turner Memorial Album: Rhythm & Blues*. The film soundtrack album *Stand By Me* features the classic Atlantic singles 'Stand By Me' (#9 Pop), which returns to the charts as a transatlantic Top Ten hit, as well as 'Yakety Yak' by The Coasters and 'Mr. Lee' by The Bobbettes.

LeVert release *Bloodline* (#8 US) and the #1 R&B single, '(Pop, Pop, Pop, Pop) Goes My Mind'. LeVert are an Ohio-based trio featuring Gerald and Sean Levert (sons of Eddie Levert of the O'Jays) and Marc Gordon. **Nu Shooz**, a duo featuring husband and wife team John Smith (guitarist/writer) and Valerie Day (vocalist), record *Poolside*, which goes gold. Their gold single 'I Can't Wait' goes to #3 Pop and #2 R&B. The follow-up, 'Point Of No Return', goes to #28 Pop. Singer **Stacey Q** (real name: Stacey Swain) releases 'Two Of Hearts', which goes to #3 Pop in the US. She also releases the Atlantic albums *Better Than Heaven* (1986) and in 1987 *Nights Like This* and *Hard Machine*.

1987 **INXS** release their biggest-selling album in 1987, *Kick* (#3 US). With sales of over six million, it includes the Top Ten singles 'Need You Tonight' (#1 Pop), 'Devil Inside' (#2 Pop), 'New Sensation' (#3 Pop) and 'Never Tear Us Apart' (#7 Pop). **Foreigner**'s *Inside Information* (#15 US), produced by guitarist, writer and group leader Mick Jones, goes platinum. The album produces their last two Top Ten hits, 'Say You Will' and 'I Don't Want To Live Without You'. Singer Lou Gramm also releases his solo debut album *Ready Or Not* (#27 US) with the hit, 'Midnight Blue' (#5 Pop). **Yes** release the platinum-selling LP, *Big Generator* (#15 US), featuring material primarily written by South African guitarist Trevor Rabin. **Tori Amos** (born Myra Ellen Amos), a prodigious talent who grew up in Maryland and won a piano scholarship to Baltimore's Peabody Conservatory at the age of five, signs to Atlantic and records her debut for the label, *Y Kant Tori Read*.

The **Modern Jazz Quartet** reform in 1982 and return to Atlantic in 1987. The album *Three Windows* marks the MJQ's 35th anniversary in this year. It is produced by Nesuhi Ertegun. *The Erteguns' New York Cabaret Music* features the music of cabaret singers and musicians that Ahmet and Nesuhi Ertegun recorded during the fifties, sixties and seventies. Featured artists include: Mae Barnes, Joe Bushkin, Barbara Carroll, Eddie Condon, Chris Connor, Jimmy Daniels, Goldie Hawkins, Greta Keller, Jimmy Lyon, Carmen McRae, Mabel Mercer, Joe Mooney, Hugh Shannon, Bobby Short, Ted Straeter, Sylvia Syms, Billy Taylor, Mel Tormé and Cy Coleman. Ahmet is executive producer. Atlantic releases **Ahmad Jamal**'s *Crystal*. **The Manhattan Transfer**'s *Brasil* features Stan Getz on tenor sax. **Yusef Lateef** returns to the label with *Yusef's Little Symphony*, which wins a Grammy for Best New Age Album Performance.

New York hard rockers **White Lion** release *Pride* (#11 US), which sells over two million copies and features the Top Ten singles 'Wait' (#8 Pop) and 'When Children Cry' (#3 Pop). **Twisted Sister** release *Love Is For Suckers*. Atlantic releases **Savatage**'s *Hall Of The Mountain King*. **Billy Joe Royal** releases the albums *The Royal Treatment* (RIAA Gold) and *Looking Ahead* in 1987. He also has a Top Ten Country hit with 'I'll Pin A Note To Your Pillow'. Abba's **Agnetha Faltskog** solos with the aptly titled *I Stand Alone*. **Nu Shooz** release *Told U So*. **Phil Collins** earns more success with the gold soundtrack LP *Buster*. **LeVert**'s gold album *The Big Throwdown* (#3 R&B, #32 Pop) includes the singles 'Casanova' (#1 R&B, #5 Pop), 'My Forever Love' (#2 R&B) and 'Sweet Sensation' (#4 R&B). Teen pop sensation **Debbie Gibson,** a singer/songwriter/pianist from Long Island, New York, debuts on Atlantic with *Out Of The Blue* (#7 US), which sells over three million and includes the hit singles 'Only In My Dreams' (#4 Pop, RIAA Gold), 'Out Of The Blue' (#3 Pop) and 'Shake Your Love' (#4 Pop, RIAA Gold).

1988 The **Modern Jazz Quartet**'s *For Ellington* is released on Nesuhi Ertegun's new label, EastWest. **David 'Fathead' Newman** records *Fire! Live At The Village Vanguard* featuring Stanley Turrentine on tenor sax. Vibraphonist **Milt Jackson** reunites with producer Nesuhi Ertegun on the EastWest album *Bebop*, featuring J.J. Johnson, Jon Faddis, Jimmy Heath and Cedar Walton. **Gerald Albright** releases *Dream Come True* and *Bermuda Nights* in 1988. The legendary **Illinois Jacquet** and his Big Band sign to the label. The album *Jacquet's Got It* earns a Grammy nomination.

Phil Collins' cover of 'Groovy Kind Of Love' goes to #1 in the UK and US. 'Two Hearts' (#1 US, RIAA Gold, #6 UK) wins the Grammy for Best Song Written For Motion Picture Or Television. The remix of Collins' haunting 'In The Air Tonight' goes to #4 in the UK. **Roberta Flack** releases *Oasis* (#24 R&B). **Mike + the Mechanics** release the gold album *Living Years* (#13 US). The title track goes to #1 in the US. **Robert Plant**'s platinum album *Now And Zen*, on the Es Paranza label (#6 US), features backing from Jimmy Page and the single 'Tall Cool One'. **AC/DC**'s *Blow Up Your Video* (#12 US) is their first studio album of all new material in three years. It goes platinum and features the single 'Heatseeker'. **Bad Company**'s *Fame & Fortune* (Atlantic) and *Dangerous Age* (Atco) go gold. **Winger**, featuring bassist/vocalist Kip Winger, Reb Beach (guitar), Paul Taylor (keyboards until 1992) and Rod Morgenstein (drums), goes to #21 on the US album chart with the million-selling *Winger*. The band also climb the singles chart in 1989 with, 'Seventeen' (#26 Pop) and 'Headed For A Heartbreak' (#19 Pop). **Kix** strike gold with *Blow My Fuse* and the Top 20 hit 'Don't Close Your Eyes' (#11 Pop). *Reach For The Sky* (#17 US) goes platinum for **Ratt**.

With the hit 'Foolish Beat', **Debbie Gibson** becomes the first teenager to write, produce and perform a #1 hit single. **LeVert** release the LP *Just Coolin'* (#6 R&B, RIAA Gold). The title track, featuring Heavy D, goes to #1 R&B and 'Gotta Get The Money' peaks at #4 R&B. A Gerald Levert discovery, the R&B vocal quintet **Troop** sign to Atlantic and debut with *Troop* (#19 R&B). London-based **Escape Club** debut with the gold album *Wild Wild West* (#27 US), while the title track races to #1. Female trio **J.J. Fad** (Just Jammin' Fresh and Def) record *Supersonic* (#20 R&B), with vocals and production by Dr. Dre. 'Supersonic' goes to #22 R&B and #30 Pop.

1989 **Nesuhi Ertegun**, the man responsible for Atlantic's extraordinary jazz catalogue over the last 40 years, dies in July.

Stevie Nicks' platinum album, *Other Side Of The Mirror* (#10 US), features Bruce Hornsby on piano and Kenny G on sax. The soundtrack album for the popular movie *Beaches* propels **Bette Midler** to #2 on the US charts and achieves multi-platinum sales. The platinum single 'Wind Beneath My Wings' goes to #1 Pop. Midler and producer Arif Mardin win the Grammy for Record Of The Year. **Ahmad Jamal** releases *Pittsburgh*. The Manhattan Transfer's lead singer **Janis Siegel** releases *Short Stories*. *…But Seriously* is another transatlantic #1 LP for **Phil Collins**. Selling over four million copies, its all-star line-up includes

Eric Clapton, Steve Winwood and David Crosby. The single 'Another Day In Paradise' (#2 UK, #1 US) sells over a million in the UK. **Pete Townshend** releases *The Iron Man: The Musical By Pete Townshend*, the soundtrack for a rock opera based on a story by poet Ted Hughes. It includes performances by John Lee Hooker, Roger Daltrey and Nina Simone. **Julian Lennon** releases *Mr. Jordan*, which features Peter Frampton on guitar and backing vocals and includes the single 'Now You're In Heaven'. **Crosby, Stills, Nash & Young**'s platinum album *American Dream* goes to #16 in the US. **Billy Joe Royal**'s *Tell It Like It Is* produces his biggest country hit on Atlantic: the title track, which peaks at #2, while the album stays in the Top 15 for over a year.

Rush's album *Presto* (#16 US) marks the beginning of a very successful relationship between Atlantic and the popular Canadian power trio, Alex Lifeson (guitar), Geddy Lee (vocals, bass) and Neil Peart (drums). **Skid Row**, a New York hard rock quintet with Toronto native Sebastian 'Bach' Bierk (vocals), Dave 'The Snake' Sabo and Scott Hill (guitars), Rachel Bolan (bass) and Rob Affuso on drums, release their debut LP *Skid Row* (#6 US) on Atlantic. Within six weeks, the album goes gold and by 1995 it has achieved multi-platinum status, selling over five million copies. Their singles '18 And Life' (RIAA Gold) and 'I Remember You' reach #4 Pop and #6 Pop respectively. The group also takes part in the Moscow Peace Festival in 1989. **White Lion**'s *Big Game* (#19 US) goes gold. Solo albums in this year include **Lou Gramm**'s *Long Hard Look*, **Mick Jones**'s self-titled release and **Tony Banks**' *Bank Statement*.

Troop's single 'Mamacita' goes to #2 R&B. *Attitude* (#5 R&B) is released and goes gold with the singles 'I'm Not Souped' (#19 R&B), 'That's My Attitude' (#14 R&B), 'Spread My Wings' (#1 R&B) and their successful cover of The Jackson 5's 'All I Do Is Think Of You' (#1 R&B), the latter three to be released in next year. Disco diva **Donna Summer** releases *Another Place And Time* with the single 'This Time I Know It's For Real' (RIAA Gold). **Debbie Gibson**'s *Electric Youth* LP goes #1 in the US. Her single 'Lost In Your Eyes' goes to #1 Pop and 'Electric Youth' peaks at #11 Pop. Dallas, Texas rapper **The D.O.C.** releases his debut platinum disc *No One Can Do It Better* on Ruthless/Atlantic, which goes to #1 R&B. It includes the hit single 'It's Funky Enough' (#12 R&B). After the release of this album his career is halted by an almost fatal car crash. **Mr. Big**, featuring instrumental heavyweights Billy Sheehan on bass and Paul Gilbert on guitar, release their debut album *Mr. Big*.

1990 LeVert go to the top of the charts again in 1991 with the #1 R&B hit 'Baby I'm Ready' from this year's gold album *Rope A Dope Style*. Sean Levert has solo success with his album *The Other Side* (#20 US). **En Vogue**, a female vocal quartet (Dawn Robinson, Terry Ellis, Cindy Herron and Maxine Jones) from the San Francisco bay area are created by the production team of Denzil Foster and Thomas McElroy. Their single 'Hold On' goes to #2 in the US (Top Ten UK). Their platinum album *Born To Sing* peaks at #21 in the US. **Linear**, a Miami trio, go to #5 Pop with the gold-selling 'Sending All My Love' and release a self-titled album on Atlantic. Louisiana-born rapper **Kyper** signs with Atlantic after the label hears one of his demos. He hits the charts with 'Tic-Tac-Toe' (#14 Pop), a self-penned song. He also releases a gold album entitled *Tic-Tac-Toe*. **Soho**, a British trio consisting of guitarist Timothy Brinkhurst and twin sister vocalists/psychiatric nurses Jacqueline and Pauline Cuff, climb the singles charts with 'Hippychick' (#14 Pop, RIAA Gold) on Atco. **Everything But The Girl**, a London pop duo distinguished by the haunting vocals of Tracey Thorn and musical constructs of Ben Watts (guitar, keyboards, vocals), releases *The Language Of Life*. Produced by Tommy LiPuma with a guest appearance by saxophonist Stan Getz, it includes the UK hit single, 'Driving'. The duo take their name from a sign in a Hull furniture store, which states: For Your Bedroom Needs, We Sell Everything But The Girl. Another gold disc for **Debbie Gibson**, *Anything Is Possible* goes to #41 Pop. Her last album for Atlantic will be *Body Mind Soul* in 1993. New York female trio **Sweet Sensation** have hits with 'Love Child' (#13 Pop) and 'If Wishes Came True' (#1 Pop). They had released the album *Take It While It's Hot* on Atco in 1988 and *Love Child* in 1990.

AC/DC come up with another transatlantic Top Ten album, *Razor's Edge* (#2 US), which sells three million copies. **INXS**'s *X* is a transatlantic Top Ten album and sells two million copies in the US. It features the hit singles 'Suicide Blonde' (#9 Pop) and 'Disappear' (#8 Pop). An important force in alternative rock, Boston band **The Lemonheads**, fronted by Evan Dando on vocals and guitar, debut on Atlantic with *Lovey*. **Robert Plant**'s album *Manic Nirvana* peaks at #13 in the US. Atlantic starts a highly successful string of reissues with a boxed set entitled *Led Zeppelin* (#18 US) featuring a career's worth of material from the group (54 tracks). The set, which sells over six million copies, is compiled by Atlantic's Yves Beauvais and produced by Jimmy Page. **Led Zeppelin**, with total album sales of approximately 39 million at this point, return to the UK Top Ten with *Remasters*, 26 tracks digitally remastered by Jimmy Page. A Florida radio station kicks off its 'All Zeppelin/All The Time' format with 24 hours of 'Stairway To Heaven'. **Rush**'s album *Roll The Bones* rocks into the #3 in the US. **Bob Geldof** releases *Vegetarians Of Love* on Atlantic. **Skid Row**'s *Slave To The Grind* becomes the first heavy metal album to debut at #1 on the *Billboard* chart. It sells over two million copies. **Ratt**'s gold album *Detonator* (#23 US), their last for Atlantic, features a guest appearance by Jon Bon Jovi. **Winger**'s Top 20 album *In The Heart Of The Young* (#15 Pop) features the hit single 'Miles Away' (#12 Pop), their last for the label. Metal band **Pantera**, spearheaded by guitarist Diamond "Dimebag" Darrell, release *Cowboys From Hell* on EastWest America/Atco. Atlantic releases **Savatage**'s *Gutter Ballet*. Another platinum album, **Bad Company**'s *Holy Water* (#35 US) includes the hit singles 'If You Needed Somebody' (#16 Pop) and 'Walk Through Fire' (#28 Pop), both to be released in 1991.

Bette Midler's *Some People's Lives* album reaches #2 in the US and sells two million copies. The platinum single 'From A Distance' (#2 Pop) earns its writer Julie Gold a Grammy for Song Of The Year. Session sax player **Nino Tempo** releases *Tenor Saxophone*. Featuring artists such as Roberta Flack and Ron Carter, the album is produced by Ahmet. Atlantic releases **Bobby Short**'s *Bobby, Noel & Cole*. **Gerald Albright** releases *Bermuda Nights*.

Phil Collins and Hugh Padgham's hit single collaboration, 'Another Day In Paradise', wins a Grammy for Record Of The Year. Collins also wins the *Rolling Stone* magazine award for Best Drummer. Single success this year includes: 'I Wish It Would Rain Down' (#3 Pop), 'Do You Remember?' (#4 Pop), 'Something Happened On The Way To Heaven' (#4 Pop) and 'Hang In Long Enough' (#23 Pop). 'That's Just The Way It Is' charts at #26 in the UK, but not in the US. The album *Serious Hits...Live!* peaks at #2 in the UK and #11 in the US and goes on to sell four million copies in the US. **Crosby, Stills & Nash** release *Live It Up*. Atlantic releases **Billy Joe Royal**'s *Out Of The Shadows*. **Laura Branigan** releases a self-titled album. **Clannad** release the gold-selling *Anam*. Singer **Alannah Myles** releases a million-selling self-titled album (#5 US). Her gold-selling single 'Black Velvet' goes to #1 Pop in the US. Later, she will release *Rockinghorse* (1992) and *Allanah* (1995), her final Atlantic album.

1991 Country artist **Tracy Lawrence** signs to Atlantic in 1991. The same day he finishes recording his debut album, he is shot four times trying to save a friend from being raped during a mugging. He recovers and by the end of 1991 his first single release 'Sticks And Stones', the title track of his album, goes to #1 on the Country chart. The album sells a million copies by 1995. **Neal McCoy**'s debut Atlantic Nashville album *At This Moment* produces the country hits 'If I Built A Fire' and 'This Time I Hurt Her More (Than She Loves Me)'.

Genesis' multi-platinum *We Can't Dance*, #4 US and #1 in the UK, includes the hits: 'No Son Of Mine' (#12 Pop), 'Hold On My Heart' (#12 Pop), 'I Can't Dance' (#7 Pop), 'Jesus He Knows Me' (#23

Pop) and 'Never A Time' (#21 Pop).Singer/songwriter **Tori Amos** comes into her own with the multi-platinum album *Little Earthquakes*. **Marc Cohn**'s soulful single 'Walking In Memphis' goes to #13 Pop in the US, driving his album of the same name into platinum sales and winning Cohn a Grammy for Best New Artist. 'Set The Night To Music', the title track of a collaborative album by **Roberta Flack** and **Maxi Priest**, goes to #6 Pop. **Mike + the Mechanics**' release *Word Of Mouth*. **Mr. Big** release the platinum *Lean Into It* (#15 US) and #1 Pop single, 'To Be With You'. **Steve Howe** of Yes releases the solo album *Turbulence*.

Lynyrd Skynyrd release *Lynyrd Skynyrd 1991* on Atlantic. The album, produced by Tom Dowd in Memphis, follows up on the success of their 1987 Tribute Tour, where the band reunite for the first time since the plane crash in 1977 which killed three of its members. In 1993, they release *The Last Rebel*. The EPs *Favourite Spanish Dishes* and *Patience & Prudence* are released by **The Lemonheads**. **Skid Row** release the self-produced gold-selling album *B-Sides Ourselves*. Featuring material recorded live at Wembley Stadium in the UK, **INXS**'s *Live Baby Live* goes platinum. *Time Space: The Best Of Stevie Nicks* goes platinum for **Stevie Nicks** and peaks at #30 Pop. **Everything But The Girl** release *Worldwide*. **Julian Lennon** releases *Help Yourself*. Paul Rodgers & **The Law** release *The Law*. Heavy metal band **Savatage** release *Streets*. **White Lion** release *Mane Attraction* and **Kix** release *Hot Wire*.

Donna Summer releases *Mistaken Identity*. **Soho** release *Goddess*. **Escape Club** release *Dollars & Sex* and the hit single 'I'll Be There' (#8 Pop). **Gerald Levert**'s solo debut *Private Line* features the singles 'Private Line' (#1 R&B), 'School Me' (#3 R&B), 'Can You Handle It' (#9 R&B) and 'Baby Hold On To Me' (#1 R&B), the latter a duet with his father Eddie. New York female rapper **MC Lyte** releases *Act Like You Know* (#14 R&B).

In a theatrical vein, acclaimed actor and singer **Michael Crawford**, known for his Tony award-winning performance in Andrew Lloyd Webber's *Phantom Of The Opera*, releases *Michael Crawford Performs Andrew Lloyd Webber*, certified platinum by the RIAA. **Bette Midler**'s soundtrack album *For The Boys* (#22 US) goes gold. She also wins an Academy Award nomination and Golden Globe award for her portrayal of a USO entertainer. Jazz saxophonist **Gerald Albright** releases *Live At Birdland West*. Guitarist **Mike Stern**'s album releases in the nineties include *Odds Or Evens* (1991), *Standards (And Other Songs)* (1992), *Is What It Is* (1993), *Between The Lines* (1996) and *Give And Take* (1997).

1992 **Stone Temple Pilots** – Dean DeLeo (guitar), Robert DeLeo (bass), Eric Kretz (drums) and Scott Weiland (vocals) – debut with *Core* (#3 Pop), which sells over seven million copies. The album goes Top 30 in the UK with tracks like 'Sex Type Thing' and 'Wicked Garden'. The Pilots win a Grammy For Best Rock Performance for 'Plush', co-written by Scott Weiland and Dean DeLeo. **The Lemonheads** get airplay with their cover version of Paul Simon's 'Mrs. Robinson'. Their album *It's A Shame About Ray* tops the college radio charts, is certified gold in the US and becomes CMJ's Album Of The Year. Atlantic's first major success in alternative music, the album also features ex-Blake Babies vocalist and future Atlantic artist, Juliana Hatfield.

AC/DC release the multi-platinum audio documentary *Live (Special Collector's Edition)* (#34 Pop). **INXS** release the million-selling *Welcome To Wherever You Are* (#16 Pop).Now a lean and mean trio consisting of Mick Ralphs, Simon Kirke and Brian Howe, **Bad Company** hit platinum with *Here Comes Trouble* (#40 Pop) and a Top 40 hit single, 'How About That' (#38 Pop). **Roger Daltrey** releases *Rocks In The Head*. Hard rockers **Dream Theater**, featuring vocalist James LaBrie, Jon Petrucci (guitar), Kevin Moore (keyboards), John Myung (bass) and Mike Portnoy (drums) release the gold album *Images And Words* on Atco. **Pantera** release the platinum album *Vulgar Display Of Power*. **Genesis** release the gold album *Live/The Way We Walk Volume One: The Shorts* (#35 Pop) which is followed next year by *Live/The Way We Walk Volume Two: The Longs* #20 Pop). **Foreigner**'s Mick Jones and Lou Gramm reunite and release *Foreigner: The Very Best And Beyond*, a million-selling album featuring three new tracks. **Everything But The Girl**'s *Acoustic* is a collection of tracks released in the US, which includes four songs from the British EP, *Covers*. **Tori Amos** releases the *Crucify* EP, which includes covers like Nirvana's 'Smells Like Teen Spirit' and Led Zeppelin's 'Thank You'.

Country singer **John Michael Montgomery** releases his first Atlantic album, *Life's A Dance*, which sells three million by 1995. It reaches the Top Five on the Country album chart and #27 Pop. His single 'I Love The Way You Love Me', a #1 Country hit, crosses over to the Pop charts. **Confederate Railroad**, originally the Danny Shirley Band, debut on Atlantic with *Confederate Railroad*, generating double-platinum sales and Country hit singles like 'Queen Of Memphis', 'Jesus And Mama' and 'Trashy Women'. Singer **Neal McCoy** releases *Where Forever Begins*. **Tracy Lawrence** is presented with *Billboard*'s Best New Country Male Artist of 1992. His second album *Alibis* quickly goes gold and then platinum. He also scores three #1 Country hits with 'Alibis', 'Can't Break My Heart' and 'My Second Home'.

En Vogue chart with 'My Lovin' (You're Never Gonna Get It)' (#1 R&B, #2 Pop), 'Give Him Something He Can Feel' (#1 R&B, #6 Pop) and 'Free Your Mind' (#23 R&B, #15 Pop) on EastWest America/Atco. **Soho** release *Thug*. **Kyper** releases *Countdown To The Year 2000*. **Right Said Fred**, an unusual British trio featuring brothers Richard and Fred Fairbrass with Rob Manzoli, release *I'm Too Sexy* which produces the inimitable international #1 Pop single 'I'm Too Sexy' and other unforgettable concoctions like 'Deeply Dippy' and 'Don't Talk, Just Kiss'.

Jean-Luc Ponty releases *No Absolute Time*. To celebrate their 40th Anniversary, The **Modern Jazz Quartet** are joined by a wide spectrum of jazz greats on *Celebration*. These include Wynton Marsalis, Freddie Hubbard, Nino Tempo, Illinois Jacquet, Phil Woods, Take Six, Bobby McFerrin, Branford Marsalis and Harry "Sweets" Edison. Mickey Roker replaces ailing drummer Connie Kay (back in full form next year) on seven of the thirteen tracks. Ahmet produces the album. A special four-boxed set retrospective of the MJQ's entire recording career, produced by Ahmet, John Lewis and Didier Deutsch, is also released to mark the occasion. The group perform a special concert at the Cafe Carlyle and the Mayor of New York declares January 14th, 'Modern Jazz Quartet Day'.

1993 The Lemonheads record the gold album *Come On Feel The Lemonheads* featuring Juliana Hatfield, Belinda Carlisle and Rick James, and the single 'Into Your Arms'. **The Juliana Hatfield Three** release *Become What You Are* on the Atlantic subsidiary, Mammoth. Singer, guitarist, bassist Hatfield, a Berklee graduate and veteran of Blake Babies, is teamed with bassist Dean Fisher and drummer Todd Phillips. **INXS**'s *Full Moon, Dirty Hearts* features guest appearances by Ray Charles on 'Please (You Got That)' and Chrissie Hynde on the title track. Bob Clearmountain and Brian Eno mix. L.A. punk rockers **Bad Religion** debut on Atlantic with *Recipe For Hate*. **The Melvins**' *Houdini* is co-produced by Kurt Cobain, Nirvana front man and a seminal figure in the Seattle 'Grunge' scene. Also Seattle-based, the Melvins release three albums for Atlantic before returning to Independent labels.

Wandering Spirit (#11 Pop), a gold album for **Mick Jagger**, is produced by Rick Rubin with back-up from Lennie Kravitz (vocals), Courtney Pine (sax), Billy Preston (keyboards), and the Red Hot Chili Peppers' Flea on bass. **Rush**'s *Counterparts* climbs to #2 on the album chart (RIAA Gold). **Mr. Big** release *Bump Ahead*. *The Best Of Bad Company Live…What You Hear Is What You Get* is released in celebration of **Bad Company**'s 20th Anniversary. **Led Zeppelin**'s *Boxed Set 2*, another repackaged collection, reaps more platinum for the label. **Savatage** release *Edge Of Thorns*. While **Yes** go through different line-ups, their gold compilation *The Very Best Of Yes* is released. The production team includes group members Trevor

Rabin and Trevor Horn, along with Yves Beauvais, Paul Clay, Tony Colton, Paul DeVilliers and Eddie Offord. **Pete Townshend** releases *Psychoderelict* and embarks on his first solo tour of North America. 1993 also marks the debut of his play *The Iron Man: The Musical By Pete Townshend* at London's Old Vic and *Tommy*'s Broadway debut, which earns five prestigious Tony awards.

Both Sides by **Phil Collins** reaches #1 in the UK and #13 in the US, with platinum sales. **David Crosby** releases *Thousand Roads*. **Tracy Lawrence** wins the AMC award for Top New Male Vocalist. His second album *Alibis* goes multi-platinum. **Bette Midler**'s 1993 platinum album *Experience The Divine – Greatest Hits* includes a previously unreleased live version of the classic 'One For My Baby (And One More For The Road)', performed on the last *Tonight Show* with Johnny Carson. In December, she plays Mama Rose in the CBS-TV production of *Gypsy* with the soundtrack album released on Atlantic. **Nino Tempo** releases *Nino*. **Michael Crawford** releases the gold album *A Touch Of Music In The Night* (#39 Pop). **LeVert** release *For Real Tho'*. **Intro** (Innovative New Talent Reaching Out), a vocal trio with Kenny Greene (lead), Clinton Wike and Jeff Sanders, record the gold-selling album *Intro* featuring the singles 'Let Me Be The One' (#23 R&B), 'Love Thang' (#28 R&B) and the crossover hit 'Come Inside' (#9 R&B, #33 Pop).

1994

Hootie & the Blowfish, a rock band originally formed at the University of South Carolina, release their debut Atlantic album, *Cracked Rear View*. The group, consisting of 'working' musicians Darius Rucker (vocals), Mark Bryan (guitar), Jim 'Soni' Sonefield (drums) and Dean Felber (bass), watch their album soar to #1 on the *Billboard* album chart, staying there for eight weeks and in the Top Ten for 55 weeks. By March of 1996, the album is certified by the RIAA as 13-times platinum, Atlantic's biggest-selling debut album. By 1999, it sells over 16 million copies and is awarded the RIAA Diamond award. The band wins Grammies for Best New Artist and Best Pop Performance By A Duo Or Group With Vocal (for the #9 Pop single, 'Let Her Cry'). The album's first single 'Hold My Hand,' with David Crosby on backing vocals, goes to #10 US. The third single 'Only Wanna Be With You' goes to #6 Pop.

Alaska-born vocalist **Jewel** (Kilcher) releases her first Atlantic album *Pieces Of You* (#25 Pop). This unpretentious debut is recorded at a San Diego coffeehouse and Neil Young's Redwood Digital studio with backing from Young's band the Stray Gators. The single 'You Were Meant For Me' goes platinum. By 1999, the album goes on to sell over 11 million copies and is certified RIAA Diamond. **Tori Amos**' album *Under The Pink* (#12 US) is a multi-platinum success, featuring the tracks 'Cornflake Girl' and 'God'. **Brandy**, a young singer/actress from Mississippi, releases her Atlantic debut, *Brandy* (#6 R&B, #20 Pop), which sells four million copies. It produces a series of hits in this year and subsequent years: the gold single 'I Wanna Be Down' (#1 R&B, #6 Pop), the platinum hit 'Baby' (#1 R&B, #4 Pop), 'Best Friend' (#7 R&B, #34 Pop), 'Brokenhearted' (#2 R&B, #9 Pop) and the platinum-selling 'Sittin' Up In My Room' (#2 Pop, #2 R&B).

It takes three weeks for **Stone Temple Pilots** to record their second album, *Purple*. It enters the US album chart at #1 and remains there for three weeks and goes on to sell over six million copies. **Collective Soul**, a progressive five-piece rock group from Georgia, release their first Atlantic album, the multi-platinum *hints allegations & things left unsaid*. The band consists of brothers Ed and Dean Roland on vocals and guitar, Ross Childress (guitar) Will Turpin (bass) and Shane Evans (drums). Hit singles include 'Shine' (#11 Pop) in 1994, 'December' (#20 Pop) and 'The World I Know' (#19 Pop) in 1995. After months recovering from a near-fatal illness, Ben Watt returns to the studio with Tracey Thorn to record **Everything But The Girl**'s *Amplified Heart*. The album goes gold in the US and UK. By the time **Donna Lewis**' demo tape reaches Atlantic, her return address has been lost after passing through so many hands. Impressed by the demo, the label is on the verge of hiring a private detective to track her down when she is finally located in England. Her first single 'I Love You Always Forever' is an international hit and certified gold in the US.

John Michael Montgomery strikes gold with his song 'I Swear'. His album *Kickin' It Up* goes to #1 on the Country chart within a month of its release and goes on to sell four million copies. **Neal McCoy** releases the platinum album *No Doubt About It*, which includes the #1 Country singles 'Wink' and the title track. **Confederate Railroad** release the album, *Notorious*, which goes platinum the following year. **Tracy Lawrence** releases his third album, *I See It Now*, which sells a million copies. Country singer **Tim McGraw** releases *Not A Moment Too Soon* on Curb/Atlantic, which goes to the top of the Pop album chart and features two crossover Country hits, 'Indian Outlaw' (#15 Pop) and 'Don't Take The Girl' (#17 Pop). The album goes on to sell over five million copies. It becomes *Billboard*'s sixth best-selling album of the year and McGraw wins Top New Male Vocalist and Album Of The Year awards from the Academy of Country Music. He is also voted Male Video Artist Of The Year at the Country Music Television Awards.

With a succession of prestigious jazz scholarships and a two-year tenure with the great Betty Carter under his belt, jazz pianist **Cyrus Chestnut** releases his first Atlantic album, *Revelation*. It spends seven weeks at #1 on the Gavin jazz chart. It holds the top spot on the Gavin and CMJ year-end charts. According to trumpeter Wynton Marsalis, saxophonist **Wessell Anderson**'s playing embodies the essence of soul, hence his nickname 'Warmdaddy'. Atlantic releases Anderson's album *Warmdaddy In The Garden Of Swing* this year. The gifted young jazz saxophonist **James Carter** earns critical acclaim with his debut, *The Real Quiet Storm*. **Gerald Albright** releases *Smooth*. Contemporary jazz trumpet player **Rick Braun** releases several albums on Bluemoon/Atlantic including *Night Walk* and *Christmas Present – Music Of Warmth And Celebration*. **The Ginger Baker Trio** release *Going Back Home*, featuring Baker (drums) with Bill Frisell (guitar) and Charlie Haden (bass).

All-4-One, a vocal quartet based in Southern California, release their debut self-titled album on Blitzz/Atlantic (#7 US). It goes double-platinum and includes their cover version of the Tymes' 'So Much In Love' (#5 Pop, RIAA Gold). It also includes the #1 Pop single, 'I Swear', written by and also a Country hit for labelmate, John Michael Montgomery. All-4-One's version goes on to become the biggest-selling single of 1994, going platinum and winning the American Music Award for Favourite New Soul/R&B Artist and the Grammy for Best Pop Performance By A Duo Or Group With Vocal. **Changing Faces**, a female urban soul vocal duo, are first heard singing in the street by Kenny Smoove, the head of Atlantic subsidiary label Big Beat's Spoiled Rotten imprint. Within a week, they are signed to the label and recording their first album, *Changing Faces* (#1 R&B, #25 Pop, RIAA Gold). The single 'Stroke You Up' (#2 R&B, #3 Pop) is certified RIAA platinum and 'Foolin' Around', written and produced by R. Kelly reaches #9 R&B. Vocalist **Robin S** releases *Show Me Love* (#37 R&B) on Big Beat/Atlantic following on the heels of the Top Ten success of 'Show Me Love' (#7 R&B, #5 Pop). **Bad Religion**'s *Stranger Than Fiction*, featuring the single '21st Century Digital Boy', is their biggest-selling album after 15 years of recording. **The Melvins** release *Stoner Witch*. **The Bottle Rockets** release their critically acclaimed debut, *The Brooklyn Side*, named after a term used in bowling. It was originally released on a small independent label before being picked up by Atlantic.

Robert Plant and **Jimmy Page** record together for the first time since the breakup of Led Zeppelin. Not surprisingly, their *No Quarter* album goes platinum (#4 US). They follow with a successful tour. **Stevie Nicks**' Modern/Atlantic album, *Street Angel*, with guest appearances from Bob Dylan, David Crosby and Andy Fairweather-Low, goes gold in the US. **Crosby, Stills & Nash** release *After The Storm*. **Clannad** releases the gold-selling *Banba*. **Victoria Williams** releases *Loose* on Atlantic/Mammoth followed by a live recording, *This Moment In Toronto With The Loose Band*. Singer-songwriter **Liz Phair** releases

Whip-smart on Matador/Atlantic. **Laura Branigan** releases *Over My Heart*. *Tonin'*, **The Manhattan Transfer**'s return to Atlantic in 1994, features guest performances by Bette Midler, Phil Collins, Smokey Robinson, Ruth Brown, Frankie Valli, Felix Cavaliere, B.B. King and Chaka Kahn. It is produced and arranged by Arif Mardin. *The Crow*, a film starring Brandon Lee, son of martial arts maestro Bruce Lee, produces a #1 US soundtrack album on Atlantic, which features music from the Stone Temple Pilots, The Cure, Nine Inch Nails and others. Atlantic releases the gold soundtrack album *Maverick* (#35 US). **Dream Theater** release *Awake* (#32 US). **Pantera** takes the album *Far Beyond Driven* to #1 in the US with platinum sales. Following the death in 1993 of co-founder and member Criss Oliva, **Savatage** release *Handful Of Rain*. The album is dedicated to Oliva's memory and co-produced by his brother Jon. 1994 marks the end of **INXS**'s tenure on Atlantic. *INXS: The Greatest Hits* is released the same year and goes on to sell a million copies.

Another milestone, Atlantic releases an album with José Carreras, Placido Domingo and Luciano Pavarotti: *Carreras, Domingo, Pavarotti With Mehta: The Three Tenors In Concert 1994*, recorded at the Dodger Stadium in L.A. Featuring the Los Angeles Philharmonic Orchestra and the Los Angeles Music Center Opera Chorus under the direction of maestro Zubin Mehta, **The Three Tenors** concert plays to an audience of 56,000 and is broadcast to an estimated worldwide audience of one billion. The album is a #1 classical hit and goes on to sell five million copies. It debuts at #4 on the *Billboard* 200 chart, the highest charting classical album ever in the rock era.

1995 **Sugar Ray**'s first album for the label is *Lemonade And Brownies* (Lava/Atlantic). The group features Mark McGrath (vocals), Stan Frazier (drums), Rodney Sheppard (guitar), Murphy Karges (bass). The album includes the tracks 'Rhyme Stealer' and 'Mean Machine', the latter made famous by the popular US cartoon duo, Beavis and Butthead. Sugar Ray goes on to perform with Korn, Cypress Hill, the Deftones and the reunited Sex Pistols. **The Corrs**, an Irish group featuring brother and sisters Jim, Caroline, Andrea and Sharon Corr, enjoy worldwide gold and multi-platinum success with their 143/Lava/Atlantic debut, *Forgiven, Not Forgotten*. It features the hits 'Runaway' and the title track. **Everything But The Girl**'s 'Missing', from their 1994 *Amplified Heart* album, is remixed by Todd Terry and becomes a worldwide hit. It reaches #2 on *Billboard*'s Hot 100 chart and #1 on *Billboard*'s Hot 100 Airplay chart in the US, where it is also certified gold. In the UK, it peaks at #3 but remains in the Top Ten for three months and is certified platinum. It also goes to #1 in Australia, Canada, Germany and stays at #1 for six weeks in Italy. Virginia rock quartet **Seven Mary Three**'s first album for Atlantic on the Mammoth imprint, *American Standard*, goes to #24 in the US and produces the single 'Cumbersome'. **Edwin McCain**'s stint as a support act for Hootie & the Blowfish brings him to Atlantic's attention. McCain's debut album on Lava/Atlantic, *Honor Among Thieves*, hits #1 on SoundScan's Top New Artist Album chart and includes the Top Ten Rock and Triple-A hit, 'Solitude', a duet by McCain and Hootie's Darius Rucker. McCain is backed by his band, Scott Bannevich (bass), Dave Harrison (drums), Craig Shields (keyboards/saxophone) and Larry Chaney (guitar). **Collective Soul** release a self-titled album (#23 US), which goes on to sell three million copies. It produces the hit 'December' (#20 Pop), *Billboard*'s #1 Hot Rock Album Track and wins the *Billboard* Music Award for Album Rock Song Of The Year – the only group to win the award two years in a row. Collective Soul also chart with 'The River Flows' and 'World I Know' (#19 Pop).

Singer-songwriter **Jill Sobule** releases her Atlantic debut album, which produces the single 'I Kissed A Girl', which gets significant airplay and is honoured as the Outstanding Song at the Seventh Annual Gay & Lesbian Alliance Against Defamation In The Media Awards. Sobule's clever 'Supermodel', also a hit, is featured in the soundtrack for the movie *Clueless*. **Juliana Hatfield**'s *Only Everything* is released on Mammoth/Atlantic. **The Tragically Hip**, a rock quintet from Canada, release *Day For Night*. **7 Year Bitch**, an all-girl band from Seattle release their debut for Atlantic, *Gato Negro*. Comic book artist Jamie Hernandez designs the album cover for an album of raw, full-bore rock'n'roll. **Skid Row** release *Subhuman Race* (#35 US). **Savatage** release *Dead Winter Dead*. **Mike + the Mechanics** release *Beggar On A Beach Of Gold*.

Gerald and **Eddie Levert** pool their many talents on the gold album *Father & Son* (#2 R&B, #20 Pop) with the Top Ten R&B single 'Already Missing You' (#7 R&B). Their cover of 'Wind Beneath My Wings' (#30 R&B) wins awards and becomes a crowd favourite on their 1995-1996 tour. Gerald also enjoys platinum success with his solo album *Groove On* (#2 R&B, #20 Pop) and **Sean Levert** also scores with *The Other Side* (#22 R&B). **All-4-One** have a hit with 'I Can Love You Like That' (#5 Pop, #40 R&B) and release the platinum album *And The Music Speaks* (#27 US), along with the seasonal LP, *An All-4-One Christmas*. Rappers **Junior M.A.F.I.A.** (Masters At Finding Intelligent Attitudes) go gold with their debut album, *Conspiracy* (Entertainment/Big Beat/Atlantic). The group members are all disciples of the Notorious B.I.G. who produces the album along with Lance 'Un' Rivera, DJ Clark Kent and Daddy-O. It includes the singles 'Get Money' and 'Players Anthem'.

Known as 'The Barefoot Diva' and 'The Queen Of Morna', vocalist **Cesaria Evora** comes from Sao Vincente off Cape Verde on the West Coast of Africa, birthplace of the Creole-Portugese Morna genre. A whisky-loving, chain-smoking grandmother whose voice is described as 'somewhere between rich chocolate and crushed velvet', Evora's self-titled Nonesuch/Atlantic album stays in the Top Five of *Billboard*'s World Music chart for over six months. **Michael Crawford** releases the Atlantic album *EFX!*, taken from the successful stage production of the same name set at the MGM Grand Hotel in Las Vegas, which features Crawford in five different roles. Pianist and vocalist **Michael Feinstein**, former archivist for Ira Gershwin, releases his first Atlantic recording, *Such Sweet Sorrow*. Atlantic earns yet another multi-platinum effort with the *Batman Forever* (#5 US) soundtrack album. **Bette Midler** releases another gold album, *Bette Of Roses*.

James Carter collaborates with jazz greats Buddy Tate and Harry "Sweets" Edison on his tribute album, *Conversin' With The Elders*. Atlantic releases **Wessell Anderson**'s *The Ways Of Warmdaddy*. **Gerald Albright** records *Giving Myself To You*. **Rick Braun** releases his breakthrough disc, *Beat Street*, on Bluemoon/Atlantic, which tops the Contemporary Jazz Airplay chart for 13 weeks and is named #1 Smooth Jazz Record Of The Year. Atlantic releases saxophonist **Nino Tempo**'s *Live At Cicada*, co-ordinated by Yves Beauvais, with executive production by Ahmet. **The Ginger Baker Trio** release *Falling Off The Roof*.

John Michael Montgomery's self-titled 1995 album goes on to sell four million copies. **Neal McCoy**'s *You Gotta Love That* goes platinum. **Confederate Railroad** releases *When And Where*. Country singer amd instrumentalist **Ricky Skaggs** releases *Solid Ground*. **Tracy Lawrence** releases *Live And Unplugged*. **Tim McGraw** releases the multi-platinum album *All I Want* on Curb/Atlantic, which produces Country hits like 'I Like It, I Love It' and 'Can't Be Really Gone'.

1996 matchbox twenty debut on Lava/Atlantic with *Yourself Or Someone Like You*, recorded with Collective Soul producer, Matt Serletic. The group features Rob Thomas (lead vocals/songwriter), Brian Yale (bass), Adam Gaynor (rhythm guitar), Kyle Cook (lead guitar) and Paul Doucette (drums). The album gains momentum as the band tours across the US and it yields a string of successful singles. The first of which is 'Long Day' (*Billboard* Mainstream Rock Tracks charts for 22 weeks). 'Push' (#1 *Billboard* Hot 100 Airplay & Modern Rock Track charts) is released next, followed by '3 am' (#3 *Billboard* Hot 100 Airplay chart) and the album also features 'Real World' and 'Back 2 Good'. *Yourself Or Someone Like You* is a multi-million-seller and, as of December 1998, had stayed in the

Billboard Top 200 album chart since its release. The album goes on to sell over 11 million copies in the US earning the group an RIAA Diamond award in 2000. matchbox twenty is also voted Best New Band in *Rolling Stone*'s annual Readers Poll, and earns a Grammy for 'Push'.

The gifted young vocalist **LeAnn Rimes** releases *Blue*, her debut on Curb/Atlantic at the tender age of 14. The album goes straight to #49 on the Country chart, making Rimes the youngest country singer to chart that high. It features the title track, written by Bill Mack, a song he had written for Patsy Cline 30 years previously. Cline died in a plane crash before recording it, so 'Blue' remains unrecorded until Mack hears Rimes perform and sends her the song. The album also includes 'Cattle Call', a duet with country legend Eddy Arnold. *Blue* is still on the charts a year later, having peaked at #3, and goes on to sell six million copies. **Tim McGraw**'s single 'She Never Lets It Go To Her Heart' from his 1996 Curb/Atlantic album *Not A Moment Too Soon* goes to #1 on both the *Billboard* and *Radio & Records* Country charts. His *Spontaneous Combustion* tour is one of the top five grossing tours of this year. **John Michael Montgomery**'s *What I Do Best* album goes on to sell over a million copies in the US. **Neal McCoy**'s gold album *Greatest Hits* is a Country Top Five chart-topper and his single 'The Shake' also reaches the Top Five. In addition he releases a self-titled album, featuring 'Then You Can Tell Me Goodbye'. Country vocalist **Mila Mason** releases her debut on Atlantic/Nashville, *That's Enough Of That*. In 1997 she releases the *Dark Horse* EP and in 1998 *The Strong One*. **Tracy Lawrence**'s *Time Marches On* album sells two million copies.

MC Lil' Kim, the only female member of the popular rap crew Junior M.A.F.I.A., goes solo with *Hard Core*. 'Not Tonight', RIAA platinum (#3 R&B, #6 Pop), her 1997 single is nominated for a 1998 Grammy award. The platinum album also becomes the highest entry ever on the *Billboard* Hot 200 Albums chart by a female hip-hop artist. Other hits from *Hard Core* include 'Crush On You' and the gold-selling #1 Rap single 'No Time' featuring Puff Daddy. The gold-selling album *Get On Up And Dance* marks **Quad City DJs** debut on Big Beat/Atlantic. It includes the hit single 'C'mon N' Ride It (The Train)' (#3 Pop, #15 R&B), which is also featured on multi-platinum *Space Jam* soundtrack. *Space Jam*, an animated film starring basketball legend Michael Jordan, yields a soundtrack that becomes the best-selling album of the first half of 1997. It features contemporary heavyweights LL Cool J, Q-Tip, Salt N' Pepa, Coolio, Quad City DJs, Seal, Robin S and R. Kelly, with production and arrangements by Todd Terry and R. Kelly. Craig Kallman is executive producer. The album sells five million copies and becomes the biggest-selling soundtrack release in Atlantic history. **Aaliyah** scores with *One In A Million*, which achieves two million sales and goes to #2 R&B and #18 Pop with the hit singles 'If Your Girl Only Knew' (#1 R&B, #11 Pop) and 'The One I Gave My Heart To' RIAA gold, (#8 R&B, #9 Pop).

Tori Amos' multi-platinum album *Boys For Pele* debuts at #2 in the US. **Clannad** release the album *Lore*, a #1 World Music hit. Singer-songwriter **Duncan Sheik** makes his 1996 debut on Atlantic with *Duncan Sheik*, produced by Rupert Hine and featuring the track 'Barely Breathing'. In 1997, Sheik's album goes to #1 on *SoundScan*'s Alternative New Artist chart and #1 on *Billboard*'s Heatseeker's chart and is certified gold. By the end of the year, 'Barely Breathing' has spent 55 weeks on the *Billboard* Hot 100 and later earns him a Grammy nomination for Best Male Pop Vocal Performance. **Donna Lewis** records her platinum debut album on Atlantic, *Now In A Minute*, co-produced by Lewis and Kevin Klein. *Billboard* ranks her at #6 in the Top New Artist chart and at the top of *Billboard*'s 200 Female Artists Of The Year. She reaches #7 on the Hot 100 Female Singles Artists chart and the Top 20 of the Overall Hot 100 Singles Artists of 1996. **Everything But The Girl** release *Walking Wounded* (#37 US), produced by Todd Terry. They also release the EP, *Everything But The Girl vs. Drum & Bass*. Britain's **Pet Shop Boys** release *Bilingual*, their debut for Atlantic. The essence of modern pop, **Fountains of Wayne** featuring Adam Schlesinger of Ivy and Chris Collingsworth, release their self-titled debut on Scratchie/TAG/Atlantic. **The Lemonheads** release the album *Car Button Cloth*. Atlantic later releases *The Best Of The Lemonheads: The Atlantic Years* in 1998. **The Tragically Hip** release *Trouble At The Henhouse*. **The Melvins** release *Stag*. Cars front man Ric Ocasek produces **Bad Religion**'s *Gray Race*. **Pantera** go to #4 on the *Billboard* Pop album chart with the gold-selling *Great Southern Trendkill*.

Tiny Music … Songs From The Vatican Gift Shop, **Stone Temple Pilots**' third Atlantic album, sells two million copies. *Coolwalkingsmoothtalkingstraightsmokingfirestoking: The Best Of Pete Townshend* is released. The 15-track album draws on material recorded by **Pete Townshend** between 1972 and 1993, and includes two previously unreleased tracks. **Rush**'s *Test For Echo* album goes gold and hits #35 on the Hard Rock album chart. It produces two singles, the title track and 'Half The World'. **Mr. Big** release *Hey Man*. *Fairweather Johnson*, **Hootie & the Blowfish**'s second Atlantic album sells three million copies and goes to #1 in the US. Their single 'Time' climbs into the US Top 20 (#14).

The Three Sopranos album is released on Atlantic, recorded at a gala performance in Los Angeles. **The Three Sopranos**, Kathleen Cassello, Kallen Esperian and Cynthia Lawrence, perform operatic medleys especially arranged by Grammy-winning composer Peter Matz Gian Carlo Chiaramello. **The Trans-Siberian Orchestra**, formed by Savatage's Jon Oliva (lead/keyboards) and Paul O'Neill (producer), release their debut on Lava/Atlantic, *Christmas Eve And Other Stories*. O'Neill combines a 60-piece orchestra, full chorus and a rock'n'roll band for this album. Trumpeter **Rick Braun** wins Gavin's Artist Of The Year and Album Of The Year.

1997

Timbaland & Magoo's debut *Welcome To Our World* is certified gold nearly two months before its release. It goes straight to #1 on *Billboard*'s Hot Rap chart, spends 29 weeks on the *Billboard* 200, reaches the Top Ten of the Top R&B Albums chart and is certified platinum. Featuring performances from Missy 'Misdemeanor' Elliott, Playa and Ginuwine, the album is actually preceded by the gold single, 'Up Jumps Da Boogie', a #4 R&B hit, which features fellow Atlantic artist Aaliyah. **Twista** kicks it into high gear on Creator's Way/Big Beat/Atlantic with the gold-selling *Adrenaline Rush*. **DJ Pooh**'s self-produced *Bad Newz Travels Fast* on Da Bomb/Big Beat/Atlantic features 'Bump Yo Speakers', 'Whoop! Whoop!' and 'Get Off'. **Changing Faces**' gold album, *All Day, All Night*, produces the hit single 'G.H.E.T.T.O.U.T.'. R. Kelly writes, produces and plays all the instruments on both the single and title track. The group's biggest hit to date, it reaches #1 R&B and #8 Pop, going platinum. *From Now On*, the second album from **Robin S.**, is produced by Eric 'E-Smoove' Miller and Todd Terry, among others. British R&B singer **Mark Morrison**'s *Return Of The Mack* album goes to #4 on the UK charts and earns four nominations for the BRIT Awards. The single 'Return Of The Mack' has been highly successful throughout Europe in 1996 and goes to #1 in the UK. The single reaches #2 in the US in 1997. Morrison writes the track in response to a prison term served in the UK. With a penchant for attracting trouble including getting a stand-in to do his community service, Morrison is back in prison in 1997 for trying to board an aeroplane with a stun gun. **LeVert** release *The Whole Scenario*, their sixth album on Atlantic. Guest artists include Yo Yo, Queen Pen, Missy Elliott and Mad Lion, with production by Gerald Levert, Marc Gordon and Edwin 'Tony' Nicholas.

Collective Soul release the gold-selling album *Disciplined Breakdown*. **Jill Sobule** continues to build a loyal following with her second Atlantic release, *Happy Town*. Singer/songwriter/violinist **Lili Haydn** releases her debut album *Lili*. She is joined by Chad Smith of the Red Hot Chili Peppers. **Kacy Crowley** debuts on Atlantic with *Anchorless*. **Poe**, a vocalist who took the name of her childhood obsession, the writer Edgar Allan Poe, records her label debut, *Hello*. The album features eight different co-writers and three producers working in seven different studios with both musicians and computers. **Ivy** release *Apartment Life*. The trio, fronted by Dominique Durand, also features Andy Chase and Adam Schlesinger (Fountains of Wayne). **Seven Mary**

Three release *Rock Crown*.

Dreamland marks the beginning of vocalist **Madeleine Peyroux**'s recording career for Atlantic. Produced by Yves Beauvais and bassist/arranger Greg Cohen, the album features fellow Atlantic artists James Carter, Cyrus Chestnut and Marc Ribot. Pianist **Cyrus Chestnut**'s *Earth Stories* earns widespread critical acclaim. Musicians include Al Vistar Garnet (drums), Steve Kirby (bass) and Anton Hart (alto saxophone). On the self-produced *Live To Love* album, saxophonist **Gerald Albright** also plays keyboards, flute and drums. **Rick Braun** releases *Body & Soul*, which quickly goes to the Top 15 of *Billboard*'s Contemporary Jazz chart and sells over 100,000 copies. It is also #3 on the NAC Smooth Jazz Album chart and leads to Braun's second Gavin Artist Of The Year award. 'Notorious', a featured album track, holds down #1 for four weeks on the NAC Smooth Jazz Track chart and reaches #1 on the year-end chart. **The Art Ensemble of Chicago** record their *Coming Home Jamaica* album at an 18-acre compound in Ocho Rios thanks to a unique sponsorship arrangement with California's Odwalla juice company. It marks the group's 30th anniversary and a return to Atlantic after a 25-year absence. In keeping with the group's idiosyncratic instrumentation, the tracks include bamboo sax, bamboo flute, whistles and gongs. To celebrate their 25th anniversary, **The Manhattan Transfer** release *Swing*, featuring Ricky Skaggs (guitars/mandolin), Stephane Grappelli (violin) and arrangements of the late Fletcher Henderson, Benny Goodman's arranger. At this point, they have produced 20 albums with worldwide sales in the millions, in addition to collecting eight Grammies. They have also won Best Vocal Group honours in both the *Down Beat* and *Playboy* jazz polls for ten years in a row (1980-1990).
The Boston Camerata record *Angels*. A completely unique and distinctively modern reinvention of chamber music, **The Kronos Quartet** – David Harrington (violin), John Sherba (violin), Hank Dutt (viola) and Joan Jeanreaud (cello) – release two albums on Nonesuch/Atlantic, *Ghost Opera* and *The Dreams And Prayers Of Isaac The Blind*. One of the world's leading classical violinists,

Maxim Vengerov releases two Atlantic albums, *The Road I Travel* and *Prokofiev And Shostakovich: Violin Concertos No. 2*. Avant-garde composer **Philip Glass** releases *Kundun: A Martin Scorsese Picture, Music From The Original Soundtrack*, which tells the story of the current Dalai Lama. Glass spent over a year on the score combining both Tibetan and Western instruments into a typically unique orchestral sound. **Angelica**, five American sopranos – Julia Bonilla, Anita DeSimone, Sewell Griffin, Lori Stinton and Rebecca Semrau – release the debut album *Angelica* on Atlantic. Changing the face of modern opera, the sopranos were matched with guitarists such as Dweezil Zappa (son of rock iconoclast Frank Zappa) and other modern musicians. Opera singer **José Cura** releases *Puccini Arias*, with Placido Domingo conducting the orchestra. Cura wins the *Opera Now* Artist Of The Year award for 1997-1998.

Moondog releases the unique album *Sax Pax For A Sax*. Recorded in Bath, England by David Lord, it features Moondog (born Louis Hardin) on bass drum and bongos accompanied by an all-saxophone orchestra featuring British reed man John Harle. Moondog originally attended the Iowa School For The Blind and later lived among the Navajo and Blackfoot Native American tribes. At one point he became a well-known attraction on New York's Sixth Avenue (actually listed in the city's guide books), playing percussion instruments of his own design, reciting poetry and dressed in full Viking costume. **The Tibetan Institute of Performing Arts** had been set up in exile to preserve the music, dance and theatre of Tibet. Atlantic releases a 1997 album of chants, folk music and translated text performed by the Institute, entitled *Dhama Suna*. **Cesaria Evora** records an album inspired by her homeland, *Cabo Verde* on Nonesuch/Atlantic. **The Gipsy Kings**, the dynamic group of singer-guitarists, release the LP *Compas* on Nonesuch/Atlantic. **Linda Eder**, the talented singer acclaimed for her role in the long-running Broadway musical *Jekyll And Hyde*, is signed to Atlantic and releases *It's Time*.

LeAnn Rimes charts with the double platinum *Unchained Melody: LeAnn Rimes The Early Years* (Curb/Atlantic), which goes to #4 on the Top 50 Country Album chart. Her 1995 release *Blue* is still on the charts. **John Michael Montgomery**'s *Greatest Hits* is still riding the Country Album charts two years after its release, while Tim McGraw's 1994 release, *Not A Moment Too Soon* is also still in the charts. **Tracy Lawrence** peaks at #29 on the Country Album chart with the gold-selling *Coast Is Clear*. **Noel Haggard** releases *One Lifetime*, **The Bottle Rockets** release *24 Hours A Day* and **Neal McCoy** releases *Be Good At It*. Country rock band **Sawyer Brown** release *Hallelujah He Is Born*. **Ricky Skaggs** releases *Life Is A Journey*. Country artist **Matt King** records *Five O'Clock Hero*.

Edwin McCain releases the Lava/Atlantic album *Misguided Roses* which is quickly certified gold in the US. The album's success is spurred by the smash single 'I'll Be'. **Genesis**, without longtime mainstay Phil Collins, who is replaced by former Stiltskin Ray Wilson, release *Calling All Stations*. **Led Zeppelin**'s album of live radio broadcasts from early in their career, titled *BBC Sessions*, is certified platinum. **Big Wreck** record their first album for Atlantic, *In Loving Memory Of…* and score a Top 20 hit on *Billboard*'s Mainstream Rock chart with the track 'The Oaf (My Luck Is Wasted)'. **Glenn Tipton**, guitarist from Judas Priest, makes his solo debut on Atlantic with *Baptizm Of Fire*. It features drummers Cozy Powell and Shannon Larkin, bassists Billy Sheehan of Mr. Big, Robert Trujillo and The Who's John Entwhistle. Canadian power trio **Widemouth Mason** release a self-titled debut on Atlantic and appear at the 1997 Montreux Jazz Festival in Switzerland.

Sugar Ray's Top 20 album *Floored* sells more that two million copies in the US. It produces the multi-format smash hit single 'Fly', featuring Super Cat, which stays at #1 for six consecutive weeks on *Billboard*'s Hot 100 Airplay chart. The song's companion video is #1 on MTV, VH1 and The Box. Their track 'Burnin' Dog (Don't Pet A)' will also appear on the 1998 Atlantic soundtrack album *The Avengers: Music From The Motion Picture*.

1998 *Spirit*, **Jewel**'s second Atlantic album is certified quadruple-platinum. Produced by Patrick Leonard, *Spirit* debuts at #3 on the *Billboard* 200 and is certified platinum out of the box. The album's first single, 'Hands', is a hit on multi-format outlets across the US and a Top Ten hit on *Billboard*'s Hot 100 chart. The success of Jewel's debut, *Pieces Of You*, keeps growing with sales in excess of 11 million by 2000. **Brandy** releases *Never Say Never*, which reaches #2 on the *Billboard* 200 and achieves sales of over five million in the US. Across the world it earns Brandy gold and platinum awards and also produces the double-platinum duet with Monica, 'The Boy Is Mine'. It reaches #1 in the US and becomes the longest-running *Billboard* 'Hot 100' single in Atlantic label history. Other singles, 'Top Of The World', the David Foster-produced 'Have You Ever?', 'Almost Doesn't Count' and 'Angel In Disguise', also enjoy chart success. Brandy earns four Grammy Award nominations, three for 'The Boy Is Mine' (Record Of The Year, Best R&B Performance by a Duo or Group with Vocal and Best R&B Song) and Best R&B Album for *Never Say Never*.

Tori Amos' fourth solo album *from the choirgirl hotel* debuts at #5 on the *Billboard* Top Current Albums chart and is certified gold a month after its release in early May and goes on to be platinum. Produced by Amos, the recording features long-time collaborator Steve Caton on guitar and Matt Chamberlain on drums. Atlantic also releases *Tori Amos: The Complete Collection: 1992-1998*, a full-length compilation of her videos. 1998 marks the release of **The Corrs**' second album on Atlantic, *Talk On Corners*. One of the tracks, 'Only When I Sleep', is co-written by the band and producer Oliver Leiber, son of the legendary songwriter Jerry Leiber. Also collaborating are Grammy-winning producer David Foster, Glen Ballard, Billy Steinberg and Rick Nowells. The album is a worldwide success, making its debut at #1 in Ireland where it has already been certified six-times platinum. It goes to #1 in the UK on six separate occasions and its momentum brings their first album, *Forgiven, Not Forgotten*, back up the UK charts to #2. The Corrs open for The Rolling Stones on their US tour. Their international hits include 'I Never Loved You Anyway', 'What Can I Do?' and 'So Young'.

Buena Vista Social Club, another eclectic musical offering from Nonesuch/Atlantic, meets with unexpected worldwide success. Produced by guitarist/singer/songwriter **Ry Cooder**, it sells over a million copies in the US alone, earning RIAA Platinum and a Grammy nomination. The group **Buena Vista Social Club**, comprised of legendary Cuban musicians from the forties, fifties and sixties, also plays a one-time-only sell-out show at Carnegie Hall in July. Recorded with two other albums in just three weeks, all three are overseen by Nick Gold. *Buena Vista Social Club* features a select group of Cuban musicians ranging in age from 14 to their late eighties. Cooder insists on the inclusion of singer/guitarist Compay Segundo on the project. After tracking down Segundo in Cuba, the producers discover that Compay had just negotiated an exclusive recording deal at 89 years old. After negotiations, Segundo is allowed to be part of the Buena Vista project. Also featured is the remarkable 77-year-old pianist Ruben Gonzalez.

Their first album together since 1994's *No Quarter* and their first collection of all new material since *In Through The Out Door*, **Robert Plant** and **Jimmy Page** release the gold-selling album *Walking Into Clarksdale*. Produced by Page and Plant and mixed by Steve Albini, the critically acclaimed album is recorded at Abbey Road Studios in just 35 days. It debuts on the *Billboard 200* album chart at #8 and is certified RIAA Gold in May. The single 'Most High' is #1 at Mainstream Rock stations across the US and a bulleted Top Five hit at Active Rock and Heritage Rock outlets. **matchbox twenty** appear on *Legacy: A Tribute To Fleetwood Mac's Rumours* (Fleetwood Music/Lava/Atlantic) with their version of 'Never Going Back Again'. The band conclude their first US tour as headliners with every date sold out. They also tour Europe, Australia and Canada. **Widemouth Mason** earn a Canadian Juno award nomination as Best New Group and a nomination for Best New Group, Rock in the annual Canadian Radio Music Awards. **Rush** releases the gold-selling triple-CD set *Different Stages* celebrating 25 years as one of rock's most enduring bands. By now, **Hootie & the Blowfish** have sold 17 million albums in the US and won two Grammy Awards. This year, they also release their third Atlantic album, *Musical Chairs*, which sells more than a million by October. It is produced by Don Gehman and features multi-instrumentalist Jon Nau who performs on guitar, organ, electric piano and harmonica.

Duncan Sheik's 'Bite Your Tongue', the first single from his new album, *Humming*, becomes the #1 most-added track at Triple-A stations across the US. The album is co-produced by Sheik. After the breakup of Stone Temple Pilots, lead singer **Scott Weiland** releases a solo album, *12 Bar Blues*. The first single from the album is 'Barbarella'. The rest of the group formed **Talk Show** with a self-titled debut album released in 1997. **David Garza** releases *This Euphoria* on Lava/Atlantic. Jason Ross, Jason Pollock and Tom Morris produce **Seven Mary Three**'s *Orange Ave.* album. **Bad Religion** release their tenth album, *No Substance*. They also launch a scholarship programme named the Bad Religion Research Fund to encourage and support new talent in the fields of cultural and natural science. **The Uninvited** release a self-titled debut on Igloo/Atlantic. The band had already won the Best Independent Album at the L.A. Music Awards and a Top Ten honour in the *Billboard* Songwriter's Contest. Producer/musician **Mitchell Froom** releases a solo album, *Dopamine*, on Atlantic. Featured artists include Sheryl Crow, David Hidalgo and Louie Perez from Los Lobos and singer-songwriter Suzanne Vega, Froom's wife. **Marc Cohn** releases his third Atlantic LP, *Burning The Daze*.

Rick Braun releases *Full Stride* and wins the Gavin award for Smooth Jazz Artist Of The Year. **Randy Crawford**'s 1998 album *Every Kind of Mood Randy, Randi, Randee* features a diverse collection of tracks produced by Mouse T (Prince, U2, Seal) and Jens Krause. Jazz saxophonist **Steve Cole** records *Stay Awhile*. **James Carter** and fellow Atlantic jazz artist **Cyrus Chestnut** team up on Carter's album *In Carterian Fashion*.

Writer, actor, producer, director **Woody Allen** showcases his clarinet playing on *Wild Man Blues*. His long-standing involvement with jazz is the subject of the documentary film of the same name. **Olu Dara**'s 1998 Atlantic release, *In The World: From Natchez To New York*, marks his debut as a bandleader. Originally with Art Blakey's Messengers and a veteran of more than 50 albums, he is joined by an eclectic group of musicians on the album including his son Nas, a popular hip-hop star. **Ahmad Jamal** releases *Nature*.

In July, **The Three Tenors**, José Carreras, Placido Domingo and Luciano Pavarotti, a worldwide musical phenomenon, perform an outdoor concert along the historic Champ de Mars in front of the Eiffel Tower in Paris. The Tenors' third consecutive World Cup musical performance billed as 'The Concert Of The Century' is televised to a worldwide audience of over two billion people across 99 countries and a live audience of hundreds of thousands. The tenors are accompanied by the Orchestre de Paris conducted by James Levine. The concert album, *Tibor Rudas Presents The 3 Tenors – Paris 1998: Carreras, Domingo, Pavarotti With Levine*, produced by Ahmet and Rudas, features Rodgers and Hammerstein's 'You'll Never Walk Alone', the closing segment from the event's dramatic 'Medley Of The World' finale. At this point, the previous two albums recorded by The Three Tenors have sold over 23 million copies worldwide, and the opera virtuosos are the top-selling classical artists of all time. Spanish tenor **Placido Domingo** records his first solo album for Atlantic, *Por Amor*. It is comprised of Latin love songs by Agustin Lara as a 100th anniversary celebration of Lara's birth. *Por Amor* is produced by Domingo's longtime collaborator, Bebu Silvetti. This year also marks the great tenor's 30th anniversary with the Metropolitan Opera of New York.

Nonesuch/Atlantic releases *Humoresque*, the label debut from the exceptionally gifted and passionate violinist, **Nadja Salerno-Sonnenberg**. Inspired by the Oscar-winning score of Hollywood legend Franz Waxman, it is among the most difficult pieces ever written for the violin. Violinist **Maxim** Vengerov releases *Brahms Violin Concerto* with support from Daniel Barenboim and the Chicago Symphony Orchestra. A new recording of composer **Steve Reich**'s *Music For 18 Musicians*, hailed as one of the ten most important works of the seventies by the *New York Times*, is released on Nonesuch/Atlantic 22 years after its original release.

Guitarist **Marc Ribot** makes his debut on Atlantic with *Marc Ribot Y Los Cubanos Postizos*. The highly regarded Ribot has worked with artists such as Wilson Pickett, Rufus and Carla Thomas, Solomon Burke, Marianne Faithfull, poet Allen Ginsberg and fellow Atlantic artist Madeleine Peyroux on her Atlantic album *Dreamland*. **Cesaria Evora**'s *Miss Perfumado* is released in 1998. Atlantic releases **Martin Sexton**'s *The American*. Irish quartet **Clannad** release *Landmarks*.

LeAnn Rimes releases the platinum album *Sittin' On Top Of The World* (Curb/Atlantic), which peaks at #3 on the *Billboard* Top 200 Album chart. **John Michael Montgomery** releases the album *Leave A Mark*. **The Great Divide**, an Atlantic/Nashville group, release *Break In The Storm*. **Confederate Railroad** release *Keep On Rockin'*, their fourth for Atlantic.

To mark its long and successful history, **Atlantic** releases the double CD compilation, *50 Years: The Gold Anniversary Collection* in March. The set features 26 legendary songs encompassing virtually all styles of modern music from R&B to soul, disco and rock'n'roll. **Storyville** release *Dog Years*, produced by Stephen Burton. During the summer, the band joins B.B. King, The Neville Brothers and Dr. John on the Blues Music Festival Tour of 1998. *Enchanted*, the digitally remastered three-CD boxed set retrospective of **Stevie Nicks**' solo career on Modern/Atlantic, is certified gold. Proving musical talent can be inherited, **Chris Stills**, son of Stephen Stills, kicks off his Atlantic recording career with *100 Year Thing*. The album showcases Stills' talents as singer, songwriter and multi-instrumentalist. A notable collaborator on the project is Ethan Johns, son of legendary producer Glyn Johns (The Who, The Rolling Stones, Led Zeppelin).

Victoria Williams releases *Musings Of A Creekdipper*. Partly recorded at the Rancho De La Luna studio in California's Joshua Tree National Park, the album is co-produced by Trina Shoemaker. **Donna Lewis** releases *Blue Planet*. Multi-talented writer/producer/arranger **Nicole Renee** records her self-titled debut with assistance from Arif Mardin and Lamont Dozier. Irish vocalist, songwriter and performer, **South Sixty** debut on the label with a self-titled album. **Sinéad O'Connor**, signs a worldwide, exclusive long-term recording contract with Atlantic.

Phil Collins releases the platinum-selling album, *Phil Collins…Hits*. Along with fifteen classic tracks, *Hits* features Collins' moving interpretation of Cyndi Lauper's 'True Colors'. At this point, Collins has sold over 80 million records around the world and earned six Grammy awards. **Monsieur Dimitri From Paris** makes his Atlantic debut with *Sacre Bleu*. Critically acclaimed in Europe, the producer has worked with Björk, James Brown and Brand New Heavies, and coordinated soundtracks for fashion shows by Jean-Paul Gaultier, Hermés and Karl Lagerfeld. **Michael Crawford** releases two albums, *On Eagle's Wings* and *In Concert (Live)*. *Dr. Doolittle: The Album*, the soundtrack to the popular Eddie Murphy film, is certified double-platinum. Jon Oliva and Paul O'Neill produce **Savatage**'s *The Wake Of Magellan*. **The Trans-Siberian Orchestra** releases *The Christmas Attic*.

Kid Rock makes his explosive debut on Top Dog/Lava/Atlantic with *Devil Without A Cause*. The phenomenally successful album goes on to achieve sales of over nine million, with smash singles such as 'Cowboy', a mainstay on Alternative and Active Rock radio, and 'Only God Knows Why', which immediately becomes the #1 most-added track on Active Rock and Alternative outlets across the US. The self-proclaimed 'Don Of Rap', **Fat Joe** debuts with the Mystic/Big Beat/Atlantic album *Don Cartegena*, which is certified gold and charts at #2 on the *Billboard* 200 and #7 on *Billboard's* 'Hot R&B' chart. The album features an all-star roster of hip-hop artists including Noreaga, Big Punisher, Jadikiss and the Terror Squad. Guest producers include Marley Marl and Puff Daddy.

1999 The Corrs release *Talk On Corners: Special Edition* on 143/Lava/Atlantic, a revised and remixed version of the group's second multi-platinum worldwide smash album. The group wins the BRIT Award for Best International Act, reflecting the worldwide success which has seen the group go to #1 in the UK, Ireland, Singapore and New Zealand; Top Ten in Germany, Australia, France, Spain, Sweden, Finland and Denmark; and 20-times-platinum in Ireland, nine-times-platinum in the UK and six-times-platinum in Spain. The November album release of their MTV special, *Unplugged*, earns the group more platinum and gold awards across the world. Atlantic releases **Sugar Ray**'s *14:59*, their third album on Lava/Atlantic. It goes on to be certified triple platinum, producing the #1 gold-selling single, 'Every Morning' and the Top Ten hit 'Someday'.

Stone Temple Pilots reform and release the group's fourth Atlantic album *No. 4*, which debuts at #6 on *SoundScan*'s Top Current Albums chart and goes on to sell over a million copies. Produced by Brendan O'Brien, all the tracks are written and performed by band members. 'Down', the album's first single, climbs to the top of the Rock Radio nationwide and Active Rock charts. At this point, Stone Temple Pilots have sold more than 20 million records worldwide. **Collective Soul** release the platinum album *Dosage*, which produces two major hit singles, 'Heavy' and 'Run'. 'Heavy' sets a new record with a 14-week chart-topping run at #1 and becomes the group's eighth #1 US rock radio hit. 'Run' is a #1 charting Triple-A track and staple on Hot AC and Triple-A outlets across the country. Atlantic releases *to venus and back*, a double-album collection from **Tori Amos**, combining a full-length studio recording with a disc of live material recorded during Amos' 1998 world tour. Certified platinum, *to venus and back* is the artist's fourth RIAA platinum-plus success. Two singles, '1000 oceans' and 'glory of the 80s' also receive significant airplay.

Los Van Van, formed back in 1969, earn a Grammy Nomination for Best Salsa Performance with the Caliente/Atlantic release, *Llego Van Van*. **Luisa** releases her self-titled debut also on Caliente/Atlantic. **Barbarito Torres** records the atmospheric *Havana Cafe*. *Jugando Con Candela* by Cuban musician and composer, **Adalberto Alvarez** is released this year. **Pedro Luis Ferrer**, a leader in the guaracha style, releases a self-titled album on the Havana Caliente imprint. **The Latin Playboys**, David Hidalgo and Louie Perez of Los Lobos, together with Tchad Blake and Mitchell Froom, releases the album *Dose*.

Russell Gunn releases his debut, *Ethnomusicology Volume 1*, for which he earns a Grammy nomination for Best Contemporary Jazz Performance. It is co-produced by Gunn with Yves Beauvais.

The iconoclastic jazz ensemble **Lester Bowie Brass Fantasy** release the ambitious, *The Odyssey Of Funk and Popular Music: Vol 1*. Popular fusion keyboardist/composer **Jeff Golub** releases *Out Of The Blue* on the Bluemoon imprint. **Willie and Lobo** — Willie Royal (violin) and Wolfgang 'Lobo' Fink (guitar) — release *Wild Heart* on the Mesa subsidiary. It is produced by Rick Braun.

Ginger Baker forges more new music on *Coward Of The County* with his group DJQ20 and with guest artist, James Carter. Warner Bros. film music executive and singer, **Gary LeMel**, records his Atlantic debut, *Moonlighting*, featuring a number of songs made famous by Bobby Darin. Darin's pianist and arranger, Roger Kellaway, provides arrangements and conducts the all-star jazz backing, which includes Elvin Jones (drums), Steve Kahn (guitar) and Michael Brecker (sax). Jazz vocal stylist **Diane Schuur** releases *Music Is My Life*, with support from Nino Tempo (tenor sax) and Alan Broadbent (piano). The album is produced by Ahmet and Yves Beauvais. Retro-swingers, **The Atomic Fireballs**, produced by Arif Mardin, release the aptly titled debut album, *Torch This Place*. **Barry Mann**, famous for his songwriting collaboration with Cynthia Weill, releases *Soul And Inspiration*, featuring Bryan Adams, Peabo Bryson and Daryll Hall. Atlantic releases *Blues, Blues, Blues* by **Jimmy Rogers**, his final album, featuring guest artists Mick Jagger, Eric Clapton, Stephen Stills and Taj Mahal.

Kid Rock's *Devil Without A Cause* remains in the US Top Five for over a year from its release. He is also nominated for a pair of American Music Awards, Favourite New Artist – Pop Rock and Favourite Artist – Alternative Music. Rock, the winner of three *Billboard* Music Video Awards and nominated for Favourite Male Musical Performer at the People's Choice Awards, travels nationwide on his *Between The Legs* tour. Rapper **Lil' Cease**, a member of Junior M.A.F.I.A. and protégé of Notorious B.I.G., releases the double-CD *The Wonderful World Of Cease A Leo* on the Queen Bee (the label belonging to Lil' Kim)/Andeas/Atlantic. It features Lil' Kim, Puff Daddy and Busta Rhymes. Atlantic boldly goes where other labels fear to tread by releasing the soundtrack album *South Park: Bigger, Longer & Uncut*. San Diego band **P.O.D.** (Payable On Death) – Sonny (vocals), Traa (bass, Wuv (drums) and Marcos (guitar) – release their platinum-selling debut album The *Fundamental Elements of Southtown* in 1999, recorded at the Gallery studios in Sherman Oaks, California. The explosive multi-influenced debut is produced by Howard Benson and mixed by Chris Lord-Alge.

Proving the seemingly limitless appeal of Atlantic's best-selling group, the label releases *Early Days: The Best Of Led Zeppelin, Volume 1*, a two-CD set that stands as the first greatest hits anthology from the hugely successful group. At this point, **Led Zeppelin** has achieved cumulative sales of over 80 million. The RIAA also named them as the top-selling hard rock act of the 20th century. **RIAA Diamond Awards** are introduced in 1999 for albums with sales of over ten million copies. Atlantic albums that win this coveted award are *Led Zeppelin IV* (22 million), *Back In Black* by AC/DC (16 million), *Cracked Rear View* by Hootie & the Blowfish (16 million), *Physical Graffiti* by Led Zeppelin (15 million), *Led Zeppelin II* (12 million), *Houses Of The Holy* by Led Zeppelin (11 million), *Pieces Of You* by Jewel (11 million), *Yourself Or Someone Like You* by matchbox twenty (11 million) and *No Jacket Required* by Phil Collins (10 million). *Turn It On Again: The Hits*, includes 18 classic tracks by **Genesis** originally released between 1973 and 1997. The release coincides with the 30th anniversary of the band's very first album. One of the world's most successful groups, Genesis has sold more than 100 million records worldwide at this point. Irish group **The Chieftains** release *The Chieftains Collection: The Very Best Of The Claddagh Years* on Claddagh/Atlantic. **Kris Kristofferson** releases The Austin Sessions on Atlantic. His first recording since 1995, he is joined by Steve Earle, Jackson Browne and Mark Knopfler to create new versions of a range of his most famous and well loved songs. **Edwin McCain** releases the gold-selling album *Messenger*.

Bif Naked releases her Lava/Atlantic debut, *I Bificus*, featuring the track 'Moment of Weakness'. With the help of producer Tom Lord-Alge, **Angry Salad** turn the group's demo – *Bizarre Gardening Accident* – into a self-titled debut on Atlantic's Blackbird imprint. **Fountains of Wayne** release the album *Utopia PKWY*, which earns critical acclaim and makes it to several end-of-year Critics' Choice lists. *Holiday From You* is the second album from **The Gufs**, with guest vocals by Rob Thomas of matchbox twenty. **The C. Gibbs Group** records the album *Twenty Nine Over Me*, featuring songs written by Christian Gibbs, formerly of the Morning Glories. Atlantic releases *Revolutions* by **The Great Divide**. **The Braids**, duo Zoe Ellis and Caitlin Cornwell debut on the Big Beat/Atlantic with *Here We Come*. Rock singer **Beth Hart** records the self-produced album, *Screamin' For My Supper*. Australian vocalist **Marie Wilson** releases *Real Life*, her US debut. **New American Shame** release a self-titled debut album on Atlantic. **Lisa Hayes and The Violets** release *Sun* on Straight Line/Atlantic. **Smoke 'N Function**, a.k.a musican and producer Cliff Sardes, debuts on the Mesa imprint with a self-titled album. **Spy** releases the album *Music To Mauzner By* on Lava/Atlantic. Swedish DJ/producer **Christian Falk** releases his label debut, *Quel Bordel*, featuring Neneh Cherry. **All-4-One** release *On And On* on Blitzz/Atlantic, with Nile Rodgers writing and producing the track, 'Keep It Goin' On'.

Neal McCoy releases the album *Life Of The Party*. **John Michael Montgomery** releases *Home To You*. **Matt King** releases *Hard Country*. Atlantic establish a Nashville-Christian division devoted to Christian and gospel music under the leadership of Barry Landis, former vice-president and general manager of Warner Resound. The label's roster includes artists such as Donnie McClurkin, The Brooklyn Tabernackle Choir, Carlton Pearson and The Higher Dimension Singers, among others.

Capitalizing on a wildly popular childhood phenomenon, Atlantic releases the platinum soundtrack album *Pokémon: The First Movie*, featuring tracks by Britney Spears, Christina Aguilera, B*Witched and Baby Spice. **Michael Crawford** releases the seasonal LP, *A Christmas Album*. **George Carlin**, one of America's most enduring comic talents whose intuitive gifts span decades and different comedic generations, is recognized with the definitive collection, *The Little David Years: 1971-1977*, a seven-CD boxed set. *You Are All Diseased* (Eardrum) is yet another brilliant and scathing live concert recording from George Carlin. Atlantic releases a 2-CD set entitled *The Civil War: The Complete Works*, an adaption of Frank Wildhorn's stage musical, featuring tracks by Hootie & the Blowfish, Patti LaBelle and Tracy Lawrence. French indie-rock artist, **Kid Loco** (a.k.a. Jean-Yves Prieur), releases his US full-length debut, *Prelude To A Grand Love Story*, on Atlantic. He releases *Jesus Life For Children Under 12 Inches* later this year.

Jewel, the multi-talented vocalist and songwriter, continues her enduring Atlantic success with the platinum album, *Joy: A Holiday Collection*. Produced by Arif Mardin, the album features the singer performing a number of seasonal songs, along with a Christmas version of Jewel's own hit 'Hands'. Jewel also makes her acting debut in director Ang Lee's *Ride With The Devil*. The soundtrack from the film is released on Atlantic and features a remixed version of Jewel's 'What's Simple Is True' (from her *Spirit* album).

2000 With eight #1 rock hits and worldwide sales in excess of seven million, **Collective Soul** release the gold-selling album *blender*, featuring 'Perfect Day', a duet between the group's Ed Roland and Sir Elton John. Recorded at Crossover Studios in Atlanta, the album is produced by Roland with Anthony J. Resta, and mixed by Jack Joseph Puig, Chris Lord-Alge and Bob St. John.

Hootie & the Blowfish release their fourth Atlantic album, *Scattered, Smothered and Covered*, featuring selections from their recorded archive of live and studio cover versions. The band looked to their internet fanbase to vote on the tracks finally included on the album and the fans also had the opportunity to choose one of three cover designs for the album's artwork. Meanwhile, Hootie guitarist **Mark Bryan** releases his solo album *30 On The Rail*.

Bad Religion's fifth Atlantic release is *The New America*, on which the band teamed up with acclaimed producer Todd Rundgren and studio legend Bob Clearmountain. The album was recorded in a rented studio in the grounds of an old sugar plantation on the Hawaiian island of Kauai. Brett Gurewitz, formerly the band's guitarist, reunites with lead Greg Graffin to co-write and appear on the track, 'Believe It'.

James Carter releases two new studio albums in 2000. Produced with Yves Beauvais, *Chasin' The Gypsy* sees Carter performing Django Reinhardt numbers like 'Nuages'. Backing on the album includes violinist Regina Carter, percussionist Cyro Baptista and drummer Joey Baron. Recorded in New York, Carter's *Layin' In The Cut* shifts in mood from Reinhardt to electric funk and features labelmate guitarist Marc Ribot and guitarist Jef Lee Johnson, who also composed some of the tracks.

Thirty-five years after the original recording of *A Charlie Brown Christmas* by Vince Guaraldi, the album is re-made by **Cyrus Chestnut** and released on Atlantic. Chestnut is joined on the album by his trio, Steve Gadd and Christian McBride, and also by Michael Brecker, Don Alias, Stefon Harris, Wallace Roney, Gary Bartz, Kenny Garrett, Pat Martino, Hubert Laws, Jerry Goodman, Steve Turre, and Steve Cole. Guest vocalists Vanessa Williams, Brian McKnight and The Manhattan Transfer also feature, and the album marks the debut of production team Ed and Guy Eckstine (sons of legendary Billy Eckstine). In addition to the original tracks is a Chestnut-composed piano interlude as tribute to the late creator of the Peanuts cartoon strip, Charles Schulz. **Steve Cole** releases *Between Us* with songs mostly written by Cole with collaborator Brian Culbertson. Featured jazz musicians on the album include Paul Jackson Jr, Gerey Johnson, Alex Al and Michael White.

With sales of over 12 million albums to his credit, **John Michael Montgomery** releases the album *Brand New Me*, which quickly goes gold. Buddy Cannon and Norrow Wilson assist Montgomery with production on the album. With sales of seven million and 16 top-selling country singles to his credit, **Tracy Lawrence** releases the album *Lessons Learned*, which he co-produces with Flip Anderson and Butch Carr.

Emmylou Harris releases *Red Dirt Girl* on Nonesuch/Atlantic. Her backing musicians include Buddy Miller, Jill Cunniff, Kate McGarrigle and Julie Miller and harmony vocals on the love lament 'Tragedy' are by Patti Scialfa and Bruce Springsteen. Produced by Malcolm Burn, the album is a powerful testament to the strength, range and talent of the artist Emmylou Harris as a performer and as a songwriter.

Sinéad O'Connor releases *Faith And Courage* on Atlantic in 2000. The controversial singer's first album of new material since 1994, her raw clear voice displays emotion and spirituality, fierce confidence, bitterness and vulnerability.

Celebrating 27 years in the business, **The Manhattan Transfer** release their eleventh studio album on Atlantic, *The Spirit Of St. Louis*, their own interpretation of the influential music by the great Louis Armstrong. The album is produced by Craig Street who gathered a top-notch team of sidemen to back the Grammy-winning quartet including, Abe Laboriel Jr. on drums, Teddy Borowiecki on keyboards, Greg Leisz on guitar, and David Piltch on bass. The album also features the talents of Jon Hassell on trumpet and Steve Berlin on baritone sax.

Martin Sexton releases *Wonder Bar*, his second outing on Atlantic.

With strong influences of classic 1970s FM radio, Sexton is joined on the album by his longtime drummer, Joe Bonadio, bassist Tony Levin and keyboardist David Sancious. The title is taken from a pizzeria in Worchester, Massachusetts where Sexton wrote many of the featured tracks.

Talented singer/songwriter **Debelah Morgan** releases *Dance With Me*, with her brother Gilho sharing production and songwriting on the 14-track album.

As one third of the band Rush with cumulative world sales of 35 million, singer and influential bassist **Geddy Lee** releases his first solo album, *My Favorite Headache* on Anthem/Atlantic. Lee is joined on the album by Ben Mink (guitar/multi-instrumentalist) and Matt Cameron (drums). Recorded in Seattle, Vancouver and Toronto, it was produced by Lee with Mink and David Leonard. **Mr. Big** release *Get Over It*, with new guitarist Richie Kotzen.

Alt-rock veterans the **Meat Puppets** sign to Atlantic subsidiary label Breaking, to release their first album for five years, *Golden Lies*. The album sees a fresh line-up around lead Curt Kirkwood, made up of Doug Sahm's son Shandon Sahm (drums), Kyle Ellison (guitar) and Andrew Duplantis (bass). Two years after their last album, **Elastica** – Justine Frischman (guitar/vocals), Paul Jones (guitar), Annie Holland (bass), Justin Welch (drums), Mew (keyboards/vocals) and Dave Bush (keyboards) – release *The Menace*, their debut on Atlantic. Fans of the Brit punk-revival band had a long wait for this album, a follow-up to their 1995 self-titled debut.

Youssou N'dour releases *Joko (The Link)*, his debut on Nonesuch/Atlantic, which is produced by Thomas Rome and David Bither. Peter Gabriel makes a guest appearance on the track 'This Dream' and the album presents the fascinating mix of themes, styles and roots of music that Youssou N'dour combines so beautifully.

The only female star of the Buena Vista Social club film and album and one of Cuba's celebrated singers, **Omara Portuondo** releases her debut album, *Buena Vista Social Club Presents Omara Portuondo* on World Circuit/Nonesuch/Atlantic. The album is recorded in Havana with backing from Buena Vista musicians including Ibrahim Ferrer and Ruben Gonzalez.

The hedonistic king of trailer park-styled hip-hop, **Kid Rock** releases the multi-platinum album *The History Of Rock*, follow up to the phenomenally successful nine million-selling album, *Devil Without A Cause*. *History* features tracks culled from Kid Rock's now out-of-print albums: 1992's *The Polyfuze Method* and 1996's *Early Mornin' Stoned Pimp*, together with previously unreleased tracks.

Uncle Kracker (a.k.a. Matt Shafer), DJ and band member of Kid Rock's Twisted Brown Trucker band, met Rock back in 1987 at an all ages DJ contest. In 2000 he releases his *Double Wide* debut album, the first non-Kid Rock record to be released on the rapper's own Top Dog/Lava/Atlantic imprint. The album, an unusual blend of influences serving up a stew of funk, rock'n'roll, hip-hop, country and southern rock, is produced by Rock and engineered by Mike Bradford. The track 'Yeah Yeah Yeah' is featured in the Jackie Chan movie, *Shanghai Noon*. Atlanta based rapper **Drama** releases his debut *Causin' Drama*, featuring 'Left, Right, Left', which peaks at #2 on *Billboard*'s Hop Rap Singles chart.

LA-based trio **opm** – Matthew (alias Shakey Lo the Kreation Kid), Casper (Geoff Turney) and John E. Necro – release their Atlantic debut, *Menace To Sobriety*, a mix of ska, hip-hop, punk and rock. Featured collaborators include DJ Malcolm Micheles, DJ Swamp and Eric Avery. **Changing Faces** release their third album, *Visit Me*. They are joined by producers R. Kelly (who wrote the title track), Bryce Wilson, Malik Pendleton, Byran-Michael Cox, Bryeyn Evans & Troy Johnson, Jazze Pha, Derek Garrett & Jonuz, Herb Middleton and Edmund Clement.

Hailing from Wales, **Catatonia** was formed in the early nineties by former busking team Cerys Matthews (vocals) and Mark Roberts (guitar/vocals). Already established in the UK, the current line-up of Matthews and Roberts with Paul Jones (bass), Owen (guitar) and Aled Richards (drums) release their Atlantic debut, *Equally Cursed and Blessed*.

Rod Stewart signs to Atlantic and proves again his powerful instincts and talent to communicate the heart and soul of a song in his album *Human*.

Hot boy-band **plus ONE** burst onto the music scene in 2000 with their own special brand of sex appeal, harmonies and Christianity. The vocal group – Gabe Combs, Nathan Walters, Jason Perry, Jeremy Mhire and Nate Cole – are teamed with David Forster, Grammy award-winning Chairman of Atlantic/143 Records and a production team which includes Buster & Shavoni, Rodney Jerkins, Eric Foster White and Brian McKnight. The result is the debut album *The Promise*, which sold over 19,000 copies in its first week of release and reached #1 on the Christian soundscan charts, also crossing over into the Pop chart.

Released on her own Queen Bee label, **Lil' Kim**'s incendiary second solo album is the platinum-selling *Notorious K.I.M.* Co-executive producer is Sean "Puffy" Combs and the album is recorded at his own New York studio, Daddy's House. Lil' Kim is joined on the album by Mary J. Blige, Lil' Cease, Cee-Lo and guest producers include Mario "Yellowman" Winans, Deric "D-Dot" Angelettie, Rated R (Coolio) & Mas, Nasheim Myrick, Rockwilder, Younglord, Jerome "Knowbody" Foster, Carlos Broady, Kanye West, Fury For The New Jeru, Darren "Limitless" Henson and Shaft.

Recorded in Atlanta and Nashville, *mad season* by **matchbox twenty** is released in May. Again featuring the production talents of Grammy Award-winning Matt Serletic, the new album is the follow up to matchbox twenty's phenomenally successful 1996 Lava/Atlantic debut, *Yourself Or Someone Like You*, which earned the RIAA's prestigious Diamond Award and sold in excess of 11 million. Their new offering quickly goes multi-platinum, and features the gold single 'Bent'. The group's lead singer Rob Thomas wins three Grammy Awards for 'Smooth', his 1999 chart-topping collaboration with Carlos Santana.

Working with producers Robert John "Mutt" Lange and Mitchell Froom, internationally acclaimed Irish quartet **The Corrs** release the143/Lava/Atlantic album, *In Blue*. It debuts at #1 on the U.K chart, as does the album's first single, 'Breathless'. The album also hits #1 in Ireland, Australia, Germany, Austria, Spain, Norway, Switzerland, Sweden and Singapore, earning an impressive array of multi-platinum, platinum and gold awards, including RIAA gold in the US. In January, all three Corrs releases were among the UK's Top 15, an unprecedented accomplishment.

Picture Credits

Images are identified by photographer and agency, and on the page clockwise from top left: (a), (b), (c), (d), etc.

ABB Archives
241 (c) Star File.

Greg Allen
448 (b) Atlantic Archives.

Kwaku Alston
485 (b) Atlantic Archives.

Amsterdam News
29 (b); **31** (a).

Matt Anker
445 (b) Retna.

AP/Wide World Photos
70 (a); **155** (a); **209** (a); **232** (a); **233** (b); **260** (d).

Archive Photos
23 (a/b); **152** (a); **310**; **350** (c).

Archive Photos/Frank Driggs
40.

Atlantic Records Archives
9 (a); **17** (c); **25** (a); **43** (a); **45** (a/b); **53**; **62** (b); **63** (a/c); **68** (b); **71**; **73** (a); **74** (a); **79** (b); **82** (c); **88**; **91** (b); **93** (a); **94** (a); **96** (a); **97**; **98** (a); **103** (a); **105** (c); **110** (c); **114** (a/b); **115** (c); **116** (a); **120** (b); **123**; **128** (c); **135**; **136** (a/b); **138**; **139** (a); **141** (b); **147** (b/c/d/e); **149** (c); **151**; **160** (b); **161** (b); **169** (b/c); **178** (a); **182** (a); **183** (a); **194** (b); **202** (b); **204** (a); **205**; **207** (a/b); **208** (a); **214** (a/b/c); **215** (a/c); **216** (b/c/d); **221** (a); **222** (c); **223**; **227** (b); **228** (d); **230** (b); **231** (b/c); **232** (b); **234** (b); **239** (c); **240** (a); **243** (c); **244** (c); **246** (b); **251** (a); **253** (b/c); **254** (b); **259** (b); **267** (b); **269** (b); **271** (a/b/c); **273** (b/c); **275** (b/c); **277** (c); **280** (b); **281** (b); **287** (b); **288** (a); **292**; **294** (a/d); **296** (a/b); **303** (b); **305**; **309** (b); **316** (a/b/c/d/f); **317** (b); **320** (a); **325** (c); **328** (c); **329** (b/c); **332** (c); **335** (a/b/c); **336** (b); **337** (b); **338** (c); **343**; **346** (a/b/c/e/f/g); **347** (d); **352** (b); **356** (a/b); **362** (b/c); **364** (a/b/c); **366** (d); **367** (a); **372** (a/b); **373** (a/d); **374**; **375** (a/b); **376** (a); **378** (a/b); **379** (a); **384** (c); **386** (a/b); **391**; **392** (f); **395** (a); **398** (c); **400**; **401** (a); **402** (a/b); **403** (a/b); **404** (c); **407**; **410** (c/e); **413** (b); **414** (b); **416** (b); **417** (a/b); **422**; **425**; **428** (a/c); **430** (a); **437**; **439** (c); **440** (a/b); **441** (c); **442** (a); **443** (b); **444**; **445** (a); **446**; **447** (b); **449** (a); **451**; **455** (b); **458**; **460** (a); **462** (a/b); **463**; **465** (a/b); **469** (a/b); **470**; **471** (a); **474** (a/b); **475** (a); **477**; **478**; **479** (b); **480** (a/b/c); **484**; **496** (b/c/d/e); **497** (a/b); **498**; **499** (a/b); **500**; **510** (a); **512** (b); **514** (b); **515**.
All album covers courtesy of Atlantic Records unless otherwise credited.

Ray Avery's Jazz Archives
9 (c); **11** (a); **30**; **41**; **43** (b); **57** (a); **91** (b); **95** (c); **134** (c); **139** (c); **143** (c); **145** (c); **153** (c); **168** (b); **169** (a); **184** (a/d); **185** (b); **199**; **202** (a/c); **225** (a); **287** (a); **441** (a); **457**; **459**; **479** (a).

Marc Baptiste
487 (b) Atlantic Archives.

Margie M. Barnes
472 (c) Atlantic Archives.

Julian Barton
489 (b) Retna.

John Bellissimo
272 (c) Retna; **413** (l/m) Corbis.

Riccardo Schwamenthal Bergamo
224 (c) Schomburg Centre for Research in Black Culture/New York Jazz Museum.

Courtesy of Joel Bernstein
257 (a); **324** (c).

Billboard
273 (a).

Jay Blakesburg Images
438 (b); **453**.

Bruno of Hollywood
50 (b) Photofest.

Courtesy of Peter Burns
78

Larry Busacca
408 (c) Retna;
412 (b) Retna;
482 (b) Atlantic Archives.

Dunc Butler
16 (a) Frank Driggs.

Paul Canty
380 LFI; **317** (c) Retna.

RJ Capak/LFI
366 (b)

John Clark
473 (b) Atlantic Archives.

William Claxton
126 (a/c); **501** (b).

Danny Clinch
483 (b) Atlantic Archives.

Rick Coleman
109 (a) David Booth/Showtime Photos, Toronto, Canada.

John Collier
392 (a) Atlantic Archives.

Fin Costello
352 (a) Retna; **285** (a) Atlantic Archives.

Paul Cox/LFI
354 (b); **367** (b).

Chris Cuffaro
512 (a) Atlantic Archives.

Jim Cummins/Star File
218 (c); **245** (a); **249** (a).

Stephen Charles La Vere, Delta Haze Corporation
14; **59** (a); **81** (d).

Deluze/Stills
442 (b) Retna.

Hulton Archive
262 (b); **303** (a).

Henry Diltz
236 (a); **237** (a/b/c); **260** (b/c); **314** (a) Corbis; **318** (b); **324** (b); **383** (b) Corbis.

Michael Dobo
259 (a); **266** (b); **270** (a); **346** (d).

Kieran Doherty
491 (a) Redferns Music Picture Library.

Tom Dowd
70 (b); **113** (a); **159**; **239** (b); **241** (d); **243** (a); **254** (a); **280** (a).

Frank Driggs Collection
9 (b); **10** (a); **18** (a/b); **19**; **20**; **21** (a/b); **25** (b); **26** (a/c); **28** (a/b); **37** (b); **44** (a); **46/47**; **48** (c); **49** (b); **51**; **52** (b); **91** (c); **99**; **101** (c); **103** (b); **110** (a); **111** (a); **118** (b); **128** (a); **140**; **161** (a).

Alison Dyer
488 (a) Atlantic Archives.

Brad Elterman
353 (b) LFI.

Sam Emerson/Atlantic Archives
339 (b); **360/361** (d).

Ahmet Ertegun Archives
4 (a); **5**; **12** (b); **16** (b); **26** (b); **350** (a); **351** (a).

Steve Finn
449 (b) Atlantic Archives.

Rob Finnis
244 (a)

Ralph Fitzgerald
404 (b) Corbis.

Ray Flerlage/Michael Ochs Archives
137 (d); **158** (a).

Dana Frank
473 (c) Corbis.

Creston Funk/Atlantic Archives
489 (a); **508/509**.

David Gahr
146/147; **168** (a); **189** (a/b/c); **212**; **220** (a); **226** (a); **228** (c); **231** (a); **246** (a); **252**; **256** (c); **258** (b); **270** (b); **275** (d); **276**; **278** (a/b/c); **279** (a/b); **286** (a); **295** (b); **297** (a/b); **302** (b); **309** (a); **313**; **324** (a); **331** (a/c); **358** (b); **359** (b); **382** (b).

Ron Galella
408 (a/b) Atlantic Archives.

Galen Gart/David Booth/Showtime Photos, Toronto, Canada
72 (a); **92**.

Gary Gershoff
394 (a) Retna.

Charlie Gillett
132 (b).

Globe Photos
100; **227** (a); **311** (b); **341**.

George Gobes
455 (a)

Star File.
José Goitia
502 (b) Canadian Press.

Marv Goldberg
55 (b).

Lynn Goldsmith
294 (c). Corbis: **289** (c); **314** (d); **326** (c); **361** (c); **406** (a/c); **443** (a:); **467** (a).

Harry Goodwin
256 (a) Star File.

William Gottlieb
4 (b/c/d); **6** (a/b); **7** (a/b/c); **10** (b/c); **11** (b); **12** (a); **13** a/b); **15** (a/b); **17** (b); **22**; **24**; **27**; **29** (a); **31** (b); **32/33**; **42** (a); **57** (c); **76/77**; **80**; **87**; **105** (b); **127** (b); **514** (a).

Steve Granitz
387 (a/d) LFI; **454** (a) Retna.

Frank Griffin/LFI
368; **369** (a/b/c/d/e); **376** (b); **392** (d); **396** (c).

Bob Gruen/Star File
192; **238** (a/c); **242** (b); **265** (c); **266** (c); **275** (a); **282/283**; **285** (b); **301** (b); **304** (a/c); **315** (a); **315** (c); **334** (a); **352** (c); **360** (b); **368** (a/b); **373** (b/c); **397** (a); **398** (a).

Sam Hain
410 (a) LFI.

John Halpern
472 (d) Atlantic Archives.

Michael Halsband
390; **392** (b/e).

Beth Herzhagt
491 (b) Atlantic Archives.

Malcolm Heywood/Atlantic Archives
370; **405**; **447** (a).

Richard Houghton/Atlantic Archives
494 (a); **495** (a).

Laurens Van Houten
236 (b) Star File.

David Hum
486 (a) LFI.

Mick Hutson
426 (a) Redferns Music Picture Library.

Icon Archives
52 (a) Photofest.

Institute of Jazz Studies/Rutger University
44 (b); **48** (a); **49** (a); **79** (a); **330** (a/b).

Images
347 (a: Robin E. Platzer); **347** (e).

Niels Van Iperen
404 (a) Retna.

Steve Jennings
399 (b) Corbis.

Armen Kachaturian
333 Atlantic Archives.

Todd Kaplan
427 (a) Star File.

D. Katzenstein
460 (b) Atlantic Archives.

King Collection
217 Retna.

Lawrence Kirsh
392 (c) Retna.

Bernd Kowalzik
482 Atlantic Archives.

James Kriegsmann/Schomburg Centre for Research in Black Culture/New York Jazz Museum
38; **102**.

Marcello Krasilcic
476 Atlantic Archives.

Ola Lager
345 (b) Atalntic Archives.

Michael Lavine/Atlantic Archives
431; **490**.

Annie Leibovitz
274.

Jean-Pierre Leloir
56 (a); **67**; **68/69** (a); **148**; **158** (b); **165** (a/b); **166**; **170** (a/b/c); **171** (a/b); **172** (a/b/c); **173** (a); **174** (a/b/c); **175** (a/b/c); **176** (a/c/d); **177** (a/b); **188** (a); **191**; **197** (a); **200** (a); **200/201**; **203**; **219** (b); **237** (d); **247** (a); **253** (a); **256** (b); **263** (b); **264** (a/d); **265** (a/c); **269** (a); **277** (a); **288** (b/c/d); **299** (a); **325** (a/b); **326** (b); **348** (a/b); **349** (a/b); **393**.

Zoz Levin
414 (a) Atlantic Archives.

Cynthia Levine
435 Atlantic Archives.

Blake Little
475 (b) Atlantic Archives.

London Features International
220 (b); **299** (b: CV); **311** (a: Maz); **312** (CV); **318** (a:US/NP); **329** (a); **339** (a); **344** (a); **354** (a/c); **365** (a: WR); **377** (a/b); **381** (LF); **382** (a); **383** (a: LF); **387** (b: UAP); **387** (c: LF); **410** (b); **448** (a).

Janet Macoska
472 (b) Retna.

Andrew MacPherson
468 (a) Atlantic Archives.

Bruce Malone
432 (a) Retna.

Eddie Maluk
396 (b) Star File.

Arif Mardin
213 (b); **251** (b); **298** (b/c).

Robert Mass
464 (a) Corbis.

Jeffrey Mayer/Rainbow Photography
198 (a); **206** (b); **216** (a); **241** (b); **266** (a); **286** (b); **298** (a); **300/301**; **349** (c); **365** (c); **427** (b); **433**.

Clay Patrick McBride/Atlantic Archives
473 (a); **486** (b); **503**; **504** (b).

Frank Micelotta Atlantic Archives
494 (b); **495** (b).

Courtesy of M.G.M. Grand
347 (c)

Courtesy of Bill Millar
132 (c); **149** (b).

Ethan Miller/Corbis
453

Chi Modu
481 (a) Atlantic Archives.

Lawrence Morano
486 (c) LFI.

Tim Mosenfelder Corbis
472 (a); **506**.

Ilpo Musto
411 (a) LFI.

Ivan Nagy courtesy of Joel Bernstein
183 (b); **293**.

Alan Nahigian
496 (a).

Randee St. Nicholas
466 Atlantic Archives.

Melanie Nissen
467 (b) Atlantic Archives.

Don Nix
130 (a/b).

Claude Nobs
196 (a: Chris Powell);
196 (b/c); **330** (d).

Veryl Oakland
258 (a); **295** (a);
320 (c).

Michael Ochs Archives
55 (a); **69** (b); **103** (c);
111 (c); **150** (c); **153** (a);
156 (b); **157 162** (a); **164**;
195 (a); **261** (a); **363**.

Steve Paley
255 (b) Atlantic Archives.

Cindy Palmano
505.

A. J. Pantsios
379 (b/d) LFI.

Dale Parent
86.

Robert W. Parent
56 (b); **81** (a/b); **82** (a);
83; **91** (a); **95** (a);
119 (a/c); **120** (a).

Don Paulsen
78 (a) Schomburg Centre for Research in Black Culture/New York Jazz Museum;
150 (a); **163** (a)

Michael Ochs Archives;
167; **207** (c); **210** (b).

Ross Pelton
504 (a) Atlantic Archives.

Penguin
113 (c) Corbis-Bettman.

Al Pereira/Star File
371; **485** (a).

Gilles Petard/David Booth/ Showtime Photos
106/107; **195** (c).

Photofest
39 (a); **65**; **93** (b); **98** (b); **101**;
108; **118** (a); **127** (a); **129** (a);
133; **152** (c); **173** (c); **180** (a);
195 (b); **208** (b); **210** (a); **213**
(a); **234** (a); **250**; **257** (b); **268**
(a); **285** (d); **301** (d); **308**; **336**
(a); **357**; **401** (b).

Photokraft
37 (a) Schomburg Centre for Research in Black Culture/New York Jazz Museum.

J. Pigozzi
395 (a).

Pictorial Press/Star File
155 (c); **197** (b).

Giuseppe Pino
304 (b); **330** (c); **331** (b); **358** (a); **359** (a).

Charlie Pizzarelli
483 (a) Atlantic Archives.

Chris Pizzello
507 Associated Press.

Doc Pomus/Sharyn Felder Archive
39 (b); **127** (c).

Neal Preston
248; **283** (b/c/d); **284** (d); **315** (b); **316** (e); **327**; **328** (b); **384** (b/d); **403** (c); **424**.

Neal Preston/Corbis
263 (a); **284** (a/b/c/e); **289** (a/b/d); **314** (b/c); **315** (d); **326** (a); **332** (a/b); **412/413** (a); **412** (c/d/g); **413** (e/f/i);

Chuck Pulin/Star File
b (a); **306/307**; **415** (b); **436**;
464 (b); **471** (b/c); **513**.

Michael Putland/Retna
182 (c); **240** (c); **272** (a);
319 (c).

Felice Quinto
347 (b).

Roberto Rabanne
185 (a) Star File.

Stuart Ramson
502 (a) Associated Press.

William 'Popsie' Randolph
62 (a) Photofest; **63** (b) Atlantic Archives;
Frank Driggs: **89** (b);
127 (e); **155** (b);
160 (a).

Daniel Ray
493 (b) Atlantic Archives.

Sheey Rayn
239 (c) Michael Ochs Archives.

David Redfern/Redferns Music Picture Library
179 (b); **416** (a).

David Redfern/Retna
187 (a); **239** (a);
345 (a) RB.

Relay Photos
219 (a).

Retna
294 (b); **304** (d).

Bill Richert
365 (b) Atlantic Archives.

Merrill Roberts
267 (a) Atlantic Archives.

John Roca
413 (c/k) Corbis.

Rock and Roll Hall of Fame
45 (c); **52** (c); **93** (c);
144; **264** (c); **385**.

Amanda Rose/Globe Photos
455 (c); **510** (c).

Lisa Rose
511 Globe Photos.

Amalie R. Rothschild
236 (c) Corbis-Bettman.

Norman Jean Roy/Atlantic Archives
488 (b); **493** (a).

Robert Hammer/Salli Sachle
235 (a) Atlantic Archives.

F. Scott Schaeger/Atlantic Archives
461; **492** (b).

Mark Scheerer
241 (a) Star File.

Duncan Schiedt
48 (b) Schomburg Centre for Research in Black Culture/New York Jazz Museum.

Schomburg Centre for Research in Black Culture/New York Jazz Museum
110 (d); **224** (c).

David Seelig
399 (a) Star File.

Tom Sheenan
394 (c) Atlantic Archives.

Andrew Southam
452 Atlantic Archives.

David Booth/Showtime Photos, Toronto, Canada
17 (a); **34**; **35**; **36**; **42** (b); **58**; **59** (b/c); **72** (b); **103** (a); **109** (b); **111** (b); **113** (b); **125**; **126** (b); **132** (a); **139** (b); **149** (a); **156** (a); **162** (b); **163** (b); **194** (a); **229**; **267** (c); **408/409**.

A.A. Spanjaard
353 (c) Retna.

Pennie Smith
281 (a); **317** (d); **323** (a); **366** (a).

Herb Snitzer
137 (a).

Robert Spencer
475 (c) Atlantic Archives.

John Springer
112 Corbis-Bettman.

Star File Photo Agency
180 (b); **226** (b).

Adele Starr
456 Corbis.

Stax-Volt/Fantasy
131.

Chuck/Charles Stewart
60/61; **85**; **90** (a); **101** (a); **106** (a); **121** (a); **142** (a/b); **181**; **186**; **202** (d); **204** (b); **218** (a); **351** (b); **419**; **421**.

D. Tann/Atlantic Archives
412 (e/f/h); **413** (b/d/g/j).

Lee Tanner, The Jazz Image
50 (a); **104**; **105** (a); **117** (a); **134** (a); **141** (a); **143** (a); **179** (a); **187** (c); **211** (a); **221** (b); **222** (a); **224** (a); **225** (b); **358** (c).

Lisa Tanner
319 (b); **322**; **323** (b); **344** (b); **353** (a); **361** (a); **362** (a); **379** (c); **384** (a); **411** (b).

Dorit Thies
487 (a) Atlantic Archives.

Katrin Thomas
492 (a) Atlantic Archives.

Hank Thompson
73 (b/c); **110** (b); **128** (b/d).

UAP
387 (b) LFI.

UPI/Corbis-Bettman
124; **154** (a/b); **237** (e).

David Wainwright
394 (d) Relay Photos

Fran Wakschal
74 (b); **75**; **428** (b).

Harry Van Walls/David Booth/Showtime Photos, Toronto, Canada
54; **57** (b).

Chris Walter
317 (a) Retna; Relay: **262** (a); **328** (a); **355**.

Matthew Welch
501 (a) Atlantic Archives.

Jerry Wexler
89 (a); **121** (d); **153** (b); **188** (b); **230** (a); **242** (a); **255** (a); **268** (b); **277** (b); **301** (c).

Bob Whitaker
206 (a) Atlantic Archives.

Lili Wilde/All Action
439 (a).

Ron Wolfson
415 (a) LFI.

Christel Wolters
438 (a) Atlantic Archives.

Charlyn Zlotnik
260 (a); **321**; **338** (a); **360** (a); **372** (c); **429**.

Vinnie Zuffante/Star File
396 (a); **432** (b).

The Publishers wish to state that whilst every reasonable effort has been made to trace the photographers of all images used in *The Atlantic Story*, any further enquiries should please be made to the Publishers' address: A Publishing Company Limited, South West House, West Street, Axminster, Devon, EX13 5NU, England.